ECONOMICS OF LABOR

THE MACMILLAN COMPANY
NEW YORK · BOSTON · CHICAGO · DALLAS
ATLANTA · SAN FRANCISCO

MACMILLAN AND CO., Limited
LONDON · BOMBAY · CALCUTTA · MADRAS
MELBOURNE

THE MACMILLAN COMPANY
OF CANADA, Limited
TORONTO

ECONOMICS OF LABOR

BY RICHARD A. LESTER

DUKE UNIVERSITY

NEW YORK · THE MACMILLAN COMPANY · 1941

To D.N.L.

For Her Interest in This Book

PREFACE

This book, as its title indicates, deals primarily with the economic aspects of labor problems. Designed as a textbook for college courses in labor, it is analytic rather than encyclopedic. The emphasis throughout the book is upon economic principles rather than upon particular events or ephemeral facts. Facts, as such, mean little until they are examined and interpreted. With labor issues on the front pages of newspapers, the public and the student may acquire many miscellaneous scraps of information about labor, but they generally lack an understanding of the underlying forces that explain the surface facts. Furthermore, the student often forgets undigested facts and detailed statistics shortly after the final examination in a course. If, however, a firm theoretical foundation is developed to which various factual material may be attached in a meaningful manner, not only is the student less likely to forget the facts but he has a basis for interpreting new data and current affairs. He then is in a position to relate new facts to old ones and to evaluate existing labor policies.

Throughout the book, including the sections dealing with historical material, emphasis is placed upon the nature of the market. In so far as possible, the new market analysis of monopolistic or imperfect competition is here applied to labor and labor problems. Knowledge of the significance of monopolistic elements in markets is absolutely essential for an understanding of the theory of wages and collective bargaining. Such a market approach is also valuable for the study of labor relations in various branches of industry. Without some understanding of market situations, students cannot fully appreciate the need for minimum-wage legislation or why some labor unions, like the stove molders, or the building trades and the truck drivers in certain localities, are strong while other labor unions, in industries having a different competitive situation, are weak. As explained with examples in Part Four, the nature of employers' markets tends to condition the attitude of employers and employers' associations toward labor unions.

In the theoretical sections on the economics of wages, hours, and employment, sharp distinction is drawn between conclusions that apply to the individual firm or industry and those that apply to the economy as a whole. Many of the errors in reasoning on labor problems result from a failure to analyze the effects both upon particular employers and upon the economy in general. Failure to draw a distinction between private and social costs is another source of erroneous conclusions on labor issues and the proper governmental policy with respect to various labor problems.

In the chapters dealing with unemployment, I have drawn extensively from recent developments in the theory of employment and business cycles, associated with such names as J. M. Keynes, Joan Robinson, Alvin Hansen, and Bertil Ohlin. In the past there has been a tendency to draw too sharp a line between the subject matter discussed in college courses covering labor on the one hand and courses dealing with business cycles, monetary theory, public finance, international trade, industrial price policies, and economic theory on the other hand. In this volume use has been made, whenever fitting, of economic principles that the student may have learned in other courses in economics.

Some of the problems in labor are so complex and complicated that simple answers are not possible. In such cases, the issues have been faced and explained. It is better for students to appreciate the weaknesses in any particular theory than for the author to side-step the issue or to offer his readers dogmatic conclusions that must be accepted on faith. Students seeking solutions to problems should be taught not only the means by which they can work out answers for themselves but also the limitations to their own conclusions. For some readers, the book may even seem to raise more issues than it settles.

At various points in the discussion, the reader may disagree with the author's point of view or his analysis of the problem. That is to be expected in a textbook that attempts to apply to labor problems the new developments in other branches of economics. Such disagreement may, however, be most desirable, for students should not be led to believe that a live subject like labor is as cut and dried as geometry, so that all the student has to do is to learn the "propositions" and their "corollaries." Indeed, I shall feel well rewarded for the effort spent in writing this volume if it can so challenge old notions and stimulate new thoughts that its readers gain a better understanding of some current labor issues and a clearer insight into the economics of labor problems.

Part Four, which deals with collective bargaining in certain industries, permits some flexibility in the use of the book. The instructor can omit some of the chapters in this Part, as well as Chapters 15 and 26, and still give a well-rounded, complete course in the subject. As explained in Chapter 27, experience indicates that the industry provides the best unit or basis for the study of labor relations. The material in Part Four illustrates how the economics of an industry may affect labor relations within that branch of business, and it permits an intensive study of a few sample industries having very different economic and market conditions.

In the preparation of this treatise on the economics of labor, I have drawn upon the writings and teachings of a large number of economists. The footnotes indicate, somewhat inadequately to be sure, how great is my debt to other authors. They fail, however, to indicate how much I have been helped by the advice and criticism of many economists who have spent long hours in reading the manuscript, a number of them at the publisher's request and expense. The suggestions of these friendly critics were very helpful in revising the manuscript, after it had been tried in mimeographed form in the author's classes at the University of Washington in 1940. In a few cases, certain suggestions were not adopted, either because they would have involved more emphasis on the legal, political, administrative, or sociological aspects of labor issues than I thought desirable in a book concerned primarily with the economics of labor or because I disagreed with the analysis or viewpoint of the critic. In one section in particular, the chapter dealing with the historical background in England, two critics thought that not enough emphasis was given to a volume published by J. H. Clapham in 1926. Personally, I am inclined to question the adequacy of his treatment of labor on the basis of selected bits of statistical material, but suffice it to say that better data are now available on real wages in England during the eighteenth and nineteenth centuries than the wage indices used by Clapham, which had been published in 1899 and 1900.

I should like to take this occasion to express appreciation to two of my teachers and former colleagues at Princeton University, Professors David A. McCabe and J. Douglas Brown, whose views on labor have had more influence upon my thinking on this subject than they might suspect from reading this book. I also want to thank Professor J. Richard Huber and Thomas E. Hogan, who taught the preliminary edition of this book at the University of Washington and offered numerous helpful suggestions. The University of Washington granted me a six-months' leave of absence in 1939 so that I could spend that period in the East, particularly at the Industrial Relations Section of Princeton University, which has an excellent collection of labor material. Two NYA workers, Jeannette Kozicki and Willy Skadsberg, have helped to type the manuscript. Above all, my wife has worked over and improved the contents of this volume.

R.A.L.

DURHAM, N. C.
January, 1941.

CONTENTS

PART FOUR. COLLECTIVE BARGAINING IN
    CERTAIN INDUSTRIES

PART FIVE. CONCLUSION

LIST OF TABLES

PART ONE

INTRODUCTION

CHAPTER ONE

LABOR PROBLEMS

Labor problems center around the purchase, sale, and performance of labor services. Labor, in the broad sense of that term, may be defined as any hand or brain work, but there are no "labor" problems when persons work for themselves and sell the articles that they produce. Labor problems arise when persons sell their services for a wage and work, as directed, on the premises of an employer. Therefore the term "labor," as used in this book, refers either to those persons who live by selling their services directly to employers or to the services that they sell. It should be clear from the context whether the discussion refers to the services or to the persons selling them.

Labor issues are of primary importance in modern America because so much of the population is either selling or buying labor, or is dependent upon such sales and purchases for a livelihood. The self-employed worker is fast disappearing from American industry. Today more than three out of every four persons who work for a living do so by selling their labor to some employer. Annual payrolls for labor services represent two thirds of the nation's money income, and normally account for at least 90 per cent of the total incomes of the wage- and salary-earners in America. Most workers who live by selling their services have few earning assets except their heads, their hands, and their jobs. Consequently, payrolls afford practically the entire support for over three quarters of the families in this country during prosperous times.

ELEMENTS IN LABOR PROBLEMS

When people sell their services and spend their working lives on the premises of the purchaser of those services, a varying amount of dissatisfaction, discontent, and industrial unrest are likely to occur. Employees are especially interested in higher wages, healthy working conditions, opportunity to advance, satisfying work, some voice in industrial affairs, and protection against loss of wages, overwork, and arbitrary treatment. From these issues arise such particular problems as unemployment, hours of work, minimum wages, work accidents, promotion, the settlement of grievances, and labor organization. Each of these particular problems grows out of the wage system, under which workers support themselves and their families by selling their labor to employers.

The specific labor issues that arise in a locality change from time to time with changes in industrial methods and in the community's attitude toward decent living standards and decent working conditions. Each shift in social aims and objectives causes some alteration in the particular problems that are currently prominent. More emphasis upon citizenship, education, and workers' welfare brings forth the demand for a shorter working day and more leisure. As workers become better educated and their work is less satisfying in a creative sense, they tend to demand a larger voice in the government of industry. As living standards rise or workers strive to raise their social status, there is pressure for higher wages. Professor Sumner Slichter has said: "The sales manager, whose job is to make us dissatisfied with our lot, is a more formidable fomenter of industrial unrest than the 'walking delegate' " of labor unions.[1]

Such issues as work satisfaction, workers' social status, and their voice in the government of industry indicate that labor problems have psychological, social, and political, as well as economic, aspects. Although labor problems arise out of the conflicting economic interests of various groups in a competitive economy, these other phases of labor issues are part of the complete picture and have an influence upon the economics of labor that cannot be overlooked. Some indication of the role that various factors play in labor problems is indicated in the following discussion. The treatment under each heading is illustrative rather than all-inclusive. Whole books have been written on such subjects as industrial psychology, human nature in industry, the social aspects of industry, and industrial democracy.

Clash of economic interests. Labor troubles in a capitalistic economy generally grow out of the conflict of interests between the

[1] Sumner H. Slichter, "What Is the Labor Problem?" in *American Labor Dynamics in the Light of Post-War Developments*, edited by J. B. S. Hardman, 1928, p. 291.

buyers and sellers of labor. Sellers of labor, like all sellers, want to
secure the highest possible price for their wares. The standard of
living of each seller depends in large measure upon the price or
wage that he receives in return for his services. No one or no group
will be criticized for attempting to improve its economic lot, for in
a business civilization such as ours a person's standing in the community and his economic importance hinge largely upon the size
of his income. In a competitive society, each group seeks to enhance its income and to enjoy a "more abundant" life by increasing
its share of the product of industry, its slice of the industrial pie.

The focal point of labor problems is the labor market, where
such issues as wage rates, hours of work, conditions of work, and
job tenure are supposed to be solved. The sellers of labor, of course,
are interested not only in hourly wage rates but also in weekly and
yearly earnings, which depend upon the hours of labor sold multi-
plied by the wage rate. They, therefore, are interested in steady
sales. Furthermore, the sellers of labor are interested in the conditions of work, such as the speed at which the machinery is run,
the attractiveness of the workshop, and health conditions there, as
well as the personality of the "boss," the possibilities of advancement, and similar matters connected with wage work. The seller
of labor may not sell himself, but he must deliver himself and spend
his working time on the property and under the supervision of the
buyer of his labor. Though the seller of a commodity normally
cares not where and how it is used by the buyer, the seller of labor
cares a great deal where he works and how he is worked. However,
the conditions surrounding a job are not readily determined by
market forces. When a sale of labor services is made, there is
usually no agreement about conditions in the workshop. The
nature of the work may change, the speed of operations may vary,
the foreman may change, or the possibilities for advancement may
alter. Most of the hundred and one conditions surrounding the
job, which are of interest to the seller of labor as well as the buyer,
cannot be settled once and for all when industrial methods are
forever changing.

At the time most sales are made, the quantity sold is not left in
doubt. But in the sale of an hour of labor, no one knows exactly
what is sold. An hour of what sort of work, and at what speed?
The worker, of course, is interested in the speed of the work, for

the industrial wear and tear on his body affects the length of his working life. The buyer, too, is interested in the output of the labor he buys. How much output did he buy when he hired the labor? And when workers are paid by the piece, how should the piece rates be determined? With any change in the technical processes or conditions of work, how should the new piece rates be set? The vague and indefinite conditions surrounding the sale of labor leave considerable room for misunderstanding, disagreement, and conflict.

1. *Division of the product of industry.* In struggling to improve their standard of living, wage-earners find that their interests come into conflict with the interests of the stockholders, the management, the firm's creditors, and other groups. Raw materials, land, labor, capital equipment, and organizing effort all play a part in the production of most articles. Where an article is the joint product of a number of productive factors, how should the dollars received from the sale of that article be divided? Who is to say how much of the total product labor produced or what part of the output capital equipment was responsible for, especially when part of it was idle?

There is no formula by which the responsibility for the production of a joint product can be allocated among the different factors of production or among the various grades of labor. In capitalistic economies, the division of the product of industry is supposed to be determined by the market. That might be a just way to settle the division of the national income between persons and functional groups, such as workers and bondholders, if all markets always operated perfectly and impartially. But many markets are partially or wholly controlled by monopolies or monopolistic elements. Market prices frequently are fixed by the producer or groups of producers rather than by the free play of demand and supply. The prices of some products, like nickel, sulphur, sulphuric acid, steel rails, Electrolux vacuum cleaners, candies, and cigarettes, have remained fixed for 10, 15, or 20 years at a time so that they could, like prices in ancient Greece, have been cut in the stone of the market place. According to Senator Carter Glass, the rates charged by bankers in this country have also been so unchanging that they could be chiseled in the marble of our Greek-temple bank buildings. In May 1933 he told the Senate that the banks, in charging "standard" rates for loans in the community, "utterly disregard the law of supply and demand." [1] Service and other charges to bank customers are determined by local bankers' associations, and every member of the association must charge the agreed-upon price.[2]

All this has a direct bearing on the conflict between the buyers and sellers of labor. The share of the total national income that sellers of labor receive depends in part upon what their money wages will buy (the prices of commodities and services, including bank services) and in part upon the share of the national income that bondholders and other capitalists obtain.

Some of the income that property-owning groups (e.g., bondholders and landlords) receive is fixed by the provisions of long-term contracts, whereas wage rates, like railway timetables, are often subject to change without advance notice. In the struggle for income that arises between creditor and wage-earner groups, there is a tendency, therefore, to protect the investment of the creditors, even though the investment may have been unwarranted or unwise, and to pinch the wage-earners rather than to put pressure upon the creditors and stockholders by squeezing the "water" out of inflated capital values. The situation would be very different if wage rates were subject to long-term contracts, as interest charges are, and if failure to live up to the wage contract would enable wage-earners to take over the business, as bondholders can in case of default on interest payments. Furthermore, there is a tendency, as has already been indicated, for interest rates to be fixed by the monopolistic practices of banks and lending institutions rather than by uncontrolled demand-and-supply forces, so that there is no way of telling what the "normal" rate of interest should be in general or in a particular case. What rate of interest is necessary to induce people to save and invest part of their income rather than spend it all for immediate enjoyment? We used to think that from four to six per cent was necessary, but during much of the last decade two and three per cent seem to have been more than sufficient.[3]

In the case of stockholders, who receive a fluctuating and residual

[1] *Congressional Record*, vol. 77, Part 4, p. 3729, May 19, 1933.

[2] *Cf.* Lester V. Chandler, "Monopolistic Elements in Commercial Banking," *Journal of Political Economy*, vol. 46 (February 1938), pp. 1–22.

[3] In this connection Professor H. A. Millis has said: "Perhaps about the usual supply of enterprise and capital might be forthcoming were their [employers'] returns sub-

income (what remains after the payment of expenses and charges), there is pressure to keep wage rates down so that profits may be maintained or increased. It is to the interest of the stockholders that every dollar of the company's payroll purchase as much in labor services as possible. That does not always mean the payment of very low wages, for low-wage labor may be so inefficient and ill-suited for the job that it is actually very costly. But obviously, with payrolls often amounting to eight or ten times the size of dividend payments, any increase or decrease in wage rates will have a marked effect on profits; a one-per-cent increase in wages may mean an eight- or ten-per-cent decrease in profits.

Although the population as a whole may have a common interest in the largest possible national product, the division of that product is a bone of contention, especially when the population is so split into definite opposing groups—the buyers of labor on the one side and the sellers of labor on the other, with the sellers striving to increase the price on which practically their entire income hinges, and the buyers striving to keep it low so that profits will not decline or disappear. Though the discussion of wage theory is reserved for later chapters, it may be stated here that the conflict between employers and employees is often difficult to settle because there is no absolute test or criterion by which to determine the share of the common national product that rightfully belongs to a particular person or productive factor.[1]

2. *Imperfect markets intensify the conflict.* Some persons say that the market and competition alone should decide the share that each

stantially reduced; for the return required depends largely upon what can be had. It is certainly no fixed and irreducible thing." *American Economic Review*, vol. 25 (March 1935) supplement, p. 11.

Neoclassical economists have even admitted that, within certain limits, a lower rate of interest might induce a larger volume of saving. *Cf.* Alvin H. Hansen, *Full Recovery or Stagnation?* 1938, pp. 19–20. *Cf.* also the discussion of saving in Chapter 9 *infra*.

[1] On this issue William M. Leiserson, when Chairman of the National Mediation Board for the railroads, said: "There is no standard of right and wrong by which wages and earnings may be determined. What income working people *ought* to receive in return for their labor is a question that cannot be answered by any ethical judgment." *Cf.* Leiserson, *Right and Wrong in Labor Relations*, 1938, pp. 67–68. In the same vein, Joseph B. Eastman, former Federal Coordinator of Transportation and member of the Interstate Commerce Commission, has written: "At one time in my history I represented labor unions in three successive and rather important wage arbitrations in the electric railway industry. Apart from the minimum wage which should be paid for any useful work, I could discover no precise abstract standard which could be applied in determining what is a just and reasonable wage." *Cf. Barron's Financial Weekly*, vol. 18 (October 3, 1938), p. 9. The question is discussed at length in Chapters 7 and 8.

group shall receive. The trouble is that markets do not work satisfactorily in settling most labor issues; that many groups, including
bankers and steel producers, do not want to permit their prices to
be established by the free action of demand and supply; and that
in some lines of business, such as public utilities and trade-marked
goods where there is but a single seller, someone must set the price,
for full competition is lacking on the supply side. The following
chapter contains a discussion of the limitations of the market in
settling many economic problems, especially labor issues, and
Chapter 5 explains in detail the peculiarities of the labor market
and how it differs from the perfect market that is postulated by
those who hail the market as the final arbiter of all economic conflict. Here it is sufficient to point out that, in the words of Professor
C. Canby Balderston, "nearly everyone who gets a pay envelope
receives for his services a price that someone else has set," and, in
setting wage rates, some industrial firms "tend to pull their base
rates out of the air with little or no study and investigation." [1]
Furthermore, as personnel executives point out, many jobs in a
firm are peculiar to its line of business and the company's type of
organization, in which case there is no "market" rate for that peculiar type of labor service except the rate that the company itself
sets.[2] The very fact that the employer sets the wage indicates that
the market is imperfect and may be subject to employer control.

With many local labor markets so imperfect and dominated by
the buyers, the sellers of labor frequently organize to protect and
promote their own interests either by economic action, such as
threats to strike and picket, or, like employers, by political pressure
upon legislatures to secure the passage of laws in their interest.
Like their employers, employees recognize that in union there is
strength. Through producers' and employers' organizations, employers attempt to control the market, including the prices for their
products and for the labor that they buy. In typical American
fashion, workers also join organizations to raise their living standards and to improve their economic lot. Instead of joining the
National Association of Manufacturers or the Iron and Steel Institute, the workingman may join the Order of Sleeping Car Conduc-

[1] C. Canby Balderston, "Wage-setting Research," *Personnel Journal*, vol. 15 (December 1936), pp. 220 and 222.
[2] W. F. Cook, "Determination of Prevailing Wage Scales," *Personnel*, vol. 14 (August
1937), p. 26.

tors; the International Brotherhood of Teamsters, Chauffeurs, Stablemen, and Helpers of America; the United Automobile Workers of America; or some other labor union, as a means of securing higher wages, better working conditions, and some measure of control over the labor market.

Psychological factors.   Labor unions usually mean more to their members than simply a device for securing higher wages, shorter hours, job tenure, and better working conditions.   Men, yes, workmen, do not live by bread alone.   There are *human* or psychological causes of labor conflict as well as material or *market* causes.   A worker's satisfaction with his job is based only partly on his wages, hours of work, or other conditions of employment. It is also based upon the extent to which he enjoys his work and feels that it is worth while.   Workers need some pride, self-satisfaction, and sense of importance.   Their work should normally afford outlet for such needs.   Especially is that true in a political democracy, based on the notion that all men are political equals and should have equal access to economic opportunities as well as an equal voice in their government.

Psychological problems in industry have increased with the growth of large-scale production, giant corporations, and extreme job specialization.   In the modern factory, division of labor has turned many jobs into monotonous, routine tasks that are uninteresting and require little thought.   The symbol of extreme specialization is the automobile worker on the assembly line who screws one nut on unfinished autos as they pass by on the conveyor belt, but much of the machine-tending work in other factories is just as dull and monotonous.   The machinery sets the pace and dominates the worker, who is a mere cog in the huge organization of industry. Under such circumstances, workers may have little interest or pride in their work, for it is devoid of importance or significance and offers no opportunity for expression of the worker's personality. The routine of repetitious operations affords little emotional outlet or satisfaction for the creative impulse of workmen.   Variety is still part of the spice of life, but industry seems to be furnishing less and less of that spice for many of its workers.

At the same time that the life of most workers seems to have become more monotonous and less thought-provoking, their education has been increased.   The number of high-school graduates has increased twenty-five times in the last half century. Whereas in 1890 less than six per cent of the persons from 14 to 17 years of age were attending high school, in 1936 about 60 per cent of them were doing so. In fact, there were well over three times as many persons attending colleges and universities in 1936 as there were in high school in 1890.

No longer does a large portion of the American labor supply consist of immigrants who are illiterate or have had practically no schooling. There has been comparatively little increase in our population from immigration during the last 20 or 25 years, so a larger and larger percentage of American labor consists of native-born workers who have graduated from our high schools, and even our colleges. Indeed, a number of the top officials in the newer unions are college-trained men. The revolt against employer paternalism and the movement for industrial democracy are tied up with the fact that many workers are well educated and resent employer domination of their working and nonworking hours.

Various studies of the factors underlying industrial unrest have pointed to labor strikes as an emotional outlet and a means of compensating for an inferior economic status, much as riots by college students serve as a sort of temporary revolt against monotony and authority in undergraduate existence. Both types of activity permit the participants to "let off steam" and also, perhaps, to "show" the authorities that the underdog will rebel against mistreatment. Professor Carleton Parker once said: "Students, disappointed and balked by the impersonal and perfunctory instruction given in American universities, compensate by an enthusiasm over athletics and student activities. . . . College athletics is a sort of psychic cure for the illness of experiencing a university education." [1] Trade-unionism and the strike may afford those who do the nation's "dirty work" some relief from the dull minutiae of industry and may help to overcome a feeling of inferiority in the lower strata of an industrial caste system.

Government of industry. The selling of labor differs from the selling of commodities. Sales of labor are more continuous and more personal. They are not made in an anonymous cash market, such as the organized markets for securities or agricultural and other staple products. The personality and social or political views

[1] Carleton H. Parker, *The Casual Laborer and Other Essays*, 1920, p. 51.

of the producer of a standardized product, such as wheat or cotton, do not affect his sales. However, they may affect a worker's ability to sell his services to an employer. Consequently, farmers selling in a general market can be much more independent than wage-earners selling their services to one employer.

The employer may influence the views and attitudes of employees through advancement and salary increases. Employees may decide that it is to their self-interest to play along with the employer and be subservient to the foreman, for the employee generally depends for his entire income upon a single buyer, his employer. The employee may hesitate to talk or act independently for fear that certain activities, even outside of working hours, may affect his employment or his prospects for advancement. One reason why some employers have resisted independent organization of their employees is that labor unions tend to increase the independence of the workers and the readiness of workers to oppose the economic and political control of employers in the community.[1]

Under the capitalistic system, employers or corporation officials are normally in a dominant economic position, and they frequently use that position to their own advantage. To a large extent, American industry is run and controlled by the owners of the means of production (or their agents, the management). They buy the raw materials and machines; they own the plants, hire the workers and the company police, and sell the finished products. They tell the workers where to work, when to work, and how to work. In some cases, the workers are subjected to many arbitrary decisions concerning their work. Often there is little free play for individualism and private initiative on the part of wage-earners at the bottom. Orders come down from the top in dictatorial fashion. The workers do not have the same opportunity to participate in the determination of their working conditions that they enjoy as citizens in the determination of their government in our political democracy. Frequently, freedom of speech and thought have been practically suppressed in industry by the worker's fear that he would lose his job if he expressed certain views.

Through labor organizations, workers attempt to restrain the

[1] Union officials, unlike union members, are not dependent upon an employer for a job. Consequently, such officials are free to talk sharply to an employer, which helps to explain why many employers believe that labor leaders are more extreme in their views than the workers whom the leaders are supposed to represent.

arbitrary and autocratic rule of industry by foremen or officials. Workers look upon their organizations as a step toward what is vaguely referred to as "industrial democracy" or "representative government in industry." To them, labor organizations are a means of obtaining some "voice" in industry and some "vote" on industrial policies that vitally affect their lives, such as the methods of production, the speed of operations, and the rules or circumstances which govern hiring, firing, lay-off, and promotion. By means of working rules negotiated between labor and employers, the workers hope to establish a common law for industry that will curb arbitrary actions of management and decrease the truckling and favoritism that have been so prevalent in certain areas of industry. Employees want to win some measure of self-government over questions that vitally concern their working lives, and, therefore, they may resent the "welfare programs" of paternalistic employers who seek to suppress independent labor organization among their employees. Such employers recognize that labor unionism acts as a curb upon dictatorial power in industry and that collective bargaining is, as Professor Hoxie explained, "a step in the process of control" of industry by workers, "an entering wedge toward industrial democracy." [1]

Labor legislation for the settlement of labor disputes, and the fixing of minimum wages by joint committees of workers and employers also tend to democratize industry. Such laws provide for the democratic determination of wages or of workers' grievances, and curb the autocratic control of industry by employers. The annual negotiation of an agreement of the West Coast paper-and-pulp industry by workers and employers has been hailed as a "parliament of industry." Such common discussion and negotiation serves also as an economic education in the problems and points of view of management and labor. Indeed, collective bargaining seems as fundamental for economic democracy as parliamentary government is for political democracy.[2]

Limitation of employer authority in industry, either through labor unions or by law, may mean a revolutionary transformation of American capitalism from autocracy, however benevolent,

---

[1] Robert F. Hoxie, *Trade Unionism in the United States*, 1917, p. 274.

[2] *Cf.* Dorothy Sells, *British Wage Boards, A Study in Industrial Democracy*, 1939, Chapter 12, especially p. 335.

toward government in industry by consultation and agreements with the workers. European democracies, especially England and the Scandinavian countries, had already moved a considerable distance in that direction before the second World War. But in this drive toward some measure of industrial democracy, toward some representation for labor in American industry, there has been, and there will be at times, labor unrest and strife in certain sections of industry. Any attempt to deprive a powerful group of some of its vested rights, of some of the absolute authority it has exercised, is likely to cause conflict. In cases where employers have had to submit to the authority of other employers (especially through employers' associations) in the management of their business, a shift of some of the control from an "outside" employers' group to the union may not reduce the authority and control of the individual employer, and the union rules may prove to be no more irksome to him than the stipulations of other employers have been.

Of course, it is possible that unionism in certain cases may mean only the substitution of one type of dictatorship for another, that a labor boss simply takes over the power wrung from an autocratic employer. Men love to exercise power, and labor unions may, like a big business, be dominated and controlled by the top executives. That is especially true of trade-unions that concentrate authority in the hands of a business agent or a top official. The clash of economic interests between the buyers and sellers of labor will continue, however, despite the nature of the labor organization.

Some social considerations. The growth of large-scale business and of corporations has tended to widen the gap between employers and employed by increasing the number of sellers of labor, decreasing the number of buyers, and by eliminating, in large part, the former personal relationship between the buyer and his employees. Approaching problems from dissimilar backgrounds and experiences, employing and employed groups often lack any understanding of each other's viewpoint and problems. Wealth alone has been an important factor in segregating the employing from the employed groups.

As industry has been marching forward on bigger and bigger corporate feet, the chance to achieve business independence, to become a businessman selling a product or service to a number of customers, has narrowed. Small independent enterprise is passing.

Small manufacturers and small shopkeepers are being crowded out by large corporations, chain stores, and national advertising. No longer can one start out on his own in many lines of business, often because the amount of capital required to set up an enterprise is so great. The relative expansion in the employed groups since 1880 is indicated by percentages in Table 1. The figures in this table and in Table 2 indicate that, in the 1930's, employees outnumbered the employers and self-employed persons by three-and-a-half or four to one.

TABLE 1. INDUSTRIAL CLASS ALIGNMENTS IN THE UNITED STATES, 1880–1939 [1]

(*percentage of all gainful workers*)

	1880	1890	1900	1910	1920	1930	1939
All employees	63.1	66.2	69.2	73.7	76.5	79.7	81.2
Wage-earners	52.7	54.4	56.5	57.1	55.0	54.3	54.3
Clerical and sales employees	6.5	7.5	8.0	11.1	14.7	17.3	18.3
Professional employees	2.8	3.1	3.4	3.7	4.2	5.2	5.6
Managerial employees	1.1	1.2	1.3	1.8	2.6	2.9	3.0
All enterprisers (self-employed or employers)	36.9	33.8	30.8	26.3	23.5	20.3	18.8
Farmers	27.8	24.6	21.4	17.6	16.0	12.7	11.8
Business enterprisers	8.0	8.0	8.2	7.7	6.5	6.6	6.1
Professional practitioners	1.1	1.2	1.2	1.0	1.0	1.0	0.9
All gainful workers	100.0	100.0	100.0	100.0	100.0	100.0	100.0

If one were to include a class called "the impartial public" in Table 1, it would presumably consist primarily of the self-employed persons in the "enterpriser" group who have no employees working for them. However, even such self-employed persons tend to be drawn by economic interests toward either the employing or employed groups. A self-employed merchant or producer may own corporate securities, or stand to lose business by a strike, or stand to gain business by an increase in wage rates in the industry or the locality.

The attitudes of various groups in the community play an important part in labor matters, and social prejudices may even influence economic forces. Much of the pressure for changed labor conditions operates through legislation, the attitude of public officials, and public opinion. Corporation labor policies are influenced by community attitudes, which in some cases may even affect

---

[1] Estimates based on census data and taken from Spurgeon Bell, *Productivity, Wages, and National Income*, 1940, p. 10.

company sales. Corporation executives usually desire social esteem, so their decisions are not governed solely by profit considerations.

It is necessary in discussing the economics of labor to bear in mind those pressures that may not operate directly through the market. Even some economic pressure is indirect or concealed. The particular wage rates paid by a corporation, for example, may be the result of pressure exerted not only through demand and supply in the labor and product markets but also by a labor union, members of the chamber of commerce, important creditors, and other persons and groups who have some influence on the policies of the corporation. In labor problems, power and pressure play a significant role.

International character of labor problems. The problems that will be discussed in this book are not peculiar to any one country or locality. They are characteristic of capitalistic countries in which much of the population works for a money wage. The struggle of wage-earners to better their living standards and working conditions is occurring in every country. In nations under a political dictatorship, strikes may be outlawed so that the clash of economic interests between the buyers and sellers of labor seldom breaks forth in the forms that are to be found in other countries. Although restricted in form, the conflict nevertheless continues to exist.

Since labor problems are common to many areas and countries, they can hardly be the product of particular persons or local conditions. Indeed, their causes, as already indicated, are much deeper and more lasting than personalities or political changes. Because they are associated with the capitalistic economy and the wage system, they may follow similar patterns in various countries. Recent experience in the railroad industry in England and America affords a striking example of such similarity.

In 1932 the British railroads were demanding a general reduction of 10 per cent in the wages of all railroad employees as the only way to solve the economic difficulties of those railroads. The labor unions countered with the claim that the British railroads were overcapitalized and that their capital values should be written down so that they would not be "carrying an excessive burden of capital which represented, to a large extent, ancient expenditure that had become unremunerative." [1] During the previous year,

[1] A. G. Pool, *Wage Policy in Relation to Industrial Fluctuations*, 1938, p. 12.

British railroad stockholders had received dividends of 3.2 per cent on the capital value of their stock and 6.1 per cent of its Stock Exchange valuation.[1]

In the middle of 1938 the American railroads were demanding a 15-per-cent reduction in wage rates. The railroad unions replied that the troubles of the railroads were due to a top-heavy capital structure growing out of financial mismanagement.[2] A 1934 report of the Federal Coordinator of Transportation had stated that "many railroads are over-capitalized, whatever test be applied," and the statistics of the Interstate Commerce Commission showed that the face value of the bonds and stocks of many railroads in 1938 exceeded by 50 per cent or more the current cost of reproducing those railroads, with allowance for depreciation. In the opinion of railroad labor, the proposed wage cut was simply a means of protecting railroad security holders at the expense of more than 1,000,-000 railroad employees, whose average yearly earnings in 1937 were $1,115.[3]

In the middle of 1938 the railroad employees were receiving an average wage rate of about 72 cents an hour, whereas the average wage rate in many branches of manufacturing, such as automobiles, petroleum, rubber tires, iron and steel, coal mining, shipbuilding, or telephone and telegraph service, was 85 cents an hour or more. Furthermore, the increase in freight rates in March 1938 was partly justified by the Interstate Commerce Commission on the basis of "increased labor costs" resulting from a five-per-cent increase in railroad wage rates in the Fall of 1937. The prices of some of the materials that the railroads buy are controlled by monopolistic elements. For instance, the price of steel rails remained absolutely fixed from 1901 to 1916 and from 1922 to 1932. In 1933 the Federal Coordinator of Transportation wrung a price cut of over nine per cent in steel rails from the four producing steel companies by threatening them with Federal investigation.[4] As for the bondholders, the average interest charge on the railroads' $12,500,000,000 of funded debt was about 4.5 per cent in 1937. Dividends amounted

[1] *The Economist*, vol. 115, Part 2 (December 10, 1932), p. 1078.

[2] *The Wages of Railroad Labor, 1938*, published by the Railway Labor Executives Association, p. 26.

[3] The argument for a wage reduction is contained in *Brief on Behalf of the Carriers*, 1938 National Railway Wage Reduction Controversy, Washington, October 17, 1938.

[4] *Cf. New York Times*, September 9, 1933, p. 19; September 26, p. 1; October 5, p. 31; October 16, p. 30; October 29, pp. 1, 29; and October 31, p. 1.

to 2.3 per cent on the par value of all stock outstanding and almost 6 per cent on all railroad stocks that were paying dividends.

The question arises, When the railroad industry is pinched, what group should be squeezed? Should an attempt be made to force down the price of materials and services that the railroads purchase? Or should creditors take a cut in the form of lower interest charges or a scaling down of inflated capital values and fixed charges through bankruptcy, receivership, reorganization, or sale? In view of the fact that profits are supposed to be a reward for assuming the risks of the business, should the stockholders take a cut in the form of smaller dividends; or should wage rates be cut, and would a wage reduction provide a lasting solution for the difficulties of our railroads? If truck competition is part of the trouble, should railroad freight and passenger rates be readjusted?

As the above examples from recent experience in the British and American railroad industries indicate, the conflict largely concerns the share of the product that capital-owning and laboring groups should receive. This conflict between jobholders and bondholders or stockholders is common to all capitalistic countries. The market, through demand and supply, may not settle such issues satisfactorily. The demand for railroad labor does not fluctuate widely over short periods of time, for many trains have to run on schedule and carry crews of a certain size. Consequently, a wage cut would not soon lead to a substantial increase in the demand for railroad labor, nor a wage rise to a substantial decrease in railroad employment. A market solution of the problem would require a very long period of time.

THE SELLERS AND BUYERS OF LABOR

With sales of labor playing such a significant role in our whole economy, it is important to know something about the buyers and sellers of labor—their numbers and their characteristics. It is the buyers and sellers of labor—the employers and employees—who are directly involved in labor problems.

Who are the workers? Detailed statistics of the working population are obtained by the decennial census. The census data show the number of persons working in different occupations and industries. The census does not, however, sharply distinguish employees from self-employed and employers in certain occupations.

Consequently, it is necessary to adjust the census figures by means
of estimates in order to obtain a picture of the supply of labor
normally offered for sale to employers. Such an estimate for 1930,
a fairly normal year, is contained in Table 2, which shows how the
persons working outside their own homes were distributed in April
of that year.

TABLE 2. GAINFULLY EMPLOYED PERSONS IN THE UNITED STATES, 1930 [1]

Employers and self-employed		10,646,294
Salaried employees		
Professional persons	2,247,276	
Managers	869,796	
Clerks and kindred workers	5,421,408	
Salespersons	1,988,050	
Skilled workers		
Foremen	547,735	
Others	5,955,327	
Semiskilled workers		
Apprentices	87,404	
Others	6,852,920	
Unskilled workers	8,286,962	
Service workers	4,266,956	
Total employees		36,523,834
Unpaid family workers		1,659,792
Total gainfully employed		48,829,920

The statistics of the working population in Table 2 have an
appearance of precision, but often it is difficult to determine whether
a worker is self-employed or is an employee. For example, insurance
agents and sharecroppers are "borderline" cases that are difficult
to classify. Furthermore, a worker may at various times during
the year be an employer, a self-employed person, and an employee.
Skilled craftsmen and farmers may, for instance, fluctuate among
those three classes, hiring others at peak seasons and working for
wages in slack periods. The author of the estimates in Table 2
believes that "the total number of persons who intermittently or
simultaneously are employers and employees is probably as high as
seven or eight million." [2] These estimates of the working population, therefore, simply present a cross-sectional picture of the situation at a certain time in 1930.

Table 2 indicates that employees outnumbered the employers

[1] W. S. Woytinsky, *The Labor Supply in the United States*, Social Science Research
Council, 1938, pp. 18–25.
[2] *Ibid.*, p. 4.

and self-employed by three-and-a-half to one in 1930, and the figure for 1940 was probably about four to one (see Table 1). If the 1930 figures were adjusted by deducting all persons engaged in farming, which means over 6,000,000 farmers who work for themselves, along with 2,700,000 farm laborers, there would remain only 4,600,000 in the employer and self-employed group, compared with 33,800,000 employees. Outside of agriculture, therefore, employees outnumbered the employers and self-employed by over seven to one in 1930.

The statistics do not permit an exact division between those persons who hire one or more workers and those who simply employ themselves, such as authors, shopkeepers who hire no clerks, keepers of boarding houses and restaurants with no employees, and professional men and women in private practice. It seems safe to say, however, that at least one half of the employer and self-employed group normally do not employ others for any length of time.[1] If that is the case, then outside of agriculture those who regularly sell their labor outnumber those who regularly buy labor by about fifteen to one.

These statistics of the number of persons selling labor (the labor supply) are of significance. They indicate not only the political importance of those who normally hire out for pay but also the extent to which the American people are dependent upon pay envelopes for their living. In earlier times, when most workers were self-employed on the farm or in small shops, the effect of a widespread breakdown in the exchange or sale of goods and services was less drastic than it is today, when three fourths of the population in our exchange economy are dependent upon the sale of their services to someone who can use them at a profit.

Table 2 indicates that the largest single group in the American labor supply consists of unskilled or common laborers, who constituted 23 per cent of the labor force in 1930. Next in numbers were the semiskilled machine tenders or operators with 19 per cent of the total, followed by the skilled manual workers or artisans, who accounted for 16 per cent of the nation's labor force. The skilled group seems to have been declining, and the semiskilled group increasing, in importance during the last few decades as American

---

[1] Cf. the 1937 employer-employee data in *Third Annual Report of the Social Security Board*, 1938, p. 172.

industry has become more and more highly mechanized. The clerks and kindred workers, together with the salespersons, make up what has been termed the white-collar class—another group that has increased in importance in the last thirty years. A majority of the service workers are domestic servants, and the rest are connected with personal-service establishments.

Women and girls constituted 22 per cent, and children under 15 years of age about 2 per cent, of the gainfully employed population in 1930. On the basis of race and nativity, the working population was then divided as follows: 72 per cent native whites, 15 per cent foreign-born whites, 11 per cent Negroes, and 2 per cent Mexicans, Indians, Japanese, Chinese, Filipinos, etc.

Who is the employer? The other party directly involved in labor problems is the employer. We are accustomed to think of the typical employer as some local businessman who hires a few workmen in his plant or store. Actually, the typical employer is no person at all but a corporation, which Chief Justice Marshall defined as "an artificial being, invisible, intangible, and existing only in contemplation of law."

It is true that in certain lines of business, like building, retail selling, or farming, most employees work for an individual who owns and manages the business. But in large-scale business, like manufacturing, mining, banking, railroading, insurance, and public utilities, practically all employees work for a corporation.[1] The man who hires or fires them does not own the company, or the governmental unit in the case of public employment. Even the president of a corporation is only an employee.

Though there are many more individual employers who own and run their businesses than there are corporations, probably two out of every three employees in this country work for a corporation.[2] This is because most corporations employ large numbers of men; the five largest American corporations employ over 1,000,000 persons. The tendency has been for corporations to take over more

---

[1] Dr. Willard Thorp estimates that in 1937 corporations accounted for the following percentages of all business in each industry: Electric light and power, 100 per cent; communication, 100 per cent; mining, 96 per cent; manufacturing, 92 per cent; transportation, 89 per cent; finance, 84 per cent; government, 58 per cent; trade, 58 per cent; contract construction, 36 per cent; miscellaneous, 33 per cent; service, 30 per cent; agriculture, 7 per cent. *Cf. Verbatim Record of the Proceedings of the Temporary National Economic Committee*, vol. 1, December 1, 1938 to January 20, 1939, p. 56.

[2] *Ibid.*, p. 55.

and more of American business. Between 1904 and 1929, the number of corporations in manufacturing doubled, while the number of manufacturing establishments owned by individuals, partners, or unincorporated groups decreased 34 per cent. In 1904 about 70 per cent of all employees in American manufacturing worked for a corporation; by 1929 corporations employed 90 per cent of all employees in manufacturing and 95 per cent of all wage-earners in mining.[1]

As more and more American business has become incorporated, the size of business concerns has increased. Employer returns to the Social Security Board under the Federal Old-Age and Survivors Insurance Benefits program show that the 37,000,000 covered employees who were reported working during the last half of 1937 were distributed as follows by size of firm: [2]

TABLE 3.   DISTRIBUTION OF EMPLOYEES BY SIZE OF FIRM, 1937

Number of employees in firm	Percentage of all covered employees
1—9	11.0
10—99	26.5
100—999	30.5
1,000—9,999	19.7
10,000 and over	12.3

The figures in Table 3 indicate that about one third of the employees were connected with concerns employing at least 1,000 workers, and half of them were in firms hiring at least 250 employees.

There is often a great deal of difference between working for a large corporation and working for an individual entrepreneur who owns and manages his own little business. In a large corporation employing tens and hundreds of thousands of workers, routine and regimentation often leave little room for private initiative in the plant or in the office. Not only is the corporation usually more impersonal and bureaucratic, but not infrequently the top officials (the hired management) treat the corporation as their personal province. There have been many instances in which corporate management or some controlling group has used the corporation for personal gain and personal profit at the expense of profits for

[1] Alfred L. Bernheim *et al.*, *Big Business, Its Growth and Its Place*, Twentieth Century Fund, 1937, p. 15.
[2] *Third Annual Report of the Social Security Board*, 1938, p. 172.

its stockholders.[1] As Berle and Means have so effectively indicated, business incorporation and corporate devices have tended to shift control from the owners of the business (the stockholders) to the managers, who may own little, if any, stock.[2] There is often a separation or cleavage between the interests of the managers, the interests of the owners, the interests of the public, and the interests of the employees.

Numerous examples could be cited to indicate how some corporate managements have disregarded the interests of the owners, labor, or the public in order to perpetuate their own power and control. Labor organization, of course, represents an important threat to the authority of corporate management. Such a challenge the officials of the corporation may meet with the expenditure of thousands and even millions of dollars of the corporation's funds. In this way, labor's attempts to obtain some industrial democracy within the corporation may be defeated at the expense of the stockholders or owners who have really supplied the means that the management uses to maintain its position and power. The following two recent cases will serve to illustrate this point.

In 1937 the managements of certain steel companies, including the Republic Steel Corporation, refused to sign written agreements with the Steel Workers Organizing Committee (a CIO union). This refusal led to the "Little Steel" strike of that year. Such agreements, involving no immediate increase in wages, had already been signed by the United States Steel Corporation and 50 other steel companies employing about half of the workers in the industry. This strike cost the stockholders of Republic Steel millions of dollars. In addition to $1,950,000 spent directly on the strike, the company was faced with some 100 damage suits totalling over $2,000,000 as a result of riots at the company's plants, in which 16 persons were killed and 323 were injured.[3] The Chairman of the Board admitted that the company lost millions of dollars of business during the strike, which he characterized as "a tremendous waste of everything." [4]

---

[1] Cf., for example, John T. Flynn, *Graft in Business*, 1931; and Exhibits 5207 and 5209 in *Hearings on S. Res. 266*, 75th Congress, third session, Part 34, 1939, pp. 13896–902.

[2] Cf. A. A. Berle and Gardner Means, *The Modern Corporation and Private Property*, 1933.

[3] Cf. *Hearings on S. Res. 266*, 75th Congress, third session, Exhibits 4670 and 4671 in Part 28, 1939, pp. 11605–10; and Exhibit 5250 in Part 34, 1939, pp. 13968–69.

[4] *Ibid.*, p. 13888.

Accused by the National Labor Relations Board of discriminating against union members and engaging in other unfair labor practices during the strike, the management of the Republic Steel Corporation carried the case to the United States Supreme Court and lost the decision in April 1940, which made the company legally liable for an estimated $5,000,000 of back pay to 5,000 discharged union members. A stockholder's suit was later filed against Republic executives, demanding that they reimburse the Corporation for an alleged $12,850,000 loss resulting from "illegal, wasteful, and improper actions" during and after the strike.[1]

During 1938 and 1939 the Metropolitan Life Insurance Company carried on an extensive and ineffective legal campaign in the courts against the New York State Labor Relations Act and Board. This court campaign, for which expensive legal talent was hired, followed an employee election, held by the Board, in which a majority of the Metropolitan's industrial insurance agents in the New York area voted for the United Office and Professional Workers (CIO) as their "exclusive" representative. The Metropolitan's management refused to recognize the union or obey the orders of the Board, insisting that the State Act could be violated because it was unconstitutional. A series of court tests upheld the constitutionality of the Act, as was to be expected in view of the U. S. Supreme Court's decision in 1937 sustaining the National Labor Relations Act. Following victory in the courts, the State Labor Relations Board found that the Metropolitan had committed a number of new "unfair labor practices," including discrimination against employees for refusing to join the company union fostered and dominated by the Metropolitan.

The Metropolitan Life Insurance Company is legally owned by some 29,000,000 persons, who hold more than 40,000,000 Metropolitan insurance policies. Over four fifths of these policies are "industrial insurance" policies, bought on the weekly installment plan by people apparently too poor to buy "ordinary" insurance policies. This wage-earners' "industrial" insurance is much more costly than ordinary life insurance. The expenditure of the policyholders' money on test cases and antiunion campaigns tends to increase the costliness of "industrial" insurance to policyholders

---

[1] Cf. New York Times, April 9, 1940, p. 20, and April 10, 1940, p. 36; and The CIO News, April 15, 1940, p. 6.

and to reduce the dividends to those policyholders. With over 80 per cent of the policyholders poor working-class people and with each policyholder entitled to one vote regardless of the amount of insurance or the number of policies he holds, the management's campaign against organized labor undoubtedly did not represent the will of a majority of the Metropolitan's policyholders and owners. It was, however, supported by the company's board of 24 directors, who were connected with 137 other corporations.[1]

In both of these cases, the management was ready to sacrifice profits or dividends so that the representatives of labor could not "tell them how to run *their* business."

It may be true, of course, that the program of the management of a labor union may no more correspond to the will of a majority of that union's membership than the labor programs of certain corporate managements seem to have reflected the attitudes and interests of a majority of the stockholders. Whether it is easier for displeased voters (owners or members) to oust the management of a corporation or of a labor union is a debatable question, with the answer depending upon the particular circumstances in each case. The carpenters' union has experienced eight straight years without any election of new officers, and the presidents of other unions, including the United Mine Workers, have had elections and votes conducted through the mails and counted by their friends at the union headquarters. The party in power in a union or a corporation can generally control the election machinery.[2]

It must be recognized, however, that a labor union is neither an employee nor an employer of labor except for its officials. Its

[1] It should be pointed out that some of the Metropolitan's directors have not attended a directors' meeting for four or five years at a time, that the persons nominated for directorships have always been elected as no opposition candidate has ever been nominated, and that less than two per cent of the policyholders eligible to vote cast ballots in the election of directors, which is only a formality without an opposition ticket. *Cf. Hearings before the Temporary National Economic Committee*, 66th Congress, first session, Part 4, *Life Insurance*, 1939, pp. 1252–53, 1274, 1279, 1286.

[2] Customarily the officials of unions are elected by vote at annual or biennial conventions of delegates, each delegate representing a certain number of members. More than one candidate is frequently nominated for an office. At annual meetings of corporations, on the other hand, few stockholders appear in person to vote; each share of stock entitles the owner to one vote; and normally there are no candidates nominated to oppose those selected by the corporation officials in power. The officers of the corporation, using company funds, send out proxy forms soliciting the vote of each stockholder, and it would require hundreds of thousands of dollars to challenge the smooth-running proxy machinery of a large corporation.

counterpart is the employers' association, which is likewise designed to control, or exert pressure upon, the market for labor. A labor union is an employee agency for securing certain economic gains for its membership, including high wages, but it does not buy or sell the services of those employees in the labor market. Slavery is the only arrangement under which one person can sell the services of another.

CHAPTER TWO

REASONING ON LABOR PROBLEMS

Factual basis for reasoning. It is very difficult to be unbiased in a discussion of any particular labor problem or of labor problems in general. One reason for this is that labor issues (such as wage rates, hours of work, or employment) are so vital to the standard of living of both capitalist and laboring groups. As stated in the previous chapter, over three fourths of all families in this country obtain practically all their living from payrolls. The standard of living of the remaining families in large part depends upon those pay envelopes, either because the family head is an employer or a large stockholder and, therefore, helps to supply the funds that go into pay envelopes, or because the family's breadwinner is an independent enterpriser whose market depends largely upon the size of payrolls. It is difficult to avoid having a class bias on labor issues if one's father has consistently been an employer, or a wage-earner dependent on pay envelopes for a living.

Furthermore, on labor issues people are likely to form their opinions primarily on the basis of their own personal experience or that of their parents or friends. In other words, the experience that forms the basis for a person's reasoning on labor issues is likely to be confined to a particular locality or to a certain period of time—usually some earlier date because opinions on vital, everyday issues are often formed in one's youth, after which the mind tends to crystallize and to accept only evidence that supports the conclusions made in an earlier period. True, people may try to broaden their experience or to bring it up to date by reading books and magazines, but not infrequently they judge the writings of an author on such a popular subject as labor problems by how closely the author's experience and conclusions conform to their own.

Students' attitudes on labor issues may be colored not only by personal experience or the experience of parents and friends but also by their own expectations—by the position in society that the student expects to occupy after he or she leaves the campus and the classroom. Those who look forward to a high position in industry are likely to take a different view of labor problems from that taken by a student who fears that he may spend the rest of his life as a wage-earning employee. Age itself may affect one's attitude toward the programs and practices of organized labor. Students are likely to criticize union practices, like seniority and the closed shop, that increase the job security of present jobholders and, therefore, tend to make it more difficult for college students to find employment during vacations or after graduation.

Because labor relations are human relations, one can support any position or opinion by citing particular cases. Human beings are of all sorts and sizes. Certain employers may be cruel, dictatorial, and antisocial in their outlook. Some workers may be lazy loafers, troublemakers, or communists who are trying to "bore from within." Consequently, any generalization can be supported by citing some particular or unusual instances, and exceptions can be found to almost every generalization in the field of labor. The student must, therefore, strive to understand the general situation—the whole picture—and not concentrate his attention on exceptional cases or the peculiar circumstances in his locality. By living in various sections of the country—in steel or coal-mining towns, in sweatshop or open-shop areas, in cities where labor-union officials have engaged in racketeering or, in league with employers, have exploited the public by eliminating all competition and boosting prices—one soon learns to what a large extent a person's opinions on labor problems are conditioned by his immediate surroundings and how difficult it is for him to expand his vision beyond the personalities and particular circumstances of the local labor situation so that he can, figuratively speaking, distinguish the forest from the near-by trees.

A further difficulty confronts the student of labor problems. Not only must he guard against drawing generalizations from exceptional local conditions, but he must also examine all factual data with a sceptical eye, for in no field of study are truth, propaganda, and rationalization more mixed together than in the field of labor.

One must bear in mind that newspaper, magazine, and book

publishers are employers, and that a number of them have, in the recent past, hired private detective agencies to spy on their employees.[1] Not only are publishers employers, but about two thirds of all newspaper income and almost 60 per cent of all the income of magazines is derived from advertising.[2] Recent history is full of cases where employing advertisers have attempted to influence or dictate the attitude that a newspaper or magazine should take on certain labor issues.[3] There can be no doubt that many of our newspapers have been prejudiced against organized labor and that labor news in the daily press has not infrequently been class-angled from the employer's point of view.[4] Unlike England, France, Australia, or the Scandinavian countries, this country has not had any important daily newspapers owned or supported by organized labor or a labor party. Furthermore, much of the news broadcasting over the radio is sponsored and paid for by employers of labor who use that means of advertising.

Because there is so much propaganda and prejudice in the field of labor, the student must study the facts, draw his own conclusions from them, and take nothing on faith. He should trust no one, not even his father, his instructor, or the author of his textbook. Though he may come from Oshkosh, Wisconsin, the student should take the objective attitude that he is from Missouri and has to be shown either by unadulterated facts or by sound economic reasoning.

UNSOUND REASONING IN ECONOMICS

Everyone believes that his own brand of economics is the only sound variety, and each person, in discussing economic questions, seems inclined to subscribe to the notion, "What's good for me is good for the country." Recently the National Association of Manufacturers and chambers of commerce covered billboard signs with

[1] Cf., for example, a report on *Industrial Espionage*, by the Senate Committee on Education and Labor, 75th Congress, second session, Senate Report No. 46, Part 3, November 16, 1937, p. 110.

[2] Cf. *Biennial Census of Manufactures*.

[3] Cf. R. S. and H. M. Lynd, *Middletown in Transition*, 1937, pp. 27, 274–84; and *Hearings on S. Res. 266 before a Subcommittee of the Committee on Education and Labor*, U. S. Senate, 75th Congress, third session, Part 24, 1939, pp. 10165–72, 10293–97.

[4] Cf. George Seldes, *Freedom of the Press*, 1935, especially Chapter 16; and William Allen White, "How Free Is Our Press?" *The Nation*, vol. 142 (June 18, 1938), pp. 693–95. The manner in which newspapers were so generally opposed to President Franklin D. Roosevelt in the 1936 and 1940 campaigns is one indication of their bias.

the slogan, "What helps business helps you." The Congress of Industrial Organizations (the CIO) replied by decorating the windows of members' autos with the slogan, "What helps labor helps everybody." [1]

Both of these slogans are of doubtful economic validity. The truth is that frequently economic benefits to one group in society may be won at the expense of other groups. A tariff restricting imports aids some domestic producers at the expense of American consumers, who have to pay prices higher than they otherwise would be, and of American exporters, whose sales eventually are correspondingly reduced by the import restrictions of the tariff. Employers in control of the labor market may acquire large profits by exploiting their labor, and labor unions in control of the labor market may raise labor costs so high as to ruin some of the employers in that line of business. Indeed, individuals or economic groups, in pursuing their own selfish interests in our capitalistic economy, are very liable to commit antisocial acts.[2] Because there is often a conflict between individual and social advantage, it is a questionable practice in economics to generalize about the social good on the basis of one's own selfish interest, or to make generalizations for the whole country from the experience of some person or private group.

Reasoning from the particular to the general. Perhaps the most prevalent cause of false conclusions in economics is the tendency for persons to apply to society as a whole conclusions that are valid only for a particular person, product, or industry. Francis Rawle, alleged to be the first writer on political economy in America, pointed to this common source of economic error as early as 1726 when he wrote: "It is false Reasoning to make general Conclusions from particular Cases." [3] Despite Rawle's warning, American writers have frequently fallen into this questionable practice, as though policies that were "sound" and appropriate for a

---

[1] *Cf. The CIO News*, September 17, 1938, p. 2.

[2] "The course which is best for each individual to pursue in his own interests is rarely the same as the course best calculated to promote the interests of society as a whole." Joan Robinson, *Introduction to the Theory of Employment*, 1938, p. 2.

[3] *A Just Rebuke to a Dialogue Betwixt Simon and Timothy, Shewing What's therein to be found*, 1726, p. 15.

Much of the discussion in this section on "unsound reasoning in economics" is based upon R. A. Lester, "Political Economy *versus* Individualistic Economics," *American Economic Review*, vol. 28 (March 1938), pp. 55–64.

part of the economy were the most fitting ones for the nation as a whole to pursue. And it is especially difficult to convince the layman that conclusions based on such reasoning are frequently unsound, because they seem to correspond so well with the lessons of everyday experience and seem to him to be simple common sense.

It has been said that economics is only common sense dressed up in technical language. But common sense, reasoning from an individual situation or particular cases, is very likely to lead one to the wrong answer for the general situation. In the words of M. S. Eccles, chairman of the Board of Governors of the Federal Reserve System, "the economics of the system as a whole differs profoundly from the economics of the individual; what is economically wise behavior on the part of a single individual may on occasion be suicidal if engaged in by all individuals collectively." [1] A number of examples will indicate the sort of errors that arise from applying to the whole economy conclusions derived from personal or business experience. The examples have been selected from a number of fields to show how widespread is the tendency to draw incorrect conclusions from particular cases. Readers who find some of these illustrations rather involved are assured that only a general understanding of this pitfall is necessary for subsequent discussions.

Illustrations. (1) The mercantilist school of economists in the seventeenth and eighteenth centuries provides the classical example of the way in which generalizing from individual experience may lead to false theories. The mercantilists believed that a nation becomes wealthy in the same way that an individual merchant does, by accumulating large sums of money or "treasure," as the mercantilists called gold and silver coins. They proposed that the country accumulate money, as a merchant does, by having total sales exceed total purchases, giving rise to a "favorable" balance of trade and an inflow of gold and silver to pay for the excess of exports over imports. Economists now recognize that it is futile for a country to pursue such mercantilistic policies, even though they may be the correct policies for its individual merchants. A large inflow of gold into a gold-standard country, by

[1] "Controlling Booms and Depressions," in *The Lessons of Monetary Experience*, edited by A. D. Gayer, 1937, p. 6.

increasing the money supply, tends to push up the country's price level, which acts to reduce exports and increase imports. With higher prices in a country, foreigners buy less and the citizens tend to purchase from abroad, both of which actions tend to cause the gold to flow out again. If the gold does not increase the money supply, but is simply kept idle in vaults under the ground, then it serves no useful purpose and becomes a burden, as our government has recently discovered. With over three fourths of the world's monetary gold stock, we had to build Fort Knox and bury the gold that the South Africans and others worked so hard to dig out of the ground.

(2) The individual who is hard up knows that his own economic difficulties would be solved if he had more money. Reasoning from his own situation, he naturally assumes that, in the same way, the nation as a whole would be better off if it had more money or currency. The nation's economic difficulties seem to him to be simply the aggregate of the difficulties of all of its citizens; and the answer to his problem seems to him to be the answer to the same difficulties suffered by others—namely, that they should all have more money. What is more natural, therefore, than to assume that, if the government or the banks would increase the country's money supply, the financial troubles of its citizens would disappear? Actually, a large increase in the money supply, such as in Germany after 1919 or in the Confederate States during the Civil War, may only increase everyone's financial troubles by causing prices to skyrocket. An individual becomes more wealthy when his money income increases faster than the money income of others.

(3) An individual gains when his product or service becomes relatively scarce. It is generally recognized that producers or sellers in a single line of business may, if the demand for their product is inelastic, gain in wealth and raise their own standard of living by restricting production and limiting supply. That is true because, as the supply of such a product is reduced, the price rises by a larger percentage, increasing the total income from sales. This so-called paradox of value was the basis of the Agricultural Adjustment Administration's crop-reduction program from 1933 to 1935. No one, however, would argue that a country with diversified industry could raise its standard of living by a general appli-

cation of a policy of reducing production. Particular restrictions may help particular groups at the expense of others, but general all-around restriction would harm everyone. On the other hand, everyone tends to gain by a greater total national output, but producers or workers in one branch of industry may lose if the output in that line increases while output in other branches of business does not.

Certain labor unions follow policies based on the notion that members' incomes will be increased if entrance to that trade and the output of that union's members are both restricted. Such practices will tend to increase members' incomes if the demand for that type of labor is inelastic, which generally is the case where the labor costs paid to that union's members are a very small proportion of the total costs of producing the finished product and where there are no good substitutes for that type of labor. One of the building crafts, the plumbers, for example, would be a good case in point. As is indicated in the discussion of restrictive practices of labor unions in Part Three, such practices are most characteristic of "sheltered," local-market lines, like the building and teaming trades, which are not producing products for a national market in competition with firms in other localities.

(4) If one producer lowers the price of his product, he is likely to sell more, but if all producers lower their prices by the same percentage (if the whole price level falls), then there may be no increase in the amount sold. In fact, a smaller total quantity may be sold because buyers expect the price to fall further and withhold their purchases in anticipation of still lower prices. Individual price movements help to adjust supply to demand, but that is not true of some movements in the general price level. Demand in general may decline as the price level falls; more goods are likely to be bought on a rising price level than on a falling one, partly because a decline in the whole level of prices is likely to lead to a decrease in money incomes. The repercussions of price changes on money incomes and total expenditures cannot be overlooked.

(5) If an individual employer raises his wage rates while other employers do not, he is likely to find that the supply of labor offered to him will increase. If all employers should raise their wage rates by an equal percentage, however, no employer would find an increase in the supply of labor offered to him. Indeed, there would

probably be a decrease in the supply of labor offered to employers, for, as real wages rise and workers' standards of living increase, they tend to demand shorter hours, their wives are more prone to give up jobs in industry, and their children remain longer in school.[1] In short, if one employer pays higher real wages, the supply of labor offered to him will increase; if all employers should pay higher real wages, the total supply of labor for sale would undoubtedly decrease. The result for a single employer is just the opposite from that for all employers.

(6) Each employer believes that a reduction in the wage rates he pays would help his business to prosper. That would be true if he could reduce his labor costs by lowering wage rates without reducing the efficiency of his labor supply, while other employers in his line of business did not reduce their labor costs. He would then, like a country which makes its products comparatively cheap to foreign purchasers by depreciating the exchange value of its currency, be in a relatively better position than he was before. But if all employers reduce their labor costs by the same percentage, no producer wins a special advantage by the wage reduction, just as no country gains a relative advantage if all countries depreciate the exchange value of their currencies by an equal percentage. All are left in the same relative position as they were before the wage reduction or exchange depreciation occurred. An all-around wage reduction is not likely to benefit any producer unless it results in a general increase in the demand for products; yet a reduction in the wage level is no more likely to increase either demand in general or the sale of labor than a reduction in the price level is likely to increase total sales or demand in general. Indeed, the chief way that reductions in the wage level are supposed to stimulate demand in general, and therefore sales, is through reductions in the price level.[2]

(7) When business in general is declining, common sense would seem to indicate that the appropriate policy for individual businessmen to pursue is one of retrenchment and curtailed expenditures. Those producers who expanded most during the preceding boom, and those enterprisers who are carrying the largest inventories, are

[1] For a more detailed discussion of the characteristics of the supply of labor, cf. Chapter 5 infra.

[2] This whole question of the relation between wages and unemployment is discussed more fully in Chapter 11. There the possibility of wage reductions increasing employment by restoring profit margins is also considered.

most likely to suffer to the greatest degree during the downswing
of the curves of general business and prices. Likewise, those banks
that expanded their credit to the largest degree during the boom
are in the most precarious position when depression sets in. The
safest policy for any individual banker or businessman during the
downswing is to become as liquid as possible. This the businessman
does by curtailing expenditures and investment and reducing inventories; the banker by calling loans, selling securities in his port-
folio, and curtailing new grants of credit so that he will not suffer
a drain of cash or reserves at the clearinghouse for checks. The
more liquid an enterpriser becomes just before and during a business recession, the more he will gain by the decline in prices, especially if he spends his liquid or cash holdings when prices have
reached the low point. To the individual during a depression it
seems sound policy to balance his budget by curtailing expenditures
as sales fall off, for during a business downswing any indebtedness
incurred because of an unbalanced budget becomes a greater and
greater real burden as prices fall and sales decline.

If demand in general is falling off, a particular producer may
be certain that any increase in his own outlays or expenditures will
not cause a corresponding increase in the market demand for his
particular product or products, though it may have a favorable
effect on demand in general. The same is true of expansion by a
particular bank during a period of general credit contraction. The
individual producer or banker, because he represents such a minute
section of the total economy, is powerless to change general business conditions merely by his own policies, or even to cause a significant increase in the demand for his own products or services.
Only a very small proportion of any increase in his payroll will
return directly to him in the form of increased sales. From the
individual's point of view, the appropriate policy seems to be to
contract rather than to expand, to swim in the same direction with
the general stream of business rather than against it. And if businessmen in general pursue a policy of retrenchment, that very fact tends
to cause general business to decline further and makes their policies
seem to have been the appropriate ones. Costs to one man are income
to others, so that the income of the whole nation is but the counterpart of all expenditures in the nation. Restriction of expenditures,
therefore, means restricting our incomes, which, in a vicious spiral,

may lead to further restriction of expenditures and so on. Businessmen, by their own policies of curtailment of expenditures, help to
deepen the depression and to intensify their own difficulties. Economy, by causing economic resources to be idle, may lead to social
waste.[1]

Though, in the face of shrinking money incomes and expenditures, further curtailment of expenditures may be individually
"sound" business, judged by its effect on society in general and
the national economy it seems essentially "unsound." Policies
that seem so sound to individuals—to reduce expenditures, to increase one's cash position, and to save although the savings lie
idle—are suicidal when followed by everyone. Though it may be
"sound" for an individual bank to contract its credit when the
banking system as a whole is contracting credit, such contraction
by banks tends to destroy part of the nation's supply of money
(checking accounts), to depress the price level, to reduce asset
values, to increase business insolvency, and to spread destruction
throughout the banking system. Not infrequently, "sound"
finance causes widespread bankruptcy.

Especially in the field of labor is reasoning by analogy from the
case of the private individual to that of the nation in general likely
to lead one to questionable conclusions. Wage rates are prices;
wage costs are a large part of the nation's income; and the relation between the demand for products and payroll expenditures is
very direct. Consequently, the whole demand-and-supply analysis,
which applies only to a single product and assumes that other
things (demand in general and all other prices) remain the same,
is well-nigh useless in reasoning on broad national policies such as
the proper wage level, the proper program to stimulate employment, or the proper expenditure program for the whole economy,
and especially the national government, to pursue.

The student should, therefore, be chary of simple, common-sense
answers to labor problems, for frequently the economics of labor
differs from the economics of some commodity such as Listerine or
linseed oil. In labor economics, the answer for the whole problem
may not be simply the sum of the separate parts, so attempts to
apply the individual approach and viewpoint in labor are likely
to prove rather fruitless and to lead to false notions.

[1] Cf. Joan Robinson, op. cit., pp. 43–49.

MARKET ANALYSIS IN LABOR [1]

Economists and the market. Economics is the study of market processes. The economist analyzes such market phenomena as demand, supply, profit, cost of production, sales, and price, which really is the heart of the market. He formulates hypotheses or economic "laws," which attempt to explain how the market operates under certain assumed conditions; and he makes realistic studies of business institutions and methods which influence market operations, in order to see how closely his assumptions correspond to present-day facts. It is from such studies of the function of markets today that the economist attempts to explain wage rates, foreign-exchange rates, the incidence and effects of taxation, internal and international trade, employment, the distribution of income, bank credit, the business cycle, savings, investment, and other economic matters. Because most things in this world have their price and enter into money transactions, market processes largely govern our economic behavior and mold our lives. Markets determine what people will work at, what plants will be idle, what will be produced, and what will not be produced. Markets set the Japanese to work making toys, the Brazilians to growing coffee, and show girls to performing on the stage; they determine whether son can go to college, whether crops will be harvested, and how much employment the man next door will have next week.

Economic analysis is built around the assumption that markets are impersonal, that all buying and selling, hiring and firing, production and employment, promotion and demotion are based on objective, economic considerations. It presupposes that demand, supply, and price are determined by impersonal market forces and are not subject to the control of any person or particular group of persons acting together in a united front, for, if the market were subject to purely personal decision, the economist could formulate no "laws" or generalizations concerning market processes. In so far as price is determined by personal fiat, or is subject to someone's arbitrary caprice, the market is not objective, and personal dictatorship rather than an impersonal market rules in economic affairs.

Economists are especially interested in the intricate relationships

[1] Part of the discussion in this section is based on Barbara Wootton, *Lament for Economics*, 1938.

between various markets. They attempt to explain how a rise in the price of one commodity or factor of production will affect the demand for other commodities or factors of production. It is, however, in this broader realm of analysis of the interrelations between markets that economic reasoning is so tenuous and so subject to some of the errors indicated in the previous section of this chapter. With an increase in the number of markets and, therefore, in the factors under consideration, any concrete problem is likely to be very complex.

Limitations to market analysis in labor. (1) Generalization is especially difficult when each problem that arises may be unique because it presents a slightly different combination of factors or a new set of circumstances. Labor problems usually involve not only a whole network of markets but also a large number of human beings, who may act or react in different patterns under varying circumstances. Consequently, there are few "pat" answers to labor issues. Indeed, sometimes the repercussions of a particular labor policy on distant markets (the secondary effects) may be more significant than the primary effects in the labor market first affected. For instance, a 15-per-cent cut in wage rates on the railroads would not only have different effects at one stage in the business cycle than at another, but such a reduction might affect the sales in various branches of industry throughout the nation. The effect of such a wage cut on purchases of commodities might be more important than its effect on the railroad industry. Consequently, broad and sweeping generalizations in the field of labor are likely to be of little practical value; most labor problems must be considered on their particular merits and on the basis of the existing circumstances.

Market analysis in the field of labor faces other limitations. Economists and laymen, either consciously or unconsciously, are inclined to assume that the market distributes economic rewards in an impartial manner and that the answer given by the action of market forces is correct. They are likely to view the market as a place in which, through competition and individual choice, the best products and most efficient producers win out. In this view, the market represents a sort of consumers' plebiscite, with each person's purchases representing a vote for products according to their merits as he sees them.

(2) In considering limitations to the market as a fair and satisfactory instrument for determining economic affairs, it is important to note that persons do not have an equal vote in the market, so that market recordings are perverted by inequalities in the distribution of wealth and income. Some people enjoy great power in the market by virtue of accumulated or inherited wealth. Consequently, the man who cares for the Pekinese puppies of an American heiress may receive in the market three times as much per week for his services as does a farm hand, but one might hesitate to say that the services of the puppy caretaker were three times as valuable to society as those of the farm hand. A plebiscite in which some enjoy plural voting may seem unfair. Though the rich frequently talk of democracy, equal opportunity, and the blessings of beginning at the bottom, they customarily see to it that their offspring have a head start in the form of a large inheritance.

(3) There are many things for which one simply cannot cast dollar votes in the market. For instance, it is almost impossible through individual purchases in the market to bring about a more equal distribution of the wealth, a stable price level, shorter working hours, more economic security, more social equality, or a system of 100-per-cent reserves behind our money, and to prevent advertising on the radio, the pollution of streams, the business cycle and unemployment, or ugliness in the form of billboards, junk heaps, unsightly buildings, and other eyesores. Such dissatisfactions cannot find ready expression through the market. Many of the broad social and economic desires of mankind, such as the desire for a larger measure of economic security, simply cannot be chopped up into small particles—the only form in which the market can handle problems. Though as individuals we may ardently wish for more security, there is no way by which we can, so to speak, bid up the value of security in the market place, so that the economic system will produce steady incomes for the working population.

(4) To many problems the market mechanism fails to supply satisfactory answers, so that reliance on the market in such cases might seem to hold up "progress." For instance, we cannot rely entirely upon the market to furnish a satisfactory educational system or sufficient library, park, and museum facilities, or the proper amount of scientific research. Our whole educational system has been, and is, subsidized from tax money and by private

philanthropy because reliance upon market forces of demand and supply would fail to furnish a well-educated and intelligent population. Children are forced to go to school, students in college are forced to take certain subjects, and the grades that they receive are determined, not by the market but by the professor. A university run on market principles would presumably support itself solely from tuition fees. The students could take whatever courses they wished and the professors could teach what they wished, with each professor's income consisting simply of so much for each student selecting his courses, or "whatever the traffic would bear." There would be no quizzes, for the market process does not require written examinations. The results of a professor's research would not be published unless there would be enough sales to make it pay.

From a purely market point of view, most economists are uneconomic and most economic research represents an uneconomic use of some of the nation's productive resources. Economists and economic studies usually have to be subsidized, at least in part, from tax money or private gifts. They could not pay their own way in a purely market economy. The market is relatively indifferent to the services of academic or learned men.

All governmental activities represent a refusal to rely upon the market. The government establishes courts, highways, a police force, credit institutions, tariff restrictions, an army, relief agencies, social services and institutions, social insurance, public works, public health services, conservation bureaus, public utility commissions, etc., because there are so many problems that market forces cannot solve or that the market does not seem to solve in a satisfactory manner. Because governmental activities are not governed by the market, the businessman, whose activities are guided by market forces, distrusts government and demands, sometimes foolishly, that governmental activities conform to business (market) rules and standards. There are, however, many business issues that are not decided by market forces, and bureaucracy is found in business as well as in the government. Advancement, demotion, and discharge in business may be determined by favoritism, personal prejudice, or office politics, and not according to economic merit. Someone at the top, not the market, must decide what the hours of work and speed of machine operations shall be. Indeed, management in business may represent personal dictatorship to the same extent as does management in the army, which is not controlled by market forces.

Many matters that are important to the worker, as W. H. Hutt states, "are not adequately determined by the market process— hours of work and conditions of work are things that intimately concern workmen and are best decided collectively." [1] Employers may not be interested in the long-run effects of hours and working conditions, because they ordinarily can recruit a new working force at any time and because employers usually lack accurate knowledge of the relationship between poor working conditions and labor turnover, or between long working hours and output. In many cases a reduction of working hours, forced by law or labor unions, has resulted in a larger output.[2] In other words, employers had been getting less for their payroll than they would have received by shortening the hours of work from 12 to 10 or from 10 to 8 a day. The market failed to lead to the most efficient work period because normally the workers in a plant must all work the same number of hours. Each worker is not free to bargain with the employer about the number of hours a day he will work, nor is the employer likely to experiment by trying working days of varying lengths, because it usually takes some time for a reduction in the working hours to improve the health, morale, and efficiency of the workers.

(5) The market is a poor provider for future generations because it fails to prevent wasteful exploitation of human and natural resources. In the case of natural resources, the government must step in to conserve our forests, our oil reserves, and our soil from wasteful practices in the cutting of timber, in the drilling of oil wells, or in the use of land. The government must prevent actions and methods of production which are most appropriate according to the market, but which cause soil erosion, dust bowls, or similar social evils.

Market forces may also result in wasteful use of human resources.

[1] W. H. Hutt, *The Theory of Collective Bargaining*, 1930, p. 107.

[2] *Cf.* Chapter 13 *infra*. J. R. Hicks writes of England: "The long hours worked in the early days of the Industrial Revolution are notorious; they were reduced, it is well known, mainly by State regulation and Trade Union action. It was found, after they had been reduced that 'the output of eleven hours' work might be greater than that of twelve.' Employers had been working at more than the output optimum, without realising it." *The Theory of Wages*, 1935, pp. 106–107.

In general, the market does not allow for human costs or human depreciation, except in a slave economy where the employer owns the worker as well as the capital equipment and must buy a new worker when the old one wears out.   In a market economy only money costs count; human costs, such as unemployment through displacement by labor-saving machinery, or deformed bodies and stunted minds resulting from child labor, work injuries, and occupational diseases, do not affect economic action and policies unless they somehow enter money costs.   For example, in deciding whether to install a new machine, the employer normally makes little or no allowance for the effects of that machine upon his workers—whether the machine may injure their health or separate some of them from their jobs.   Prior to the passage of unemployment-insurance laws, unemployment resulting from the introduction of labor-saving machinery was not a money cost to the employer, though it represented a cost to society and to the workers displaced.   With the rise of the factory system in early nineteenth-century England, market forces resulted in widespread employment of young children in factories for 12 to 16 hours a day.   As is indicated in the next chapter, the government had to pass restrictive factory legislation because free markets were tending to make some of the English workers into a deformed and uneducated group.   From a national or social point of view, child labor and sweatshops, by stunting the development of body and intellect, may mean an uneconomic use of the nation's human resources.

The state is even more interested in the proper development and use of human resources than it is in natural resources.   It is interested in improving its man power and in developing good citizens.   The labor union, through educational activities and by encouraging an independent spirit amongst wage-earners, may help to produce more independent and self-respecting citizens.[1]

[1] Alfred Marshall, the noted English economist, wrote: ". . . the Unions have an effective answer to the argument, recently given, that any check to the growth of capital caused by a rise of wages at the expense of profits is likely to be cumulative. If they do what they can to make labour honest and hearty, they can reply that an addition to the wages of their trade is as likely to be invested in the Personal Capital of themselves and their children, as an increase in profits is to be invested in Material Capital: that from the national point of view persons are at least as remunerative a field of investment as things: and that investments in persons are cumulative in their effects from year to year and from generation to generation." *Elements of Economics of Industry*, vol. 1 (second edition), 1898, p. 419.

(6) Often markets are not objective but are under the control of some person or group of persons. Only where the market is perfect can it be objective and impartial. A perfect market is one in which a homogeneous or standardized product is bought and sold by so many buyers and sellers acting independently that the actions of any buyer or seller have only a negligible effect upon the market or the market price. Such perfect markets are rare. Practically the only markets closely approaching a perfect market are our organized commodity exchanges, like the Chicago Board of Trade, and the security exchanges, like the New York Stock Exchange. In the case of all trade-marked commodities there is but one seller of the product. In villages and rural areas there may be but one retailer of a product or but one seller of banking services. In company towns there may be but one buyer of labor services— the company. In most localities there is but one seller of telephone, gas, electric, and water services. Frequently there is but one seller of transportation services (train or bus) between two towns. Often the seller of labor services (say a locomotive engineer, machinist, or printer) can find but one or two buyers of that particular service in his vicinity. Where there are few buyers or sellers, the market is imperfect; and the more imperfect the market, the more it is likely to be subject to personal domination and control. In short, imperfect markets contain monopolistic elements, which can make the market or market price perform more or less as they wish.

Some of our most imperfect markets are labor markets. The imperfections and monopolistic elements in such markets are discussed in detail in Chapter 5. Here it is sufficient to repeat that there are probably 15 times as many sellers as regular buyers of labor and to point out that often there is but one buyer of a certain kind of labor service in a given locality—a buyer's monopoly or monopsony. Not only are local buyers of labor frequently few in number but, as Adam Smith pointed out long ago, they may not engage in competition with one another for workers by bidding up wage rates. The employer quotes the price he will pay for labor, and the wage rate he sets is usually what he considers to be "the prevailing rate" in the locality for that type of work, or it may be a rate somewhat below "the prevailing rate." As wage investigations indicate, there are often wide and illogical variations in the payment for identical work in the same locality and sometimes in the same plant.[1]

Such widespread variations in price would not occur in an organized commodity market. There is often a great deal of difference between selling a product one makes and selling one's labor, even though Justice Sutherland in *Adkins* v. *Children's Hospital*[2] maintained that "in principle there can be no difference between the case of selling labor and the case of selling goods." The sale of goods in the open market leaves the seller a relatively free and independent individual, but the sale by a wage-earner of his whole working time to one employer leaves him dependent upon one buyer who "bosses" him at work.

Though, as Alfred Marshall pointed out, it matters not to the seller of bricks whether they are used in a palace or in an odorous sewer, it matters a great deal to a seller of labor, such as a bricklayer, where and how his services are used, for labor services are inseparable from the laborer's person. Conditions affecting the use of his labor also affect him as an individual; his future fortune partly depends upon the use or abuse of his person by the buyer. This is one of the reasons that labor leaders deny that "the labor of a human being is a commodity or article of commerce."[3] State statutes providing that labor be paid for in cash or negotiable checks have been upheld as constitutional by the U. S. Supreme Court, including Justice Sutherland, but it is inconceivable that he or the Court would uphold a law forbidding the purchase of plows with store orders, merchandise, or other substitutes for cash.

The reasoning that applies to a commodity may not always apply so effectively and without modification to labor. Labor markets are often more imperfect than commodity markets. Generally, it is easier for buyers to dominate the labor market and control the price of labor than it is for them to control the markets and prices

[1] *Cf.*, for instance, *Variations in Wage Rates under Corresponding Conditions*, U. S. Department of Labor, Women's Bureau, Bulletin 122, 1935, p. 2, and p. 4 where it is stated: "Even when allowance for all factors that might cause the variations had been made, comparisons made in plants under conditions as nearly identical as obtainable showed differences in payment so marked as to be attributable only to lack of wage standards." *Cf.* also Chapter 5 *infra*.

[2] (1923), 261 U. S. 525.

[3] The Clayton Act, passed by Congress in 1914, states: "The labor of a human being is not a commodity or article of commerce" and the covenant of the League of Nations affirms the proposition that "labour is not merely a commodity."

of standard commodities. Control of labor markets is, indeed, the normal thing, whether workers are unorganized or organized.

It is because of these limitations and imperfections of the market that the state legislatures and the Congress pass labor legislation. It is because the market either does not settle many vital issues or is dominated by employers that workers organize for collective bargaining. The failure of the market to function satisfactorily has led to legislation on social security, minimum wages, maximum hours, industrial accidents, occupational diseases, and labor relations, as well as to agreements between labor unions and employers limiting the employer's right to hire, fire, and work his men as he pleases.

The very fact that we have widespread unemployment for long periods of time indicates that the market is not functioning perfectly. If people do not buy commodities and services with their dollars, or if they cast their dollar votes only slowly, the whole exchange mechanism breaks down, for in a market economy each person is dependent for a livelihood upon the purchases of others. When buying stops, selling stops also, for every purchase is a sale. In countries where the market no longer dictates to industry, like Russia and, to some extent, Germany, and in those spheres of activity not governed by the market, such as housework or the army, there is no involuntary unemployment. One of the advantages of personal dictatorship and control of all industry is that it does not involve reliance upon the money votes of many persons in the market place in order to keep the wheels of industry whirling. Of course, dictatorship is generally accompanied by many social and personal disadvantages, including limitations on personal freedom.

SHORT- AND LONG-RUN ANALYSIS IN LABOR

In reasoning about labor problems it is necessary to state clearly whether one's conclusions apply to the immediate future or are valid only after a period, sufficient for complete adjustment to the economic change, has elapsed. Frequently, the conclusion for the immediate future (the short run) may be quite different from the conclusion for the long run, when the employer and the employees have had time to make full adjustments to such a change as a decline in price. In the long run, adjustments can be made through changes in the investment or productive capacity of the industry, whereas short-run adjustments involve changes in production at existing capacity. Costs that are fixed in the short run may be varied in the long run, and circumstances that would bankrupt an employer over a long period of time might not do so in the short run.

Because labor represents a cost to employers, it is important that the student of labor understand the nature of costs. In general, costs may be classified as either fixed costs, which are a constant total sum regardless of the rate of output up to full capacity of the plant, and variable costs, the total amount of which varies directly with the number of units being produced. Fixed or overhead costs are such charges as interest on bonds and debts, depreciation, property taxes, property insurance, and the salaries of night watchmen and certain executives—charges that would have to be met even if the plant were closed up. Variable costs, on the other hand, are such charges as the cost of raw materials, of power, light, and heat, and of labor engaged directly in producing or selling the product—costs that a company could eliminate by shutting up the plant. The importance of this distinction in costs will be indicated presently.

Under our profit-and-loss system, each producer, whether a monopolist or an independent businessman with many competitors, normally strives to obtain the largest net return or maximum profit from the business, or he strives to minimize his losses when profits disappear. A producer will increase his output up to the point where the addition to total cost involved in producing the last unit (his marginal cost) is as great as the increment to his total income caused by producing that unit (his marginal receipts). He will strive to increase his output as long as marginal receipts exceed marginal cost, but he will not knowingly expand output to a point where marginal cost exceeds marginal receipts.

In the short run, of course, only variable costs alter with output changes; fixed costs cannot be avoided but must be met whether the company is operating or not. Consequently, in determining how much to produce in the short run, the employer will consider only variable costs and will strive to increase his rate of output as long as the addition to variable costs from producing another unit (his marginal variable cost) is less than the amount that another unit of product will add to his total income (his marginal receipts). Normally, the doors of no plant will be closed as long as total receipts exceed total variable costs, so that something is left over to pay on the fixed or overhead costs. Indeed, plants may be operated at full capacity for considerable periods of time even though they are being run at a loss in the sense that the returns are not large enough to pay all the overhead costs.[1]

Over a long period of time, of course, fixed costs may alter as changes are made in the amount of investment in plant and equipment. As the equipment wears out, it may not be replaced, or new purchases of equipment may exceed the rate of depreciation of the old equipment. Even in the short run, fixed costs may be changed. Whenever a company defaults on its indebtedness because of failure to earn its overhead costs, the company's financial structure is overhauled, and overhead costs are usually reduced in the process. Bondholders may become stockholders, wiping out the fixed interest charge represented by their bonds. Such a writing down of fixed-cost liabilities and asset values usually occurs whenever over a period the price of the company's product has been so low or demand so slack that overhead costs could not be met. But bankruptcy, receivership, and reorganization of the capital structure are financial matters and do not, in themselves, change the character of the physical plant or equipment. Like a sale, they simply change the ownership of the physical assets of the company.

In time, costs get into line with selling prices. This occurs through changes in the demand and supply of the product in case variable costs are out of adjustment with selling prices, or by the writing up and down of asset values where the valuation of the physical equipment of the company is out of line with present market values as determined by the prospective income of the company and the rate of interest. Indeed, costs are only prices and are determined in the same way as are other prices. Eventually cost prices become adjusted to selling prices because the action of demand and supply either causes cost prices to change, or selling prices to change, or both.

Because the rate of operations of employers is governed by marginal variable costs, it may be possible for selling prices to fall, or

[1] For a more detailed treatment of marginal costs, receipts, and output, the reader may consult one of the following: A. M. McIsaac and J. G. Smith, *Introduction to Economic Analysis*, 1937; A. I. Meyers, *Elements of Modern Economics*, 1937; E. Chamberlain, *The Theory of Monopolistic Competition* (third edition), 1938; Joan Robinson, *The Economics of Imperfect Competition*, 1933.

for employees to force a rise in wage costs, without reducing the employer's rate of operations at all. Normally, employers are meeting overhead costs and making some profit. If the employer cannot substitute land or machinery for men without completely revising his plant or his business policies, it is possible for wage rates to be increased in the short run until his total variable costs are nearly as large as his total receipts, wiping out his profits and leaving but a small sum toward his fixed costs. Even so, he would try to operate at full capacity as long as his marginal variable costs did not exceed his marginal receipts. Indeed, there are cases where an employer would try to continue operations for a time even though his marginal receipts were less than his marginal variable costs. That would be true of producers who expected a rise in the price of their product in the near future, or whose business assets (especially going-concern and good-will items) would drop in value if customers were not served and advertising ceased, or whose physical property (such as farm land, a coal mine, or certain types of machinery) would depreciate more rapidly if it were not operated than if it were in use. An employer must take all such factors into account in deciding whether to lock out his employees or to permit them to go on strike. In such cases, the employer's loss may be much greater than simply the loss of profits and the total sum of overhead costs during the period of the strike.

In the long run, of course, employers can, within limits, substitute land or machinery for men, and the productive facilities in the industry may be altered. No new money would be invested in a business that has not been earning profits or has poor prospects of earning profits in the future; and, without new investment, productive capacity in the industry would decline as existing equipment wore out. But one must bear in mind that profits may appear through the writing down of fixed debts or a reduction in the interest rate on debts as well as by a cut in variable costs. Bankruptcy or refunding of debt at a lower interest rate frequently makes profits possible. Though before 1930 a return of around six per cent was considered necessary to attract new money for investment in bonds and mortgages, plenty of money has recently been seeking investment in fixed-interest securities at figures as low as a three-per-cent yield. The same is true of profits, which seem to have no particular "normal" rate. In short, sufficient new investment might occur throughout American industry, even though interest and profit rates should be considerably below the figures which seemed "normal" to our fathers. With interest and profit, "normal" may simply be the rate to which we become accustomed.[1]

HISTORICAL APPROACH TO LABOR PROBLEMS

It is easier to understand and to judge the present after a study of the past. From history one learns how the economic system has developed from a simple economy of local markets to a complex, class-divided economy of nationwide and international markets. Not only is the student's understanding aided by such a study of the evolution of economic society from simple to complex forms, but he learns the relations between the development of economic organization and institutions on the one hand and economic doctrines on the other. False theories can only be understood in their historical setting.

From past experience the student learns the "lessons" of history; he discovers the mistakes and mistaken notions of our forefathers. Such an historical background is especially advantageous in the study of labor problems because many practical men, who distrust what they call "theory," often subscribe unconsciously to the ancient, disproved doctrines of former days. Knowledge of past periods, when the economic structure was entirely different, also gives the student a basis for viewing modern economic matters with some degree of detachment, if not with a critical eye. Finally, an understanding of past trends and experience, both here and abroad, places him in a better position to foretell what the future has in store.

It is with such purposes in mind that the next two chapters, dealing with labor history in Europe and America, were written. Other chapters will, to be sure, contain historical material, but these two introductory chapters, covering the period up to the middle of the last century, are designed to give a broad historical background for the study of American labor problems and labor relations.

[1] For further discussion of this point, see J. M. Keynes, *The General Theory of Employment, Interest and Money*, 1936, especially pp. 202–204 and 375–76; and Chapter 12 *infra*.

CHAPTER THREE

HISTORICAL BACKGROUND: ENGLAND

That free markets alone will not bring about the economic millennium is evident from the experience of England and France during the first half of the nineteenth century, when the doctrine of laissez faire was tried and found wanting. The period from 1810 to 1840 stands out in European history as the epoch during which there was the least amount of governmental intervention in economic affairs. The leading men of the time argued that market forces of demand and supply should have free reign to work their magic. They thoroughly believed that complete freedom for individual initiative and self-interest would result in the greatest social good, and they were convinced that any government interference or labor legislation would be both vicious and futile, because it would run counter to "natural law." So firmly were the people of England convinced of these economic superstitions that they repealed all laws safeguarding the workers, restricting the spread of factories, and limiting the rise of capitalism.

From bitter experience, however, the English soon learned the limitations of markets as final arbitrators of economic matters. Before long Parliament was forced to pass a new set of labor laws called Factory Acts in order to eliminate the most glaring evils and abuses that developed under this "natural order" of laissez faire. An understanding of this epoch in economic history is so important for a student of labor, as well as for advocates of the individualistic ideal who oppose labor organization and legislation, that this chapter is devoted to a discussion of labor in England during the early nineteenth century and the failure of laissez faire as an economic policy.

EARLY GOVERNMENT REGULATION

Trade practices, prices, and wages in English industry were subject to a high degree of government regulation from the eleventh to the nineteenth century, first by the medieval guilds and, after the fifteenth century, by an all-powerful national government in the hands of the Tudors. Much the same was true in France where, following regulation by the guilds, Colbert instituted, in the middle of the seventeenth century, a series of national acts regulating practically every detail of economic life.

Guilds. The merchant and craft guilds in the Middle Ages made regulations to control all sales and production within the town or city. Markets from the eleventh to the sixteenth century in England were mostly local. These guild rules or fair trade practices forbade usury, speculation, cornering of the market, or profiting by resale at a higher price. The guild in each line of business established a fixed "just" price for the product, and journeymen workers had to be paid a set "just" wage. The quality of the product was maintained by regulations governing the materials to be used, the hours of work, and working conditions in the master's shop, together with the requirement that the worker serve a certain period of apprenticeship in order to qualify as a master or member of a particular guild. These municipal rules of the guilds—mostly the common law of that time—were enforced upon all business establishments by the guild wardens.

Under the guild system there was a fair degree of economic and political equality. Every master craftsman was a worker who possessed his own productive equipment; none was permitted to become merely a middleman or a capitalistic employer. Each master had to produce his own wares—from raw material to finished product—and the products were sold directly to the consumer from the master's own home, which served as a store, workshop, and dwelling. Under these circumstances, no one producer could obtain a major share of the local market. Each businessman had to make his product himself and to sell it at the established "just" price; he could not introduce a change in the technique of production without the permission of the guild. With such restriction on competition and avarice, each guildsman was practically assured of some work, and there was no unemployment problem.

Along with a large measure of economic security, the medieval craftsman had personal pride in his product—though it was a long time before cobblers discovered that there is a difference between the left and the right foot. The craftsmen got personal satisfaction in creating and selling a praiseworthy product. The guilds also played an important part in the social life of the town, and guild funds were used to assist widows, orphans, and the poor.

As trade and the use of money increased, local markets expanded into nationwide markets, so that the regulating function gradually was transferred from the local guilds to the national government. In the sixteenth century under the Tudors, a series of national acts were passed in England similar to the former guild regulations. These acts were directed against the new and expanding capitalism that was destroying the old guild system.

The guilds declined because they could not meet the competition of a new class of middlemen, known as merchant capitalists. The old spirit of religion, which had served to enforce "just" prices and "just" wages, gave way before the pursuit of profit by these first capitalists. So characteristic was the merchant capitalist of this time that, when in 1712 a pamphleteer depicted an English clothier talking cloth prices and termed him "John Bull," the name and character were adopted as symbolic.

Domestic system. These merchant capitalists first hired craftsmen to make products at home (hence the term, domestic system); such products the merchant capitalist then sold to consumers. In this way the worker craftsman was separated from the consumer market for his product. Before long, the merchant capitalist was furnishing the worker with raw materials and machinery and splitting up the old crafts into their component processes, with workers concentrating upon only one operation. With such a division of old crafts, unskilled workers and their families began to take over work formerly done only by master craftsmen. After the merchant capitalist had acquired control of the raw materials, the tools of production, and the market for the product, the craftsman became merely a "hired hand" dependent upon an employer for most of his livelihood. Whenever the capitalist found it unprofitable to hire him, the specialized worker had to fall back upon his small plot of land, for he was now out of touch with the market, owned no capital equipment, and was trained in but one stage in the production of a single commodity. With specialization and production by a wage-earning class, periodic depressions commenced to occur, and unemployment for the first time became a troublesome national problem. The worker was dependent upon the capitalist for work and wages, and the operations of the capitalist fluctuated with a wayward market for the product.

National regulation of industry. The new capitalism was strenuously opposed by English authorities when it first appeared. To prevent the concentration of industry in the hands of capitalists and the rise of a destitute proletariat, Parliament passed laws regulating industry and industrial relations. These laws prohibited the pursuit of certain occupations in areas outside the jurisdiction of the guilds, restricted the movement of workers away from the towns, and limited both the number of weavers a clothier might hire and the number of looms per weaver. The Statute of Artificers (1563) forbade any person to practice a recognized craft or occupation within the realm of England who had not served a seven-years' apprenticeship, and also provided that all wages should be fixed yearly by the justices of the peace in every shire and by mayors or others in each city. In 1773 Parliament likewise passed the Spitalfields Weavers Act under which the mayor and justices were "to settle and regulate the wages of persons employed in Silk Manufacture" in London.

During the seventeenth century, wages were regularly fixed each year under the Statute of Artificers, designed to assure the payment not merely of a living wage but of real wages as high as those earned before the rise in prices. These governmentally decreed wage rates were apparently accepted by employers, but during the eighteenth century the fixing of wages by the justices and mayors became less regular. By the time that Adam Smith published *The Wealth of Nations* (1776), such wage-fixing by government agencies was of little significance. Upon petition of the clothiers, an act was passed in 1757 exempting the woolen trade, England's greatest industry, from the Statute of Artificers, and in 1813 the wage-fixing clauses of the Statute were entirely repealed.

During this same period of national regulation of industry, England pursued the trade policy called mercantilism. Laws were passed to regulate imports, exports, and shipping, so that England would have a "favorable" balance of trade (commodity exports exceeding commodity imports) with imports of precious metals making up the trade deficit. This English policy of mercantilism was one of the important factors that gave rise to the American Revolutionary War.

THE TRIUMPH OF LAISSEZ FAIRE

Contemporary authorities from Daniel Defoe to Adam Smith refer, with some exaggeration, to the period from 1700 to 1775 as a veritable golden age for industrial labor in England. Yet during the next half-century from 1775 to 1825, when methods of production were so changed and improved that the period is known as the Industrial Revolution, the lot of a part of the English laboring class apparently failed to improve.

Industrial Revolution.   Studies of modern labor problems usually begin with this period of rapid industrial change in England that ushered in the factory system. Between 1775 and 1785 the steam engine and spinning and weaving machines were invented and firmly established in English manufacturing. Consequently, the cost of making yarn fell more than 85 per cent between 1779 and 1812.[1] By 1813 as many as 2,400 power looms were in use in England, and in 1833 there were 85,000.[2] The increased use of machinery after 1770 is also indicated by the following figures showing the annual production of pig iron in Great Britain: [3]

1720	25,000 tons
1770	32,000
1800	156,000
1830	653,400
1860	3,826,700

By 1800 the steam engine was in use in 84 cotton mills, 30 coal mines, 22 copper mines, 28 foundries, and 17 breweries.[4] Yet this new machinery, designed to free men's bodies and to increase their living standards, tended in some cases to injure their bodies, to depress their wages, and to force entire families to work in factories from 12 to 17 hours a day. Of course, the adverse effects of the Industrial Revolution were felt directly by only a part of the working population, because a majority of the working people even in 1830 were still domestic or workshop workers. However, working and living conditions for most workers seem to have been little

[1] A. P. Usher, *An Introduction to the Industrial History of England*, 1920, p. 310.
[2] *Ibid.*, p. 302.
[3] W. Bowden, M. Karpovich, and A. P. Usher, *An Economic History of Europe Since 1750*, 1937, pp. 119, 385.
[4] L. Huberman, *Man's Worldly Goods*, 1936, p. 179.

better in the early decades of the nineteenth century than they were half a century earlier under the domestic system.[1]

Repeal of statutory safeguards. The suffering of certain working groups was intensified during the Industrial Revolution in England because the old statutes, which afforded some protection to the workers, were repealed. Until well past the middle of the eighteenth century, it was generally believed desirable for the government to regulate economic behavior for the purpose of promoting the general welfare of the nation. In the latter part of the century, however, a new social theory and philosophy of government swept over the western world. According to this new philosophy, the general welfare was best served when the government kept its hands off economic matters and permitted each individual to pursue his own selfish interests, subject only to the forces of competition in a free market. Men became convinced that government action in the economic realm was both futile and vicious in that it would be contrary to "natural" law and "natural" forces.

This new social philosophy first arose in France as an extreme reaction against the excessive state regulation of industry begun by Colbert. In France during most of the eighteenth century, industry was minutely regulated by codes, which dictated the kind, quality, and price of each commodity produced and were enforced by an army of state inspectors. The abolition of such hampering restrictions and the freeing of trade was advocated by the first "school" of economists, the French Physiocrats, under the leadership of Francis Quesnay, who died two years before Adam Smith published his *Wealth of Nations*. The eighteenth century worshiped nature, and physiocracy means "the rule of nature." The Physiocrats believed that natural laws governed human societies as well as the physical world and that, in the "natural order," there was a harmony of interests between men, whereas government interference was artificial and caused conflict. Consequently, they adopted the motto of "laissez faire"—let alone.

This theory of laissez faire—let the market, not the government, control—along with the doctrine of economic harmonies, was adopted by Adam Smith directly from the Physiocrats, some of

[1] *Cf.* J. L. Hammond, "Industrial Revolution and Discontent," *Economic History Review*, vol. 2 (January 1930), pp. 215-28. For a conflicting view, *cf.* J. H. Clapham, *An Economic History of Modern Britain, The Early Railway Age 1820-1850*, 1926, Chapter 14, especially pp. 561, 602.

whom he had known personally. Smith believed that when "all systems either of preference or of restraint" are completely abolished, "the obvious and simple system of natural liberty establishes itself of its own accord," and he thought that each man pursuing his own self-interest is "led by an invisible hand to promote an end which was no part of his intention"—the general welfare of the nation. It is easy to understand why parts of the *Wealth of Nations* soon became the businessman's bible, though not the part in which Smith pointed out that high wages increased the efficiency of labor so that "where wages are high, we shall always find the workmen more active, diligent, and expeditious than where they are low."

With the spread of this doctrine of the supernaturalism of the "natural" order and "natural" forces, the government began to cease interfering with the relations between masters and men, and statutes regulating industry were abolished. In 1814 the famous Statute of Artificers was repealed; in 1815 the Assize of Bread in London, regulating baking and retail trade, was withdrawn; and in 1816 the income tax was abolished as an unwarranted interference with the natural liberty of individuals, at a time when about half of the laborer's wages went for taxes.[1] In 1799 and 1800 laws were passed prohibiting any labor organization or union of workers to protect themselves, for such organizations were considered to be a violation of natural liberty and contrary to the "laws" of economics. When the economist David Ricardo, as a member of Parliament, demanded the repeal of the Spitalfields Act regulating the wages of silk weavers, he said: "The principles of true political economy never changed, and those who did not understand that science had better say nothing about it." The Act was repealed in 1824.

This was an age in which economic "laws" were considered immutable and were supposed to work with mechanical precision. Probably in no other period of history were economists and their doctrines so popular, and with good reason, for their theories were so comforting to the conscience of the wealthy. Malthus, in theorizing about population, subtly suggested that the poor themselves were responsible for their poverty and that misery was the medicine of nature for eliminating surplus people. In fact, Darwin drew important elements of his theory of natural selection from Malthus,

---

[1] A. Toynbee, *Lectures on the Industrial Revolution of the Eighteenth Century in England,* new impression, 1928, p. 107.

who used the very phrase "struggle for existence" in his *Essay on Population*. Both Malthus and Ricardo explained that wages tended always to remain close to the level of subsistence. "The natural price of labor," wrote Ricardo, "is that price which is necessary to enable the labourers to subsist, and to perpetuate their race without either increase or diminution." The pay for labor was supposed to be fixed by such "natural laws"—Ricardo compared his economic laws to the law of gravity. Any attempt to increase the share of the national income going to laborers, it was argued, would inflict injury upon the workers themselves. No wonder this dogma of despair earned for such political economy the title of "the dismal science."

This economic doctrine of complacent pessimism was well received. The names of Malthus and Adam Smith were as familiar in Parliamentary discussion as the names of Cicero and Virgil. The best of English society extended a warm welcome to the apostles of this economic fatalism. Ladies of distinction popularized the doctrines of Ricardo and Malthus in newspaper articles, popular stories, and in conversations with a certain "young Caroline," which had a wide vogue. In fact, a contemporary of Ricardo wrote that distinguished ladies, before engaging a governess for their children, would inquire about her competence to teach political economy.[1]

A number of contemporary economists sharply criticized the edifice of dreary doctrine erected by Malthus and Ricardo and embellished by McCulloch and Mill. In the two decades following the publication of Ricardo's *Principles of Political Economy and Taxation* (1817), a number of writers severely attacked his teachings and put forth theories of their own which contained much of the modern doctrines of marginal cost, marginal utility, and marginal productivity. But these more modern doctrines, put forth by such writers as John Craig (1821), Samuel Bailey (1825), Professor M. Longfield (1833), and Sir George Ramsay (1836), were branded as unorthodox; and their writings were disregarded and neglected until unearthed almost a century later by Professor E. R. A. Seligman.[2] Such critics were ignored in their day because they wrote

[1] C. Gide and C. Rist, *A History of Economic Doctrines*, translated by R. Richards from the 1913 revised edition, undated, p. 119.

[2] "On Some Neglected British Economists," *Economic Journal*, vol. 13 (1903), pp. 335–63 and 511–35.

that high wages and high profits were in fact frequently coexistent, because they questioned the existence of any "natural or necessary price of labour" or of any fixed wage fund which would not permit an increase in total wages, and because they pointed out that the real cause of variations in wages and profits was the productivity of labor and industry. As Professor Seligman says, they had virtually "the modern theory of the economy of high wages," but such doctrine was unpopular at a time when people believed in "a strange system which would give as little as possible to by far the most numerous body of all, the labourers." [1]

There is a struggle for existence and survival in the realm of ideas as well as in the physical world, and the most fitting doctrines generally win out—those which fit best into the prejudices of the ruling groups in society. Employers found no difficulty in believing economists when they said that "the capitalist, who consults his own interest, always works for that of the nation." [2]

Class bias of classical economics. The effects of environment upon economic doctrines are perhaps best illustrated by Malthus and Ricardo. Ricardo's father was a stockbroker, and, following in his father's footsteps, Ricardo made a fortune on the London Stock Exchange. Malthus was a churchman whose heart and home were in the country. His education and environment gave him both a familiarity with agricultural needs and a keen interest in the prosperity of landowners and land cultivators. Both believed in the same "law" of land rent, which they independently discovered and which is known as the Ricardian theory of rent. Reasoning on the basis of this rent doctrine, Ricardo (the city man) concluded that "the interest of the landlord is always opposed to that of the consumer and the manufacturer" (all other groups in the state); whereas Malthus (the country preacher and professor), protesting against Ricardo's conclusion, asserted "that the interest of no other class in the state is so nearly and necessarily connected with its wealth and power, as the interest of the landlord"— "the prosperity or adversity of the one [the landlord] involves the prosperity or adversity of the other [the state]." [3]

[1] *Ibid.*, pp. 355 and 523.

[2] S. de Sismondi, *De la Richesse Commerciale*, vol. 2, 1803, p. 152.

[3] T. R. Malthus, *Principles of Political Economy*, 1821, pp. 160, 176. For a discussion of this point see "Malthus and Ricardo" in Simon N. Patten, *Essays in Economic Theory*, edited by R. G. Tugwell, 1923, pp. 19–32.

Neither Ricardo nor Malthus had any vital connections with the laboring groups, so they could also agree in their general notions about wages. Both were convinced that labor unions were a foolish, if not a wicked, resistance to the natural and inexorable laws of the economists. Both believed that wages depend upon the ratio between population and capital. Ricardo, on the basis of Malthus' generalizations concerning population, thought that the condition of the laboring classes was certain to become worse in the future with population increasing faster than capital. Ricardo presumably was led to this erroneous conclusion by the fact that the real wages of some working groups had been falling in England. For example, the real wages of artisans in London fell more than 15 per cent between the decades 1780–1790 and 1810–1820.[1]

Malthus, on the basis of this same ratio between population and capital, proposed the famous wage-fund doctrine, the superstition which was used by economists, manufacturers, and politicians from Malthus' time until 1870 to prove the folly of trade-unionism and the viciousness of any agitation for higher pay or shorter hours. There are also traces of the wage-fund doctrine in Ricardo's writings. According to this doctrine, wages are paid only from a fund created by past accumulations of capital, which presumably meant food, clothes, and other consumers' goods. At any particular time, this amount of stored-up capital, resulting from savings and destined only for the employment of labor, was assumed to be fixed by causes beyond the control of either the employer or the workers. As J. S. Mill put it: "More than that amount it is assumed that the wage-receiving class cannot possibly divide among them; that amount and no less, they cannot possibly fail to obtain. So that the sum to be divided being fixed, the wages of each depend solely on the divisor, the number of participants."[2] The workingman was looked upon as a divisor and not as a multiplier or producer. The only hope that the leading English economists held out to the workers for over 50 years was that, since the workingman could not increase the dividend, he should strive to reduce the divisor—the working population.

This wage-fund myth, the stock reply to all demands of workers,

[1] Rufus S. Tucker, "Real Wages of Artisans in London, 1729–1935," *Journal of the American Statistical Association*, vol. 31 (March 1936), pp. 78–79.

[2] Mill, "Thornton on Labour and Its Claims," *Fortnightly Review*, vol. 11 (May 1869), p. 515. The various theories of wages are discussed more fully in Chapter 7 *infra*.

was attacked as early as 1825. In that year Thomas Hodgskin wrote: "As far as food, drink, and clothing are concerned, it is quite plain that no species of labourer depends on any previously prepared stock, for, in fact, no such stock exists; but every species of labourer does constantly, and at all times, depend for his supplies on the co-existing labour of some other labourers." He also questioned the validity of any rigid law of wages under capitalism where, with division of labor, the output is the joint product of a number of factors so that "there is no longer anything which we can call the natural reward of individual labour." [1] But Hodgskin's attack was disregarded, as was that of John F. Bray, who in 1839 also criticized the wage-fund theory.

The falsity of the wage-fund theory was first generally recognized after J. S. Mill, its most distinguished advocate, confessed in 1869 that the theory was erroneous. Mill wrote: "The doctrine hitherto taught by all or most economists (including myself) which denied it to be possible that trade combinations can raise wages, or which limited their operations in that respect to the somewhat earlier attainment of a rise which the competition of the market would have produced without them—this doctrine is deprived of its scientific foundation, and must be thrown aside." [2]

In view of the theories of the classical economists from Adam Smith to J. S. Mill and the use to which they were put by dominant social groups in England, it is no wonder that the working population became wary of economic doctrines and came to consider political economy a weapon of the wealthy against the workingman. In 1873 the economist J. E. Cairnes pointed out that economics had been a tool of the vested interests, when he wrote:

Political Economy too often makes its appearance, especially in its approaches to the working classes, in the guise of a dogmatic code of cut-and-dried rules, a system promulgating decrees, "sanctioning" one social arrangement, "condemning" another, requiring from men not consideration, but obedience. Now when we take into account the sort of decrees which are ordinarily given to the world in the name of Political Economy—decrees which I think I may say in the main amount to a handsome ratification of the existing form of society as approximately perfect—I think we shall be able to understand the repugnance, and even violent

[1] H. S. Foxwell, "Introduction" to Anton Menger's *The Right to the Whole Produce of Labor*, 1899, pp. lviii, lx.
[2] Mill, *op. cit.*, p. 517.

opposition, manifested toward it by people who have their own reasons for not cherishing that unbounded admiration for our present industrial arrangements which is felt by some popular expounders of so-called economic laws. When a workingman is told that Political Economy "condemns" strikes, . . . looks askance at proposals for limiting the hours of labour, but "approves" the accumulation of capital, and "sanctions" the market rate of wages, it seems not an unnatural response that "since Political Economy is against the workingman, it behoves the workingman to be against Political Economy." [1]

Adam Smith, Malthus, Ricardo, and Mill are among the great names in economics. Their economic teachings probably exerted more influence upon contemporary opinion and practices in England and elsewhere than have the writings of other economists in later periods. Knowledge of their theories is necessary in order to understand how statesmen and economists who considered themselves friends of the people could view so serenely the bad working and living conditions of many factory workers during the early years of the Industrial Revolution in England. One must study the intellectual currents of the period when the western world embraced the doctrine of laissez faire in order to appreciate the prevailing fatalism and opposition to corrective measures. Such a study indicates the influence that environment has on economic doctrines and the forces that determine the predominant economic theology of a period. It also helps to explain why workers are inclined to be wary of economic doctrines, and even consider much economics to be mere apologetics. Finally, with such an historical background, one is better able to evaluate the arguments of those who advocate government inaction and noninterference with business or labor relations. Their arguments are often refined or watered-down versions of the natural philosophy and economic dogmas which had their heyday 100 years ago in England and France.

THE CONDITION OF THE WORKERS

The skilled craftsmen. Thousands and thousands of skilled journeymen and masters petitioned Parliament, complaining that they were robbed of property rights and investment in their trades by repeal of protective legislation like the Statute of Artificers, which required a seven-years' period of apprenticeship for most

[1] *Essays in Political Economy*, 1873, pp. 260, 261.

industrial occupations. The craftsmen considered it "clearly unjust to take [away] the whole of the ancient established property
and rights of any class of the community, unless, at the same time,
the rights and property of the whole commonwealth should be dissolved, and parcelled out anew for the public good." [1] Skilled
workers questioned the constitutionality of Parliament's one-sided
action in repealing the ancient statutes. The watchmakers passed
a resolution in 1817 stating "That the pretensions to the allowance
of universal uncontrolled freedom of action to every individual,
founded upon the same delusive theoretical principles which fostered the French Revolution, are wholly inapplicable to the insular
situation of this Kingdom, and if allowed to prevail, will hasten
the destruction of the social system so happily arranged in the
existing form and substance of the British constitution, established
by law." [2]

The new machinery and minute division of labor did away with
the demand for the old craft skills of many artisans. With machines,
the work became so light that women and children could be employed on a large scale in the factories. Children had worked long
hours in unhealthy workshops under the domestic system, but now
their employment was systematized, concentrated, and made more
visible. Under the early factory system in England, the employment
of women and children was the foundation of certain branches of
industry. Three independent estimates for the years 1833, 1835,
and 1839 indicate that almost half of the factory workers in England
were children under 18 years of age—one quarter of the workers
in the cotton mills were under 14 years of age. [3] About 55 per cent
of all factory employees in the 1830's were women, and nearly one
half of the female employees were under 18 years of age. In woolen,
silk, and flax mills, 70 per cent of all "operatives" in 1839 were
women. A census of 1841 showed that 27 per cent of the workers
in British mines (coal, iron, tin, etc.) were under 20 years of age,
although only 3 or 4 per cent were females. [4] One of the most important arguments against this widespread use of the labor of

[1] A. E. Bland, P. A. Brown, and R. H. Tawney, *English Economic History: Select
Documents*, 1914, p. 589.

[2] *Ibid.*, p. 590.

[3] *Supplementary Report of the Factory Commission*, 1834, Part I, p. 138; Andrew Ure,
Philosophy of Manufactures, 1835, p. 481; and Frederick Engels, *The Condition of the
Working-Class in England in 1844*, 1892, p. 142.

[4] Engels, *op. cit.*, p. 241.

women and children was that it disturbed "the order of nature," ejecting males from the workshop to fill their places with women and children, who should be in the home.

Hours and child labor. The new machinery had a number of other effects. Factory owners wanted to operate their costly equipment as continuously as possible in order to keep down the overhead cost per unit of output and to get as much as possible out of the machinery before a new invention made it obsolete. The normal working day for women and children as well as men was from 12 to 14 hours for six days a week, and at rush seasons factories sometimes ran day and night on one shift. Children, who in rush seasons worked 18 hours a day with only four hours for sleeping, often fell asleep at meals "with the victuals in their mouths."[1] A West Indian slave master, upon hearing of the hours children worked in English factories, remarked: "I have always thought myself disgraced by being the owner of slaves, but we never in the West Indies thought it possible for any human being to be so cruel as to require a child of nine years old to work twelve and a half hours a day, and that, you acknowledge, is your regular practice."[2]

Working weeks from 72 to 108 hours for children tended to deform their bodies and legs and made workers old at 40. To force child laborers to perform their stint, foremen sometimes strapped them. Children of six, seven, and eight years of age worked in coal mines where, for 12 or 14 hours a day, girls in their teens, crawling on all fours, would drag a car or tub of 300 or 400 pounds of coal by a chain attached to a leather band around their waists.[3] Economists, in estimating the gain from the new factory system, generally failed to allow for the suffering and the wear and tear on human bodies that such toil at tender ages involved. It was the literary writers like Dickens, Carlyle, Coleridge, Charles Kingsley, Charlotte Brontë, Byron, Thomas Hood ("Song of the Shirt"), and Elizabeth Barrett Browning ("Bitter Cry of the Children") who pointed to the human and inhumane aspects of the early factory system. Almost without exception, the authors in the period from 1760 to 1850 who are remembered today were opposed to the capitalism of the time.

[1] Bland, Brown, and Tawney, *op. cit.*, pp. 510–13.
[2] J. L. and B. Hammond, *The Town Labourer, 1760–1832*, 1920, p. 160.
[3] Bland, Brown, and Tawney, *op. cit.*, pp. 516–17; and E. P. Cheyney, *An Introduction to the Industrial and Social History of England* (revised edition), 1920, pp. 243–44.

In France, where laissez faire was also the ruling philosophy, the general working day averaged 15 hours, and in 1828 it was believed that French children and youths were gradually becoming enervated by exhaustive toil for such long periods. There too the thong for the punishment of working children appears as an instrument of production.[1]

Wages. In many cases, children were forced to toil long hours in factories because their fathers could not obtain employment, or because the men's earnings were too meager to support their families.[2] The well-known French economist, J. B. Say, from his travels in England in 1815, declared that a worker with a family, despite efforts often of a heroic character, could earn no more than three quarters, and sometimes only one half, the sum needed to support his family.[3] According to a writer in 1820, real wages (wages reckoned in commodities) had fallen 33 per cent from 1760 to 1820.[4] A recent study of the real wages of artisans in London from 1729 to 1935 indicates a decline of 30 per cent between the decades 1760 to 1769 and 1810 to 1819.[5] According to this study, it was only after 1850 that the real wages of London artisans in the nineteenth century began to surpass those paid 100 years before—and that despite the rapid advances in English industry. Other studies indicate that real wages differed widely in various regions and that they tended to rise in the north and fall in the west during the latter part of the eighteenth century.[6]

From contemporary writings and available statistical evidence, one must conclude that the wage-earners failed to receive a large share of the increased production during the period of the Industrial Revolution from 1775 to 1825. In fact, during that half-century, production and the real wages of some groups seem to have gone in exactly opposite directions. Apparently, most of the increased productivity was used to increase capital equipment in Eng-

---

[1] Gide and Rist, *op. cit.*, pp. 171–72.

[2] J. L. and B. Hammond, *op. cit.*, p. 157.

[3] "De l'Angleterre et des Anglais," in *Oeuvres*, vol. 4, p. 213.

[4] J. Barton, *Inquiry into the Depreciation of Agricultural Labour*, 1820, p. 11. *Cf.* also A. Toynbee, *op. cit.*, p. 106.

[5] R. Tucker, *op. cit.*, pp. 78–79.

[6] *Cf.* E. W. Gilboy, *Wages in Eighteenth Century England*, 1934. Some of the evidence regarding real wages during the early decades of the nineteenth century is contradictory. Certain fragmentary statistics even indicate that the level of real wages, especially for unskilled workers, rose during that period. *Cf.* Clapham, *op. cit.*, pp. 561, 602.

land and to expand capital investment abroad. It was from 1795 to 1835 that the problem of pauperism reached its most extreme and acute form, and that the term "labouring poor" became such a common expression.[1] In a book published in 1836, P. Gaskell said: "Upwards of a million of human beings are literally starving and the number is constantly on the increase. . . . It is a new era in the history of commerce that an active and increasing trade should be the index, not to the improvement of the condition of the working classes, but to their poverty and degradation."[2] Under such circumstances it is easy to understand why Ricardo had a subsistence theory of wages rather than a productivity theory—the real wages of many workers were falling with increased productivity—and why he thought that the condition of the laboring classes would continue to decline.

It was during this very same period that a new class of large employers made sizeable fortunes. Indeed, the cotton industry, in which fortunes seem to have been acquired most readily, was the industry in which wages and working conditions were the least satisfactory.[3] The factory system and the cost of machinery tended to create a wide social cleavage between workers and their employers. As employing units increased in size, employers could take little or no part in the actual work in their factories, and the "cash nexus" took the place of the old human ties between master and workmen. Factory workers tended to dwell in separate areas or sections of a city, frequently inhabiting company houses and having to buy at the company store. England had become, to quote Disraeli, "Two nations: between whom there is no intercourse and no sympathy; who are as ignorant of each other's habits, thoughts, and feelings, as if they were dwellers in different zones, or inhabitants of different planets; . . . THE RICH AND THE POOR."[4]

Industrial depressions. A part of the laboring population also suffered from a series of business crises and depressions, which involved a large number of bank and business failures as well as periodic unemployment. Along with large-scale production and expanded markets, the Industrial Revolution seems to have intensified business cycles. In 1814 a crisis, accompanied by an ava-

[1] Toynbee, *op. cit.*, p. 74.
[2] *Artisans and Machinery*, 1836, Preface.
[3] J. L. and B. Hammond, *op. cit.*, p. 141.
[4] *Sybil or the Two Nations*, 1845, pp. 68–69.

lanche of commercial failures, shook the English market. Thereafter there were depressions in 1819–1820, 1825–1826, 1836–1837, and the early 1840's, and in 1847–1848 there was a great crash.[1] That period became known as the "hungry forties." Norman J. Siberling finds that in these years there were fluctuations in business and "recurrent conditions of overproduction and underproduction, liquidation, and overborrowing, pessimism and optimism, and falling and rising markets, which make up the business cycle."[2] Laissez faire proved to be no cure for business cycles and depressions.

Suppression of trade-unions. Large-scale operations in the new factories, by massing workers together, made common or organized action by workers much easier. But any combined action by workers in defense of their own interests was outlawed by the Combination Acts of 1799 and 1800. Combinations of workmen to better their conditions were declared illegal as early as the fourteenth century, and there were reported to be as many as 40 special laws against combination on the Statute Book in 1800. But these earlier laws against labor combinations were justified on the grounds that it was the business of the state itself to regulate industry and working conditions, and that combinations of workers to influence wages and working conditions would be encroaching upon the province of Parliament. The triumph of laissez faire, by removing the protection of the state, should have removed the objection to labor combinations. Instead, combinations were condemned as a violation of natural liberty, an interference with the freedom of employers and employees to make whatever bargains they pleased. In France, under the Napoleonic Code, not only were trade-unions and strikes outlawed, but employers' organizations were permitted, and common action by employers to lock out their workers was subject merely to a slight fine or punishment. There was a widespread notion that the employer could do no harm and that, if the state should look after the capitalist, the capitalist would look after the workers.[3]

Although the English Combination Acts on paper forbade combinations of employers, the employers combined freely, even ar-

---

[1] Gide and Rist, *op. cit.*, pp. 171–72; and N. J. Siberling, "British Prices and Business Cycles, 1779–1850," *The Review of Economic Statistics*, vol. 5 (October 1923), supplement 2, pp. 237–38.

[2] Siberling, *op. cit.*, pp. 246–47.

[3] J. L. and B. Hammond, *op. cit.*, p. 220.

ranging for large concerted reductions in wages; yet they were not punished.[1] Apparently the bias of the judges, a number of whom were large employers, partly accounts for the one-sided administration of these Acts. Workers who refused to work, either because low-wage employers would not raise wages to the general level or because their employers reduced wages as much as 50 per cent, were imprisoned for combination when numbers of them quit.[2] The Combination Acts proved a great aid to employers in reducing wages. For persons who believe that trade-unions are largely responsible for unemployment and industrial difficulties, the experience in England during this period should be especially instructive.

In 1824 the English Combination Acts were repealed—even Malthus and Ricardo favored their abolition—but their repeal was recommended on the expectation that "if left alone combinations would soon cease to exist." Instead, labor organizations increased, even though Parliament in 1825 restricted lawful combinations to those for the purpose of affecting wages and hours of work. For a long time, labor unions were opposed by the leading economists as futile according to the orthodox doctrine of wages and, therefore, "in the long run as injurious to the working man as to the employer." Leading economists (including Ricardo, Lauerdale, and Nassau Senior) also supported the opposition of manufacturers to legislation limiting the hours and conditions of work for children and women—the so-called Factory Acts. To these economists such hours laws were "contrary to all principles of sound legislation" and to "that great principle of political economy, that labour ought to be left free." [3]

RETURN TO GOVERNMENT REGULATION OF INDUSTRY

Factory legislation. A few years after the last Tudor statutes on wages and apprenticeship were swept away in 1813 and 1814, England began to rebuild piecemeal a new industrial code, which soon controlled the free play of individual action even more effectively than had the former code of the Tudors. This new factory

---

[1] *Ibid.*, p. 65.
[2] *Ibid.*, pp. 130, 256.
[3] J. L. and B. Hammond, *op. cit.*, p. 167; and W. J. Ashley, *The Economic Organization of England*, 1922, p. 166.

code was designed to remedy some of the evils that had developed under laissez faire.

The first Factory Act, passed in 1802, applied only to poorhouse children, who were bound out by the state to cotton manufacturers. The sad life of these poor or pauper apprentices, supposed to be cared for by the employer, was called to the attention of Parliament by Sir Robert Peel, himself an employer of nearly 1,000 of them. The Act did not apply to most child labor, which consisted of "free" children, living with their parents. This "Health and Morals of Apprentices Act" prohibited the binding out of children under nine years of age, limited the working time of children above nine years to 12 hours during the daytime, and required that the employer provide his pauper apprentices with some schooling.

In 1819, the Cotton Factories Regulation Act applied to "free" children the hours provisions of the 1802 Act, forbidding the employment of children under nine, and limiting to 12 the hours of children of nine to sixteen. Opposition to this Act was led by the economist Lauerdale, who maintained that "the employer was the person most likely to be acquainted with the different degrees of strength possessed by his workmen, and most likely to avoid overworking them with a view to his own advantage." [1] It is significant, however, that a number of employers were willing to support even more drastic provisions for limiting the working hours of children in cotton factories. In 1833, an Act extended the prohibitions of the 1819 Act to all textile trades, and also limited to eight a day the hours of children between nine and thirteen years of age. For the first time, a staff of inspectors was created to see that these Acts were enforced.

In 1842, the state proceeded to interfere with the free market for the labor of adult women by excluding them from work in underground mines. An Act passed in 1844 (1) provided for the proper fencing of machinery for workers' safety; (2) restricted the labor of children to a half day, requiring their attendance at school during the other half day; and (3) limited the hours of adult women to 12 a day, also prohibiting night work for them. It was in opposition to such limitation of the working day by legislation that Nassau Senior, Professor of Political Economy at Oxford, attempted to "prove" that hours could not be reduced further because in a mill

---

[1] J. L. and B. Hammond, *op. cit.*, pp. 200–201.

employing persons under 18, which by law could operate only 11½ hours a day, "the whole net profit is derived from the last hour," so that a reduction of the working day by one hour would destroy the entire net profit, whereas an increase to 13 hours would double the net profit.[1] Hundreds of millowners supported this hours legislation for women, 300 of them signing a petition for limiting female labor to 10 hours a day. That step was taken in 1847, when the "Ten Hour Act" restricted the working day of young persons and women to 10 hours. This Act, it is estimated, applied to over 360,000 workers, or at least three fourths of all persons employed in textile industries.[2] With its passage, the chief outlines of the factory code in England were formed.

Credit for passage of the Factory Acts is partly due to the landowning aristocracy, the Tories, who took this means of revenge against the capitalists and millowners for aiding in the repeal of the high tariffs on agricultural products (the Corn Laws). But many businessmen themselves revolted against the doctrine of laissez faire when they saw its effects in the deformed bodies of children, the impairment of health and life, and the poverty of hard-working families. As time passed, opposition to the Factory Acts gradually withered away. The evil effects on British industry, predicted by those who opposed the passage of the Acts, failed to materialize, and many of the strongest opponents of the factory legislation eventually acknowledged its benefits.

Actually the Factory Acts proved advantageous from an economic point of view. Evidence from studies by factory inspectors after 1844 proved that "the output of eleven hours' work might be greater than that of twelve" and that long hours, far from being productive, resulted in spoiled work, inefficiency, and breakdowns.[3] By 1860 public opinion had completely changed; the belief that shorter hours necessarily meant lessened production "had long been exploded"; and the Ten Hour Bill of 1847 was hailed as "something of which all parties might well be proud."[4] When in 1867 the proposal was made to extend the operation of the Factory

---

[1] N. W. Senior, *Letters on the Factory Act as It Affects the Cotton Manufacture*, 1837; quoted also in Bland, Brown, and Tawney, *op. cit.*, pp. 606–607.

[2] E. P. Cheyney, *op. cit.*, p. 237.

[3] B. L. Hutchins and A. Harrison, *A History of Factory Legislation* (third edition), 1926, pp. 122–26.

[4] *Idem.*

Acts from textile factories to all factories and workshops, it "was received with general favour" and an act to that effect was passed in 1867 without opposition.[1]

The question arises: If shorter hours were economical, why didn't English employers discover it instead of being forced to take such economic action by law? As early as 1820 a few enlightened employers, like Robert Owen, did begin to experiment by reducing hours from 14 to 12 to 10 a day with favorable results. Why didn't competition by enlightened employers force a reduction in the hours of work? In the first place, the enlightened employers were so few in number that competition was ineffective; practically all employers simply followed the prevailing practice. But most of all, competition is likely to be a poor method for accomplishing long-run results. It takes time for the beneficial effects of an hours' reduction upon the productivity of workers to appear in a company's profit account. The same is true of action to eliminate unhealthy and hazardous conditions in workshops. As English experience in the early nineteenth century indicates, absolute individualism in the labor market is frequently uneconomic.

Summary. The different stages in the regulation of industry were adjusted to the size of the market for products. It is the size of the market that determines the appropriate type of economic organization, including the size and structure of business units. The guild regulations afforded protection to worker-enterprisers producing for a local market. The Tudor or national regulations attempted to extend guildlike controls to a market that had expanded with improved transportation facilities, so that it no longer was confined to the boundaries of the town or city. Further expansion of the market, and accumulation of capital through trading ventures and commercial dealings, permitted additional specialization of production in the form of the factory system. The Factory Acts were designed to regulate production in factories in order to prevent abuses that seemed detrimental to society in general.

With the changes in the structure of industry that arose as the markets for products expanded, the worker-enterpriser of the guild system gradually was separated from the product market, from the market for raw materials, from ownership of the means of production, and from all but one of the various stages of production. From

[1] *Ibid.*, p. 123.

an independent entrepreneur, the worker was reduced to a dependent wage-earner, who, if not employed by a merchant capitalist or in a factory, was in no position to engage in production on his own, for he had no customers, no equipment, and no knowledge of the sources of raw materials or the various stages in the production of the article on which he had been working.

Having been reduced to economic dependency through loss of control over markets and production, workers sought later to achieve some degree of economic control through labor organization. Labor organizations have attempted to exert control mainly in the labor market rather than in product markets. Essentially, they have represented an attempt by workers to increase the economic power and control of the wage-earning groups. To that extent, they presented a challenge to the authority and control of employing groups, whose economic power tended to expand as the dependency of the workers increased.

CHAPTER FOUR

HISTORICAL BACKGROUND: AMERICA

Colonial regulation of industry. In many respects, the story of industrial and labor development in this country parallels that of England, the mother country. Most of the colonists emigrated from Great Britain at a time when the domestic system was emerging there and national regulation was replacing the old guild regulation of industry. There was some lag of industrial development in this country behind that in England, however, because in the mother country transportation facilities were better and markets were larger. Except for staple agricultural exports, markets in the colonies were mainly local. Consequently, colonial industry was in the handicraft stage, with master craftsmen and their apprentices. The master owned his own tools and shop, combining in one person the functions of capitalist, worker, and merchant. Indeed, in 1648 the Massachusetts legislature granted charters to the Boston shoemakers and coopers (barrelmakers) giving them privileges similar to those held by craft guilds in England. Officers of these American guilds were given the authority to regulate trade practices and craft membership and to enforce craft rules by levying penalties.[1]

Colonial legislatures passed laws that regulated industry to an extreme degree. Following English precedent, our colonial ancestors regulated the weight, size, and price of a loaf of bread, the quality of woolen cloth, the processes in the manufacture of leather, the size and quality of containers and building bricks, as well as the price of beer, leather, iron, sugar, and shoes.[2] It was against the assize of bread, so common in the colonies, that the New York bakers, who were entrepreneurs and not wage-earners, struck in 1741.[3] These laws were designed to protect the consumer and to

[1] J. R. Commons *et al.*, *History of Labour in the United States*, 1918, vol. 1, p. 46.
[2] V. S. Clark, *History of Manufactures in the United States*, 1929, vol. 1, pp. 64–66.
[3] Commons *et al.*, *op. cit.*, p. 53.

promote sales abroad by upholding the quality of workmanship. They were administered by "viewers" or inspectors, who were either appointed by public authorities or chosen by the craftsmen themselves.

There were also colonial statutes regulating the fees charged by tanners, blacksmiths, grain- and sawmill owners, cartsmen, and others. It was against a municipal ordinance fixing the price for removing a cartload of dirt from the streets that the New York teamsters (also entrepreneurs) struck in 1677.[1] Because prices for services seemed "excessive" in the colonies, some of these early statutes fixed maximum fees as a means of keeping down wage rates. From 1630 to 1635, the Massachusetts legislature attempted to fix maximum wage rates for "Carpenters, Joyners, Brickelayers, Sawers, Thatchers, Wheelewrights, Tylers, Mowers, Master and inferior taylors, and labourers," stipulating a fine for all offending employers.[2] In 1638 the towns of Massachusetts were given authority to fix "the prices & rates of all workmen, laborers, & servants wages." Records show that in 1651 a worker was hailed into court for "taking excessive wages."[3] Such legislative action was taken in Massachusetts because the "excessive rates" charged by workmen had become "a general complaint."

"High American wages" date from the founding of Jamestown and Plymouth. In 1625, a colonial treasurer in Virginia declared that the wages paid were "much in excess of the sum paid to the same class of persons in England." In 1630 the Governor of Massachusetts complained that the "scarcity of workers caused them to raise their wages to an excessive rate."[4] In all the colonies at various dates, from 1633 to 1776, there were complaints that "Labour is dear," and, according to statements in 1651 and 1698, wages in the northern colonies were from two to three times as high as in England.[5] A committee of the Pennsylvania legislature stated in 1752 that immigrating workers soon set up for themselves, which "keeps up the Price of Labour, and makes it more difficult for the old Settler to procure working Hands." This committee concluded: "For

---

[1] *Ibid.*, p. 25.

[2] *Ibid.*, pp. 51–52; and U. S. Bureau of Labor Statistics, *History of Wages in the United States from Colonial Times to 1928*, 1929, Bulletin No. 499, p. 9.

[3] U. S. Bureau of Labor Statistics, *op. cit.*, pp. 9–10; and Commons *et al.*, *op. cit.*, p. 50.

[4] U. S. Bureau of Labor Statistics, *op. cit.*, pp. 7–8.

[5] Clark, *op. cit.*, p. 156.

so long as Land can be easily procured for Settlements between the
Atlantic and Pacific Oceans, so long will Labour be dear in America." [1]

Though apprenticeship was almost as familiar in the colonies as
in England and was regulated by numerous colonial statutes, the
scarcity of labor caused the term to be reduced below the seven-
year requirement in the mother country. For example, the City of
New York adopted an ordinance in 1680 providing that "coopers,
carpenters and smiths &c., serve five years before being allowed to
set up business" for themselves.[2] A French writer noted that just
before the American Revolution all American mechanics served a
regular apprenticeship.[3]

There is plenty of evidence that our colonial forefathers, like their
English and French contemporaries, believed in government regulation of industry and labor to promote the welfare of the community.

Rise of the merchant capitalist. By the time of the American
Revolution, cities had grown, and markets had expanded so in size
that master craftsmen were employing numbers of journeymen in
central workrooms or in the worker's home, where the whole product was made. Consequently, the number of wage-earners was increasing, and the worker gradually lost control over the customer
market and the raw material. As competition displaced custom in
economic affairs, price became more important than the reputation
of the craftsman, especially in "shop" work for a general or distant
market. With the widening of markets toward the end of the eighteenth century, a class of wholesale merchants arose who bought the
products of different workshops and sold them to retailers in the
same or distant localities.

These wholesale merchants soon became merchant capitalists,
who did not engage in production but were marketing specialists
who bargained with shop employers for their products, or furnished
raw materials to home workers doing piecework. The master employers gradually became dependent upon this merchant capitalist
for the sale of their products. By playing one craftsman-employer
against another, either in the same city or in different cities, the

---

[1] *Pennsylvania Archives*, eighth series, vol. 4, p. 3520.
[2] Commons *et al.*, *op. cit.*, p. 46.
[3] M. St. J. de Crèvecoeur, *Lettres d'un Cultivateur Américain*, III, 1784, pp. 487–88.

merchant wholesalers put considerable pressure upon master employers to reduce their costs of production.

Such competition between employers and communities led to attempts to reduce the wages of skilled workers and caused master employers to subdivide the work of their shops in order both to speed up the output and to use cheaper unskilled workers—even women and children—on some phases of the work. The apprenticeship system began to disintegrate in the first two decades of the nineteenth century as one former trade became half a dozen separate tasks. In this way, many "green hands" could be hired, who had not served an apprenticeship. In some lines of manufacture, such as textiles, merchant capitalists supplied farmers' wives and daughters with the raw materials and tools for making cloth and garments. In shoemaking, not only was there a tendency for a craftsman to specialize on one operation, such as heeling or stitching soles, but he frequently worked at home, with the aid of his family, on raw material furnished by the merchant capitalist. This merchant-capitalist stage began in some industries in the first decades of the nineteenth century. By then there was a distinct wage-earning class, which frequently did not own the hand tools it worked with. As David Saposs puts it: "From an independent producer the Lynn shoemaker was reduced to a dependent wage-worker." [1]

It was this resort to wage-cutting and the use of "green hands," under the bargaining pressure of the merchant capitalist, that led to the first real conflicts in this country between employers and employed. The first strike of wage-earners seems to have been that of the journeymen printers in Philadelphia in 1786 against a reduction of wages below six dollars a week.[2] To combat such competition, the skilled craftsmen tried to establish a wage below which no one could work, irrespective of the quality of his product. They also demanded strict observance of apprenticeship rules, which would automatically eliminate the competition of unskilled workers as well as women and children.[3] But, unlike the situation in England prior to 1814, there were no statutes of apprenticeship to be enforced by law after the Revolution. Apprenticeship in the United States was only a custom, its enforcement depending upon the strength of the craftsmen's organizations. All that the skilled crafts-

---

[1] Commons et al., op. cit., p. 102.   [2] Ibid., pp. 25, 123.   [3] Ibid., p. 164.

men could do was to refuse to work in the same shop with a man who had not served an apprenticeship, and complain that their skill, acquired by apprenticeship, was "a thing of property" which must be protected if they were to support their families.[1]

Early trade-unions. This competition and conflict, accompanying the rise of the merchant capitalist, led to the first formation of trade-unions by skilled workers, such as printers, shoemakers, tailors, carpenters, etc. It was this same kind of competition that led to the formation of the first labor unions in other countries, which were also organizations of skilled, and not unskilled, workers. The first continuous organization of wage-earners for the purpose of maintaining or advancing wages was that of the shoemakers in Philadelphia, organized in 1792.[2] These first unions were formed to protect the standard of living and jobs of the skilled craftsmen from the competition of lower grade and lower paid workers. As the New York printers complained in 1811, skilled craftsmen were being "turned out of their places by miserable botches because they will work for what they can get." [3] The result was that the wages of the unskilled tended to rise, and the standard of living of the skilled craftsmen to fall. Such, for example, was the case from 1800 to 1810.[4] At this time the lot of the unskilled was improving, so it was only the skilled who formed unions to protect their interests and living standards.

Around the turn of the century, a number of craft organizations or companies were organized and incorporated in the large cities along the Atlantic seaboard. These protective organizations adopted a scale of minimum wages (a "book of prices") below which they would not work, and attempted to force employers to hire only members of the organization, who had served an apprenticeship. Members of the shoemakers' organizations around 1800 pledged one another "not to work for any employer who did not give the wages, nor beside any journeyman who did not get the wages." [5] Most of these craft protective organizations included employing, as well as employed, master craftsmen and, like the European guilds, had benefit features such as accident, sick, and death benefits to protect members and to aid widows and orphans. Prior

---

[1] *Ibid.*, p. 449.   [2] *Ibid.*, pp. 108–109.   [3] *Ibid.*, p. 114.

[4] *Ibid.*, p. 105; and J. B. McMaster, *A History of the People of the United States*, 1895, vol. 3, pp. 510–13.

[5] Commons *et al.*, *op. cit.*, p. 121.

to 1827, however, they were all local craft organizations and many of them were short-lived. Employers' organizations in opposition to labor unions, "to break them up altogether, root and branch," were formed as early as 1798 amongst employer-shoemakers in Philadelphia.[1]

As in England, the employers in this country soon used the law and the courts against these workers' organizations. From 1806 to 1815, shoemakers' organizations were prosecuted in six cases under the English common-law doctrine of conspiracy, which the courts ruled was also the law in this country. In four of these first six cases of conspiracy, the journeymen shoemakers were found guilty and were given slight fines, but not imprisoned as in England. In the first decision of 1806, the defendant shoemakers were held to be "guilty of a combination to raise wages." This decision called forth a vigorous protest, the Jeffersonian democrats attacking both the Federalist judges and the English common law, while the workers complained that other groups, including employers and merchants, had their associations and meetings to affect wages and the prices of goods. In the succeeding conspiracy cases, the judges changed the emphasis in the law, declaring that combinations to raise wages were illegal only when unlawful means, such as coercion or intimidation, were used or when the workers conspired to injure a third person, such as a nonmember, by trying to secure a closed shop. Two of these early conspiracy cases were closed-shop cases.

From 1821 to 1827 there were four more conspiracy cases. In 1821 the shoemakers tried unsuccessfully to prosecute employers for conspiring to reduce wages. The court held that it was lawful for masters, who were forced by employees to raise wages, to combine in order to restore them to their "natural level," but that "it would have been criminal" if the employers had combined to depress the wages of journeymen below what they would be if there were no resort to artificial means by either side.[2] In the other cases, two against tailors and one against hatters, the workers were found guilty. From 1828 to 1842, there were eight additional prosecutions for conspiracy, but only two convictions. The workers again claimed that they were forced to combine in self defense, "by combinations of Bankers, of Merchants, and dealers in all exchangeable commodities."[3] In the famous case of *Commonwealth* v. *Hunt* in 1842,

[1] *Ibid.*, p. 133. [2] *Ibid.*, p. 163. [3] *Ibid.*, p. 373.

Judge Shaw of the Massachusetts Supreme Court stated that strikes for the closed shop were legal, if conducted in a peaceful manner.[1]

The factory system. The first successful factory operated by water power was the cotton mill established by Samuel Slater in Rhode Island in 1790. Slater transplanted English labor precedents in America by hiring seven boys and two girls between the ages of 7 and 12 to operate this first mill. In 1801 Josiah Quincy reported that Slater's mill was run by one superintendent and over 100 children from 4 to 10 years old, earning 12 to 25 cents a day.[2]

The factory system began to make rapid strides in textiles after the installation of the first power loom in 1814, which reduced labor costs per unit of output by over 50 per cent in a few years. The expansion of factories in cotton manufacture is indicated by the following figures for the number of spindles in cotton factories:[3]

1810	87,000 spindles
1815	130,000
1820	about 300,000
1830	1,246,503
1840	2,284,631

The years from 1814 to 1840 also witnessed a rapid expansion in iron production, another indication of the increasing mechanization of American industry. The estimated production of pig iron was as follows:[4]

1810	55,000 tons
1830	190,000
1840	300,000
1850	600,000

In 1810 only two per cent of the cloth made in America was produced in factories, but by 1820 textile manufacture had moved from the fireside to the factory. As V. S. Clark puts it: "Hitherto sailors had been about the only people who left their homes to maintain them; now women were withdrawn from the domestic circle to recruit the mobile forces of manufacturing labor."[5] With the introduction of steam engines in 1830, the "transition from mother-and-daughter power to water-and-steam power" was completed.

[1] *Ibid.*, p. 412.

[2] "Account of Journey of Josiah Quincy, 1801" in *Proceedings of the Massachusetts Historical Society*, second series, vol. 4, p. 124.

[3] Clark, *op. cit.*, p. 544; and E. L. Bogart, *Economic History of the American People*, 1930, pp. 408, 412.

[4] Estimates based on the data in Clark, *op. cit.*, p. 500.

[5] Clark, *op. cit.*, p. 529.

Power-driven machinery soon reduced the labor costs of weaving by as much as 80 or 90 per cent, permitting the use of the cheaper labor of women and children. As the man who first applied power to the weaving of woolen cloth later explained: "We got rid of 60 weavers, the most of them men who in those bygone days were intemperate and exceedingly troublesome, and substituted for them 30 girls, who were easily managed and did more and better work." [1]

Indeed, in cotton factories in America, as the economist Henry Carey pointed out in 1835, a much larger proportion of the workers were women than was the case in England. A report of a Congressional committee in 1816 gives the following estimates for persons employed in cotton mills in that year: [2]

Males from seventeen up	10,000
Women and female children	66,000
Boys under seventeen	24,000
Total	100,000

In general, only about one tenth of the workers in cotton factories during the first half of the nineteenth century were able-bodied men. In some cotton mills as many as 90 or 95 per cent of all workers were girls and women. For the country as a whole, women employees represented 68 per cent in 1831, and 64 per cent in 1850, of all workers in the American cotton industry. [3] In Massachusetts, where the cotton mills employed mostly farmers' daughters between 17 and 24 years of age, these figures for women workers were 80 per cent in 1831 and 70 per cent in 1845.

Working conditions in the Massachusetts and New Hampshire mills, using the so-called Waltham system of factory organization, were considerably better than in the mills in Rhode Island, New York, New Jersey, Pennsylvania, and Maryland, which followed the English precedent of employing whole families including very young children. Millowners in these latter states would, for example, advertise in the newspapers as follows: "Ten or twelve good respectable families consisting of 4 to 5 children each, from 9 to 16 years of age, are wanted to work in a cotton mill in the vicinity of Providence." [4] It was also the custom to pay these families, not in

[1] U. S. Bureau of Labor Statistics, *op. cit.*, pp. 85–86.
[2] E. Abbott, *Women in Industry; a Study in American Economic History*, 1915, p. 89.
[3] *Ibid.*, pp. 90, 102.
[4] J. K. Towles, *Factory Legislation of Rhode Island*, Publications of the American Economic Association, third series, 1908, vol. 9, p. 10.

cash, but with provisions and other articles from the company store.

Under the Waltham system, the companies hired mostly young women from the country, who lived at rather respectable boarding houses provided by the company. Before 1850, these girls usually came from high-class homes, and some of them were well educated. In 1840 the "mill girls" in Lowell, Massachusetts, began the publication of the first magazine in the world written exclusively by women or by factory girls. The lives of these girls were, however, controlled by a vigorous company paternalism, which dictated the time of going to bed and the rules of social intercourse. The girls not only lived in company boarding houses, but attended company churches and usually spent their earnings at company stores, many of them being paid in orders on a company store rather than in cash. Payment in orders led to abuses such as overcharging and falsification of accounts. Payment in cash was instituted at the Fall River mills only after a young lady, the company's best weaver and the daughter of a stockholder, demanded that she be shown the account books and found that articles like suspenders and rum were charged against her.[1]

Child labor. The early protectionists, in arguing for tariffs to protect our "infant" industries, stated that factory work did not demand able-bodied men but was better "done by little girls from six to twelve years old." [2] America's "infant" industries were, in many cases, operated by infants. Some states followed the English practice of binding poorhouse children to factories as pauper apprentices, although this was never done on such a large scale as in England. It was estimated in 1830 that two fifths of all workers in factories were children between 7 and 16 years of age, and in 1831, over one eighth of all employees in cotton mills in New England were children under 12.[3] A Senatorial investigating committee found in 1838 that one fifth of all hands employed in cotton mills in Pennsylvania were under 12 years of age, and that, of the employees under 18 in cotton mills, no more than one third could either read or write.[4] Even as late as 1900, almost one seventh of all workers in the cotton industry were children under 16.[5]

---

[1] Abbott, *op. cit.*, p. 273.   [2] *Ibid.*, p. 51.
[3] Towles, *op. cit.*, pp. 10–11. *Cf.* also Commons *et al.*, *op. cit.*, p. 173.
[4] J. L. Barnard, *Factory Legislation in Pennsylvania: Its History and Administration*, Publications of the University of Pennsylvania, Series in Political Economy and Public Law, 1907, pp. 11, 14.   [5] Abbott, *op. cit.*, p. 357.

These young children worked from 12 to 15 hours a day—from dawn till dark—in the factories. Testimony before the Senatorial committee in Pennsylvania in 1838 brought out that the youngest children were often too exhausted to eat after work and would fall asleep the minute they reached home at night.[1] Children sometimes fell asleep standing up at their work, to be awakened by a dash of water or a box on the ear. There are reports in Rhode Island and Pennsylvania of the use of leather straps for whipping factory children, but strapping apparently was much less frequent here than in England.[2] In some cases, parents who had a number of children in a mill and wanted to send some of them to school were not "allowed to withdraw one or more, without withdrawing the whole." [3] In 1853 a member told the Rhode Island House of Representatives: "The most superficial observer cannot have failed to notice the palid countenances, apparently diseased forms, and heavy steps of those children, who through the cupidity of their parents or their employers, are doomed to such unremitting and long-continued toil as is detailed in the report on your table. I am credibly informed that there are mills wherein, owing to the present active sale of their goods, the operatives work from two, three, and four o'clock in the morning until nine in the evening." [4] An experienced doctor told the Pennsylvania Senatorial committee in 1838 that the health of children was most seriously impaired by such labor, especially in cotton factories.[5]

Hours and wages. The working hours in early factories in America were the same as those on the farm—from sunrise to sunset, and sometimes even after sundown. Since the presence of sunlight, rather than the condition of the workers, generally determined the hours of factory labor, the working day varied with the seasons. In 1832 the yearly average for New England mills was stated to be 13 hours a day.[6] A writer in 1839 estimated the average hours throughout a year at $73\frac{1}{3}$ a week for New England factories and $75\frac{1}{2}$ a week for the mills in the Middle and Southern

---

[1] Barnard, *op. cit.*, p. 11.
[2] Barnard, *op. cit.*, p. 13; and Abbott, *op. cit.*, pp. 346–47.
[3] Commons *et al.*, *op. cit.*, p. 184.
[4] Towles, *op. cit.*, p. 24.
[5] Barnard, *op. cit.*, p. 12.
[6] S. M. Kingsbury, *Labor Laws and Their Enforcement with Special Reference to Massachusetts*, 1911, p. 13.

States.[1] At that time, English factories, limited by the Act of 1833, were working only 69 hours a week. One worker said in 1833: "The blacks of the South enjoy more leisure, time, and liberty, and fare quite as well as the operatives in the northern and eastern manufactories." [2]

For these long hours, workers got what seems to us now to be very low wages, yet there were many complaints about "the high price of wages." Informed persons stated around 1790 that the money wage rate for common labor was much higher here than in England, though that was not true of the wages of skilled craftsmen.[3] A number of wage comparisons around 1825 indicate that the average pay for unskilled laboring men in America was about $1.00 a day, or 35 per cent above comparable rates in England calculated at the current exchange rate, and that the wages of women and children factory "hands" at times were as much as 20 per cent above the English level for such workers. However, in some cases factory pay in America was lower than in Great Britain. The weekly wages of women and girls in the Waltham spinning rooms averaged $3.23, while those in Manchester, England, were from $2.50 to $3.75.[4] In many American mills, wages were lower than at Waltham. Around 1825 there are statements that the wages in Massachusetts woolen mills and some American cotton mills were no higher than in England.[5] It was about this time that President Monroe, in an annual message, congratulated the manufacturers on the "fall in the price of labor, apparently so favorable to the success of domestic manufactures."

According to a study of wages by the United States Bureau of Labor Statistics, there is sufficient consistent evidence to justify the conclusion that by 1810 "wage standards had become fairly fixed for the respective crafts, and [the data] suggest about the same differences in wages between geographic localities and trades that we find today." [6] The highest wages were in New England, New York, New Jersey, Pennsylvania, and Ohio, and the lowest were in the South, with the territory west of Ohio holding the middle ground. In these belts, wages were higher inland than near the seaboard, which appears to support the statement of the committee of the

---

[1] *Ibid.*, pp. 23–24.   [2] Commons *et al.*, *op. cit.*, p. 358.   [3] Clark, *op. cit.*, p. 389.
[4] *Ibid.*, p. 395. Calculations based simply on the current exchange rate between English and American money.
[5] *Cf. Ibid.*, pp. 392–97.   [6] U. S. Bureau of Labor Statistics, *op. cit.*, p. 56.

Pennsylvania legislature in 1752, that free land kept up the price of labor.

Statistical evidence seems to indicate that the real wages of common laborers and skilled craftsmen did not increase from 1800 to 1820, and probably even declined somewhat during that period.[1] The wages of skilled workers, of course, tended to decline relative to those for unskilled workers. An index of real wages for this country since 1820, constructed on a 1913 base by Professor Alvin Hansen, is summarized by decades in the following table: [2]

1820–29	46.1
1830–39	47.6
1840–49	55.8
1850–59	52.0
1860–69	52.9
1870–79	76.5
1880–89	85.3
1890–99	102.5
1900–09	103.0
1910–19	102.4

Such data seem to indicate that the workers failed to receive a major share of the increased production from 1800 to 1870.

During decades when real wages remained fairly stable in the nineteenth century, many industrialists made large profits. According to V. S. Clark, early cotton manufacturers acquired comfortable fortunes, and individual manufacturers, in spite of temporary reverses, accumulated fortunes of half a million dollars.[3] For example, the fortune of Samuel Slater, who arrived in America without funds and hired nine children from 7 to 12 years old to operate his first mill in Rhode Island, was inventoried in the midst of the 1829 crisis at over $690,000.[4] Rates of profit from 20 to 50 per cent a year were not uncommon, and, judging from numerous but scattered profit figures, the return on funds invested in factories probably averaged 12 per cent before 1850. Twenty-four New England corporations with a nominal capital of $20,000,000 averaged 10 per cent for the decade ending 1849, and the cotton mills controlled by Boston capitalists averaged 14-per-cent profits during the five years up to 1850.[5] These years included the long depression from 1839 to 1843 and the mild depressions of 1846 and 1848.

[1] Ibid., p. 58; McMaster, op. cit., pp. 510–13; and H. A. Millis and R. E. Montgomery, Labor's Progress and Some Basic Labor Problems, 1938, p. 80.

[2] "Factors Affecting the Trend of Real Earnings," American Economic Review, vol. 25 (March 1925), p. 32.

[3] Clark, op. cit., pp. 374–78.   [4] Idem.   [5] Ibid., p. 375.

Depressions. Even in this early period, business depressions tended to occur at about the same time in various countries. There were depression conditions in this country during the years 1816–20, 1829, 1834, the early 1840's, and 1848.[1] In most of these years, England also suffered from depressed business conditions, indicating that depressions then were often international phenomena, perhaps transmitted by means of an international monetary standard. The effect of business fluctuations on the workers is illustrated by statements in the New York newspapers in 1829, telling of "thousands of industrious mechanics," who, "with tears on their manly cheeks, confessed their inability to provide food or clothing for their families," and of "hundreds and thousands of shivering applicants for charity, who thronged" the almshouses.[2]

Labor organizations. By the early 1820's, the workers in factories began to organize, and were the first to use the word "union" in the title of their organizations. In 1825 the first strike conducted solely by women occurred. In 1827, a strike by Philadelphia building trades workers for a 10-hour day led to the formation of the first effective city-central organization of local unions in separate trades known in the world—the Philadelphia Mechanics' Union of Trade Associations. This coordinated organization of wage-earners in separate trades represented action by workingmen as a class for a common purpose and seems to have antedated similar organizations in England by three years.[3] In that same city in 1828, there began the publication of the first trade-union journal in the world, the *Mechanics Free Press*. Trade-unionism in this country apparently was a purely American-made product rather than a foreign importation.

The world's first city-central organization in Philadelphia in 1827 led to what is claimed to be the first labor party in the world. This was the "Working Men's Party," which began in Philadelphia in 1828 and flourished in New York, New England, and Ohio from 1829 to 1832. During these years there were city and state conventions, and a number of the Party's candidates were elected to state and local offices. The Party, of course, included independent craftsmen and farmers as well as wage-earners. By August 1830 no

[1] *Cf.*, W. L. Thorp, *Business Annals*, 1926, pp. 94, 116–25.

[2] Commons *et al.*, *op. cit.*, pp. 170–71.

[3] *Ibid.*, p. 169; and J. R. Commons (Ed.), *Documentary History of American Industrial Society*, 1910, vol. 5, pp. 21–22.

less than 20 newspapers are said to have "come out fearlessly in the advocacy of the principles of the Working Men's Party," and at one time or another as many as 50 newspapers in 15 states expressed approval of the movement.[1] Among the chief principles of the party were: (1) free public education for all, (2) the 10-hour day, (3) abolition of monopolies and restrictions on banks as "privileged monied institutions," (4) more equal and just taxation, and (5) opposition to protective tariffs, for, as the *Mechanics Free Press* put it, "of all others, tariff protected manufacturers are most prone to reduce the wages of their workmen." In some cases, as in New York, the Working Men's Party declared itself in favor of the equal division of all property, including land and capital. Even in Vermont, Working Men's Societies pointed out that the producers of the wealth in the country were becoming poorer, while the nonproducers were growing richer, and they demanded a more equitable distribution of the nation's production for the producers of wealth.[2] But the first and foremost demand of the Party was for a free and universal system of tax-supported schools to educate and elevate the children of the workers—the capitalless, wage-earning class. The need for such an educational system is indicated by an estimate in 1833 that over 1,000,000 (or one out of every three) children in the United States between the ages of 5 and 15 were not in school.[3] This period of political activity and reform proposals has been called the "hot air" epoch in American labor history.

Gradually the strength of the unions increased. In 1829 the 10-hour day was adopted for skilled trades in New York City, and by the end of 1835 labor had made the 10-hour day the standard for skilled craftsmen in most of the large cities. At that time, the membership of trade-unions in this country was estimated at 300,000.[4] The first national federation of trade-unions existed from 1834 to 1837, and in the same period the first five national organizations of local unions in one trade were formed. The National Typographical Association in printing, for example, was organized in 1834 to combat the introduction of "green hands" in printing. It levied dues on, and issued union cards to, local member unions.

Although labor organizations suffered a setback during the depression following the panic of 1837, the movement was fully re-

[1] Commons *et al.*, *op. cit.*, p. 286.
[2] *Ibid.*, pp. 236–37, 292, 522.
[3] Bogart, *op. cit.*, p. 432.
[4] Commons *et al.*, *op. cit.*, p. 424.

stored by the early 1850's. Employers were also organized at that
time. By 1853

a tacit understanding in some trades amounted in effect to an employers'
association as far as the payment of wages was concerned. Hence the
journeymen found that, while they were ostensibly dealing with individual employers, they were in reality dealing with employers' associations, and this for the most part in an arbitrary way, i.e., before any
employer would give his reply to a demand for increased wages, he would
confer with his fellow employers and would reach some agreement with
them.[1]

This situation caused the unions to give up the method of dealing
with individual employers separately, and led to the introduction
of the trade agreement, accepted by a number of employers and
local unions in an industry and in an area. By 1854 most of the
strong unions in the eastern cities had made such collective agreements with employers or employers' associations.[2]

Factory legislation. The establishment of a factory code in
this country to protect weaker members of the wage-earning class
from exploitation was aided considerably by the example of, and
experience under, the Factory Acts in England. The first child-
labor laws, such as the Connecticut law of 1813 and the New Jersey
law of 1816, like the first Factory Acts in England, stipulated that
the factory officials provide employed children, especially pauper
apprentices, with instruction in the three R's. The next batch of
child-labor laws, enacted by various states from 1842 to 1853, either
forbade the employment of children under 10 or 12 years of age in
factories, or limited the working hours of children to 10 a day, along
with a requirement that child employees must have had some previous schooling. In the debates on these laws, the example of England was frequently cited.

These early child-labor laws, however, made no provision for
factory inspectors to enforce them, as did the English Factory Act
of 1833. Though they represented public recognition of the evils of
child labor and the right of the government to regulate the relations between employer and employee, these laws were, for the
most part, "unenforceable threats," which employers did not obey.
For example, a Connecticut law passed in 1857 forbade the em-

[1] *Ibid.*, p. 605.
[2] *Ibid.*, p. 606. The history of labor organization after the 1850's is contained in
various chapters of Part Three *infra*, especially Chapter 20.

ployment of children under 10, yet hundreds of children from 8 to 10 years of age were employed in Connecticut from 1870 to 1887, and a Connecticut official reported in 1866: "If I were to attempt to execute the present [child-labor] law, this village would be too hot to hold me." [1] About one fourth of the employees in Connecticut cotton factories in 1870 were children under 16. Though New Jersey passed a law in 1851 forbidding employment of children under 10 in "any factory," the hiring of "mere infants in shops" continued, for a factory inspector found in 1884 that the "average age" at which child employees had begun work was 9 years.[2]

It was only in the 1880's that states like Massachusetts, Rhode Island, Connecticut, New York, New Jersey, and Pennsylvania really began strict enforcement of their Factory Acts, usually by means of a staff of factory inspectors. By that time, the hours of factory labor for minors had been limited to 10 a day in many states and the minimum age for factory labor had been raised to 12 or 13 years of age. In this country, enactment of legislation limiting the hours of work for women and regulating factory conditions (heat, light, ventilation, sanitation, etc.) occurred much later than in England. Though the 10-hour day on Federal public works was adopted in 1840, and some states around 1850 passed laws making 10 hours the legal working day unless otherwise stated by contract, it was only in the 1870's and 1880's that states began to limit by law the working hours for women to 10 a day or to pass legislation regulating working conditions in factories.

One reason why this country was much later than England in enacting an effective Factory Code was that the factory system was not established here on a large scale as early as it was in England. As late as 1850 there were two-and-a-half times as many farmers and agricultural workers as there were wage-earners in factories and handicraft industries in this country. Another reason was the hesitancy of one state to take action for fear that its industries would be handicapped in interstate competition. However, the greatest obstacle to effective factory legislation in this country was the doctrine of laissez faire, which colored all discussions and arguments on the subject.

[1] A. M. Edwards, *The Labor Legislation of Connecticut,* Publications of the American Economic Association, 1907, third series, vol. 7, No. 3, pp. 9, 14, 30, 34.

[2] A. S. Field, *The Child Labor Policy of New Jersey,* Publications of the American Economic Association, 1910, third series, vol. 11, No. 2, pp. 14, 35.

The national and state governments and their constitutions were established at a time when the doctrine of natural rights and the philosophy of laissez faire were in vogue, both here and in Europe. In addition, there still existed in industrial centers the spirit of frontier individualism. Therefore, it is not surprising to find state legislators arguing that hours legislation for women and children would be "foreign to the spirit of our government," or that it was "the established policy of the State from its foundation" to allow "every adult person to govern his own conduct and his own contracts." [1] It was also argued that "competition is the best guarantee the laboring man can have that he will be properly dealt" with; that hours legislation would be an "infringement of the natural rights of the laborer"; that, if a shorter working day was a good thing, it would be adopted by natural means without legislation; and that such restrictions would injure business within the state and, therefore, would cause the laborers to suffer.[2] A bill to raise the age limit for children in factories to 14 years was even considered "socialistic."[3]

Employers as a unit were opposed to legislation lowering the hours of labor. They even thought that legislation to shorten the working hours of children in factories to 10 a day would have an "unhappy influence," for, by fostering idleness, it would provide the Devil with little workshops. Dr. Towles believes that the millowners in Rhode Island were sincere in their conviction that a 10-hour day by legislation "would do great harm to the laboring class," and he adds:

There seems to be much logic in the contention of the pragmatists that our opinions are based upon our interests; that a man's ideas of what is true and worth while are relative concepts and vary with his position in society. It is interesting to note in this connection that some of the men most active in opposing the ten-hour day for women and children were among the founders of the Society for the Prevention of Cruelty to Children.[4]

American economists did not enjoy the reputation nor exert the influence on legislators that Malthus, Ricardo, and Mill did in their day in England. Their doctrines were not cited by opponents of state factory legislation. Though many college professors, out of touch with economic conditions at home, taught the classical doctrines of Malthus and Ricardo, most American economists, influ-

---

[1] Barnard, *op. cit.*, p. 4; and Towles, *op. cit.*, p. 68.
[2] Kingsbury, *op. cit.*, pp. 51, 79; and Towles, *op. cit.*, p. 68.
[3] Edwards, *op. cit.*, p. 36.   [4] Towles, *op. cit.*, p. 69.

enced by this favorable environment, vigorously attacked the gloomy theories of these English economists, which one American charged strove "to apply, as a universal condition of human being, the miserable results of local misrule." [1] While some academic economists preached "Great is the laissez faire of the Ricardians," other economists in this country opposed laissez faire, many advocating government intervention to encourage industry, especially in the form of protective tariff legislation. Some American economists recognized that there frequently is a conflict between individual and social interests, and thought that poverty was due, not to the niggardliness of nature, but to a faulty distribution of wealth and income, which one of them proposed to remedy by having all property divided equally among the people at least once in every generation. Though the most widely used college textbook prior to the Civil War preached the wage-fund doctrine, in 1876 that doctrine was fully exploded by Professor Francis Walker, who held that production furnishes the true measure of wages. [2] It is easy to understand why these doctrines of the American economists, which failed to fit the predilections of contemporary capitalists, were not used as ammunition against factory legislation.

It is true that Professor W. G. Sumner of Yale in the early 1880's argued against labor organizations as a bootstrap device, which could have absolutely no effect on wage rates because wages are determined solely by demand and supply, but Professor Sumner as an ardent free trader was hardly an advocate for the industrialists.

When the employers claimed that factory legislation would ruin the state's business to the benefit of industry in other states, the proponents of child-labor and hours legislation pointed out that the same objection had been strenuously urged in England against the Ten Hour Act of 1847 and other English Factory Acts, yet there the result had been just the opposite. England's experience with factory legislation, they pointed out, had been a success; neither production nor wages had been lessened by such laws, and English manufacturers admitted the good effects of England's hours legislation. [3] It was claimed that a reduction in hours would even increase

---

[1] A. Walker, *The Science of Wealth* (fourth edition), 1866, p. 452.

[2] For a discussion of the doctrines of early American economists, *cf.* J. R. Turner, *The Ricardian Rent Theory in Early American Economics*, 1921, especially pp. lxiii, 22–26, 31, 40, 48–52, 61–64, 67–69, 77, 84, 113, 115, 146–49, 155, and 170–73.

[3] Barnard, *op. cit.*, p. 8; and Kingsbury, *op. cit.*, pp. 81–84.

the profit of employers, for workers "would be more vigorous and better able to work, from having had suitable time to rest." [1] In the first half of the nineteenth century, a number of doctors had stated that the long hours of labor for women and children were seriously impairing their health. [2] Finally, a legislative committee in Massachusetts pointed out in 1850 that the legislature had "destroyed the natural relations" between employer and employee by passing incorporation acts, which "created immense artificial persons, with far larger powers than are possessed by individuals." These large corporations, in the words of the committee, "all act substantially in concert in dealing with laborers and avoid all competition in overbidding for labor," which enables them "to fix inexorably, without consultation with the laboring class, all the terms and conditions of labor." The committee, believing fully in the doctrine of laissez faire under normal circumstances, maintained that artificial strengthening of the power of capital by state interference in the form of incorporation laws made necessary action to "protect the interest and welfare of the laborers." [3]

Such arguments, along with the evident evils resulting from failure of state legislatures to protect women and child workers, finally led to the enactment of factory codes in the various states. As in England, experience in American factories proved laissez faire impractical and costly to the community through wasteful exploitation of human resources. Dire predictions of ruin to American manufacturers from factory legislation were disproved by successful experience.

More recent labor legislation is discussed in subsequent chapters dealing with minimum wages, hours of work, social insurance, and labor relations. Chapter 20 discusses the history of labor organization from the middle of the nineteenth century to the present time. This chapter was designed to give the broad sweep of labor history, to explain the background of labor legislation, to indicate how public policy has fluctuated between laissez faire and government regulation of the labor market, and to explain the competitive conditions that gave rise to the first labor unions. [4]

---

[1] Commons *et al.*, *op. cit.*, p. 541; and Barnard, *op. cit.*, p. 15.

[2] Kingsbury, *op. cit.*, p. 52; and Barnard, *op. cit.*, p. 12.

[3] Kingsbury, *op. cit.*, pp. 79–80.

[4] An excellent little history of labor in America is Mary R. Beard's *The American Labor Movement, A Short History*, 1935.

PART TWO

LABOR'S ECONOMIC PROBLEMS

CHAPTER FIVE

THE LABOR MARKET

People generally believe that wage rates, like other prices, are determined in the market by demand and supply. But they usually are at a loss to explain the nature of the demand schedule and the supply schedule for labor in various markets. For this they can hardly be blamed, because economists have given too little attention to the characteristics of labor markets, especially the imperfections in such markets. In this chapter the characteristics of labor markets will be discussed, and the nature of the demand and supply schedules for labor will be examined. Often buyers of labor are in a dominant position in the market and, therefore, it is possible for them to "exploit" the sellers of labor unless the sellers organize or the government intervenes by some such action as the passage of minimum-wage laws. Chapter 6 discusses the possible effects of employer organizations and labor unions upon the labor market. The economic aspects of minimum-wage laws are treated in Chapter 12.

General remarks. Before discussing the imperfections in the labor market, a few general observations should be made on the nature of the market. The labor market is essentially a local market. The market place is customarily at the buyer's place of business, so that there may be as many market places as there are buyers. Sometimes public and private employment exchanges or trade associations or trade-unions aid in the selection and placement of workers, but in the end the sale normally occurs on the buyer's premises. Therefore, when the sale takes place, there is only one buyer in the market place, though there are usually many sellers of labor offering their services for sale.

Not only must the sellers sell at the buyers' places of business, but they normally can sell to only one buyer and in only one market place at any one time, and they have only their own labor to sell.

93

Because the worker sells his own services, which require his presence on the buyer's premises during working hours, the worker may be unable to shop around in other markets during the working day. Furthermore, hours of labor cannot, like certain commodities, be stored up and accumulated until a later date when the price is higher.

IMPERFECTIONS IN THE LABOR MARKET

The nature of the labor market can best be explained by contrasting that market with what has come to be called a "perfect market," which organized commodity and security markets, such as the Chicago Board of Trade and the New York Stock Exchange, closely approximate. In this way the imperfect elements in the labor market may be clearly discerned.

Six characteristics of a perfect market will serve as the basis for this contrast. Parts of the following discussion may seem to emphasize obvious facts, but in theoretical writings on wages the obvious has frequently been overlooked or disregarded.

1. The first requisite of a perfect or purely competitive market is that the commodity or service be homogeneous or standardized, so that no buyer will prefer any particular seller and no seller will prefer any particular buyer. It is immaterial to the buyer, for example, from what person he purchases a certain share of stock or grade of wheat or rubber. An hour of labor, however, is not a standarized or homogeneous unit; it varies with the hour of the day, the working facilities, the management, the worker's experience, and many other circumstances. Buyers prefer certain sellers for personal as well as economic reasons. Also, a seller of labor services will normally prefer certain buyers, perhaps because of their reputation for fair dealing, the steadiness of their employment, the possibility of advancement, the human quality of the supervision, the location of their plants, the physical conditions in their factories, the effect of employment in these firms upon the social status of the employee, or for some other reason.

2. With pure or perfect competition, such as is found in organized stock and commodity exchanges, there is but one price for a given article in the market at any one time. Sellers are not able to sell their services or commodities above that price, nor are buyers able to purchase below that price. Whether one applies the term labor

market to a buyer's place of business or to a local area which includes several buyers, he finds that there is not a single wage rate for each class and grade of labor that clears the market and leaves no qualified sellers unable to sell at that rate. Instead of one price for each occupation and grade of labor, there is a whole range of prices. The same buyer may pay unequal rates for the same work by workers of the same efficiency for such reasons as differences in length of service, sex, race, or personality of workers. It is possible for a buyer to discriminate and pay different rates for the same service by persons of the same status because of the secrecy that frequently surrounds the terms of employment of various workers, especially where the workers are unorganized. Such discrimination is, however, more characteristic of firms employing few workmen than of large enterprises, which normally have standard or set rates for each class of labor just as they have fixed prices for their products. When higher than standard rates are secretly paid to some workers in a certain classification, the employer may receive additional service, such as spy work or pace setting, or he may make the additional payment in order to keep the natural leaders in his labor force friendly toward the firm.

Wage studies indicate that in the same locality rates of pay for one grade of labor in a well-defined occupation vary considerably among employers.[1] Such variations cannot be fully explained or justified by differences in effort or quality of service, but must be explained on such grounds as imperfect competition or a desire on the part of the employer to be considered favorably by the laboring groups in the community. Executives of 60 important firms stated at a recent conference that some of these differences in wage rates between firms could be explained "only on grounds of one employer's ability and willingness to pay more than other employers for apparently comparable services" and by the "inability or unwillingness of some employers to pay more than absolutely necessary

[1] Cf., for example, R. Larue Frain, "Two Errors in Interpreting Wage Data," *American Economic Review*, vol. 19 (September 1929), pp. 378–92; and by the same author, "Wage Levels between Firms," *ibid.*, vol. 21 (December 1931), pp. 620–35. Cf. also, *Variations in Wage Rates under Corresponding Conditions*, U. S. Department of Labor, Women's Bureau, Bulletin 122, 1935, p. 4, where it is pointed out that there are marked variations in wage rates in the same occupation in a given locality and in the same plant, and "even when allowance for all factors that might cause the variations had been made, comparisons made in plants under conditions as nearly identical as obtainable showed differences in payment so marked as to be attributable only to lack of wage standards."

to hold crews together." [1] In other words, it is possible in the labor market for a given buyer to lower his offer, while other buyers continue to pay the same rates, without being eliminated from the market by the disappearance of his entire labor supply. Sellers do not shift in mass with every change in the relative rates of wages offered by different employers, and buyers will not hire all qualified labor offered at their wage rates.

3. In a perfect market the number of buyers and sellers is so large that any one seller or buyer will have a negligible effect upon the total supply or demand and, therefore, no seller or buyer can influence the market price by his own actions. To each seller the demand curve for his product or services appears to be a horizontal line at the prevailing price (no matter how much he sells in the market, his sales will be too insignificant to affect the market price), and to each buyer the supply curve in the perfect market seems to be a horizontal line so that he can buy as much or as little as he wishes without affecting the price in the market.

On the sellers' side of the labor market there may be such atomistic competition because each seller can sell no more than his own services. For all practical purposes, the amount of labor he does, and can, offer for sale is relatively fixed. Where a special skill or training is necessary for the job, it is possible, of course, that there may be only a few qualified sellers in the locality, in which case the sellers' side of the market contains elements of imperfection. Often sellers are, after a period of employment with a particular firm, better qualified for certain types of work in that firm than they would be for work in any other firm, in which case there would be a seller's monopoly or oligopoly (a few qualified sellers) bargaining with a buyer's monopoly. This situation is treated more fully later in this chapter.

Though there are usually large numbers on the sellers' side of the market, normally there is but a restricted number on the buyers' side. As was indicated in Chapter 1, half of the 37,000,000 employees covered by the Federal Old-Age and Survivors Insurance

[1] John W. Riegel, *Wage Determination*, Bureau of Industrial Relations, University of Michigan, 1937, pp. 8–9. Professor Balderston has also explained that the wage level within a labor market is not a single line but a "broad band," because some companies "consciously adopt the policy of paying more than the market average, whereas others pay below it" and because of a lack of knowledge of what the market rates really are. *Cf.* C. Canby Balderston, *Wage Differentials*, *A Study of Wage Rates in Philadelphia Metal Plants*, 1939, p. 13.

Benefits program are in firms with 250 or more employees, and in American industry as a whole the sellers of labor probably outnumber the regular buyers of labor by at least fifteen to one.

The situation on the buyers' side of the labor market (in the sense of a local area and not the market place) may range all the way from monopsony (a buyer's monopoly), to oligopsony (a few buyers), to, in very rare cases, a sufficient number of small buyers to constitute pure or perfect competition. In many localities, such as company towns or one-industry areas, there is practically a monopoly on the buying side of the market. In such coal, steel, lumber, or textile towns, the buyer may realize, of course, that his short-run supply curve of labor is more vertical than horizontal.[1] Even where there are a number of buyers in a local market area, some of them may be so large that they exert considerable influence on the market situation. In industrial cities from 25,000 to 100,000 in population, it is not at all infrequent to find that one fifth of all wage and salary workers in the city are working for a single firm, and often three or four firms in such cities employ about one half of the employees in the city. The influence that a single firm may exert in the local market area for labor is noticeable when a company closes its factory or threatens to move out of the locality. Where a firm accounts for a considerable part of total employment in a locality, the management of that firm, instead of taking the price of labor as given and adjusting to it after the fashion of buyers in purely competitive markets, is liable to consider the effect of its actions upon the price of labor services and to have what is called a wage policy.

To a buyer of labor, the supply curve will be tipped (not horizontal) whenever that buyer realizes that he cannot purchase more labor without bidding up the price of labor; that is, he is such an important element on the buying side of the market that changes in the amount that he purchases do affect the market price. The difference between the demand curve as seen by a seller in a perfect market and a seller in an imperfect market is illustrated by Figures 1 and 2. The seller in a perfect market assumes that he can increase the quantity that he sells from 10 to 50 without affecting the price in the market, whereas the seller in an imperfect market realizes, as indicated in Figure 2, that he can sell larger quantities only at decreasing market prices. On the supply side, the same con-

---

[1] The nature of the supply of labor is discussed later on in this chapter.

trast between conditions in perfect and imperfect markets is illustrated in Figures 3 and 4. The buyer in a perfect market assumes that
the supply is perfectly elastic to him at the market price, that his supply curve is a horizontal line permitting him to increase his pur-

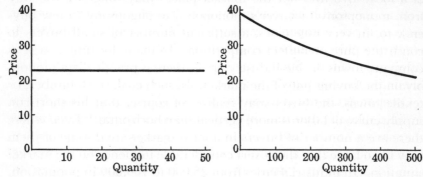

FIG. 1. Horizontal Demand Curve for   FIG. 2. Tipped Demand Curve for a
  · a Seller in a Perfect Market.   Seller in an Imperfect Market.

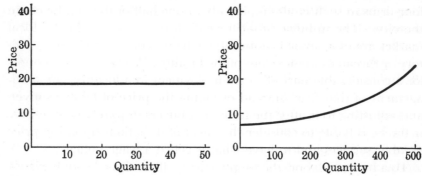

FIG. 3. Horizontal Supply Curve for a   FIG. 4. Tipped Supply Curve for a
  Buyer in a Perfect Market.   Buyer in an Imperfect Market.

chases from 10 to 50 without affecting the market price. The buyer
in an imperfect market, on the other hand, faces a tipped supply
curve, because his purchases are so significant in the market that
they do affect the market price. The quantity he purchases can be
increased only by bidding up the market price.

4. In a perfect market both buyers and sellers must possess full
knowledge of market conditions and opportunities in other markets. The buyers of labor services usually do have rather full
knowledge of the market, especially the larger buyers. It is a common practice for companies, trade associations, local employers'

associations, or chambers of commerce to make periodic surveys of the wage rates paid by employers within a locality or industry for workers of various classes or occupations and to make that information available to the employers. Companies sometimes offer their figures in exchange for wage figures of other firms; or one firm, such as the telephone company, may act as a clearinghouse for wage data; or companies may be members of trade associations which give their members wage information for that trade in many different localities. Such wage surveys are customarily used in determining the company's wage policy.

Companies are not accustomed to make known to their employees or the public the information obtained from their surveys of the labor market. Such surveys are usually kept confidential, and it has been found that, if a company's workers are engaged in making such a wage survey, "other employers decline to furnish wage information for fear that the sources of such information may become known to unauthorized persons." [1] Employees, therefore, usually know relatively little about the labor market even in their locality, to say nothing of other localities, for, as J. W. Riegel points out, "employees of different companies cannot furnish comprehensive wage statistics to each other, as can employers." [2] Such data are all the more necessary for a seller of labor because an intelligent choice of a job involves so many factors, including such items as working conditions in the plant, the supervision, the cost of living in the locality, the speed of operation in the plant, and the possibility of future employment and advancement. Ignorance of market conditions and outside opportunities on the part of labor tends to make an employer's supply curve of labor relatively inelastic to wage-rate reductions by causing a "pool" of labor to be more or less attached to him.

5. Above all there must, in a perfect market, be no cooperation nor collusion among sellers or among buyers. It is obvious that a labor union represents an attempt at cooperation on the sellers' part, but it is less widely recognized that cooperation and collusion on the buyers' side is frequent and often more effective. Adam Smith wrote in his *Wealth of Nations:* [3]

The masters, being fewer in number, can combine much more easily; and the law, besides, authorizes, or at least does not prohibit their com-

[1] Riegel, *op. cit.*, p. 11.   [2] *Ibid.*, p. 9.   [3] Everyman's Edition, 1924, p. 59.

binations, while it prohibits those of the workmen. We have no acts of parliament against combining to lower the price of work; but many against combining to raise it . . .

We rarely hear, it has been said, of the combinations of masters, though frequently of those of workmen. But whoever imagines, upon this account, that masters rarely combine, is as ignorant of the world as of the subject. Masters are always and everywhere in a sort of tacit, but constant and uniform combination, not to raise the wages of labour above their actual rate. To violate this combination is everywhere a most unpopular action, and a sort of reproach to a master among his neighbours and equals. We seldom, indeed, hear of this combination, because it is the usual, and one may say, the natural state of things, which nobody ever hears of. Masters, too, sometimes enter into particular combinations to sink the wages of labour even below this rate.

What Adam Smith wrote in 1776 is still true. In the purchase of labor all enterprisers have a common interest as buyers, whereas in the market for most commodities and services some firms are buyers and some are sellers. The products of one firm may be the raw materials, merchandise, or equipment of another firm; and most firms buy transportation, communication, power, and other services from outside companies. Therefore, the labor market is practically the only market in which business firms and businessmen are all on one side of the market. On probably no other price would enterprisers be so united by self-interest.

It is not surprising then to find, as Adam Smith found in his day, that employers tacitly cooperate to keep wage rates down in the localities where their plants are established. For example, there is considerable pressure upon the telephone company not to pay more than "the prevailing rate" in any locality where the telephone company hires workers. When Henry Ford adopted the five-dollar day with a 48-hour week in 1914 he discovered that, to use his own words, "Many employers . . . condemned us because we were upsetting standards—violating the custom of paying a man the smallest amount he would take." [1] Without any concerted action by employers' associations or formal agreements by firms with regard to wages, there may be considerable pressure upon employers to keep their wage rates down, even outside of those localities where attempts are made to attract industry by offering employers low-price

[1] Henry Ford in collaboration with Samuel Crowther, *My Life and Work*, 1926, pp. 126–27.

labor.[1] Because of the pressure brought to bear upon employers to keep wage rates down, most large firms follow the practice of paying "the average of prevailing rates in the community" and attracting the better workers by means other than price competition, such as recreation and welfare programs, group insurance, etc. The wage policies of large firms are more fully discussed in a later section of this chapter.

Apparently labor markets have been subject to practically all of the collusive practices that have been condemned by economists and the law when they have been used in the commodity and security markets. Not only has there been concerted action on wages by members of trade associations or employers' associations, but there have been gentlemen's agreements not to spoil the market by bidding or competing with one another for labor, and in some industries there seems to have been what might be called a practice of following the leader. That, for example, was the case during the early years of the depression in the steel industry, and a similar situation has existed at various times in the oil industry and in shipping on the Pacific Coast. Other firms in the industry have tended to change their wage rates as the U. S. Steel, or the Standard Oil of New Jersey, or the San Francisco shipowners altered their wage scales.[2] In his 1934 presidential address to the American Economic Association, Professor H. A. Millis made the following statements about collusion in, and control of, local labor markets by employers:

. . . Furthermore, the economic theorist assumes in much or in all of his analysis that there is no element of monopoly or concerted control in the demand for labor or in fixing wages. This is by no means true. An employer, or a group of employers acting in concert or just individually fearing to create problems, may dominate the employment situation in a community. So it was in the mining of anthracite coal between the middle seventies and the turn of the century. Wages were pegged; payment for

[1] In 1926, when the Canadian National Railway Company proposed to pay a two-cents-per-hour supplementary wage to shopmen in certain regions for the whole-hearted manner in which they had accepted and operated the union-management cooperative plan, the Canadian Pacific Railway Company objected and, in consequence, the Canadian National dropped any attempt to share the gains of cooperation with the workers by additional wage payments and instead adopted in 1928 the method of one week's vacation with pay. *Cf.* Louis A. Wood, *Union-Management Cooperation on the Railroads*, 1931, pp. 238–41 and 248–50.

[2] *Cf. Iron Age*, vol. 128 (October 1, 1931), p. 894; vol. 129 (May 12, 1932), p. 1082; and vol. 132 (July 20, 1933), p. 34; and *Proceedings before Federal Mediation Board of the United States Government*, 1934 (unpublished, original in Library of Congress), vol. 3, pp. 271, 281, 285, 296–97, and 303.

timbering and "dead work" was reduced or eliminated altogether; coerced purchases at company stores charging high prices, and powder sold at a profit of 200 per cent, took the larger part of the earnings of the miners. Even in a city like Chicago, an industry may dominate a large community and the firms engaged in it may control the situation within rather wide limits. Going beyond this, I could cite a number of instances where associations of manufacturers or merchants have fixed scales or, indeed, maximum wages to be paid and have enforced them more successfully than any American state has enforced its minimum wage standards.[1]

6. Finally, in a perfect market both the buyers and the sellers must have free entry and access to the market. A closed-shop agreement, of course, restricts such freedom of any person to enter the market, as does the black-listing of union leaders or workers who have certain political views.

Free access to the labor market is also restricted where the worker fears he may be discharged if his present employer learns that he is shopping around in the market. Such fear may prevent the worker from canvasing the market situation in an intelligent manner, and it is strengthened by the practice among employers of asking former and present employers for their opinions of the worker's ability and industry. The worker's freedom of access to the market is also restricted when an employer hesitates or refuses to hire any workers employed by certain other firms because the employer (or officials of that company) does not wish to antagonize those other firms. It may be that these other firms are customers of that employer, or they may cooperate with his company in certain ways, or the owners and management of these other firms may be in a position to injure that employer in a financial or personal manner. Even without any possibility of injury to an employer who may bid away the employees of other firms, there is, as Joan Robinson indicates, a strong convention "that it is a dastardly act for one employer to lure away labour from another by the offer of higher wages," [2] and that convention acts to restrict competition in the market. Any such influence or pressure restraining a trader from acting for his own best interests in that market is, of course, interference with the freedom of the market.

[1] "The Union in Industry: Theory of Collective Bargaining," *American Economic Review*, vol. 25 (March 1935), pp. 6–7. The question of the influence of employers' associations on the labor market is treated in detail in the next chapter.

[2] *Essays in the Theory of Employment*, 1937, p. 14.

In commodity or stock exchanges, persons trading in the market frequently switch from the buying to the selling side and *vice versa* as the price changes. They are not consistently and continually sellers regardless of the price. In the labor market, however, the sellers seldom, if ever, change over to the buying side, nor do the buyers frequently switch to the selling side of the market. It is, of course, practically impossible for most employees to start in business as enterprisers in those lines of business in which they have worked. The present-day capital requirements for establishing most businesses act as a complete barrier to any attempt by a seller of labor to become a buyer whenever the market value of labor services falls appreciably. That is especially true in such lines as banking, insurance, metals, the public utilities, government service, oil, tobacco, rubber, and other branches of business that require a considerable amount of capital.

That the market for labor is imperfect is indicated by the behavior of wage rates. Customarily they do not move by very small fractions (such as one eighth of a cent), as do prices on commodity or stock exchanges, but change by five-cents-per-hour intervals. Wage rates are not the constantly fluctuating prices that have traditionally been associated with free and perfect markets. Furthermore, wage rates may lag far behind movements in the general level of prices, or fail to follow price-level movements at all. Both of these phenomena are evident in the period during and directly following both the Civil War and the first World War.[1] Indeed, it is not at all infrequent to find that hourly wage rates in various classifications have remained the same in localities for years at a time, though other prices and the general price level have fluctuated widely or moved to a considerable degree either upward or downward.

Such facts seem to indicate not only that there are elements of imperfection and monopoly in the labor market, but that custom and other noneconomic factors, some of which were mentioned in the foregoing discussion, play an important role in the determination of wage rates. It would seem that often, in the past, hourly wage rates might have been somewhat different from what they

[1] "Some firms went through the entire war and post-war periods of inflation without raising more than a few scattered rates." Sumner Slichter, *Modern Economic Society*, 1931, p. 618.

were without any noticeable effect on the demand for, or supply of, labor. Such an implication is involved in the conclusions of Marshall and Edgeworth "that there is a degree of indeterminateness, or arbitrariness, about the fixing of wages—even when combination is absent" from both sides of the labor market.[1]

NATURE OF DEMAND AND SUPPLY

Many people who assert that wages should be determined by demand and supply fail to appreciate the complicated nature of the demand for, and supply of, labor services. Such an assertion may be rather meaningless where, as in the case of labor, it is possible that the demand curve crosses the supply curve at two or more prices, or corresponds exactly with the supply curve over a whole range of prices, or fails to intersect the supply curve at any price.

The difficulties involved in even attempting to construct demand and supply curves for labor are formidable. Perhaps, strictly speaking, it is invalid to draw up composite supply and demand curves for labor, because no two workers are exactly alike, and the same worker varies in effectiveness from hour to hour and with each particular set of circumstances. How is one to establish a uniform or homogeneous unit for labor when labor varies so in effectiveness and when the price itself may react upon the efficiency of the worker? Should money units or real units be used for the price scale? Such difficulties can, however, only be suggested here and must of necessity be largely disregarded in the discussion that follows.

Supply. There seems to be rather general agreement that at least a part of the nation's supply curve of labor has a pronounced negative slope, which means that the higher the price paid for labor the less labor will be supplied.[2] In this respect, the supply curve for labor as a whole is unlike other supply curves, for they are positively sloped throughout; that is, the amount supplied increases as the price rises. From statistical studies, Professor Paul Douglas concludes that the short-run supply curve of labor in this country has

[1] *Cf.* J. R. Hicks, "Edgeworth, Marshall, and the Indeterminateness of Wages," *Economic Journal*, vol. 40 (June 1930), p. 215.

[2] *Cf.* Paul Douglas, *The Theory of Wages*, 1934, pp. 269–314; Erika H. Schoenberg and Paul Douglas, "Studies in the Supply Curve of Labor: The Relation in 1929 between Average Earnings in American Cities and the Proportions Seeking Employment," *Journal of Political Economy*, vol. 45 (February 1937), pp. 45–79; Joan Robinson, *op. cit.*, pp. 162–68; and Slichter, *op. cit.*, pp. 620–27.

an elasticity of -0.24 to -0.33, which signifies that an increase in real hourly wages of one per cent would normally cause a decrease of from a quarter to a third of one per cent in the number of man-hours offered for sale.[1] The short-run supply curve of labor in general has this peculiar negative slope because, as the family's real income rises, workers press for a shorter work week and more leisure; women become less eager to secure wage-paying employment; and the working life of the average employee is shortened at both ends—by a longer period of education and earlier retirement from gainful employment.[2]

The majority of English mercantilists in the seventeenth and eighteenth centuries believed that the short-run supply curve of labor was negatively inclined, for they thought that with higher wages workers would be less willing to work and would, therefore, waste more time in idle pursuits, while lower wages would cause workers to work more hours during a week in order to eke out an existence. For extremely short periods of time, the negative slope of the supply curve of labor is probably not pronounced, because it may take a little time for a new wage level to affect the labor supply. Over a long period of years, the supply of labor in general is, of course, governed largely by changes in the total adult population within the area.

Though for the nation as a whole more units of labor would be supplied at a lower price, provided it is above bare subsistence, than at a higher price, the same would only be true for any particular area or occupation, if there were absolute immobility of labor or if the price of labor in various areas should move always by the same percentage and in the same direction. Fundamentally, therefore, the slope of the supply curve of labor in any area or for any employer depends upon the mobility of labor, because a supply schedule for one employer or area assumes that wage rates elsewhere do not change. It is not necessary, of course, that all labor be mobile in order that adjustments can be made to market changes. Such market adjustments may readily occur if

---

[1] *Cf.* previous footnote.

[2] Though the total supply curve may have a negative slope, certain factors making the slope of the total curve negative would affect some occupations more than others because of the existence of noncompeting groups. An increased supply of women's and children's labor, with a general decline in real earnings, would have little effect on the labor supply in the highly skilled trades.

a sufficient portion of the labor supply in each classification and area is highly mobile. Where a sufficient section of the labor supply is very mobile, the supply curve of labor for the whole country might have a negative slope, yet the supply curve of labor for any particular area, industry, occupation, or employer might have a positive slope, as do supply curves for commodities. On the other hand, the short-run supply curve of labor in a relatively isolated area, such as a company town, might be similar to the short-run supply curve for the country as a whole. The same might be true for occupations that are difficult to learn, so that the labor supply consists of some noncompeting groups.

It has been said that absolute immobility of labor would lead to a negative supply curve of labor for every area and employer, because at lower real wages workers attempt to work longer hours and more members of the family seek wage-paying employment. If the supply curve of labor for an employer or an area should be positively sloped, the factors increasing labor's immobility, along with the fact that labor is perishable and cannot be stored by the supplier, would tend to make any such positive supply curves relatively inelastic.[1] For a number of reasons, labor is relatively immobile and does not readily move from employer to employer, from occupation to occupation, or from area to area, even where the differences in hourly wage rates are considerable.

In the first place, it is usually costly and inconvenient for workers to move from one locality to another, and they may lose working time in making any change of jobs. Therefore, an employer in a locality may enjoy what has been called a "spatial monopoly." This would be especially the case in an isolated company town. The recent trend toward decentralization in such industries as hosiery, rubber, autos, and auto accessories tends, of course, to increase the spatial monopoly of such employers in the purchase of labor.

Secondly, workers are frequently ignorant of their opportunities in other markets, and a job is such a complex of factors that it may be difficult for the worker to determine whether he would really

[1] Absolute inelasticity exists when changes in price have no effect upon the amount supplied—at a higher or lower price the same amount would be offered for sale. Perfect elasticity exists when changes in quantity supplied can occur without any change in price. The former would be represented by a vertical line, and the latter by a horizontal line, on an ordinary price-quantity graph.

be better off if he were working for another firm in another area. He has to consider noneconomic as well as economic factors and to consider the long-run as well as the immediate prospect.

Thirdly, there are many restrictions on shopping around in other labor markets. The worker sells his services, which require his presence on one buyer's premises during working hours when the process of hiring normally occurs. Therefore, a worker may be unable to look elsewhere for work without quitting his present job. Furthermore, he is usually unable to acquaint other buyers with the real quality of his wares (services), for the present buyer is the only one who knows the present quality of the worker's services, and the present buyer only knows what their quality is under his particular working conditions. Any other buyer may not be able to judge accurately the value of such services until he has begun to purchase them.

Fourthly, unemployment may be an obstacle to mobility. If there is any unemployment in another market, a worker will hesitate to move to that other market to seek work as an "outsider," even though real wages there may be higher. As Joan Robinson has pointed out, it is probable "that workers are influenced almost entirely by the chance of finding a job, and that relative real wages exercise only a slight pull upon movements of labour." [1]

Fifthly, the worker knows that by moving from one employer to another he will lose any seniority rights or privileges as well as any good will or other elements of value connected with his present job that he cannot transfer to a new job. As a new employee in another firm he may be the first one to be laid off. Especially would a worker not change employers if he had acquired considerable skill and knowledge that is peculiar to and valuable to the firm for which he works, such as knowledge of company policy and procedures, but which would be of little or no value to other employers. This might be true of supervisors, management, some white-collar employees, and some highly skilled workers.

Sixthly, recent practices and attitudes of employers reduce the mobility of labor. Where employers have the practice of hiring workers early in their working lives with the notion that they will remain for the rest of their working days, the mobility of labor is reduced. The practice in industry of having a hiring deadline under

[1] Joan Robinson, *op. cit.*, p. 54.

40 or 50 years of age has the same effect of preventing older workers from changing their employers. Pension programs, group insurance, and other employer devices for attaching employees to one particular firm likewise contribute to reducing labor mobility and turnover. Mobility and labor turnover also tend to be reduced by any feeling on the part of employers that a worker who has changed employers frequently is likely to be an undesirable employee, by money debts that the employee owes to his employer, by employment contracts entered into by workers for an entire season, by the practice of not paying workers in full upon demand, or by other means of control of the worker by the employer. Finally, there are all the difficulties already discussed that confront any worker attempting to set up in business for himself. Such limitations to mobility vary in importance from locality to locality and from occupation to occupation, being perhaps most significant in a company town and the highly skilled trades.

All of these factors limiting the mobility of workers tend to make the labor-supply curve for any market area or any employer conform rather closely to the supply curve for the country as a whole. Indeed, it is not at all unlikely that a section of the labor-supply curve for some market areas has a negative slope. It is also probable that the supply curve of labor for many employers is absolutely inelastic within narrow ranges of wage rates and that, with a slight lowering of rates, an employer would experience no reduction in his labor supply. It is also true, of course, that employers can increase the supply of labor services offered to them without any change in wage rates by such devices as advertising for workers, importing labor from other localities, and engaging in welfare programs.

Various hypothetical supply curves of labor for the whole nation and for employers in different market situations are illustrated in Figures 5, 6, and 7. Figure 5 shows a negatively sloping supply curve for the total labor supply in a nation or other territorial unit. Figure 6 indicates a possible supply curve for an employer who, for a number of reasons including his rather isolated location, is unable readily to attract new, qualified workers to his plant. The opposite situation is shown in Figure 7, which represents the labor-supply conditions for an employer who is able to attract many new, qualified workers by slight increases in the wage rates he offers.

Demand.   Although there have been attempts to determine "the probable elasticity of demand for labor as a whole" in terms of real-wage rates and money-wage rates, the results are of very questionable validity.[1]   The difficulty is that real and money wages make up a large portion of the nation's real and money income, so that changes in wage rates are likely to change the total demand for all employers' products.[2]   There seems to be just as much support for the argument that a general reduction in money wages will reduce the demand for labor in the short run as there is for

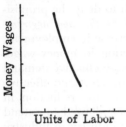

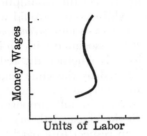

Fig. 5. Supply Curve of Labor for the Whole Nation.

Fig. 6. Supply Curve of Labor for an Employer in an Isolated Area.

Fig. 7. Supply Curve of Labor for an Employer in a Metropolitan Area.

the contention that a reduction in the level of money wages will increase the demand for labor.[3]   The same conclusion would seem to hold in the case of a reduction in real wages.   Therefore, in a closed system,[4] the demand curve for labor as a whole might have a positive or a negative slope depending upon the particular circumstances, especially those determining the rate of spending in the community.

In attempting to derive the demand for all labor one cannot simply use the demand-and-supply analysis that is applied to single firms or products, which assumes that all other things (other prices and wage rates as well as incomes and the rate of spending) remain the same or constant.   Here is another illustration of the error

[1] *Cf.* Paul H. Douglas, *The Theory of Wages*, 1934, pp. xviii, 151–52, 488–89; and A. C. Pigou, *The Theory of Unemployment*, 1933, pp. 88–106.   *Cf.* also, S. E. Harris, "Professor Pigou's Theory of Unemployment," *Quarterly Journal of Economics*, vol. 49 (February 1935), pp. 301–23.

[2] *Cf.* R. A. Lester, "Political Economy *versus* Individualistic Economics," *American Economic Review*, vol. 28 (March 1938), pp. 55–64.

[3] *Idem;* and *Report of the Director*, International Labour Office, 1937, pp. 29–34. This point is discussed in later chapters, especially Chapter 11.

[4] A closed system or an isolated economy is assumed in order to avoid consideration, at this point, of the effects of wage changes upon international trade.

involved in applying to a general situation the conclusions and methods of analysis that are appropriate only for particular parts or small segments of the economy. As J. M. Keynes has pointed out,

> . . . the demand schedules for particular industries can only be constructed on some fixed assumption as to the nature of the demand and supply schedules of other industries and as to the amount of the [total] aggregate demand. It is invalid, therefore, to transfer the argument to industry as a whole unless we also transfer our assumption that the aggregate effective demand is fixed. Yet this assumption reduces the argument to an *ignoratio elenchi*. For, whilst no one would wish to deny the proposition that a reduction in money-wages *accompanied by the same aggregate effective demand as before* will be associated with an increase in employment, the precise question at issue is whether the reduction in money-wages will or will not be accompanied by the same aggregate effective demand as before measured in money, or, at any rate, by an aggregate effective demand which is not reduced in full proportion to the reduction in money-wages. . . . But if the classical theory is not allowed to extend by analogy its conclusions in respect to a particular industry to industry as a whole, it is wholly unable to answer the question what effect on employment a reduction in money-wages will have. For it has no method of analysis to tackle the problem.[1]

Professor Z. C. Dickinson makes the same point when he explains that "the demand for labor as a whole is not external to labor, since fundamentally most of each man's labor constitutes a demand for labors of other persons" and, therefore, "the notion of elasticity of demand, which is so often applied without qualification to labor in general, does not make sense as it would when applied to a particular kind of labor in a given market."[2]

In the following discussion of the demand for labor by particular employers, it should be clear that the effects upon the general situation of the changes made by a particular employer in his demand for labor are disregarded. The employer's demand for labor services will be considered as of any given moment of time, and no allowances will be made for changes or shifts in employers' demand schedules caused by alterations in consumer demand over a period of time.[3]   Shifts in demand schedules or curves with changes in

[1] J. M. Keynes, *The General Theory of Employment, Interest and Money*, 1936, pp. 259–60.

[2] Z. C. Dickinson, "Recent Literature on Wage Theory," *Quarterly Journal of Economics*, vol. 49 (November 1934), p. 140.

[3] ". . . and some are ready to discuss the shape of the demand curve for labour in general. There is, however, no such thing as a demand for labour in general. More-

incomes and wage levels are discussed in Chapter 11 on Wage Rates, Employment, and the Business Cycle. In this chapter we are examining not the general situation but particular markets from the individualistic viewpoint of single buyers.

An individual employer's demand for labor is not solely a function of the real- or money-wage rate. According to what might be called the standard or orthodox explanation, an employer's demand for labor depends primarily upon (1) the elasticity of his marginal-receipts curve,[1] (2) the marginal-cost curve of labor to him, (3) technical conditions in that line of production, and (4) the supply curves of the other factors of production.[2] Each of these four factors will be explained.

(1) According to the traditional explanation, an employer will hire additional labor as long as the additional labor adds more to his receipts than to his costs. The amount that an additional laborer adds to his employer's receipts depends upon the resulting increase in the employer's output and upon the elasticity of the employer's marginal-receipts curve.[3] The employer's marginal-receipts curve in turn depends upon the demand curve for his product (his average-receipts curve). In a perfect market an employer's average-receipts and marginal-receipts curves are the same horizontal line at the prevailing price, but the average-receipts curve of an employer is tipped where the market for his product is imperfect, as it would be if he were one of a few large producers of a standard product or were producing a trade-marked

over if there be demand curves for particular types of labour, during a business cycle the shifts in the curves are at least as important as their shapes. Indeed, the essential point of the purchasing power argument may be formulated as the affirmation that a wage reduction itself provokes a shift in the demand curves for particular types of labour." E. Ronald Walker, "Wages Policy and Business Cycles," *International Labour Review*, vol. 38 (December 1938), p. 764.

[1] Elasticity is the rate of change in quantity demanded or sold with slight changes in price. If, with a slight change in price, there is a more than proportionate increase or decrease in the quantity demanded, the demand is elastic. Elasticity, on the demand side, is measured from unity, which is the condition when price times quantity demanded always equals a constant dollar sum. Inelasticity of demand occurs when the dollar sum increases with a slight rise in price, and a demand curve is elastic when the total dollar sum decreases with a slight rise in price.

[2] *Cf.* Joan Robinson, *The Economics of Imperfect Competition*, 1933, pp. 235, 245, and 257.

[3] Marginal receipts is the increase in total receipts from the sale of an additional unit of output.

A reader who has difficulty with this terminology and these concepts might consult an elementary textbook in economics such as A. L. Meyers, *Elements of Modern Economics*, 1937, or A. M. McIsaac and J. G. Smith, *Introduction to Economic Analysis*, 1937.

product. If an employer's average-receipts curve is a straight line (other than a horizontal or vertical one), the rate of fall of the marginal-receipts curve is twice the rate of fall of the demand curve for his product.[1] The reason for this is that a lowering of the price of his product in order to sell one more unit will lower the price of all the units of the product that the employer sells. The sale of one more unit will increase his marginal receipts by the price of the extra unit sold minus the price reduction in all the other units that occurs because that extra unit is sold. Marginal receipts will be less than the price. Consequently, the employer, by hiring another unit of labor, will add to his receipts a sum somewhat less than the price at which the employer's additional output is sold, and the employer will hire additional workers, not according to the price received for the added product they produce, but according to his marginal-receipts curve.[2] Since, with a tipped straight-line demand curve for his product, an employer's marginal-receipts curve will have a slope twice as steep as the demand curve for his product, the demand curve for labor will

[1] This statement may be illustrated by the following hypothetical example:

Price at	Units bought at that price	Total receipts	Marginal receipts (addition to total receipts)
$2.00	0	0	0
1.90	1	$ 1.90	$1.90
1.80	2	3.60	1.70
1.70	3	5.10	1.50
1.60	4	6.40	1.30
1.50	5	7.50	1.10
1.40	6	8.40	.90
1.30	7	9.10	.70
1.20	8	9.60	.50
1.10	9	9.90	.30
1.00	10	10.00	.10
.90	11	9.90	−.10
.80	12	9.60	−.30

Average receipts (total receipts divided by the number of units bought) corresponds to the price, and the average-receipts curve represents the demand curve for the product of the individual firm. The reader will notice that, whenever the average receipts (see price) decline by 10 cents, marginal receipts decline by 20 cents.

For further discussion of the relationship between demand curves and curves marginal to them, cf. Joan Robinson, op. cit., Chapter 2, especially pp. 30–35.

[2] Whenever an employer's demand curve is inelastic (has an elasticity of less than unity) his marginal receipts will be minus, for the total sum of price times quantity demanded decreases with the reduction in price necessary to sell the additional output. Increases in price where the demand is inelastic will, of course, increase the employer's total receipts from sales and his net profit, so a rational monopolist would always raise his price at least to the point where his demand curve became elastic.

tend to be more inelastic than the demand curve for his product under such circumstances, and labor will be paid a wage less than the additional product that it produces valued at the market price.

In so far as an employer's own costs affect the sale of his own product, the elasticity of his marginal-receipts curve at any point will be tied up with the purchasing power of his own payroll. A company town or construction camp run by an employer, where an employee must buy practically everything from the company, are extreme examples of this relationship.

(2) Another factor affecting the demand for labor is the nature of the labor market. Where the labor market is imperfect for any of the reasons discussed above (especially where the number of buyers is small or there is not sufficient mobility of labor between purchasers), an employer may have to raise the price of his labor (wage rate) in order to buy more, or he may be able to reduce the price of his labor by buying less. Under such circumstances, his demand curve for labor may not vary in direct relation to his marginal-receipts curve. This is so because, if the employer must offer a higher wage rate in order to obtain more labor, any additional unit of labor will add to the employer's cost an amount considerably more than simply the wage of that unit. The employer, in demanding more labor, is bidding up the price he has to pay for it. An additional unit of labor would increase the employer's costs by the wages of that new unit of labor plus the rise in the wage rate for all the labor that the employer is already hiring to do the same work. In such cases, an employer's marginal cost of labor far exceeds the wage of an additional worker. Even though the market for the employer's product may be a perfect market, so that the demand curve for his product is a horizontal line, if he has to raise his present rate of wages to his workers in order to obtain more labor, the employer is liable to refrain from employing an additional unit of labor, despite the fact that its price (wage) may be somewhat below the employer's marginal receipts from the product of that additional unit of labor. As Sumner Slichter puts it, "the present level of wages is quite as real a determinant of the demand for labor as the value of additional men." [1]

[1] *Modern Economic Society*, 1931, p. 620.

(3) The technical conditions of production help to determine the amount of labor relative to other factors of production that an employer uses to manufacture his product. Where the plant is already constructed and the equipment is installed, this ratio may be relatively fixed in the short run. If it is not possible to vary the ratio of the factors used, then the employer's demand for labor is bound to be less elastic than the demand for his product, because a reduction in wage rates will only reduce total costs by the fraction that wage costs are of total costs. In the mass-production industries, wage costs are generally less than one fifth of the total costs of production of a single employer.[1] With an employer's wage costs at 20 per cent of his total costs, a reduction of five per cent in wage rates would mean a reduction of but one per cent in his total costs. In this case, the smaller the percentage that labor costs are of total variable costs in the short run or of total costs in the long run, the more inelastic an employer's demand curve for labor would be.

D. H. Robertson believes that, as the result of the installation of elaborate, expensive, and durable plants, there is no possibility for the employer to vary or "dose" his labor force until the point is reached where the net value to the employer of the efforts of the last worker hired just equal that worker's wages. In highly mechanized industries, where there is a close and intimate coordination between the plant and the size of the labor force required to operate it, the demand curve for labor is, according to Robertson,

. . . a kind of bastard compound between a long-period and a short-period curve, which may well, so far as it can be conceived of as having any real existence, be of a highly disquieting shape,—nearly flat for part of its length, and then suddenly dropping almost vertically. A completely rationalized world might turn out to be one in which, if organized so as to obtain their *de facto* economic worth, a certain proportion of workpeople could find employment at very high wages, while the remainder could hardly find it on any terms at all.[2]

(4) The elasticity of the supply of other factors of production, as well as their prices, affects an employer's demand for labor whether the proportion of factors can or cannot be altered. If the proportion of each factor used by the employer cannot be altered, a decrease in wage rates will not cause much increase in employment

---

[1] Wages and salaries were 21 per cent of the total value of the product in manufacturing in 1937. *Cf. Biennial Census of Manufactures, 1937*, 1940, p. 20.

[2] D. H. Robertson, *Economic Fragments*, 1931, pp. 50–51.

because, without substitution, total costs might not be reduced much by a wage reduction. With a rigid proportion of factors, the more inelastic is the supply of other factors of production, the less will an employer's demand for labor change with changes in wage rates.[1] If the proportions are not fixed and, for example, capital equipment can be substituted for labor, then an employer's demand for labor depends, in part, upon the extent to which he can substitute capital equipment for labor with any increase in wage rates or will substitute labor for capital equipment with a decrease in wage rates. The greater the ease of substitution, the more elastic will be an employer's demand curve for labor. Such substitution, however, normally takes time and is, in general, a long-run rather than a short-run factor affecting an employer's demand curve for labor.

Furthermore, a general rise in wage rates would, by raising the variable costs of equipment producers, raise the price of capital equipment, so the effect of wage-rate changes upon the price of substitute capital equipment must be considered in any discussion of the effect of substitution upon an employer's demand schedule for labor. An increased demand for capital equipment, of course, means an increased demand for labor to construct it, so that the effect of this demand for labor to construct machinery upon the supply curve of labor for the employer buying the machines may depend upon whether the plant of the producer making the machines is located in the vicinity of the plant of the buyer of machines or at some distance away.

The foregoing discussion has been concerned with the question, What effect would changes in an employer's labor costs have upon his demand for workers? To sum up, it has been found that an employer's demand for labor would generally be more inelastic, (1) the more inelastic is his marginal-receipts curve, (2) the smaller is the ratio of his labor costs to his total costs, and (3) the more difficult it is for him to substitute capital equipment or land for labor and, in such circumstances, the more inelastic is the supply of the other factors of production. As a result of any of these factors, increases or decreases in an employer's labor costs would tend to cause but minor, or comparatively small, changes in his total employment.

[1] Joan Robinson, *The Economics of Imperfect Competition*, pp. 258–62.

Possible market situations. The above discussion indicates that the short-run demand of an employer for labor may be extremely inelastic, at least in certain sections of the employer's demand curve for labor. The short-run supply curve of labor may be absolutely inelastic or even have a negative slope. With absolute inelasticity of demand and supply, an employer's demand and supply schedules might be identical or equal over a whole range of prices, so that there is no one price that alone clears the market.

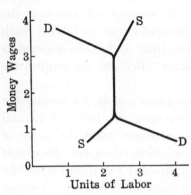

FIG. 8. Demand and Supply Coinciding over a Range of Wage Rates.

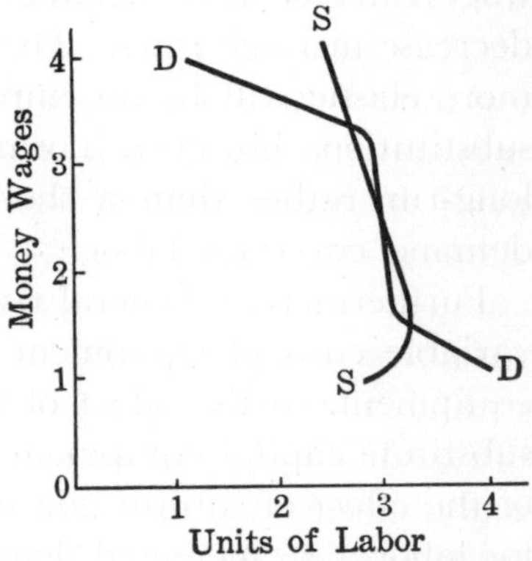

FIG. 9. Demand and Supply Intersecting at Three Wage Rates.

When the supply curve is negatively inclined, it is possible that the demand curve might cut the supply curve at three or more points. Such possibilities are illustrated in Figures 8 and 9, in which *DD* represents the demand curve and *SS* the supply curve.

It may be in some cases that there is no price that will clear the market. Failure of the demand and supply curves to intersect might occur for a number of reasons. Employers will not hire all qualified labor offered at the firm's present wage rates, nor will they always reduce wage rates because it is possible to hire other qualified workers at a cheaper rate, nor are they likely to dismiss their working force and to hire a new staff of workers simply because a new staff could be purchased at a lower wage rate.

Some modifications. The above discussion of the demand for labor and possible market situations is based on the traditional orthodox explanation, which assumes that employers know their marginal-receipts and their marginal-cost curves and that they always pursue a policy of expanding operations to the point where marginal receipts equal marginal variable costs. How unreal such assumptions are is indicated in the discussion of the marginal-productivity theory of wages in Chapter 7. The fact is that the appropriate marginal-receipts curve would be the one that the employer thinks will exist in the future when the products of the added labor are finally sold. Furthermore, unless he experimented with a whole series of selling prices every little while during a business cycle, an employer selling a trade-marked product would not know the present nature of his marginal-receipts curve. Many employers, such as gasoline companies, assume that the demand for their products is inelastic to price reductions, because competitors would cut prices too and it takes some time for general price reductions to stimulate demand, and that the demand for their products is very elastic for price increases, partly because all competitors may not raise prices. When an employer assumes that the demand curve for his product has such a "corner" at the prevailing price, his marginal-receipts curve would have a gap at the prevailing price, falling from a positive to a negative figure.[1] If marginal-revenue and marginal-cost curves are discontinuous, as is likely to be the case under imperfect and monopolistic competition, there may be many points of equilibrium between demand and supply, with bargaining power often the deciding factor.[2]

One may also question whether the management of business corporations is guided solely or even primarily by the principle of maximizing profits, at least in the short run. Other considerations, such as maintaining customers, preserving the firm's trade position, or raising the management's prestige, may play an important part in production policies. And even though an employer were attempting to maximize profits, it is long-run considerations rather than immediate profits that would generally guide his decisions on operations.

[1] *Cf.* Paul M. Sweezy's discussion in "Wage Policies," *American Economic Review*, vol. 28 (March 1938) supplement, p. 156. *Cf.* also, Paul M. Sweezy, "Demand under Conditions of Oligopoly," *Journal of Political Economy*, vol. 47 (August 1939), pp. 568 73; and M. Bronfenbrenner, "Applications of the Discontinuous Oligopoly Demand Curve," *Journal of Political Economy*, vol. 48 (June 1940), pp. 420–27. Marginal receipts are negative wherever the demand is inelastic (less elastic than unity) so that total receipts decrease as price decreases.

[2] *Cf.* Benjamin Higgins, "Indeterminacy in Non-Perfect Competition," *American Economic Review*, vol. 29 (September 1939), pp. 468–79; and Raymond F. Mikesell, "Oligopoly and the Short-Run Demand for Labor," *Quarterly Journal of Economics*, vol. 55 (November 1940), p. 166.

There are a number of circumstances under which an employer might continue to employ workers for a while even though marginal receipts were below marginal costs. That might be true whenever his property would depreciate at a more rapid rate if unused than it would if in use. Coal mines, farm lands, and certain kinds of machinery, for instance, tend to depreciate rapidly in value if left continually idle for any length of time. Also, an employer might continue to employ men for a short period of time even though his marginal costs exceeded his marginal receipts if continued operation were necessary to prevent the loss of the company's good will or its value as a going concern. Rather than have a strike and lose part of his market to competitors, an employer might temporarily pay employees a wage rate that caused his marginal costs to exceed his marginal receipts. The same policy might be pursued by an employer who wanted to keep his labor force intact.

Generally, however, the situation is reversed. Especially during depressions, an employer's marginal receipts are likely to be above his marginal costs, yet he will not employ more workers. That, for example, might be the case if the employer wished to conserve cash in order to meet future commitments, if he expected prices to decline in the near future, or if an increase in output would involve additional investment in capital equipment and it did not seem desirable to make such an investment at that time.

Importance of price policies and pricing systems. Employers with price policies are not likely to lower prices to stimulate demand for their products even though it might be immediately profitable for them to do so. Producers who maintain their selling prices at a certain figure from year to year, permitting production and employment to fluctuate with changes in consumer demand, simply are not operating according to the principle of expanding production until marginal variable costs equal marginal receipts.[1] In such cases, changes in the elasticity of an employer's marginal-receipts curve may have little or no effect upon his demand for labor. Especially would this be true in industries where employers do not feel free to change their prices but are forced to follow the

[1] There are cases where marginal receipts cannot equal marginal costs because there is a gap in the marginal-receipts curve. There would be such a gap in a marginal-receipts curve whenever the demand or average-receipts curve over a range of prices was absolutely inelastic.

prices established by trade-association policies or by concerted action. For a number of reasons an employer might be reluctant to reduce his selling price and increase his output even if marginal receipts exceeded marginal costs. He might fear that a price reduction would lead to a price war, to smaller marginal receipts than he had estimated, to customer ill will from losses on inventory, or to resentment by consumers later on, if it seemed desirable to restore the price to the former level. Larger short-run profits might be at the expense of smaller profits in the long run.

In cases where local retail outlets of large firms are selling the firm's nationally advertised products, the price is likely to be the same all over the country, although costs and profits may vary from locality to locality. The firm, however, is not likely to lower prices in a particular locality in order to expand operations up to the point where marginal variable costs equal marginal receipts. Officials of the Teamsters' union in the West have repeatedly pointed out that, despite the high wages for truck drivers, delivery men, and other union employees in, say, the city of Seattle, Washington, the prices of nationally advertised products delivered at one's home in Seattle are no higher than they are in other localities, such as the deep South, where wage rates are much lower.

Large firms are accustomed to pay uniform or fixed prices for their raw materials. Repeatedly, purchasing agents of such firms receive identical bids from would-be suppliers of materials. Such price uniformity occurs whether the firm is buying lead for the manufacture of paint, malt for the manufacture of beer, fiber tubes for use in making radios, cement for various kinds of construction, newsprint for the publication of newspapers, or steel for the production of automobiles. Various pricing methods or systems have been used so that producers of standardized products may quote identical prices to all buyers. These arrangements for securing unity of action with respect to price include the basing-point system, the "freight-allowed" method of price quotation, the establishment of price zones, and the exchange of prices through some organization such as a trade association.[1] Exchange of in-

---

[1] The widespread use of these different pricing methods in various branches of American industry is indicated in an analysis by the Temporary National Economic Committee, which explains the geographic price structure for hundreds of commodities. This analysis is contained in *Price Behavior and Business Policy*, Monograph No. 1, Temporary National Economic Committee, 1940, pp. 286–345.

formation to secure price uniformity may occur even in retail selling. In some cities of the Far West, for example, retail automobile and lumber dealers have followed the practice of reporting to a central exchange all bids made on used cars or on lumber in house construction, giving the name and automobile license number of the prospective customer. The buyer then is confronted at every retail outlet in the area with the same price for his used car or for lumber to build his house.

Under the basing-point system, price uniformity is achieved by having all producers of the product quote their prices to buyers at a single point or at a few points throughout the country, despite the fact that the producing mills are located at varying distances from the basing point or points. In this way, a buyer may be unable to take advantage of his location near a mill, and the "prevailing price" is the same for all purchasers in the area covered by the same basing point. In the case of the "freight-allowed" method, all sellers may quote the same list prices to all buyers wherever the buyers are located, for the seller pays the full cost of transporting the product to the buyer's place of business.[1] This arrangement is designed to permit uniform delivered prices so that no buyer can, as in the case of purchases of labor, take advantage of his location to obtain cheaper prices than his competitors.

During depression periods, it is probably normal for marginal receipts to exceed marginal variable costs in those firms that follow rather rigid price policies. In some cases, marginal variable costs per unit of output might decline if the factory or factories were operated at a larger percentage of capacity. A recent study by the Brookings Institution indicates that, for a large firm in heavy manufacturing and with no bonded indebtedness, total cost per unit of output would decline about 25 per cent with an increase of operations from 40 per cent of capacity to full capacity, and would decline 16 per cent by increasing operations from 60 to 100 per cent of capacity.[2] Of course, a part of this decline in unit costs is accounted for by the distribution of the firm's fixed costs over a larger number of units of output. Some economists believe, however, that the variable costs per unit of output may not increase, and may even

[1] *Cf.* Vernon A. Mund, "The 'Freight Allowed' Method of Price Quotation," *Quarterly Journal of Economics*, vol. 54 (February 1940), pp. 232–45.

[2] *Income and Economic Progress*, 1935, p. 151. This assumes, of course, that there is no change in wage rates or the prices of other elements in the cost of operation.

decrease, with an expansion of production toward full capacity in certain industries operating on a part-time basis.[1]

Under various pricing systems such as delivered prices with "freight allowed," the basing-point method, or price zones, the net receipts of the seller vary with the distance of the buyer's property from the seller's mill, for the seller pays or "absorbs" the freight charges. Under such circumstances, producers would presumably govern their operations by average, and not marginal, receipts. It would simply be impossible for the seller to draw up a marginal-receipts curve or schedule, since marginal receipts vary with the location of each buyer.

Employers' demands for labor and other factors of production may also be governed by average, rather than marginal, costs. That presumably would be true where, as just explained, the costs per unit of production in a firm would not increase as operations are expanded from 40 or 60 per cent of capacity to full capacity. Where employers pay overtime rates of time-and-a-half for one seventh to one half of all employee hours, their purchases of labor are also apparently governed by average, and not marginal, costs.[2] A number of economists have recently emphasized the importance of average costs in employers' calculations and employment policies.[3] Where employers follow rather rigid price policies, each employer's rate of operations and demand for labor will be largely determined by the general state of trade, and his total employment may have no close and direct relationship to changes in wage rates. Consequently, the employer's demand for labor would appear to be inelastic under such circumstances, for it would not vary much with marked changes in wage rates.

With the widespread use of certain price policies and special

[1] For further evidence and opinion on this point, cf. H. M. Oliver, Jr., "Does Wage Reduction Aid Employment by Lowering Prices?" *Southern Economic Journal*, vol. 6 (January 1940), pp. 335–36; Jacob Viner, "Mr. Keynes on the Causes of Unemployment, A Review," *Quarterly Journal of Economics*, vol. 51 (November 1936), pp. 149–50; and John P. Miller, "The Pricing of Bituminous Coal: Some International Comparisons," in *Public Policy*, edited by C. J. Friedrich and Edward S. Mason, 1940, p. 150.

[2] On the Pacific Coast in the first half of 1940 between one third and one half of the hours in longshoring and one seventh of the hours in pulp mills were paid for at overtime rates of time-and-a-half. Cf. Chapter 8 *infra*.

[3] Cf., for example, Viner, *loc. cit.*; Paul H. Douglas, "Wage Theory and Wage Policy," *International Labour Review*, vol. 39 (March 1939), p. 356; Theodore J. Kreps, "Business-Controlled Prices," Chapter 13 in *Economic Problems in a Changing World*, 1939, edited by Willard Thorp, p. 282; and Norman S. Buchanan, *The Economics of Corporate Enterprise*, 1940, p. 290

methods or systems of price quotation, the factors stressed by the standard or traditional analysis, such as marginal-receipts and marginal-cost curves, may be of minor significance in the determination of an employer's demand for labor, especially in the short run. Through widespread application of schemes for maintaining price uniformity over large areas, employers have tended to make invalid the simple marginal-costs-equal-to-marginal-receipts explanation of an employer's demand for the factors of production.

RESTRAINT OF COMPETITION BY BUYERS

Concerted action by employers of labor to keep down wage rates has already been discussed under (5) in the section on imperfections in the labor market, and that discussion need not be repeated. It indicated that concerted action on wage rates by the buyers of labor has not been infrequent in the recent or distant past. Indeed, the buyers' side of the labor market normally contains many monopolistic elements. The same thing may be true on the sellers' side of the market under union organization and control.

Even without any concerted action or definite agreement by the buyers of labor, there exists a convention that it is not cricket for employers to bid or compete against one another for labor services. This convention may well be based on the experience that, by bidding up the price of labor, employers are only tending to reduce the supply of labor available to them, whereas, in general, reductions in wage rates tend to increase the supply.

The very fact that the buyers quote the price in labor markets which are not affected by labor organization is an important factor in strengthening the market position of the buyer, partly because labor is so immobile and the labor market so imperfect. With buyers quoting the price, there will be no price rise without specific action on price by the buyers. The prevalent practice is for buyers to pay "the average of the prevailing prices" for that class of labor in the locality.[1] Such an average of "prevailing rates" is discovered by the wage surveys, already mentioned, and becomes the basis for

[1] On public work it is also the practice for government units to pay the prevailing wage (the weighted average of all the rates being paid for the same occupation, or the rate which is paid to the largest number of workers in that classification) in the locality. Governments may also pay less than "the prevailing rate." They, therefore, tend to lend support to any existing "exploitation" by private employers.

a company's entire wage scale. The representatives of 60 large companies recently "reported that their firms adjust wage rates with reference primarily to local conditions" so that "firms with scattered plants have several wage scales." [1] In other words, large firms tend to adjust their wage policies so that any existing inequities resulting from imperfect labor markets will be perpetuated and so that, as large buyers of labor, they will not disturb or "spoil" the local labor market. It becomes a nice question whether, if all firms in a locality always pay the average "prevailing wage," the same average prevailing wage would not always prevail. That would certainly be the case unless the supply situation changed considerably, which is not so likely to occur in view of the nature of the supply of labor, its immobility, and other imperfect elements in the labor market.

Instead of engaging in price competition for labor, large firms have attempted to attract and hold the high-grade employees by means of such inducements as steadier employment, good working conditions in the plant, group insurance, pension plans, and other welfare programs. The fact that the employee has built up seniority rights by working for the firm over a period, or the fact that he has certain knowledge or skills that are valuable only to that particular company, tends to attach him to that firm. With increasing specialization and diversification, much of the knowledge and training learned on one job with a certain firm may not be transferable, so it would not be of the same value to any other concern. In such cases, the buyer is in a much stronger market position than the seller, for he may suffer very little loss if he must dispense with any one of 10 to 100 similar employees, whereas he is the only buyer to whom such employees can sell exactly those services. Of course, if the employee is unique in certain respects, as might be the case with some of the officers of a company, then the situation is one of "bilateral monopoly" (only one seller and one buyer), for which there is no single solution. In such a case, the wage rate is indeterminate, just as it tends to be indeterminate where labor services are so peculiar to a firm that only that one firm buys exactly that type of labor services.

Indeed, as personnel directors freely admit, "Many jobs are peculiar to a given plant, and no comparable rates can be found in

[1] Riegel, *op. cit.*, p. 22. *Cf.* also pp. 2 and 14.

other companies." [1] In 1937 W. F. Cook of Kimberly-Clark Corporation said: "In any given company, and ours is no exception, there are many jobs which are peculiar to our business and type of organization. There are no 'market' rates for such kinds of service in our communities." [2] Under such circumstances there is a buyer's monopoly (monopsony) for that particular type of work, and also a seller's monopoly to the extent that workers have a special training that sets them off as a special group for whom there is no readily available substitute.

POSSIBILITIES OF EXPLOITATION

"Exploitation" is a word that is widely used in labor discussions but is seldom defined. Two definitions of labor exploitation have been proposed recently. According to one definition, labor is exploited whenever it is being paid less than the wage rate that would prevail if the labor market were a perfect market. In other words, exploitation occurs whenever labor is paid less than the full money value of an additional unit of labor to the employer, disregarding the effect that the hiring of an additional unit will have upon wage rates in the market or upon the rate of wages paid to some or all of the employees already working for the employer. As indicated under (2) in the discussion of demand, where the employer's cost curve for labor is not horizontal but is tipped upward because he is important enough in the labor market to influence the market rate by his own purchases of labor, he is not likely to bid up the price of labor to a point where the value of the services of the last laborer is equal to the price of that laborer's services.

A second definition of labor exploitation includes the nature of the market for the employer's product. [3] According to this definition, if the market for the employer's product is imperfect and consequently his selling price is higher than it would be were his product market a perfect market, the consumers of the product may be exploited. In so far as such exploitation of consumers reduces real wages (the purchasing power of workers' cash income), it might

[1] V. S. Karabasz, "Certain Difficulties in Determining the 'Market Rate' of Wages," *Personnel*, vol. 13 (May 1937), p. 148.

[2] "Determination of Prevailing Wage Scales," *Personnel*, vol. 14 (August 1937), p. 26.

[3] *Cf.* Joan Robinson, *The Economics of Imperfect Competition*, pp. 281–304. For a criticism of Mrs. Robinson's definition, *cf.* Edward Chamberlain, *The Theory of Monopolistic Competition* (third edition), 1938, pp. 182–83.

be said that the wage-earners are subject to exploitation when commodity markets are imperfect. However, it seems preferable to refer to this latter condition as consumer exploitation and to define labor exploitation only in terms of the labor market.

The difficulties involved in attempting to apply this labor-market test of labor exploitation in concrete instances are evident from the discussion of imperfections in the labor market in this chapter. Labor markets simply are not perfect markets and probably could not be made into perfect markets under any circumstances. However, a rather impractical test or concept of exploitation is better than none at all. Applying the test of the perfect labor market does help to give definite meaning to the term, and also aids one in understanding the various ways in which the exploitation of labor may occur.

On the basis of such a definition, it is evident that there is considerable possibility of labor exploitation in view of the imperfections in the labor market and the character of the general supply curve for labor as well as the supply curve for individual employers. With the general supply curve of labor negatively inclined and the supply curve of labor for most employers highly inelastic at various points, there is little pressure from the supply side to force up the price of labor, unless the sellers of labor take concerted action or the government passes maximum-hours or minimum-wage laws. The very fact that employers frequently employ men overtime at one-and-a-half or two times the regular wage rate to do normal (not emergency) work also indicates the possibility of exploitation.[1]

It is possible for some employers to pay wage rates well below the average of "the prevailing rates" for that grade of labor in the locality because employers paying the average prevailing rate do not stand ready to take all qualified labor offered to them at their wage rates. Therefore, some employers may exploit the market situation, even though other employers do not follow suit. Exploitation is likely to occur in the lower grades of labor, especially in the case of the labor of women and children. As real wage rates fall, it is the supply of low-grade labor, including women and children workers, that expands most rapidly, and it is the women and children that presumably are most immobile. Indeed, once the price of labor, especially in the lower grades, begins to fall, there is

[1] For a further discussion of overtime wage rates, *cf.* Chapter 8 *infra*.

a tendency, because the general supply curve for most classes of labor is negatively inclined, for that price fall to become cumulative instead of self-limiting or corrective. Given the supply situation in most labor markets, the employers have an opportunity to exploit that situation by concerted action or even by individual action.

Workers are, of course, likely to be exploited when employers act in concert to restrain competition and to keep wage rates down. The same result is likely to occur when buyers follow certain conventions and practices, such as payment of the average of the prevailing wages in the locality. The numerous imperfections in the labor market are also conducive to exploitation, and, though expansion of the activities of public employment exchanges or a law to prevent concerted action by buyers to restrain competition could help to make the labor market more perfect, the imperfections cannot be entirely eliminated. There might still be market situations such that any one of a number of possible wage rates would clear the market, or perhaps three or four rates in the same market for the same grade of labor at the same time would also clear the market. Under such circumstances, the possibilities for exploitation would continue to exist.

The existence of such possibilities for exploitation is the primary justification for labor unions. It is also the chief justification for minimum-wage laws. Because of the imperfections and peculiarities of the labor market, it may often be the case that a rise of wage rates, as the result of trade-union action or enforcement of minimum-wage laws, may not reduce the volume of employment at all, even assuming no increase in effective demand for the product as a result of the wage increase. Indeed, if labor is being exploited (the last worker taken on is being paid a wage less than his full value to the employer measured by the amount he alone adds to the employer's receipts), the employment of labor might be increased by an appropriate increase of wage rates through action by a trade-union or a minimum-wage board.[1]

[1] To illustrate this point, assume that an employer is hiring 30 workers at $5.00 a day. Suppose that the hiring of five additional workers would increase the employer's total receipts by $5.50 per worker or $27.50 a day but that the employer would have to offer wages of $5.20 a day in order to attract additional workers with the proper qualifications from other areas or other pursuits. He cannot pay new employees $5.20 a day without also paying his regular employees $5.20 a day, which would increase his total costs by $6.00 a day (20 cents × 30 workers). Therefore, the five additional workers would add each day to his total receipts $27.50 ($5.50 × 5) and to

The reader may ask how exploitation of labor can occur when the company's creditors are only receiving a "normal" interest rate and the stockholders are only enjoying a "normal" dividend rate on their stock. The opportunity for exploitation of labor would, of course, tend to be capitalized; that is, it would, by permitting large profits, tend to increase the capital or asset value of the enterprise. With sufficient writing up of capital values, the rate of return on total capital value would not be above the average. Furthermore, if the capital values had been inflated in one way or another (through stock-watering, extravagant and unwise investment, wasteful construction of facilities, or a drop in the price level), a "normal" rate of return on such capital investment might be possible only because labor is exploited. One must bear in mind that capital values frequently should be written down, if for no other reason than that the price level has declined or the investment was unwise. Under such circumstances, a company might be earning a very low rate of return on inflated asset values, yet recapitalization to an appropriate figure would show that the return to the owners actually was above the national average, partly because the laboring force was being exploited. And, as indicated in Chapter 2, it is very difficult to say what the "normal" rate of return on capital investment should be.

his total costs $32.00 ($5.20 × 5 + $6.00 a day additional to the regular force). Consequently, the employer would not hire additional workers if he had to pay $5.20 a day to attract them. If, however, a trade-union or the government forced wage rates to rise to $5.20 a day for all workers in that class, then the employer would hire the additional five workers because they would add $27.50 a day to his total receipts and only $26.00 a day to his total cost ($5.20 × 5). In such cases, a forced increase in wage rates leads to the employment of more workers by an employer, *other things remaining the same*. In this connection, *cf.* Joan Robinson, *The Economics of Imperfect Competition*, p. 295. The whole issue is discussed more fully in Chapter 12 *infra*.

CHAPTER SIX

ORGANIZATIONS AND THE LABOR MARKET

The discussion in the previous chapter indicated that the buyers of labor are likely to dominate, if not control, the labor market wherever the sellers do not resort to concerted action. This chapter deals with attempts by both buyers and sellers to gain a greater measure of control over the labor market through cooperation and organization. Many of the practices and policies of employers' organizations and labor unions are for the purpose of affecting demand, supply, or price in the labor market.

EMPLOYERS' ORGANIZATIONS

There are few industries in this country which do not have at least one organization formed or fostered to promote the employer's interests in labor matters. The Department of Commerce in 1938 listed more than 7,000 associations of employers. Some of these organizations are local, such as the Associated Employers of Indianapolis or the Employers Association of Detroit; some are state-wide, like the Illinois Manufacturers Association or the Associated Industries of Vermont; and some extend throughout the nation on a craft or industry-wide basis, like the National Founders' Association or the National Cotton Manufacturers' Association.[1]

To a certain extent, the organizations of employers parallel the organizations of labor. Not only are employers' associations local, regional, and national, but the National Association of Manufacturers has, through the "National Industrial Council," created a permanent federation of the local, state, and national employers' associations located in all parts of the country. In 1938 the National Industrial Council, which in some respects resembles the AFL and the CIO, consisted of 185 industrial associations and,

[1] For an extensive list of such employers' associations, *cf. Hearings before a Subcommittee of the Committee on Education and Labor of the U. S. Senate on S. Res. 266*, 75th Congress, third session, Part 17, Employer Associations and "Citizens' Committees," pp. 7522–28.

together with the National Association of Manufacturers, represented 40,000 different employing concerns with between 6,000,000 and 7,000,000 employees, producing about 75 per cent of the manufactured goods of the country.[1] The Industrial Council and its affiliated organizations enable employers to secure "industrial unity" and "a united front in presenting the case of industry." [2]

The operations of employers' associations generally are not known by the public, partly because economists have been more prone to study labor organizations than employers' organizations and partly because some of the activities of employers' associations, such as industrial espionage, have been kept under cover to prevent adverse publicity. Unlike European associations of employers, industrial associations in this country have operated to a large degree in secret. Furthermore, many of the activities of employers' organizations do not directly affect the labor market, and it is such activities for the general benefit of the locality that receive the most publicity. That is true, for example, of the various chambers of commerce— local, state, and national. Yet the chambers of commerce in such cities as Los Angeles, Cleveland, Rochester, and San Francisco attempted during the 1920's to control labor relations and to affect the labor market in those cities by promoting "the American Plan" of the open shop. Not infrequently the local chamber of commerce has been interested in keeping wage rates low and eliminating labor unions as a means of attracting industry to the locality.

In some industries there may, of course, be little need for employer combinations because one company itself is large enough to constitute an "employer trust." As Alfred Marshall pointed out, "each large employer is in his own person a perfectly firm combination of employing power," so that "a combination of a thousand workers has a very weak and uncertain force in comparison with that of a single resolute employer of a thousand men." [3] The American Telephone and Telegraph Company or the Western Union Telegraph Company alone control a very large portion of the possible demand for the services of telephone or telegraph operators.

[1] Albion G. Taylor, *Labor Problems and Labor Law*, 1938, p. 607. *Cf.* also, National Labor Relations Board, *Governmental Protection of Labor's Right to Organize*, Bulletin No. 1, August 1936, p. 53. The activities of the National Association of Manufacturers and the National Industrial Council are fully discussed in Parts 17 and 18 of the *Hearings on S. Res. 266.*

[2] *Hearings on S. Res. 266*, Part 18, pp. 8059, 8061.

[3] *Elements of Economics of Industry* (second edition), 1898, vol. 1, pp. 398–99.

Furthermore, they may exert some measure of control over other employers of telephone or telegraph operators. In the past, Western Union has forced large companies leasing its wires to cease dealing with the Telegraphers' union and to stop employing union members, through a clause in its wire leases stating that operators hired by the wire lessees "shall be subject to the approval of and satisfactory to the company leasing the wires." [1] The greater the proportion of the total industry controlled by one company, the less, obviously, is the need for an employers' association or combination in that industry.

Employers' associations are formed primarily to provide collective action on the part of employers in handling labor problems. The National Metal Trades Association, an employers' organization representing some 950 plants of machinery, iron, and automobile concerns, has established 26 district branches "for the purpose of providing concerted local action."[2] Such concerted action may be political or economic. Activities of employers' associations which do not directly influence the labor market, such as lobbying, publicity campaigns, and labor spying to destroy unions, are discussed in Part Three, especially Chapter 23. Here we are interested in the collective actions of employers that are designed to affect demand, supply, or wage rates in the local labor market.

1. *Policies affecting demand.* Employers' associations may control or change the demand for certain kinds of labor in a locality by various devices. One method is to shift the production to another locality, having an employer's orders filled by other members who may return the profit to him. For example, the constitution of the National Founders' Association, an employers' association in the machinery branch of the foundry industry, provides relief for a member in case of a labor dispute by, among other things, "having the work done for him elsewhere to the extent of 70 per cent of the amount [he] produced at the time of the last quarterly report." [3] In the face of labor trouble or a threatened strike, an employers' association may arrange for an industry-wide lockout or the closing

---

[1] *Cf. Investigation of Western Union and Postal Telegraph Cable Companies*, Senate Document No. 725, 60th Congress, second session, pp. 40–42.

[2] *Hearings before a Subcommittee of the Committee on Education and Labor pursuant to S. Res. 266*, 75th Congress, first session, Part 3, p. 1004.

[3] Clarence E. Bonnett, *Employers' Associations in the United States*, 1922, p. 39. This device was once used by the Stove Founders' National Defense Association.

of plants in a locality, which obviously reduces the demand for certain kinds of labor in that area.[1]

The activities of the Industrial Association of San Francisco from 1921 to 1935 illustrate how absolute the control of an employers' organization over the demand for labor in an industry may become. The Industrial Association was formed by the San Francisco Chamber of Commerce in July 1921 after the labor unions, through the Building Trades Council, refused to accept an arbitration award reducing wage rates in 17 building crafts by 7.5 per cent for a period of six months beginning May 9, 1921, and after the building employers' organization, the Builders' Exchange, with a membership of more than 1,000 building contractors and dealers, had enforced a lockout from May 9 to June 13, 1921.[2] The program of the Industrial Association was to force all building workers, not just the 17 crafts, to accept a 7.5 per cent reduction in wage rates; to enforce the open shop by preventing any union-shop agreements or any agreements between employers and labor organizations; and, finally, to make certain that no changes in wages, hours, or working conditions occurred in San Francisco except such changes as the Association itself or its "Impartial" Wage Board decreed.[3] To this program the employing interests (merchants, bankers, contractors, and building-materials producers) pledged not only their support but a sum of $1,250,000, every bank in the city except one contributing from $5,000 to $25,000.[4] The rules and regulations formulated by the Industrial Association were enforced throughout the San Francisco market for building labor by means of a permit system, an employment bureau, a training school for building workers, a series of agreements with various local employers' associations, and a plan to reimburse contractors or owners for losses incurred because they followed the instructions of the Industrial Association.

Of interest from the demand side is the permit system, which

---

[1] *Cf.*, for example, Frederick L. Ryan, *Industrial Relations in the San Francisco Building Trades*, 1935, pp. 154–55.

[2] *Ibid.*, pp. 152, 154, 155, 167, 168.

[3] *Ibid.*, pp. 169–70.

[4] William Haber, *Industrial Relations in the Building Industry*, 1930, pp. 418, 432. Almost $1,800,000 is said to have been collected by the Industrial Association from 1921 to September 1925 (Ryan, *op.cit.*, p. 174, note 18). Early in 1926 the Association again asked for funds, and it is estimated that $1,000,000 was contributed by merchants, bankers, and industrial leaders (*ibid.*, p. 189).

required every building employer to abide by the rules and regulations of the Industrial Association before the important building materials would be furnished to him. These rules included the open shop, the payment of the Association's wage scale, and the use of the materials only on the job to which the permit applied. Violation of the rules, detected by the Association's inspection service and its system of daily reports, meant withdrawal of the permit and stoppage of the flow of materials to that job; members of employers' organizations who violated the rules were subject to fine or expulsion from the organization. From 1921 to 1925 some 28,000 permits were issued, without which it was practically impossible for persons in San Francisco to buy most building materials from dealers or manufacturers, because the wholesalers and manufacturers were supporting the Industrial Association. A few building employers maintained the union shop and attempted to obtain building materials from Los Angeles or from Salt Lake City or other out-of-state cities, but the Industrial Association frequently prevailed "upon building material dealers in other cities to cancel orders destined to 'independent' employers in San Francisco, with the understanding that the Association would reimburse such dealers for the losses sustained." [1] Where union-shop contractors paying higher wages were the low bidders on a job, the Industrial Association also induced owners to accept the higher bids of non-union contractors, reimbursing such owners for the difference between the bids.[2]

Despite the fact that the employers' combination forced a uniform wage reduction of 7.5 per cent in 1921 and kept building wage rates in San Francisco much below the prevailing rates in other American cities of comparable size from 1923 to 1932, it kept up the prices of building materials. One method by which employers' organizations can influence the demand for labor is by controlling the prices of the other elements of production or the prices of finished products. Many employers' combinations, by fixing the prices of their products, really tend to determine the volume of sales and, therefore, the demand of the combination's members for labor. The Industrial Association claimed to have eliminated "monopolistic combinations" of building labor in San Francisco, but it did so by establishing a monopolistic combination of em-

---

[1] *Ibid.*, p. 175.   [2] Haber, *op. cit.*, p. 419.

ployers on the demand side of the market for building labor in that
city.

In 1923 the U. S. Department of Justice brought suit against the
Industrial Association, the Builders' Exchange, various employers'
associations, and others for using the permit system and combining
in violation of the Federal antitrust laws. "Aside from the general
operation of the permit system, the attorneys for the government
asserted that the material dealers' combination had been guilty of
collusively bidding and refraining from bidding against each other
in the sale of building material and in the erection of buildings, for
the purpose of raising prices; of arbitrarily determining the persons
who should furnish material and erect buildings; of circulating
blacklists against contractors who were not in the combination,
and of agreeing with banks, trust companies, and other moneyed
corporations to refuse loans and to call in loans made to individuals
who were not in the combination." [1] In April 1925 the U. S. Supreme Court, reversing the U. S. District Court, upheld the use of
the permit system, even though it might interfere with the free
flow of building materials between states, on the grounds that the
design or "motive for conspiracy" was monopolistic control of the
local market, the restraint of interstate commerce being "purely
incidental" to accomplishing that local purpose, and that "imported" building materials, warehoused and mingled with the
general goods of a state, ceased to be articles of interstate commerce
and subject to Federal jurisdiction. [2] Following a carpenters' strike
late in 1926, the Industrial Association agreed to suspend the operation of the permit system after February 7, 1927 as long as the open
shop in the building trades continued and the wage rates decreed
by the Association's "Impartial" Wage Board were fully enforced
by other means. [3]

2. *Policies affecting supply.* Employers' organizations may influence
the local supply of certain kinds of labor in various ways. The Associated Employers of Indianapolis, for example, has attempted to
prevent a reduction of the labor supply in that city by preventing
employers in other cities, especially automobile manufacturers,
from "stealing" laborers away from Indianapolis. This the Asso-

---

[1] *Ibid.,* p. 177.
[2] *Industrial Association of San Francisco* v. *United States* (1925), 268 U. S. 64.
[3] Ryan, *op. cit.,* pp. 193–96.

ciated Employers has done by bringing pressure upon local newspapers so that they would refuse to accept "help wanted" advertisements from out-of-town concerns.[1] It also has induced a national
advertising agency to withdraw street-car advertisements calling
for 4,000 men to fill jobs in another city.[2] On the other hand, the
Associated Employers has attempted to affect the labor supply
offered to any employer in Indianapolis by having several hundred
employers sign pledges stating that they will strive to reduce "labor
turnover" or the mobility of labor within the city.

Not only may employers' organizations prevent the "exportation"
of labor from the locality, but they may subsidize the "importation"
of labor into an area. The Industrial Association of San Francisco
operated an employment bureau, advertised in newspapers in other
cities for nonunion building craftsmen, brought them to San Francisco under an agreement which bound them to work under the
conditions established by the Association, and rented a hotel in
which to house them. By 1928 the Industrial Association had
brought "approximately 5,000 nonunion men" to San Francisco,
which led to the charge that it had flooded the labor market in
that city with a large number of building workers in order to keep
wage rates down in building.[3]

From 1922 to April 1925, the so-called Citizens' Committee to
Enforce the Landis Award upon the Chicago building unions
brought more than 25,000 nonunion building workers to Chicago
by advertisements, by the maintenance of employment offices in
other cities, by the sending of printed material to workers elsewhere, and by other means. This Citizens' Committee was organized by the Chicago Chamber of Commerce, the Illinois Manufacturers' Association, and other employer groups; was directed by
eight employers not in the building industry; and was supported
by many merchants, bankers, and architects. It proceeded to put
economic pressure upon building contractors, forcing them to conform to the rules it established. The Committee's expenditures of
$2,000,000 during the first three years of its existence were financed
by a one-per-cent levy on all construction work done in Chicago.[4]

The constitution of the National Metal Trades Association, whose

---

[1] Bonnett, *op. cit.*, p. 505.   [2] *Idem.*   [3] Ryan, *op. cit.*, pp. 172 and 190.
[4] *Cf.* Royal E. Montgomery, *Industrial Relations in the Chicago Building Trades*, 1927,
pp. 279–81, 293.

members are manufacturers using the products of steel mills, provides that every local branch maintain "an Employment Department," in order to aid in supplying workmen to employer members of the Association. In case of a strike, the Association advertises for workers and supplies them to its members, paying the cost of "recruiting strike-breakers," the expense of their transportation to the member's plant, and, if necessary, the cost of housing and feeding them. Such recruits are given a certificate of recommendation guaranteeing them preference in employment by members of the Association.[1] The Association also pays the "extra compensation" above the member's normal wage rates necessary to obtain workers "for service of this character."[2] In pointing out the advantage of membership in the Association, the Secretary of the Cleveland branch stated in 1934: "In times of strike it would seem to me that the national aspect of our organization enabling us to secure men from all points in case of need and also the influence which we can bring about through national contacts to help a member keep its business in case of a strike, should carry a great deal of weight."[3]

According to its constitution, the National Founders' Association will, as one method of relief to a member in case of a strike, procure "workmen for him to the extent of 70 per cent of the average number he employed" prior to the strike. This Association also maintains in its employ under yearly contract a body of high-grade "contract molders," who normally work in the shops of some members of the Association and who, in case of a strike, can be sent wherever the Association directs, to work and to instruct green hands in the arts of high-grade molding of cast-iron products.[4]

The establishment of training schools for skilled craftsmen is another method of increasing the local supply of workmen in certain skilled trades. The Industrial Association of San Francisco established a system of trade schools for bricklayers, plasterers, plumbers, paperhangers, etc., and by 1928 had trained more than

[1] William O. Weyforth, *The Organizability of Labor*, 1917, p. 213.

[2] *Cf. Hearings before a Subcommittee of the Senate Committee on Education and Labor, pursuant to S. Res. 266*, 75th Congress, first session, Part 3, pp. 848, 1005, and Part 15-A, p. 5496. In 1937, following these hearings, parts of the constitution of the National Metal Trades Association were so changed that its activities in the labor market may follow a different pattern in the future.

[3] *Ibid.*, Part 15-A, p. 5470.

[4] Bonnett, *op. cit.*, p. 74; and Weyforth, *op. cit.*, p. 213.

1,700 boys in these various crafts.[1] The Citizens' Committee to
Enforce the Landis Award in Chicago also established a training
school to teach youngsters the building trades.[2]

3. *Control of wage rates.* In a number of ways, employers' organizations may control wage rates. During the period from 1921 to
1932, the Industrial Association of San Francisco and the Builders'
Exchange, by exerting the power of economic life or death over
builders through the permit system and financial control, forced
building employers to pay the wage rates set by the Association's
"Impartial" Wage Board. The Board's announced rates became
not only the minimum rates but usually the maximum rates as
well.[3] In this way, building wage rates in San Francisco were prevented from rising during the period from 1922 to 1926, although
such wage rates rose all over the country and there was a building
boom in San Francisco. In 1927 building wage rates in San Francisco were almost 10 per cent below the average for 23 cities and
were among the lowest rates in the United States for cities of comparable size.[4]

A similar situation occurred in the construction industry in
Chicago after the arbitration award of Judge Kenesaw Landis in
1921, which reduced wage rates 20 per cent or more in many building trades, so that the real wage rates in Chicago after the award
apparently were 25 per cent below the 1914 level.[5] The Citizens'
Committee to Enforce the Landis Award, by various kinds of economic pressure including the expenditure of $2,000,000 and the
hiring of a corps of private detectives and inspectors, forced this
severe wage reduction upon the Chicago building workers from
1921 to 1924, and in some trades to 1926, despite the fact that there
was an unprecedented building boom in Chicago during that
period.[6] Through extensive advertising and the circulation of lists
of employers adhering to the Landis "maximum" wage rates, requests were made that no building jobs be given to contractors
paying more than the Landis wages.[7]

Early in 1921 the American Shipowners' Association decided to
force a reduction of at least 15 per cent in the base wage rates of

[1] Ryan, *op. cit.*, pp. 172–73, 188.   [2] Montgomery, *op. cit.*, pp. 282, 294.
[3] Ryan, *op. cit.*, pp. 183, 189.   [4] *Ibid.*, pp. 182, 189, 195–97.
[5] Montgomery, *op. cit.*, p. 259; and Haber, *op. cit.*, p. 388.
[6] Montgomery, pp. 281, 284; and Haber, p. 393.
[7] Haber, *op. cit.*, pp. 388 and 393.

seamen and to abolish all pay for overtime, which together would effect a reduction of 30 to 35 per cent in the wages of sailors. The U. S. Shipping Board immediately gave its full support to the wage-reduction proposals of the owners. Indeed, the chairman of the U. S. Shipping Board ruled that no ship operator using any of the Board's 1,400 vessels could make an agreement with any union to pay wages above the rates that the Shipowners' Association had decided upon, and threatened to withdraw all government vessels from companies signing men on at higher wages.[1] In regard to this action by a Federal agency in support of the American Ship-owners' Association, Senator Robert M. La Follette told the United States Senate in July 1921: "Even where shipowners were willing to pay these men the then-existing [higher] wages and continue them, the power of the Shipping Board was exerted everywhere with the shipowners who desired to secure the allocation of Ameri-can [Government] ships to prevent their paying the men according to their own idea of what was fair."[2] As an indication of the pressure that the Shipowners' Association was exerting to force the wage reduction, Senator La Follette read the following excerpt from a telegram from the executive officers of the Seamen's Union in San Francisco:

Seafarers' union interviewed Frey of steamers *Yale* and *Harvard*. Is paying [union wage] scale and overtime as of 1920 and in some instances more. Not member of American Shipowners' Association. Stands alone in that respect on Pacific Coast. Is desirous of meeting all demands of [our] organization but fears to sign 12 months' agreement on account of Chamber of Commerce in Los Angeles and San Francisco who would bring influence to have his fuel supply stopped. Immense pressure is being brought to bear on Vice President and General Manager Frey from American Shipowners' Association and other sources as shown us by telegrams.[3]

The National Metal Trades Association states in its Declaration of Principles that "this association will not countenance any conditions or any rates of compensation which are not reasonable or just." Where an employer member "is not paying proper wages" or "is not paying wages that are comparable to the going rate of the community," the Association calls the member's attention to

[1] *Proceedings of 25th Annual Convention of International Seamen's Union of America*, 1922, p. 17.
[2] *Congressional Record*, vol. 61, Part 5, p. 4241.   [3] *Idem.*

that fact, stating that the condition should be corrected or, in case of labor trouble, the Association will refuse to assist that member.[1] It is for such assistance that the member has been paying his dues into the Association's $200,000-to-$300,000 Defense Fund, and any company is naturally reluctant to forfeit its stake or investment in the Association by failing to follow the Association's dictates.[2]

An employers' association has various means of attracting members and keeping the membership in line with its dictates. Should a member fail to follow orders, the association may fine him or collect the cash where members bond themselves for amounts ranging from $2,500 to $25,000 or more as a guarantee that they will comply with the association's principles and rules.[3] An employers' organization may, through its membership, help to maintain the market for a member's product. Members may also hesitate to disobey the association's orders for fear of losing the advantages of the association's plan for "strike insurance," by which members are reimbursed for losses sustained in strikes. An employer might very well hesitate to go it alone for fear that he would have to meet singlehanded the full power of a labor union, while his competitors were busy capturing his market.

Nonmembers may also become convinced, by threats of loss of sales to members or, as in California, by threats to cut off the supply of building materials or of fuel for ships, that it is to their advantage to obey the association's dictates. Wage rates in the various ports on the Pacific Coast were kept in line with the San Francisco rates during the 1920's by threats of shipowners to boycott any ports failing to follow the suit of San Francisco, the center of employer-controlled wage changes. In the hearings before the Federal Mediation Boards in the Pacific Coast dispute of 1934, various employer and employee witnesses explained that the Shipowners' and Waterfront Employers' Associations in San Francisco determined wage rates for the whole Coast.[4] One witness explained how, after

[1] *Hearings on S. Res. 266,* Part 3, pp. 826, 843.
[2] *Cf. ibid.,* p. 951.
[3] *Cf.* Weyforth, *op. cit.,* p. 216; and Haber, *op. cit.,* p. 351.
[4] *Proceedings before Federal Mediation Board of the United States Government,* March 28 through March 31, 1934, vol. 3, pp. 271, 281, 285, 296–97, 303; and *Proceedings before the National Longshoremen's Board, Sitting as a Board of Arbitration to Arbitrate Controversies between Marine Service Bureau and International Longshoremen's Association, Local 38, of the Pacific Coast District,* 1934, vol. 21, p. 1755, and vol. 22, p. 1793. (Originals in the Library of Congress, Washington, D. C.)

complaint by the workers in the port of Tacoma, Washington, against a cut of 10 cents an hour in wages, the Tacoma waterfront employers stated that, though in their opinion only a cut of 5 cents an hour was justified and they regretted that the San Francisco shipowners had decided upon a more drastic cut, nevertheless they were powerless to oppose the 10-cent cut and were forced to follow the orders from San Francisco.[1]

EMPLOYEES' ORGANIZATIONS

Employee organizations or labor unions, like their employer counterparts, usually attempt to influence or control the labor market for the services of their members. Indeed, organized groups generally strive to improve the living standards of the members and to protect them from so-called "unfair" or "cutthroat" competition. This frequently means the exercise of some control over the actions of members by the association, for the purpose of restricting supply or of achieving some price stability through restraint of price-cutting. For much the same reasons that steel companies prefer steady, uniform prices for their products, most workers and some employers (like building contractors) want stability and uniformity in the wage structure. Through trade associations or other organizations, employers in an industry may develop a set of working rules, sometimes called "codes of business" or "practices in the industry," which tend to limit the nature and methods of competition in that branch of business. In much the same manner, employees, through trade-unions, frequently develop "working rules" and devices that tend to restrict the scope of competition in the labor market and to restrain wage-cutting.

In 1940 there were about 170 national labor unions in the United States, with a combined membership of around 8,700,000 workers, or less than one fourth of the total labor supply. In some industries, however, like coal mining, railroading, printing, clothing, and building, a large percentage of all workers were union members.

1. *Policies affecting supply.* Labor organizations try, by various means, to restrict the supply of labor available in a particular occupation and in a particular area. The supply of labor includes, of course, not only the total hours of work offered in the market but the output or work done during the period of employment.

[1] *Proceedings before Federal Mediation Board*, vol. 3, p. 281.

The employer really buys labor output, and limitation of labor output may occur either by a reduction in the number of sellers of a certain type of labor, or by a reduction in the number of hours each seller offers for sale, or by restrictions upon the daily output of each seller.

There is some merit to Professor Solomon Blum's claim that labor unions cannot, like large industrial corporations and combinations, limit "the absolute total supply in order to stimulate higher prices."[1] True, the *total* supply of labor is fairly fixed in the short run; it cannot be withheld from the market and stored, a customary monopolistic practice, nor can trade-unions have "superfluous" workers dumped into the ocean like "superfluous" vegetables, nor plowed under like "superfluous" cotton, nor killed off like "super-fluous" pigs. But, though they are unable to control the *total* labor supply of a country, they sometimes have been able to exert a measure of control over the *local* supply of labor in certain occupations or over the output of labor in certain trades. Even in the restriction of output, George Soule claims that "capitalistic monopolies are far more effective than are labor organizations."[2]

The services of skilled craftsmen command a high wage because such services are relatively scarce. One method by which a union may attempt to maintain or stimulate such scarcity is through the enforcement of apprenticeship rules, which may discourage youths from entering the trade by requiring that all learners serve an apprenticeship of, say, three years in a union shop, and which may limit the number of apprentices permitted in any shop. Nowadays, however, it is very difficult for a union to control entrance to a trade because most trades can be learned in a nonunion shop, at a vocational school, in prisons, and elsewhere. Usually, once a worker has learned the trade every effort is made to induce him to join the union, unless practically all the work is controlled by the union in union shops. Where the employers in a locality employ only union workers, the union may restrict the available labor supply by union initiation fees in the hundreds of dollars and by very high monthly dues, or, as sometimes occurs in the building trades, by a system of temporary permits in boom times, which

---

[1] S. Blum, *Labor Economics*, 1925, pp. 341–42, 360, 363.
[2] *Annals of the American Academy of Political and Social Science*, vol. 184 (March 1936), p. 5.

force the holder out of the union as soon as his last permit expires.[1] Especially during slack periods, certain local unions have been closed, for a time, to new members. Of course, restrictions on entrance to the union are effective only when the union has some measure of control over the jobs in a locality either because employers agree to hire only union workers or because they find it profitable to hire their workers through the union.

The strike really represents an attempt to withhold all, or a certain portion, of the labor supply from the market. Supply is simply the amount offered *at a certain price or prices*. If the strike concerns wage rates, it simply represents an attempt to withdraw the supply of labor represented by the strikers from that particular labor market until the wage rate demanded by the strikers is established. Through picketing, the striking employees hope to prevent the employer from having free access to the labor supply on the market, and, by means of the boycott, they hope to restrict his access to the commodity markets.

Labor unions, if they are able to establish a shorter work day or work week, really reduce the amount of labor that is offered by each seller at a certain price. The employer, in order to buy a larger number of hours from any seller, is forced to pay punitive overtime rates of one-and-a-half or two times the wage rate for normal working hours.[2] A shorter work week for all workers reduces the total number of hours of labor offered for sale at various wage rates.

It is among the building-trades locals in certain cities that one finds probably the greatest degree of monopoly control over supply by labor unions. The building-trades unions are in an especially good position to exercise such monopoly control because their members are highly skilled and the market is local, so that building costs and wages in one locality may be very high with little threat of outside low-cost competition. As yet few buildings are shipped into a city ready-made. Consequently, the conditions in building vary widely from locality to locality, and the building trades are frequently an exception to generalizations that apply primarily to labor unions in industries manufacturing products for a national market.

[1] Ryan, *op. cit.*, p. 99; and Haber, *op. cit.*, pp. 203–204.

[2] Overtime work is prohibited outright in most of the women's and men's clothing industries, and in other industries it is frequently prohibited during designated dull seasons.

Not only have some local building unions enforced rigid apprenticeship rules and charged union entrance fees as high as $100 to $500,[1] but they have sometimes restricted output by establishing a "daily stint" or a fixed quota for a day's work. For instance, the local union may forbid members, if they are plasterers, to handle more than 12 barrels of lime a day; if lathers, to tack on more than 30 bundles of lath a day; if composition roofers, to lay more than so many square feet of roofing a day; if bricklayers, to lay more than, say, 1,000 bricks a day.[2] Building-trades unions have also restricted output by rules prohibiting the use of paint brushes more than four or four-and-a-half inches in width, or the use of paint spray machines, or the use of a stone pick in stonecutting, or the laying of bricks with both hands, or the placing of mortar for bricks with a shovel—the trowel is the tool of the trade; the shovel is too crude and, incidentally, might speed up operations. These restrictions upon output not only reduce the supply of work (in terms of output) offered by union members, but tend to increase the number of hours of labor demanded by the employer in order to complete a job. Especially if the demand for the services of the members of the union is fairly inelastic, the membership may gain in both money and real income by practicing a restriction of output. Indeed, restriction of output to maintain or raise prices is a common business practice, and it is widely used by unorganized as well as organized workers.[3]

2. *Policies affecting demand.* Union restrictions upon the introduction of labor-saving machinery, including minor labor-saving devices such as wide paint brushes, tend to keep up the demand for the services of the skilled workers in the union, if practically all employers hire union members. The same is true of restrictions that prevent a subdivision of the craftsman's job so that unskilled or semiskilled workers can perform a portion of it. All union regulations that protect the craft from invasion by untrained workers, or protect the jobs of craftsmen by preventing the introduction of labor-saving devices, help to sustain the demand for the services of the craftsmen concerned.

Unions adopt various other rules in order to influence the em-

---

[1] Haber, *op. cit.*, pp. 202–204.
[2] Ryan, *op. cit.*, pp. 96, 100; and Montgomery, *op. cit.*, p. 158.
[3] *Cf.* S. B. Mathewson, *Restriction of Output among Unorganized Workers*, 1931.

ployment of their membership. They may insist that certain specified jobs require the hiring of a crew of at least two or three skilled journeymen.[1] Some building unions prohibit the contractor from working on the job.[2] Structural steel workers may require that they handle all steel from the unloading point to the building site, thus doing laborers' work at high cost. Plumbers' unions have sometimes forbidden the use of assembled plumbing supplies or the installation of fixtures partly put together at the shop or plant. Painters have been forbidden to work on cabinets partly finished at the factory. A painters' union, under threat to picket on the opening night, forced the owner of an ice arena in Cleveland to hire union painters to run dry brushes over the seats for a few days prior to the opening of the arena because the seats were purchased already painted from an out-of-town firm. Printers in certain cities have insisted on the "dead-horse" rule against the use of "borrowed matter"; that is, any advertisements set up in one newspaper shop cannot be run in another newspaper without being completely reset by printers in the shop of the second newspaper. Such restrictive "working rules," most characteristic of highly skilled crafts in which labor organizations are relatively strong, are designed to increase the demand for the services of union members and to afford more employment to union members in a seasonal industry like building.

3. *Control of wage rates.* Economic groups combine primarily in order to influence price by eliminating the undercutting forces of competition. An employer combination or association may, through its control over the buyers' side of the market, restrict or prevent competitive bidding for workers. The control that a labor union may exert over the wage rates paid for certain types of work in a community depends upon the extent to which the union controls the various possible sources of supply. The union's control is also partly dependent upon the influence it can exert over the demand for an employer's products. Union members may not only refuse to work for employers who do not pay the wage scale demanded by the union, but they may also refuse to patronize an employer who does not employ union workers at the wage scale set by the union. The ability to put the union label on one's products

---

[1] *Cf.* Montgomery, *op. cit.*, p. 180.
[2] *Ibid.*, pp. 161, 182; and Ryan, *op. cit.*, p. 101.

is especially important to producers whose goods are sold directly to consumers in low-income classes, such as beer, certain printed matter, overalls, and other kinds of clothing.

The union attempts to maintain or to increase wage rates through cooperative or collective selling. That is usually the purpose of other cooperative selling groups, including sellers' associations. Where most of the employees of a certain employer or in a certain trade are members of one union, they may, by united action, prevent competitive underbidding of the union wage scale by individual workers. Indeed, individual members of a union are customarily fined or otherwise punished for infraction of the union's rules against undercutting of the union rate. Through the enforcement of a standard work day and a "daily stint," the union tends to prevent any attempt to cut wage rates indirectly by lengthening the hours or by stimulating an increase in output. The concerted or unified action of a union that dominates the supply of a certain kind of labor in an area prevents the employer from playing one worker off against another in order to find out the lowest wage rate he needs to offer. With a strong union controlling the supply side of his labor market, the employer may be faced with the choice of having all the union members he wants to hire at the union scale or of having no labor supply at all if he tries to pay a lower rate. Like other monopolistic elements in the market, the labor union selects a wage rate and attempts to force that rate upon the market through collective action on the part of some or all of the sellers.

If a union demands an increase in wage rates, the employer is usually faced with two alternatives: either he must pay a wage scale somewhat higher than he would otherwise have paid, or he must sustain the losses in earnings that accompany a strike—the overhead expense of idle equipment and the profits unearned during the strike as well as the loss of customers to competitors and the effect on employee morale, both of which may affect his profits long after the strike is over. In either case, the employer is in a worse position than he would have been had his employees not combined in a union. For this reason alone, wage rates are likely to be higher where the employer has to deal with an aggressive union than would be the case if no union existed. Since exploitation (as defined in Chapter 5) may occur in the better paid as well as in the poorer paid trades, it is clear that collective action by the sellers of labor may result in higher wage rates than would be established by free and unrestricted competition on the sellers' side of the market.[1] Concerted action by sellers may not only establish a higher price but may, if the demand schedule for their services is inelastic, result in a greater money, and even real, income for them. Frequently it pays monopolistic groups to fix upon a price above the one that would prevail under unlimited competition.

JOINT CONTROL BY EMPLOYERS' AND EMPLOYEES' ORGANIZATIONS

In some cases employers' organizations have cooperated with employees' organizations to restrain competition on both sides of the labor market and sometimes, also, on the supply side of the employers' commodity market. In return for a promise by the employers' combination that union members will have a monopoly of the combination's work, the union assures the employers' combination that competing employers who do not join the combination will not procure the services of union members. Union officials may even resort to further action to prevent the production and sale of articles by employers who are not members of the combination. In return for high wage rates, the union may also aid the employers' combination to maintain fixed prices and to obtain "good" profits. Such two-sided monopoly, established by union-employer agreement, may operate to the disadvantage of all those outside of the two cooperating groups: nonunion workers, independent employers, and the general public, which buys the products.

Union-employer cooperation to regulate competition has occurred, for instance, in building construction in various cities, in the photoengraving industry, in the clothing industry, and in industries such as laundry, dry cleaning and pressing, baked goods, and general trucking in certain cities in the Pacific Northwest where the Teamsters' union has been powerful. In such industries, price-cutting and wage-cutting are likely to occur to an extreme degree because there is a large number of small employers in the industry, it is so easy to enter the business, and wages are such an important item in total costs. In building construction, for example, contractors desire some organization to enforce stability and com-

[1] *Cf.* J. R. Hicks, *The Theory of Wages*, 1935, pp. 82, 136–58. This point is discussed more fully in Chapter 8 *infra*.

petitive equality in wage rates, so that they can bid on jobs without being subject to the risk of sharp and sizeable increases in wages. Unregulated competition in building construction has not infrequently led to the elimination of efficient and scrupulous contractors, because more speculative and unscrupulous employers have bid extremely low on jobs and then have cut wages, rushed workers, and encouraged poor workmanship in order to squeeze some profit out of their low bid. The consuming public often has failed to gain by such low bidding, because constant labor strife, frequent failures among contractors, and bad workmanship were the result.[1]

In building. Alliances between contractors' associations and building unions, to gain monopoly control of the local building market, have occurred in certain cities like Chicago, Boston, and New York.[2] Unions and employers' associations have connived to eliminate outside competition through exclusive agreements, under which the union agrees to work only for contractors affiliated with the employers' association upon assurance that the contractors in the association will hire only members of the union. In other cases, the union may promise not to install the goods of any manufacturer not a member of the employers' association in return for a pledge that the employers' combination will employ only union labor or will not furnish materials for jobs on which nonunion labor is employed. Such union-employer agreements permit wages and profits to be raised by exacting higher prices from the public. This may be done through various devices for price-fixing or price control, such as the exchange of information about bids by members of the combination, control over the prices submitted in bids, or the allotment of certain work or areas to certain members of the association. General contractors in the employers' association may agree to subcontract only to members of the organization, and unions may put pressure upon employers to join the "bosses' association," by suggesting such affiliation as a means of avoiding labor difficulties.

In 1921 the Lockwood Committee in New York discovered "every article entering into building construction to be under the control of merciless, gouging, monopolistic combines," and the

---

[1] *Cf.*, for instance, Ryan, *op. cit.*, pp. 22–24.

[2] Most of the material in this and the following paragraph is based upon Montgomery, *op. cit.*, pp. 187–208; and Haber, *op. cit.*, pp. 232–33, 368–69.

Dailey Commission in Chicago declared that the contractors there "dictate their own prices, and the consumer has no alternative but to submit to prices arbitrarily fixed by the members of the organization." During the period from 1910 to 1930, a number of unions and contractors in Chicago were prosecuted and convicted under the Federal antitrust laws for combining, especially through union-employer agreements, to restrain competition and fix prices. It is only fair to add that many national labor unions in the building trades prohibit, by constitutional provisions, such exclusive agreements between locals of the union and employer associations. Nevertheless, a new wave of antitrust prosecutions in the building trades occurred in 1939 and 1940.

In photoengraving. Beginning with the Chicago locals in April 1915, the American Photo-Engravers' Association and the International Photo-Engravers' Union made an arrangement whereby the union got a closed shop and wage increases in return for a promise that union members would work only for firms that were affiliated with the local units of the American Photo-Engravers' Association and that maintained the Association's "standard scale" of uniform, minimum base prices, based on high costs and intended to provide a good profit. Before 1915, the industry had suffered from "ruinous competition" and price-cutting, so that the minimum wage rate for photoengravers, who are highly skilled craftsmen and make distinctive products on order, was but $30 a week in New York as late as November 1917. Because about 70 per cent of the factory costs in photoengraving are labor costs, the union determined to prevent competition that resulted in wage cuts and to "force the manufacturers to make money" by enforcing uniformity in the selling price of the product. In New York City, for example, the president of the local union wrote to various employers as follows: "Enclosed herewith find 'minimum selling base for photo-engravings' as adopted by the members of this union for their protection, the disregard of which will result in our requesting the withdrawal of our members from your employ."[1]

[1] Most of the material given here on the photoengraving industry has been taken from "In the Matter of American Photo-Engravers' Association *et al.* and the International Photo-Engravers' Union of North America *et al.*," *Federal Trade Commission Decisions*, January 30, 1928, to June 11, 1929, vol. 12, 1930, pp. 29–69. *Cf.* also, John A. Fitch, "The Guild Reappears in Industry," *The Survey*, vol. 41 (November 16, 1918), pp. 192–93; and Herman Feldman, *Problems in Labor Relations*, 1937, pp. 10–11.

The American Photo-Engravers' Association, with some 33 state and city locals, represented from 75 to 90 per cent of the commercial (not newspaper) output of photoengravings in the United States. Its local affiliates (called clubs) generally could inspect the books of all member employers and could fine, suspend, or expel employers who undercut the "standard scale," which the Association was attempting to make the uniform minimum price for plates throughout the country. A "Johnny B. Good" Fund was collected from members in 1917 for the purpose of "educating" employers to adopt the Association's price scale. The International Photo-Engravers' Union of North America, of which Matthew Woll had been president for some time, contained in the early 1920's over 90 per cent of the 7,500 workmen in the industry.

To make certain that all employers maintained the Association's enhanced scale of prices so that the employees might be given the desired wage increases, the locals of the Photo-Engravers' Association and of the union in 32 large cities had, by 1917, incorporated the following famous Clause 10 in written agreements between the local employer and union organizations:

Clause 10.—In order that the Union may secure the adoption and carrying out by all photo-engraving concerns in [city] of the scale of wages and working conditions herein specified, and have the responsibility of said [employers'] club for their observance and performance, the union hereby requests, and the club hereby agrees, that the club will admit to its membership all reputable photo-engraving concerns in [city] and in consideration thereof and of the assumption of the responsibility by the club for any and all violations of said scale of wages and working conditions by every member of the club, the union agrees that its members will work only for such photo-engraving concerns as are members of the club, provided that the club shall not arbitrarily or for any but good cause, refuse admission to or deny retention of membership in the club.

This series of agreements containing Clause 10, adopted in about 50 cities from 1915 to 1922, put the full united strength of the unions and the employers' organizations behind the price-fixing wage-raising program. The officers of the union and the employers' association had made every effort to see that Clause 10 was incorporated in all union-employer agreements. As the president of the Photo-Engravers' Association said in 1919, "our employees are working with us and not for us, and are, in reality, our business partners; and woe betide the pirate who preys unfairly on us; for he will now find a united front arrayed against him." The president of the international union declared that the union had no alternative but to withdraw men from the shops of employers who refused to join the employers' organization or were expelled from it because they had engaged in price-cutting, a sufficient cause for suspension by the employers' organization according to the union's resolutions and the precepts of its officers. Indeed, strike pressure was brought to bear by the unions against photoengraving concerns in some cities in order to enforce the Association's uniform price scale.

In an address in 1917, President Woll described the Clause 10 as the one means to protect the business from the evil of price-cutting by organizing both employers and employees to maintain prices, a fair profit for the employer, and a fair wage for the employee. The president of the Photo-Engravers' Association congratulated the union on having leaders so capable of safeguarding the interests of union members, and stated in 1920 that Clause 10 had so stabilized prices and profits that the members of the Association had received a "very splendid return" for the wages paid. The price increases in that year alone added about $6,000,000 to the sales income of American photoengravers. So strong was the arrangement that it prevented price-cutting even in times of business depression.

Though Clause 10 was eliminated from agreements in most cities during 1921 and 1922 because of formal complaints that it violated various antitrust laws, the local unions cooperated with the employers' association by threatening to enforce that section of the general laws of the national union authorizing the executive council, if necessary, to withdraw union men from shops engaged in "unfair, unjustified, or unwarranted competition for trade." The president of the Photo-Engravers' Association reported, a year after the abandonment of Clause 10, "We in New York today are getting very close together—very close . . . we are going right back where we were."

The market for photoengraving is mainly local, and the Photo-Engravers' Association attempted to localize it more completely by discouraging solicitation of business in other cities. In its magazine, letters from engraving firms turning down out-of-city business were published and highly praised as "evidence of existing cooperation." In some areas there were gentlemen's agreements not to solicit business in another firm's territory, and the various local associations of photoengravers made understandings that, in quoting prices to buyers in other cities, their members would conform to the prices and rate of discount prevailing in that territory.

From 1914 to 1925, items in the Association's standard scale of minimum prices showed an increase from 100 to 650 per cent. In 1925 the photoengraving firms made an average net profit of about 12.5 per cent on a $14,000,000 investment—partly overinvestment. The high prices had resulted in many new firms entering the industry, so that production capacity far exceeded the possible demand at prevailing prices; yet even with the increased costs of so much idle capacity, profits were high and the wage rates in photoengraving came to be among the highest in the country. Apparently the demand for photoengraving is fairly inelastic, despite the fact that there are other processes of reproducing pictures and designs, such as lithography and rotogravure.

By the Seattle Teamsters.[1] In the city of Seattle, Washington, the various units of the Joint Council of Teamsters (Local 28) have helped to enforce what has facetiously been called "Dave Beck's voluntary NRA"—Mr. Beck has been president of the Joint Council and the West Coast Representative of the International Brotherhood of Teamsters, Chauffeurs, Stablemen, and Helpers of America. In essence, it represents an arrangement whereby the union and the employers' associations cooperate to pay high wages, to charge "standard" prices, and to restrain or regulate competition. The lines of business so "stabilized" and controlled are petty trades like cleaning and dyeing, baking, trucking, and laundry, in which price wars are common. In such lines, there are well over 100 firms in Seattle, and competition would, unless controlled by some "stabilizing" force or price-fixing arrangements, tend to result in all sorts of price-cutting and price discrimination. In the baked-goods industry, for instance, most products have to be sold soon, for nothing is so worthless as last week's cream puff. In trucking there are

---

[1] Much of the material in this section on the Seattle Teamsters is based on an unpublished Master's thesis by Carl Gustaf Westine on *The Seattle Teamsters* (1937) in the University of Washington Library, and Richard L. Neuberger, *Our Promised Land*, 1938, Chapter 8. Part of the data the author himself has collected from interviews and discussions with residents of Seattle.

many small operators, some with only a single truck, so trucking rates are frequently disorganized and uneconomic, the same firm often quoting different rates to different buyers.[1] In cleaning and pressing, despite the vigilance of the employers' association and the "voluntary NRA," secret cutting of prices below the "standard" price scale has occurred at times for established customers.

The Teamsters claim jurisdiction over "everything on wheels"— all drivers and delivery men, including auto salesmen and garage employees—and have about 20,000 members in and around Seattle. The closed shop is maintained by fining members for working with expelled members or nonunion men, or for teaching the work to a man without a union clearance card. With drivers and delivery men 100 per cent organized, the Teamsters' union can prevent any employer from receiving supplies or delivering his product. Economically, a city is very dependent upon transportation, especially where distances are great as in the Far West. By controlling transportation, the union controls the local market and holds a whip hand over any erring industrialist. This power has been used to "organize the boss," by causing enterprisers to join employers' associations, like the Laundry and Dry Cleaners' Association, the Truck Owners' Association, the Garage Owners' Association, the Milk Dealers' Association, or the Bakers' Association, which collect "dues" and are sometimes administered by former union officials. These associations, to which employers may give power of attorney over labor matters, make blanket agreements with the union covering all employers in the association. The associations and the union cooperate to raise and regulate wages and prices, and to follow a policy of controlling competition and of organizing concerns so that they will charge the "standard" price. The union may refuse to handle goods produced by employers not in the association or that are for sale at less than the "standard" price. Members of the union may be expelled or fined for failing to "come out" of a firm declared unfair by the union.

The head of the Seattle Teamsters believes that "labor cannot prosper unless business men and invested capital are given reasonable and adequate protection," "that labor cannot receive a fair wage from business unless business receives a fair profit on its in-

---

[1] Since 1935, interstate trucking has been under the jurisdiction and regulation of the Interstate Commerce Commission.

vestment." Because the union has helped to guarantee good profits, many businessmen in Seattle have had "confidence in" the Teamsters' organization, and the local chamber of commerce has been decidedly friendly toward that union. As Mr. Beck has explained, "labor is working in very close harmony with the industrial organizations in Seattle." In the past, the Teamsters' union on the West Coast has made agreements with employers containing or implying such provisions as the following:

It is mutually understood by all parties of this Agreement and agreed that in order to maintain the ability to pay the schedule of wages and hours specified in this Agreement and otherwise perform the provisions of this Agreement, the employer must be able to obtain and maintain adequate prices for the bakery products sold, and the failure of the employer to obtain such prices . . . will jeopardize the interests of the members of the Union employed in the baking industry. The employer, therefore, agrees at all times in the life of this Agreement to maintain prevailing adequate prices for bakery goods sold or handled, and not to begin or engage in any price war to cut the prices of any bakery products below that generally charged for the product in that trade area, or to engage in any other trade practice or act which may tend to disrupt the baking industry in that area and thus adversely affect the ability of the employer and other employers to maintain adequate wages and satisfactory working conditions in the State of Oregon, and the members of Local 499 agree to cooperate to the fullest extent with the employers to create and maintain the conditions herein specified, in order to maintain a stabilized condition at all times.[1]

In "stabilizing" the various industries in which the Teamsters' members have been employed so that union wage scales could be maintained, it has been necessary to regulate and control competition. In this connection, the head of the union has said:

[1] Section 23 in an agreement signed in the middle of 1937 between the Wholesale Drivers' and Salesmen's Union, Local 499, Portland, Oregon, and the Portland bakeries. Cited in Neuberger, *op. cit.*, p. 186; and Carter Brown, *The Teamsters' Union in Seattle*, June 1938, p. 52, an unpublished Bachelor's thesis in the Reed College Library.

In the June 1938 issue of the Official Magazine of the Teamsters' union, the international president of the union warned against price-fixing agreements with employers' associations as in violation of the Federal antitrust laws. He admitted a dislike for the "cutthroat employer that cuts prices below the regular price" but maintained that the union should "keep within the law."

In regulating competition, the head of the Seattle Teamsters insists that he has never entered into price-fixing agreements. The commissions of the drivers for laundry, pressing, and dry-cleaning establishments are computed from a standard uniform price list, so that all teamsters receive the same standard commission for delivery work. The employers, though forced to pay all Seattle drivers the same fee, can, according to Mr. Beck, vary their prices from the union's standard price list.

There are too many filling stations in Seattle. More are threatened. We're going to close some of them. First, I advise promoters against starting new stations. If that doesn't work, the Teamsters' union simply will refuse to serve them. They won't last very long.[1]

It has been charged that labor is operating a racket in the milk industry. If we let milk come into the Seattle market without restriction every dairy in Seattle would be bankrupt in two weeks.[2]

The union thus helps to protect employers already established and indirectly assists the larger employers to win out over small independents. Admitting that his union had put a stop to the shipment of autos by caravan and the hauling of citrus fruit from California to Seattle by drivers paid very low wages, Mr. Beck stated in a speech in January 1938: "Railroads and responsible trucking companies couldn't meet such competition, so we put a stop to it. Was that racketeering? Why, we were doing work that properly belongs to the chamber of commerce." [3] Union members, presumably under an agreement with the Truck Owners' Association, have also protected the trade of the large trucking firms by forceably preventing farmers from trucking produce other than their own into or out of Seattle. In defense of this policy Mr. Beck has said:

A man who buys a truck for a few dollars, collects farm produce and sells it in Seattle, and then picks up a load of cement or something else to drive back and sell, is not a farmer. He is a peddler and legitimate business cannot face that competition and pay union wages.[4]

Consequently, employers, regardless of what they may say to complaining customers about the union, have generally been pleased with a situation that permits them to maintain satisfactory prices and profits and prevents certain types of new competition from entering their field.

The union and employers have been able to raise wages and prices primarily because the market for laundry service, taxicab service, cleaning and pressing, local trucking, garage work, baked goods, and milk delivery is a local one that firms outside the area cannot capture. Such services and products cannot be shipped into Seattle on a large scale by outside concerns in order to take advantage of Seattle's high prices. If an outside firm tried to

[1] Neuberger, *op. cit.*, p. 184.
[2] *Seattle Post-Intelligencer*, January 27, 1938, p. 5.
[3] *Idem.*
[4] *The Washington Teamster*, vol. 1 (April 1940), p. 4.

take advantage of the high prices, the local teamsters might refuse to deliver its product or services. Consequently, the cost of laundry, cleaning, pressing, taxicab, and garage service in Seattle may get out of line with the cost of such service in cities 100 miles away. For most of those services the demand is fairly inelastic, although the level of laundry prices in Seattle reduced the volume of business so that the union accepted a cut in the weekly wages of laundry drivers after 1931 from $40 to $30 a week. In 1938 their wages were increased to $35 a week. The prices for pressing, cleaning, and laundry service in Seattle have probably been as high as they are anywhere in the country.[1]

In the laundry business, the cooperation between the union and employers has been so close that few laundries have dared to charge less than the "union" or standard price scale. Four wholesale establishments, which handle practically all of the cleaning done in Seattle, would undoubtedly refuse to perform work for a retail firm that openly cut cleaning prices, and the Teamsters' union might refuse to deliver for the price-cutter or "chiseler." The union, which includes small entrepreneurs in its membership, may act as an enforcement agency to uphold the prices agreed upon.

The prices of most nationally advertised products are no higher in Seattle than elsewhere, and rents are fairly low for a city of that size. The proportion of the total costs of nationally advertised products that goes to truck drivers in Seattle is, of course, very small. The wages of Seattle teamsters would have a significant effect only in industries like taxicab service, laundry, milk, etc., where drivers' wages are an important item in total costs. Nevertheless, the fact that many nationally advertised products sell for the same price all over the country, regardless of whether the plant or retail store is in a high-wage or a low-wage locality, indicates that there may be little direct relationship between labor costs and prices. Large producers of branded products may really make most of their profits from operations in certain localities.

In his unpublished study, *The Seattle Teamsters*, Carl Westine

---

[1] Early in 1939 the "official" price throughout Seattle was 65 cents for pressing and $1.00 for cleaning a man's suit, $1.00 to $1.75 for cleaning dresses, and 75 cents for pressing and $1.25 for cleaning overcoats. For laundry the prices were: 20 cents for men's shirts, 25 cents for pajamas and nightgowns, 7 cents for a pair of socks, and 10 cents for stockings. In some of the Chinese hand laundries, prices in 1938 and 1939 were at times about 25 per cent below these prices.

states that in the laundry, cleaning, and pressing business "union wage gains have, in practically every instance, been followed by increased prices" to the consumer. In baked goods he found that "virtually every year [in the 1920's] there were wage increases until Seattle's bakeries paid top wages for their line of work in the United States." [1] In 1937 the average union wage for truck and delivery drivers throughout the country was 77 cents an hour; in Seattle all drivers, except general teamsters on small trucks, were receiving from 80 cents to $1.00 an hour. [2] In 1937 Seattle teamsters, with weekly earnings ranging from $35 to $46 for a 40- or 48-hour week, were receiving the highest wages paid for teamsters in any city of that size in the United States. Such wages were only possible, as the head of the Seattle Teamsters frankly admits, through cooperation with employers' organizations to "stabilize" the industry. An alliance or understanding between employer and employee organizations, which can successfully control prices in a local market, may raise wages without reference to wage rates for the same work in other localities or the wage rates for other types of work in the same locality.

In the clothing industry, the unions and employers' associations have, through joint control, succeeded in regulating the industry and limiting competition in order to permit higher wages. The methods used to "stabilize" the clothing industry are discussed in Chapter 30.

General remarks. Parts Three, Four, and Five of this book contain further comments on the practices of employers' associations and labor unions. The need for the "stabilization" of certain industries by unions is discussed in these later Parts, where the broad social implications of such private regulation of industries by labor and employer organizations are also considered.

This discussion of organizations in the labor market is included at this point to provide some background for the treatment of wages in the following two chapters. The discussion in this chapter should give the reader a better basis for criticizing wage theories and analyzing the factors that affect wage rates. Of course, the examples that were selected for illustrative purposes represent rather extreme cases. Such stress on monopolistic elements in the labor market is

[1] Westine, *op. cit.*, p. 55.
[2] *Monthly Labor Review*, vol. 46 (March 1938), p. 745.

necessary, however, because economists have been too prone to overlook the important part that labor and employers' organizations and agreements play in the labor market. In formulating wage theories, they have tended to neglect the influence of monopolistic power and economic pressure.

CHAPTER SEVEN

WAGES:
A PARADE OF THEORIES

The two preceding chapters have explained some of the factors that influence the actual determination of wage rates in different branches of industry. This chapter contains a discussion of the various theories of wages that have been in vogue from time to time during the past three centuries. In the following chapter, some of the material in this and the preceding two chapters is synthesized into what, it is hoped, represents a satisfactory explanation of the way wage rates are determined in our modern economic society.

Most people consider theory to be something that will not work in practice. Unfortunately, too many of the theories in economics have been open to that criticism. Essentially, however, a theorist is one who reasons things out, and theory is the result of reasoning from past experience. Economic theory simply consists of generalizations about facts; it explains the relations, especially the cause and effect relationships, between economic facts, thereby deepening our understanding of economic affairs. The student uses facts to discover, and to test the validity of, economic theories; any theories that fail to fit the facts should be discarded as unsound or amended so that they do provide an adequate explanation.

One of the purposes of this discussion of various wage theories is to see how well the leading wage theories of the past meet the test of fact. A study of the weaknesses in such theories should help to develop a healthy skepticism and should aid in understanding how economic doctrines evolve and change with changes in economic structure and economic institutions. Such a study should also enable the student to classify contemporary notions concerning wages. He will be surprised to find how little there is that is new under the sun. John Maynard Keynes indicated the importance of studies of economic doctrines when he wrote:

. . . the ideas of economists and political philosophers, both when they are right and when they are wrong, are more powerful than is commonly understood. Indeed the world is ruled by little else. Practical men, who believe themselves to be quite exempt from any intellectual influences, are usually the slaves of some defunct economist. Madmen in authority, who hear voices in the air, are distilling their frenzy from some academic scribbler of a few years back. I am sure that the power of vested interests is vastly exaggerated compared with the gradual encroachment of ideas . . . . soon or late, it is ideas, not vested interests, which are dangerous for good or evil.[1]

In the past, eminent economists have made errors by assuming that the characteristics of their times would be permanent and by drawing universal generalizations from transient economic conditions. Economic theories have frequently been influenced by contemporary economic interests, and economic explanations have often become justifications for current economic conditions. Consequently, the different theories of wages can be fully understood only by placing them in their appropriate historical setting. The reader should, therefore, bear in mind the historical material presented in Chapters 3 and 4, which, it will be recalled, also contained some discussion of wage-level changes and wage theories, especially during the first half of the nineteenth century. It will be necessary, in some cases, to explain also the economists' notions about interest, rent, and profits, for wage theories frequently are not independent of theories concerning the reward going to the other factors of production.

SUBSISTENCE THEORIES

The mercantilists. A group of nationalistic economists, who wrote in England and France between 1630 and 1775, propounded some false notions about wages and economic policy that may still be heard in certain quarters. The mercantilists, as they are called, believed that wages should be kept at the minimum necessary for physical subsistence of the workers and their families. As a matter of fact, the wages of unskilled workers were near the subsistence level during most of the mercantilist period, and some of the mercantilists even maintained that the "laborers of all countries and all times would inevitably receive subsistence wages." [2] The almost universal agreement amongst the mercantilist writers that cost of

[1] J. M. Keynes, *General Theory of Employment, Interest and Money*, 1936, pp. 383–84.

[2] *Cf.* E. S. Furniss, *The Position of the Laborer in a System of Nationalism, A Study in the*

subsistence was the norm for wages was their closest approach to a theory of wages.

The other fundamental notion of the mercantilists concerning wages was that the labor cost of producing articles determined their price in domestic, and even in foreign, markets. This notion that the only costs of production are money costs for wages and that expenses for wages determine prices is a typical shopkeeping point of view and could only have arisen in the domestic-system or cottage stage of economic development, in which capital equipment and capital costs played a very minor role. Such a point of view, of course, fails to take account of social or human costs, costs to the nation from destructive use of natural and human resources. It is likewise typical of the merchant, who always strives to cover his costs, to believe that costs determine selling prices—as though there never is unsound investment and the product of any whittler is bound to bring a price that fully compensates for all the hours he spent on it. This mercantilist labor-cost, or wages, theory of market values furnished an historical precedent for the labor-value theories of Ricardo and Marx more than a century later.

That wages should conform to mere physical subsistence and that market prices, even abroad, conform to domestic wage costs, were considered by the mercantilists as truisms requiring no proof. Another proposition that seemed to them self-evident was that higher money wages always meant higher prices, and that lower money wages in England would mean lower prices for English products sold abroad. They failed to see that high wages might be consistent with low prices where the productivity per worker was high for such reasons as an abundance of natural resources, improved methods of production including machinery, or a highly efficient body of workers.

The mercantilists believed that national well-being was founded on a country's export trade, that a nation, like an individual merchant, became rich by acquiring money (gold and silver) through a "favorable" balance of trade (an excess of commodity exports over commodity imports, with gold imports covering the deficit). The mercantilists argued that England's balance of trade suffered

Labor Theories of the Later English Mercantilists, 1920, pp. 185, 194, and 205–21. Much of the material in this section on mercantilism is based upon Chapter 7 (Theories of Wages) of Professor Furniss' book.

because competing countries, paying lower wages, could undersell England in foreign markets. As one writer put it in 1763, "The high price of labor is a fatal stab to the trade and manufactures of this country." [1] The mercantilists wanted to keep the laborers poor so that the nation might become rich through a favorable balance of trade. They frequently proposed that the real wages of the laboring classes be reduced, for "if the price of labor is continually beat down, it is greatly for the public good." [2] One mercantilist writer argued that the standard of life among the English laborers should be reduced to that of the competing nation with the lowest wage rates.

The mercantilists supported various policies which, it was thought, would depress the price of labor and reduce labor's share of the national income. They wanted to increase England's population because with "many laborers, labor will be cheaper." [3] Immigration was encouraged in various ways for "by this means, the price of labor is continually beat down, combinations of journeymen against their masters are prevented, industry is encouraged and an emulation excited." [4] Poor relief to employed workers, as a supplement or "allowance in aid of wages," was to act as a sort of subsidy to the export trade by permitting lower wages so that the English manufacturer might sell his product abroad at reduced prices and capture the foreign market.

The doctrines of the mercantilists conformed to the preconceptions, and supported the interests, of the traders and merchant capitalists who were in a controlling position in England during that period. Their self-interest was put forward as the national good; the mercantilists' doctrines explained how national necessity required exploitation of their laboring countrymen. It benefited the workers of that period not at all that economists later exposed the falsity of such notions. It is now generally recognized that a country does not gain by depressing the standard of living of most of its citizens or by selling its exports abroad as cheaply as possible; that both trading nations, as well as both individual traders, gain by exchanging goods, whether the nations or individuals be poor or rich; that an increased supply of money in a country only increases prices, thereby tending to reduce exports; and that a large supply of precious metals, as Midas learned and we are rapidly learning,

[1] *Ibid.*, p. 174.   [2] *Ibid.*, p. 132.   [3] *Ibid.*, p. 141.   [4] *Ibid.*, pp. 142–43.

is a barren burden which may be costly to a country because it has to be stored, protected, and paid for with useful goods.

Ricardo and his followers. Adam Smith's *Wealth of Nations* contains elements of various wage theories including the subsistence, the wage-fund, the exploitation, the bargain, and the productivity theories. With regard to subsistence, Smith wrote: "The wages paid to journeymen [workers] and servants of every kind must be such as may enable them, one with another, to continue the race of journeymen and servants, according as the increasing, diminishing, or stationary demand of the society may happen to require." [1] Forty years later this notion was expanded into a complete subsistence doctrine by Ricardo, who wrote: "The natural price of labor is that price which is necessary to enable the laborers, one with another, to subsist and to perpetuate their race, without either increase or diminution." [2]

The wage doctrines of Smith and Ricardo, like those of economists in other periods, were the product of their times. In those days the mass of the workers were receiving wages that barely furnished subsistence; the rich and the employers were wont to look upon the working groups as one would look upon a slave or a draft horse—that their natural cost consists of the expenses for their upkeep. In short, Ricardo applied his cost-of-production theories to human beings as well as to goods when he contended that the normal price for labor was the minimum cost of producing men.

According to Ricardo, the market price for labor might vary from the "natural price" for but a short time, because economic forces would act to restore the price (wages) to the "natural" level at subsistence. If "the market price of labor exceeds its natural price," such high wages stimulate an increase of population according to the population doctrines of Malthus, and with such an increase in the supply of laborers "wages again fall to their natural price, and indeed from a reaction sometimes fall below it," in which case the labor supply is reduced somewhat by increased mortality due to the lack of sufficient subsistence. Population adjusts so that "the supply of labourers will always ultimately be in proportion to the means of supporting them." [3] Ricardo and his followers compared

---

[1] Adam Smith, *The Wealth of Nations* (Everyman's Edition), 1931, p. 72.
[2] David Ricardo, *Principles of Political Economy and Taxation*, 1817, p. 90.
[3] *Ibid.*, p. 194.

economic laws to the laws of physics. The position of physical objects is the resultant of certain mechanical forces including gravity, and such forces act to restore a physical object to its former equilibrium position whenever it is disturbed. In the same way, Ricardo and his followers argued, the play of economic forces will cause market price to settle down toward the equilibrium or "normal" price of subsistence.

Ricardo indicated that this "natural" or equilibrium level of wages was not absolutely fixed and constant, but might be raised slightly in time if custom and habit increased the quantity of food, necessaries, and conveniences that seemed indispensable for the worker's existence. However, Ricardo's followers tended to disregard this qualification, and the master himself held out little hope for any permanent advance in the condition of the laboring class since subsistence established by habit might be revised downwards as well as upwards. Ricardo's "iron" or "brazen" law of wages, as it has frequently been called, was a comfort to the rich, for, by emphasizing that changes in the labor population brought wages back to subsistence, it made the workers, as parents, themselves responsible for the condition of the working class.

There are two other phases of Ricardo's views on labor that are of interest here. Some of his sentences foreshadow the wage-fund theory, for he states that wages depend upon the demand for labor represented by capital, especially "the quantity of necessaries to be allotted to labor," and the supply of labor in the form of the number of workers. He also held a labor theory of value, for he believed that the exchange value of products corresponded to the value of the labor, including capital as "accumulated labor," which was necessary for their production. As we shall see, Karl Marx soon used such widely accepted views of Ricardo to prove that the laboring class was being "exploited." Frequently, in the past, the classical theories of the masters have been applied by others to substantiate conclusions that would horrify the original exponents of the theory.

WAGE-FUND AND "EXPLOITATION" THEORIES

The wage-fund theory. In his discussion of wages Adam Smith wrote of "the funds destined for the payment of wages" and "the funds destined for maintaining labourers" as "the demand for labourers." Such "funds," he said, consisted of "surplus" income of landlords, monied men, and enterprisers above what they needed to maintain their families or to carry on their "own work" or trade. This "surplus" in excess of their own needs was used to employ workers and pay wages in advance of the sale of the product. Smith concluded that "the demand for those who live by wages cannot increase but in proportion to the increase of the funds which are destined for the payment of wages." [1] Similarly, Ricardo spoke of "the quantity of necessaries to be allotted to the laborer" and maintained that the demand for labor increased "in proportion to the increase of capital," which "consists of food, clothing, tools, raw materials, machinery, etc. necessary to give effect to labour."

Despite the fact that the wage- or wages-fund theory was accepted as gospel by the outstanding English economists (Malthus, Ricardo, J. R. McCulloch, James Mill, Nassau Senior, and John Stuart Mill) for half a century, parts of the doctrine remained vague and ambiguous. For instance, though the fund was supposed to increase by savings and diminish with increased taxes on the rich or reductions in savings, it was considered to be a predetermined amount that at any particular time could not be changed. Influenced perhaps by the yearly period of production in agriculture, some of the economic writers gave the impression that the wage fund, consisting mostly of food, was fixed for a year at a time. They maintained that the wage-receiving class could not possibly receive more nor less than the exact amount of the fund that capitalists had determined to spend as "wage-advances" to workers. Therefore, said the economists, wages depend solely "upon the relative amount of capital and population," and the level of wages is determined simply by dividing the wage fund (the demand) by the number of workers (the supply). Any successful effort to raise wages by legislative or trade-union action would simply reduce the amount received by other wage-earners without changing the general level of wages. Such wage increases were, it was assumed, at the expense of other workers and not at the expense of the capitalist—a comforting doctrine to the employer. Likewise, the economists considered it "idle to suppose that the efforts of capitalists to cheapen labor can have the smallest influence on its medium

---

[1] Smith, *op. cit.*, p. 61.

price" or the average rate of wages. What one wage-earner lost, another was supposed to gain. The wage-earners as a whole could only be harmed by actions which reduced the wage fund, such as taxes on capitalists which decreased their capital funds. Therefore, it was considered of primary interest to workers that the income of the capitalists be increased and not decreased—also a comforting notion to the capitalists.

The wage-fund theory was a rigid demand-and-supply explanation of wages, which assumed that the supply of labor at any time was fixed or absolutely inelastic, and that the demand for labor consisted of a fixed sum determined by the intentions of capitalistic employers. As indicated in Chapter 3, Hodgskin and Bray vigorously attacked the theory in 1825 and 1839 respectively, but their assaults, though sound, were disregarded. It required the pens of F. D. Longe, W. T. Thornton, and Francis A. Walker, writing in the decade after 1865, to puncture the wage-fund myth.[1] These writers pointed out that the demand for labor arises not so much because the employer has to get rid of a surplus fund but because consumers demand the product of industry. It is consumer demand that ultimately employs labor, and workers may be sustained out of the current product of industry or their own savings as well as by advances from funds accumulated by employers. Furthermore, the demand for labor, by individual employers or all employers, does not always have unit elasticity so that the price of labor times the amount purchased will equal a constant dollar sum. The wage fund is really indeterminate since the demand for labor and the amount paid out for wages vary with the price of labor; no employer is bound to spend a fixed sum regardless of the wage rate. The total amount paid out in wages might increase with an increase in the efficiency, or the number, of workers, even though there was no increase in capital funds. Therefore, both the demand for, and supply of, labor (in the sense of output) are not "independent variables," but may fluctuate with changes in the rate of wages.

The fallacies of the wage-fund theory are so apparent that it is surprising the doctrine was widely and enthusiastically preached in England and America for half a century. "Undoubtedly," as Professor Lewis H. Haney says, "in the long and widespread sway

---

[1] Longe, *A Refutation of the Wages-fund Theory of Modern Political Economy* (1866); Thornton, *On Labour* (1869); and Walker, *The Wages Question* (1876).

of the wages-fund doctrine is to be seen the influence of class bias." [1] Though the doctrine in its rigid form has been discredited, it exists, consciously or unconsciously, in the minds of many people.

The exploitation theory. At the beginning of his chapter on "The Wages of Labour," Adam Smith suggests the basis for an exploitation theory of wages. He writes:

> In that original state of things, which precedes both the appropriation of land and the accumulation of stock, the whole produce of labour belongs to the labourer. He has neither landlord nor master to share with him. . . .
>
> But this original state of things, in which the labourer enjoyed the whole produce of his own labour, could not last beyond the first introduction of the appropriation of land and the accumulation of stock. . . .
>
> As soon as land becomes private property, the landlord demands a share of almost all the produce which the labourer can either raise, or collect from it. His rent makes the first deduction from the produce of the labour which is employed upon the land . . . . profit makes a second deduction from the produce of the labour which is employed upon land.
>
> The produce of almost all other labour is liable to the like deduction of profit. [2]

It was such notions of Adam Smith's that Karl Marx used to develop his "exploitation" theory of wages. Marx, a contemporary of Mill, drew more extensively, however, from the writings of Ricardo and his followers. From Ricardo he adopted such ideas as the labor theory of value, the Ricardian theory of rent, and the notion that wages and profits increase only at the expense of one another. Marx took the accepted doctrines of the classical economists and derived from them his own "natural laws." His theories are the direct descendants and the final consequence of the dreary doctrines preached by the leading economists of the early nineteenth century.

Starting with Ricardo's notion that labor creates all value, Marx contended that profits, interest, and rent are unwarranted deductions from the product that labor alone creates. [3] Under capitalism, he explained, the exchange value of products is determined by the average amount of socially necessary labor time spent upon their production. In addition to current labor time spent in producing

---

[1] *History of Economic Thought* (revised edition), 1932, p. 524.

[2] Smith, *op. cit.*, pp. 57–58.

[3] *Cf.* Marx, *Capital, A Critique of Political Economy*, especially Parts 3 through 6.

an article, allowance is made for previous labor time embodied in any capital equipment used in producing the article. The wages that the workers receive are assumed to be only as much as is necessary for their maintenance—the "cost of reproducing the labor power" used. According to Marx, the capitalist compels his employees to work for more hours a day than is necessary in order to produce their subsistence. The difference between the exchange value of the workers' product and the subsistence wages they receive is the "surplus value" that is "expropriated" by the capitalists and distributed as profit, interest, and rent. In short, Marx assumes that laborers produce an "expropriated" amount in addition to their subsistence and that the capitalists, through superior bargaining power, can force the workers to perform that additional work. The capitalists enjoy bargaining superiority because they own the means of production, without which it is impossible for workers to produce, and because there is a large "reserve army of unemployed" workers. Here Marx touches on the bargaining theory of wages which is discussed in the next section.

Marx's wage theory is subject to a number of objections. The doctrine of "surplus value" assumes that the labor theory of value and the subsistence theory of wages are valid. The labor theory of value, by basing value on the labor time spent rather than the utility of the product, obviously puts the cart before the horse. The subsistence theory of wages has already been discussed. It fails to make sufficient allowance for population trends, for increases in per-capita productivity, or for the strength of competitive forces. As explained in Chapter 5, recent theories of "exploitation" emphasize the monopolistic elements or imperfections in labor and commodity markets.

RESIDUAL AND BARGAINING THEORIES

Residual-claimant theory. Adam Smith, in the statements quoted in the previous section, explains that rent and profit constitute the first and second deductions from the produce of labor, which implies that labor receives what is left after such deductions. There are, therefore, traces of a remainder or residual theory of wages in Smith's writings.

It was Francis A. Walker, the American economist, who in 1875 worked out a residual theory of wages, based upon the proposition that the worker was "the residual claimant to the product of industry." [1] Rent he believed was fixed by the differential principle of the Ricardian rent theory, profits by the relative degree of skill of the enterpriser according to the same principle, and interest by the return necessary to induce saving for capital accumulation. Rent, profits, and interest being independently determined and deducted from the product of industry, "the whole remaining body of wealth, daily or annually created, is the property of the laboring class, their wages, or the remuneration of their services. So far as, by their energy in work, their economy in the use of materials, or their care in dealing with the finished product, the value of that product is increased, that increase goes to them by purely natural laws, provided only competition be full and free." [2] Walker optimistically believed that inventions and progress "immediately" inured to the benefit of workers, because the reward for other factors was definitely limited, whereas the reward for labor was "enhanced by every cause, which increases the product of industry."

Professor F. W. Taussig's theory of discounted marginal productivity is in a sense a residual theory for, like Walker, he explains that rent and interest, which are determined by independent principles, are subtracted first. "The product of labor is discounted [in advance] by the capitalist employers." [3] Other economic writers, like E. von Böhm-Bawerk and C. J. Bullock, have maintained that wages cannot rise so high that they will tend to discourage enterprisers and capitalists by permanently reducing the proportion of the product paid out in profits and interest. [4] However, the very fact that the residual-claimant idea has been applied by economists to the other shares of distribution, especially profits, is sufficient to cause one to question its validity as a theory of wages.

The bargain theory. Adam Smith's writings also contain traces of a bargaining theory of wages. He states that the employers have the advantage in disputes over wage rates because they "can com-

---

[1] F. A. Walker, *Political Economy* (third edition), 1888, p. 250.
[2] *Ibid.*, pp. 250–51.
[3] F. W. Taussig, *Principles of Economics* (third edition), 1930, vol. 2, p. 214.
Alfred Marshall in the first edition of his *Principles* (p. 548) approaches a residual theory of wages when he states that wages tend to equal "the net product of a man's labour" or "the value of the product which he takes part in producing after deducting all the other expenses of producing it."
[4] *Cf.*, for example, Böhm-Bawerk, "Macht oder ökonomisches Gesetz" in *Zeitschrift für Volkswirtschaft*, 1914; or Bullock, *Introduction to the Study of Economics*, 1897, pp. 414–15.

bine much more easily" (the law then prohibited combinations to raise wages but not those "to lower the price of work"), and because employers have more resources so that they "can hold out much longer," thus forcing their workers "into a compliance with their terms." Employers, Smith believed, "frequently make better bargains with their servants in dear than in cheap years," for in years of scarcity workers are "more humble and dependent" and "many are willing to take [employment] upon lower terms than ordinary." [1]

Adam Smith also observed the wide and irrational range in wage rates for comparable work concerning which some recent comments by employers were quoted in Chapter 5. Smith said: "The price of labour, it must be observed, cannot be ascertained very accurately anywhere, different prices being often paid at the same place and for the same sort of labour, not only according to the different abilities of the workmen, but according to the easiness or hardness of the masters." [2]

Various economists since Adam Smith have emphasized bargaining power as a factor in wage determination. W. T. Thornton, attacking the wage-fund theory in 1869, explained that the sellers of labor are at a disadvantage in bargaining with employers because they cannot afford to postpone their sales nor can they store their labor, whereas the employers, having greater resources, can hold out longer, and, being few in number, can combine more readily to depress wages.[3] In 1898 Professor John Davidson published his book on *The Bargain Theory of Wages*, in which a bargaining theory of wages is developed at some length. A more recent discussion of the bargaining theory is to be found in Maurice Dobb's little book on *Wages* (new edition, 1938).

Proponents of the bargaining theory of wages, like Davidson and Dobb, maintain that there is no single principle or economic force that alone determines wage rates. Any simple theory, they claim, is not adequate to explain the complex of interacting forces at work in the labor market. The various forces in the labor market act and react upon one another; a rise in wage rates may reduce the labor supply or increase the efficiency of the workers con-

---

[1] Smith, *op. cit.*, pp. 74–75.
[2] *Ibid.*, p. 69.
[3] W. T. Thornton, *On Labour, Its Wrongful Claims and Rightful Dues*, 1869.

cerned. Bargaining theorists do not believe that each wage rate is definitely determined by demand-and-supply forces operating independently and that only this one wage rate can prevail. They explain that there usually is a whole range of possible wage rates between the "upper and lower limits," between the highest wage the employer will pay and the lowest wage the workers will accept. These theorists attempt to discover the various elements behind demand and supply in the labor market. A wit once said: "Teach a parrot to say 'supply and demand' and you have an economist." The proponents of the bargaining theory might add: "Teach an economist to say 'supply and demand' and you have only a parrot."

According to these theorists, the "upper limit" to wage rates depends upon a number of things, including the productivity of the workers, the investment of the employer in capital equipment, the cost of borrowing new money for operations, the competition of other firms in the industry, and the possibility of substituting machinery or land for labor in production. Presumably there is a wage limit beyond which the employer would simply refuse to hire a certain group of workers, and, if necessary, might prefer to close his plant. Workers, on the other hand, have a lower limit or "supply price" below which they may refuse to work. This lower wage limit is flexible and varies with circumstances. It is affected by the worker's own self-respect, the opinions of others, his knowledge of conditions elsewhere, trade-union policies, labor legislation, etc. Where the actual wage rate will fall between these two limits depends, according to the theory, upon the bargaining strength of the sellers and the buyers.

Bargaining power is a rather vague term and is influenced by a variety of factors, some of which are noneconomic, such as custom and public opinion. A worker's bargaining strength is weakened by any conditions that prevent him from holding out for a certain wage. Such conditions include lack of reserves, family responsibilities, and lack of opportunities for work elsewhere. Alternative opportunities serve as limits to unfavorable treatment by one's present employer. Bargaining theorists stress the fact that workers have few alternative ways of making a living today except by selling their labor, because it is becoming increasingly difficult for a worker to start in business for himself. These theorists also explain that the worker is handicapped by circumstances that decrease his mobility (such as home ownership, local ties, lack of funds for moving expenses, employer policies that attach workers to the firm, etc.), and that thereby prevent threats to move as a means of safeguarding the worker's interests. Indeed, the proponents of this theory hasten to point out that the wage-earning class is so poor that any reductions in wages tend to produce the conditions (increase in the supply of labor hours offered for sale, willingness to offer labor services at a lower supply price, etc.) which will perpetuate that lower wage rate. Thus, "poverty breeds poverty."

Bargaining power presumably is strengthened by combination and collective bargaining through labor unions. No worker is indispensable to an employer; but the larger the group of workers, the more indispensable it will be. Labor unions also have reserve funds with which to support workers who are holding out for the union wage rate. The pressure of public opinion on the side of the workers may cause employers to pay higher wage rates to avoid social disapprobation. The example set by the government in hiring men may establish certain labor standards that will be followed by private industry. Labor legislation, such as minimum-wage and unemployment-insurance laws, may help to maintain the "lower limit" or the supply price of labor at a certain level.

It is apparent that trade-unionism is to some extent based on the bargaining theory of wages. United action through unionism helps to prevent any tendency by individual workers to underbid one another for employment and so reduce the "lower limit." The union, by threatening the employer with various losses connected with a strike, may even raise his "upper limit." By covering the whole competitive area or all employers in an industry, a national union may eliminate any competition in wage rates within the industry and thus, perhaps, also raise the "upper limit" of individual employers in that industry by raising wages for all employers in the same proportion and at the same time. In such cases it may be presumed that at least a part of any wage increase brought about by national collective bargaining will be passed on to the consumers of the product.

It is sometimes argued that the wage-earners as a whole do not gain in real wages whenever wage advances result in increases in the prices of the products that they purchase as consumers. This curious modern echo of the wage-fund theory is, however, erroneous. With a general advance in money wages, the selling prices of the products affected would presumably rise by a smaller percentage than wages were increased, unless labor costs were the only cost of producing the article. Consequently, advances in the general level of money wages will increase the real wages of workers to the extent that labor costs fail to constitute the total costs. Real wages in such a case are presumably increased largely at the expense of those who receive nonwage incomes and who must pay higher prices although their money incomes have not increased. Where the money wage increase is confined to one industry, the real wages of wage-earners as a whole would be increased unless all of the product was purchased by wage-earners. Some wage-earners would, of course, gain at the expense of the buying power of other wage-earners as well as the buying power of those purchasers of the product who receive a nonwage income. It is the reduction in the buying power of the nonwage-earner purchasers that is transferred to the wage-earning group as a whole by the wage increase.

Most bargaining theorists believe that there are certain monopoly gains from patent rights, trade-marks, and property ownership, which may be squeezed out by a wage increase without causing an increase in the price of the product. Some of them believe that an increase in wages at the expense of profits and interest might have little or no effect upon the supply of capital or investment [1] and, therefore, no appreciable effect upon the amount of capital devoted to the employment of labor. Bargaining theorists usually do not relate changes in wage rates to changes in employment. They are likely to maintain that employers' demand curves for labor, at least in the short run, are generally inelastic over most of the range of wage rates between the "upper and lower limits." That might be the case, for example, because technical conditions in the industry do not permit the substitution for labor of other factors of production, because present production methods and capital equipment require a certain labor force for any operations, or because the employer follows a policy of price maintenance,

[1] This argument is based on the idea, discussed in Chapters 1, 8, and 12, that there may be no fixed "normal" rate of return which is necessary in order to maintain a sufficient supply of new capital equipment.

permitting production and employment to fluctuate, instead of adjusting his selling prices according to the principle of equating marginal receipts to marginal cost.

Even if the employer should follow the principle of adjusting marginal receipts to marginal cost, it may well be that the other factors of production are really receiving a reward larger than the minimum required in order to obtain their services. In such a case, an increase in wage rates might lead to unemployment because other things (including the excessive reward to other factors) remain the same. In that event, as Maurice Dobb says, "it would be as true to say that the high level of interest or profits which capitalists were demanding was a 'cause' of this unemployment as to say that it was the unique result of the level of wages." [1] If, as has been suggested,[2] a hoarding tax were placed upon idle funds, which would penalize capitalists when they hold out for a higher reward (a so-called strike of capital), then employment would increase with the reduction in the reward for capital brought about by the hoarding tax. Such are the grounds for the bargaining theorists' assertions that "the position of any claimant may improve, or become worse, without any alteration in itself, merely by an alteration in the relative strength of another claimant," and that the claims to income are "admitted by rival claimants only because they are forced to admit them." [3] Bargain theorists would deny the contention of the productivity theorists (discussed in the next section) that the reward for any factor of production can be measured by the increased output when an additional unit of that factor is used. Additional units of air, water, light, and other free agents, they point out, may increase the total output, but no share of the output is granted to such agents for their "contribution."

MARGINAL-PRODUCTIVITY THEORY

Adam Smith started his chapter on "The Wages of Labour" in *The Wealth of Nations* with the statement that "The produce of labour constitutes the natural recompense or wages of labour." Following this lead, a number of economic writers in the nineteenth century pointed out that wage rates were related to "the

[1] M. Dobb, *Wages* (new edition), 1938, p. 131.

[2] *Cf.*, for example, Arthur Dahlberg, *When Capital Goes on Strike*, 1938; or Irving Fisher, *Stamp Scrip*, 1933.

[3] John Davidson, *op. cit.*, pp. 122, 124, and 126.

productive power of labor." But, as Professor Seligman has stated, the reputation of Ricardo and other "great names was such that any deviation from the accepted doctrines was branded as unorthodox," and those English writers who emphasized the importance of productivity were largely overlooked and neglected.[1] In fact, the German economist, T. H. von Thünen, summarized the modern theory of marginal productivity very well in 1826. Pointing out that, with a given quantity of capital, each increase in the number of workers leads to smaller and smaller additions to the total output, he concluded that the wage for all workers of equal skill and industry was determined by the addition to a firm's output for which the last worker alone was responsible. "Since there cannot be unequal wages for equal services," he said, the wages of any class of workers are "equal to the increased product which results from the last worker hired."[2] This part of von Thünen's work was, however, completely ignored by other economists.

The notion that wage rates are related to productivity began to be accepted in England during the 1850's, when, to the astonishment of all, the Factory Acts and the Ten Hour Law,[3] instead of ruining English industry as was expected, actually stimulated it. The increased efficiency that followed the extension of the Factory Acts from textiles to other industries led to the downfall of the hitherto accepted doctrine of the economy of low wages. Proof of the validity of the doctrine that high wages might lead to greater output, as Adam Smith had said, was to be found in the statistics showing the unexpected results from reducing hours under the Factory Acts. Such astonishing results in practical affairs led to a change in wage theory; the old purely mechanical notions about wages now began to be questioned. In answer to the claims that high wages hurt English industry in foreign trade, it was pointed out that international differentials in real wages were based upon differences in output or productivity per capita. The notion that high wages and large output per worker were causally connected came to be accepted, but there was some disagreement concerning

---

[1] E. R. A. Seligman, "On Some Neglected British Economists," *Economic Journal*, vol. 13 (1903), p. 535.

[2] T. H. von Thünen, *Der Isolierte Staat* (third edition), 1930, Part 2, pp. 569, 577, and 584.

[3] These Acts were discussed toward the end of Chapter 3, *supra. Cf.* also John Davidson, *op. cit.*, pp. 102–104.

whicn was cause and which was effect. Did high wages lead to a larger output or a larger output to higher wages? Though this question may seem to resemble the conundrum, "Which came first, the chicken or the egg?" there developed a rather general opinion that the causal connection was from output to wages and not *vice versa*.

American writers on economic subjects early emphasized that wages are dependent to some extent upon the productivity of the worker. Professor Francis Walker declared in 1876 that wages are paid ultimately out of the product of industry and that it is production which limits them.[1] Toward the end of the nineteenth century a number of European and American economists, of whom John Bates Clark was the most influential, rediscovered independently the theory of diminishing productivity and the marginal-productivity theory of wages. Undoubtedly, as Professor F. A. Fetter has stated, the theories of marginal utility and marginal productivity, which were elaborated by economists toward the end of the nineteenth century, were designed to answer the "exploitation" theory of Karl Marx as well as to fill the void left by the downfall of the wage-fund doctrine. The disproving of Marx's theories was probably the major pastime of economists at that time. The leading exponent of the marginal-productivity theory, J. B. Clark, had suggested in his early writings a bargaining theory of wages with some exploitation of labor, but he ended up with a "natural law of wages," which proved that labor's "product and its pay are identical."[2]

The theory. The marginal-productivity theory of wages explains that employers will continue to hire workers until the value of the product of the last worker hired in that classification is equal to the wages paid to that additional worker. So long as workers' wages are less than the amount by which their services will increase the incomes of employers, it will pay employers to expand their employment and production. By hiring more workers, employers tend to make labor scarce and to bid up wage rates, while at the same time the added output of the new workers hired tends to depress the selling prices of the articles that they help to produce.

---

[1] *Cf.* F. A. Walker, *The Wages Question*, 1876.

[2] *Cf.* Paul T. Homan, *Contemporary Economic Thought*, 1928, pp. 28, 38, 59, and 60; and J. B. Clark, *Distribution of Wealth*, 1895, Preface.

Competitive forces, therefore, cause wage rates to approximate the exchange value or "productivity" attributable to the last worker hired (the marginal worker) in any homogeneous group of workers. The wage rate for identical workers would tend to be identical. In this way, the theory attempts to explain not only the general level of wages but also the differentials in wages for various grades of labor.

The marginal-productivity theory is used to explain not only the rate and amount of wages paid to labor but also the remuneration received by the other factors of production, including capital equipment and business enterprise. The theory assumes that the employer will continue to hire each of the productive factors up to the point where the cost of the last additional unit (the marginal unit) of each factor equals the value to him of the additional product (the marginal net product) which he thinks that the marginal unit of the factor alone creates. The marginal productivity of a factor establishes the limit to the price that it is profitable for employers to pay for a certain quantity of that factor, and it is assumed that employers will distribute their business expenditures amongst the various factors of production on the basis of their marginal productivity.

The theory may seem very simple, but its simplicity is deceptive. As a demand theory of wages, the marginal-productivity theory fails to make full allowance for the peculiar nature of supply curves for labor. It assumes the existence of perfect labor markets, perfect product markets, and increasing costs for additional units of output. It also assumes that an employer can calculate the "net marginal product" for each factor of production and for each class of workers. The assumptions upon which the theory rests will be examined in detail following a discussion of the definition of the "marginal product" and an explanation of various factors that may affect the size of the "marginal product."

Meaning of marginal productivity. "Marginal net product" is a term that must be defined. It may mean (1) the extra physical product yielded by the additional unit of labor after somehow making allowance for the expenses (such as bookkeeping expenses, extra raw materials, or capital equipment) involved in employing that labor. The term may also refer to (2) the value of that extra physical product represented by its present market price or the price at which it is sold, or to (3) the increase in the employer's total receipts (marginal receipts) that occurs from the hiring of the additional unit of labor. Items (2) and (3) would be the same dollar figure in a perfect market. However, the monetary difference between definitions (2) and (3) would be marked whenever an employer has a distinct product so that the demand curve for the product is tipped, because then the selling price of the marginal product always exceeds marginal receipts (the selling price of the marginal product minus the loss resulting from the reduction in the price of all the other units of product sold). Wherever the demand curve for an employer's product has unit elasticity,[1] marginal receipts are zero, and whenever it is inelastic (less elastic than unity), marginal receipts are a negative figure, because additional units of the product can only be sold at such a reduction in price that the employer's total income from sales would decline. Although there is still considerable confusion concerning the term, definition (3) (marginal receipts) is now the generally accepted definition of "the marginal product." To determine the marginal "net" product, allowance must be made for the additional expenses of hiring the marginal unit of labor, including some interest charge for the payment of wages in advance of the sale of the marginal product.

Perhaps the reader is beginning to appreciate how difficult it would be to calculate the "marginal net product" in any particular instance. Indeed, it may be practically impossible in many cases to "unravel the web of the social product, tracing each thread to its source" by means of the marginal-productivity theory. Where a product is the result of a combination of two or more factors (such as labor, capital equipment, and business enterprise), there may be no way of telling what portion or part of the physical product was produced by each factor. What happens to the output when a unit of labor is added or withdrawn is largely determined by technical conditions, and any increase or reduction in the output may really be due in part to the productive power of other agents. Certainly machinery alone might have no product at all. Especially is it difficult to determine the portion of the output contributed by a single unit of labor in the mass-production industries,

---

[1] Unit elasticity of demand exists where slight changes in price cause offsetting changes in the amount purchased so that price times quantity sold gives a constant dollar sum.

where there is minute subdivision of labor, where operations and sales units are highly integrated, and where workers are hired or laid off in gangs.

Even in such a relatively simple case as the harvesting of farm crops, it is not at all clear what the workers' marginal productivity is. Certainly, without the services of the hired hands the ripe grain, fruit, or vegetables would rot. In harvesting, the last worker taken on presumably should receive a wage equal to the marginal receipts or the proceeds from the sale of, say, the fruit he picks, assuming that the fruit is sold at once and no equipment is necessary for picking it. Of course, farmers do not pay pickers any such wage.

The term "productivity" has been used in an ambiguous way by certain economic writers. Should the term include noneconomic factors that may not increase the firm's sales income, such as the worker's personality, his political beliefs, or his race? Should it include any "psychic income" that an employer may derive from an agreeable and attractive secretary? If productivity is measured simply by the amount of money wages a worker receives, it may bear little or no relation to his own efforts. In fact, it would be affected by any change in the supply of workers in his line, by a variation in the general rate of spending, by a change in the price of the product, or by any alteration in other prices that might affect the demand for the product or the supply of the factors of production in that industry.

Factors affecting "productivity." In attempting to estimate the "net" productivity of a worker, the employer has to take for granted all the other expenses connected with hiring him. If there should be an increase in these other expenses, the worker's "productivity" might decline. Also, the "productivity" of workers could be increased by any one of the various ways of affecting demand or supply through trade-union action that were discussed in the previous chapter. Furthermore, a worker's "productivity" may be increased by improvements in the management and administration of the business.

If "productivity" is to be measured by the resulting addition to the employer's total receipts, it would be increased by a reduction in the total physical output whenever the demand for the product was inelastic above the prevailing market price, for then a reduction in the quantity for sale would cause such a rise in price that there would be an increase in the total receipts of employers in that industry. Whenever the demand is inelastic, idleness may increase the total income of producers in the industry, as the experience with crop reduction under the New Deal's Agricultural Adjustment Administration indicates. In such cases, employers' income is increased by restrictive practices, by "soldiering" on the job, and even by idleness in the industry, but it is questionable whether such inactivity should be called "productivity."

Further examples will indicate why this theory might be called the "maximum-profits" theory of wages rather than the "marginal-productivity" theory. Expenses for selling campaigns may be profitable to the individual employer because they attract business from his competitors, but such shifts in demand, from one cigarette or gasoline brand to another, may not increase total physical output or consumer satisfaction. Indeed, by causing a much larger number of gasoline filling stations or cigarette companies to exist, they may result in higher costs and prices, in a smaller demand and smaller total output, and in a waste of capital and labor resources.[1] Activities that increase the income of an employer seem "productive" from the individual point of view, but may be "unproductive" from the social point of view. In figuring the appropriate size for a gang to hold up a certain bank, the leader may add to his group until the last burglar taken on just equals the additional loot expected from that burglar's services, but no part of the gang's income would be considered "productive" from a social point of view.

Limited to capitalistic enterprise. Not only is the marginal-productivity theory an individualistic theory, but it can be applied only to businesses operated for a profit. It cannot be used to explain the wages of workers in governmental activities that are not "self-liquidating" through sales in the market. Therefore, it cannot be applied to such fields as education, social service, or other non-profit activities that are not dependent upon sales in a market and are not operated according to the principle of maximizing money

[1] In cases where selling costs result simply in a shift in demand from one concern to another, Professor Edward Chamberlain believes that the "net marginal product" is "zero" (*The Theory of Monopolistic Competition* [third edition], 1938, p. 186). He is, however, confusing the individual with the social point of view. The marginal-productivity theory is an individualistic theory and from the individual employer's point of view selling costs must add to his total revenue or he would not incur such costs.

profits. Also, the theory cannot be used to explain the wages of domestic help or of craftsmen who perform services for the final consumer, such as work in and around his home.[1] Although perhaps a majority of the academic economists are proponents of the marginal-productivity theory, it is questionable whether the wages or salaries of professors are governed by that doctrine. At least, professors of economics do not customarily request the university authorities for a raise in salary on the grounds that their "marginal productivity" has increased. They generally use the arguments that trade-unionists are criticized for using: that the cost of living has risen, that their family responsibilities have increased, that salaries in other occupations are higher or have risen, that their period of service with the university has been sufficiently long to warrant a raise, etc. An offer from another institution is, of course, a most effective argument. And, although economics professors at times have advised trade-unionists to accept a wage cut in order to stimulate the demand for their services, academic economists have not generally urged salary cuts as a means of stimulating demand in their own line of work.

There are innumerable difficulties in attempting to apply the marginal-productivity theory to clerical workers and those engaged in managing businesses. It is also difficult to apply the theory to that portion of a firm's wage bill that represents fixed cost, such as watchmen's wages, some executives' salaries, etc. Fixed costs are based on long-run considerations, especially the relation between expected return and the rate of interest, and are not governed directly by the principle of expansion until marginal variable cost equals marginal receipts.

Assumptions. The marginal-productivity theory is based upon a number of assumptions that frequently fail to fit the facts of modern economic life. Perhaps the most important and least valid assumptions underlying the theory are that labor and product markets are perfect markets and that employers decide their production and employment policies according to accurately known marginal-

---

[1] Professor Chamberlain would also exclude selling and advertising from the province of the theory because he says: "To hold that factors employed in selling activity are paid in accord with the value of their marginal products would be a manifest absurdity" (*op. cit.*, p. 187). As indicated in the previous footnote, he arrives at this conclusion because he is judging selling activities from a social, and not an individual, point of view.

cost and marginal-receipts curves. The main assumptions of the theory are contained in the following postulates:

1. That the labor supply consists of groups of homogeneous units, so that it is a matter of indifference to the employer which units of labor in the group he buys. Such homogeneity is necessary in order to draw up demand, supply, and marginal-cost curves and to apply to labor the marginal principle of adding or subtracting little bits or increments of labor at the margin.

2. That labor and the other factors of production are sufficiently mobile so that workers will change from one employer to another as soon as any differentials in wage rates arise. The discussion of mobility in Chapter 5 indicates the questionable character of this assumption in the case of labor, and existing capital equipment cannot often be transported or used for making other products.

3. That the factors of production, including labor, have infinite continuity and that any factor can be readily and completely substituted for any other factor, at least up to the margin. Infinite continuity and elasticity of substitution are necessary if the marginal curves are not to be discontinuous and full of gaps. The marginal analysis breaks down, for example, where the technique of production requires a certain fixed crew of workers, or where, with operations at technical full capacity of equipment, marginal revenue may exceed marginal variable cost, because additional production would require the building of another plant. Investment in new plants depends not so much upon present profits as upon the relation between the rate of interest and expected future profits during the lifetime of the new plant.

4. That there is no excess capacity so that additional units of output can only be produced at increased costs per unit. As indicated in Chapter 5, variable costs per unit of output may be larger at 40 or 60 per cent of capacity than they are at 100 per cent of capacity, in which case employers presumably would not govern their operations by marginal costs when they were operating under the full capacity of their capital equipment.

5. That an employer knows what is the "marginal productivity" of each unit of every factor in his business, including labor. In order to figure out such "marginal productivity," he would have to know the exact shape of his marginal-receipts curve, the exact shape of each cost curve, and the net cost to him of employing each

unit of each factor. Much of the allocation of joint costs, even to different divisions of a firm, must be done arbitrarily. The appropriate marginal-receipts curve would be the one that would exist in the future when the products attributed to the additional units of labor or capital finally were sold in the market. Unless he experimented with a whole series of selling prices every little while during a business cycle, an employer selling a branded product in an imperfect market would not know the exact nature of his marginal-receipts curve. Indeed, it is the subjective marginal-receipts or sales curve in the mind of the producer that is of primary importance, and such a curve may be uncertain and indefinite, for it would be influenced by the expected attitudes and reactions of competitors to changes in the producer's price or sales.[1]

If the employer follows certain common pricing methods, his net receipts will vary with the distance of each customer from his plant. Under such circumstances, it is not possible to draw up marginal-receipts curves, and average receipts may be the governing factor. In determining wage and production policies, employers are undoubtedly influenced primarily by the profitability of their operations as a whole, and not by any calculation of the profitability of hiring additional units of labor alone.

6. That the employer in an imperfect market will always reduce his price to increase his sales, whenever such action may add to his short-run profits. Employers following a price policy based on long-run considerations may not wish to sacrifice future profits in order to maximize present profits, especially when price reductions might antagonize customers or lead to a price war. It is not clear from the theory what production and employment policies an employer is assumed to pursue when there is a difference between the policy that would maximize profits in the short run and one that would maximize profits in the long run.

7. That the market for labor is a perfect market, so that the employer will not affect the wage rate no matter how much labor he himself hires. The larger firms grow in size, the more imperfect labor markets will tend to be. Whenever the employer is important enough in a labor market to realize that his purchases affect wage rates, he will try to avoid bidding up wages against himself. If new

[1] *Cf.* Robert Triffin, *Monopolistic Competition and General Equilibrium Theory*, 1940, pp. 62–66.

purchases involve wage raises to the present staff, he will not hire new workers up to the point where their wage equals the marginal receipts attributable to their services. As the discussion in Chapter 5 indicated, labor markets are far from being the perfect markets assumed by the theory. They frequently contain all sorts of monopolistic elements, such as trade-unions, employers' associations, and tacit agreements between buyers, as well as the type of collusion between labor and employer organizations discussed in Chapter 6. Seldom do the buyers or the sellers engage in full and free competition.

8. That no element of monopoly has entered into the determination of the prices for the other factors of production. The prices of other factors, of course, are an important element in the determination of the marginal productivity of labor and an employer's demand curve for labor services.

9. That employers' demand curves for labor correspond to the marginal-productivity curves of their workers and that the total demand curve for all labor is the sum of all employers' individual marginal-productivity curves. This assumption was criticized under the discussion of demand in Chapter 5, and that criticism need not be repeated here. Suffice it to say that an individual employer's marginal-productivity curve is drawn up on the assumption that all other prices and wages remain fixed. Such an assumption, though largely correct for partial analysis in a very small section of the economy, breaks down when the economy as a whole is under consideration. In economics, the whole is not the sum of all parts separately determined on the assumption that no change occurs in any other part of the economy.

Statistical and factual evidence clearly indicates that these assumptions do not hold water today. Hourly wage rates, instead of varying in direct proportion to each worker's efficiency, are generally uniform throughout the plant for all workers classified in a certain grade. Instead of fluctuating constantly as the workers' "productivity" changes, wage rates usually move in jumps or in steplike fashion by intervals of two-and-a-half or five cents an hour. Instead of a uniform wage rate for the same type of work by comparable workers in the same locality, there frequently is a whole range of rates for what presumably is the same "productivity." This range of rates is sometimes explained as the difference between "good" and "bad" employers.[1] In many localities, women and Negroes are paid lower wage rates than white men for comparable work. Large corporations, hiring similar workers in widely scattered localities, generally pay the prevailing local rate or rates, so they may be paying different rates for the same work by comparable workers in different localities. There may also be wage differentials based on length of service or seniority.

The fact that wage rates frequently lag far behind changes in the price level, as they did during the first World War for example, indicates that many other factors influence wage rates besides marginal productivity. Furthermore, the marginal-productivity theory can hardly explain the payment for overtime work of wage rates amounting to one-and-a-half or two times the regular hourly wage where the work is of a normal, and not an emergency, nature.

It is evident from such facts that the marginal-productivity theory does not contain a complete explanation of wage rates in our economy. Faced with these facts, proponents of the marginal-productivity theory have modified the doctrine in various ways. They state that marginal productivity "measures" or "regulates" wage rates, but does not "determine" them.[2] Some of them admit that "wage rates over short periods" do not adjust to the marginal productivity of labor, but contend that there is "a tendency toward long-run correspondence" between wage rates and marginal productivity.[3] Because of employers' price and wage policies, adjustments in the short run may take place through increases or decreases in output and employment rather than through changes in wage rates.

It is doubtful, however, whether there is a closer long-run correspondence between marginal productivity and remuneration to the factors of production than exists in the short run. One must bear in mind that a long-run period is simply composed of a series of short-run periods. Certainly employers cannot calculate the long-run marginal productivity of any factor of production as closely as they can its "productivity" in the short run. The more distant future is full of uncertainties. Furthermore, as already mentioned, the same policy might not maximize profits in both the short

---

[1] Cf., for example, J. R. Hicks, *The Theory of Wages*, 1932, pp. 55–56.

[2] Cf., for example, Hicks, *op. cit.*, p. 86; and D. H. Robertson, *Economic Fragments*, 1931, p. 43.

[3] H. A. Millis and R. E. Montgomery, *Labor's Progress and Some Basic Labor Problems*, 1938, p. 204.

run and the long run. Profits may be sacrificed in the near future, for example in a lockout or a strike, in order to increase profits in the long run. In addition, it is questionable whether the management of business corporations, even in the long run, is guided solely by the principle of maximizing profits. It may be influenced by other purposes, such as a desire to perpetuate itself in office, to maintain its authority, to preserve the firm's trade position, and to expand the size of the business.

Although the marginal-productivity theory has certain weaknesses as a realistic explanation of wage determination, it does explain some of the forces and factors that influence money wages. To point out the limitations of the theory in modern industry is not to deny that the forces it stresses play an important role in determining the wage rates paid in certain sections of the economy, where competition is highly effective and industry operates under small-scale conditions. Where they are not blocked by such factors as market imperfections, employer and employee associations, or employer price policies, the forces emphasized by the marginal-productivity theory would cause money wage rates to gravitate toward the theoretical "marginal productivity" of the workers. And certainly physical productivity is the most important element in determining the level of real wages in a country.

Many advocates of the theory have, however, failed to examine its assumptions carefully, so that they might understand the weaknesses and limitations of the theory. They have attempted to use the marginal-productivity theory as a basis for reasoning upon economic policy, especially the appropriate wage policy during the downswing of a business cycle. They have, for example, argued that the existence of unemployment proves that wage rates are above the marginal productivity of the workers and that full employment can be attained merely by sufficient reductions in money wage rates. The questionable character of such reasoning is more fully explained in succeeding chapters.[1]

[1] One reader states that, although the assumptions of the marginal-productivity theory may "not always be realized in practice," the theory is of significance as an analytical tool, and he insists that it is so used in the discussions involving the concept of "exploitation" in Chapters 12 and 13 *infra*. The discussions referred to, as well as the definition of "exploitation" in Chapter 5, are based on a comparison with the conditions that would exist in a perfect market. This reader's insistence is, therefore, correct only if the marginal-productivity theory is considered to be merely synonymous with one of its assumptions, the concept of a perfect market.

SUMMARY REMARKS

During the last two or three centuries, wage theory has gone through a strange cycle of evolution, with the alleged responsibility for wage rates shifting from workers to employers and back to workers again. According to the subsistence theory, the sex instinct of the workers, by increasing the labor supply, is the chief factor in wage determination. The wage-fund theory, although still retaining the notion that workers are responsible for the supply, placed the emphasis on the demand side, with the demand for labor depending largely upon the intention of capitalist employers. These early theories were also supposed to work with a mechanical rigidity; it was assumed, for example, that the wage fund, in conjunction with the size of the population, established a fixed and definite limit to an increase in the wage level.

The "exploitation" theory of Karl Marx places the responsibility for wages and the wage level upon the capitalist employer, emphasizing his power to exploit the workers. The residual-claimant and bargaining theories, in turn, place a part of the responsibility for wage determination upon the workers. Under the bargaining theory especially, there is no one important factor that is repeatedly emphasized; the theory is broad, nonmechanical, and rather indefinite. The marginal-productivity theory has been used to place the primary responsibility for employment and wages upon labor itself. Especially has labor been considered master of its own economic destiny by those theorists who have thought of "productivity" as almost synonymous with the workers' efficiency. Such a notion, of course, overlooks the part that improved methods and expert management play in production and fails to appreciate that "productivity," in the sense of marginal receipts, may be increased by restricting production. Furthermore, the marginal-productivity theorists, like J. B. Clark, come to much the same conclusion as the classical economists, like Ricardo and Mill, that the workers are not likely to be exploited by their employers—at least, not in the long run!

This discussion of wage theories indicates that as fast as one theory was overthrown and discarded, a new one sprang up to fill the breach. The human mind is unsettled and upset without definite answers to problems, and generally it seeks the simplest possible solutions to complex issues. Hence the quest for a single principle to explain the determination of wages. Theoretical economists are especially anxious to prove that their principles provide a single, unique answer to a question, that their theoretical apparatus will give a "determinate" solution to a problem.

It is natural, therefore, that the reader should ask, "What is the truth?" Which of these various wage theories is correct? The only frank reply is that no one of them is absolutely correct. Each one may contain some truth, but none of them alone covers the whole ground and explains all the facts. Too much faith in the absolute determining power of a single principle lays one open to the criticism that Hamlet made to his friend from Göttingen: "There are more things in heaven and earth, Horatio, than are dreamt of in your philosophy." In the next chapter an attempt will be made to select the significant elements from some of the theories discussed in this chapter and to weave them, along with some additional elements, into an explanation of the forces that actually determine wage rates in the American economy today. Such an "eclectic" theory will not provide a neat, simple answer to the wage problem, but economic reality itself is not simple.

CHAPTER EIGHT

AN ANALYSIS OF WAGE RATES

A theory of wages can explain only those forces that generally play a major part in the determination of wage rates. It is, of course, futile to try to explain every factor that may, in any particular instance, exert some influence upon wage rates. In such a complicated matter, it is impossible to find perfect answers or generalizations that will be completely accurate in all cases. The most that can be done is to explain what might be called the "key" factors in the problem, those forces or factors which seem to play an important role in many instances. Such fundamental factors or relationships, indeed, must be found if one is not to wander around lost in the seeming chaos of surface reality.

Although a study of principles and key factors is essential if one is to gain any understanding of economic reality, it is necessary to recognize that any one factor alone can give but a one-sided statement or answer to the problem and that the various factors involved may interact upon one another. It is one of the limitations of much "mathematical" economics that it assumes the strict independence of the various factors and, therefore, cannot be qualified and modified to square with the complexities and interrelations that exist in the real world. Furthermore, employers' expectations and estimates of future demand are important in our economy, yet they can hardly be represented by a mathematical formula.

It is necessary also to bear in mind that wage theory is individualistic and is part of the theory of distribution, which explains how the national income is divided among the various factors of production. Wage theory attempts to explain how the price of labor is determined in our present capitalistic economy, which depends primarily upon decisions by the managements of individual firms for its operation. Such theory is not, therefore, directly concerned with what wage rates ought to be, or with what wage policy should be

followed in a country in order to increase employment. Those issues will be discussed in Chapters 11 and 12; they are national, not
individual, questions. Much the same is true of theories of unemployment, which are discussed in Chapter 10; they are *general*
theories. Wage theory, as such, should be kept separate from the
theory of unemployment, for we are here interested in how wage
rates are actually determined rather than in how those rates may
affect employment. The factors that determine the amount of employment and the size of the national income are discussed in the
chapters that follow. Therefore, the effects of wage increases or decreases upon the national income or upon the general demand for
products will not be considered in this chapter.

It is, of course, evident that an increase in the volume of unemployment may put downward pressure upon wage rates by causing
workers to accept jobs at lower wages and to underbid prevailing
wage scales in order to obtain work. But unemployment or underemployment is one of the factors that affect the supply schedule of
labor. This aspect of unemployment is included along with other
factors affecting the supply of labor in the summary discussion of
wage theory that follows.

GENERAL ANALYSIS OF WAGES

Significance of markets. The nature of the market is a most
important factor in any analysis of particular prices. In the case of
wage rates, the nature of two markets must be considered: the local
market for that grade of labor and the market for the employer's or
employers' products. In this section dealing with the influence of
market factors on wage rates it will only be necessary to refer in a
summary fashion to the discussion and conclusions contained in
Chapters 5 and 6.

1. *The labor market.* Generally speaking, labor markets are by
their very nature some of the most imperfect markets in our economy. Workers are dissimilar, so the article for sale, labor services,
is not uniform. Without the possibility of complete substitution
afforded by uniformity, the market cannot be perfect and an
element of monopoly or uniqueness is present. An extreme illustration of this uniqueness is the case of a president of a large
corporation drawing a salary of, say, $200,000 a year. Generally
speaking, he and his associates, not the market, fix that salary.

His value to the corporation, in large part, may depend upon his knowledge of the corporation's property, personnel, and markets.

On the supply side of the labor market there may be a considerable degree of immobility, generally fostered by employers' policies. Partly because of such immobility, supply schedules in certain individual markets may be inelastic at certain wage rates or may even have a negative slope within a range of wage rates. The fact that the short-run supply curve for labor in general has a negative slope is of profound importance in the determination of wage rates. Wage cuts, instead of causing a reaction in the form of a decrease in supply, tend to stimulate an increase in the total hours of labor supplied. Consequently, there is a tendency for the supply of labor to adjust itself in a way that tends to cause any wage, once established, to continue.

On the demand side, one or more buyers may dominate the labor market. Large employers generally have wage policies, which indicates imperfection in the market. In a perfect market, like the Chicago wheat pit, market forces, not certain individuals, set the price. In the labor market, however, employers or bargaining groups usually name the price. Employers may follow the practice of paying "the prevailing wage" in the locality, or the convention of not bidding labor away from other employers. A large employer is likely to realize that in bidding up wage rates he may be bidding against himself. In many localities the competition for labor is restricted because a few large employers follow a common policy with regard to wage rates or because employment in the locality is largely controlled by one firm, as is usually the case in the mill villages of the South, company towns in the North and West, and in some of the smaller cities in various parts of the country. In small towns and cities, the monopolistic fixation of wages is much more readily accomplished than in large metropolises, which may help to explain why, generally speaking, the larger the city, the higher are money wage rates. The prevalence of mill villages in the South probably plays a small part in the Southern wage differential.

These characteristics of the demand and supply in labor markets act to perpetuate whatever wage is established and to prevent any change from "prevailing rates." Undoubtedly, they help to explain why movements in wage scales are by jumps, and frequently lag far behind the movements of most prices.

2. *The product market*. Where the market for his product is not a perfect market, the producer-employer generally has a price policy. If that policy involves the maintenance of selling prices in the face of falling demand, the result is likely to be considerable fluctuation in production and employment. In a business recession, fixed prices throw part of the risk and burden of adjustment upon employees in the form of reduced employment. For reasons already mentioned in Chapters 5 and 7, employers who control the prices of their products may not reduce selling prices in order to equate marginal receipts and marginal variable cost. Fluctuations in employment with fixed prices may exert downward pressure upon costs, especially wages, through increasing unemployment and idleness during a depression. Though unemployment may cause more labor to be offered for sale at lower prices and may lead to wage cuts, such wage reductions are not likely to result in an expansion in an employer's production and employment unless there is an increase in his sales at the fixed price.

As indicated in the last part of Chapter 6, the success of any attempt of employer and employee organizations, through cooperation or collusion, to raise wages and prices depends upon the nature of the market for the employer's product or service. Such collusion is most successful in what the British call the "sheltered trades," which are not subject to outside competition. Some of the products or services that were mentioned in this connection in Chapter 6 were baked goods, building, photoengraving, dry cleaning, pressing, trucking, and taxicab and delivery service. The demand for some of these services, like trucking and delivery, may be inelastic, because there is no good substitute or because the services form such a small part of the total cost of products. Without the limiting factors of good substitutes or outside competition, local prices and wage rates in such "sheltered trades" may deviate widely from similar prices and wages in other localities.

It is interesting to note that variations in wage rates between localities are especially marked in those sheltered industries that are well organized in some cities. On June 1, 1938, union wage rates for motor-truck drivers in different localities ranged all the way from under 35 cents to over $1.10 an hour, and union rates for plumbers and electricians varied from under $1.00 to over $2.00 an hour.[1]

Importance of organizations and bargaining agencies. In any imperfect market, the economic power of persons may affect the price. This is especially true in a market, such as the labor market, where employers or organizations name the price and where demand and supply may meet over a whole range of prices or may not meet at all. Under such conditions, the market may be cleared by a number of prices instead of one standard price. Actual studies of labor markets show that in many instances there are different wage rates in the same locality for the same kind of work by comparable workers. Such discrepancies, which are explained by the existence of "good" and "bad" employers, could be corrected by economic pressure on the "bad" employers. The short-run supply curve of labor also lends itself to the use of economic power, for a wage rate once attained by bargaining strength tends to become the new equilibrium rate; a negatively sloping supply schedule adjusts itself in an appropriate manner to any change in wage rates.

In the actual process of bargaining, an individual employee alone may have little economic power, especially if he is unskilled or is one of a large number of similar employees working for a large corporation. Labor unions are founded on the principle that a considerable amount of economic power may be gained by the combined action of a large number of individual workers who, acting separately, would be weak. The union frequently forces the employer to choose between paying all his employees a certain wage scale or facing the consequences of a strike. Under such circumstances, the employer is not permitted to add workers to his staff, one at a time, until the last one taken on establishes the wage for all, in line with the marginal-productivity theory. The union, in effect, tells the employer: "You can hire as many workers as you wish at the union rate, but if you don't pay the union rate we will use every effort to prevent you from hiring any workers."

There are some monopolistic selling practices that unions generally do not use. A seller with a monopoly can discriminate between buyers, charging them different prices for the same goods in

[1] *Cf.* "Union Scales of Wages and Hours of Motortruck Drivers, June 1, 1938," *Monthly Labor Review*, vol. 48 (March 1939), p. 683; and "Union Scales of Wages and Hours in the Building Trades, June 1, 1938," *Monthly Labor Review*, vol. 47 (November 1938), p. 1100.

the same market, or he may "dump" products by selling them more cheaply in distant markets. As has been indicated, it is a common practice to quote uniform delivered prices for a price zone or the whole country, which means that the seller receives smaller net receipts on the sales to more distant buyers. The monopolistic seller may not only fix his price as he pleases but he may also fix the quantity that the buyer must take at that price if the buyer is to purchase any of the product. It is true that certain unions have full-crew rules or rules regarding the number of workers for a particular task. However, unions do not attempt to force employers to hire a certain total number of hours of labor at the union rate. Generally, unions let employers determine how many hours of work they will buy. Unions, of course, may not have control of the supply of labor in a certain line, and even if they do have all the eligible workers in the union, all union members may not act in unison during a strike.

Labor unions may exert pressure, both political and economic, in various ways. A full discussion of trade-union tactics must be reserved for Part Three. An illustration of the effect of economic pressure by a trade-union upon wage rates will be sufficient for present purposes.

On the West Coast, the International Brotherhood of Teamsters, Chauffeurs, Stablemen, and Helpers of America has recently been organizing eligible workers in such former open-shop cities as Los Angeles and, along with the organizing campaign, has, of course, been forcing some employers to pay higher wages to laundry, milk, and other delivery drivers, taxicab drivers, and garage employees. Banks, merchants' and manufacturers' associations, and other employer organizations have brought pressure to bear upon employers not to sign union agreements. The union, in turn, uses its economic strength to force employers to sign on the dotted line. The Teamsters' representative for the 11 Western states, Dave Beck, tells those business concerns in Los Angeles having branches throughout the West that, if the management will not sign an agreement for its Los Angeles establishments, the union will decide not to work for or patronize any of its branches outside Los Angeles. Chain stores and large firms with numerous branches cannot afford to resist such economic pressure, for the union is very strong in many Western states, whereas the Los Angeles businessmen's organizations have little economic or political influence outside the city. The Teamsters, through their control of transportation in many areas, may practically prevent an employer from receiving materials or delivering his product. They may refuse to transport any product that has been handled by an antiunion employer. As the largest AFL union, with a membership around 400,000, the union may also make certain that its members as consumers discriminate against the products of opposing employers.

In slack periods, employers frequently attempt to cut wages before reducing other costs. When an employer says that wages will have to be reduced, Mr. Beck asks to have a certified accountant study that employer's books to make sure that there has been no financial manipulation in the past, such as the writing up of assets, the distribution of stock to "insiders," or the payment of excessive salaries or dividends. If the accounts of the firm are satisfactory, he then demands that all those who receive significant shares of the employer's total costs—the landlord, the creditors, the raw-material suppliers, etc.—meet in a conference and each accept some cut in their incomes if the workers are to agree to take a reduction.[1] Unless some other cost items are reduced, the union will resist a wage cut with all its "economic pressure." Such union activity cannot help but have a significant effect upon wage rates.

Various statistics compiled by the U. S. Bureau of Labor Statistics indicate the effect of labor organization upon wage rates. For example, a study of wage rates in the building trades in 1936 indicated that in 31 building occupations union rates were invariably higher than nonunion rates.[2] On the average, hourly earnings for nonunion workers in construction were about 30 per cent lower than the rates for union members. Even in the same cities, union wage rates were generally from 20 to 30 per cent higher than nonunion wages for the same kind of work in the building trades. Perhaps a part of this differential between union and nonunion workmen may be explained on the grounds that union workers in each trade are more skilled and that large cities are more highly organized, but most of the wage differential is undoubtedly due to union organization and action.

[1] The *Biennial Census of Manufactures* for 1937 shows that only 21 per cent of the total sales income of firms in manufacturing went for wages and salaries to the firm's employees, whereas 59 per cent went for materials, fuel, and electric energy produced by other firms and the remaining 20 per cent went for other costs and for profits.

[2] *Cf.* E. P. Sanford, "Wage Rates and Hours of Labor in the Building Trades," *Monthly Labor Review*, vol. 45 (August 1937), pp. 281–300.

A study of the wage rates paid to street-railway workers in more than 130 cities during 1914, 1930, and 1933 reveals that wage rates for the same job were from 10 to 15 per cent higher for unionized street railways than for nonunionized railways in cities of comparable size.[1] Surveys of the meat-packing and furniture industries in 1937 and of the boot and shoe industry in 1939 showed that hourly earnings were between 10 and 15 per cent higher in organized plants than in unorganized establishments.[2]

In industry after industry, changes in wage rates relative to the general wage level have gone hand in hand with changes in the organized strength of the union in that industry. In 1921, able seamen in our intercoastal trade received an average monthly wage rate of $85. Two years later, after an unsuccessful strike, with the membership of the Seamen's union reduced from 103,300 to 18,000 and company unions with practically closed-shop arrangements in some important ports, the wages of able seamen were but $49 a month.[3] The disappearance of collective bargaining in the industry probably accounted for a good part of this drop in wages. Much the same thing happened in bituminous-coal mining during the 1920's. As the union membership in the bituminous-coal industry declined from around 400,000 in 1922 to about 125,000 in 1930, hourly earnings fell from an average of 85 cents in 1922 to 63 cents in 1929, or 26 per cent.[4] On the other hand, average hourly earnings in bituminous coal increased from 41 to 77 cents or almost 90 per cent during the period from 1933 to 1936, when membership in the union increased more than threefold.[5] The average monthly wages of able seamen increased from $47 in 1933 to $68 in 1937, or about 45 per cent, while the membership of the Seamen's union increased almost fourfold.

Certainly the whole structure of wages in this country has been affected to a considerable degree by the activities of labor unions

[1] Cf. Emerson P. Schmidt, "Union and Non-Union Wages and Hours in the Street Railway Industry," Journal of Political Economy, vol. 42 (October 1934), pp. 654–59.

[2] Cf. Jacob Perlman, "Extent and Causes of Differences in Hourly Earnings," Journal of the American Statistical Association, vol. 35 (March 1940), pp. 8–10.

[3] Cf. Merchant Marine Statistics, Bureau of Navigation, U. S. Department of Commerce; and Leo Wolman, Ebb and Flow in Trade Unionism, 1936, p. 187.

[4] Cf. Wages and Hours in Bituminous-Coal Mining: 1933, U. S. Bureau of Labor Statistics, Bulletin No. 601, 1934, p. 4; and The Effect of Labor Relations in the Bituminous Coal Industry upon Interstate Commerce, National Labor Relations Board, Bulletin No. 2, June 1938, p. 39.

[5] Monthly Labor Review, vol. 47 (July 1938), p. 146.

and the practice of settling wage rates through negotiation and agreement between organizations of workers and employers. By covering all employers in an industry (the whole competitive area), the union is able to raise wage rates much higher than it could if only a few employers were unionized in an industry having national distribution for its products. In the latter case, unionized employers would face the competition of nonunion employers in the industry, who were paying lower wages. If all employers in the industry were unionized, however, the only competition would be that of possible substitute products, such as the substitution of oil, gas, and electricity for coal as fuel. If the market is a local one, as in building, baked goods, and delivery service, a strong labor organization may raise wages in the locality with little fear of low-wage competition from other areas.

A temporary effect of unions upon wage rates may be observed during strikes. In the 1922 shopmen's strike on the railroads, strike-breaking shopmen were paid 10, 15, and sometimes 20 cents an hour more than the wages that the railroad executives vowed would break the railroads if paid to the regular, experienced shopmen. Such expenditures in opposition to the union may be considered by corporation officials an "investment" of the stockholders' money, which will benefit the stockholders in the long run. During the Little Steel strike of 1937, leaders of the back-to-work movement were paid wages of $600 to $1,300 a month by the Republic Steel Corporation, whereas their normal monthly wages before and after the strike were from $200 to $300 a month.[1] These back-to-work leaders received such wages without working at all in the plant; the workers in the plant during the strike also received extraordinarily large earnings.

As indicated by the examples cited in Chapter 6, organizations of employers may exert considerable control over the labor market and can, under certain circumstances, practically force wage reductions. Such organizations may keep wages down below the wages for the same work in other cities of comparable size, as happened in the San Francisco building trades during the 1920's, or they may reduce wage rates below the wages for comparable work in other industries, as happened in shipping on the West Coast during the

[1] *Cf. Hearings on S. Res. 266*, 75th Congress, third session, Part 32, Exhibit 5138, p. 13357.

1920's. On the other hand, through collusion with workers' organizations, the employers may pay relatively high wages and reap good profits by charging consumers comparatively high prices.

Role of productivity. Physical productivity per worker is important in the determination of real wages (the purchasing power of money wages), because it sets a limit to the total output, and therefore the total real income, of a country. The national income, or the total consumption of a country, can amount only to (1) total domestic production of goods and services, plus (2) imports, minus (3) wasted products and (4) exports, which are sent abroad and cannot, therefore, be consumed at home. The physical productivity of workers, as is explained in a subsequent section of this chapter dealing with regional wage differentials, depends mainly upon natural resources, the technique of production, the methods of industrial organization, and transportation facilities, rather than upon their own efforts and skill.

Although the total physical output of goods and services largely determines the total real income of a country, it does not explain the division of that income among the various factors of production. In the determination of rates of wages, interest, and profits, it is the "value productivity" rather than the physical productivity of each factor that is significant, and "value productivity" may be increased by fixing prices, influencing demand, or reducing physical productivity and supply when the demand curve for the product is inelastic. The discussion of the marginal-productivity theory in the previous chapter indicated, however, some of the important limitations to value productivity as a factor in wage determination. Available statistics fail to show a close correspondence between the real earnings of workers and physical productivity, or between wages and value productivity.

Various statistical series indicate that since 1900 increases in real earnings have lagged behind increases in physical product per employee and, therefore, that real wages have lagged behind the total real income of the country. For example, Professor Paul Douglas discovered from a detailed statistical analysis that, in all manufacturing in this country, real earnings increased 30 per cent from 1899 to 1925, whereas physical productivity per employee increased 54 per cent.[1] Similar percentages for railroads and street railways

[1] Paul Douglas, *Real Wages in the United States*, 1930, p. 510.

were practically the same as for manufacturing.[1] In the manufac-
tured-gas and the electrical industries, physical output per employee increased around three and four times as rapidly as did real
earnings during that period.[2] Only in the telephone industry and
coal mining were real wages slightly (three and nine per cent)
above physical product per employee in 1924 compared with 1902.[3]
Of course, the increase in the units of capital equipment relative to
the units of labor used in industry during this period helps to account for the lag of real earnings behind average productivity per
employed person. Despite this lag, real wages apparently increased about 400 per cent in the century between the 1820's and
the 1920's, the greatest increases in real wages from decade to decade since 1800 occurring in the decades after the Civil War, and the
first World War.[4] During those periods, prices declined sharply,
while wages sank more slowly.

From 1899 to 1914 and from 1914 to 1921, workers' earnings in
manufacturing rose more rapidly than did the value product added
per wage-earner in manufacturing. On the other hand, yearly
earnings per worker only rose 12 per cent from 1921 to 1929, compared with a rise of 38 per cent in the value added per wage-earner
in manufacturing.[5] During this same period from 1921 to 1929, the
distribution of the total value added by manufactures changed as
follows: wages and salaries dropped from 57.5 to 48.6 per cent,
while overhead and return to capital increased from 42.5 to 51.4 per
cent, of the total value added by manufacturers.[6] It is from such
facts that Professors H. A. Millis and R. E. Montgomery conclude
that "the individual employee in manufacturing experienced a relative loss" during the 1920's.[7]

Presumably the value productivity of business executives or top
management should be measured by the rate of profits or the return
on investment in the firm. A recent study of some 100 companies
listed on the New York Stock Exchange, the presidents of which received an average of over $100,000 in 1929 and over $65,000 in

---

[1] *Ibid.*, pp. 518–20.   [2] *Ibid.*, pp. 522–23.   [3] *Ibid.*, pp. 516, 521–22.

[4] H. G. Moulton, *Income and Economic Progress*, 1935, pp. 181–82.

[5] *Cf.* Ethelbert Stewart, "Ratio of Value of Production to Wages and Their Purchasing Power in Manufacturing Establishments, 1849 to 1929," *Monthly Labor Review*,
vol. 31 (December 1930), pp. 1330–31.

[6] E. F. Gay and Leo Wolman, in *Recent Social Trends*, 1933, vol. 1, p. 231.

[7] H. A. Millis and R. E. Montgomery, *Labor's Progress and Some Basic Labor Problems*,
1938, pp. 170, 203.

1936, showed little, if any, correlation between executive compensation and relative earnings of these companies during the period from 1929 to 1937.[1] Even for 59 large corporations with assets over $100,000,000, "no significant relationship or correlation could be discovered between executive compensation and earnings."[2] It would be difficult to explain such executives' remuneration by the marginal-productivity theory or to maintain that there is a "prevailing" or "market" rate for executives' services. Many chief executives, in their dual position, aid in establishing their own compensation, and some executives have given themselves large bonuses (up to $1,000,000 a year) during a period of years when common stockholders received no dividends at all.[3]

Effects of institutions and laws. Wages are influenced not only by economic factors but also by custom, public opinion, legislation, and certain institutions. Convention has helped to maintain some of the various differentials in wage rates that are discussed in the following section of this chapter. Public opinion also may cause employers to offer higher wages than they might otherwise pay. The fact that the government as a purchaser requires that certain wages be paid on public works and in the manufacture of government supplies may be of considerable significance to the country's wage structure, for employers cannot readily switch from higher wages on government contracts to lower wages on articles for private purchasers. Under the Federal Walsh-Healey Public Contracts Act of 1935, the Secretary of Labor has set minimum rates of pay for work on government contracts, which have benefited almost 5,000,000 workers in manufacturing establishments, according to an estimate late in 1938.[4]

A system of public employment exchanges helps to adjust labor demand and the labor supply in various localities and throughout the country. Knowledge of work opportunities and wages elsewhere aids in ironing out inequalities in wages and in reducing local shortages of labor. Unemployment compensation, by affording out-of-work benefits to jobless workers for as long as three or four months, tends to relieve the downward pressure upon wage rates that arises when unemployed workers are in desperate need of some

[1] John C. Baker, *Executive Salaries and Bonus Plans*, 1938, pp. 104, 183, 261.
[2] *Ibid.*, p. 184.
[3] *Cf.* John T. Flynn, *Graft in Business*, 1931, pp. 196–202.
[4] *Monthly Labor Review*, vol. 47 (December 1938), p. 1358.

income. State minimum-wage laws and national minimum-wage legislation, like the Fair Labor Standards Act, have, of course, a direct effect upon wage rates at the bottom of the country's wage structure. Later chapters are devoted to a detailed discussion of minimum-wage and unemployment-compensation laws and their effects upon wage rates. They are mentioned here only because economists have been too prone to disregard such institutional elements in discussing factors that determine wage levels and the wage structure.

ANALYSIS OF WAGE DIFFERENTIALS

This section deals with various types of wage differentials: the differentials between regular and overtime hours; between the sexes, races, and age groups; between various occupations; between particular industries; between certain districts and regions within the country; and, finally, between different nations. In the regulation of wages by minimum-wage legislation or trade-union action, wage differentials are of considerable practical importance.

Overtime rates. It is now a widespread practice, especially where union agreements prevail, for workers to receive one-and-a-half or two times the regular hourly rate for work outside the normal working hours or on Sundays and holidays. A few unions even forbid their members to work overtime. During the nineteenth century it apparently was not a general practice in this country for nonunion employers to pay higher wage rates for overtime hours; but the NRA codes stimulated the adoption of higher overtime rates during 1933 and 1934, and the Federal Fair Labor Standards Act of 1938, which applies to firms in interstate commerce, requires the payment of one-and-a-half times the regular wage rate for all hours worked in excess of 40 during any seven-day period, unless the industry is exempt from this provision.

The practice of paying higher or punitive wage rates for overtime work raises some interesting economic questions. Do workers gain by the practice of charging higher overtime rates? Does it pay employers to hire workers at punitive overtime rates? If it does, is the hourly rate being paid to such workers for the normal day below the net value of their labor (their marginal productivity) to the employers? The last units of labor hired for the day presumably are the overtime hours, which in many cases might be considered to be the marginal units of labor. Economists have generally held that the marginal unit tends to establish the price for all the units sold in that classification. Is the labor market an exception to that rule?

There is a difference of opinion whether the motive of workers and their organizations in establishing overtime rates is to reduce the actual working day, thus reducing the supply of working hours offered in the market, or whether it is to increase actual earnings and average daily wages in those lines of business in which employers are unable to avoid any overtime work for some employees. Probably the answer depends upon the circumstances. The railroad executives charged that the workers wanted the eight-hour day before the first World War in order to increase their earnings, because their "runs," and therefore their working hours, could not be reduced in some cases without operating the trains at excessive speeds.

It is evident that price discrimination exists when the charge for hours beyond the normal working day is one-and-a-half or two times the normal hourly rate. In most markets, the more one buys from a particular seller, the lower the average price is likely to be. But in the labor market, the more one buys from a particular seller beyond the normal day, the higher is the average price one is paying, and the highest rate is being paid for the overtime hours, which invariably represent less efficient labor than the normal working hours.

Employers frequently pay overtime rates for work during emergency situations—in order to repair a breakdown or to eliminate a "bottleneck." It may also prove profitable for employers to hire workers at overtime rates under certain other circumstances, such as where the employer will be financially penalized if he fails to complete a job at a certain date; where he has a large amount of costly equipment that is idle much of the year in highly seasonal lines of business; where overhead costs are so large, as in shipping, that it pays to load and unload the ship fast in order to increase the amount carried annually by the ship and to avoid high dock charges, or where a manufacturer, already operating at full capacity during normal hours in good times, would lose customers, whose patronage is desired in dull times, if he failed to fill their orders during peak periods. In all such cases, regular employees are hired for overtime work because no good substitutes are available at a lower cost, including the cost of breaking them in and keeping separate records for them.

Generally employers hire workers at overtime rates for short-run considerations, in which case it may pay them to do so if marginal receipts exceed marginal variable costs. In an industry like the longshore industry, however, the loading and unloading of ships is so much a normal part of the business that the payment of over-time rates may be considered a long-run matter. On the Pacific Coast in the latter part of 1939 and the first half of 1940, between 40 and 50 per cent of the hours worked by longshoremen each month were overtime hours, paid for at the rate of $1.40 an hour, compared with 95 cents an hour for the regular hours.[1] Various explanations have been offered for the fact that over 40 per cent of all longshore work was being paid for at an overtime rate almost one-and-a-half times the regular rate for a normal six-hour day. These explanations include the special terms of the agreement with the union, the organization and strategic position of the longshore-men, and the employers' desire to keep their ships in operation, es-pecially with a shortage of ships. In the pulp mills of the Pacific Coast, over 14 per cent of all hours worked were overtime hours during 1940, paid for at time-and-one-half. The mills were oper-ated continuously, and Sunday work was considered overtime.

It may well be that, when employers hire workers to do normal work at punitive overtime rates, they are paying those workers less than their full marginal productivity for the regular working hours, that the marginal productivity of the workers is closer to the over-time rate than it is to the normal wage rate. Perhaps in such cases firms are employing workers according to average wage rates rather than according to the marginal principle.

In *Capital*, Karl Marx cites a number of cases, taken from Parlia-mentary investigations of English factories in the middle of the last century, where it was the practice to pay higher overtime rates for what was obviously normal, and not emergency, work. Marx com-ments as follows on this practice of "extra pay" for regular work during overtime hours: "The increase in the price of labour with the extension of the working-day beyond a certain normal limit, takes such a shape in various British industries that the low price of labour during the so-called normal time compels the labourer to

---

[1] *Cf.*, for example, *Longshoremen: Pacific and Atlantic*, International Longshoremen's and Warehousemen's Union, Seattle, 1940, pp. 10–11.

work during the better paid overtime, if he wishes to obtain a sufficient wage at all." [1] There can be little doubt that exploitation of the workers did occur in such cases.

The payment of overtime rates may indicate not only the existence of normal wage rates below the full marginal productivity of workers in some cases but also it may indicate, where overtime rates are paid for emergency reasons, that the employees are gaining by such price discrimination, which separates the normal from the emergency demand, charging higher prices for the latter more inelastic demand. In such an event, the emergency demand and the emergency supply may be considered as a separate labor market, in which the employees are able to charge more than they do or could receive in the long run for their services in the market for normal working hours.

It is another question whether an employer gains in the long run by hiring some or all of his working force to work overtime at punitive rates. If account is taken of the inefficiency of employees during overtime hours as well as the immediate and ultimate effects of overtime work upon an employee's work during normal working hours, there is a possibility that it has not paid employers, in some instances, to hire their employees to work overtime at punitive rates. [2]

Sexes, races, and age groups. 1. *Women's wages.* Various studies indicate that women's earnings are from 30 to 50 per cent lower than those of male workers in this country as well as abroad. [3] Part of this differential in earnings is to be explained by the fact that a larger percentage of the women workers are concentrated in the lower paid, unskilled occupations. Even where men and women are working in the same occupation, however, there is frequently discrimination against women in the form of lower wage rates. About one fourth of the NRA codes, for example, included provisions for differentials by setting up lower minimum scales for women. [4] Wage studies by the U. S. Bureau of Labor Statistics in

---

[1] Karl Marx, *Capital* (Modern Library edition), pp. 598–99.

[2] For evidence on this point see the heading, "hours and efficiency," in Chapter 13 *infra*.

[3] *Cf.* U. S. Census Bureau, *Special Report on Manufactures*, 1905, Part IV, p. 65; M. Leven and W. I. King, *Income in the Various States*, 1925, pp. 79–80; National Industrial Conference Board, *Wages in the United States*, 1930, p. 52; M. Leven, *The Income Structure of the United States*, 1938, pp. 54–55. For foreign statistics, *cf.* J. H. Richardson, *A Study on the Minimum Wage*, 1927, p. 136.

[4] *Cf.* Mary E. Pidgeon, *Employed Women under N. R. A. Codes*, U. S. Department of Labor, Women's Bureau, Bulletin No. 130, 1935.

various industries, such as the cigar and cigarette, paper-box and fiber-container, textile and bread-baking industries, indicate that women's average hourly wages for the same type of work tend to be from 10 to 30 per cent lower than men's, although in a few occupations the average hourly earnings of women exceeded those of men by a slight margin in certain areas.[1] It is possible that in some cases men's and women's work within the same occupation may be somewhat different and, therefore, not absolutely comparable.

Various explanations have been offered for the differential between women's and men's wages. In the first place, women workers are generally younger and more inexperienced. The majority of employed women are under 30, which means that most of them become married and abandon their jobs early in life. Furthermore, the average female worker reaches the peak of her earning power by 30, or about 10 years ahead of the average male worker.[2] In many occupations, women over 30 or 35 are considered less desirable as employees.[3] For various reasons, including the fact that women generally are in industry but a few years, female workers have not been well organized and have lacked bargaining strength. During the 1920's, no more than three or four per cent of the gainfully employed women were members of labor unions.

The characteristics of demand and supply have much to do with the lower hourly earnings of women workers. On the demand side, many occupations are closed to women either because female workers are ill-suited for the work or because they are excluded from the occupation by custom or public opinion. On the supply side, an increasing percentage of the women over 15 years of age have been entering the labor market during the last half century, so that the percentage of all gainfully employed workers represented by women has increased each decade from 15 per cent in 1880 to 22 per cent in 1930.

A number of economists believe that the supply curve of female labor in any given locality begins at a very low wage rate, because the supply price, or wage that women are ready to work for, is gen-

---

[1] Cf. Leven, op. cit., pp. 53–60, 157–61.

[2] Ibid., pp. 58–59. Cf. also, Commissioner of Labor, Women and Child Wage-earners, 1910, vol. 18, p. 26; and U. S. Women's Bureau, Bulletin No. 85, 1931, pp. 11–12, 74–80.

[3] Cf. Virginia Pope, "Future of Women Workers," New York Times, March 13, 1932, Section 9, p. 5; and Annual Report, 1930, U. S. Secretary of Labor, pp. 123–24.

erally lower than the wage for men. These economists also believe
that the supply curve of female labor is very inelastic at the higher
wage rates.[1] Such characteristics of the female labor supply in a
locality are partly explained by the pressure of financial need upon
families in which the husband's or father's earnings are insufficient
or irregular, and partly by the immobility of female labor because
of family attachments. Almost 30 per cent of the women workers in 1930 were married and most of the others lived with their
families, so any increases in the earnings of male labor are likely
to cause a decrease in the supply of female labor. There are
grounds for believing that the general supply curve of female
labor may have a negative slope for changes in women's wages
as it certainly does have in response to changes in men's wages,
which cause married women to enter or withdraw from the labor
market.

The nature of the local supply curve of female labor may help to
explain why, with the wage differential, women workers are not
substituted for men in those lines where both men and women are
employed.[2] Professor S. Florence points out that, with such a supply schedule, an employer would have to pay much higher wages
to attract many more women workers, which might cause that employer to "fall foul of his fellow-employers in the same district and
possibly his male employees," both of whom "seem to have definite
views of what a woman *should* earn." [3] Also, any offer of higher
wage rates to new female workers would probably cause a like increase in the wage rates paid to the women he already employs and
possibly an increase in the wages of his male employees. Because
women workers are not as a rule graded into skilled and unskilled
classes or differentiated into separate crafts,

> . . . it is difficult for any employer to raise the wages of women in
> one group which he wants to increase without raising the wages of all

---

[1] *Cf.*, for example, S. Florence, "A Statistical Contribution to the Theory of Women's
Wages," *Economic Journal*, vol. 41 (March 1931), pp. 31–32; and M. Dobb, *Wages*
(1938 edition), pp. 157–61.

[2] "Even in the industries which employ both men and women we nearly always
find the sexes sharply divided, in different departments, working at different processes
and performing different operations," and "in the vast majority of the cases these
several departments, processes and operations are mutually complementary, and there
is no question of sex rivalry." S. and B. Webb, *Industrial Democracy* (1919 edition),
p. 496.

[3] Florence, *op. cit.*, p. 35.

the women he employs. The additional profit obtained by substituting additional women for men may thus be offset by the addition to the wages of women he employed originally and whose service he could have continued to obtain at the original wage.[1]

Furthermore, women's wages generally bear a definite relation to those for skilled and unskilled men, so it might prove difficult for an employer to increase women's wages without altering the wages of his male employees. On the basis of such considerations, Professor Florence concludes that "there is a sort of unilateral buyer's monopoly in the sense that there is a limit, tacitly agreed upon, to the price offered in any local market for women's labour," which "is not met by a corresponding sellers' monopoly or ladies' agreement on the part of the women." [2]

2. *Race.* Some of the same factors that explain the wage differential between women and men help to explain the differential that tends to exist between white workers on the one hand and Negro and oriental workers on the other. Studies by the U. S. Bureau of Labor Statistics indicate that, in the North, Negro and white laborers generally receive the same wage rates when they perform the same work, and this seems to be true for a majority of the firms in the South. Out of 534 Southern plants covered in a study of entrance rates for common laborers in 20 industries in 1937, almost 70 per cent reported the same entrance rates for both races, 28 per cent reported higher rates for whites, and about 2 per cent reported higher rates for Negroes.[3] In certain Southern states, however, the differentiation between entrance rates for colored and white labor was particularly observable. Consequently, although the entrance rates averaged practically the same for whites and Negroes in the North, a simple average of such wage rates in the South showed the Negroes about 10 per cent below the whites.[4] Studies of various industries by the U. S. Bureau of Labor Statistics also indicate that the average hourly earnings of Negroes are generally below those of white workers in the same occupations.[5]

As in the case of female workers, such differentials in hourly

[1] *Idem.*   [2] *Idem.*
[3] *Cf.* Jacob Perlman and Edward K. Frazier, "Entrance Rates of Common Laborers in 20 Industries, July, 1937," *Monthly Labor Review*, vol. 45 (December 1937), p. 1498.
[4] Leven, *op. cit.*, p. 162.
[5] *Ibid.*, pp. 163–64.

earnings are due partly to differences in skill and ability,[1] partly to discrimination which limits the jobs open to colored workers, and partly to lack of organization amongst colored workers. The disproportionately large number of Negroes on relief in the North during the depression years of the 1930's indicates that Negroes are generally at a disadvantage in the labor market. It is estimated that less than two per cent of all Negro workers belonged to labor unions in 1929. That percentage is, of course, higher today. While the CIO unions have as a rule taken Negroes and orientals into the same local unions with white workers, a number of AFL unions have followed the practice of segregating both Negroes and orientals on the West Coast into separate locals of the national union, and some of the craft unions have openly or indirectly closed their doors to colored workers.

3. *Age.* Productivity, and therefore earnings, are affected by the worker's age. A study of the income of employed workers in Michigan in 1934 showed that the income of women workers reached a peak at about 30 years of age, the income of male skilled and unskilled workers at around 40, the income of clerical workers at around 45, and the income of professional workers at about 50.[2] During the years between 18 and 30, incomes increase rapidly. The income of unskilled workers doubled between 18 and 40 years of age, while for all employed workers it increased about two-and-a-half times. After each group reached the peak of its earning power, individual incomes tended to decline. Averaging all employed workers in Michigan in 1934, those at 20 and 70 years of age received about half the income of those at 40, the peak age of earning power for the group as a whole. Custom and advancement by seniority also affect the earnings of workers in various age groups.

Occupational and industrial differentials. In connection with the decennial census of population, the Bureau of the Census

---

[1] For a summarizing article on the relative efficiency of Negro and white workers, indicating that Negroes are equally efficient, *cf.* Robert C. Weaver, "The Efficiency of Negro Labor," *American Federationist,* vol. 41 (December 1934), pp. 1327–31.

[2] *Cf.* State Emergency Welfare Commission, "Total Income during 1934 of Gainful Workers," *Michigan Census of Population and Unemployment;* and Leven, *op. cit.,* pp. 51, 58. Statistics of the average annual earnings of over 30,000,000 workers covered by old-age insurance in 1937 show the same tendency for earnings to decline after the workers have reached 45 or 50 years of age. *Cf.* John J. Corson, "Insurance Against Old-Age Dependency," *Annals of the American Academy of Political and Social Science,* vol. 202 (March 1939), p. 63.

uses a list containing over 20,000 occupational designations. Although many of these separate designations are duplications in the sense that they really belong to the same occupation, still that figure gives some indication of the variety of occupational pursuits followed by American workers.

It is primarily from the supply side that differences in wage rates between callings and occupational groups in the same locality must be explained. A large number of factors may affect the supply of qualified workers seeking jobs in any particular occupation or line of work. Among the most important factors, the following might be mentioned: (1) the distastefulness or danger connected with the job, (2) social attitudes toward the occupation, (3) the regularity or irregularity of employment in that line, (4) the expense of training or education for that kind of employment, and (5) the scarcity of persons with natural qualifications for the work. Opera singers, home-run kings, and movie actresses receive abnormally large salaries because there are few persons well qualified for such jobs. Occupations that require a long period of apprenticeship or education, such as the skilled crafts or the professions, as a rule are also well paid. Although the hourly wage is frequently high in some lines that are irregular or seasonal in nature, such as the building trades, in other lines where the work is very casual, such as picking crops, hourly earnings may be relatively low. The same is true of dangerous and disagreeable work. Prize fighters, drivers of racing cars, and strike-breakers receive relatively high wages, whereas the wages of timber workers, garbage collectors, and sewer cleaners are relatively low. Low wages are found chiefly in lines that require little skill.

Occupational differences in wages persist because workers are divided into "noncompeting groups"; that is, groups that cannot be substituted for one another. The street cleaner cannot take the place of the doctor, nor the university janitor the place of a certain professor, even though some students might consider that a step in the right direction. Occupational stratification in the form of noncompeting groups also tends to perpetuate itself in a world where the cost of training for any occupation or calling must be borne by the individual worker or his parents. In general, only those with higher incomes can afford the cost of training for highly skilled and professional jobs, so differences of wages once established influence supply conditions in the different grades of labor in a way that tends to preserve prevailing wage differentials.

Various artificial restrictions upon the supply of labor in an occupation may increase occupational differentials in wage rates. The establishment of certain requirements for admission to the occupation, like those fixed by medical and bar associations or those determined by common practice, such as the Ph.D. degree for college professors, affect the supply of eligible labor in an occupation. The same is true of various other artificial barriers to entrance into a trade, like those set up by labor unions, such as a required period of apprenticeship, the closed union with a closed-shop agreement, and restrictions upon the hours of work and upon output. Various means whereby labor unions can affect the supply of, and even the demand for, the services of their members, thereby maintaining high wage rates in the occupation or craft, were discussed in detail in Chapter 6.

Differences in wage rates between industries can largely be explained by occupational differences, together with such factors as the skill required and the sex, color, and age of the workers. The average wage rate for an industry means very little, for in 1935 wage rates ranged from 30 cents to $3.50 per hour in the iron and steel industry and from 15 cents to $2.50 an hour in building construction.

It simply is not possible to eliminate occupational, geographic, and other differentials from the wage figures for various industries. Perhaps the figures that come closest to representing purely industrial differentials are the hourly entrance rates for common laborers in various industries in a certain area. Such figures are given in Table 4.

TABLE 4.   HOURLY ENTRANCE RATES OF ADULT MALE COMMON LABORERS IN NORTHEASTERN-CENTRAL STATES: AVERAGE, HIGHEST, AND LOWEST RATES, JULY 1935 [1]

Industry	Average	High	Low
Lumber (sawmills)	32.2 cents	42.5 cents	27.5 cents
Leather	38.0	45.0	30.0
Brick, tile, and terra cotta	40.8	80.0	35.0
Foundry and machine shop products	41.1	62.5	30.0
Paper and pulp	42.2	52.0	32.0
Slaughtering and meat packing	45.0	47.5	40.0
Cement	45.5	60.0	40.0
Iron and steel	45.6	48.5	37.0
Petroleum refining	52.5	56.0	52.0
Automobiles	55.4	75.0	38.0

[1] Paul H. Moncure, "Entrance Rates Paid to Common Labor, July 1935," *Monthly Labor Review*, vol. 42 (March 1936), pp. 704–705. The northeastern-central states include Illinois, Indiana, Michigan, Ohio, and Wisconsin.

The wide range between high and low rates for automobile firms and brickyards (in contrast to the narrow range for petroleum refining) in the same region seems to indicate that different grades of common labor are required by the same industry and also by the different industries. The type of performance demanded of common labor in the automobile or petroleum-refining industries undoubtedly differs considerably from that required of common labor in sawmills, for example.

Geographic differentials. To a greater degree than is generally appreciated, geographic differences in wage rates are really due to occupational and industrial differences. The working population of the South, for instance, is largely employed in agriculture and textiles, both of which are low-wage industries wherever located and in both of which wage-earners are, for the most part, of the common-labor type. Furthermore, it is real wages that are important in examining geographic differentials. Money wages may differ considerably between two localities, and yet, because of lower costs of living in the lower wage locality, real wages may be much the same in both areas. The cost of food, housing, etc., for example, tends to be lower in rural districts, where money wages are also generally lower, than in metropolitan centers.

Geographic differentials in wage rates will be discussed under three general headings: differences between urban and rural areas, differences between regions within the country, and differences between nations.

1. *Rural-urban differentials.* There are a number of reasons why money wages are lower in rural than in urban areas. In the first place, the differences in cost of living between metropolitan and rural districts, already mentioned, are an important element in such differentials. In the second place, such city-country contrasts are partly due to occupational differences. The rural wage-earners or laborers generally are less highly skilled. Table 5 shows, by size of community, the estimated average income per year for some 9,500,000 wage-earning families in this country who were not on relief from July 1935 through June 1936—the period to which the estimates apply. Occupational differences undoubtedly help to explain why the average yearly income per family in rural communities was but 62 per cent of the average income in metropolises in 1935–1936.

TABLE 5. AVERAGE ANNUAL INCOMES OF WAGE-EARNING FAMILIES IN FIVE
TYPES OF COMMUNITY, 1935–1936 [1]

Metropolises:	
1,500,000 and over	$1,626
Large cities:	
100,000 to 1,500,000	1,414
Middle-sized cities:	
25,000 to 100,000	1,263
Small cities:	
2,500 to 25,000	1,261
Rural communities	1,004

Occupational differences are, to some extent, eliminated in
Table 6, which shows the average hourly entrance rates of adult
male unskilled workers in cities of various size. These statistics
indicate that average hourly wage rates for unskilled labor in
cities under 10,000 are from 80 to 90 per cent of such wage rates
in cities 500,000 or over in population.

TABLE 6. AVERAGE HOURLY ENTRANCE RATES OF ADULT MALE COMMON
LABORERS IN 20 INDUSTRIES, BY SIZE OF CITY, JULY 1937 [2]

Cities	Country as a whole	Northern and Western states	Southern states
500,000 and over	59 cents	60 cents	45 cents
100,000 to 500,000	50	56	40
50,000 to 100,000	48	54	38
25,000 to 50,000	50	53	39
10,000 to 25,000	52	55	35
Less than 10,000	48	53	39

The size-of-city differentials are not so large for unskilled labor
as they are for those skilled trades that are highly unionized and
enjoy a local market little affected by out-of-city competition, such
as building and newspaper printing. Figures in Table 7 indicate
that, in cities with 40,000 to 100,000 inhabitants, the average union
wage per hour in building and newspaper printing is about 75 per
cent of the average wage in large cities over 1,000,000 in population. A part of the size-of-city and rural-urban differentials in

[1] *Consumer Incomes in the United States, Their Distribution in 1935–36*, National Resources
Committee, Washington, 1938, p. 27. *Cf.* also, State Emergency Welfare Relief
Commission, "Total Income during 1934 of Gainful Workers," *Michigan Census of
Population and Unemployment*, 1936, p. 3, which indicates that the yearly incomes of
employed workers in rural townships in Michigan ranged from 46 per cent (for professional workers) to 66 per cent (for clerical and skilled workers) of the incomes of similar
workers in cities with over 40,000 inhabitants.

[2] Jacob Perlman and Edward K. Frazier, "Entrance Rates of Common Laborers in
20 Industries, July 1937," *Monthly Labor Review*, vol. 45 (December 1937), p. 1499.

TABLE 7. AVERAGE HOURLY WAGE RATES FOR UNION MEMBERS IN THE BUILDING TRADES AND IN NEWSPAPER PRINTING IN THE NORTHERN AND PACIFIC STATES, JUNE 1, 1938 [1]

Cities	Building trades	Newspaper printing
Over 1,000,000	$1.50	$1.39
500,000 to 1,000,000	1.31	1.28
250,000 to 500,000	1.29	1.26
100,000 to 250,000	1.15	1.13
40,000 to 100,000	1.12	1.08

wage rates is undoubtedly due to the greater degree of labor unionism among workers in the city than in the country and in the large cities than in small cities.

Another factor affecting the labor supply, besides labor organization, is the fact that the population in the cities has not been replacing itself, so that a considerable portion of the labor supply in urban areas has to be recruited or drawn from rural communities with less than 2,500 inhabitants, which accounted for 44 per cent of our population in 1930. In that year the net reproduction rate per generation for the white population of this country was 1.47 for rural areas and 0.87 for urban communities. The net reproduction rate generally declines as the size of the city increases, so that it is over twice as high for rural farm areas as it is for cities above 250,000. [2] Consequently, wage rates in the cities must be higher, in order to attract to the cities a sufficient supply of workers, who will make up the deficit resulting from the low fertility rates in urban areas. Inhabitants of rural areas who value the attractions of country life can only be drawn to the cities by high wage differentials, especially when, in the cities, they may be more subject to loss of earnings through unemployment or to discrimination in the form of seniority rules.

2. *Regional differentials.* Statistics indicate that, by 1810, wage standards had become fairly fixed and showed "the same differences between geographic localities and trades that we find today." [3] J. B. McMaster, the historian, reports that wage rates then were high-

[1] "Union Scales of Wages and Hours in the Printing Trades, June 1, 1938" and "Union Scales of Wages and Hours in the Building Trades, June 1, 1938," *Monthly Labor Review*, vol. 47 (December 1938), p. 1372 and (November 1938), p. 1109. *Cf.* also Jacob Perlman, "Extent and Causes of Differences in Hourly Earnings," *Journal of the American Statistical Association*, vol. 35 (March 1940), pp. 6–7.

[2] Frank Lorimer and Frederick Osborn, *Dynamics of Population*, 1934, p. 28.

[3] *History of Wages in the United States from Colonial Times to 1928*, U. S. Bureau of Labor Statistics, Bulletin No. 604, 1934, p. 56.

est in the New England and New York-to-Ohio area, and lowest in the South, with the territory west of Ohio holding the middle ground.

The Southern wage differential has been explained on many grounds. Of fundamental importance in all regional and national differentials in real wage rates is the population-resources ratio—the natural resources per capita. The South is not rich in minerals, and its soil has been depleted and eroded. In the past, cotton farmers have tended to use up the land and to move on, so that the center of cotton culture has moved westward from the Atlantic seaboard to the Mississippi River. That helps to explain why economic productivity, measured by money income, is much lower for Southern agriculture than for agriculture in other regions of the country. In 1929 the income of farmers in California averaged 10 times that of farmers in South Carolina; yet almost one half the working population in the South depends on agriculture for its support. Indeed, over half the farmers in the country are in the South. Undoubtedly, the system of tenant farming also helps to explain this low-income yield in Southern agriculture and the waste of soil resources. The income differential between the South and the rest of the country is greater in agriculture than in other lines of economic activity.

The quality of the region's population or human resources is also an important factor in economic productivity. Not only does the climate affect output per capita, but the Southern states have the highest rates of illiteracy, and Negroes constitute over one third of their working force. Also, lately some of the youth is being drained away so that the population of the South is heavily weighted by elderly persons. It is, therefore, understandable that the particular industries which employ the largest number of workers in the South are industries that use mostly unskilled or semiskilled labor. Half of the industrial workers in the South are concentrated in textiles and lumber, and both of these industries, wherever located, are low-wage industries because they generally employ a relatively low grade of labor. It is in the unskilled occupations that the wage differential between Southern industry and industry in the rest of the country is the largest. In some highly skilled occupations, like the railroad shop crafts and the building trades, the differential is at a minimum and in some cases practically disappears.[1] This is

[1] *Cf.* Clarence Heer, *Income and Wages in the South*, 1930, pp. 58–62.

true of union as well as nonunion workers. Table 8 indicates the
wage rates for skilled and unskilled building workers in various sections of the country.

TABLE 8. AVERAGE HOURLY WAGES OF BUILDING WORKERS BY REGIONS IN
PERCENTAGE OF THE AVERAGE FOR THE WHOLE COUNTRY, 1936 [1]

State areas	Common laborers	Bricklayers	Carpenters	Plasterers
New England	117	93	94	98
Middle Atlantic	104	107	111	110
East North Central	119	101	108	103
West North Central	115	98	95	95
South Atlantic	84	92	89	90
East South Central	66	92	81	84
West South Central	70	87	84	82
Mountain	96	98	104	93
Pacific	122	103	100	103

The low return in Southern agriculture makes it possible for industries in the South to attract workers from the farms by wage
rates that would fail to attract labor from rural areas in the North.
Furthermore, rural labor is not generally qualified to enter skilled
trades in industry, which helps to explain why the geographic
differential is largest in unskilled work. Table 9 indicates the
Southern differential in hourly rates for unskilled workers in various
industries.

TABLE 9. AVERAGE HOURLY ENTRANCE RATES OF ADULT MALE COMMON
LABORERS IN VARIOUS INDUSTRIES, JULY 1938 [2]

Industry	North and West, cents	South and Southwest, cents	South in percentage of North and West
Brick, tile, and terra cotta	48	29	60
Cement	56	41	73
Chemicals	60	36	60
Fertilizers	47	27	57
Foundry and machine shop	51	35	69
Glass	53	44	83
Iron and steel	60	44	73
Leather	51	39	76
Lumber (sawmills)	55	24	44
Paints	54	33	61
Paper and pulp	51	40	78
Petroleum	68	57	84
Slaughtering and meat packing	58	50	86

[1] Edward P. Sanford, "Wages and Hours in the Building Trades," *Monthly Labor
Review*, vol. 45 (August 1937), pp. 284–87.

[2] Edward K. Frazier and Jacob Perlman, "Entrance Rates of Common Laborers,
July, 1938," *Monthly Labor Review*, vol. 48 (January 1939), p. 168.

The Southern differential for common labor in the middle of 1938 ranged from 56 per cent in the case of lumber to 14 per cent in slaughtering and meat packing, with the average differential about 30 per cent.   In the highest paying lines, which presumably attracted the best quality of common labor in the South, the differential between the North and the South generally was the smallest.

The importance of productivity in regional wage differentials is also brought out in statistics for the lumber industry. Hourly wage rates in logging and sawmilling were about twice as high in the West as in the South in the early 1930's. The amount of lumber produced per man-hour worked was, however, over twice as great in the West as in the South. This difference in productivity of the workers in the two regions is largely explained by the advantage that the West enjoys in the size of logs, the average timber stand per acre, and the degree of mechanization and horsepower available per worker. As a consequence of the high productivity per worker in the West, the labor costs at the mill during the first quarter of 1934 were $5.11 for logging and milling 1,000 board feet of West Coast Douglas fir compared with similar labor costs of $7.58 per 1,000 board feet for Southern pine. Comparative labor costs for shipping and selling by the mills were also lower for the West than for the South.[1]

Various other reasons have been offered to help explain the Southern wage differential. Such reasons include the fact that there are no cities with as many as 500,000 inhabitants in the South, the lower cost of living in the South, the higher freight rates there, the lack of competition for labor in Southern mill towns, the lack of organization amongst Southern workers, the fact that the South sells much of its products abroad and buys many of its goods from our tariff-sheltered industries in the North, and the lack of mobility of Southern labor, especially the unskilled. Perfect mobility of labor would, of course, tend to iron out all geographical differentials.

The average hourly wage in the cotton-textile industry in the

[1] Cf. Peter A. Stone et al., Economic Problems of the Lumber and Timber Products Industry, National Industrial Recovery Administration, Work Materials No. 79, March 1936, pp. 152, 322–23. In 1940, experts estimated that in Washington and Oregon about 16 man-hours were required for logging and milling 1,000 feet of lumber compared with 29.5 hours per 1,000 feet of Southern pine. Cf. also "Technology, Productivity, and Employment in the Lumber Industry," Monthly Labor Review, vol. 51 (July 1940), p. 60.

South during August 1938 was 36.5 cents, which was 18 per cent below the Northern average of 44.6 cents. Some Southern mills, however, were paying rates as high as Northern mills, although Northern mills in general hired more skilled labor and had a higher output per man-hour. This cotton-textile differential had been as high as 39 per cent in 1924, gradually declining to 17.5 per cent in 1935.[1] A study based on the data of the Biennial Census of Manufactures in 1935 indicates that the average differential in hourly wages between comparable industries in the North and the South was then about 15 per cent in manufacturing.[2] This same census shows that, in terms of average "value productivity" per man-hour by wage-earners, Northern and Western manufacturers exceeded Southern manufacturers by 25 per cent or more.[3]

Even within the South itself there were wage differentials. The average hourly wage for the "Lower South" was 18.4 per cent below the wage for similar manufacturing industries in the North; for the "Upper South" the differential was 13.7 per cent, and for the Southwest, 12.8 per cent.[4] Wage rates in manufacturing seem to have had much the same pattern in the New England, the Middle Atlantic, and the East North Central states during 1933 and 1935, but were 5.5 per cent below the Northern average in the West North Central states during 1935.[5] The wage scales for the industry groups in the West conformed very closely with the composite wage scales for the country as a whole.

3. *National differentials.* As indicated in Chapter 4, wage rates in English money were higher in the American colonies than in the mother country a few years after the first settlement, and a differ-

[1] *Cf.* N. A. Tolles, "Regional Differences in Cotton-Textile Wages, 1928 to 1937," *Monthly Labor Review*, vol. 46 (January 1938), pp. 36–37; and A. F. Hinrichs, *Wages in Cotton-Goods Manufacturing*, U. S. Bureau of Labor Statistics, Bulletin No. 663, 1938. In 1925 the New England states had over half of all cotton-spinning spindles in the United States; in 1938 New England had less than one third of such spindles.

[2] A. F. Hinrichs and A. F. Beal, "Geographical Variation in Hours and Wages 1933 and 1935," *Monthly Labor Review*, vol. 47 (July 1938), p. 134. Relatives were calculated from the basic data for each industry and then combined into a weighted index in order to eliminate, in so far as possible, the influence of high-wage and low-wage industries in the two regions.

[3] *Ibid.*, p. 125.

[4] *Ibid.*, p. 141. The "Upper South" includes Delaware, Maryland, District of Columbia, West Virginia, Virginia, North Carolina, Kentucky, and Tennessee; the "Lower South" includes South Carolina, Georgia, Florida, Alabama, Mississippi, Arkansas, and Louisiana; the Southwest includes Oklahoma and Texas.

[5] *Ibid.*, p. 140. The West North Central states include Minnesota, Iowa, Missouri, North Dakota, South Dakota, Nebraska, and Kansas.

ential seems to have persisted since then between real wages here and abroad. As early as 1623 there were complaints of the excessive cost of labor in Virginia and in New England. A few years later a colonial writer was urging impoverished Englishmen to come to Maryland, where they could "live plenteously well." [1] A committee of the Assembly of Pennsylvania correctly stated in 1752 that the ease with which "the industrious Poor obtain lands . . . keeps up the Price of Labour." [2] Undoubtedly the man-land or population-resources ratio plays a most important part in the determination of value productivity per worker in a country.

Fundamentally, it is physical productivity per worker that explains national differentials in the level of real wages. In national wage comparisons, the total real income of the nation is generally more important than the share of that total going to wage-earners. Indeed, international comparisons of average per-capita incomes and of real wages generally show about the same percentage differentials between countries. [3] Various studies by the International Labour Office indicate that in 1930 real wages (measured by the purchasing power of money wage rates in terms of food, fuel, light, and soap) were about as follows in percentage of real wages in the United States: Canada 82 per cent, Sweden and Denmark 58 per cent, England 53 per cent, Holland 43 per cent, Germany 38 per cent, France 31 per cent, and Italy 21 per cent. [4] None of these percentages, except that of France, would be increased if allowance is made for the changes in the International Labour Office's index of real wages from 1930 to 1938. In fact, the percentages for Germany and Holland would be decreased considerably by such adjustment for more recent figures.

Productivity per worker in a country is affected not only by the ratio of population to available natural resources but also by the skill and ability of the workers, the methods of production, the size of the product market, the available power facilities, and a number

---

[1] Cf. T. V. Wertenbaker, *Labor Costs and American Democracy*, Alumni Lectures, Princeton University, 1938, p. 4.

[2] *Pennsylvania Archives*, eighth series, vol. 4, p. 3520.

[3] Cf. J. W. Angell, *The Recovery of Germany*, 1929, p. 321, and *Undersökningar Rörande det Samlade Skattetrycket i Sverige och Utlandet*, Statens Offentliga Utredningar, Stockholm, 1936:18, pp. 132–34, for statistics of per-capita real income in various countries.

[4] *International Labour Review*, vol. 21 (April 1930), p. 560, and vol. 22 (October 1930), p. 545; subsequent issues contain an index of real wages, on a 1929 base, for these various countries.

of other factors. Of course these factors are interrelated; machine methods are used where labor is scarce, and labor scarcity is largely determined by the population-resources ratio.

The question of regional and national differentials in wages is also involved in the discussion of regional and national labor standards in Chapter 19.

CHAPTER NINE

INCOME AND CONSUMPTION

This chapter is devoted to a discussion of wage and income statistics and their bearing upon consumption and investment. Statistics are generally dull, but income figures are so startling that politicians frequently quote them to their constituents. A study of actual earnings and income distribution is necessary in order to attempt an answer to a number of interesting questions, such as the following: Have wage-earners been gaining or losing as compared with other classes? Has there been a tendency for income to become concentrated in fewer hands? What really is "the American standard of living"? Are most wage-earners receiving enough to provide their families with a decent living? Do taxes bear more heavily upon the poor than the rich? Are we suffering from underconsumption? Has investment kept pace with savings, or have savings been wasted by hoarding? What effect does investment have upon consumption? Would further redistribution of income through taxation aid economic progress?

Statistics alone will not provide answers to all of these questions. It will, of course, be necessary to interpret the figures and to fit them into some theoretical pattern. In doing so, caution will be required, for the statistics are only indexes and estimates—some perhaps are little more than intelligent "guesstimates." In certain cases, they may permit of various interpretations or lend support to different theories. Consequently, the analysis and conclusions based upon such figures may be subject to error and certainly should not be accepted as the final, absolute truth.

Nature of the national income. The nation's income fundamentally consists of the net volume of goods and services consumed within the country during any period such as a year. It is evident that there may be a difference between the nation's total income produced—the "heap" of goods and services made available for consumption in any one year—and the total amount of goods and services actually consumed during that year. Not all of the national income produced may be consumed in the same year, so that the income produced may exceed the income consumed. Also, the income consumed may exceed the income produced during any one year, because the people have drawn more from the store of goods (both consumers' goods and capital goods) accumulated in previous years than they have added to that store.

Available estimates of our national income do not attempt to measure the total income consumed by the nation. Rather, they represent the national "income produced" or the aggregate "income paid" to individuals in connection with production, both measured in terms of that common denominator in our economy, the dollar. In any year the national "income produced" (the market value of the net product of goods and services) may differ in amount from the aggregate money "income paid out" to individuals in the process of production, because firms may retain some income as surplus or business savings, or they may draw upon accumulated surplus by disbursing more money than the firm received during the year, in which case there would be a deficit or negative business savings. Total "income paid out" may be divided into various categories either according to the type of payment (wages, interest, rent, profits, etc.), or according to the size of a person's or a family's total income from various sources. Classification by productive function or type of payment is known as functional distribution. These two aspects of income distribution will now be treated in turn.

FUNCTIONAL DISTRIBUTION OF THE NATIONAL INCOME

The broadest classification of the national income on functional lines consists of a division between labor compensation (wages and salaries) on the one hand and compensation to capital (including entrepreneurship) on the other hand. Table 10 indicates the relative share of the national income allotted to each of these claimant groups, labor and capital, during various years.

In interpreting this table there are a number of things that the reader must bear in mind. In the first place, these percentages are only estimates. A recent estimate of the national income and its component elements shows total employees' compensation as

TABLE 10. PERCENTAGE DISTRIBUTION OF NATIONAL INCOME BETWEEN LABOR
AND CAPITAL IN VARIOUS YEARS [1]

	Labor	Capital
1900	53	47
1910	56	44
1920	63	37
1925	62	38
1930	65	35
1932	64	36
1935	67	33
1938	68	32
1939	68	32

69.2 per cent of national income in 1920 and practically the same
figure, 69.5 per cent, in 1930.[2] These recent figures also indicate
that the entire increase in the percentage figure for labor from 1930
to 1935 was brought about by relief payments of various sorts.
The "capital" item, as indicated in the footnote to the table, includes some "labor income," represented by the labor that enterprisers like farmers and small businessmen perform themselves.
The more that employees are hired to perform such work, the more
the capital percentage would decrease.

The most important factor in this increase in the share of the
national income going to employees has been the expansion in the
number of employees relative to enterprisers or independent businessmen during this period. According to the estimates in Table 1,
total employees increased from 69 to 81 per cent of the gainfully
employed population between 1900 and 1939. Professor W. I.
King has estimated that the number of wage-earners and salaried
employees increased from 24,410,000 to 35,572,000 between 1909
and 1927, while the number of entrepreneurs or independent businessmen declined from 9,845,000 to 9,801,000.[3] The reduction in
the number of independent businessmen, as the corporation takes
over more and more of our industrial life, accounts for most of the
decline in the income of entrepreneurs (independent businessmen)

[1] Estimates for 1900 to 1925 from M. Leven, H. G. Moulton, and C. Warburton,
America's Capacity to Consume, 1934, pp. 157, 158; and for 1930 to 1939 from Robert R.
Nathan, "National Income at Nearly 70 Billion Dollars in 1939," *Survey of Current
Business*, U. S. Department of Commerce, vol. 20 (June 1940), p. 9. "Capital" includes
interest, dividends, rents, royalties, corporate savings, and entrepreneurial returns,
which represent "labor income" of entrepreneurs as well as return on owned capital.

[2] Simon Kuznets, *National Income and Capital Formation 1919–35, A Preliminary Report*,
National Bureau of Economic Research, 1937, Table 6, pp. 24–25.

[3] *The National Income and Its Purchasing Power*, National Bureau of Economic Research,
1930, pp. 56, 60, 62.

from 21 to 13 per cent of the national income between 1920 and 1935, while interest and corporation dividend payments rose from 10 per cent of the national income in 1920 to almost 17 per cent in 1932, declining to 13 per cent in 1935.[1]

It is only by bearing in mind the relative expansion in the employee groups that one can reconcile the percentage figures in Table 10 with the fact that a concentration of income into fewer hands, to the relative disadvantage of workers, occurred during the decade of the 1920's. It might also be well to compare Table 10 with Table 1, which shows that in 1939, when the total employees' share of the national income was estimated at 68 per cent, employees represented about 81 per cent of the working population of the country.

If one lumps wages, salaries, and returns to individual enterprisers together and compares such an "earned" income share with what might be called the "passive" share, representing the return on investment and property, he finds that there was practically no change in the percentages for these two shares between 1909 and 1929; the "passive" share accounted for 24.5 per cent of the national income in 1909 and 24.8 per cent in 1929.[2] In the latter year there were around 2,000,000 income recipients who were not gainfully employed. Most of them presumably were living on income from property.[3]

Income shares in the business cycle. The working class as a whole generally loses more than the other economic groups during a depression. The proportion of the total national income received by employees as compensation for labor tends to decline during the downswing of the business cycle. That was apparently the case, for example, from 1920 to 1921 and from 1929 through 1933.[4] On the other hand, the relative share received for property ownership tends to increase under adverse business conditions. From 1929 to 1933, for instance, interest payments received by individuals showed a relative increase from 6.5 to 10.3 per cent of the total national income. Interest charges are customarily fixed costs, which means that the relative share going to interest receivers expands as the total national income contracts. Interest receipts sometimes represent an "unearned" return in the sense that they

---

[1] Simon Kuznets, *op. cit.*   [2] Leven, Moulton, and Warburton, *op. cit.*, p. 159.
[3] *Ibid.*, p. 26.   [4] *Cf.* Simon Kuznets, *op. cit.*

continue to be paid, out of surplus if necessary, upon capital goods long since worn out or obsolete.

A study of corporation disbursements for interest, dividends, and wages as well as corporation profits, during the period from 1922 to 1935, has been made by Professor T. J. Kreps. Professor Kreps' study shows that, although corporate disbursements to labor (wages and salaries) kept pace with corporate disbursements to stockholders and creditors from 1922 to 1924, there was an increase of almost 65 per cent in disbursements to stockholders and creditors between 1924 and 1929 compared with a 20-per-cent increase in the disbursements for labor. Furthermore, the corporation statistics for the period from 1929 to 1934 show that the "wages of capital are not cut as easily as the wages of labor." [1] Professor Kreps indicates how corporation policies may influence the functional distribution of income when he concludes from his study "that corporate security holders not only profited most from the boom in the twenties, but suffered least from the depression in the thirties," and that factory payrolls, while increasing considerably under the various economic and governmental influences after 1932, had not in 1933 and 1934 "reached the levels (in terms of 1923–1925) at which dividend payments, interest payments, and compensation of officers" were maintained during those early years of the New Deal. [2]

Wages, prices, and functional distribution. Some writers have argued that an increase in wage rates for a certain group of workers will not change the functional distribution of income, because a rise in wages will only result in a proportional rise in the price of the product; consequently, the wage dollars of all workers will buy correspondingly less, so that the real income of the wage-earning class remains exactly the same. Such an argument is, however, based upon a number of questionable assumptions. Presumably product prices would rise by the same percentage as wage rates only if all costs in the industry were wage costs or if the return to capitalists always increased in proportion to increases in workers' earnings. Furthermore, it assumes that workers buy enough of the

---

[1] T. J. Kreps, "Dividends, Interest, Profits, Wages, 1923–35," *Quarterly Journal of Economics*, vol. 49 (August 1935), p. 575.

[2] *Ibid.*, p. 599. Estimates by Simon Kuznets show that between 1923 and 1929 the amount paid out by business to workers increased 22 per cent whereas the amount paid out to capital, as interest and dividends, increased by 50 per cent. *Cf.* Kuznets, *op. cit.*, pp. 62–67.

product so that the wage increase is exactly offset by the additional sum that they have to pay to buy the same amount of the product. As long as people receive some income for ownership and not labor, any increase in wage rates is not likely, in itself, to cause a proportionate change in prices. Consequently, increased money wage rates would tend to increase the share of the nation's income received by workers, unless such higher rates caused employment to decrease by an offsetting amount.

PERSONAL DISTRIBUTION OF THE NATIONAL INCOME

This section deals with the distribution of income to family groups and to single individuals. It draws extensively from a study made by the National Resources Committee of consumer incomes during the 12 months from July 1935 through June 1936.[1] At that time there were in this country 29,400,300 families, representing 116,000,000 persons (nearly 91 per cent of the population), and about 10,000,000 single persons living alone or not attached to any family group. Many of these families, of course, contained several wage-earners; the total family income includes the earnings of all members of the family as well as income from other sources such as investments, boarders, relief, etc.

The percentage distribution of the national income among all families and single individuals combined is indicated in Table 11.

TABLE 11. PERCENTAGE DISTRIBUTION OF FAMILIES AND SINGLE INDIVIDUALS BY NUMBER AND BY AGGREGATE INCOME, 1935-1936 [2]

Income level	Number	Aggregate income
Under $500	17.01	3.48
$500—750	14.63	6.10
$750—1,000	14.90	8.65
$1,000—1,250	12.65	9.42
$1,250—1,500	9.49	8.62
$1,500—2,000	13.14	14.98
$2,000—2,500	7.50	11.09
$2,500—3,000	3.74	6.76
$3,000—5,000	4.60	11.21
$5,000—10,000	1.51	6.91
$10,000—25,000	0.66	6.43
$25,000—50,000	0.13	2.96
$50,000—100,000	0.03	1.53
$100,000—500,000	0.01	1.36
Over $500,000	Less than 0.005	0.50

[1] National Resources Committee, *Consumer Incomes in the United States, Their Distribution in 1935–36*, 1938. The estimates of income received by families and individuals in this study are based upon a nationwide sample of about 300,000 families.

[2] National Resources Committee, *op. cit.*, p. 6.

This table shows the difference between the percentage that the various classes represent of the nation's consumer units (families and single persons) compared with the percentage that such classes receive of the nation's total income. For example, families and individuals with incomes under $1,000 represented about 47 per cent of all consumer units, yet they received but 18 per cent of the total national income. Indeed, 5 per cent of the consumer units in the highest income groups received 27 per cent of the national income, or as much as 60 per cent of the consumer units at the lowest end of the scale. And the highest 1 per cent of the consumer units, with incomes of $9,100 and over, received 14 per cent of the nation's income—only a trifle less than did the lowest 40 per cent of the consumer units. The extreme inequality in income distribution may be stated in another way. One tenth of the nation's income went to the top one half of one per cent of all consumer units and another tenth served to support the lowest third of the families and single individuals. Relief receipts accounted for some of the income of about 30 per cent of the consumer units in this lowest-third group.

During this 12-month period from the middle of 1935 to the middle of 1936, half of all the families received less than $1,160, and half of the single individuals received less than $830. The average or mean income for all families was $1,622, and for all single individuals $1,151.

Economic equality. The inequality of income was greater in the 1920's than in the 1930's. It is generally recognized that extremes in the distribution of money income are greatest during prosperous periods. This is so because profits rise rapidly during booms, and the rich become much richer, mainly through larger profits. Various statistical studies indicate, for example, that there was a distinct tendency toward a more extreme concentration of income during the decade of the 1920's.[1] Some authors, from less precise statistical material, conclude that there was a progressive increase from 1910 to 1929 "in the proportion of individuals in the higher income groups."[2] Estimates by the Brookings Institution

[1] *Cf.*, for example, *Concentration and Composition of Individual Incomes, 1918–1937*, Monograph No. 4, Temporary National Economic Committee, 1940; Leven, Moulton, and Warburton, *op. cit.*, p. 126; and Rufus S. Tucker, "The Distribution of Income Among Income Taxpayers in the United States, 1863–1935," *Quarterly Journal of Economics*, vol. 52 (August 1938), p. 586.

[2] Leven, Moulton, and Warburton, p. 106.

for the year 1929 show that 6.6 per cent of the total national income went to consumer units (families and single individuals) with incomes of $500,000 or over, compared with 0.5 per cent in Table 11 for the same income classes in 1935–1936.[1] At the other end of the income curve, 17.3 per cent of all consumer units received between $500 and $1,000 in 1929, while 29.5 per cent of all consumer units received incomes of $500 to $1,000 in 1935–1936. Allowance should be made, of course, for the 15-to-20-per-cent decline in wholesale prices and the cost of living between 1929 and 1935–1936.

Inequality in the distribution of wealth, in large measure, accounts for the inequality in incomes. A study based on the Federal income-tax figures for 1920 indicates that, while those with incomes between $1,000 and $2,000 derived 82 per cent of their income from labor service and 18 per cent from property, those with incomes between $500,000 and $1,000,000 obtained 94 per cent of their income from property, and those with incomes over $2,000,000 got 99 per cent of their income from property.[2] Such figures indicate the direct relationship between the concentration of wealth and unequal distribution of income. The inequality in the ownership of wealth is even greater than that for income. An estimate at the end of 1921 showed that the richest 2 per cent of the population, those with $40,000 or more in property, owned 40 per cent of the total national wealth, whereas the poorest 65 per cent owned only 16.6 per cent of the nation's total wealth.[3]

There is also some evidence that inequality in the distribution of wealth has increased during the last century.[4] Such inequality is perpetuated, of course, through inheritance from parents to offspring. Many well-to-do persons, although they make public statements strongly in favor of equal opportunity and starting at the bottom, start their own children near the top by willing them sizeable inheritances.

Great extremes in the distribution of income and wealth are characteristic of large industrial countries like the United States, England, or Germany. This is true mainly because large market

---

[1] *Ibid.*, p. 230.   [2] O. F. Boucke, *Principles of Economics*, 1928, vol. 2, p. 180.
[3] W. I. King, "Wealth Distribution in the Continental United States at the Close of 1921," *Journal of American Statistical Association*, vol. 22 (June 1927), p. 153.
[4] *Cf.* H. A. Millis and R. E. Montgomery, *Labor's Progress and Some Basic Labor Problems*, 1938, pp. 265–71, for a summary of the available data on this point.

areas are necessary in order that huge fortunes may be amassed. Under the medieval guild system, with local markets and restrictions on competition, it simply was not possible for one townsman to become many times more wealthy than most of his fellow townsmen. Nowadays the largest fortunes are in the largest countries. In smaller industrial nations, like Sweden, Denmark, or Switzerland, the standard of living of the people may be fairly high, but market areas, and therefore the size of business units, are too small to permit accumulation of dollar fortunes in nine digits. One can readily see that it would have been impossible for Ford or Rockefeller to have acquired their large fortunes from the automobile and oil industries had they set up in business in one of the smaller industrial countries.

It is one of the greatest paradoxes of our civilization that the inequality in the distribution of wealth and income shows no sign of lessening, despite the fact that political and civil equality have been practically achieved for a considerable period of time and that educational differences are gradually being reduced with the recent developments in public education. Why economic inequality should persist in the face of these other equalizing tendencies is difficult to explain. Certainly in a business civilization that tends to evaluate persons mainly by the amount of income and wealth they possess, such extreme economic inequality gives rise to considerable discontent and class antagonism.

INCOME AND LIVING STANDARDS

"The standard of living" is a popular phrase with a variety of meanings and connotations. To some it signifies actual living conditions; to others it suggests some "ideal" or desirable level of living that people "ought" to enjoy. When persons talk of "the quantum of goods and services necessary for decent existence" or of a wage sufficient to provide "an American standard of living," they have in mind some norm or minimum level, which they are using as a measuring stick. Such standards for measuring the adequacy of family incomes, of course, change with economic circumstances, rising with any increase in the quantity and variety of goods available per person. A decent and healthy standard of living for an American worker's family today is quite different from a similar standard for a wage-earner's family 50 years ago, before the widespread use of automobiles, radios, moving pictures, electric lights, furnaces, well-equipped bathrooms, etc. Twenty-five years ago an automobile would have been considered a luxury by most Americans; the same is true of many other articles that now are a part of the everyday life of the workingman.

Preceding discussions of wage and income figures have indicated that there are occupational, regional, and other differences in the real income of working-class families in America. The level of living is generally different for common laborers and railroad engineers with families of the same size. The standard of living amongst the poor whites or Negro sharecroppers in the South is totally unlike that of the residents of Park Avenue, New York City, or Hollywood, California. Actually, there is no single American standard of living. As the income estimates in Tables 11 and 12 testify, levels of income, and therefore standards of living, range all the way from most extreme poverty to extreme luxury.

TABLE 12.   PERCENTAGE DISTRIBUTION OF FAMILIES AND INDIVIDUALS BY INCOME LEVEL, 1935–1936 [1]

Income level	All families [a]	All families not receiving relief	Wage-earning families not receiving relief	Single individuals
Under $250	4.0	2.8	3.0	9.6
$250–500	10.3	7.8	7.5	15.6
$500–750	12.9	11.3	12.0	19.6
$750–1,000	14.6	13.4	16.2	15.9
$1,000–1,250	13.2	13.2	16.2	11.0
$1,250–1,500	9.8	10.8	12.7	8.7
$1,500–1,750	8.0	9.1	9.8	5.4
$1,750–2,000	6.5	7.3	7.4	4.0
$2,000–2,500	8.4	9.5	8.0	4.9
Over $2,500	8.1	14.8	7.2	3.6
Average income	$1,622	$1,781	$1,289	$1,151
Median income	$1,160	$1,285	$1,175	

[a] All families represented 29,400,300 families or 116,000,000 persons; nonrelief families included 24,913,200 families; wage-earning families not receiving relief included 9,459,300 families; and single individuals, 10,058,000 persons.

Levels of living. Assuming that an annual income of $750 in 1935–1936 was, in most localities, too low to maintain a family of four on a level of normal health and working efficiency, Table 12 indicates that over one fifth of all nonrelief families failed to reach even such a substandard or "poverty" level. The standard of living

[1] National Resources Committee, *Consumer Incomes in the United States*, 1938, pp. 18, 22, 27, 30.

of a family can be roughly ascertained by the percentage of the family budget represented by expenditures for food. At a $750 income level, fully half of the family's income would generally be used to buy food.

It has been estimated that at least $1,000 was necessary in 1935–1936 to provide a family of four with the bare essentials or basic necessities of life, with food costs approximating 40 per cent of the family budget, and housing, along with fuel and light, accounting for an additional 25 per cent.[1] Table 12 shows that two fifths of all wage-earners' families not receiving relief failed to achieve such a "subsistence" standard of $1,000 in 1935–1936. In this same period, an income of $1,500 would, under most circumstances, have been necessary in order to provide the average family of four with a "health-and-decency" standard of living. Such a standard would include, besides a minimum amount of food for healthy existence that would consume 35 per cent of the family's income, such elementary social necessities as medical care, clothing compatible with self-respect, and a few recreation and "sundry" items such as a newspaper and a fortnightly movie. Only one third of all families not on relief had incomes of $1,500 or more in 1935–1936. Indeed, well over two thirds of all wage-earners' families not on relief failed to enjoy such a health-and-decency standard during those years.

A larger income would have been needed to provide for families of more than four persons at each of these standards—"poverty" ($750), "subsistence" ($1,000), and minimum "health-and-decency" ($1,500). Yet there is no evidence that the largest families enjoy the largest incomes. Indeed, although 21 per cent of all non-relief families were below the $750 level, 23 per cent of all families containing seven or more persons were below that level, and the percentages were 13.4 and 14.8 respectively for the $750-to-$1,000 income class. Apparently the largest families in the lower income brackets live on smaller incomes than families containing from three to six persons.[2] The largest families probably do not enjoy above-average incomes because the principal breadwinner in working-class families generally earns from 80 to 85 per cent of the total family income, with 10 to 15 per cent being provided from the

---

[1] For a discussion of the measurement of various living standards, cf. Millis and Montgomery, op. cit., pp. 61–72.

[2] Ibid., pp. 21–22.

wages of other family members including boarders and 5 per cent being furnished from various other sources.

Even in the prosperous year of 1929, according to estimates by the Brookings Institution, over one fifth of all families in America received incomes below $1,000; over two fifths had incomes of less than $1,500; and three fifths were below the $2,000 income level.[1] In 1929 living costs were higher, so the "poverty" level was around $1,000 for a family of four, and the minimum "health-and-decency" level was between $1,750 and $2,000. The Brookings Institution study considered $2,000 as necessary, at 1929 prices, to provide the basic necessities for a family of five. There is no doubt, however, that for the country as a whole the standard of living rose considerably during the decade ending in 1929. It is estimated that in 1919 as much as 33 per cent of all consumptive expenditures were for food and nonalcoholic beverages, compared with a percentage of 23.5 for 1929.[2]

TAXATION AND LIVING STANDARDS

Although we have fairly good estimates of the way income is originally distributed, estimates of the way that consumption is divided between various economic classes and persons are somewhat less satisfactory. Consumption of goods and services may differ from income because the government, through taxation and expenditures for public services, may really be taking from some persons and giving to others. Also, people may save or hoard their money incomes, which would mean that their income would exceed their consumption during such a period. Such savings and hoarding tend to vary with changes in the business cycle. Finally, people, by purchasing on credit, may also consume more dollars' worth of goods and services than their dollar incomes, especially if they fail to pay their debts.

A recent estimate of consumer expenditures does indicate that during 1935-1936 the highest one third of the nation's consumer units (families and single individuals) spent 2.7 times as much for food, 3.6 times as much for housing, 5.4 times as much for clothing and medical care, and 13 to 14 times as much for education and

[1] Leven, Moulton, and Warburton, *op. cit.*, p. 54.
[2] C. Warburton, "How the National Income Was Spent 1919–29," *Journal of the American Statistical Association*, vol. 30 (March 1935) supplement, p. 177.

automobiles as did the lowest one third of the nation's consumer units.[1] Indeed, the consumer units with incomes over $10,000, although accounting for less than one per cent of all consumer units, spent as much for current consumption in 1935–1936 as did the lowest one fifth of the consuming units.[2] Even though the rich were saving two fifths of their incomes, their expenditures on consumption were large in dollar figures.

It is not possible to determine the extent to which governmental activities cause a difference between consumption and income originally received. In the first place, it is impossible to estimate exactly how much of the total tax burden rests upon each income group or class. Certain taxes, such as sales taxes, may be shifted to the buyer of a product, so that the person who pays the tax money to the government does not really bear the tax burden; he passes that burden along to others through higher prices for products. In the second place, it is not possible to estimate exactly how much of the total benefits of governmental expenditures each income group receives. How would one allocate between income groups such public expenditures as those for the army and navy, the police, the schools, the courts, legislatures, etc.? There is no doubt that the government, generally speaking, exerts an income-equalizing influence through taxation and public expenditures; but the extent of that influence depends upon the type of taxes levied and upon the kinds of expenditures. Progressive taxes, like income and inheritance taxes, take relatively more from the incomes of the rich than the poor;[3] expenditures for public relief increase the consumption of the poor much more than expenditures for interest on government bonds. On the other hand, taxes like sales, excise, and general-property taxes are regressive in effect, which means that they take a larger percentage of the incomes of the lower classes than of the upper classes. This is true even though the tax rates are uniform, because the lower classes spend a larger proportion of their income upon the taxed commodities and because the more valuable a piece of property is, the more likely it is to be underassessed.[4]

[1] National Resources Committee, *Consumer Expenditures in the United States, Estimates for 1935–36*, 1939, p. 51.

[2] *Ibid.*, p. 48.

[3] *Cf.*, for example, Maxine Yaple, "The Burden of Direct Taxes as Paid by Income Classes," *American Economic Review*, vol. 26 (December 1936), pp. 691–710.

[4] Professor Herbert D. Simpson estimated in 1928 that property taxes absorbed eight-and-a-half per cent of the entire net income of classes with incomes of less than

In 1937 personal income and inheritance taxes accounted for about 15 per cent of the country's total tax bill of Federal, state, and local taxes. Property taxes represented about 36 per cent, and sales taxes of various sorts amounted to about 30 per cent, of the nation's total tax bill.[1] By way of contrast, personal income and inheritance taxes accounted for 42 per cent of total national and local tax revenue in Great Britain in 1934 compared with 7.7 per cent for the United States. Certainly, our tax system has been heavily weighted with regressive taxes compared with the tax systems of most large industrial countries. Taxes based on personal ability have played a minor fiscal role in this country.

Distribution of the tax burden. Most generalizations concerning the tax burden that rests upon different income classes cannot be taken seriously because they are based upon very questionable assumptions. For instance, tax-reduction advocates try to prove that the poor bear very heavy tax burdens by quoting figures based upon the assumption that most of the total tax burden really "falls on the dollars you spend as a consumer." Actually, well over half of the tax revenue in this country is raised by taxes levied on home-owners, noncommercial automobiles, inheritances, personal incomes, corporation net income, etc., which are not, according to experts in tax incidence, shifted to any consumer through prices. A recent study by various economists indicates that our tax system is regressive in effect for incomes of $2,000 and below, but is progressive for the upper income brackets, which are subject to the Federal income tax. On the basis of a series of assumptions (a family of four, residing in New York or Illinois, owning a home and a car, using tobacco, and bearing the burden of certain taxes which, it is assumed, are shifted to such a family), it was found that in 1936 taxes took the percentages of the total family income in each class indicated in Table 13 (the range represents the variations that arise when five different sets of assumptions are used).

$2,000. The percentage decreased with higher income classes until, for the largest incomes, property taxes amounted to but one-and-three-fourths per cent of entire net income. *Cf.* "Borrow—Don't Tax," *Survey Graphic*, vol. 23 (September 1934), p. 431.

[1] *Cf.* Twentieth Century Fund, *Facing the Tax Problem*, 1937, pp. 9–27. Sales taxes in the above percentage include retail sales, gasoline, tobacco, liquor, customs, and other Federal taxes on commodities and services.

TABLE 13.   TOTAL TAX BURDEN AS PERCENTAGE OF FAMILY INCOME IN
NEW YORK AND ILLINOIS, 1936 [1]

Occupation and income	Percentage
Farmer with $500	11 to 19
Farmer with $1,000	10 to 15
Farmer with $2,000	8 to 13
Wage-earner with $1,000	15 to 19
Wage-earner with $2,000	14 to 18
Salaried worker with $5,000	18 to 21
Salaried worker with $20,000	27 to 37
Corporation official with $100,000	38 to 60

The tax burden is regressive (the percentages in Table 13 decline
as the family income increases) for incomes under $2,000 primarily
because the percentage of full assessment is generally higher for
small properties than for large properties and because the smaller
income groups save little or nothing, so that they have a higher
ratio of expenditures to income.

A recent study of the tax burden on income classes for the entire
country during the 12 months from July 1938 through June 1939
shows results roughly similar to the figures in Table 13.[2]   Total
taxes borne were estimated at 22 per cent of the incomes of persons
receiving under $500 a year, at approximately 17 per cent for
those in income classes from $1,000 to $5,000, and at increasingly
higher percentages for those with incomes above $5,000. For the
last income class ($20,000 and over) total taxes borne were esti-
mated to be 38 per cent of total income received. This same 1938–
1939 study also shows that a large portion of all taxes (60 per cent)
is paid by persons with incomes under $3,000 a year, who spend
practically all of their incomes for consumption.[3]   It has been
estimated that three out of every four tax dollars in 1936 represented
a reduction in consumption expenditures and only one out of

[1] Taken from Twentieth Century Fund, *op. cit.*, p. 232. For a more complete discussion of this question of the distribution of the tax burden and the basis of the above
estimates, *cf.* Mabel Newcomer, "Estimate of the Tax Burden on Different Income
Classes" in *Studies in Current Tax Problems*, Twentieth Century Fund, 1937. For an
estimate of the distribution of income by income classes after deductions for Federal
income taxes and savings, *cf.* M. Leven, *The Income Structure of the United States*, 1938,
pp. 103–104. For estimates of the direct tax burden on low-income families based on
a study of such families in nearly 300 American cities, *cf.* J. M. Leonard, *The Direct
Tax Burden on Low Income Groups*, National Municipal League, 1939, 36 pp.

[2] *Who Pays the Taxes?* Monograph No. 3, Temporary National Economic Committee,
1940, p. 6.

[3] *Ibid.*, pp. 28–30.

every four tax dollars came from the stream of savings.[1] Four corporation presidents in a recent book propose that the nation's tax burden be altered so that less government revenue will come from consumption and more from savings.[2]

The effects of governmental expenditures upon the real income of various income classes are even more difficult to estimate. Expenditures for the public debt (interest and principal) may help to increase the incomes of those in the higher income brackets; public expenditures for relief, playgrounds, public health, libraries, and schools favor the lower income groups. Around half of all public expenditures, however, have been for such items as general government, the army and navy, police and fire protection, highways, and sanitation, which cannot be classified as definitely and consistently partial to high- or low-income groups.

INCOME AND SAVINGS

Inequality in the distribution of income affects the total volume of savings. Generally speaking, as a family's income rises, the percentage it spends for food decreases and the percentage of its income saved increases. For example, it is estimated that families with an income of $30,000 a year or more saved 40 to 50 per cent of their income in 1929, whereas families receiving less than $1,250 a year saved nothing at all.[3] Estimates for 1935–1936 agree, in general, with these 1929 figures.[4] Therefore, the more unequal is the distribution of income, the greater will be the percentage of the national income that is saved. There was a tendency for the percentage of the aggregate income that was saved to increase during the period from 1900 to 1930, particularly during the postwar years.[5] The reader will recall that during the first three decades of this century there was likewise a tendency for income to be more unequally distributed and that the purchasing power of the average income was also increasing.

According to an estimate by the Brookings Institution, total savings in 1929 amounted to $20,000,000,000, or over one fifth of

[1] H. S. Dennison, L. Filene, R. E. Flanders, and M. E. Leeds, *Toward Full Employment*, 1938, pp. 185–87.

[2] *Ibid.*, pp. 188, 201.

[3] Leven, Moulton, and Warburton, *op. cit.*, pp. 95–96.

[4] *Cf.* National Resources Committee, *Consumer Expenditures in the United States, Estimates for 1935–36*, 1939, pp. 20 and 48.

[5] Leven, Moulton, and Warburton, *op. cit.*, Chapter 9.

the total national income. It is estimated that family savings contributed $15,100,000,000, that the savings of unattached individuals contributed an additional $2,700,000,000, and that savings caused by corporations' adding earnings to surplus instead of paying them out as dividends to stockholders accounted for the remaining $2,200,000,000. Two thirds of the $15,100,000,000 savings by families was done by those with incomes of over $10,000 a year, who were but two per cent of the population in 1929. On balance, those families receiving incomes under $1,500 spent more money than they received, so that they used up some of the savings of others. These relationships between savings and family income are indicated in Table 14.

TABLE 14. SAVINGS OF NONFARM FAMILIES BY INCOME CLASSES, 1929 [1]

Income class	Percentage of income saved
Under $1,000	−22
$1,000 to 1,500	1
1,500 to 2,000	6
2,000 to 3,000	9
3,000 to 4,000	13
4,000 to 6,000	17
6,000 to 10,000	24
10,000 to 20,000	36
20,000 to 50,000	39
50,000 to 100,000	44
100,000 to 250,000	49
250,000 to 1,000,000	56
$1,000,000 and over	66

Personal savings are the difference between one's income and his expenditures for current consumption. There are various reasons why a person may not spend all of his income. Many of these reasons are unrelated to the interest rate or to the rate of return from investment. Most saving occurs more or less automatically. People buy life insurance, or set money aside for a "rainy day" or for their old age. Some persons attempt to increase their economic power and prestige through saving, in which case saving may be its own reward. Such motives for saving may be so strong that much saving might take place without the payment of an interest return. In fact, a number of economists and businessmen believe a lower

[1] Leven, Moulton, and Warburton, *op. cit.*, p. 95. For a criticism of these estimates for the income brackets above the $250,000 class, *cf.* Henry H. Villard, "Dr. Moulton's Estimates of Savings and Investment," *American Economic Review*, vol. 27 (September 1937), p. 482.

rate of interest, down to a certain minimum, might serve to stimulate a larger volume of savings.[1]

It has been asked, "If savings are supplied so freely by the well-to-do, why does not the rate of interest fall to zero?" The point is that the rate of interest represents a reward for not hoarding, a reward for parting with money in return for a less liquid security. A preference for liquidity, or a propensity to hoard, may arise whenever persons expect prices to fall, expect interest rates to rise so that security prices may fall, or expect consumption to decline so that investments may be less profitable. Under such conditions, the interest rate might rise, yet people would prefer to hoard their savings rather than lend or invest them and run the risk of losing their money.

No one claims that in recent decades our economic difficulties have arisen from lack of sufficient savings to meet the needs of industry for new capital equipment. On the contrary, the rate of expansion in the country's capital investment may be slackening as its rate of population and manufacturing growth begin to slow down. Yet industrial maturity may not reduce the inequality in income distribution or the propensity of persons to save. Consequently, generous savings, which provided for rapid and, for the most part, healthy expansion in the youth of a country, "may tend to be unwholesome fat" after it reaches industrial maturity.[2]

In the past, some people have attempted to justify extreme inequality in the distribution of incomes on the ground that it promoted savings, and some economists have argued that it is dangerous for a country to put heavy taxes on large incomes because such taxes might dry up the source of funds for capital accumulation and expansion. But, as Joan Robinson has pointed out, "it is an

---

[1] Cf., for example, Alvin Hansen, *Full Recovery or Stagnation?* 1938, pp. 19–20; and Dennison *et al.*, *op. cit.*, pp. 191–92.

Professor J. M. Clark has stated: "Changed interest rates, within the usual range of such changes, do not have any great effect in stimulating or retarding savings. In fact, they may even have the reverse effect to the one that is required to bring about equilibrium. For a lowering of interest rates results in raising the market values of existing investments, and creates a profit from appreciation on the holding of outstanding securities, aside from the cash earnings they yield from current production. Thus it tends actually to attract savings into this field. There seems, therefore, to be insufficient reason for expecting the automatic machinery of the market to bring about the desired perfect equilibrium and prevent any possible oversavings." *Economics of Planning Public Works*, 1935, p. 48.

[2] Dennison *et al.*, *op. cit.*, p. 199.

extremely uneconomic method of getting saving done to fatten up a certain number of people to the point at which saving is no effort to them." [1]   Furthermore, large savings under existing circumstances may not be socially desirable.   An expansion of consumption in the form of better living conditions for the poorest groups in the community may be preferable to increased savings, especially if such savings fail to result in the creation of more capital equipment and simply "run to waste."

SAVINGS AND INVESTMENT

It has been the traditional view in economics that savings automatically result in new investment—in an addition to inventory or capital equipment. Such a view is correct whenever, as in a self-sufficient economy, the saver and the investor are the same person. The fisherman saves by devoting part of his time and resources to the making of a boat; the farmer saves by setting aside some of his harvest as seed for next year's crop or by building fences, which he obviously cannot consume, so that his cows will not collide with automobiles on the highway.

In our modern money economy, however, the saver is seldom the builder, so the act of saving does not in itself cause a corresponding increase of investment in capital goods, such as factories, machinery, railways, and agricultural implements. Money saved by well-to-do persons is used to construct new plants and to manufacture new equipment only when it pays some employer to make such investment in his business. When prospects for profit are not good, money saved tends to lie idle in banks or elsewhere. Capital equipment is not increased, nor are men given construction jobs, if the money saved is used to pay off bank debts, thereby decreasing the money supply in the form of checking accounts, or is used to bid up the price of existing securities, or is simply hoarded in the bank or in the home. Hoarding has been defined as a decrease in the rate of spending of money (cash and checking accounts) for the purchase of goods and services.[2] Saving that serves to keep money from circulating has also been called a "strike of capital," because persons who have cash and checking accounts decline to use their money.

[1] Joan Robinson, *Introduction to the Theory of Employment*, 1938, p. 47.
[2] D. H. Robertson, "Saving and Hoarding," *Economic Journal*, vol. 43 (September 1933), p. 401. The indirect effect of reducing the rate of expenditure is, of course, to diminish aggregate money income.

From a national point of view, the function of savings is to increase the country's productive facilities so that a greater amount of consumption goods may be produced in the future. Savings without any corresponding expenditures for capital equipment or for current consumption cause a reduction in the nation's total demand and represent a social waste. Some English economists have pointed out that, because all incomes are derived from expenditures of one sort or another, unspent savings reduce the incomes of people by a corresponding amount, and with reduced incomes people cannot save so much, with the net result that the hoarding of savings will continue to reduce the community's income until a point is reached at which all savings are being invested and no new savings are being hoarded.

Such a process apparently took place during the slump of the early 1930's. Businessmen struggled to build up money balances by reducing their investment in inventories and capital equipment. Such actions, if successful, represented saving without any corresponding spending for investment or other purposes. The result was a reduction in spending, in money incomes, in total demand, and in production, until production became adjusted to the smaller total sums that were being spent. Such hoarding of savings also helps to account for the fact that from 1930 to 1936 the investment of savings was not sufficient even to maintain the existing capital equipment and business inventories in this country.[1] Our capital equipment depreciated faster than replacements and repairs occurred during that period.

In such depression periods it seems that savings, if one includes hoarding in savings, increase as the rate of turnover of money slows down and funds are used to repay bank loans, thus extinguishing checking-account money. Actions that keep money from circulating, or reduce the money supply, tend to cause individual savings to exceed actual investment. For any brief period of time, therefore, the amount of voluntary savings may be greater than the amount of investment, but such a situation cannot continue, because persons' incomes are derived from expenditures either for consumption or investment. When some peoples' savings result in less being spent, other persons' incomes or earnings are reduced by a corresponding amount, so that they cannot save as much as they

---

[1] *Cf.* Kuznets, *op. cit.*, p. 48.

formerly did. Consequently, savings unspent by some cause other persons whose incomes are reduced to save less, and the more people strive to get in a "liquid" position by hoarding money, the more all money incomes are reduced. Unspent savings will cause incomes to be reduced until a point is reached where all current savings are being invested—where savings equal investment. In terms of real phenomena, saving and investment are always equal, since savings not invested run to waste.

CONSUMPTION AND CAPITAL FORMATION

In a specialized economy such as ours, funds not spent for consumption (savings) will be spent for new plants and capital equipment only when some business firm invests the money for such capital goods. Business firms borrow and invest only when there is some expectation of a future profit from such investment. The prospect for profitable investment, in turn, depends upon the firm's estimates of the future demand for its products, upon expected demand for consumption goods. In an exchange economy, capital equipment is of value only if it turns out other goods at a profit, so that, in the final analysis, all value and all new investment hinge upon expected consumption. In such an economy, in which borrowers and not savers actually invest the funds in capital equipment, the following dilemma may arise: Savings occur by keeping, or by reducing, expenditures for consumption below one's income; yet a net expansion in capital investment will generally be made only when there is some likelihood that consumption will increase in the future. J. M. Keynes has well expressed this dilemma in the following words:

An act of individual saving means—so to speak—a decision not to have dinner today. But it does *not* necessitate a decision to have dinner or to buy a pair of boots a week hence or a year hence or to consume any specified thing at any specified date. Thus it depresses the business of preparing today's dinner without stimulating the business of making ready for some future act of consumption. It is not a substitution of future consumption-demand for present consumption,—it is a net diminution of such demand. Moreover, the expectation of future consumption is so largely based on current experience of present consumption that a reduction in the latter is likely to depress the former, with the result that the act of saving will not merely depress the price of consumption-goods and leave the marginal efficiency [rate of return over cost] of existing capital unaffected, but may actually tend to depress the latter also. In this event it may reduce present investment-demand as well as present consumption-demand.[1]

Professor Keynes goes on to point out that employment of labor and other productive resources is based upon the expectation of consumption, so saving, which involves abstaining from present consumption without any simultaneous order for future consumption, may have a depressing effect upon employment.

Although it is generally recognized that capital equipment is not a self-contained entity, unrelated to consumption, there is no agreement amongst economists concerning the relationship between expenditures for consumption and expenditures for capital creation. The classical view, based on the assumption of full employment of all economic resources, has been that an increase in the expenditures for consumption would cause a decrease in the production of capital equipment, and, *vice versa*, an increase in expenditures for capital equipment would necessitate a reduction in consumption. More recent theories, assuming some unemployment of economic resources, state that investment and consumption tend to expand and contract together. Available statistics seem to support this recent view. Apparently in only 3 of the 13 years from 1901 to 1914 and in only 2 of the 14 years from 1919 to 1933 did the production of capital goods move in the opposite direction from the production of consumption goods.[2] It seems clear from our industrial history that changes in consumption are generally accompanied by similar changes in investment, especially during downswings of the business cycle. Certainly, capital expansion does not occur year after year when consumption is declining. An increase in the production of capital goods could, of course, take place without any increase in total expenditures for consumption if there were a shift in demand to a new product or if some new invention should reduce costs of production enough to cause existing capital equipment to be scrapped. Without a new product or a new cost-reducing invention, an expansion in total expenditures for capital

---

[1] J. M. Keynes, *The General Theory of Employment, Interest and Money*, 1936, p. 210.
[2] *Cf.* H. G. Moulton, *The Formation of Capital*, 1935, pp. 44–46. *Cf.* also figures for the period from 1921 to 1938 in Alvin Hansen, *op. cit.*, p. 293. Consumers' goods consist of articles destined for individual or personal use; capital goods are articles used to produce consumers' goods or other capital goods.

goods is not likely unless there is an increase in expenditures for consumption.

There is, however, a question as to which leads the way. Some economists believe that an increase in capital expenditures precedes an increase in consumption expenditures in a business cycle; certain economists contend that consumption expenditures lead and investment expenditures follow; while other economists believe that change in either investment or consumption may cause a change in the other. The problem of which class of expenditure really precedes is complicated by the fact that expected changes may be the causal factor and by the fact that, once a general movement is under way, there is interaction between changes in investment and in consumption. From a survey of business fluctuations in this country since the Civil War, Harold G. Moulton concludes that, in most cases, changes in business conditions, especially business recoveries, seem to begin with changes affecting the production or sale of consumption goods rather than of capital goods.[1]

The "acceleration" and "multiplier" principles. These two principles attempt to explain the relationship between consumption and capital investment. The acceleration principle is a statement of the effects of changes in consumption expenditures upon investment expenditures, and the multiplier principle is a statement of the effects of changes in investment upon income, consumption, and employment.

According to the acceleration principle, any change in the rate of expansion of consumers' goods production is likely to cause a greater percentage change in the rate of investment. That is true because capital investment each year is but a small percentage of the value of all existing capital equipment. A simple example will illustrate this point. Suppose that 10 out of every 100 units of capital equipment must be scrapped and replaced each year so that, with no change in total consumption or in production methods, annual capital investment might amount to 10 per cent of existing capital equipment. Under such conditions, a 10-per-cent increase in consumption, assuming no excess capacity, might necessitate an annual expansion in the production of capital equipment up to 20 per cent of existing capital equipment—one half of the production for replacements and the other half for new equipment to sup-

[1] Moulton, *op. cit.*, pp. 71, 73.

ply the 10-per-cent increase in consumption. In such a case, a 10-per-cent increase in consumption would have resulted in a 100-per-cent increase in capital investment. Should consumption again flatten out, investment might decline to the 10-per-cent-replacement level—a drop of 50 per cent. A 10-per-cent decline in consumption, under this same set of circumstances, might even lead to a complete cessation of all investment, since then there might be no need for the 10-per-cent replacement of old equipment. Consequently, changes in consumption tend to be magnified backward to the capital-goods industries and to cause larger percentage changes in investment in capital goods, although the relationship between changes in consumption and investment is not rigid. It may be modified by the existence of excess capacity, by the possibility of postponing capital replacements, by changes in production methods, and by changes in employers' expectations regarding future business conditions.

The multiplier is an expression of the effects that changes in investment may have upon income and, through income, upon the rate of consumption and employment. An increase in the rate of investment, by increasing people's incomes, will tend to increase the rate of consumption and employment. How much consumption will be increased depends upon the percentage of any additional income that people spend for consumption and how rapidly such expenditures take place. The multiplier may, therefore, be defined as either the ratio between additional investment and the increase in total income that results, or the ratio between the additional investment and the consequent increase in total consumption, or the ratio between additional employment in the capital-goods industries and the increase in total employment that follows. If, for instance, employment in the consumption-goods industries should increase by two workers with each increase of one worker employed in the capital-goods industry, the employment multiplier would be three. The multiplier is discussed further in Chapter 15. Of course, it also operates to reduce consumption and employment with decreases in investment.

INEQUALITY OF INCOMES AND ECONOMIC PROGRESS

It has frequently been argued that inequality in the distribution of income results in some persons being so poor that there is bound to be a deficiency in demand. Lack of purchasing power, it is said, leads to underconsumption and overproduction.

Some economists have attempted to answer this "lack of purchasing power" argument by pointing out that every cost is also an income and that the receipts from a sale equal the selling price. It is argued that, since firms disburse all their income in one way or another, enough purchasing power is continually being paid out by business to permit the purchase of the products of business. Furthermore, as long as the money supply is not reduced or the price level raised, there can hardly be a general lack of purchasing power, although it may well be that some persons with purchasing power are not spending their money at the normal rate. Finally, if our economic difficulty were a deficiency in purchasing power rather than a failure to use purchasing power, it is hard to understand how such a "deficiency" is ever overcome, so that economic recovery can take place. The "deficiency" theory may seem to explain the downswing, but is of little use in explaining the end of a business slump. A theory based upon changes in the spending of purchasing power can, however, be used to explain both the downswing and the upswing of business.

Changes in the rate of spending may be caused by hundreds of different factors, one of which is economic inequality. As has already been indicated, there is a general tendency for savings to increase more rapidly than consumption expenditures as a person's income rises. Consequently, a large part of any addition to income in the upper income brackets is likely to be saved, whereas practically all additions to the incomes of persons in the low-income groups would be spent for current consumption. This is clear from the percentage-saved figures in Table 14. Of course, the percentage of his total income that a person spends for current consumption may be influenced by factors that affect his willingness to save, and the rate of income expenditure for low-income groups may even change with different phases of the business cycle.

There seems to be a general tendency for families in income groups above $1,000 a year to increase their consumption as their income increases, but not by as much as the increase in their income, so that there will be a gap between income and consumption. This tendency or "psychological propensity" has been called by

J. M. Keynes the "propensity to consume." [1] From statistical studies, such as that in Table 14, there is evidence that the gap between income and consumption expenditures tends to increase, as a rule and on the average, the higher up the family is in the scale of income levels. At least the percentage of total income saved seems generally to increase with the size of the family income between the $1,000 and $100,000 income levels. The investigations of Professor C. C. Zimmerman of rural and urban families in Minnesota led him to conclude that, especially for farm families, there is a distinct tendency for savings to increase more rapidly than consumption expenditures with a rise in the family income.[2] Of course, the relationship between family income and savings or consumption expenditures is not uniform for all families with the same income nor the same for a family under all circumstances.

Actual and expected consumption, along with the rate of investment, determine the volume of output and employment. As Keynes points out, the more wealthy a community is, the weaker is the propensity to consume likely to be and, therefore, the wider will be the gap between consumption and income.[3] A poorer community is much more prone to spend most of its income for consumption goods. Also, the problem of providing sufficient new investment to fill the gap between income and consumption may be more difficult in a country already well developed. There may not be the same opportunities to invest savings in new capital equipment in a well-to-do community and in a mature economy that there are in new, less developed areas that are growing rapidly in population. At least, the decline in total demand or the general rate of spending may be much greater, in percentage terms, in a comparatively rich country, so that the difference between actual and potential production may be more marked in such countries.

[1] "There is ambiguity as to the precise meaning Keynes attaches to the phrase 'propensity to consume.' Sometimes it appears to mean the relation between the absolute level of income and consumption, and sometimes the relation between changes in these categories [a *marginal* propensity to consume]; sometimes to the actual consumption out of actual income; and sometimes to the anticipated consumption out of an increase in incomes." Lauchlin Currie in *The Economic Doctrines of John Maynard Keynes*, National Industrial Conference Board, 1938, p. 18.

[2] *Cf. Consumption and Standards of Living*, 1936, Chapter 13, and *University of Minnesota Bulletin*, Nos. 253 and 255. *Cf.* also, Elizabeth W. Gilboy, "The Propensity to Consume," *Quarterly Journal of Economics*, vol. 53 (November 1938), pp. 120–40; and "The Propensity to Consume: Comment and Reply," *ibid.* (August 1939), pp. 632–38.

[3] J. M. Keynes, *The General Theory of Employment, Interest and Money*, p. 31.

The problem of unemployment and idle equipment, which has popularly been termed "poverty in the midst of plenty," seems to be directly tied up either with insufficient propensity to consume, or insufficient inducement to invest, or both.

The problem of unemployment troubled Thomas Malthus early in the nineteenth century. In 1821 he said: "We see in almost every part of the world vast powers of production which are not put into action, and I explain this phenomenon by saying that, from the want of a proper distribution of the actual produce, adequate motives are not furnished to continued production." [1] Improper distribution of income, he thought, would cause too much saving, which might "be prejudicial to a country," because excess saving impairs "the usual motives to production." In his own words: "If every person were satisfied with the simplest food, the poorest clothing, and the meanest houses, it is certain that no other sort of food, clothing, and lodging would be in existence." [2]

A century earlier Bernard Mandeville, in an allegorical poem entitled the *Fable of the Bees*, had expressed similar fears that a prosperous exchange economy might be brought to a state of stagnation and widespread unemployment through frugal saving and a reluctance to spend freely. In the comment following his poem Mandeville stated:

As this prudent economy, which some people call *Saving*, is in private families the most certain method to increase an estate, so some imagine that, whether a country be barren or fruitful, the same method if generally pursued (which they think practicable) will have the same effect upon a whole nation, and that, for example, the English might be much richer than they are, if they would be as frugal as some of their neighbors. This, I think, is an error.[3]

The classical economists reasoned with Adam Smith that "what is prudence in the conduct of every private family can scarce be folly in that of a great Kingdom." They thereby fell into the error, discussed in Chapter 2, of reasoning by analogy from the individual to society in general. Because persons can better their economic positions by economizing and accumulating savings, it was assumed that society as a whole would better itself by pursuing the

---

[1] A letter from Malthus to Ricardo, dated July 7, 1821.

[2] Malthus, *Principles of Political Economy* (second edition), 1836, Preface, pp. 8, 9.

[3] "Remark Q," *The Fable of the Bees: or, Private Vices, Public Benefits* (sixth edition), 1732, vol. 1, pp. 197–98.

same principle—by economizing and being thrifty. But if every
one in a community should economize by reducing his expenditures for consumption, it might prove disastrous for the economy.
Certainly if there was a general decline in the demand for consumers' goods, it would not be profitable to save and invest in capital equipment—to increase the power to produce more consumption goods.

Because some individuals, through credit devices, lived beyond
their means in the 1920's and had to default on their debts, many
persons became convinced that people in general must be content
with simpler and lower living standards. As the Brookings Institution economists indicate, such a notion, based on reasoning from
the particular to the general, confuses two distinct issues: the level
of expenditures that particular persons can support out of the share
they receive of the country's total income, and the general level of
consumption that our productive resources are capable of supporting if people, in general, spend and invest their incomes rapidly
enough.[1] It is not economy, but waste, to reduce expenditures so
that capital equipment and man power are idle. In a true economic sense, the community can afford to consume all that can
possibly be produced without impairing its capital equipment.

The austere doctrine that a community cannot afford to live as
well as possible is rooted in traditional teachings concerning the
virtue of individual thrift. Widespread saving may be harmless,
even socially desirable, in periods of economic expansion, when economic resources are not idle and opportunities for profitable investment are never lacking. But in a period when unemployment is
widespread, increased savings may be wasteful, and "sound" precepts of personal finance may lead to general bankruptcy.

It is trite to say that our economic troubles are due, not to a lack
of productive capacity, but to faults in the distributive or market
mechanism. Some of these distributive difficulties, without doubt,
arise out of the wide inequality in the distribution of income. It
has been argued that economic progress might be stimulated by
greater equality in incomes and wealth. Some economists believe
that more equitable distribution of incomes would tend to stabilize
the rate of spending and also to speed up spending by increasing the
community's propensity to consume. Of course, the rate of spend-

[1] H. G. Moulton, *Income and Economic Progress*, 1935, pp. 60–61.

ing in a community is affected by many other factors, including the general expectation concerning economic conditions; but the possibility and likelihood that some expenditures will be postponed is much greater, the more unequally the total income of the community is divided.

One of the chief social justifications for great inequality in wealth and incomes has been that the savings of the rich were required for capital accumulation and expansion. But, as Keynes concludes, "in contemporary conditions the growth of wealth, so far from being dependent on the abstinence of the rich, as is commonly supposed, is more likely to be impeded by it." [1] Up to the point where full employment prevails, the growth of capital depends, in considerable measure, upon increases in expenditures for consumption. The inducement to invest is related to the propensity to consume. Measures that tend to equalize incomes are likely to raise the propensity to consume and, by increasing the rate of expenditures for consumption, tend to stimulate economic prosperity and the growth of capital.

[1] Keynes, *op. cit.*, p. 373.

CHAPTER TEN

THE THEORY OF UNEMPLOYMENT

Unemployment represents a failure to make a sale of labor services. Failure to sell such services may arise for any one of a large number of reasons. Consequently, the alleged "causes" of unemployment are almost innumerable, and some of the stated causes are mutually inconsistent. For example, the following factors are mentioned among various "causes of unemployment" in a recent textbook on labor: inflexible or monopolistic prices that are kept too high, falling prices that perpetuate the "vicious spiral of deflation," "continued insistence on high wage rates," taxes that "seem unduly high," "high profits to employers or large stockholders," "inequality in income distribution, which leads to over-saving," and lack of sufficient demand for consumers' goods.[1]

Generally speaking, it is rather difficult to understand how costs such as wages and taxes could be too high at the same time that profits were also too high. Likewise it might seem somewhat inconsistent to say that both high prices and rapidly falling prices cause unemployment, or to state that wages are too high and in the same breath to complain that the rich are receiving such large incomes that too much is being saved and too little spent for consumers' goods, or to assert that lower wage rates, by restoring or preserving profit margins, would lead to more employment, while at the same time it is stated that a more equitable distribution of income is needed to reduce unemployment.

It is possible that some or all of these seemingly contradictory statements can be reconciled. For any such reconciliation, however, a framework of analysis is required in order to discover what role each factor plays in a complete theory of unemployment. Without such a framework for analyzing the unemployment problem,

[1] Carroll R. Daugherty, *Labor Problems in American Industry* (fourth edition), 1938, pp. 76, 86–88, 90, and 94.

the student, faced with hundreds of alleged causes of unemployment, would find himself, like the drunk who was unable to stagger past two trees, "lost in an impenetrable forest."

In the development of such a frame of reference, the chief problem is to integrate monopolistic-competition theory with monetary theory. These two types of economics have developed more or less independently, so they seem to be two worlds of theory almost completely divorced from one another. Monopolistic-competition theory, which was discussed briefly in Chapter 5, is concerned with the adjustment of individual firms to market situations. From such individual-firm analysis is derived the theory of monopoly, the principle of maximizing profits, the theory of individual prices and wage rates, and the theory of income distribution. The fundamental weakness of partial analysis of the individual-firm or particular-product type is that it is static theory based on the assumption that demand in general remains unchanged, that every individual continues to spend or invest all his income. Consequently, conclusions based upon partial analysis tend to emphasize expenditures as costs rather than as income or purchasing power and to stress the need for reducing costs in order to maintain profit margins.

Monetary theory, on the other hand, is concerned with changes in the aggregate money demand for all goods and services. It is dynamic theory, dealing with general changes that affect all industry, such as fluctuations in the money supply, in the rate of monetary turnover, in the rate of interest, in the rate of investment, and in the general price level. Monetary analysis, therefore, applies to the economy as a whole and cannot, like partial analysis of the individual-firm type, be based on the assumption that all other things (especially total effective demand) remain unchanged. Because he deals with factors affecting the general rate of spending, the monetary theorist is likely to look at larger expenditures as a means of speeding up the circulation of money and of increasing incomes, rather than as an increase in costs, and his conclusions may seem "unsound" to individual businessmen, who usually reason from the particular case to the general situation.

This distinction between monetary or general analysis and individual or partial analysis in economics can perhaps be explained best by an illustration. Failure to sell a particular product may result from the fact that its price is too high compared with the prices of competing products. Sales of that product could be stimulated by a relative reduction of its price, in which case its market would expand at the expense of sales of other products. A widespread or general lack of sales, however, can hardly be because all prices are too high. To high relative to what? Total purchasing power represented by the money supply? Total money incomes? Total demand as indicated by aggregate money expenditures? Furthermore, if all prices were reduced by the same ratio, no product would gain at the expense of other products and it is questionable whether such a general reduction would result in the sale of a larger volume of goods and services. A lower price level might simply mean proportionately lower incomes.[1] Movements of individual prices relative to one another may help to adjust the supply of a product to the demand or *vice versa*, but movements in the general level of prices may only aggravate a maladjusted situation, goods generally being purchased more readily and rapidly on a rising price level than on a falling one.

To which of these two realms of theory the problem of unemployment belongs has been an unsettled question. It will be necessary in this chapter to indicate the role that actions of individual firms play in determining the volume of unemployment and to explain the influence upon employment and unemployment exerted by general monetary considerations that affect all firms. Some sort of a synthesis between monetary and monopolistic-competition theory is required in order to analyze the problem of unemployment, because there are interactions and interrelations between the policies pursued by individual firms and changes in total money incomes and expenditures. In working out such a synthesis, it may be well to start with a discussion of certain historical and factual material, which will serve as a guide to straight thinking on the question of unemployment.

SOME PERTINENT FACTS

Under the guild system in England, before the guilds became exclusive and began to decline in importance, the townspeople were not troubled by periodic and widespread unemployment. The guild

---

[1] As indicated in the next section, incomes were so reduced in Norway and Denmark during the period from 1925 to 1928 when the price level was reduced about 50 per cent.

restrictions on competition, on control of the local market, on subdivision of the work, and on changes in technique helped to assure
each guildsman of some share of the orders of customers. Consequently, there was no wide inequality in income and wealth in the
towns. Because his sales income was not split up into various costs
(rent, wages, interest, etc.) and profits, the guildsman did not close
up his shop whenever a profits share, amounting to, say, 10 per
cent of his total yearly receipts, disappeared. Like the present-day
farmer, he would have thrown himself out of a job by shutting up
the business or even by reducing the scale of his operations to, say,
40 per cent of capacity.

However, with the development of a money and exchange
economy, accompanied by the rise of a merchant capitalist class,
periods of widespread unemployment began to plague the English
economy. With production for a profit and production in advance
of sales in a wide market, variations in market conditions caused
periodic fluctuations in sales, in the rate of production, and in the
employment offered to the wage-earning class, who were dependent
upon their specialized jobs for a livelihood. During the reign of
Queen Elizabeth in the latter half of the sixteenth century, unemployment and poverty had become so widespread that a series of
poor laws were passed to meet the problem.

Depressions. There were severe business depressions in this
country as early as 1720 and 1730.[1] The depression of 1720–1723
caused a "general damp" of trade in all the Middle Colonies except New York, which seems to have avoided the depression through
previous currency issues and by being the only Middle Colony on
a paper-money standard. In Pennsylvania, New Jersey, and Delaware, there was widespread complaint about "miserable markets,"
the "stagnation" of trade, and the scarcity of coins which were
"hoarded up." According to a writer at that time, Pennsylvania
had "never been under such low circumstances for want of trade
and money." "Both artificers and traders" migrated from the
Middle Colonies "in search of employment" and shipyards were

---

[1] The facts and quotations in this and the following paragraph are taken from two
articles on colonial currency issues and depressions, written by the author. *Cf.* "Cur-
rency Issues to Overcome Depressions in Pennsylvania, 1723 and 1729," *Journal of
Political Economy*, vol. 46 (June 1938), pp. 324–75; and "Currency Issues to Overcome
Depressions in Delaware, New Jersey, New York and Maryland, 1715–37," *Journal of
Political Economy*, vol. 47 (April 1939), pp. 182–217.

"almost empty," so that shipbuilders and carpenters nearly "starved for want of work." Currency issues in these colonies in 1723 and 1724, however, did "much good by increasing trade," so that "artificers found employment" and shipbuilders again enjoyed "full employment at their trade."

"Hard times" returned to the Middle Colonies in 1729 and 1730, when markets again were "glutted with goods" and people were "pinched by a stagnation of the currency." Once more "honest and industrious tradesmen were reduced to poverty for want of employ," and again currency issues stimulated business, causing a more "speedy" circulation of the money. This early American experience indicates that over 200 years ago, when our population was relatively sparse and before a large wage-earning class and large business corporations were in existence, the country suffered periodically from business depressions during which producers and merchants could not sell their wares and craftsmen could not sell their labor. Writers at that time blamed the depressions and dull markets on the "scarcity of money" and the tendency to hoard coins.

A detailed study of business cycles in a number of countries since 1790 shows that periods of depression seem to occur rather generally throughout the world at about the same time.[1] Therefore, any explanation of depressional unemployment apparently would have to be based on conditions common to all countries rather than on circumstances peculiar to any one. This tendency for depressions to seize most countries in the same year seems to have been especially marked in the decades just before the first World War, when practically the entire world was on the gold standard.

Since the first World War, the pattern of depressions throughout the world has been somewhat less regular. Finland completely avoided, and Germany, Austria, and France in large measure escaped from, the 1921 depression through paper-money issues and currency inflation.[2] Denmark and Norway brought on a very severe

[1] Cf. Willard L. Thorp, *Business Annals*, 1926, especially Chart 6, pp. 94–95. This chart, indicating business cycles in a large number of countries, shows that the following were periods of general depression in various countries: 1797–1799, 1816–1820, 1837–1843, 1847–1849, 1857–1859, 1866–1868, 1874–1878, 1883–1886, 1893–1896, 1907–1909, 1913–1914, 1920–1922.

[2] Cf. R. A. Lester, "The Gold-Parity Depression in Norway and Denmark, 1925–28," *Journal of Political Economy*, vol. 45 (August 1937), pp. 462–64; and "A Rejoinder," *Journal of Political Economy*, vol. 45 (December 1937), pp. 810–13.

depression in 1925–1928, when the rest of the world was enjoying a period of prosperity, by returning to the gold standard at a figure representing the prewar gold content of the Danish and Norwegian crowns.[1] This meant almost doubling the gold value of these currencies. The Danish and Norwegian price levels dropped almost 50 per cent, but these countries were no better off with a lower price level because incomes had, in general, fallen by a corresponding amount. By being on a silver standard, and because silver was falling in value, China escaped for two years the "world-wide" depression of 1929, which affected adversely all gold-standard countries. All the business indexes in China continued to rise until toward the end of 1931, when the price level began to fall as silver appreciated in value.[2] Such facts seem to indicate that money, monetary standards, and price-level movements play a significant role in the business cycle and that monetary theory must be an important element in any explanation of depressional unemployment.

Generally speaking, the countries that recovered first from the depression of the early 1930's were the countries like Sweden, Japan, Australia, and England that left the gold standard first. Commenting on the "lessons of the slump" in his annual report for 1937, the Director of the International Labour Office at Geneva stated:

If the depression has shown one thing more clearly than anything else it is that economic prosperity and social security depend more on monetary policy than on any other single factor. . . .

. . . The demonstration that in one country after another the upturn in business and employment coincided not with the reduction of wage-rates, the cutting of costs or the deterioration of working conditions but with the abandonment of deflation and the adoption of monetary expansion has made a deep impression upon the world.[3]

He also found from a study of the movement of wage rates and employment in eight representative countries from 1929 to 1937 that there is no simple and direct relationship between the level of wage rates and the volume of unemployment. Indeed, the

[1] *Cf.* Lester, "The Gold-Parity Depression in Norway and Denmark, 1925–28," pp. 433–65.

[2] *Cf.* Sir Arthur Salter, "China and Silver," *Economic Forum*, vol. 2 (Spring 1934), Section 2, pp. 1–117.

[3] *Report of the Director*, International Labour Office, 1937, pp. 13, 41.

experience of some countries seemed to contradict the theory that wage-cutting would tend to prevent unemployment. In Sweden and the United Kingdom "there was little or no decline in wage rates, and yet in both countries employment fell relatively little and made an excellent recovery" and, "in the United States, when wage rates fell employment fell also, and when wage rates rose employment also rose—a double denial of the theory." [1]

For the benefit of those who believe that high wage rates in comparison with prices are the cause of recent depressions, Professor Paul Douglas points out that the two major depressions of 1920 and 1929 occurred at a time when the prices of manufacturing services were increasing much more rapidly than were labor costs and that, therefore, from the wage-price standpoint, conditions were favorable to the capitalistic groups—at least in the manufacturing sector of our economy. From 1919 to 1920, the average price received by manufacturers for fabricating and processing increased 32 per cent compared with a 15-per-cent increase in labor costs per unit of output. From 1927 to 1929, the price of fabricating and processing rose 3 per cent in the face of a 4-per-cent fall in labor costs. The latter condition, Douglas believes, "is presumptive evidence of a large degree of imperfect competition, quasi-monopoly, and oligopoly." [2]

Concentration in capital-goods industries. Depressional unemployment is much more extreme in producers' or capital-goods industries than in consumers' goods industries, partly perhaps because of the acceleration principle. Cyclical fluctuations in employment, in production, and, to some extent, in prices seem to be wider in range the further the industry is from the consumer and the more durable (long-lived) is the product. Wholesale prices fluctuate more than retail prices; raw-material prices are more flexible than the prices of finished products. The physical volume of production of durable products contracted three fourths between 1929 and 1932 compared with a drop of one fourth for nondurable products. Between the same two years, the physical volume of agricultural production declined but 1 per cent compared with a 38-per-cent decline in mining, a 44-per-cent decline in manufacturing, and a 68-per-

[1] *Ibid.*, pp. 29–32.

[2] Paul H. Douglas, "The Effect of Wage Increases upon Employment," *American Economic Review*, vol. 29 (March 1939) supplement, pp. 156–57.

cent decline in construction.[1] A considerable proportion of all agricultural products are, of course, consumers' goods, some of which are not durable. Table 15 indicates the percentage of the labor force that was unemployed in different sectors of the economy at certain times.

TABLE 15. PERCENTAGE OF LABOR FORCE UNEMPLOYED BY MAJOR INDUSTRIES [2]

	Jan. 1930	March 1933	Sept. 1937	May 1938
Agriculture	10.5	14.5	2.7	10.2
Forestry and fishing	14.0	53.0	26.0	39.1
Extraction of minerals	1.5	41.4	24.1	37.3
Manufacturing	8.0	40.3	8.3	27.7
Construction	24.1	73.3	42.0	55.0
Transportation	5.6	39.7	22.5	37.1
Public utilities	0.4	29.0	22.1	27.2
Trade, distribution, and finance	—	22.9	13.8	18.5
Service	—	16.2	1.3	1.8
Miscellaneous	4.0	33.2	12.8	24.2

Professor Douglas believes that the capital-goods industries are much more subject to monopoly, duopoly, triopoly, and oligopoly than are the consumers' goods industries, and he cites some figures showing that from 50 to 100 per cent of all output is controlled by one, two, three, or four firms in the following lines of production: automobiles, beef products, cans, cigarettes, copper, corn binders and planters (agriculture implements), plate and safety glass, iron ore, steel, and whisky.[3] It is questionable, however, whether there is less concentration of economic control in consumers' goods industries than in capital-goods industries. In the above list, beef products, cigarettes, and whisky are consumers' goods. Some consumers' services, such as electricity, telephone, and natural gas, are subject to monopoly control. Furthermore, the effects of monopoly are partly achieved in the sale of consumers' goods through the

[1] Cf. J. K. Galbraith and J. D. Black, "The Maintenance of Agricultural Production during Depression: The Explanations Reviewed," Journal of Political Economy, vol. 46 (June 1938), p. 305. This article examines the reasons for the maintenance of agricultural production during depressions.

[2] Taken from Reports on Public Assistance to the Administrator, Works Progress Administration for the City of New York, March 14, 1939, Table 4, pp. 36–37. The source of these statistics is the National Industrial Conference Board.

[3] Cf. op. cit., p. 150; and Verbatim Record of the Proceedings of the Temporary National Economic Committee, vol. 1 (December 1, 1938 to January 20, 1939), Bureau of National Affairs, Inc., 1939, pp. 80–81. It is interesting to note that labor unions have been strong for some time in bituminous coal and women's clothing, in which the largest four companies control 10 and 2 per cent respectively of total output.

branding of food products, such as cereals, coffee, crackers, etc., and partly through legal restrictions upon price flexibility, such as resale price-maintenance laws. The explanation for the more steady employment and production in consumers' goods and consumers' services industries is to be found, not so much in the price policies of employers and their control over the markets for their products, as in the fact that a certain minimum production of consumers' goods and services is necessary to sustain the present population. The same statement is not, however, true of the production of capital goods. As was indicated in the discussion of the acceleration principle, capital construction might decline almost to zero with little or no drop in the production of consumers' goods, but the production of consumers' goods could not drop off in the same fashion without widespread misery and starvation.

Persistent, large-scale unemployment. A striking characteristic of the 1920's and 1930's was the phenomenon of widespread unemployment for long periods of time. Table 16 indicates how significant was this problem of wholesale unemployment in England during both decades and in the United States after 1929. As

TABLE 16. AVERAGE YEARLY PERCENTAGE OF LABOR FORCE UNEMPLOYED IN GREAT BRITAIN AND THE UNITED STATES [1]

Years	Great Britain	United States
1851–1860	4.8	
1861–1870	5.4	
1871–1880	3.7	
1881–1890	4.9	
1891–1900	4.5	
1901–1910	5.0	6.1
1911–1920	2.1	5.1
1921–1930	12.0	4.8
1931–1939	15.8	17.5
1930	16.1	7.8
1931	21.3	16.3
1932	22.1	24.9
1933	19.9	25.1
1934	16.7	20.2
1935	15.5	18.4
1936	13.1	14.5
1937	10.9	12.0
1938	12.6	18.8
1939	10.3	16.7

[1] Figures for Great Britain represent the percentage of unemployed among trade-union members (1851–1925) and the percentage of workers covered by unemployment insurance who were unemployed (1926–1939). *Cf.* Wladimir Woytinsky, *Three*

explained in the footnote to this table, the percentage figures for both countries are not comparable and those for the United States are more conservative than some other estimates. The table shows that unemployment in Great Britain averaged over 14 per cent between 1920 and 1939, or three times the pre-1920 average, and that it continued above 10 per cent in the latter part of the 1930's when England was supposed to be enjoying a great prosperity boom. Much the same situation has prevailed in the United States since 1929. The business boom of 1936–1937 failed to reduce unemployment below 13 per cent of the labor supply. It is a strange situation to find one out of every seven or eight workers unemployed during periods of so-called prosperity in the two wealthiest countries of the world.

Any theory of unemployment must attempt to account for the existence of long-time underemployment or economic stagnation during recent periods. Some English economists have tried to explain the existence of a large volume of unemployment in Great Britain from 1925 to 1929 (over one tenth of all persons covered by unemployment insurance were unemployed during those years) on the grounds that restoration of the currency to prewar gold parity in 1925 meant a 10-per-cent deflation for the English economy, but others have questioned whether equilibrium with widespread underemployment in England during that period can be explained primarily by monetary policy.[1]

THE EQUILIBRIUM THEORY OF UNEMPLOYMENT

As has been indicated, economists differ in their diagnosis of unemployment. Such differences in diagnosis arise, in large part, out of the type of analysis used in attacking the problem. Two fundamentally different methods of approach have been applied. They might be called the "equilibrium" approach and the "monetary"

Sources of Unemployment, International Labour Office, Studies and Reports, Series C, No. 20, 1935; and current issues of the International Labour Review. Figures for the United States represent a conservative estimate of the percentage of the whole labor force that was unemployed during these years. Cf. Reports on Public Assistance to the Administrator, Works Progress Administration for the City of New York, March 14, 1939, Table 1, p. 28; and National Industrial Conference Board, The Conference Board Economic Record, vol. 2 (March 20, 1940), p. 78.

[1] Cf., for example, J. M. Keynes, Essays in Persuasion, 1932, Part 3 (The Return to the Gold Standard), especially section 5; and Rufus S. Tucker, "Mr. Keynes' Theories Considered in the Light of Experience," in The Economic Doctrines of John Maynard Keynes, National Industrial Conference Board, 1938, pp. 29–35.

approach. An economist's reasoning and conclusions on the problem of unemployment are bound to be influenced by his approach—
his preconceptions, frame of reference, and methods and instru-
ments of analysis. For instance, the "equilibrium" economists have
been prone to place most of the blame for the "extra" or "excessive" unemployment in England during the late 1920's, not upon
monetary conditions (an overvalued currency resulting from return
to the gold standard), but upon wage rates, which, over a wide
area, had been set at a level considered "too high" to allow an
"equilibrium between the demand for and the supply of labor." [1]
It was suggested that labor unions and intervention by the government in the form of minimum-wage legislation and unemployment
insurance, which strengthened the bargaining power of unions,
were responsible for the abnormal volume of unemployment by
maintaining wage rates above the "economic" or "equilibrium"
level.

The concept of equilibrium. The notion of equilibrium or
balance of forces represents a mechanical analogy applied to economic affairs. In mechanics, disturbing forces will cause an object
to move along the line of the resultant until it again comes to rest.
In like manner, it has been argued, changes in the economic forces
of demand and supply will cause prices to move and come to rest
at the point where demand and supply are again adjusted, where
the volume demanded and supplied is equal so that the price clears
the market. Only some "artificial" interference or restraint can
prevent this "natural" norm of equilibrium from being reestablished
after each "disturbing" change.

Such an equilibrium analysis must explain the existence of unused resources or unemployment in terms of "disturbances" to
equilibrium, "friction" and "maladjustments" during periods of
transition from one equilibrium to another, or "artificial" restrictions, which prevent price movements from establishing equilibrium. Consequently, equilibrium economists, in discussing unemployment, stress the maldistribution of economic resources, the lack
of mobility of labor, the existence of monopoly and rigidities in the
price system, and governmental interference that serves to prevent
prices and wage rates from falling. With the perfectly flexible

[1] *Cf.*, for instance, A. C. Pigou, "Wage Policy and Unemployment," *Economic Journal*,
vol. 37 (September 1927), pp. 355–68.

prices of the perfect market, considerable unemployment, in the opinion of these economists, could occur only from the failure of labor to move fast enough into new firms, new industries, or new localities, with changes in consumer demand and the structure of industry.

Equilibrium analysis may be applied to only a small part of the economy—to one firm, one industry, or one area. It has also been applied to the economy as a whole. Partial equilibrium analysis attempts to explain the short-run and long-run adjustments that will take place to restore equilibrium locally when, for instance, industry in one locality is put at a relative disadvantage by an increase in local property taxes, an increase in local wage rates, or a drop in the price of the locality's most important product. Such partial analysis assumes no change in economic conditions outside the locality with local adjustments—no general change. General equilibrium analysis attempts to explain the effect of various disturbances upon the system as a whole. It assumes that, at a certain set of relationships among all prices (including wage and interest rates), demand and supply will be equalized in all lines. This "solution," which clears all markets and permits the full employment of all factors of production, is, according to this type of analysis, the norm toward which economic forces are directing the economy.

Criticism of equilibrium analysis. The equilibrium approach assumes that there is a price or set of prices which will clear the market, and that economic forces are tending to push prices toward such an equilibrating norm.

1. *Aggravating price movements.* In reality, price movements may so alter the general situation that it is erroneous to assume that price changes are "tending" to restore or maintain any mechanical sort of equilibrium. For instance, a rise in the price of a security on the stock market may stimulate an increase in demand, leading to a larger rather than a smaller volume of sales, and so on in a cumulative fashion.[1] In some cases, as was indicated in Chapter 5, there may be no price or wage that will clear the market. Failure of demand and supply to meet at any price or wage may result when the demand and the supply curves are sloping in the same direction

[1] For a further discussion of price movements that tend to perpetuate disequilibrium under certain conditions and the formulation of the "cobweb theorem" with regard to such phenomena, *cf.* A. M. McIsaac and J. G. Smith, *Introduction to Economic Analysis*, 1937, pp. 378–84.

or when employers maintain the same fixed staff of workers for technological and other reasons. Again, as indicated in Chapter 5, demand and supply may meet at a number of prices or over a whole range of prices. Emil Lederer points out that a firm may also be in equilibrium at several points whenever, because of the existence of excess capacity or certain technological conditions, it can produce at diminishing unit costs, so that profits will be equally large with high prices and a small output or low prices and a large output.[1]

The rate of interest has been cited as a price whose movements do not tend to clear the market. As indicated in Chapter 9, it is possible that a fall in the rate of interest, down to a certain minimum, might increase the supply of savings, partly because security ownership becomes more profitable as outstanding securities rise in price when they are being discounted at a lower market rate of interest. It is on such grounds that Professor J. M. Clark concludes that changes in the level of interest rates may not tend to maintain equilibrium or to prevent "oversaving." People save very largely for security, which is not the chief motive that induces businessmen to borrow and invest in new capital equipment. Consequently, uncertainty or risk, which may make businessmen hesitate to invest, may cause savers to try to save more and, therefore, act as "a potent engine of disequilibrium."[2] The actions of every individual in the economy tend to affect the rate of interest, for it influences decisions to save rather than to spend money for consumption and, as the premium for not hoarding, it tends to influence hoarding and the rate of investment.

Although individual price movements may tend to adjust demand to supply so that the market is cleared, general price movements, such as changes in the price level, the level of wage rates, or the level of interest rates, frequently aggravate a maladjusted situation rather than correct it by restoring balance or equilibrium. A sharp downward movement in the price level, instead of stimulating demand, may lead to hoarding, smaller incomes, and a smaller volume of sales—a vicious spiral of deflation. That, for example, was what happened in Norway and Denmark from 1925 to 1928 when the price level was reduced almost 50 per cent. Incomes, employment,

---

[1] *Technological Progress and Unemployment*, International Labour Office, Studies and Reports, Series C, No. 22, 1938, p. 132.

[2] J. R. Hicks, "Mr. Keynes' Theory of Employment," *Economic Journal*, vol. 46 (June 1936), p. 250.

and production declined because production for a cash market is, in part, a speculation on the general level of prices when the finished product is sold.

As the discussion in Chapter 5 indicated, the short-run supply curve for labor as a whole has a negative slope, which means that at lower wage rates a larger supply of hours of labor will be offered for sale. Under such circumstances it is possible that there would be some unemployment at any conceivable level of wages, for movements in the wage level call forth just the reverse response from the supply side to that necessary for a restoration of equilibrium between the aggregate demand and the total supply.

2. *Hoarding and equilibrium.* Hoarding has already been defined as a decrease in the rate of turnover of cash and checking accounts. People hold their money instead of spending or investing it. By reducing the rate of circulation of money, hoarding reduces money incomes during a period of time and, therefore, leads to sales reductions and price declines.

Equilibrium economists generally have failed to appreciate that hoarding causes total receipts to be less than total costs during a period of time, because a portion of the funds paid out by producers as costs is withheld from the market and is not used for the purchase of products. Although under these circumstances the price level may fall, such a price-level decline may stimulate further hoarding and lead to a "vicious spiral of deflation," or it may at least result in equilibrium at underemployment of economic resources. Some equilibrium economists, overlooking the fact that reductions in the rate of spending mean reductions in incomes, have maintained that "stable underemployment equilibrium" is only possible when there is "cost rigidity (including wage rates) and monopoly control of supplies." [1] Presumably they believe that reductions in the rate of spending are not possible under conditions of perfect competition and perfect markets. They overlook the fact that price-level changes can occur under perfect competition and that such changes are likely to alter the rate of spending and the size of money incomes. Money may be held as a speculation against such contingencies as changes in the price level, in interest rates, or in money incomes.

[1] *Cf.* Alvin H. Hansen, "Mr. Keynes on Under-Employment Equilibrium," *Journal of Political Economy*, vol. 44 (October 1936), p. 680; and H. Gordon Hayes, "Hoarding and the Competitive Equilibrium," *American Economic Review*, vol. 28 (March 1938), pp. 89–91.

Such speculative hoarding may, indeed, give rise to a cumulative tendency for incomes and the price level to decline, which, in turn, enhances the value of the hoarded dollar.

Professor Wesley Mitchell has pointed out that the proper conception of equilibrium is that of an income and expense statement, showing the difference between aggregate receipts and aggregate expenditures during a period of time and from one period to another.[1] When these two aggregates are out of balance, there may be no more tendency for economic forces to restore a balance than there is a tendency for businesses suffering losses one year to be restored to the profits column the next year.

3. *The concept of a cumulative process.* As early as 1898, Thorstein Veblen raised the question, "Why is economics not an evolutionary science?"[2] Veblen believed that economic theory should concern itself primarily with the process of economic development in terms of an unfolding sequence and cumulative change.

Recently a group of Swedish economists have been working on theories of the general process of economic expansion and contraction, as Veblen suggested.[3] Theirs is a sequence analysis of the general or "monetary" type, dealing with total income and output, the money supply and its rate of circulation, consumption expenditures, savings and investment, and the interaction among these factors, which are assumed to remain constant under partial equilibrium analysis. These economists point out that changes in the economic system as a whole cannot be explained by applying an equilibrium concept to each section of the economy separately, any more than changes in a person's health can be determined by studying each part of the body (arms, legs, and inner organs) separately. There are interactions among parts of the economy and general or "monetary" factors, so that an explanation of the total economic development cannot be derived by adding up the explanations of the development in each separate part of the economy, based on an equilibrium concept.

These younger Swedish economists point out that general equilib-

---

[1] *Cf. Business Cycles, the Problem and Its Setting,* 1928, pp. 186–88.

[2] *Cf. Quarterly Journal of Economics,* vol. 12 (July 1898), pp. 373–97.

[3] *Cf.,* for example, Erik Lundberg, *Studies in the Theory of Economic Expansion,* 1937; and Bertil Ohlin, "Some Notes on the Stockholm Theory of Savings and Investment," *Economic Journal,* vol. 47 (March and June 1937), pp. 53–69 and 221–40. This discussion of recent sequence analysis in Sweden rests largely upon these two publications.

rium analysis, based on a system of simultaneous equations which are supposed to give a "solution" that clears all markets, not only is a rather mystical and sterile method of analysis but falsely assumes that all actions and reactions occur simultaneously throughout the whole economy. Time and the speed with which reactions and interactions take place are very important in any analysis of the processes of economic change; ultimate consequences may be more significant than immediate effects. The longer is the period necessary for all interactions to work out completely, the greater will be the changes in total income and other general factors. Such changes would alter the demand and the supply schedules assumed for various products and upset any tendency toward equilibrium in a section of the economy. Also, buyers' plans, their expectations with regard to incomes and prices, and their readiness to purchase may be affected by the speed with which, and the manner in which, a certain series of reactions and adjustments take place.

Sequence or process analysis represents an altogether different approach from equilibrium analysis. It does not assume that the economic system is always tending toward some theoretical equilibrium. Whereas equilibrium analysis explains changes in the volume of unemployment by reference to monopoly and "friction" or lack of complete mobility, process analysis explains unemployment in terms of changes and circumstances that affect psychological reactions, which, in turn, determine the velocity of circulation of money and, therefore, total realized incomes. For instance, a large crop may cause the price of wheat to fall. Wheat farmers, anticipating lower incomes, may reduce their purchases, resulting in a decline in the demand for certain industrial products long before the drop in wheat prices lowers the retail price of wheat products. Smaller purchases by wheat farmers may lead to smaller incomes and receipts for industrial firms selling products to farmers. As a consequence, employment and investment may decline in such industrial lines, with unfavorable repercussions upon other segments of the economy, causing still smaller purchases and incomes. The importance of the effects of the decline in wheat prices upon the rest of the economy depends, of course, upon the rapidity with which such unfavorable reactions are transmitted to other branches of the economy through reduced purchases and incomes.

On the other hand, purchases and incomes may expand in a

cumulative fashion. Such an expansion might be caused by the expectation of a war boom. The more money people spend, the greater are total incomes, and the more people can spend. It is not true for the individual that the more he spends the more he will have to spend, but that is true for all people in the economy as a whole because collectively money incomes come from expenditures.[1] The expenditures of some persons make up the incomes of others; when some people spend less money, other people earn less money. A person's money holdings at the beginning of a period plus his money income during the period, along with his borrowing capacity, set the upper limit to what he can spend during the period. His plans and his expectations with regard to incomes, prices, etc., determine his willingness to spend up to that limit. The closer he and all others come to spending their limit during the period, the greater, of course, will be their incomes during that period—the more money they will be able to spend. Equilibrium analysis, because it assumes simultaneous change and neglects the time lag between the receipt and the expenditure of money, is not well adapted for a study of dynamic and cumulative changes. In an exchange economy, the rate of turnover of money and goods is an important element in the economics of unused resources. The expectation of a decline in sales at the end of a war may cause persons to decrease the rate at which they spend their money, thereby bringing on a business slump.

The role of monopoly. It has been assumed that monopoly also plays a significant part in any explanation of the unemployment or nonemployment of men, money, and machines.

Under perfect competition, price tends to equate demand and supply, but that is not true under monopoly. As Professor Edward Chamberlain and others have pointed out, excess capacity, unsold supply, and production below capacity may be permanent and normal characteristics of the equilibrium adjustment under monopoly or monopolistic competition (comparatively few firms producing special brands of the same product).[2] Unless there are so many

[1] As J. M. Keynes points out, "this is the significant difference between the theory of economic behavior in the aggregate and the theory of the behavior of the individual unit, in which it is assumed that changes in the individual's own demand do not affect his income." Cf. *The General Theory of Employment, Interest and Money*, p. 85.

[2] Cf. E. Chamberlain, *The Theory of Monopolistic Competition* (third edition), 1938, pp. 109 and 171; also, J. M. Cassels, "Excess Capacity and Monopolistic Competition,"

firms in an industry that no firm produces more than a negligible amount of the total output, price and production patterns tend to resemble those of monopoly rather than those of perfect competition.

As was indicated in Chapter 5, the price and production policies of a producer in a monopolistic or semimonopolistic position are governed more or less by the nature of his marginal-receipts curve, which has a downward slope in contrast with the horizontal marginal-receipts curve of a firm selling in a perfect market. And, if the demand curve for his product is a straight line sloping downward, the producer's marginal-receipts curve will fall twice as fast as the demand curve. It would seem that, with such demand conditions, the production of a commodity would be only half as large under monopoly as under competition, and half of the productive factors, including labor, would be unemployed. Joan Robinson, in discussing "a world of monopolies," maintains, however, that it is absurd, when production is generally operated under conditions of monopoly or semimonopoly, to assume that all outputs would be thus restricted. She states:

When we are considering one industry in isolation, we can find the monopoly output with the existing demand curve, but if output is restricted in all industries all demand curves will alter. The method which applies to one industry separately cannot be applied to all taken together.[1]

Mrs. Robinson is correct in maintaining that one cannot discover the effect of monopoly or semimonopolistic conditions in many industries upon unemployment simply by discovering what would happen to unemployment in one industry if that industry were changed from a position of perfect competition to one of monopoly or semimonopoly. Here again, the whole truth may not be simply the sum of the results found from studying each part (industry or firm) separately. Although she does not attempt to analyze the issue fully, Mrs. Robinson seems to assume that widespread monopoly would generally lead to larger monopoly profits and exploitation, through a reduction in the return to the factors of production like labor, rather than to a decrease in employment.[2] Yet she also writes:

Quarterly Journal of Economics, vol. 51 (May 1937), pp. 426–43. Excess capacity, as used here, means that some portion of all the factors of production are unused in the industry and, therefore, in the community.

[1] *Cf*. Joan Robinson, *The Economics of Imperfect Competition*, pp. 310 and 314.

[2] *Cf. ibid*., pp. 310–26.

It may be that a sudden and widespread introduction of restriction schemes [under monopoly] will lead to very prolonged and perhaps permanent unemployment. And it may be that the very imperfect mechanisms by which full employment can be re-established under competitive conditions would be even less effective under a régime of monopoly.[1]

Imperfect markets and monopolistic elements in industry may tend to reduce the total amount of employment in a closed economy [2] for four reasons. First, under monopoly, employment tends to be smaller because a firm's employment policy is governed by its marginal-receipts curve, which declines more sharply than the demand curve for the product. Second, large units of production and monopolistic conditions tend to reduce the possibility for the establishment of new firms or self-employment. Third, if monopoly leads to the exploitation of labor (larger profits and lower wages), it may make incomes more unequal and reduce total expenditures for consumption. Finally, it is possible that monopoly and rigid prices may stimulate and prolong depressions by preventing a balanced adjustment between selling prices and cost prices. As indicated in the discussion of the decline in wheat prices, a cumulative downward tendency may occur if prices decline and production is maintained in lines (like agriculture) having an inelastic demand at the same time that prices are maintained in industrial lines dominated by monopoly.

Prices are inflexible in imperfect markets for a number of reasons. Producers of branded products or oligopolists (a few producers of the same product) may maintain prices in order to avoid catalogue revisions, price wars, retaliatory actions by competitors, or a step that might offend dealers or customers.[3] They may believe, as automobile manufacturers do, that sales volume is governed largely by the trend and level of consumers' incomes and that price reductions would be ineffective in stimulating sales.[4] It has been con-

---

[1] *Ibid.*, p. 325.

[2] The assumption of a closed economy is made here in order to avoid, until the next chapter, an analysis of the effect of price and wage changes upon international trade.

[3] *Cf.* Chamberlain, *op. cit.*, p. 106, where he writes: "Business or professional 'ethics' are another factor. It has long been considered unethical in the professions to compete on the basis of price."

[4] *Cf. The Dynamics of Automobile Demand*, General Motors Corporation, 1939, pp. 4, 122. On p. 135 of this publication a General Motors official writes: "The fact of the matter is that the usual theory of the law of supply and demand frequently works in reverse, that is, when buyers believe prices will rise, buying increases. It is significant

cluded from an elaborate statistical study that the elasticity of demand for automobiles is somewhere between 0.65 and 2.5.[1] An elasticity of two would mean that a one-per-cent reduction in price would increase the quantity sold by two per cent. Assuming a demand elasticity of two, an official of General Motors Corporation has figured that a typical firm, breaking even in 1937, would lose money if it had reduced prices by five or ten per cent (assuming other firms followed suit), because the costs of producing the additional cars would have been greater than the additional income.[2] With wages around 12 per cent of total variable costs (or 10 per cent of total costs) [3] in the automobile industry, it is not likely that new employees would be taken on by an automobile concern, even at zero wages, if prices would have to be lowered to sell their added output. Certainly, whenever conditions approach unit elasticity (an elasticity of one) in the automobile industry, the added cost of more output would far exceed additional sales income, so that it would not pay to expand production and employment, although new workers could be had for nothing.

This discussion may indicate why industrial firms, instead of reducing prices in the face of falling demand, simply permit production and employment to fluctuate in a manner that tends to cause a cumulative contraction throughout the whole economy. It may also explain why employers with price policies may not continue to employ workers until wage rates rise to full "marginal productivity." Certainly it explains why, in industries dominated by monopolistic elements, employment cannot be increased much by wage reductions during a depression. Exactly how much monopolistic elements in our economy restrict the demand for labor is difficult to say.[4] But the existence of monopolistic policies helps to explain why the monetary demand for labor is not sufficient to prevent widespread unemployment.

that business activity is usually the greatest when prices are rising. When prices begin falling, however, most purchasers stop buying which makes a bad matter worse. Accordingly, I recommend that the proponents of the flexible prices theory give consideration to designing some scheme whereby all prices will promptly rise further when a depression begins so as to induce a scramble for the available supply of goods and thus arrest the developing depression!"

[1] Ibid., p. 123.   [2] Ibid., pp. 127, 131.

[3] Calculated from the figures in ibid., pp. 124, 127; and Biennial Census of Manufactures, 1935, 1937, p. 1150.

[4] For another discussion of this matter, cf. Price Behavior and Business Policy, Monograph No. 1, Temporary National Economic Committee, 1940, pp. 42–43, 51–52.

A GENERAL THEORY OF UNEMPLOYMENT

For the most part, a theory of unemployment must be a general or monetary theory rather than one built upon partial analysis and "frictions" or immobility. Labor, as a factor in production, really represents output in general rather than simply a particular kind of output. Consequently, there cannot be too much labor in the same sense that there can be too much cotton compared to other commodities.

A general theory of employment or unemployment must be based largely upon buyers' psychology and monetary demand. In that sense, the theory that is developed here is a demand theory, although any general theory of unemployment must take into account the characteristics of the labor supply as a whole. The discussion in this section rests heavily upon recent writings centered around J. M. Keynes' book on *The General Theory of Employment, Interest and Money*. It should help to draw together various parts of this and the preceding chapter.

Supply. As indicated in Chapter 5, the short-run supply schedule for labor as a whole, at least over part of its range, is negatively inclined. Consequently, the volume of employment and of unemployment may both be increasing or decreasing at the same time. Such a situation of more employment with more unemployment might be caused by married women and youths entering, and withdrawing from, the labor market. It might also arise simply because there will be during the next decade, as there has been during the past decades, a net addition to the labor supply of about 500,000 persons each year. Because the labor-supply curve has a negative slope, it is possible that "full" employment might occur at a number of levels of total employment.

Demand. In an exchange economy, total employment depends upon total expenditures or aggregate demand for goods and services. Aggregate demand may be divided into expenditures for consumption and investment expenditures for capital equipment. All production for a cash market is dependent upon consumption expenditures and investment expenditures, which represent an increase in productive equipment for the purpose of supplying goods and services during some future period. Investment is based upon the expectation of a certain sum of future expenditures for the product of the capital equipment, and, therefore, ultimately rests on expected expenditures for consumption.

Most incomes are derived from the production of goods and services designed either for consumption or to increase capital equipment. Generally speaking, production (costs and profits from production) furnishes the total incomes out of which aggregate money demand for goods and services arises. Aggregate demand is simply another name for total expenditures. These primary relationships in a market or exchange economy are indicated in the following diagram:

THE NORMAL FLOW OF MONEY IN AN EXCHANGE ECONOMY

production for $\left\{ \begin{array}{l} \text{consumption} \leftarrow \text{consumption} \\ \text{investment} \leftarrow\!\!\!-\!\!\!- \text{investment} \end{array} \right\}$ expenditures $\leftarrow\!\!\!\!\rceil$

└─────⟶ total income ─────⟶ aggregate demand ──────┘

The rate of speed with which money makes this circuit tends to determine total money incomes, the volume of sales, and total employment in the productive enterprise of the exchange economy. The velocity of circulation of money around this circuit, in turn, is determined largely by the plans and expectations of consumers and producers, upon their disposition to spend and invest (spend for capital equipment). Decisions to consume and decisions to invest together determine total money incomes and total employment. Hoarding (not spending, or delaying expenditures) slows down the normal flow of money, thereby decreasing money expenditures and incomes.

People's willingness to spend for consumption and nondurable goods depends, for the most part, upon consumers' income expectations, upon the relation between their realized income and the income they expected to receive, and upon expected changes in the price level. The disposition of producers in consumers' goods industries to invest in capital equipment or to produce more than is currently being sold (to produce for stock) depends largely upon their expectations concerning future profits, which are tied up with the expected expenditures for consumption, the future level of prices, the future interest rate on borrowed money, and anticipated changes in the technique of production. A producer investing at present would be at a disadvantage should the price and interest level fall or a new labor-saving machine be invented, so that competitors could obtain better capital equipment or the same equipment at a lower cost. For the most part, activity in the consumption-goods industries is governed, however, by current receipts and by the acceleration principle, which tends to determine investment in such industries.

Activity in the capital-goods industries may be less closely related to current expenditures. Long-term investments, such as the construction of railroads, ships, and commercial buildings, depend upon long-term expectations, which may be correlated not so much with short-term fluctuations in incomes as with expected changes in the growth of population and in the rate of interest. An increasing population stimulates long-term investment by practically assuring enterprisers of an expanding market for transportation services and building space. Consequently, an expanding population tends to increase employment by stimulating construction. A reduction in the rate of interest for loanable funds sharply reduces the yearly carrying costs of a building or other long-term investment, for interest on borrowed funds generally accounts for a large part of total carrying costs. An investor in capital equipment is interested in the rate of net return on the investment. A reduction in the rate of interest tends to increase the net return on capital investment and to make profitable investments that would be unprofitable at higher interest rates. New inventions and the development of new products may also promote new investment, partly by making existing capital equipment less valuable. Indeed, any striking "disequilibrium" arising from a shift in demand to different products would initiate and stimulate new investment. In such a manner, "disequilibrium" may create more employment.

Current production for a cash market and capital investment are both speculative in the sense that they are based on expectations; but investment, because it is a long-time proposition, is more risky and venturesome. That is one reason why capital investment fluctuates so widely during a business cycle. Once an investment in capital equipment has been made, the money has been "sunk" in the sense that the investment cannot be withdrawn if conditions and expectations change later on. The alternative to investing or spending one's money income is to hold on to it. Such hoarding of money is a particularly good speculation when there is a likelihood that the price level will fall. Holders of money balances gain from falling prices, while persons with debt commitments and durable equipment tend to suffer a relative loss. Money, because it represents generalized purchasing power and has little, if any, carrying cost, is a desirable asset in periods of uncertainty or economic slump. In one sense, interest is the reward that has to be offered to people for not hoarding, which, by slowing down the circulation of money, simply reduces money incomes. Consequently, unused savings may start a cumulative contraction in money incomes.

The expectations of consumers and enterprisers, through the acceleration and multiplier principles, may cause a cumulative expansion or contraction in money incomes and total employment. It is difficult to predict how changes in circumstances will affect consumers' and producers' expectations and, hence, the general rate of spending. Consequently, one cannot predict with positive assurance the effect on total employment of any particular action or program in an exchange economy, where all buyers can spend their money when and as they see fit. An action that stimulates both consumers and producers to spend rapidly would be the most effective in inducing an expansion in employment, although stimulus to either the consumption-goods or the capital-goods branch of industry is likely to be transmitted to the other branch because there is the cumulative interaction suggested by the acceleration and multiplier principles. Furthermore, if a substantial improvement in economic conditions is expected by people generally, it will tend to be realized, because such an expectation would lead to actions that would increase spending, incomes, and employment.

Either consumers or producer-employers can slow down the speed with which money moves around the circuit of the "normal flow." As already indicated, the expenditures of consumers practically determine the total volume of employment in the consumers' goods industries, especially for nondurable goods and for services. In such lines, an employer is likely to govern his cost expenditures by his sales income. That is also true, to a considerable extent, of employers in capital-goods industries, but the buyers of capital goods are themselves employers producing goods, so the relationship between capital-goods production and ultimate consumption expenditures is rather flexible, with leads and lags of varying lengths. Purchases of capital goods can generally be postponed. Consequently, although everyone is dependent upon the spending of everyone else in an exchange economy, the expectations and decisions of producer-employers are of much greater significance to the capital-goods than to the consumer-goods industries. In both branches of industry, of course, seasonal variations in purchases may lead to seasonal fluctuations in production and employment.[1]

The existence of partial monopoly, monopolistic competition, and very imperfect labor markets may affect the rate of spending of employers. With monopolistic elements in the economy, there may not be the same stimulus to expansion that exists when markets are more perfect. As indicated in Chapter 5, firms large enough to have tipped demand curves for their products and sloping supply curves for their labor factor are not likely to hire workers up to the point where workers are receiving their full marginal productivity. Consequently, employment in an industry is likely to be increased by eliminating monopolistic elements. Furthermore, in industries dominated by a few large firms, investment may be restricted through various pressures and threats by firms already in the industry. The prevalence of a policy of noncompetition in price and of price rigidity, along with the tendency toward bureaucracy and conservatism in large firms, has a dampening influence upon enterprise and, therefore, upon business spending and economic expansion.

Business spending, especially for capital equipment, is based, not so much upon cold calculation of mathematical expectation, as upon a "feeling" concerning the future that has been called "business confidence." The more economic power and business decisions are concentrated in the hands of a group of professional managers of large firms, the more will waves of optimism and pessimism affecting that class tend to cause waves in total business spending. In an exchange economy with production for profit, employers, for the most part, have to swim with the general stream of business, and the most successful ones are likely to be those who correctly anticipate which way the average person will move. In such an economy, the employer who expects a slump will not expand production and employment. Indeed, he may begin to curtail operations, which would, if widely practiced, help to bring about cumulative contraction and a business slump. In an economy where people are free to spend or hoard as they see fit, uncertainty of the future may cause business

[1] For a statistical analysis of seasonal fluctuations in employment and unemployment, cf. W. S. Woytinsky, *Seasonal Variations in Employment in the United States*, 1939.

managers to hesitate to hire more people or to make long-term commitments. Such hesitancy or inaction may reduce the rate of spending and investment, and result in hoarding, or a so-called "strike of capital."

In countries under a dictatorship, the general rate of spending may be more stable than in free, democratic countries, either because the psychological reactions of the people can be more closely controlled, or because the possibilities for hoarding or other anti-social inaction are more restricted, or because people are more prone to spend their money—to have a feast today rather than in the future. As the area in which individual initiative and freedom reign is reduced, the possibility for central control of the rate of spending is likely to increase. In so far as the government can cause private employers to hire workers and to produce more goods, even at a financial loss, it can also exert control over the rate of spending and employment. Where the central government owns important sections of the total economy, it may be in a better position to prevent marked changes in total expenditures. The government can continue to produce at a considerable loss, which it can cover by taxing the people. The rather complete control that the government has over business enterprise in Russia, for example, explains in large measure why that country was not plagued during the 1930's by widespread unemployment as were the more democratic, capitalistic countries.

In capitalistic countries, people can spend or hoard freely. They can pile up claims to goods and services which they may never utilize. They may forego dinner today without ordering one or two additional dinners on any future date. Consequently, total spending fluctuates, and expenditures may not be spread over time in a way that will create sufficient inducement or opportunity to invest in capital equipment so as to absorb rapidly all the funds that are not spent right away for consumption goods. In certain cases, it may seem desirable for the government to absorb idle funds and increase public investment by engaging in a public-works program. If there were political and practical difficulties preventing such a public-investment program, J. M. Keynes suggests that, rather than perpetuate idleness by doing nothing, it would be better to speed up the rate of spending by putting dollar bills in old bottles, burying them, say, in abandoned coal mines, and then permitting private enterprise to dig up the dollar bills at a profit. Such activity would increase employment and incomes, he points out, in the same manner as does gold mining—a pretext for digging holes in the ground that is approved as sound finance.[1]

[1] Keynes, *op. cit.*, pp. 129–30.

CHAPTER ELEVEN

WAGE RATES, EMPLOYMENT, AND THE BUSINESS CYCLE

As the discussion in the previous chapter has indicated, anything that serves to reduce total expenditures during a period of time may reduce total employment and, therefore, cause unemployment. That is why the alleged causes of unemployment seem innumerable. In a country with an expanding labor supply, factors preventing a corresponding expansion in total employment may also be said to cause unemployment. An analysis of the process of economic expansion and contraction is, therefore, essential for an understanding of the economics of unused resources or operations at undercapacity in all lines of production.

This chapter is devoted to a discussion of some alleged causes of unemployment and the probable effects of various wage policies during different phases of the business cycle. The "causes" of unemployment that will be discussed at length are "high" wage rates, labor-saving machinery, "excessive" population, and "high" taxes.

SOME ALLEGED CAUSES OF UNEMPLOYMENT

Wage rates and unemployment. Many businessmen and some economists maintain that labor is unemployed because the price of labor is too high. The way to sell more labor, they say, is to reduce wage rates.[1] Professor Willford I. King expressed this view in 1939 when he wrote:

Merchants the world over know that the way to stimulate sales is to cut prices. What is true of soap or shoes is equally true of the labor used in making the soap or shoes. . . .

In the last analysis, it can truthfully be said that unemployment is,

[1] It is interesting to note that, though business executives may generally favor wage reductions during a depression, they are somewhat reluctant to see their own salaries reduced. From 1929 to 1932, while payrolls in all manufacturing firms fell 59 per cent, executive salaries (excluding bonuses) fell only 10 per cent in 100 large industrial companies. *Cf.* John C. Baker, *Executive Salaries and Bonus Plans*, 1938, p. 25.

in the main, caused by wage costs being so high as to make it impossible to market the entire output which industry can conveniently turn out.[1]

Such an argument for wage reduction as a stimulus to employment is based on the common-sense fallacy of reasoning by analogy from the particular to the general.[2] As is indicated more clearly in the following quotation from an eminent English economist, such reasoning assumes that what is true for one industry taken separately is true of all industry as a whole:

In a particular employment, provided demand for its product is elastic, more persons can be employed if they will work for less remuneration. In all employments taken together, demand is indefinitely elastic, and consequently indefinite numbers can be employed if they do not ask for too high a remuneration. General unemployment appears when asking too much is a general phenomenon.[3]

It is on the same basis of partial or particular-industry analysis that some economists have claimed that the salaries of university professors should have been reduced or reduced further during the early 1930's. Statistics indicate that tuition fees rose over 21 per cent for state universities and over 11 per cent for private universities from the school year 1928–1929 to the school year of 1936–1937.[4] During the period from 1931 through June 1934 there was a decline of nine per cent in total student enrollment in all institu-

---

[1] W. I. King "Wage Rates, Wage Costs, Employment, Wage Income and the General Welfare," *American Economic Review*, vol. 29 (March 1939), pp. 39 40. Professor Sumner H. Slichter expressed the same view when he wrote in an article on "Selling More Labor" (*Atlantic Monthly*, vol. 158, p. 324) in September 1936: "In any event, our common sense should have warned us that raising the price is not likely to increase the sales of any article and that there is no reason to expect labor to be different in this respect from all other articles. It is not likely to be the one and only thing which can be sold in greater volume by increasing the price."
Contrast these statements with the views of the General Motors official quoted in Chapter 10, p. 265, footnote 4.

[2] A. P. Lerner also points to "the danger of taking propositions that have been established as true when applied to sections of the economy and illegitimately applying them to the economy as a whole." He writes: "What is true of a firm or of a particular industry or a set of industries need not be true of the economy as a whole. To draw attention continually to such relationships between the parts and the whole is probably the most distinctive function of the economist." "The Relation of Wage Policies and Price Policies," *American Economic Review*, vol. 29 (March 1939) supplement, p. 158.

[3] Edwin Cannan, "The Demand for Labour," *Economic Journal*, vol. 42 (September 1932), p. 367.

[4] Taken from a statistical survey of 200 colleges and universities made by the General Education Board and reported in *Newsweek*, April 3, 1939, pp. 32–33. Enrollment figures are from the *Biennial Survey of Education 1932–1934*, U. S. Office of Education Bulletin (1935) No. 2, Chapter 4, p. 31.

tions and a similar drop in the number of faculty members. It is argued that the high salaries of university professors, by preventing tuition fees from falling, caused this reduction in student enrollment, in the same way that the maintenance of high wages for anthracite miners and railroad workers helped to reduce the sales of anthracite coal and the traffic on railroads by about 50 per cent.[1] If faculty salaries had been reduced sufficiently, so the argument runs, student enrollment would have kept up or increased and the employment of instructors would have expanded instead of contracting.

1. *Wage cut in one line.* It is true, of course, that a reduction of wage rates in a single industry, if it resulted in a reduction in the price of the product, would tend to increase the sales of that product and lead to the employment of more workers in that industry. So far as an individual firm or industry is concerned, the effect of a wage cut upon the demand for the firm's or industry's products can generally be disregarded. The workers in the automobile or the shoe industry, for example, buy such a small percentage of all the automobiles or shoes they manufacture that a reduction in their wage incomes has little effect upon the total sales of automobiles or shoes. From the point of view of a single firm or a single industry, there would undoubtedly be a stimulus to expansion from a reduction in labor costs, which explains why so many people are convinced of the economic wisdom of wage cuts.

In an analysis of general expansion and contraction, however, the effects of a wage cut in the automobile or shoe industry upon the sales of all products could not be disregarded. If a wage-price cut in a single industry did not increase the general rate of spending, the advantage to that branch of industry would have been gained largely at the expense of other branches, and the increase of employment in the favored industry would probably be balanced by a reduction of employment elsewhere. "Any one man in a crowd can get a better view of the procession by standing on a chair, but if they all get up on chairs no one's view is improved." [2] In examining the effects of a wage-rate change in a single industry, one must take into account the repercussions in other branches of the economy, the effects upon total expenditures for consumption and

---

[1] *Cf.* Sumner H. Slichter, "The Changing Character of American Industrial Relations," *American Economic Review*, vol. 29 (March 1939) supplement, pp. 128–29 for a statement regarding the coal miners and the railroad workers.

[2] Joan Robinson, *Introduction to the Theory of Employment*, p. 51.

investment. Wage cuts may lead to strikes, reduce political confidence, cause popular discontent, stimulate hoarding, and have other adverse effects upon the economy. Taking a general point of view, some economists, including Professor J. M. Clark, believe that "lower wages may in their immediate effect do more to decrease the effective demand for labor than to increase it" and so "may defeat their own end by reducing the immediate volume of spendings." [1]

Under conditions of monopolistic competition, price is frequently above marginal variable costs. That may be true, for example, when production is at a rate far under capacity. As indicated in Chapter 5, a number of economists, on the basis of certain statistics, believe that variable costs per unit of output may decrease as the volume of output expands from 60 or 80 to 100 per cent of capacity.[2] Price may remain above marginal variable costs for long periods of time when producers keep up their prices for fear that price reduction would "spoil the market" or lead to a price war. During periods of depression, the demand curve for their produce may seem to employers in semimonopolistic positions to be inelastic or, in some cases, even inversely elastic, which really means that less will be demanded at a lower price because the price fall causes the demand for the product at various prices to decline with a leftward shift in the whole demand curve. When employers maintain prices, more workers might not be hired even at zero wages. The difficulty generally lies in the market for the product rather than in costs. In lines where selling prices remain fixed and price is often above marginal variable costs, shifts in the volume of employment generally will arise from shifts in demand (the volume of expenditures) and not from shifts in the level of costs. Furthermore, conditions are so changed by a depression that many employers could not know the shape of their marginal-receipts and marginal-

[1] J. M. Clark, *Strategic Factors in Business Cycles*, 1934, p. 141.

[2] *Cf.* pp. 120–21. A comparison of the man-hour employment figures of the U. S. Bureau of Labor Statistics with the production index of the Federal Reserve Board indicates that, after 1933, man-hour output frequently varied directly with total production.

A study of the accounting records of a paper company for the Temporary National Economic Committee revealed that "changes in the volume of output had the greatest effect on labor costs, and as a result changes in labor costs were quite out of proportion to those in wage rates. Unit labor costs increased as volume fell and declined as volume expanded." The results were much the same for the International Harvester Company. *Cf. Industrial Wage Rates, Labor Costs and Price Policies*, Monograph No. 5, Temporary National Economic Committee, 1940, pp. xix and xx.

cost curves, and, hence, their policies would probably be governed primarily by the profit-and-loss statement.

Certainly the relationship between wage rates and employment is far more complex, indirect, and uncertain than persons reasoning on the basis of the marginal-productivity theory of wages and particular-industry analysis have assumed. Economists reasoning on such bases have generally argued that high wage rates lead to greater use of, and demand for, capital equipment. But unused machinery and plant facilities are as characteristic of depressions and of even so-called prosperous periods as is unused labor. Consequently, the problem of unemployment is a general one of widespread idleness of men and machines in the midst of want and hunger—a much broader issue than simply wage rates alone.

2. *Wage-level and price-level cut.* In discussing the theory of the connection between the level of wages and unemployment, it is necessary to distinguish between cases where wage cuts result in price cuts and cases where wage reductions do not lead to a reduction in the selling price of the product. Because wages are only a part of total variable costs, product prices normally would not be reduced by as large a percentage as wage rates were reduced. With payrolls only about 20 per cent of the total costs of individual firms in manufacturing, a wage-rate reduction of, say, 25 per cent would generally allow for a price reduction of but 5 to 8 per cent. Consequently, a wage reduction with lower prices tends to reduce the real incomes (the buying power) of wage-earners and to increase the real incomes of owners, creditors, and landlords, who, with the same money incomes, can buy more. The question is, Will they buy more? If a reduction in wage rates is to increase employment, total money expenditures for consumption goods and investment goods must decline less than the drop in the price level. Is that likely to happen?

Since wages are a form of income that generally is spent rapidly, a wage-rate reduction is likely to reduce the rate of spending and total expenditures. Especially are total expenditures likely to be reduced by a transfer of buying power from wage-earners to owners during a depression, when there is little likelihood that owners will invest such transfers or gains in new capital equipment. Also, should consumers and investors expect further wage-price declines, general economic contraction might begin or continue. In such an event, the fall in wages, instead of lessening unemployment, would have increased it.[1]

A lowering of wage and price levels alone would tend to lower the rate of interest by reducing the demand for money in trade. At lower prices less money is needed to carry on the same volume of transactions. But the demand for money to hold or hoard may offset the reduced demand for money in trade and, thus, prevent any reduction in the rate of interest. Lower interest rates, as already indicated, have a tendency to stimulate investment and, therefore, economic expansion.[2] If a general wage-rate reduction should give rise to the expectation of more wage-price cuts, accompanied by a further decline in the volume of consumers' purchases, interest rates might rise by a premium representing the increased risk of investment in securities or capital equipment.

It is possible, of course, that a reduction in the wage level would, at first, have a favorable effect on "business confidence," because businessmen, reasoning falsely from the particular to the general, would expect larger sales in the future. Unless the volume of sales did expand, profits would not increase when price declines were accompanied by wage reductions. As has just been indicated, an expansion in sales volume is unlikely to accompany wage-price cuts, and, without such an expansion, business optimism would probably not lead to new investment, especially when present production was at a rate well under capacity. Professor E. M. Bernstein concludes that

Because the favorable effects are likely to operate on a very small scale, and because there is a possibility of unfavorable psychological effects that may operate on a large scale, a general reduction in wages cannot ordinarily be regarded as a desirable remedy for unemployment.[3]

[1] Cf. M. Mitnitzky, "Wage Policy Today and Tomorrow," International Labour Review, vol. 32 (September 1935), p. 355.

[2] In a recent book, four corporation presidents state that in their "considered business opinion" the rate of interest has but a very limited bearing on decisions to invest in capital goods except in certain lines like public-utility or apartment-house construction. They write: "The man in the operating end of business cannot but be convinced that the demand for fresh capital is correlated primarily with increases in effective demand for products. He builds additions to his plant or starts new projects in response to demand or, more rarely, in anticipation of it. When he cannot anticipate an effective demand no interest rate is low enough ordinarily to affect him." H. S. Dennison et al., Toward Full Employment, 1938, p. 192.

[3] "Wage-Rates, Investment, and Employment," Journal of Political Economy, vol. 47 (April 1939), p. 226.

3. *Wage-level cut without price reduction.* Economists who argue for
wage reductions to stimulate employment often are consciously or
unconsciously assuming the validity of the marginal-productivity
theory of wages for all industry and, therefore, assume that prices
will decline also. Some economists, however, advocate wage reductions on other grounds. They admit that, under conditions of
imperfect competition and unused capacity, the level of wages is
strongly influenced by the profitability of employers' operations as
a whole and little, if at all, by calculations of the marginal contributions of labor to output.[1] They also recognize that many producers keep selling prices fixed, that demand rather than the level
of costs normally tends to determine employment in consumers'
goods industries, and that production costs constitute the incomes
out of which demand arises. However, they rely upon a wage reduction to stimulate investment before the wage reduction has had
time to produce unfavorable effects upon total demand and total
sales.

The argument for a wage reduction without a simultaneous fall
in prices runs somewhat as follows.[2] A large part of a business
firm's expenditures are assumed to be postponable in the sense that
the firm can defer those expenditures (for capital equipment and
inventories, for example) without losing customers to competing
firms. It is further assumed that operations at a loss will cause
such business expenditures to be postponed, because the chief
factor governing them is presumed to be the current earnings of
the business compared with earnings or losses in the preceding
period. It is believed that wage reductions during a depression,
by restoring profit margins, will restore the "investment morale"
of businessmen and give firms a credit status that will enable them
to finance any investment they may wish to make. Such a profit
margin will lead to expenditures to restore depleted inventories and
to replace inefficient equipment. This increase in postponable expenditures, assuming a lag before wage reductions would reduce
sales, is relied upon to increase payrolls sufficiently and soon enough
to more than offset the deflationary or contractive effects of wage
cuts. The supporters of this doctrine believe that there is a "rea-

---

[1] *Cf.* Jacob Viner, "Mr. Keynes on the Causes of Unemployment, A Review,"
Quarterly Journal of Economics, vol. 51 (November 1936), p. 150.
[2] Taken chiefly from *ibid.*, p. 162. *Cf.* also M. Mitnitzky, *op. cit.*, pp. 356–57.

sonable probability" that, under certain conditions, the expansionist tendencies will overcome the negative consequences of the wage reduction.

Such a wage reduction, unaccompanied by a change in the price level, amounts to a transfer of some purchasing power from workers to owners or perhaps to creditors. It may simply postpone the process of writing down capital values rather than increase postponable expenditures. Profit is a percentage return on capital values, and, during a depression, production becomes profitable in many cases through reorganization and reduction of asset values and liabilities, which processes usually involve some immediate reduction in creditors' incomes.

Should the wage-rate saving not be passed on to creditors but be retained by owners, it is still questionable whether they would spend it for investment in a way that would more than counterbalance the reduction in the expenditures of the wage-cut workers. Capital expenditures, as four corporation presidents[1] and the acceleration principle explain, tend to correlate primarily with increases in effective demand (expenditures) for the firm's products. Without some increase in consumption expenditures and with operations well under capacity, new investment for capital expansion is unlikely to be stimulated by a wage reduction. In certain phases of the business cycle, it is possible that the expectation of greater profits from a wage reduction would cause businessmen to produce for stock and to expand capital expenditures at the same time that wages were reduced. But such expansion is not likely to occur before businessmen are convinced that the bottom of the downswing has been reached. During a depression, wage cuts are likely to cause wage-earner consumers to curtail expenditures, in so far as possible, and to lead producers to anticipate some reduction in consumers' purchases. Expectation of still further wage cuts, if not some price reductions eventually, might start a spiral of declining demand. Under certain conditions, wage cuts simply involve a transfer of purchasing power from spenders to savers and hoarders.

Recent studies of the financial records of eight firms in four industries indicate that during the 1930's price changes were not based primarily on wage-rate changes and that, in most companies,

---

[1] *Cf.* the quotation in this chapter, p. 279, footnote 2.

costs apparently are far less important in immediate price-policy decisions than businessmen are accustomed to believe. Apparently it is more usual for price changes to bring about wage changes than for wage changes to induce price changes. Falling prices are frequently followed by wage cuts, since labor costs often constitute the one cost element that is largely within the control of the individual producer and, therefore, capable of immediate reduction. As wages are usually a small percentage of an employer's total costs, changes in labor costs would seldom be sufficiently great to cause a significant change in prices, although they may make a big difference in profits or in the cash position of a company. These studies indicate that the wage policies of companies are influenced to a considerable degree by their financial position.[1]

4. *International aspects.* The belief that wage cuts have beneficial effects upon employment rests in part upon the assumption that most countries are on an international gold standard. The foreign-trade argument for wage and price reductions is less valid when countries are off gold so that exchange rates may fluctuate freely.

The price levels of all countries on gold are linked to the value of the yellow metal, for each country guarantees to exchange its currency for gold, or gold for its currency, at a fixed price. Under such circumstances, if one country's price level does not decline as rapidly as the price levels of other gold-standard countries, that country will find its exports decreasing (because with relatively high prices it is a poor country from which to buy) and its imports increasing (because its inhabitants tend to buy from abroad where prices are lower). Domestic currency can be converted into gold to be shipped abroad and there the gold can be converted into foreign currencies with which to pay for the increased imports, thus causing the domestic money supply to contract and the money supply of foreign countries to expand. Consequently, a high price level in a gold-standard country, by causing a decrease in exports relative to imports and a condition of tight money, tends to reduce money incomes and employment. Conversely, wage and price reductions, by stimulating exports and an increased money supply through gold imports, tend to cause employment in the country to expand, partly at the expense of other countries on the gold stand-

---

[1] *Cf. Industrial Wage Rates, Labor Costs and Price Policies*, Monograph No. 5, Temporary National Economic Committee, 1940, pp. x, xi, xvii, xx, xxv.

ard. By undercutting its neighbors, the country hopes to transfer its unemployment problem abroad. Competitive wage- and price-level cuts by a country on gold have essentially the same effects internationally as wage-price cuts by single firms or industries have on the domestic economy. Likewise such wage-price cuts by gold-standard countries are on all fours with a deliberate policy of exchange depreciation by countries off gold for the purpose of stimulating exports and retarding imports.

The gold standard tends to foster international competition in wage and price reductions, which may lead, as in the early 1930's, to a vicious spiral of deflation. On the other hand, wage and price reductions are of little or no international advantage to countries with free currencies and fluctuating exchanges. In such a country, a 50-per-cent reduction of wages and prices, for example, might result in a 100-per-cent rise in the exchange value of the country's currency, which is possible because the currency's exchange value is determined by demand and supply without regard to gold. Therefore, even though domestic prices were cut in half, they would be the same for foreigners who would, at the new exchange rate, have to pay twice as much foreign money for a unit of the country's currency. Under such circumstances, wage cuts would not increase employment in a country by transferring unemployment abroad.

5. *The proportion of productive factors.* Some economists argue that a high level of wages increases unemployment by causing employers to substitute machines for men, to use more labor-saving devices and less labor. Such an argument assumes that an increase in capital equipment causes the displacement of labor and results in "technological unemployment." The effects of technological change and labor-saving devices upon unemployment are discussed in the next section. Here it is only necessary to point out that it seems somewhat inconsistent for economists to claim, in answer to the technocrats, that advances in technique and capital equipment increase employment and in the next breath to state that high wages, by stimulating the use of labor-saving devices and more capital equipment, decrease employment.

Those who state that high wage rates will cause a substitution of capital for labor often overlook the fact that a general rise in the level of wages would also raise the cost of machines and that increased purchases of capital equipment would increase employment in the capital-goods industries, which, through the multiplier principle, might cause employment in general to expand. There is no reason to believe that additional capital investment, which increases the equipment per worker, would necessarily lead to less employment.

Actually, changes in wage rates would probably not cause any substitution of capital for labor, or *vice versa*, during a depression when much existing capital equipment is lying idle. Wage reductions in a depression are not likely to lead employers to replace machines by men. The ratio of workers to equipment is largely fixed by technical considerations and the character of existing equipment, so that a change in the proportion of factors would not be likely to occur until new equipment was purchased to replace existing plant facilities. Wage levels, therefore, may influence the proportion of factors and the technique of industry only very gradually and, for the most part, only during periods of peak production when expansions in plant generally take place. Even then wage rates are only one of many considerations, including the interest rate, recent advances in technique, and forecasts of future technical changes, that influence the decisions concerning the ratio of men to machines in any firm or industry.

That the relationship between wage rates and unemployment is not direct and clear-cut is indicated by experience in this country following the first World War. In the three-year period from 1920 to 1923, real wages rose over 16 per cent, partly because of a sharp drop in the cost of living, yet the percentage of the total labor supply unemployed in 1923 was no more, and was probably less, than in 1920, despite the return of a large number of soldiers to industry during that time.[1]

Machinery and unemployment. The effect of labor-saving devices upon the demand for labor has been discussed ever since the English textile workers rioted in the eighteenth century, smashing the new machinery that seemed to be robbing them of their jobs.[2] That new machines, new productive processes, and new methods of management may cause skilled workers to suffer a rel-

---

[1] Paul H. Douglas, *Real Wages in the United States*, 1930, pp. 108, 427, and 458.

[2] For a complete survey of theories regarding labor-saving devices and employment, cf. Alexander Gourvitch, *Survey of Economic Theory on Technological Change and Employment*, National Research Project, Work Projects Administration, May 1940.

ative loss, through obsolescence of particular skills or displacement by unskilled workmen, is not denied. The issue here is whether technical progress and increasing productivity create idleness, whether machinery and improved methods decrease the total demand for labor, thereby increasing the total volume of unemployment.

As proof that technical improvements cause unemployment, the "technocrats" in the early 1930's pointed to striking examples of "machines doing the work of men," such as the "electric eye," the teletype machine, and the New Jersey rayon factory that would "eventually require the services of but a single man," thus bringing employment in that plant "as close to zero as possible."[1] In this way, according to the technocrats, mechanization has been shutting one door after another to human labor and causing widespread permanent unemployment.

It is evident that the arguments of the technocrats are based upon particular examples, from which they draw broad generalizations—the old, familiar fallacy. For a complete analysis it is necessary to examine the effects of changing technology upon the economy as a whole, upon the total demand for labor in all lines. That one-firm and one-industry analyses give only an incomplete knot-hole view is indicated by the experience of the 1920's. From 1920 through 1929 there was practically no expansion of total employment in the whole group of basic industries, which includes manufacturing, mining, construction, transportation, agriculture, forestry and fishing, communication, and electric light and power. As a matter of fact, the number of wage-earners in manufacturing declined during that decade. Yet from 1920 through 1929 there was an expansion of almost 50 per cent in employment in the service industries (trade, personal and public service, the professions, recreation, and amusements), so that total employment for the whole economy increased about 15 per cent during that decade, despite an increase of about 25 per cent in the productivity per worker.[2]

If technological improvements cause a decrease in total employ-

[1] Howard Scott, "Technocracy Smashes the Price System," *Harper's Magazine*, vol. 166 (January 1933), pp. 135–36.

[2] *Cf.* David Weintraub and Harold L. Posner, *Unemployment and Increasing Productivity*, Works Progress Administration, National Research Project on Reemployment Opportunities and Recent Changes in Industrial Techniques, 1937, pp. 20 and 27–28.

ment, one would expect to find a cumulative increase in unemployment following the introduction of the factory system, which has resulted in a progressive expansion in physical productivity per worker. Yet the trend of total employment has been rising ever since 1800, and there is no evidence of a progressive increase in the percentage of unemployed persons during the nineteenth century and the first three decades of the twentieth century (see Table 16).

Certainly technological improvements are not the primary cause of depressional unemployment. Improvements in technique are occurring constantly and not simply during the downswing of the business cycle. In fact, the rate of installation of new machinery and capital equipment declines sharply during business slumps, for then much existing equipment is idle.[1] Consequently, economies during periods of curtailed production are achieved primarily by labor-saving methods rather than by the purchase of new labor-saving machines.

It is true that some business-cycle theorists claim that changes in the technique of production (new inventions, new processes, new goods, and the discovery of new resources) are the impelling forces behind business fluctuations. But these theorists believe that such innovations, by opening up new opportunities for investment in fixed capital, initiate an upswing of the business cycle. In a sense, technological advance performs a function similar in effect to an earthquake, by making existing capital equipment of little value and opening up new areas for profitable investment. Increased purchase of machinery provides additional employment and income for workers in the capital-goods industries, which spreads to other branches of industry according to the multiplier principle. Some theorists claim that business depressions are mostly a consequence of a decline in the capital-goods industries and consider it a bad sign that the capital-goods industries did not expand as fast during the 1920's as in earlier periods.[2] This relative decline in the

---

[1] "From 1914 to 1933 it was demonstrated over and over that technological change occurred at *times* when employment was rising; technological change was most rapid in *industries* where employment was rising; technological change was most rapid in *areas* where employment was rising." Edna Lonigan, "The Effect of Modern Technological Conditions upon the Employment of Labor," *American Economic Review*, vol. 29 (June 1939), p. 248.

[2] David Weintraub and Irving Kaplan, *Summary of Findings to Date, March 1938,*

rate of growth of industries producing capital goods was mostly offset by rapid expansion in the service industries.

1. *The traditional analysis.* The long-familar argument of economic theorists is that improvements in machinery or managerial efficiency lead either to lower prices for consumers or to higher profits for employers, thereby enabling one of these groups to increase their demand for goods or services, so that displaced workers can expect to be reabsorbed soon into employment. As B. M. Anderson, Jr., explains, "in economic theory the matter is very simple" [1]—in fact, much too simple.

According to the orthodox explanation, there are three possible situations, depending upon the demand for the product and price changes in the industry. It is assumed that, in a competitive industry, selling prices will promptly fall by an amount corresponding to the reduction in cost of production caused by the improvement in technique. The first case is that of a competitive industry with a product enjoying a highly elastic demand, so that at a lower price a larger sum of dollars is spent by consumers on that product. In this case, Professor Anderson claims that "more labor will speedily be employed in the same industry than before the new invention came." [2] Actually there might be cases where, because the new machine saves so much labor per unit of output, fewer workers would be employed in an industry after the installation of a major labor-saving machine, even though that industry's product had a demand that was more elastic than unity. Professor Ander-

Works Progress Administration, National Research Project on Reemployment Opportunites and Recent Changes in Industrial Techniques, 1938, p. 117.

With regard to technological change and unemployment, Professor Sumner Slichter has written: "The displacement of labor which is likely to be most troublesome in the future is not displacement by technological changes. Rather it is displacement by the slowing down in the rate of industrial growth. In fact, the effect of technological changes will probably be to reduce displacement rather than to increase it, because technological changes will help sustain the demand for capital goods. Indeed, from the standpoint of maintaining employment, technological changes are likely to come too slowly rather than too rapidly in the immediate future." *Cf.* "Implications of the Shorter Hour Movement," *Proceedings of the Academy of Political Science*, vol. 15 (January 1934), pp. 70–71.

[1] B. M. Anderson, "Technological Progress, the Stability of Business, and the Interests of Labor," *The Chase Economic Bulletin*, Chase National Bank of New York City, vol. 17 (April 13, 1937), pp. 16–17.

Good summaries of the traditional theory are also to be found in Paul H. Douglas, "Technological Unemployment," *American Federationist*, vol. 37 (August 1930), pp. 923–50; and Alvin H. Hansen, "Institutional Frictions and Technological Unemployment," *Quarterly Journal of Economics*, vol. 45 (August 1931), pp. 684–97.

[2] Anderson, *loc. cit.*

son also neglects to explain what happens to employment in other industries now that more money is being spent for the cheaper products of this industry.

The second case is that of a competitive industry with a product having an inelastic demand, such as wheat or salt. In this case employment in the industry may be reduced, but lower prices enable consumers to purchase the same quantities of the product with a smaller sum of money, thus releasing some of these consumers' funds so that they can increase their demand for other products. As labor is required to produce these additional products, the demand for labor will expand in these other lines, permitting the displaced workers to be reabsorbed into industry. It should be noted that the argument in this case rests upon the assumption that purchasers will at once spend their savings from cost-price reductions for other goods or services, so that the total volume of expenditures does not decrease. Even if total expenditures in the economy do remain constant after the decline in price, there is no assurance that the number of workers finding new jobs in other lines will exactly balance the number thrown out of employment by the technological improvement.

In these cases, in which the price is reduced and money is released to buy more than the quantities of products previously purchased, it is assumed that there is no decline in the total amount of money or in the speed with which it is spent. A decline in the rate of spending would occur if consumers increased their idle balances instead of immediately spending all their gain from price declines, or if the displaced workers should spend less rapidly than formerly any money remaining from their previous incomes. Any redistribution of income resulting from the introduction of labor-saving devices may change the velocity of circulation of money.

The third case is that in which, because of monopolistic elements in the market, it is more profitable to maintain the price of the the product at or near its former figure after installing the new method or machine. In this case, the lower costs yield larger profits to the employers adopting the labor-saving devices. It is assumed that these increased profits "must be spent or invested" by the employers or stockholders and, thus, must "lead to demand for labor." [1] There is no assurance, however, that such an increase

[1] *Idem.*

in the purchasing power of employers at the expense of reduced incomes for workers will be spent rapidly enough to prevent a reduction in total expenditures. Even with the same volume of total expenditures, total employment would decline. Without a reduction in price, the same quantity of goods would be sold as before; but, with the new technique, fewer workers are needed to produce that quantity of goods.

A recent illustration of this third case is to be found in the steel industry. During the last decade or so there has been a widespread introduction of the new, hot-strip rolling mill to replace the old "hand" sheet rolling mill. It is claimed that 15 men on a new strip mill can produce as much steel as 100 men on hand mills, so that the strip mill reduces the total labor cost required to produce tin plate, one of the major steel-mill products, from $36 to $14 a ton, or 61 per cent.[1] Despite the fact that well over half of all tin plate was produced by strip mills in 1939, the price of tin plate was no lower then than it was in 1926 when the strip mill was first introduced. The obvious effect of such a combination of policies is to increase total unemployment. This illustration explains why so-called "technological unemployment" has sometimes been referred to as inflexible-price unemployment.

2. *Impossbile to isolate.* There is no way to determine, in quantitative terms, the net effect of a technological improvement upon total employment in the economy. A change in technique may tend either to reduce or to increase employment in the same or other industries. The stimulating effects upon employment of technological change are generally felt, in the first instance, in the capital-goods industries, even when a new product or a new industry develops from the new invention. Generally speaking, the question is how the change affects total expenditures during the period and, therefore, the demand for labor.

The complexity of the interrelationships among industries, products, and markets makes it impossible to isolate the effects of technical changes upon employment and to separate so-called "technological unemployment" from the total volume of unemployment at any one time. Many of the effects of labor-saving in-

[1] Harold J. Ruttenberg, "85,000 Victims of Progress," *New Republic*, vol. 94 (February 16, 1938), pp. 37–38, and by the same author, "The Big Morgue," *Survey Graphic*, vol. 28 (April 1939), pp. 266–69.

novations are indirect, so their full consequences upon all the factors that influence total employment cannot be traced. For instance, technological improvements may direct production away from competing plants in the same industry; they may, by improving the product or lowering its price, reduce the demand for another commodity and for labor to fabricate that commodity; they may reduce the demand for materials and fuels used in the production of the product; or they may improve the quality of the product so that less labor is needed for its upkeep. Under such circumstances, it does no good to ask unemployed workers or the employers who laid them off whether or not their unemployment is the result of technological change. If the demand for the employer's product was declining partly because of technical improvements in other lines, neither the employer nor his laid-off workers would know to what extent their unemployment was due to labor-saving devices. Furthermore, firms generally install labor-saving equipment during an upswing, when employment is expanding. The effect then is that not so many new workers are hired in that industry as otherwise would be the case; but, because no workers are laid off as a consequence, no person is liable to hold such a technological improvement responsible for his continued unemployment.

Although the net effect of labor-saving machines and methods upon total employment cannot be discovered, some persons know that their own jobs have been abolished by such devices. An individual is less interested in broad effects upon the general level of employment than he is in the consequences to his own job and income. The fact that his unemployment may be accompanied by an expansion of employment in the capital-goods industries or an increase in the demand for unskilled labor is of little consolation to a skilled worker displaced by a new machine. Various studies of displaced workers indicate that the average time lost between lay-off and a new job may be four or five months—older workers may never obtain regular employment again—and most of the displaced workers receive lower wages on their new jobs.[1] People see such displacement of men by machines happen in the community. Some persons experience it. They can hardly be blamed if they draw false general conclusions from their own particular limited experience.

[1] For a summary discussion of these studies, *cf.* Weintraub and Posner, *op. cit.*, Section 5, "What Happens to Displaced Workers?" pp. 58–69.

Population and unemployment. The relationship between population and unemployment is a subject concerning which much is said and little is known. Some people claim that an increasing population brings increasing unemployment and that a reduction in the population would be one solution to our unemployment problem. Others maintain that "it is actually easier to employ an expanding population than a contracting one," because a growing population, by assuring businessmen of more consumers and expanding markets, gives a powerful stimulus to business and especially to investment in capital equipment, such as houses, ships, and factories.[1] It has been said that the introduction of labor-saving devices did not create a large unemployment problem before the first World War because the domestic market was expanding so fast with the rapid increase in population.[2] There is some question whether the results will continue to be the same now that the rate of growth of our population is declining rapidly, and many recent inventions seem to require very little capital investment.

A survey of the world during the 1930's reveals no correlation between unemployment and density of population. The most densely populated countries have not had the largest percentages of unemployment. As was indicated in Chapter 10, the Middle Colonies had severe depressions and unemployment early in the eighteenth century when the population of New Jersey, Pennsylvania, Delaware, and Maryland all together amounted to only about 200,000 persons. Changes in population trends are so slow and gradual that they could hardly be the cause for sharp increases in unemployment during any particular depression.

Certain economists do maintain, however, that a decline in the rate of population growth may prevent the attainment of full employment by narrowing down the outlets for new private investment.[3] There has been, for example, a close relation between the

[1] J. R. Hicks, "Mr. Keynes' Theory of Employment," *Economic Journal*, vol. 46 (June 1936), p. 252.

[2] During the last century, our population was increasing by about one third each decade. During the past decade the increase did not amount to one thirteenth. The statisticians predict a stationary population by 1970 or 1980.

[3] *Cf.* Hans Staudinger, "Stationary Population—Stagnant Economy?" *Social Research*, vol. 6 (May 1939), pp. 143–46; and Alvin H. Hansen, "Economic Progress and Declining Population Growth," *American Economic Review*, vol. 29 (March 1939), pp. 7–10.

construction of new houses and the increase of population. With a declining rate of population growth, some savings formerly invested in homes must be spent or invested in other ways if the gap between income and consumption expenditures is to be filled. It may be that in the future a larger percentage of all funds will be spent on personal services, which do not require a large investment in capital equipment.

Professor Alvin Hansen estimates roughly that the growth of population in the last half of the nineteenth century was responsible for about 60 per cent of the capital formation in the United States.[1] Without such an expansion in population, he says, the rate of technological advance and the development of new industries must be speeded up in order that there may be sufficient investment opportunities to maintain full employment. Yet, under monopoly control, the introduction of new machinery may be held back until the value of the old machine falls below the economies of the new technique. Professor Hansen believes that "the combined effect of the decline in population growth, together with the failure of any really important innovations of a magnitude sufficient to absorb large capital outlays, weighs very heavily as an explanation for the failure of the recent recovery [ending in 1937] to reach full employment."[2]

Taxes and unemployment. The effect of taxes upon employment and unemployment is also a subject concerning which there is no consensus of learned opinion. The diversity of views arises, in part, from the fact that various taxes have different economic effects, so it is often necessary to specify the tax under discussion. Certain taxes, such as a high income tax without deductions for capital losses, may discourage investment in new and risky ventures by causing investors to prefer a safe, steady income. Enterprise may also be affected adversely if, as in the case of the undistributed-profits tax of 1936, business managers became unduly alarmed[3] and upset their own "business confidence" in the process. It is said that taxes may reduce employment by driving some firms into

[1] Hansen, *op. cit.*, p. 8. One may, of course, question the assumptions upon which this estimate was made.

[2] *Ibid.*, p. 11.

[3] *Cf.* James G. Smith, "Economic Significance of the Undistributed Profits Tax," *American Economic Review*, vol. 28 (June 1938), pp. 305–10; and H. S. Dennison *et al.*, *op. cit.*, pp. 226–33.

bankruptcy; but bankruptcy is concerned only with ownership, and business equipment generally continues to be operated until it is worthless, no matter who owns it. High taxes in one community may cause industries to shift to other localities, but such shifts, in themselves, should not affect the total volume of employment in the country as a whole.

On the other hand, taxation and public expenditures may increase employment. By redistributing income and reducing economic inequality, as explained in Chapter 9, taxes may increase expenditures for consumption. Also, the government may spend the money collected in taxes faster than the taxpayers would have spent it, in which case running the money through the public treasury may speed up the rate of spending and thus increase total expenditures and total money incomes.

It is said that high taxes increase unemployment by reducing a country's exports. This is not the place to discuss the whole theory of international trade, which is based on comparative (not absolute) advantage.[1] The principle of comparative advantage explains why a country with poor resources and productive facilities continues to export, selling abroad those commodities in which, compared to the rest of the world, that country has the least disadvantage. A high level of taxation, as such, would not affect the range of comparative advantage of a nation's various industries. Furthermore, should high taxes raise prices—income, inheritance, and land taxes have no direct effect upon the prices of commodities— the whole mechanism of international finance would operate to counteract such a rise in the country's price level. As explained in the subsection on international aspects of wage rates, relatively high price levels in gold-standard countries are reduced by a change in the export-import ratio, an outflow of gold, and a reduction in the money supply. In countries with a free currency, price-level rises are offset by a decline in the exchange value of the country's currency—foreign money buys more of that nation's currency.

To sum up, although particular taxes may have adverse effects upon employment by discouraging investment, especially of the

[1] For a discussion of international-trade theory, cf., for example, P. T. Ellsworth, *International Economics*, 1938. Certain aspects of international trade are discussed more fully in Chapter 19 *infra*.

pioneering type, the general level of taxes as such should have no more effect upon the total volume of employment in a country than the general level of prices has.

WAGE POLICY AND THE BUSINESS CYCLE

Recently there has been considerable discussion of the effects upon the business cycle of the price and wage policies of large firms, and the wage policies of trade-unions.[1] The discussion in this section builds upon the brief treatment of price and wage policies in Chapter 5.

Wage policy. As indicated in Chapter 5, it is the general practice for large firms to pay what is considered the average "prevailing rate" of wages for that type of work in the locality. Individual business firms hesitate to pay more than such a "market" rate for fear of "unstabilizing" wage relationships and arousing employer antagonism.

For a number of reasons, a firm may also hesitate to cut wages, or to be the first one to reduce wages in the industry. A "good" wage policy may be good advertising or a good investment. A creditable reputation amongst customers or in the labor market may help to maintain sales and to assure the firm an efficient labor supply. The "extra cost" of a good wage policy may be chargeable to advertising, especially if a large portion of the firm's customers are working-class people. An employer may also feel that sharp wage reductions will have such an adverse effect on employee morale, and therefore on output, that the "extra cost" of a stable wage policy is a good investment, assuring him a more efficient working force then and in the future. If a wage reduction would lead to labor strife, especially a strike, the employer may believe that the resulting loss would exceed any gain from wage reductions. For all these reasons, there is a tendency for employers to maintain existing wage scales, to pursue a policy of rather stable wage rates.

---

[1] *Cf.*, for example, Arthur Feiler, "Adjustments of Prices and Costs as a Means of Stabilization," *Social Research*, vol. 6 (May 1939), pp. 207–21 and 237–41; Donald H. Wallace, "Monopoly Prices and Depression," in *Explorations in Economics*, 1936, pp. 346–56; Sumner H. Slichter, "The Changing Character of American Industrial Relations," *American Economic Review*, vol. 29 (March 1939) supplement, pp. 121–37; and the series of three articles on wage policy and industrial fluctuations in *International Labour Review*, vol. 38 (December 1938), pp. 758–93, and vol. 39 (January and March 1939), pp. 1–33 and 319–59.

In industries where firms follow a uniform stable price policy, there is a further reason for maintaining wage scales. Wage reductions by one firm might spread to others and soon lead to price-cutting, which might "spoil the market" and upset competitive relationships in the industry. Price cuts improve a firm's position primarily at the expense of competitors who are forced to take retaliatory action, which may lead to a price war and losses for the whole industry. Consequently, there may be a strong desire for stable prices and stable wages, especially in an industry where there are a few large firms. Stable wages may help to assure stable prices by affording the industry a good excuse or reason in reply to public pressure for price reductions. In some industries, special devices are used in order to enlist employee support for stable or higher prices for the industry's product. In the copper and silver industries, for instance, wage rates are increased or decreased by 25 or 50 cents a day with each stipulated increase or decrease in the price of the metal.[1]

Even without any special arrangements tying wage rates to prices, organized labor in an industry may realize that it is to the self-interest of the workers to see that fairly stable prices are maintained for the products of the industry. When there was a flurry of price-cutting in the steel industry in 1938, the union leaders twice expressed opposition to price-cutting in steel on the grounds that "price-cutting always leads to wage-cutting." [2]

Many economists maintain that during a business slump it would be profitable for industrialists to lower prices and that it would be to the self-interest of the working class to reduce wage rates.[3] Professor Sumner Slichter believes that "most employers under conditions of monopolistic competition put the price of their products too high" and that most labor-union officials underestimate the elasticity of the demand for the services of union

[1] Cf. "Development of Collective Bargaining in Metal Mining," Monthly Labor Review, vol. 47 (September 1938), pp. 594–95. This practice of basing wages on the price of the metal mined was started by the Anaconda Copper Company in 1907. Similar arrangements have existed in the British coal-mining and iron-and-steel industries for 50 or 60 years. (Cf. A. G. Pool, Wage Policy in Relation to Industrial Fluctuations, 1938, p. 99.) The same system, based on wool export prices, is used for shearers and wool-shed workers in New Zealand.

[2] Cf. New York Times, January 26, 1938, pp. 1 and 6; and Edward S. Mason, "Price and Production Policies of Large-Scale Enterprise," American Economic Review, vol. 29 (March 1939) supplement, p. 67.

[3] Cf., for example, W. I. King, op. cit., pp. 39–47.

members.[1] As one example, he cites the building-trades unions which he says "have seriously misjudged their market and are pursuing a price policy that is not only injuring their members but is substantially reducing the ability of private industry to absorb the savings of the community." [2] Professor Slichter would have the wage reductions he recommends occur as "isolated cuts," for he believes it "particularly important" to avoid "general and sweeping wage changes," which "will arouse an expectation of still further cuts and thus induce postponement of commitments." [3]

The question arises whether the steel workers and, say, the plumbers or the plasterers would increase their incomes by accepting a sharp wage cut apart from any general reduction in wages. Would such "isolated" wage cuts, by reducing product prices, stimulate sales and employment in those lines enough to more than offset the wage-rate reduction and, thus, increase the income of those workers? The answer generally is "No!" The industrialists and trade-unionists know their own self-interest better than do these economists.

The demand for most steel products and for the services of any one of the building trades is likely to be very inelastic. This is because steel is generally merged with so many other commodities in the making of a final product and because the wages of plumbers or plasterers are but a small percentage of total building costs and there are no good substitutes for their services. For example, about $80 worth of steel goes into the average automobile, and wages to steel workers are around 30 per cent of the total value of steel products. Consequently, a 100-per-cent reduction in wages in the steel industry would cause only a 30-per-cent reduction in steel prices, which in turn would reduce automobile prices by but $24, or about 3 per cent. A reduction in the price of nails would have only an infinitesimal effect upon the cost of building, and hence would do

[1] Slichter, "The Changing Character of American Industrial Relations," *American Economic Review*, vol. 29 (March 1939) supplement, p. 131. Professor Slichter maintains that business enterprises have not adequately recognized that "there is a marked difference in the elasticity in the demand for most products with the lapse of relatively short periods of time." *Ibid.*, p. 126, footnote.

[2] *Ibid.*, p. 133. Union wage scales in building did decline about 17 per cent from 1931 to 1933, but in 1938 they were 12.5 per cent above the 1929 level. (*Cf.* "Union Scales of Wages and Hours in the Building Trades, June 1, 1938," *Monthly Labor Review*, vol. 47 [November 1938], p. 1097.)

[3] *Ibid.*, p. 135.

little to stimulate the demand for nails. Wages to plumbers or plasterers generally constitute only one to two per cent of total building costs (not including land) in residential or apartment-house construction.[1]

It is clear from these illustrations that the demand is very inelastic for many products used only in conjunction with other goods, and for the services of many skilled workers who work on only a small portion of the finished product. Generally speaking, the smaller the percentage of total costs represented by a particular kind of labor or type of material, the more inelastic will be the demand for that labor or material—the more difficult it is to stimulate sales by restricted wage and price reductions. Consequently, individual industries, like the nail industry, or a body of craftsmen, like the plumbers, are likely to lose by "isolated" price or wage reductions. They could profit from price or wage cuts only if the rest of the building-materials producers and the other building-trades workers reduced prices and wages at the same time and by a corresponding amount.[2] But such uniform action by all groups concerned is not likely to occur voluntarily and might, by spreading throughout the economy, lead to the very vicious spiral of deflation that Professor Slichter wishes to avoid.

There may be some question whether one can speak of *a* wage policy in a highly specialized capitalistic economy where producers and workers are generally but a small part of a large productive process and where each group aims at furthering its own self-interest rather than at aiding the general good of the whole community. In such a competitive society, some workers gain by increasing the prices charged to other workers, and one finds the coal-miners' union condemning the development of cheap hydroelectric power (a substitute product) under such auspices as the Tennessee Valley Authority.

[1] *Cf.* "Labor and Materials Costs in Small-House Construction," *Monthly Labor Review*, vol. 48 (May 1939), pp. 1058–61. An article in *Fortune* (vol. 17, June 1938, p. 92) shows that a 25-per-cent reduction in all building wages (from an average of $1.15 to 86 cents an hour) in the construction of Knickerbocker Village (a housing development in the slum area of the lower East Side in New York City) would have reduced total costs, including land, but 5 per cent, so that rentals to the 1,600 white-collar workers and their families living in Knickerbocker Village would have been lowered only 3½ per cent, allowing for taxes and operating expenses.

[2] *Cf.* Paul H. Douglas, "The Problem of Unemployment in Unemployment Insurance," in *Social Security in the United States, 1937*, Tenth National Conference of the American Association for Social Security, 1937, p. 119.

The term "policy" may imply a greater degree of central control than exists in democratic countries. Perhaps it is only in countries controlled by dictators, who can force general or isolated reductions in wages and prices, that one can properly speak of *a* wage policy. In democratic countries, wages are not generally set by a single authority except under minimum-wage laws. Nevertheless our Federal administrations do attempt to influence the course of wage rates. The Roosevelt Administration tried, by various New Deal legislation, to raise the general level of wages on the ground that such a rise would "increase purchasing power"; and it also attempted, simultaneously and unsuccessfully, to bring about a reduction in the hourly wages of building workers. This Federal policy was predicated upon certain notions concerning the effects of wage rates upon the business cycle.

Proper wage policy in depression and prosperity. This discussion of the appropriate wage policy during different stages of the business cycle must, of necessity, be in very vague, general terms. Economic policy is an art that cannot be practiced according to any simple foolproof formula. An economic policy may work out very differently in different countries, and the effects may vary in the same country depending upon the circumstances and the social climate. Especially is that true in democracies, in which economic matters are governed primarily by the voluntary actions of all citizens. In such countries, the psychological effects of a policy are extremely important. Consequently, no rules can be propounded to cover all possible situations. In this section we can only discuss some of the important factors to be considered and make a few general remarks by way of conclusion.

One matter should be made clear at the outset. Wage policy cannot be based upon the marginal-productivity theory of wages. The discussion in Chapter 7 indicated how valid this theory is in our present-day economy. It is especially ill-fitted for application to business-cycle conditions. The shape of demand curves for products may change rapidly during a business cycle, yet the employer knows but one point on such curves—the demand at his present price.[1] Past data on the volume of his sales at various prices

[1] Employers with price policies generally believe the demand for their product to be very elastic above the present price and very inelastic below that price. An employer believes this largely because he assumes that competing firms will lower prices to meet any price reduction but will not raise prices if he does so.

are out of date. Consequently, an employer cannot calculate a marginal-receipts schedule and marginal-cost curves at various possible outputs. There are good grounds for believing that employers during much of the business cycle are guided by other considerations—the profitability of their operations as a whole, average costs, or the maintenance of prestige [1]—rather than by calculations of the marginal contribution of labor to output.

The objective of wage policy presumably should be to maximize employment, production, and consumption over a complete business cycle. The controversial issues concern the means of obtaining that desired goal. In general, the division of opinion on means arises from a difference in the business-cycle theory used as the basis for judging wage policy. One group of theorists holds that prosperity collapses because costs, including wages, become too high and diminish the prospect for profit. This group, which may be called the wages-as-cost theorists, also believes that depression continues because wage rates remain too rigid, so that costs are not deflated enough to restore profit margins. The opposing group of theorists maintains that the boom bursts because wages are too low and profits too high, which permits investment to outrun consumption. This second group, which we shall designate the wages-as-income group, believes that prosperity can be restored only by increased expenditures and that wage reductions will serve only to decrease total expenditures and to set in motion a deflationary spiral of demand and price reductions. The wages-as-income group emphasizes the importance of maintaining the market for consumers' goods.

These two types of theory lead to opposite conclusions with regard to wage policy. On only one matter do they both agree: that wage rates should be increased at some stage in the upswing. The wages-as-cost theorists would prefer that such wage increases occur at a time when recovery is well established but before the limit of bank credit and other resources is approached.

Little purpose would be served by extensive and detailed comment on these theories. The discussion of wage rates and unemployment in the first section of this chapter answers some of the

[1] Cf., for example, Jacob Viner, *op. cit.*, p. 150; E. Ronald Walker, "Wages Policy and Business Cycles," *International Labour Review*, vol. 38 (December 1938), pp. 776–77; and Paul H. Douglas, "Wage Theory and Wage Policy," *International Labour Review*, vol. 39 (March 1939), p. 356.

arguments in favor of wage-level reductions as a means of expanding employment. The wages-as-costs theorists overlook the fact that the expectation that incomes are going to sag, say, two per cent in the coming year is roughly equivalent in effect to a rise of two per cent in the amount of interest payable for the same period and that a lower price level increases the real burden of private and public debt and, hence, taxation.[1] Professor Keynes states that a policy of flexible wage rates might "cause a great instability of prices, so violent perhaps as to make business calculations futile." [2] The wages-as-income theorists point out that the percentage of profit or return on capital may be increased by deflating capital values, which were overexpanded during the boom period, rather than by deflating wage rates.

Both sides can cite illustrations from past experience to prove their case. The wages-as-income theorists point out that in the recovery of the 1890's wages began to rise in the United States and Great Britain before wholesale prices reached their lowest point,[3] that distribution to consumers was well maintained in the short-lived depression of 1921 because wage reductions were less severe than during previous depressions,[4] that a policy of maintaining wages was followed in Sweden during the depression of the early 1930's, helping Sweden to experience a most remarkable recovery after 1933 with labor shortages in 1935 and 1936,[5] and that no other country made such drastic and wholesale cuts in wages and other costs as the United States made between 1930 and 1933, yet no country suffered more intensely from that depression.[6]

The wages-as-costs theorists would question some of these interpretations of business-cycle experience. They would add that the rise in wage rates brought about by the New Deal was responsible for the widespread unemployment after 1933 and especially the recession of 1937, and they would point to the case of Australia, where in 1931 a general reduction of 10 per cent in real wages was

[1] J. M. Keynes, op. cit., pp. 264–65.   [2] Ibid., p. 269.
[3] Wesley Mitchell, Business Cycles, 1913, pp. 464–66.
[4] Millis and Montgomery, op. cit., vol. 1, p. 214; and Emmett H. Welch, "The Relationship between Wage Rates and Unemployment," Journal of the American Statistical Association, vol. 28 (March 1933) supplement, p. 58.
[5] Arthur Montgomery, How Sweden Overcame the Depression, 1938, pp. 52–53.
[6] A. G. Pool, Wage Policy in Relation to Industrial Fluctuations, 1938, p. 147.

introduced as a recovery measure, along with other actions, and recovery followed soon thereafter.[1]

Movements in wage rates affect total employment and aggregate expenditures (total income) by affecting such items as the money supply, the rate of interest, the expected yield on capital investment, the rate of spending or hoarding, and the country's export-import balance. This list indicates how complex and involved the whole problem of wage policy may be. If, for example, the money supply changes directly with decreases in wage rates, little will be gained from wage cuts; whereas, with an unchanged money supply, wage reductions may free a part of the money supply and thus reduce interest rates, provided that the wage cuts do not stimulate hoarding. Other factors must also be considered in such a case. Wage cuts may shatter confidence by increasing strikes and labor strife; they may increase the instability in the price level; and they may also have international repercussions if the country is on the gold standard. Professor Keynes points out that monetary policy may be a desirable alternative to wage policy. For example, the same effects on the rate of interest that are achieved by reducing wage rates while the money supply remains constant may be produced by increasing the quantity of money while leaving the level of wages unchanged.[2] The government has much greater control over the money supply than it has over wage rates, some of which may be fixed for years by trade or joint agreements.

Because of the difficulties and dangers in any attempt to control the business cycle through wage-level changes, a number of economists believe that the maintenance of a stable general level of money wages is the most advisable policy to pursue, especially if international adjustments are to be secured by means of fluctuating exchange rates.[3]

Many economists do, however, favor a depressional wage policy of reductions for special groups of workers in the capital-goods industries, especially in the building trades.[4] Such a partial or relative

[1] For a discussion of this policy, cf. W. B. Reddaway, "Australian Wage Policy, 1929–1937," *International Labour Review*, vol. 37 (March 1938), pp. 314–37. It is also discussed more fully in Chapter 12 *infra*.

[2] Keynes, *op. cit.*, p. 266.

[3] *Cf.*, for example, *ibid.*, p. 270; and E. R. Walker, *op. cit.*, pp. 791–93.

[4] *Cf.*, for example, Sumner H. Slichter, *op. cit.*, pp. 133–35; H. M. Oliver, Jr., "Wage Reductions and Employment," *Southern Economic Journal*, vol. 5 (January 1939), p. 315; E. M. Bernstein, "Wage-Rates, Investment, and Employment," *Journal*

wage cut should be distinguished from a general wage reduction. The aim is to stimulate the demand for certain capital goods by a relative reduction in wages and prices while, presumably, the level of all other wages and prices remains unchanged. The construction industry suffers severely during some depressions, and it is argued that investment will be stimulated more by a reduction in building wages than it would be, for example, by a cut in the wages of retail clerks.

This argument for a wage reduction in the machine-making or construction industries has been accepted by advisers to the Roosevelt Administration and by economists who are strongly opposed to general wage slashes. Some of them maintain that the demand for most capital goods is elastic (greater than unit elasticity), although there is no agreement among economists on this point.[1] Indeed, some insist that during a depression, when much existing capital equipment is idle and consumption is not increasing, there would be little or no new investment even if money could be borrowed at a zero rate of interest.[2] The economists favoring wage reductions in the depressed capital-goods industries, where average wages are normally at least 20 per cent above the average in consumers' goods industries, argue that the repercussions on consumption will be slight because only a small portion of the working population is employed in the construction and machine-making industries. In the meantime, they say, consumption will be stimulated by the increase in employment brought about through the multiplier principle following the increased production of capital goods. They advocate a policy of easy money and low interest rates, to act, along with the reduced price for capital goods resulting from the wage cuts, as an inducement to businessmen to increase investment during the depression.[3]

Sample statistics for apartment and small-house construction

of *Political Economy*, vol. 47 (April 1939), pp 227–31; Emil Lederer, "Industrial Fluctuations and Wage Policy," *International Labour Review*, vol. 39 (January 1939), p. 30; A. P. Lerner, *op. cit.*, p. 169; and E. R. Walker, *op. cit.*, p. 791.

[1] Professor Donald H. Wallace thinks it "probable that elasticity of demand for many capital goods becomes very much less in depression." *Op. cit.*, p. 352.

[2] The bankers seem to agree with this notion, for they argue that the demand for loanable funds during a depression is very inelastic, even though such funds represent generalized purchasing power for which the elasticity of demand should be greater than it would be for most particular investment projects to be financed by borrowed funds.

[3] *Cf.* Bernstein, *op. cit.*, p. 231.

indicate that about two thirds of all construction costs are for materials and that the remaining one third goes for payrolls to labor working on the site of the building. When allowance is made for land costs, taxes, interest charges, and operating expenses, labor costs for construction may be less than one fourth of the complete costs, including carrying charges, of a residence or an apartment house. Consequently, wage reductions in the building trades alone are not likely to cause a significant reduction in the total cost of owning and operating a new home or a new apartment house. In order to cause a significant reduction in housing costs, building-materials prices must also be reduced, which might mean wage cuts in the materials industries. But the further the wage cuts are spread, the more consumption and the general rate of spending may be affected. Some economists maintain that the stimulus to recovery must first come, as it generally has in the past, through an increase in consumption which will spread to the capital-goods industries through the acceleration principle. They believe, therefore, that the proper policy is to stimulate consumption by means of public spending and measures tending to equalize incomes, which will increase the propensity to consume in the community.

CHAPTER TWELVE

GOVERNMENT REGULATION OF WAGES

Governments regulate wage rates and fix legal minimum wages for various social and economic purposes. Whether the objective is to raise the standard of living of low-wage groups or to modify the swings in the business cycle, purposeful regulation of wages by governments represents a definite policy. This chapter on wage regulation, therefore, continues the discussion in the previous chapter on wage policies and illustrates how wage regulation has worked in practice. In fact, the most outstanding attempt to control the business cycle by wage policy occurred in Australia during the 1930's under the machinery for fixing minimum wages.

In 1939 minimum-wage legislation in some form was to be found in at least 16 different countries, including France, Germany, Poland, and Canada. It was first adopted in New Zealand and Australia over 40 years ago. Both England and the United States have followed, to some extent, the principles and methods developed in Australia. For a study of the problem of wage regulation in capitalistic countries, the experience in Australia, New Zealand, Great Britain, and the United States is probably of most significance. This discussion of the principles, problems, and results of minimum-wage regulation will, therefore, be confined to developments in those four countries.

MINIMUM-WAGE REGULATION ABROAD

Because there has been such a close correspondence between the development of minimum-wage laws and policies in Australia and their development in New Zealand, the experience of these two countries will be handled under one heading.

Australia and New Zealand.[1] In the early 1890's in both

[1] This subsection is based primarily upon the following publications: *The Minimum Wage, an International Survey*, International Labour Office, 1939; J. Henry Richardson, *Industrial Conciliation and Arbitration in Australia and New Zealand*, 1939 (mimeographed);

Australia and New Zealand, legislation was passed establishing machinery for fixing minimum wages. The legislation was supported by the Liberal and Labour parties and was opposed by employers. The machinery consisted of flat minimum rates fixed by law for factory workers and a system of industrial courts or wage boards. Its purpose was to end the sweating of labor by long hours and miserable pay and to provide for the compulsory arbitration of labor disputes. As the system developed, the industrial courts, set up primarily for the settlement of disputes, took over most of the task of fixing minimum wages, maximum hours, and conditions of work.

In Australia the administration of minimum wages has been complicated by a conflict of jurisdiction between the industrial tribunals in the six states and the Federal Commonwealth Arbitration Court. It is possible for a building employer in some states, for example, to have his carpenters and laborers subject to the wage awards of the Federal court and his bricklayers and plasterers under the awards of the independent state tribunal. Unions in some states prefer the state tribunal and in other states, the Federal court, which deals with disputes extending beyond the boundary of one state. Workers may, therefore, attempt to "spread" the dispute into the Federal court if it is more liberal. About one half of the workers affected by minimum-wage awards come under the jurisdiction of the Federal court in Australia. The overlapping of jurisdiction and conflict in policies between the Federal and state tribunals have recently been eliminated in part. This jurisdictional difficulty has not been present in New Zealand, where there has been but one Arbitration Court, national in scope and covering over 250,000 workers. More than two thirds of all employees in Australia and over half of all employees in New Zealand have been under the jurisdiction of the arbitration tribunals and, therefore, subject to their awards.

In neither country has the national court been given any definite principles to follow in fixing minimum wages, hours of work, and overtime rates, or in determining the conditions of work. In both countries the whole structure of minimum wages rests upon the

W. R. Maclaurin, *Economic Planning in Australia, 1929–1936*, 1937; W. B. Reddaway, "Australian Wage Policy, 1927–1937," *International Labour Review*, vol. 37 (March 1938); E. J. Riches, "The Restoration of Compulsory Arbitration in New Zealand," *International Labour Review*, vol. 34 (December 1936); and by the same author, "Conflicts of Principle in Wage Regulation in New Zealand," *Economica*, vol. 5 (August 1938).

basic or living wage awarded for the lowest grade of unskilled labor. This "basic wage" is determined, at least in part, by the cost of a reasonable living for a family of four or five. For women the basic wage in Australia is about 54 per cent as large as the basic wage for men, and generally must be sufficient to support an adult female in "a fair and average standard of comfort."

On the foundation of this "basic wage" are built the minimum wages for other grades of labor. The specific "margins" above the basic wage are determined according to the degree of skill of the job. Consequently, when the basic wage is raised or lowered, all the other minima for the more skilled workers are generally increased or decreased by the same amount (not percentage).

In both countries the first general wage award of the national courts occurred in 1907. The "Harvester Judgment" in Australia, made after a study of living costs, set 42 shillings a week (approximately $10.20 in American money at the 1907 exchange rate) as a fair and reasonable basic wage. That wage was about 27 per cent above the average unskilled wage in 1907, but the sharp increase had no perceptible effect on employment. Following the "Harvester Judgment," the court in New Zealand established a basic living wage that the president of the court considered to be about 27 per cent above the existing minimum there.

From 1907 on, changes in the basic wage by the national courts in both countries were based mainly upon alterations in the cost of living. The basic wage was kept up to date in Australia by an adjustment every three or six months for cost-of-living changes. As a means of providing "a reasonable living wage," the New Zealand court practically pegged the basic wage to the retail price level from 1912 to 1923. The court awards in New Zealand normally run for three years, but retail prices soared so rapidly from 1918 to 1923 that the court, during that period, was given the power to alter the wage level throughout all trades at regular intervals, which it did every six months by proclaiming a bonus determined by changes in a price index for household expenditures. Consequently, real-wage rates were maintained with little change during the boom and the slump that followed the first World War.

Notions as to the capacity of industry to pay wages also played a part in some of the decisions of the New Zealand court on basic wages prior to 1930. Furthermore, the margins for skill have, at times, been permitted to decline somewhat on grounds that industries did not have the capacity to pay such high wages, or that the skilled workers were less in need of state protection. After 1918 the New Zealand court followed the practice of setting three basic wages: one for unskilled, one for semiskilled, and one for skilled labor. The employer, of course, has always been free to pay more than the minima the court sets.

The method of adjusting wages by movements in living costs, which for the most part prevailed in both countries from 1907 to 1930, was disrupted by the sharp fall in the prices of Australia's and New Zealand's exports beginning in 1929. The economies of both countries are very dependent upon exports, for about 30 per cent of Australia's production, and about 40 per cent of New Zealand's production, is exported. Wool and wheat account for over half the total value of Australia's exports, and three fourths of New Zealand's exports are wool, butter, and meats. These commodities dropped so sharply in price compared to the prices of their imports that Australia and New Zealand were forced to send much more of their products abroad than formerly in order to buy a certain quantity of imports. For example, the buying power of New Zealand's exports in terms of imports fell over 40 per cent from 1929 to 1932.

A country's standard of living is determined by the volume of internal production minus exports plus imports. Consequently, although the volume of production in New Zealand remained almost constant from 1929 to 1933, exports increased 30 per cent and imports decreased about 40 per cent, so that the volume of goods available for consumption in New Zealand in 1932 and 1933 was only about 68 per cent of the 1929 figure.[1] The decline was not so sharp in Australia. There the available real income in 1931 and 1932 was about 85 per cent of the 1929 level.[2]

There was a feeling in Australia that this loss in the national income, arising primarily from the change in foreign markets, should be distributed equitably amongst all classes in the community. Most of the economists in Australia advocated a 10-per-cent cut in real wages, a reduction in interest rates, and a policy of allowing foreign exchange to find its "natural price." Influenced by the

[1] Cf. Economic Journal, vol. 47 (March 1937), p. 194.
[2] Cf. Colin Clark and J. G. Crawford, The National Income of Australia, 1938, p. 65.

economists' reasoning, the Commonwealth Arbitration Court in January 1931 awarded a reduction in real wages of 10 per cent (representing a total money-wage cut of 26 per cent since 1929), and in the same month the exchange value of the currency declined 11 per cent (making a total decline of 23 per cent since 1929). In the middle of 1931, interest rates on Federal bonds, mortgages, and other obligations were reduced by 22.5 per cent.

It is estimated that the Federal court's award of a 10-per-cent cut in real wages directly affected one fifth of all wage-earners, and that by 1933 about one half of the wage-earners in Australia had had their wages reduced by the full amount of the Federal court's 1931 award. Some of the state courts were slow to follow the lead of the Federal court, so at times there were fairly wide discrepancies between the state and Federal basic wages. These discrepancies were, however, narrowed down during the succeeding recovery period. With economic recovery, the Federal court in 1934 restored part of the 1931 cut. Influenced by the advice of economists, the Federal court raised wages by a "prosperity loading" of four to six shillings in 1937, which restored real wages to the 1929 level. It was argued that increased wages would serve as a check on the tendency toward overexpansion and unhealthy boom conditions and that a wider distribution of the increased national income would lead to steadier progress. The boom was, however, checked by a decline in 1937 in the price of Australia's important exports.

It is clear that during the 1930's the Federal court in Australia tried to modify the business cycle by wage policy. That, however, is difficult for the court to do, for it has no control over monetary and fiscal policy, the exchange rate, or the foreign demand for Australia's exports. Economic conditions in Australia have been largely determined by changes in the foreign markets for Australia's exports. Therefore, it has been argued that variations in the exchange rate may be a more desirable method of adjusting the Australian economy to changes in external conditions than are variations in the wage level. An Australian economist who has served as adviser to the Federal court says:

. . . a policy of exchange depreciation with stable, or slightly reduced, money wages would bring all the benefits that could be expected from cutting wages. Such a policy would probably lead to somewhat lower real wages, . . . It would have many advantages: the relief to the exporters would be direct and immediate, while with lower wages it came only slowly as the wage reductions led to lower charges for goods; there would not be the grave complications about debts which arise when all prices are reduced; dealers would not be faced with a series of losses as they sold stocks bought at a higher price level; above all, in this instance, there would have been none of the friction arising out of the different wages declared by the various tribunals.[1]

The course of events during the 1930's was rather different in New Zealand. The level of real wages there remained two or three per cent above the 1929 figure from 1930 to 1936. In June 1931 the court did award a general reduction of 10 per cent in money wage rates, but the critics of the court continued to insist that wages were being maintained at an artificially high level. In 1932, at the instance of organized farmers and employers, a coalition government practically limited the powers of the court to wage awards for women only. The Labour Government, which came into office in 1935, restored and strengthened the power of the court in 1936.

The suspension of the court's authority in 1932 was to facilitate the lowering of wages and to make wages more flexible. It is interesting, therefore, to note that during this suspension period the decline in the general index number of wage rates was less than 10 per cent—in fact, less than the decline in the cost of living, so that real wages actually rose during the period. The fact that women's wages fell slightly less than the wages of men, who were better organized, has been cited as evidence that the right of appeal to the court, which women workers retained during that period, afforded them some real protection.

In July 1936 all the cuts in money wage rates imposed by the New Zealand court during the depression period were restored, which raised the level of real wages almost nine per cent above the 1929 figure. By January 1933 the New Zealand currency had depreciated to the level that the Australian currency had maintained since December 1931. From the available evidence, such as statistics of production, consumption, and unemployment, the recovery in New Zealand up to 1939 seems to have been as rapid and as substantial as the recovery in Australia.

In both New Zealand and Australia the arbitration courts, in

[1] W. B. Reddaway, *op. cit.*, pp. 330–31.

deciding wage cases, have often vacillated between the two conflicting principles of social need for the workers and economic capacity of industry to pay wages. Both these criteria are indefinite and elastic. Usually the need for a "reasonable" living wage has been stressed in awards of basic rates for unskilled workers, whereas the condition of industry has been given more weight in setting "fair margins" for skill. In Australia since 1930 the stress has been primarily upon economic or business conditions. The workers, of course, have generally favored the living-wage principle rather than a nebulous capacity-to-pay notion that seems to work against them under most circumstances.

Although there have been some exceptions, the New Zealand and Australian courts have generally followed the principle of considering wage-paying capacity in terms of industry as a whole and have shown little inclination to give special concessions to depressed industries. The New Zealand court, for example, has expressed the opinion that "if an industry cannot pay the workers engaged in it a reasonable wage it is in the interests of the community that it should cease operations and that such workers should become absorbed in some other and more profitable industry." The Federal court in Australia has made similar statements. Although in New Zealand the fact that a particular industry is enjoying unusual prosperity has not been considered a reason for awarding rates above the standard minima, in certain cases in Australia the Federal court has granted industry, or "prosperity," allowances to workers in an industry which was particularly prosperous at the time.

The results of minimum-wage regulation in Australasia are difficult to determine because the influence of one factor cannot be completely isolated in a complex situation. In both countries the national income is, to a considerable degree, dependent upon external trade. Some conclusions can, however, be drawn. "Sweating" has been eliminated.[1] The system has favored unskilled and other workers whose bargaining power is weak. The various wage rates for unskilled workers in Australia and New Zealand have been much higher than, for example, in Great Britain. Comparison with the differential rates for skill in England indicates that the

---

[1] "Sweating" involves taking advantage of the weak economic position of workers by working them for long hours at unduly low wages in cheap, unhealthy "sweatshops."

advantages of wage regulation in Australasia have not been so great for the more skilled workers. Furthermore, wage rates have been made uniform for each grade of work, and wage movements have been standardized. The rise in the level of real wages in Australia from 1907 to 1936 was not so great as it was in Britain.

It has been claimed by some that the wage-award system has widened the gap between wage rates in tariff-sheltered industry and unsheltered agriculture, but there was no tendency for this gap to close in New Zealand during the period of suspension in the 1930's, and it is probable that the trade-unions in the sheltered industries could achieve as much without state wage regulation. In both countries a majority of the citizenry favor such regulation, even though it involves some red tape and loss of time. In both countries the court's friends and enemies have shifted sides at times. Labor leaders generally believe that the system provides a higher level of wages, especially for the unskilled and weaker working groups. They also believe that it fosters union member-ship because the court's jurisdiction is limited to disputes involving registered unions of workers. Through such wage regulation, em-ployers obtain protection against competitive wage-cutting and adjustment of wage disputes with little open strife and few strikes. There is no doubt that the settlement of wage issues by a political authority rather than by economic force stimulates political activity by labor groups.

Great Britain.[1] In 1909 Great Britain passed a Trade Boards Act applying to trades in which wage rates were "exceptionally low as compared with other employments." This Act was patterned after the 1894 law of the Australian State of Victoria, which pro-vided for trade boards composed of representatives of employers, employees, and the public, as a means of fixing minimum wages in certain "sweated" trades. By 1918 British experience had indicated the desirability of extending the minimum-wage machinery be-yond "sweated" trades to industries lacking adequate employer-employee organization for wage regulation. It was felt that in-dustrial harmony required some machinery to prevent a sudden

[1] Material for this subsection has been gathered chiefly from the following: *The Minimum Wage, an International Survey*, International Labour Office, 1939; Dorothy Sells, *British Wages Boards, a Study in Industrial Democracy*, 1939; and Sir Hector Hether-ington, "The Working of the British Trade Board System," *International Labour Review*, vol. 38 (October 1938), pp. 472–80.

fall in wages after the first World War. Consequently, the 1918 amendment empowered the Minister of Labour to set up a trade board wherever "no adequate machinery exists for the effective regulation of wages throughout the trade." Nine boards were set up under the 1909 Act, and by 1922 a total of 52 boards had been established under the 1918 amendment. In 1924, the wages-board system was extended to agriculture. It is estimated that in 1939 almost 2,000,000 workers (about nine per cent of the working population) belonged to trades covered by the boards established under these acts. About 70 per cent of the workers covered by boards in industry were women.

The laws contain no clear definition of the principles to be followed in determining minimum wages. In general the following criteria are used, but with no agreement as to the relative weight of each: (1) a rate sufficient for maintenance so that the reproach of "sweating" is avoided, (2) a rate more or less equivalent to rates paid in comparable occupations, and (3) a rate which market conditions will permit the industry to pay. In actual practice, the resulting rates are largely a consequence of bargaining and compromise between employer and employee members on the boards. They are, however, subject to the approval of the Minister of Labour. Changes in living costs do, of course, constitute good grounds for a request for a change in rates. During the depression of the 1930's, one half of the boards reduced their minimum rates by varying amounts.

The rates set by each board apply only to that one industry or trade, with provision sometimes for regional differentials. Besides a general minimum rate for men and for women, special minimum rates for skilled workers are fixed in some cases. The minimum rates for women are about 57 per cent of the rate for men in unskilled work. As in Australasia, the boards fix the normal working week and overtime rates and also grant special exemptions from the general minimum rate for workers of subnormal productive capacity, such as learners, juveniles, and injured or infirm workers.

In many trades, wage rates were raised considerably with the first introduction of the minimum wage by a wage board. In some cases minima were established at almost double the previous wage in certain localities. There is some statistical evidence that in the 1920's and 1930's real wages were relatively higher in the covered industries than in trades not subject to minimum-wage regulation.[1]

It has been claimed that, especially in agriculture, minimum wages at times were fixed at a level higher than the industry could bear. The Cave Committee, appointed in 1922 to investigate the workings and effects of the Trade Boards Acts, considered it possible that some of the boards had contributed to the volume of unemployment during the sharp decline in prices and trade in 1920 and 1921, but no special or statistical investigation was made to determine the issue. An investigation in 1923 of trades in which such complaints had been made revealed that in each case the unemployment was due to causes more profound and more far-reaching than the minimum wage.[2] It is interesting to note that during the depression of the 1930's "No cry was raised against minimum-wage legislation, in spite of the fact that Trade Board rates maintained remarkable stability during that period."[3] Of the nine industrial groups showing over 20 per cent of unemployment in December 1937, only two were subject to a legal minimum wage. At that time the average minimum rates in Britain were roughly equivalent to $16 a week for adult male workers in industry, $10.75 for adult males in agriculture, and $9 a week for adult female workers in industry.[4] In some lines there has been a definite tendency for the rates fixed by the Trade Boards to become the prevailing rates for that class of workers, although a number of workers may receive better pay.[5]

Not only has the English system of minimum-wage boards abolished "sweating" and improved labor relations considerably in the covered industries, but it has tended to stimulate efficient management and improvements in working methods. Some employers have praised the legislation for that reason. In 1922 the Trade Board Inspector in Charge of Special Enquiries testified that the

---

[1] Cf. D. Sells, op. cit., pp. 270–90.

[2] Dorothy Sells, The British Trade Boards System, 1923, Part 4, and "The Economic Effects of the British Trade Boards System," International Labour Review, vol. 8 (August 1923), pp. 191–220.

[3] Sells, British Wages Boards, op. cit., pp. 300–301.

[4] Ibid., p. 281. These figures may be compared with $12 a week, which is now the minimum wage for all industrial workers covered by the American Fair Labor Standards Act of 1938, and with $16 a week which will be the minimum under that Act in 1945, except for industries granted a lower minimum by the administrator. The reader should bear in mind that comparisons of minima in different countries fail to allow for differentials in standards and costs of living.

[5] Ibid., p. 288.

enforcement of minimum rates had "resulted in most employers acquiring a greater knowledge of the details of their business" and that "many employers frankly welcome the fixing and enforcing of minimum rates because they provide a basis for equitable competition by materially reducing, if not eliminating, that element of the trade which previously 'cut' market prices by 'trimming' the wages of workers." Indeed, the Banking Trade Board recently established was first proposed by organized bankers who argued that they should be protected against unorganized competitors who were paying low rates. A writer with long experience as chairman and member of trade boards stated in 1938:

The system has produced stability without rigidity. Many businesses which could maintain themselves only by the payment of sweated wages have been forced out of existence. But, on the whole, they have been replaced by more efficient units which have been able to support the higher rates. Wages have risen; employment has not diminished; and there are few trades which would readily return to the unregulated position of pre-Board days.[1]

ECONOMIC THEORY OF THE MINIMUM WAGE

The case for minimum-wage regulation on economic grounds rests primarily upon the nature of the labor market, including the supply curve of labor. Other economic arguments include the effects of minimum-wage regulation upon workers' health and productivity, upon the distribution of income, and upon employment

The labor market and "exploitation." The discussion in Chapter 5 indicated that most labor markets are a far cry from the perfect market as envisioned by economists and that there are situations in which a number of wage rates may clear the market or in which no rate will equate demand and supply. Part of the difficulty arises from the fact that the general supply curve for labor, at least in some sections, has a negative slope and, therefore, tends to parallel the demand curve.

Numerous studies have brought out the imperfect character of most labor markets. The New York State Department of Labor, for example, found that the wages of women laundry workers in 32 New York municipalities showed a complete lack of standardiza-

[1] H. Hetherington, *op. cit.*, pp. 479–80.

tion in May 1933. There were marked differences in rates for the same type of work in the same locality. The hourly rate for flat workers ranged from 13 to 50 cents; the full-time weekly earnings of press operators varied from under $6 to $20; and the actual weekly earnings of hand ironers ranged from under $3 to $28. Average weekly earnings were $3.67 in one plant and $15.12 in another. The highest median (middle) rate per week ($14.64) was found in cities from 50,000 to 100,000 inhabitants and the lowest median rate ($10.34) in cities 10 times as large (from 500,000 to 1,000,000). It is no wonder that the New York State Laundry-owners' Association complained of the chaotic condition in the industry and urged, in 1933, the enactment of a state minimum-wage law. The Industrial Commissioner in New York concluded from this 1933 study of the laundry industry that "wages are in many cases fixed by chance and caprice" and "bear no relation to the fair value of the service rendered." [1]

In 1934 the Women's Bureau of the United States Department of Labor analyzed data from various studies showing variations in wage rates paid under corresponding conditions.[2] Efforts were made to assure that the material used in making comparisons was comparable in every possible respect. Factors such as differentials between men's and women's wages, or variations in the hours worked, in the type of product, or in the size of the city were taken into account. A study of 20 cotton mills in North Carolina in 1932 showed the median wage for women in the highest paying plant was double the median in the lowest paying plant. A survey of 129 shirt factories in 19 states in the Summer of 1933 revealed that the median week's earnings of women differed as much as 200 or 350 per cent between plants in the same state. Hourly wages in 11 large laundry plants in Ohio in May 1933 ranged from a median of 13 cents in one plant to 28 cents in another. A number of studies also showed some male and female workers receiving hourly wage rates double those of other employees doing identical work in the same plant. The conclusion from such comparisons, made under

[1] *Cf.* New York State Department of Labor, *Report of the Industrial Commissioner to the Laundry Minimum Wage Board Relating to Wages and Other Conditions of Employment of Women and Minors in the Laundry Industry, New York State,* 1933 (mimeographed), pp. 44, 67–69, and Letter of Transmittal.

[2] *Cf.* Mary Elizabeth Pidgeon, *Variations in Wage Rates Under Corresponding Conditions,* U. S. Department of Labor, Women's Bureau, Bulletin No. 122, 1935, pp. 1–10, 41.

conditions as nearly identical as possible, was that variations in wages paid for essentially the same work were so wide and marked as to be attributable only to a lack of wage standards—to imperfections in the labor market.

In his classic article opposing minimum wages for women, Professor F. W. Taussig admits that their weak bargaining power "causes much to depend on the temper and character of the individual employer" and that "the conditions of their employment are such as to lead easily to 'unfair' wages—wages kept low by taking advantage of timidity, ignorance, lack of mobility, lack of bargaining power." [1] Yet, although he recognizes that "divergent rates of pay under similar conditions point strongly to haphazard influences of this sort," he argues that there is one price which "alone clears the market." Indeed, his economic reasoning is based on the assumption that the labor market is a perfect market, that wages are determined by marginal productivity, and that the supply curve of female labor is "peculiarly elastic" and positively sloped.[2]

In what is perhaps the most complete theoretical study of state regulation of wages, Professor A. C. Pigou also analyzes the problem on the basis of the marginal-productivity theory, assuming both that the supply curve of labor is positively sloped and that, if workers are "mulcted of part of their possible earnings by the greater strategic strength" of employers, it will make no difference to the rate of spending or to the size of the total national income.[3]

If one thing is clear from the analysis of the labor market in Chapter 5, it is that the marginal-productivity theory does not furnish an adequate basis for reasoning on the effects of minimum-wage regulation. Chapter 7 pointed out some of the weaknesses in that theory of wages, which rests on the assumption of perfect markets and free competition between employers. It cannot be too strongly emphasized that minimum-wage regulation is needed primarily because labor markets are so imperfect, because the supply of labor apparently has a negative slope, and because "exploitation" of labor can and does occur,[4] although there are so many

[1] F. W. Taussig, "Minimum Wages for Women," *Quarterly Journal of Economics*, vol. 30 (May 1916), pp. 430, 431.

[2] *Ibid.*, pp. 420, 422, 434, 441.

[3] A. C. Pigou, *The Economics of Welfare*, 1920, p. 516. Public regulation of wages is discussed in Part III, Chapters 11, 13, 15, 16, and 17 of Pigou's book.

[4] *Cf.* the discussion of exploitation in Chapter 5 and the footnote at the end of the section on the marginal-productivity theory in Chapter 7, where it was pointed

imperfections in the labor market that the full extent of such exploitation is difficult to determine. The analysis of income, consumption, and employment in Chapters 9 and 10 indicates how questionable is Pigou's assumption that the exploitation of workers (paying them wages below the rates that would prevail if the labor market were a perfect one) will have no effect upon total incomes and the total volume of employment.

Professor Pigou mentions that in many parts of England before the first World War the wages of agricultural laborers were kept down by tacit understandings among farmers and a fear of adverse local opinion by those who would otherwise willingly raise wages.[1] In such cases of exploitation he recognizes that "the legal enforcement of a higher wage would [increase] the number of labourers in a way unambiguously advantageous to the national dividend" or national income.[2] Higher wage rates for workers in one industry or one firm would, therefore, cause employment in the firm or industry to expand, so that workers' incomes would rise more than in proportion to the increase in wage rates.

This situation of employment expanding because of a forced increase in wage rates confined to a particular firm or industry arises out of monopolistic elements in the purchase of labor and was illustrated by a mathematical example in a footnote at the end of Chapter 5.[3] In that example an employer did not hire more units of labor at $5.20 a day, although the marginal receipts from each new unit of labor would have been $5.50 a day, because the hiring of more workers would have forced the employer to increase the wage of all his labor force in that group from $5.00 to $5.20 a day. The necessary wage increase for the existing force, if $5.20 had to be paid for new workers, would have made the marginal costs of hiring new workers exceed the marginal receipts from each new unit of labor ($5.50 a day).

Supply, demand, and profits. What the government may do through minimum-wage legislation is to eliminate the possibility of employers' keeping the wage rate low by not bidding up the wage in order to hire more workers, or the possibility of depressing wage rates by hiring fewer workers. When the government es-

out that the explanations involving exploitation in this and the following chapter are based on the concept of a perfect market rather than the other assumptions and implications of the marginal-productivity theory.

[1] Pigou, *op. cit.*, pp. 513–14, 517.   [2] *Idem.*   [3] *Cf.* p. 126.

tablishes an effective **minimum** wage, it actually makes part of the supply curve of labor to an employer horizontal at that minimum wage, as it would be in a perfect market. As a result, the employer loses the possibility of hiring workers at a rate below the minimum. The change brought about by a uniform minimum wage is illustrated in Figure 10, in which *LS* represents the total hours of labor

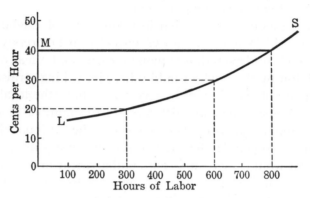

FIG. 10. Effect of Minimum Wage upon Employer's Labor Supply.

offered to an employer in an imperfect market at various wage rates and *MS* represents the supply curve of labor in that same market after a minimum wage of 40 cents an hour has become effective. The employer in this example no longer has the choice of buying 300 hours of labor at 20 cents an hour, 600 hours at 30 cents an hour, or 800 hours at 40 cents an hour. After the minimum wage has been established, he must pay at least 40 cents an hour for all of his labor. Under such circumstances, he is likely to employ more workers, because he cannot obtain labor at a wage below 40 cents an hour by hiring less than 800 hours. A reduction in his demand for labor below 800 hours would then have no effect upon the wage rate.

The reader will observe that Figure 10 contains no demand curve. It is possible that a particular employer might eventually be forced out of business by a minimum wage of 40 cents an hour. His elimination might occur through bankruptcy, in which case creditors might take over the firm. If, however, wages remained so high that the return on newly invested capital in the firm would be well below the average rate of return in all industry, it is possible that capital might gradually be withdrawn from that firm as the equipment was permitted to wear out without replacement. It may be difficult and costly, however, to withdraw capital gradually until plants become worthless, and, as will be explained presently by an example from the rubber industry, the officers of corporations are not likely to let plants run down and to cease reinvesting earnings simply because the firm has been earning a return below the average for all industry.

One of the reasons that a demand curve has not been drawn in Figure 10 is that the employer's demand for labor at various wage rates is likely to be changed (probably increased) by the minimum wage, especially if the minimum-wage administration fixes a uniform minimum that affects the wages paid by competing firms in that industry, by firms in industries manufacturing substitute products, and by firms competing with the employer for local labor. No longer would firms in a locality be able to keep wages below 40 cents an hour by following the practice of paying a prevailing wage below that figure. In case some of the wages paid by all firms in an industry are affected by the minimum wage, one firm may not have its labor costs increased relative to the labor costs of its competitors. Then the question becomes one of how a labor-cost increase in an industry may affect sales, employment, and profits in that industry. If the labor-cost increase should affect all industries to an equal degree, reasoning concerning its effects must be on a general, all-industry basis. In so far as the effects of minimum wages are distributed unequally among firms or among industries, some firms and industries may gain at the expense of those affected most adversely.

It was pointed out in the discussion of women's wages in the section on wage differentials in Chapter 8 that one of the factors depressing women's wages and preventing the substitution of lower wage female workers for male workers is the fact that higher wages for newly hired women would probably necessitate a like increase in the rates paid to all women in that firm because women workers are not as a rule differentiated into separate crafts and wage classes.

No one knows how prevalent the exploitation of workers is and the extent to which an increase of wage rates forced upon the low-wage firms in a particular industry might cause an increase, or at least no decrease, in the employment offered by such firms either in the short or the long run. That the establishment of minimum wages would not cause a decrease in employment in many industries and localities seems to be indicated by the various wage-rate and labor-market studies conducted by the Women's Bureau of the U. S. Department of Labor and the state minimum-wage administrations, some of which have been mentioned.

If employers do not compete with one another, but instead have mutual agreements or understandings not to raise wages above a given point, there may be no market force causing wages to increase. As Professor Paul Douglas explains, there is a considerable body of evidence that employers frequently do make and observe understandings on wage policy.[1] Some employers in smaller cities hesitate to raise wage rates for fear of becoming unpopular among their associates, which helps to explain why the smaller the city, the lower wage rates tend to be. In towns dominated by one firm, such as the mill villages of the South or the company towns (in steel, coal, metal mining, lumber, etc.) of the North, it is obvious that there may be little or no wage competition for labor in the local market. Furthermore, as Professor Douglas points out,

> . . . in a very large percentage of cases, movement from one town or small city to another merely means moving into another place where wages are set more or less authoritatively by the big employer or employers of the new locality. How much, for example, will a Southern mill-worker benefit himself by moving from one mill village to another? The same question may be raised for wide areas in the North, Middle West, and West, of the United States. All too often a worker merely moves from one place where the wage is monopolistically set to another place where it is similarly set.[2]

Under such circumstances, some wage rates may be well below theoretical marginal productivity or the rate that would prevail were the labor market a perfect market. The competition between employers, which in our economy is supposed to assure the payment of full marginal productivity, simply does not exist.[3]

Professor Taussig contends that, if the employers take "no more than the competitive capitalists' toll," low wage rates are not due

---

[1] Paul Douglas, "Wage Theory and Wage Policy," *International Labour Review*, vol. 39 (March 1939), p. 342.

[2] *Idem.*

[3] *Cf.* Paul Douglas, "The Economic Theory of Wage Regulation," *University of Chicago Law Review*, vol. 5 (February 1938), p. 214.

to "oppressive exercise of bargaining strength by the employers," that no exploitation of workers is occurring if employers' profits are not "above the usual or competitive level." [1]

Various investigations of rates of profit, however, fail to reveal that profits tend toward any usual, normal, average, or minimum level.[2] Wide variations in profits occur between firms and between industries, and a certain group of firms and industries may consistently show extremely high profit rates year after year. Differences exceeding 100 per cent between the average profit rates earned by considerable groups of corporations may persist for a decade or more. Such statistical studies of profits indicate that most business firms continue to produce as much at low as at high rates of profit. There is, therefore, no right level of profits, any more than there is one correct level for interest rates or wage rates.[3] In such cases, the level that industry becomes accustomed to may seem the most appropriate one. Furthermore, the rate of profit on capital investment may be increased or decreased by writing capital values down or up. This is one of the reasons why it is extremely difficult to find agreement amongst economists and accountants as to just what the rate of profit really is in any particular case. Consequently, one simply cannot, as Professor Douglas suggests, test the capacity of industry to pay higher minimum wages by observing how high profit and interest rates are.[4] Indeed, the rate of profit might seem low for any one of a number of reasons, including the inflation of capital values as a result of capitalizing the advantages derived from exploiting labor.

Labor supply and efficiency. The nature of the supply curve for labor in general and for female workers in particular is such that there generally is little pressure through market forces on the supply side to cause wage rates to increase. Consequently, wage rates, once established, tend to continue. In fact, if real wages are declining, not only does the supply of labor tend to increase but

---

[1] Taussig, *op. cit.*, pp. 429–31.

[2] *Cf.*, for example, David Friday, *Profits, Prices and Wages*, 1920, pp. 36–38; and Ralph C. Epstein, *Industrial Profits in the United States*, 1934, pp. 101–11 and pp. 579–87. Professor Epstein attributes the lack of a central tendency in profits partly to the imperfect character of competition, to the prevalence of trade-marks, special designs of products, quasi monopoly, and advantages of all sorts, which prevent producers from manufacturing identical products for sale (pp. 111–12).

[3] *Cf.* the discussion of interest rates in Chapters 1 and 9.

[4] *Cf.* Paul H. Douglas, "The Economic Theory of Wage Regulation," *op. cit.*, p. 202.

the workers' efficiency tends to fall off with the reduction in their real income, and such a drop in efficiency may decrease the nation's product or income. The effect tends to be cumulative, because at a lower level of wages workers are in a weaker bargaining position. On the other hand, to quote Professor Pigou,

> If exploitation is prevented and wages are forced up to a fair level, the benefit to efficiency will start an upward movement exactly analogous to this downward movement. High earnings will lead to greater efficiency; greater efficiency will lead to the power of obtaining higher earnings, both because the workers' services are worth more and because, being better off, they are in a stronger position for bargaining.[1]

It is necessary to add that such an increase in efficiency alone would not cause money wage rates to rise and to continue at a higher level. It is because the increase in wages is likely to decrease the total number of hours of labor offered for sale that the higher wage rate tends to stick.

Sidney Webb explains that the establishment of a minimum wage tends to increase the physical productivity of the workers affected, because higher wages build the worker up physically by raising his standard of living, stimulate management to adopt new processes and improved methods, drive business away from the least competent employers, and lead to the selection of only the best workers.[2] Of course, all firms cannot have the pick of the labor supply, so the effect of the last-mentioned factor is lessened the more general and uniform is the application of the minimum wage.

Mr. Webb contends that higher wage standards, like the more humane conditions forced upon employers by the English Factory Acts (limiting hours of work and laying down certain safety and health requirements) prove profitable to employers and advantageous to the community by making industry steadily more efficient and productive.[3] As with the Factory Acts, many employers in Britain overhauled their methods and equipment when minimum

---

[1] Pigou, *op. cit.*, pp. 549–50.

[2] Sidney Webb, "The Economic Theory of a Legal Minimum Wage," *Journal of Political Economy*, vol. 20 (December 1912), pp. 978–84. Such first-hand research as the investigations of the Ratan Tata Foundation in England bear out this view that the fixation of legal rates will increase efficiency of operation and management. *Cf.*, for example, R. H. Tawney, *The Establishment of Minimum Wage Rates in the Tailoring Industry*, 1915, pp. 160–65; and M. E. Bulkley, *The Establishment of Minimum Wage Rates in the Boxmaking Industry*, 1915, pp. 50–53.

[3] Webb, *op. cit.*, pp. 985–90.

wages were first introduced with results that pleased and astonished a number of employers who, at the outset, were not in favor of setting a floor to wage rates by law.[1] He points out that factory sanitation, safety, and hours laws, which some employers opposed at first because they involved additional expense, place more limits on business management than do minimum wages, which only bring an employer up to the wage level of other employers.

Conservation of human resources. Some people argue that it is against public policy to permit an employer, in normal times, to pay workers wages that are insufficient to provide the minimum amount of food, shelter, and clothing without which they cannot continue in good health. These people contend that the minimum wage is necessary in order to conserve our human resources and to improve the well-being of our population.

Minimum wages, like shorter hours, may prove to be a good investment—at least for the community as a whole—by improving the health and efficiency of underfed and poorly housed workers or by speeding up the rate of spending; but it is not likely that employers would voluntarily adopt such a program. In the first place, it takes time for what has been called the "steam-engine theory" to work—for increased wages (more fuel) to produce more efficient workers (more power)—and an individual employer may hesitate to make such an investment in workers, because there is no assurance that he would continue to retain the services of employees whose wages he might increase. The nation's capital stock of labor is, so to speak, offered for rent to the employer without any specific charges for rapid depreciation or deterioration. If some workers become run down because of low pay and abuse on the job, the employer can generally replace them by others drawn from the common pool.

Furthermore, an employer's sales are primarily dependent upon the payrolls of other employers, so that low or reduced wages for his workers will have little effect upon the demand for his product. If all employers could and did follow such a low-wage policy, however, it is likely that total expenditures would be decreased and that cyclical fluctuations in spending would increase, to the detriment of the community as a whole. Such general effects of extremely low wages upon total incomes, expenditures, and consump-

[1] Pigou, *op. cit.*, p. 517.

tion are no less real because they are difficult to determine and to measure. These general aspects of the question will be discussed more fully after the following analysis of the circumstances under which a forced increase of hourly wage rates in one firm or one industry alone will not cause a reduction in the total hours of employment offered by that firm or industry.

Possible situations in particular firms or industries. Previous discussion in this section has already indicated that a forced rise in wage rates will increase a firm's total employment, both in the short and the long run, if the firm has been "exploiting" those employees affected by the minimum wage and if the minimum wage is not above their full marginal productivity or the rate that would prevail were the labor market a perfect market. Such "exploitation" of workers may occur because of market imperfections, especially monopolistic elements on the buying side of the labor market. One must bear in mind that a forced rise in wage rates is likely to increase workers' marginal productivity because it tends to reduce the supply of labor hours offered for sale and it also tends to increase the efficiency or effectiveness of the workers.

Even without any previous "exploitation" of workers, there are circumstances under which a forced increase in wage rates would not decrease that firm's employment in the short or long run. A firm's unit costs of output would not be increased if the rise in wages should cause an expansion of production per worker by as large a percentage as the increase in total costs resulting from higher hourly wage rates. Such an expansion in production might occur because of an improvement in the efficiency of the workers or an improvement in production methods brought about by the wage rise. Whether the additional output would depress the price of the product would depend upon conditions in the product market. Under the assumptions of a perfect market, the increased output of any one firm would be too insignificant to affect the selling price. Therefore, if output per worker is increased as rapidly as total costs, so that costs per unit of output remain the same, employment in the firm presumably would not decrease. For a firm selling in an imperfect market, the increase in output per worker would have to be great enough so that the consequent reduction in unit costs would offset the decline in marginal receipts due to the downward-tipped or sloping demand curve for the product.

In the rare case of a competitive industry with an absolutely inelastic demand, an increase in costs and selling price would not decrease employment in the industry but might do so elsewhere by causing more funds to be spent for that industry's product. This situation would not occur under monopoly or monopolistic competition because a monopolist, unless restrained by law, would continue to increase his profit by raising his price until he had reached the point where the demand curve for his product became elastic (more elastic than unity). Under conditions of monopoly or imperfect competition, where firms have sloping instead of horizontal demand curves, an increase in wage rates that increased unit costs of production would tend to cause the point of maximum profit to occur at a smaller output and volume of employment.

As the discussion in this and the previous chapter has indicated, employers may not, in many cases, hire workers according to the marginal-productivity theory. Employers are probably influenced mainly by such considerations as average costs, rates of profit, and the firm's market position. Because there is no minimum rate of profits and firms losing money may continue to operate at full capacity, it is possible for wages to be forced up at the expense of profits, even in an individual firm, without causing a reduction of employment and investment in that firm either immediately or within one or two decades. Studies of the profits of many corporations show that firms invest new capital in spite of the fact that their rate of profits is lower than that obtaining in other lines of industry, where profits are not only higher but are increasing.[1] The flow of investment funds does not always follow the dictates of profit, partly because decisions to reinvest profits or depreciation reserves are made by corporation officials and directors, and not by each individual stockholder acting independently. Firms earning less than average profits generally do not cease all new investment. Indeed, a recent study shows that, during the 14 years from 1922 to 1936, the rate of profit on stockholders' investment in the rubber-tire industry was not much more than half the average rate of profit for all manufacturing industry.[2] Yet between 1927 and 1929, in the face of a poor dividend record, low earnings, and

[1] R. C. Epstein, *op. cit.*, pp. 583–87.
[2] Lloyd G. Reynolds, "Competition in the Rubber-Tire Industry," *American Economic Review*, vol. 28 (September 1938), pp. 464–65.

declining profits, there was an increase in plant construction that expanded the capacity of the rubber-tire industry by 50 per cent. The author of the rubber-tire study comments as follows on these facts:

It is very well for the calculating outsider to suggest that a business should be allowed to stagnate or waste away when it no longer yields normal returns on investment. To an official within the institution, however, such a proposal seems somehow treasonable. The corporation is a petty state whose borders, if they cannot be extended, must at least be maintained.[1]

This discussion indicates how complex and complicated is the question of the effect of minimum-wage regulation upon employment, even when, as in this subsection, the analysis is limited to the individual firm and no account is taken of effects upon total demand through changes in the rate of spending. The difficulty is that so many factors and conditions affect the problem that one cannot reason on the basis of a few simple assumptions. Consequently, definite and absolute answers are not possible.

Some possible effects. The discussion in the previous chapter of the effect of higher money wages upon employment applies with equal force here. Minimum wages may cause the use of more machinery and more economical methods of production; but, as already stated, such developments may increase employment by stimulating the capital-goods industries. It is strange that those who are so ready to explain that there is no need to fear technological advance are often the first ones to condemn wage regulation on the grounds that it will stimulate such advance.

It is claimed that minimum-wage regulation by one state will cause an exodus of industry from that state. That such state regulation may have a tendency to cause some industry gradually to shift its location is possible, although many of the low-wage service industries must be near their market. Chapter 19 contains a more extended discussion of this question of the effect of state and national labor standards upon the location of industry. The answer is somewhat different for states within a nation having a uniform currency system than it is for national regulation, where adjustment may occur through exchange rates. The migration of industry as a whole is not an argument that applies to national wage

[1] *Idem.*

regulation. The effects of higher wages upon international trade were treated in the previous chapter, and that discussion need not be repeated here.

In particular instances, the fixing of minimum wages by law may cause a company to change some of its personnel. For example, men may replace women or juvenile workers. An illustration of this is the famous case of the 21 scrubwomen at Harvard University who were fired without notice just before Christmas in 1930, because the Minimum Wage Commission of Massachusetts finally threatened to place "fair Harvard" upon its list of "unfair employers." [1] It seems that in 1921 the Commission had decreed a minimum of 37 cents an hour for office and building cleaners, which decree Harvard had evaded for nine years, paying the cleaning women in Widener Library only 35 cents an hour or $1.75 for a five-hour day. Rather than pay the two cents an hour more, the Harvard authorities decided to replace them by male scrubbers, to the chagrin of some alumni who raised a fund for the old mop squad, some of whom had scrubbed Widener for 25 or 30 years.

Such replacement hurts some persons and helps others, but presumably it does not reduce the total demand for labor. Sidney Webb claims that productivity and the national income are increased by the selection of the best workers, in which case, however, it may be difficult to justify exemptions and lower minima for handicapped workers. It is also claimed that minimum wages increase the national income by reducing labor troubles and labor strife.

There is no agreement concerning the general effects of minimum-wage legislation. Its advocates claim that it tends to speed up the rate of spending by causing a more equitable distribution of income and that it will serve to prevent a vicious spiral of wage-cutting and price deflation during a business slump. An increase in the incomes of low-wage groups presumably would result in an increase in expenditures for consumption, and an expansion of the consumers' goods industries might spread to the capital-goods industries according to the acceleration principle.[2] The general

---

[1] Cf. Monthly Labor Review, vol. 30 (March 1930), pp. 558–59; "Rub in Scrubbing," Survey, vol. 63 (March 15, 1930), p. 695; and "Scrubwomen: Finale," Survey, vol. 65 (February 15, 1931), p. 559.

[2] Cf. V. F. Coe, "Minimum and Fair Wage Legislation—The Economic Aspect," in Industrial Relations, papers presented at a conference on industrial relations sponsored by Queen's University, September 14–17, 1938, Kingston, Ontario, 1938, pp. 73–74.

effects on spending, incomes, and employment would, of course, depend a great deal upon the objectives and the nature of the wage regulation. Certain economists believe that, under most circumstances, minimum wages will so increase the incomes of low-paid workers, and hence increase consumption expenditures, that employment in general would be stimulated to a greater extent than the resulting increase in costs would tend to depress the level of employment.[1]

It should be clear that the fixing of minimum rates generally does not affect the best paying firms. The purpose is rather to raise the lowest paying firms up to the standard or level attained by the majority. Firms already paying more than the minimum rate will presumably continue to do so for the same reasons (better pay means more output, etc.) as before. That the minimum does not generally become the maximum rate for covered workers is indicated by Australian, English, and American experience.[2] If the minimum is a flat rate not adjusted for changes in living costs, there may be a tendency for the differential above the minimum to decrease in periods of falling prices and wages and to increase in periods of rising wage and price levels. There is no question but that the minimum rate should be somewhat flexible during periods when the price level declines by 30 per cent or more, as it did, for example, from 1920 to 1921 and from 1929 to 1933.

As a general principle, the minimum wage should apply uniformly to all industries, with no exceptions. One purpose in passing minimum-wage laws is to make all industry conform to certain minimum standards. Permitting a few exceptions, based on the financial capacity of particular firms or industries, will only lead to more exceptions, because there is no logical basis for discriminating in favor of certain producers. Discrimination under minimum-wage legislation, like a government subsidy or a tariff, tends to aid inefficient and uneconomic sections of the economy at the expense of other firms that are competing for the consumers' dollars. By the same token, there is little justification for discrimination against more prosperous firms or industries by requiring them to

---

[1] Cf., for example, Weir M. Brown, "Some Effects of a Minimum Wage upon the Economy as a Whole," American Economic Review, vol. 30 (March 1940), pp. 98–107.

[2] Cf. Barbara N. Armstrong, Insuring the Essentials, 1932, p. 164.

meet a higher set of minima for workers of the same quality.[1] If particular firms or industries seem to be making excessive profits, the remedy lies with the state's taxing power and not with the minimum-wage administration.

EXPERIENCE WITH WAGE REGULATION IN THE UNITED STATES

At the outset, employers have generally opposed the introduction of minimum wages on the grounds that business would be injured or ruined. After a few years of experience with such wage regulation, however, most of them become convinced that minimum-wage laws may be beneficial to them and to society. That, for instance, occurred in both Australia and England, where employers who had predicted direful consequences later supported the legislation establishing minimum wages.[2] The experience in this country has followed much the same pattern. For example, a majority of employers in California and Oregon apparently were certain that the minimum-wage laws passed in those states in 1913 would prove ruinous to their businesses. Years of experience, however, changed their opinions, and a decade later the various employers' associations in·both states came out strongly in support of the minimum wage.[3] Employer sentiment toward Federal regulation of wages in this country under the Fair Labor Standards Act of 1938 appears to be following the same course. When the Act was before Congress it was criticized by employers' associations as being "inharmonious with American philosophy" and "a step in the direction of communism, bolshevism, fascism, and naziism."[4]

The American experience with governmental regulation of wages will be treated under two headings: state regulation and Federal regulation. In each case the structure, development, and economic consequences of the wage regulation will be discussed. In many instances the results are difficult to assess with accuracy, partly because the experience of the Federal government and of all but two

[1] In Australia, the Federal Commonwealth Arbitration Court and the minimum-wage authorities in Queensland have, at times, been guilty of establishing extra high minima for certain prosperous industries. *Cf. ibid.*, p. 160.

[2] *Cf.* Millis and Montgomery, *op. cit.*, vol. 1, pp. 285, 292, 294, and 314.

[3] *Cf.* Barbara N. Armstrong, *op. cit.*, pp. 151, 152, and 154.

[4] *Cf.* statements by the president of the Cotton Textile Institute and the spokesman for the National Association of Manufacturers in the *New York Times*, June 11 and 12, 1937.

states has been brief and interrupted by court decisions invalidating the laws establishing wage regulation.

State regulation. There are two types of state laws for the regulation of wages paid by private firms: laws establishing minimum rates of pay for public work done under contract and laws fixing minimum rates for women and children in private employment.

In 1940, a total of 35 states had laws requiring certain minima—usually the "current" or "prevailing" rate in the locality—for work on public projects, such as buildings and roads. All but five of these laws were passed during the decade ending in 1939. In 1940, a total of 26 states and the District of Columbia had minimum-wage laws applying to women and minors in certain private employments. The Connecticut law also applies to men. Most of these state minimum-wage laws follow a general pattern.

1. *Provisions of state laws.*[1] The first state act, which was passed in Massachusetts in 1912, followed the precedent of the British Trade Boards Act of 1909 by providing for wage boards with an equal number of employer and employee representatives and one or more disinterested persons to represent the public. Such wage boards or conferences usually determine the minimum wage for the industry, and an administrative agency of the state generally issues the wage orders or decrees and enforces them. In only two states, Nevada and South Dakota, are flat minimum wages fixed by the legislature and stated in the law. The Arkansas Act, passed in 1915, contains a flat minimum rate but provides that the Industrial Welfare Commission may raise or lower the flat minimum for any occupation or industry after investigation and public hearings.

The principles that wage boards are to follow in determining minimum wages vary somewhat between states. The laws of 12 states provide that the minimum-wage rates must be adequate to supply the necessary cost of living. Of the other 12 states with "flexible" laws, six provide for wages "fairly and reasonably commensurate with the value of the service rendered," five combine

---

[1] The data in this subsection are taken primarily from Florence P. Smith, *State Minimum-Wage Laws and Orders, An Analysis*, U. S. Department of Labor, Women's Bureau, Bulletin No. 167, 1939; "Minimum-Wage Legislation as of January 1, 1940," *Monthly Labor Review*, vol. 50 (April 1940), pp. 891–909; and *The Minimum Wage, An International Survey*, International Labour Office, 1939.

the principles of cost of living and fair value for the service, and one, Rhode Island, combines the "fair-value" standard with the "wages the industry can afford to pay." In these 12 states the wages paid for work of comparable character by employers voluntarily maintaining fair minimum standards may also be considered by the wage boards. Considerations of constitutional law, rather than of economic theory, have guided the selection of the principles that are contained in the state laws.

By 1939, over 100 wage orders had been issued in the minimum-wage states. These orders applied to approximately 1,000,000 women out of a potential coverage estimated at 4,000,000 women in the 25 states. Some gainfully employed women, such as domestic servants, farm workers, and professional women, are excluded from most minimum-wage laws. The orders apply mostly to service trades that are primarily local, intrastate employments, such as laundry and dry cleaning, retail trade, beauty shops, hotels and restaurants, canning, and office work. These orders, most of which can be revised once a year, fixed minimum rates ranging in 1938 from 13.02 cents an hour for waitresses in Ohio cities under 5,000 in population to $18 a week or 50 cents an hour for experienced "beauty culturists" in Washington, D. C., and $32 a week for registered pharmacists in Oklahoma cities of 40,000 or more inhabitants. As many as 74 per cent of all the rates set under state minimum-wage laws for women were for 30 cents or more an hour in 1938.[1] Practically all states authorize rates below the minimum for minors, apprentices, and handicapped employees. Generally, public hearings are held before the rates go into effect, and appeal can be made to the courts against any wage order. The diversity in minimum rates between states and between industries within the same state are due largely to the weight given to the different principles or criteria, to the relative bargaining strength of employer-employee representatives on the wage boards, and to differences in the attitude of public representatives on the various boards.

2. *Course of development.* Although influenced at first by precedents abroad, the development of minimum-wage legislation in this country has been determined largely by decisions of the U. S. Supreme Court and by business conditions.

The chronology of state wage regulation can conveniently be

[1] Florence P. Smith, *op. cit.*, p. 2.

divided into three periods: 1912–1923, 1924–1932, and 1933–1941. During the first period, minimum-wage laws were enacted in 15 states and the District of Columbia, despite opposition of business-men and discouragement by outstanding economists. Furthermore, organized labor opposed the legal regulation of men's wages, on the ground that higher wages should be obtained by collective bargaining and not by law. These first minimum-wage laws were all of the "cost-of-living" type, specifying that the minimum rates established should be sufficient to meet the necessary cost of health-ful living. Although the Supreme Court, by a four-to-four decision in the Oregon Case in 1917,[1] seemed to uphold this principle, the constitutionality of all existing minimum-wage legislation became questionable when the Court in a five-to-three decision in 1923 in-validated the District of Columbia minimum-wage law.[2]

The second period begins with the District of Columbia or Adkins decision. From 1924 to 1933, no state minimum-wage laws were enacted. In fact, during that period 10 state laws were either in-validated or repealed, and in two other states the laws were never put into operation. Only in Massachusetts and California was some attempt at enforcement made during this period. The Massachu-setts law at that time was presumed to be constitutional because the only penalty for disobeying a minimum-wage decree was publicity, and any individual employer could be exempt if he could show financial inability to comply with the minimum rate. None, however, applied for such exemption.

In California continued enforcement of the minimum-wage law, including the collection of thousands of dollars for noncompliance, was made possible through the voluntary cooperation of employers' associations and large employers who found the minimum wage of advantage to business. Such support was given to the minimum wage in spite of the fact that the California minimum after 1919 was $16 a week, which was considerably above the minima in most states. The smaller employers were forced to obey the law, although it was considered unconstitutional, because no small em-ployer wished to incur the cost of carrying a case to the U. S. Supreme Court.[3]

[1] *Stettler* v. *O'Hara* (1917), 243 U. S. 629.
[2] *Adkins* v. *Children's Hospital* (1923), 261 U. S. 525.
[3] *Cf.* B. N. Armstrong, *op. cit.*, pp. 152–55.

By 1933 the interest in minimum-wage legislation revived, for the depression had led to wage-cutting and to the spread of sweat-shop conditions. Passage of the National Industrial Recovery Act by Congress also lent support to the minimum-wage movement. Seven states enacted minimum-wage laws in 1933, and nine more state laws were passed during the following five years. These laws were based on the "fair-value" principle, because in the District of Columbia decision in 1923 the Court had said that "a statute requiring an employer to pay the value of services rendered would be understandable." It was a surprise, therefore, when the Court in June 1936 invalidated the New York State law enacted in 1933 and based on the "fair-value" concept.[1] One writer has figured out that actually a majority of 10 out of the 17 judges participating in the first three minimum-wage cases (Oregon in 1917, District of Columbia in 1923, and New York in 1936) declared such legislation constitutional, but the conservative judges, by remaining on the bench longer, were able to determine the decisions.[2] In March 1937 the U. S. Supreme Court overruled the District of Columbia case by declaring constitutional the 1913 minimum-wage law of the state of Washington, based on a cost-of-living standard.[3] Whether the Supreme Court in this five-to-four decision upholding minimum-wage legislation was following the returns of the November 1936 election or was influenced by President Roosevelt's proposal for changing the number of judges on the Court is not known. In its decision the Court said:

The exploitation of a class of workers who are in an unequal position with respect to bargaining power and are thus relatively defenseless against the denial of a living wage is not only detrimental to their health and well-being but casts a direct burden for their support upon the community. . . . The community is not bound to provide what is in effect a subsidy for unconscionable employers.[4]

Following this favorable decision, a number of states enacted new legislation or amended existing statutes, and there was a marked increase in the number of wage boards established and wage orders issued.

[1] *Morehead* v. *New York ex rel. Tipaldo* (1936), 298 U. S. 587.
[2] *Cf.* Irving Dillard, "A Supreme Court Majority?" *Harper's Magazine*, vol. 173 (November 1936), p. 598.
[3] *West Coast Hotel Co.* v. *Parrish* (1937), 300 U. S. 379.
[4] *Idem.*

3. *Effects of state wage regulation.* Attempts to estimate the net effects of minimum-wage legislation are handicapped by the fact that few laws have had an opportunity for unhampered development. Except in Massachusetts and California, the laws have had relatively brief periods of enforcement. Also, it is difficult to relate cause and effect in the welter of economic change. Nevertheless, sufficient evidence has already been collected to indicate that minimum-wage legislation has increased the earnings of women workers, that the minimum has not become the maximum, that minimum-wage regulation has not caused a relative reduction in the level of employment for women, and that there has been no widespread tendency for men to replace women as a result of raising women's wages by law.

The following experience indicates some of the effects of minimum-wage regulation upon the level of women's wages: [1] Women's wages in California showed an abrupt rise each time the minimum there was increased. A survey in 1922 revealed that the median weekly earnings of women in manufacturing, laundries, and stores in California were from 15 to 25 per cent above the median earnings of women similarly engaged in Ohio and New Jersey, which then had no minimum-wage laws. The median weekly earnings of women in Massachusetts laundries increased more than 11 per cent from 1920 to 1921, following a minimum-wage decree, despite the fact that prices and wages were falling during that period. In the minimum-wage states of California and Wisconsin, the minimum hourly rates for the canning industry in 1932 were 25 cents and 22.5 cents, respectively, compared with a rate of not more than 12.5 cents in approximately three fourths of the plants of 43 New York canneries, where no minimum-wage law was then in existence.[2] New York passed such a law in 1933. A study of 131 laundries in New York and 116 in Pennsylvania, a state then having no minimum wage, showed that hourly earnings of women in New York increased from 25.4 cents to 31 cents (22 per cent) between 1933 and 1935, compared with an increase from 21.8 cents

---

[1] Unless otherwise indicated, the statistical data in this subsection have been taken from Mary E. Pidgeon, *Women in the Economy of the United States of America*, U. S. Department of Labor, Women's Bureau, Bulletin No. 155, 1937, pp. 101–109; and *The Effect of Minimum-Wage Determinations in Service Industries*, Women's Bureau, Bulletin No. 166, 1938, pp. 3–5.

[2] *Cf. The Benefits of Minimum Wage Legislation*, U. S. Department of Labor, Women's Bureau (mimeographed), March 1937, p. 4.

to 25 cents (15 per cent) in Pennsylvania. In November 1935 not 1 per cent of the women workers in New York laundries were earning less than 27.5 cents an hour, whereas over 73 per cent of the women in Pennsylvania laundries were receiving less than that hourly rate. The increase in the average weekly earnings of women workers in New York laundries during the period following the minimum-wage order was 29 per cent, compared with 17 per cent for all manufacturing industries in the state.

The experience in California, Massachusetts, and other states seems to indicate that the percentage of women workers receiving more than the minimum has not been reduced by the enforcement of minimum-wage orders. Of the women workers covered by minimum wages in California, 47 per cent were receiving above the minimum in 1920 and 60 per cent in 1923, despite the fact that prices fell sharply between those two years.[1]

Apparently the raising of women's wages by law has not caused a significant reduction in their opportunities for employment. In 1920 California raised the minimum wage from $10 to $16 a week, yet the proportion of women employees in all manufacturing industries (laundries included) increased from 20 per cent in 1918 to almost 27 per cent in 1921. In Massachusetts, the percentage of total employees represented by female workers remained practically the same from 1912 to 1924, notwithstanding minimum-wage legislation and regulation.[2] In New York State, women continued to form 60 per cent of the employees in laundries after the establishment of the minimum wage, and there was "no indication that the increased wage for women resulted in the displacement of women by men in the laundry industry."[3] In Rhode Island, the hourly earnings of women and minors in 54 firms manufacturing wearing apparel rose over 14 per cent during a one-year period that included the effective date of the minimum-wage order for the industry, yet there was a slight increase in the proportion of women employed by those 54 firms.[4]

[1] Cf. Ralph Broda, "Minimum Wage Legislation in the United States," International Labour Review, vol. 17 (January 1928), p. 36.
[2] Ibid., p. 42.
[3] Mary E. Pidgeon, op. cit., p. 109.
[4] State of Rhode Island, Comparison of Hours and Wages of Employees in 54 Identical Firms in the Manufacturing of Wearing Apparel and Allied Industries in the State of Rhode Island, June 1938 (mimeographed).

This evidence points to three possible factors. Either the market for women's services has been so imperfect that they have been subject to exploitation, or their productivity has been increased through increased efficiency and improved management, or men are not good substitutes for women workers in the industries affected by minimum wages, perhaps because the wages of men also rise at the same time. Judging from the studies of the labor market discussed in the previous section on the economic theory of the minimum wage, it seems probable that the imperfect character of the labor market is the most important factor permitting women's wages to be forced up in low-wage industries without decreasing their employment opportunities.

Federal regulation. National regulation of wages by the Federal government began in 1933 with the enactment of the National Industrial Recovery Act. Other Federal acts containing provisions for the regulation of wages are: the Guffey Coal Act of 1935, the Walsh-Healey Public Contracts Act of 1936, the Merchant Marine Act of 1936, the Sugar Act of 1937, and the Fair Labor Standards Act of 1938. The National Industrial Recovery Act and the Guffey Coal Act were invalidated by the Supreme Court.

The Sugar Act and the Merchant Marine Act require that sugar producers and shipowners meet certain minimum-wage standards as one of the conditions for receiving government benefit payments in the case of sugar and a government "operating-differential" subsidy for ships. Similar legislation was enacted in England in the 1925 British Sugar (Subsidy) Act. As early as 1909, the British Parliament passed the Fair Wages Clause requiring government contractors to pay wage rates no less favorable than those prevailing in the district where the work is performed.

1. *The Public Contracts Act.* This Act applies the Federal regulation of wages to concerns that receive government contracts in excess of $10,000. All persons employed by the contractor in the manufacturing or furnishing of materials, supplies, articles, or equipment under such contracts must pay not less than the prevailing minimum wage in the locality for such work, that wage to be determined by the Sectetary of Labor. In practice, the Department has interpreted the "prevailing minimum wage" to mean that wage, lying in the lower part of the wage structure,

which predominates and has "superior force and influence" in the industry in that geographic area.[1]

Certain cases cited by the Administrator of the Public Contracts Division of the Department of Labor indicate the possible effects of wage determination under this Act.[2]   For many commodities, ranging all the way from cotton garments to hats and shoes, the government paid less for goods of the same specifications after the minimum wage had been established than it had paid during the preceding year.   For example, firms receiving government contracts for cotton shirts, shorts, and socks had paid employees in their plants as low as $5 a week, 3 cents an hour, and $8 a week, respectively, in 1936 and 1937.   When, in 1937, the minimum was set at $14 and $15 a week in the manufacture of cotton shirts, 37.5 cents an hour for cotton shorts, and $18 a week for socks, the government bought the identical garments for approximately 20 per cent less than before the minimum-wage determination.

2. *National Recovery Administration.*[3]   The National Industrial Recovery Act, passed in May 1933, provided for codes of fair competition by industries, which fixed maximum hours of labor, minimum rates of pay, and other conditions in the trade or industry. It represented the first application of minimum-wage regulation to men in private employment and the most extensive experiment in wage regulation up to that time.   In August 1934 as many as 22,000,000 employees were covered by 517 codes and about 2,000,-000 more were under the President's Re-employment Agreement, a voluntary code designed to apply to all industrial employments until a separate code was established for the industry.

The President's Re-employment Agreement proposed a minimum wage of 40 cents an hour for factory and mechanical workers, unless the hourly rate for that work had been less than 40 cents on July

---

[1] For a good discussion of the economic issues that have arisen in the administration of this Act, as well as the economic problems involved in the general application of minimum-wage legislation, *cf.* O. R. Strackbein, *The Prevailing Minimum Wage Standard,* 1939.

[2] These cases are cited in L. Metcalfe Walling's article, "Public Contracts Act Procedure," in *Wage and Hour Reporter,* June 26, 1939, pp. 7–8, published by the Bureau of National Affairs, Inc., Washington, D. C.

[3] In writing this subsection the author has drawn primarily upon the following publications: Leverett S. Lyon *et al., The National Industrial Recovery Administration, an Analysis and Appraisal,* 1935; Ruth Reticker, "Labor Standards in NRA Codes," *Annals of the American Academy of Political and Social Science,* vol. 184 (March 1936), pp. 72–82; and C. F. Roos, *NRA Economic Planning,* 1937.

15, 1929, in which case the July 1929 rate would obtain if it was not below 30 cents an hour, the absolute minimum. The minima under the codes varied tremendously, because each industry was considered "different." In some codes the minimum rates were as low as 15 cents an hour; at the other extreme was the 70-cent minimum for New York City in the wrecking and salvage code. An analysis of over 500 codes, however, shows that almost 40 per cent of the employees were under codes with minima of 40 cents an hour for unskilled male workers, about 45 per cent of the employees were covered by codes with minima between 30 and 40 cents an hour, and only about 4 per cent of all employees in "coded" industries were under codes with minima below 20 cents an hour.

Wage differentials and exemptions were also provided. Codes with flat minima for the whole country covered only one fifth of the employees under codes. Some two thirds of all covered employees were under codes with geographic differentials in wage rates, and a number of codes also provided for size-of-city and sex differentials. In most codes, exemptions from the minimum rates or subminimum rates were permitted for old and handicapped workers, learners or apprentices, and office girls and boys.

The Supreme Court ended the life of the NRA, as it was called, in May 1935, two days after its second birthday. The lack of consistent policy and uniform practice as well as its short life make it difficult to estimate the effect of wage regulation under the National Recovery Administration. There seems to be general agreement that the Act served to halt the spiral of wage-cutting and resulted in material increases in the money wage rates received by the lowest paid workers in industry. The codes apparently effected some equalization of earnings among employees in the same firm by raising the minimum-wage standards, and also tended to reduce regional wage differentials. Probably the reduction of wage differentials put some economic pressure upon small towns and Southern industry, but the existence of the Recovery Administration was too short to have much effect upon such matters as the location of industry or technological change. There was a considerable increase in industrial employment during the lifetime of the NRA, but how much of the increase was due to that program and how much to other factors, such as devaluation of the dollar, public-works expenditures, and the agricultural program, cannot be determined.

3. *Fair Labor Standards Act of 1938.* This Act, known also as the Wage and Hour law, is designed to accomplish for persons employed in interstate commerce or in the production of goods for interstate commerce three of the objectives of the National Industrial Recovery Act: a ceiling for working hours, a floor for wages, and the abolition of child labor. Like the President's Re-employment Agreement, its aim is a minimum wage of 40 cents an hour and a 40-hour week. The Wage and Hour law provides that the standard work week for covered firms shall be 40 hours after October 24, 1940, with the payment of one-and-one-half times the regular rate for overtime. From October 24, 1939 to October 24, 1945 the minimum wage in covered employment is 30 cents an hour, and thereafter 40 cents an hour unless the Administrator permits a lower minimum for a particular industry. Children under 16 years of age cannot work in manufacturing or mining, and minors of 16 or 17 may not work in occupations declared to be particularly hazardous or detrimental to their health or well-being.

It is difficult to determine the exact coverage of the Wage and Hour law because the courts have not yet delimited the processes and employments "necessary to the production" of goods for interstate commerce. The Administrator of the Wage and Hour Division estimated that 550,000 were affected by the increase from a 25- to a 30-cent minimum in October 1939 and that 11,000,000 employees will eventually be covered by the Act, for it applies to men as well as to women and children. Agriculture is specifically excluded, so far as the wages and the hours sections of the Act are concerned.

It is the stated purpose of the Act to eliminate as rapidly as practicable "labor conditions detrimental to the maintenance of the minimum standard of living necessary for health, efficiency, and general well-being of workers" in the covered industries, "without substantially curtailing employment or earning power." This purpose is to be accomplished primarily through statutory minima (30 cents an hour before, and 40 cents an hour after, October 24, 1945) and through wage orders issued by the Administrator following recommendations from special industrial committees or wage boards having equal employer and employee representatives along with representatives of the public. These wage orders are designed to raise the minimum for particular industries above 30 cents, and to 40 cents, an hour as soon as that can be done "without substantially curtailing employment." The intention is to reach, "as rapidly as is economically feasible, the objective of a universal minimum wage of 40 cents an hour" in all of the covered industries. But the Administrator may at any time, upon recommendation of an industry committee, issue an order fixing a minimum wage for a specific industry between 30 and 40 cents an hour, if such action "is necessary in order to prevent substantial curtailment of employment in the industry."

In determining and recommending the highest minimum rate (not in excess of 40 cents an hour) which will not substantially curtail employment in each industrial classification, the following among other relevant factors are to be considered:

1. Competitive conditions as affected by transportation, living, and production costs.

2. The wages established for work of like, or comparable, character by genuine collective bargaining.

3. The wages paid for work of like, or comparable, character by employers who voluntarily maintain minimum-wage standards.

No minimum-wage rate is to be fixed solely on a regional basis, and no differentials are to be made on the basis of age or sex. Learners, apprentices, messengers, and handicapped workers may be certified for wages below the minima for regular workers.

Although the provision forbidding the fixing of minimum-wage differentials solely on a regional basis seems to bear heavily upon some Southern industries, regional differentials are still possible because freight rates average higher in the South than in the North and the costs for the same level of living are generally a little lower in the South.[1]

A consideration of the factors mentioned shows how complex and involved are the problems that face the industrial committees, a number of which have already made recommendations. Mountains of statistical material will not enable a committee to determine whether a particular minimum rate will "substantially curtail employment in the industry." It is impossible to tell from statistics to what extent workers are being exploited or how much productivity will, immediately and eventually, be increased as a result of the effects of a wage rise upon employee efficiency, production methods,

[1] Cf. the study made by the Works Progress Administration, *Intercity Differences in Costs of Living in March, 1935, 59 Cities*, 1937.

and the supply of labor. The effect of a wage rise in one industry upon employment depends, in part, upon the trend of wages and prices in other industries and upon changes in the money supply and general business conditions. In practice, the minimum rate recommended by the committees, which the Administrator may accept or reject but not modify or alter, seems to be determined largely by bargaining within the committee, and such minimum rates will probably be altered by the committees as experience seems to indicate. In some cases, the courts may have to decide whether a certain minimum wage has "substantially" curtailed employment in the industry.[1]

The problem of the relationship between wage rates and employment was discussed in the previous chapter. There it was pointed out that the issue cannot be confined to the particular industry directly concerned, as it is in the Fair Labor Standards Act. The essential question is, Does the particular minimum rate tend to decrease total employment, not in the particular industry, but in all industry? An increase in wage rates in a declining industry, for example, might help to curtail employment in that line of business, but should such an industry enjoy special consideration and a lower minimum than other industries? A special decrease in the minimum rate might retard the introduction of labor-saving machinery into an industry producing a product with an inelastic demand and, thus, help to prevent a substantial reduction in employment opportunities in that industry, at least for a short time. If the minimum wage is not decreased in that industry, is it substantially curtailing employment in the industry?

That minimum-wage rates should be determined by general considerations is indicated by the experience in October 1938, when the Act became effective. The Administrator estimated that between 30,000 and 50,000 persons (less than one half of one per cent of the workers affected by the law) lost their jobs then for reasons probably traceable to the Act. Practically all of these lay-offs were in a few industries in the South, such as pecan shelling, tobacco stemming, lumbering, and logging. In his interim report to Congress, submitted in January 1939, the Administrator stated:

[1] For a summary discussion of experience in administering the Act, *cf.* "Two Years of the Fair Labor Standards Act," *Monthly Labor Review*, vol. 51 (September 1940), pp. 551–63.

It is very difficult to determine how many lay-offs reported at that time followed rapid building up of inventories, how many were seasonal shutdowns or reductions, and how many were actually a consequence of the newly-established minimum wage. Many shutdowns were for only a few days or weeks. . . . Estimated total employment of employees covered by the Act showed slightly more than a seasonal increase from September to November.[1]

In minimum-wage regulation, the chief need is for uniformity throughout industry and flexibility over a period of time. The absolute minima contained in the Fair Labor Standards Act are based upon the assumption that the price level will not change. Past experience does not justify that assumption, and experience abroad indicates the desirability of relating the level of the minimum wage to the level of the cost of living.

[1] Mimeographed press release reported in part in the *New York Times*, Jan. 16, 1939, p. 1.

CHAPTER THIRTEEN

HOURS OF WORK

The length of the work day and the work week are of importance to workers and to society. Long hours of toil may affect the worker's health and reduce the length of his working life. Such hours may also stunt his growth as a citizen by failing to permit him sufficient time for social, cultural, and political activities. Besides these social aspects, the hours question has a number of economic implications. The wage the worker receives depends, in part, upon the available supply of qualified labor services. That supply, in turn, depends upon the number of hours each worker offers for sale in a given period of time. The supply of labor hours in the market also has some bearing on the problem of unemployment. Furthermore, the employer as a buyer of labor is not interested in purchasing mere hours; he is concerned with the worker's output, although no specific output per hour is mentioned when workers are hired on a time basis. The length of the working day will affect the worker's output per hour or per week.

For an understanding of the relationship between hours and output, hours and wage rates, and hours and unemployment, it is necessary to examine both the theoretical and the historical aspects of the hours problem. Therefore, this chapter contains a survey of past experience with changes in working hours and an analysis of the economics of shorter hours, together with a discussion of governmental regulation of hours in this country.

Before examining past experience, however, certain terms should be defined. There is a difference between "actual hours worked" and the "nominal," "basic," or "full-time" day or week. In slack times the actual hours worked per day or week may fall far short of the nominal or full-time day or week. During boom periods, on the other hand, actual hours may exceed the nominal day or week, in which case punitive rates are generally charged for the excess or "overtime" hours. It has been claimed that workers demand reductions in the "basic" day in order to obtain the higher overtime rates for some of their actual working hours.

PAST EXPERIENCE

This section explains the trend in working hours during the past century and gives a cross-sectional picture of the present situation. Consequently, it is concerned primarily with facts and figures.

The trend of working hours. As indicated in Chapters 3 and 4, working hours in English and American factories averaged about 13 a day and 75 a week around 1830. The work day was not fixed but varied with the seasons. Machines were operated from sunrise to sunset in order to run them as continuously as possible, and long hours were generally favored as a means of eliminating idleness and "improvident practices." When the movement for a 10-hour day began to rise in this country around 1825, employers labeled it "an evil of foreign growth." The reader will recall that one of the important planks of the Working Men's Party, which flourished around 1830, was the 10-hour day.

The trend in the average hours of labor in American industry since 1840 is indicated in Table 17. The figures for the nineteenth century probably underestimate the average for all industry, since they are drawn largely from establishments where reduced hours made an earlier appearance than they did in the mass of American workshops. The statistics in Table 17 represent the actual hours worked during those years. The nominal or full-time hours per week since 1890 are indicated in Table 18.

TABLE 17. AVERAGE HOURS OF LABOR PER DAY IN MANUFACTURING, 1840–1920 [1]

1840	11.4	1890	10.0
1850	11.5	1900	9.8
1860	11.0	1910	9.4
1870	10.5	1920	8.5
1880	10.3		

The figures in these two tables indicate a continuing downward trend in both actual and nominal working hours. In the past century, for example, the full-time week of printers and blast-

[1] Data from T. S. Adams and Helen Sumner, *Labor Problems*, 1905, p. 518; and P. H. Douglas, *Real Wages in the United States, 1890 to 1926*, 1930, p. 116.

TABLE 18. AVERAGE FULL-TIME HOURS PER WEEK IN MAJOR BRANCHES OF
INDUSTRY, 1890–1937 [1]

	Manufacturing	Building	Bituminous coal
1890	59.9	55.2	60.0
1899	59.6	52.6	52.7
1909	56.8	46.0	51.6
1914	55.1	44.9	51.8
1919	50.8	44.1	48.4
1929	50.6	43.1	48.5
1932	47.9	40.6	48.6
1937	40.8	38.9	35.0

furnace operators has apparently been reduced by 50 per cent.[2]
Table 18 shows that the scheduled week in bituminous-coal mining
has declined over 40 per cent in the past half century. It is also
apparent from this table that marked reductions in full-time hours
in manufacturing occurred during the first World War and during
the depression of the 1930's. The figures for bituminous-coal mining show similar reductions during the same periods, along with a
sharp reduction in the 1890's after the United Mine Workers
union was formed.

Between 1890 and 1933, nominal hours in the building trades
were considerably lower than those for industry as a whole. Such
lower hours have undoubtedly been due to the strength of the labor
unions in building, which also accounts for the fact that hours reductions in the building trades follow a separate pattern, with only
minor reductions during the first World War and the depression
of the 1930's. The influence of labor organization can also be seen
in the hours figures for bituminous coal after 1919. As the United
Mine Workers declined in strength and membership from 1920 to
1932, there was a one-per-cent increase in the average nominal
hours of bituminous miners. As the union recovered rapidly in the
New Deal period following 1932, the full-time week was reduced
as much as 28 per cent in two years (1932 to 1934).

During the prosperous 1920's, the nominal hours of labor generally increased. A substantial number of employees who had their
hours reduced during the first World War surrendered part of their

[1] Taken from Leo Wolman, *Hours of Work in American Industry*, National Bureau of
Economic Research, Bulletin 71, November 27, 1938, Table 1, p. 2. Although correctly indicating the trend, these figures are not, in some cases, exactly comparable for
all years. For such limitations to the data, *cf.* Wolman's footnotes.
[2] *Ibid.*, p. 1.

gains in the following decade. From 1921 to 1929, for example, the proportion of workers in manufacturing with full-time hours of 48 or less a week fell from 51.5 to 45.9 per cent.[1] As indicated in Chapter 9, there was a tendency in the 1920's for the distribution of income to become more unequal, and corporation disbursements to stockholders and bondholders expanded much more rapidly than did corporation payments to labor. Advocates of the shorter work week have seized upon such facts as proof of their theory that shorter hours are necessary in order to create a scarcity of labor, to raise wage rates, to reduce the proportion of the national income going to profits and property, to increase total consumption, and to put an end to booms and depressions.[2]

Hours differentials. As with wage rates, there are various differences or differentials in the length of normal working hours.

1. *Differentials between union and nonunion hours.* The influence exerted by labor organization upon the hours of labor has already been mentioned in the previous comments upon the trend of hours during the past three or four decades. An exact measure of the differential between union and nonunion hours is difficult to obtain because such conditions do not generally exist side by side, in the same area and in the same industry. In Table 19 the average full-time hours per week in union establishments in six industries are compared with the average for seven industries classified as "non-union."[3] The two manufacturing industries that, according to the Biennial Census of Manufactures, had the lowest average for

TABLE 19. AVERAGE FULL-TIME HOURS PER WEEK IN "UNION" AND "NONUNION" MANUFACTURING INDUSTRIES, 1890–1925

	Union industries	Nonunion industries
1890	54.4	63.1
1900	53.0	62.7
1910	50.1	60.5
1920	45.7	54.2
1925	45.9	53.0

[1] *Ibid.*, p. 4.

[2] *Cf.*, for example, Hugo L. Black, "The Shorter Work Week and Work Day," *Annals of the American Academy of Political and Social Science*, vol. 184 (March 1936), pp. 62–67.

[3] Data from Paul H. Douglas, *op. cit.*, pp. 112, 114. The "union" industries include only the unionized sections of the metal trades, granite and stone work, book and job printing, newspaper printing, planing mills, and bakeries. The "nonunion" industries include cotton and woolen textiles, hosiery and knit goods, sawmills, iron and steel, boots and shoes, and slaughtering and meat packing. In calculating the average for nonunion industries, the weights on p. 94 of Douglas were used.

full-time weekly hours during the 1920's were men's clothing and women's clothing, both highly organized industries.[1]

Probably the most comparable statistics on this issue are those that were obtained from a survey of the building trades in 105 cities throughout the country made by the United States Bureau of Labor Statistics in the Fall of 1936. The results of that survey, covering 126,000 union and 60,000 nonunion workers, are summarized in Table 20. Less than four per cent of the union workers had a normal work week exceeding 40 hours in 1936, whereas the full-time weekly hours of half the nonunion workers were above 40. These figures may be somewhat influenced by the fact that unions are strongest in large cities where hours tend to be shorter.

TABLE 20. FULL-TIME WEEKLY HOURS OF UNION AND NONUNION WORKERS
IN THE BUILDING TRADES, 1936 [2]

Week of	Percentage of union workers	Percentage of nonunion workers
40 hours or less	96.3	50.7
41 to 48 hours	3.6	41.4
Over 48 hours	0.1	7.9

The tendency for labor organization to shorten the work week is indicated by such statistics, showing that full-time hours have generally been more reduced in union than in nonunion industries and, within the same industry, in union than in nonunion establishments.

2. *Regional differentials.* In part, regional differences in hours are a reflection of the differences between union and nonunion hours, because unions are stronger in certain areas than in others. For instance, the building industry is more highly organized in the cities of the East, the Middle West, and the Pacific Coast than it is in the South. The 1929 census of the construction industry showed that 55 per cent or more of the wage-earners in the Northeast and the Pacific Coast states had full-time hours of 44 or less a week.[3] On the other hand, half of the building workers in the Southern states east of the Mississippi River had full-time weeks of 55 hours

[1] Wolman, *op. cit.*, pp. 8, 11.
[2] *Cf.* "Hours of Labor in the Building Trades, 1936," *Monthly Labor Review*, vol. 45 (October 1937), p. 798.
[3] *Cf.* Wolman, *op. cit.*, p. 16.

or more. In manufacturing, much the same situation prevailed in 1929. The average full-time week for factory employees in the Northeast and on the Pacific Coast was 49 and 50 hours compared with 54 hours for the South. For 56 per cent of the Southern factory workers, the full-time working week was over 54 hours, whereas only about 20 per cent of the factory workers in the North and the Far West had a normal working week in excess of 54 hours.[1] As in the case of regional wage differentials, longer normal hours in the South are partly due to the fact that a large portion of Southern manufacturing consists of low-wage, long-hour industries, like cotton textiles and lumber.

Complete statistics on full-time hours in various regions unfortunately are not available for the period since 1932. But the situation in that year, as far as concerns regional differentials in hours, was about the same as it had been in 1929. The highest average full-time hours per week for such industries as cotton textiles, woolen and worsted goods, hosiery, furniture, sawmills, and machine shops were in the Southern states, especially Georgia, while the Northeastern states and particularly the Pacific states had the lowest average hours in those industries.[2]

3. *International differentials.* The shorter working week was attained earlier in Australasia and in the industrial countries of Europe than in the United States. The eight-hour day was enjoyed by a large percentage of the industrial workers in Australia in the 1890's and by a majority of the industrial workers in Russia by 1918, in England and Germany by 1920, and in France by the early 1930's. Until 1933, government intervention had played a much greater role in the reduction of the hours of men abroad than in this country.

Table 18 indicates the sharp drop in full-time hours in this country following 1932. No other country, with the possible exception of France, experienced such a rapid reduction in normal working hours during the 1930's. In 1938 the normal hours of work in industry in New Zealand, France, and the United States were approximately 40 a week. In New Zealand and France they were fixed at 40 by law. In Canada, Australia, and Argentina, the average seems to have been about 44 hours a week. In Great Britain, Sweden, Belgium, and Brazil, 48 hours was the rule, al-

[1] *Ibid.*, p. 14.   [2] *Cf. ibid.*, p. 15.

though the hours in the building trades in Britain generally ranged from 44 to 47.[1]

Hours and efficiency. Despite the marked decline in working hours during the past century in this country, the physical productivity per worker per day has continued to increase. Reduction in the work day has not been accompanied by a reduction in real income. For example, between 1914 and 1925 the normal hours of work in manufacturing were reduced about 10 per cent, yet the productivity per employee in manufacturing increased 33 per cent during that 11-year period.[2]

The precise effect of shorter hours upon output and total costs is, however, difficult to determine. The available evidence consists primarily of data on total output or costs before and after the hours change. It does not, therefore, make full allowance for current changes in other conditions of production besides the length of the work period, such as changes in the technique or methods of production, in the personnel, in the quality of the product, in materials and other costs, in the psychology of the workers, etc. Furthermore, it takes time for shorter hours to affect a worker's efficiency and output. Professor H. M. Vernon found, for instance, that it required more than a year for a reduction from 12 to 8 hours a day in open-hearth steel furnaces to work out its full effects in increased output.[3] Consequently, the test period must be sufficiently long if the total effects of the hours change are to be measured.

In spite of such limitations, the evidence does indicate that the total output of workers will decrease in most industries if the work day is increased beyond 8 or 10 hours. As indicated in Chapter 3, studies by factory inspectors after passage of the English Factory Act of 1844 proved that "the output of eleven hours' work might be greater than that of twelve" and that long hours resulted in spoiled work and breakdowns. Experiments with the effects of hours reductions upon output were made by the British Industrial Fatigue Research Board during the first World War in the British munitions factories. With no change in the character or speed of machinery or in the nature and quality of the product, it was found that the total weekly output of women performing certain operations

[1] For statistics, *cf.* issues of the *International Labour Review* and the *Year-Book of Labour Statistics*, issued by the International Labour Office.

[2] Douglas, *op. cit.*, p. 510; and Wolman, *op. cit.*, p. 2.

[3] *Cf.* H. M. Vernon, *Industrial Fatigue and Efficiency*, 1921, pp. 36–37.

increased 13 per cent when their actual hours of work fell from 60 to 48 a week, and the output of men in similar work increased 19 per cent with a reduction in actual hours from 58 to 50 a week.[1] A study of three British steel mills during that war showed that the hourly output of men rolling red-hot tin-plate bars increased 11 per cent with a change from the eight- to the six-hour shift and declined over 11 per cent when these mills returned to the eight-hour shift.[2] That overtime may result in inefficiency and reduced output is indicated by the experience of the Zeiss Optical Works in Germany. One Fall the workers were eager to work overtime in order to earn more money for Christmas. It was found that the addition to their total output as a result of overtime work began to decline in a week, and that by the fourth week they were producing practically the same output as before the increase in hours.[3]

A few instances may be cited from the experience in this country. When the work day was reduced from 10 to 8 hours in the bituminous-coal industry in 1897, the average output per worker per day increased, even in states where the proportion of coal mined by machine decreased.[4] A study of a number of paper mills by the United States Tariff Board showed that the labor costs per ton of output decreased almost 15 per cent with the change from a 12- to an 8-hour work day in 1909. The Chief Statistician of the Board stated that the increased output per hour "was due largely to the increase of personal efficiency of the workers under the shorter day," which resulted in fewer breakdowns and work stoppages.[5] In a survey made by the National Industrial Conference Board in 1929, approximately 68 per cent of the 94 companies that reduced hours in changing to the five-day week reported no reduction in output. Indeed, 18 of these companies reported an increase in output with the change from five-and-a-half or six days to five days a week.[6]

[1] *Ibid.*, pp. 38–42.   [2] *Ibid.*, pp. 54–55.
[3] Ernst Abbe, *Gesammelte Abhandlungen*, vol. 3, 1906, p. 223.
[4] *Cf.* Report of the United States Industrial Commission, *Final Report*, vol. 19, 1902, pp. 767–72.
[5] *Cf.* United States Tariff Board, *Report on Pulp and News Print Paper Industry*, 1911; and *Fourth Report of the New York State Factory Investigating Commission*, vol. 5 (February 15, 1915), pp. 657–59.
[6] *Cf.* National Industrial Conference Board, *The Five-Day Week in Manufacturing Industries*, 1929, p. 41.

For further evidence indicating "superior output in shorter hours," the reader is referred to *The Case for the Shorter Work Day* by Felix Frankfurter and Josephine Gold-

Professor P. Sargant Florence concludes from a study of a large amount of European and American statistical data that a reduction of hours will increase hourly output, and in most cases, daily output, until the eight-hour day is reached. He qualifies this conclusion by stating that reduction of hours to eight increases the daily output in occupations where speed depends mainly upon the human factor, as in coal mining, or in factories where the speed of operations depends fairly equally upon the human and mechanical factors. Probably where machinery predominates in setting the pace, as in steel mills, or where the completion of the operation depends on chemical processes, a reduction of hours may result in a reduction in total daily output per worker. Reductions of hours below eight a day will not increase hourly output sufficiently to prevent a decline in the daily total unless the speed of operations depends mostly upon the human factor and the work is of a heavy type. Reduced hours decrease the absence from work because of sickness, the number of accidents per hour, and the percentage of defective output. Increases of normal working hours have the reverse effects.[1]

Such conclusions, however, do not fully answer the question, What is the effect of hours reductions upon the total costs per unit of output? From a social point of view the increased sickness, injuries, and mortality resulting from longer hours would also have to be taken into account in determining whether shorter hours were economical. Even the costs of private firms are increased by such items as breakdowns, defective output, sickness, and increased accidents, which raise the employer's premium under workmen's compensation insurance. Consequently, hours reductions may reduce total costs per unit of output even though the worker's daily output does not increase.

There is another factor to be considered. Reduced hours may produce more unemployment for machinery, or in some circumstances reductions of hours may increase the employment of capital equipment. A change from an eight-hour shift to two six-hour

mark, containing 200 pages of examples from the experience of this and other countries. These two volumes of the *Brief for Defendant in Error in the Case of Bunting* vs. *Oregon,* Supreme Court of the United States, October Term, 1915, have been reprinted by the National Consumers' League. *Cf.* vol. 2, pp. 636–46.

[1] *Cf.* P. S. Florence, *Economics of Fatigue and Unrest,* 1924, pp. 229, 348; and also H. M. Vernon, *op. cit.,* pp. 62–76.

shifts increases the use of capital equipment from eight to twelve hours a day, whereas a change to one six-hour shift would reduce by two hours the daily use of such equipment. The effect of increased or decreased daily use of equipment upon total costs per unit of output depends, in part, upon the important factor in the depreciation of the equipment. If the significant factor in its decline in value is obsolescence (time), then reduced use of the equipment during any period of time would tend to increase the cost of capital per unit of output. On the other hand, if its depreciation were due solely to wear and tear from use, capital costs per unit of output might not be increased much by a shorter operating period each day. Of course the factor of interest on the investment in capital equipment would have to be taken into account in such calculations.

THE ECONOMICS OF SHORTER HOURS

As indicated in Chapter 3, well-known English economists a century ago tried to prove that the whole profit of a textile factory, operating 12 hours a day, was derived from the last hour of work and that an additional hour of labor each day would double the firm's net profit. The Manchester school of economists, including John Bright and Richard Cobden, opposed governmental restrictions upon hours under the Factory Acts in the 1840's as certain to bring ruin upon English manufacture. Almost the opposite conclusions can, however, be drawn from various statistical data. Professor Florence found, for example, that output per hour in American munition plants during the first World War decreased about six per cent on the day that two-and-two-thirds hours of overtime were added to the normal day of 10 hours and that the hourly output declined about four per cent on the normal work day following a day of overtime. Taking the two days together, hours would have been increased 13.33 per cent and output but 7.25 per cent. At time-and-a-half for overtime, the 7.25-per-cent increase in output would have cost 20 per cent more in wages. Professor Florence concludes that "since overtime is usually paid at a higher rate of wage, the cost is out of proportion to the gain in total output." [1]

Social vs. private interest. From the social point of view, the desirable length of the work day is that which will maximize the

[1] *Cf.* Florence, *op. cit.*, pp. 230–32, 349.

output of workers throughout their working lives and not the work day or week which will give the largest total output for a short period of time.[1] Individual employers, of course, need not be guided by the long-run effects of working hours upon their present working force, since they can generally replace abused or worn-out workers by others.

Throughout this book the differences between total social cost and total private cost have been emphasized. Employers may not pay, or at least may not pay fully, for the effects of long hours of hard or monotonous work upon workers' health and mental development, and upon the length of their working lives. The hours issue is, therefore, broader than simply the question of the effect of reduced hours upon the total costs of employers or upon total output in the short run. The hours problem is involved in the conflict between private and social interests which arises in a capitalistic economy where people live by selling goods and services to others and production is motivated by private profit. Labor sellers in any occupation may strive for shorter hours as a means of raising the price of their labor and of preventing capital owners from "hogging" the gains from progress, as appeared to be the case during the 1920's.

In a Robinson Crusoe type of economy, workers consume the product of their own labor; workers' income and output are identical. Similarly, the real income of society as a whole is its total output. But, for individuals and groups in an exchange economy, income may not vary directly with output. In such an economy men work, not for their own output, but for the value of their output. That is to say, they work for money with which to acquire little bits of other people's output.

As indicated in Chapter 5 on the Labor Market, the sellers of any type of labor service are generally so numerous that an individual seller normally accounts for but a minute fraction of the total supply of that type of labor. In this respect, labor markets may differ from product markets, which are sometimes dominated by one or more large corporations. With a large number of sellers of

---

[1] Even the maximum product may not be the appropriate test. David Ricardo, the classical English economist, wrote: "Happiness is the object to be desired, and we cannot be quite sure that, provided he is equally well fed, a man may not be happier in the enjoyment of the luxury of idleness than in the enjoyment of the luxuries of a neat cottage and good clothes." *Letters of David Ricardo to Thomas R. Malthus, 1810–1823*, edited by James Bonar, 1887, pp. 138–39.

labor, variations in one worker's hours may have only a negligible effect upon the wage for that kind of work, so that his income does tend to fluctuate directly with the hours he works. But that may not be true for the group of labor sellers as a whole. One should be careful not to commit the fallacy of composition by arguing from the individual to the group.

A large producer or group of workers may gain by restricting the supply if the demand for the product or type of service is inelastic. The discussion of wage policy and the business cycle in Chapter 11 indicated why the demand for the services of particular groups of workers, like plumbers, plasterers, and railroad employees, may be very inelastic. Under such circumstances, the income of the group may be increased considerably by group action to reduce the total man-hour supply of labor in that line of work. This is the economic basis for the famous trade-union couplet: "Whether you work by the piece or the day, decreasing the hours increases the pay." The income of the group is increased because employment in that occupation does not decline as rapidly as the average wage rate rises. The reverse is also true. Should the total man-hour supply be increased by lengthening the hours of work, it would mean a much lower wage rate and a lower total income for the group, if the demand for its services were inelastic.

To sum up, generally there is a direct relationship between the income of the individual seller of labor services and his hours of work. Frequently there is an inverse relationship between the income of a whole group of workers in a special occupation and their total hours of work or their total output.[1] A group which works longer and adds more to the country's total output (real income) may receive less of the nation's total product, and a group which reduces its total hours and output, hence diminishing the nation's total of goods and services, may receive an enhanced share of that total. If the income of the group is increased by a common restrictive policy, each worker in the group would lose if all were to abandon the restriction, yet each would gain if he alone could succeed in evading the common restriction. It is such conflicts of interest between the individual, the group, and society as a whole that make agreement on social policy so difficult to achieve.

[1] For a further discussion of this point, cf. Lionel Robbins, "The Economic Effects of Variations of Hours of Labour," *Economic Journal*, vol. 39 (March 1929), pp. 25–40.

International aspects of shorter hours. The analysis just applied to industrial groups within a country also applies to the exchange of products between countries. Restrictions may raise the world price of a country's exports enough to outweigh any reduction in quantity sold. That has been the basis for various valorization schemes, such as the British or Stevenson Plan for controlling the output of crude rubber during the 1920's. In such a case, the nation's income and the total world income in terms of goods and services might move in opposite directions.[1] Most countries differ, however, from industrial groups within a country, in that they export a large number of commodities, many of which are also produced in other countries, so that the exports of any one country are not likely to enjoy an inelastic demand. Nevertheless, it must be recognized that a country may improve its terms of trade (the ratio between the prices of its exports and of its imports), and thus obtain more imports from a given quantity of exports, by practicing restrictive policies.

There is no basis in international trade theory for a belief that a country will be injured in international trade if its citizens decide that they prefer shorter working hours to an increase in real income. Even should the nation's total output be decreased by shorter hours, that would not cause its imports or its exports to cease. Presumably, with a general reduction of, say, 50 per cent in production, a country would have about the same ratio of exports to total production as before.

International trade is based upon ratios of productive efficiency in various lines within the country compared with similar ratios for the rest of the world. It is, therefore, comparative, not absolute, ability to produce various commodities that is significant. Iceland exports mutton and imports peaches, not because Iceland can produce mutton better than other countries but because, compared with the rest of the world, Iceland is the least inefficient in mutton and because Iceland can consequently obtain more peaches by selling mutton abroad and buying peaches with the proceeds than she could obtain by growing peaches in Iceland.

The argument that a country's export trade would be handicapped or destroyed if shorter hours result in higher costs overlooks not only the fundamental basis for international trade (ratios of

[1] *Cf. ibid.*, p. 37.

comparative advantage) but also the mechanism of international adjustment which was explained in Chapter 11. A relative increase in costs and prices within a gold-standard country soon leads to gold outflows, which tend to cause the money supply, and hence the level of prices in the country, to decline and which tend to bring about the opposite results in the countries receiving the gold. When countries are on paper-money standards, the adjustment takes place through changes in exchange rates. Higher domestic costs and prices can be completely offset by a corresponding decline in the exchange value of the country's currency. It is on such grounds that the Irish economist J. E. Cairnes wrote in 1874: "A rise or fall of wages in a country, so far forth as it is general, has no tendency to affect the course of foreign trade." [1] A higher level of wage costs does no more to hamper foreign trade than does a higher level of profits, rent, interest, or taxes.[2]

Possible situations in particular firms or industries. This title corresponds to one in the previous chapter. The reasoning there applies with full force here because the basic argument against shorter hours, as against increased wage rates under governmental regulation, is that labor and total costs per unit of output are thereby enhanced. Considerations of social cost will be disregarded here, and the discussion will be confined to employers' costs.

As was indicated in the subsection on hours and efficiency, reductions in the length of the working day generally increase the hourly output of workers and may, depending on the circumstances, cause no decline in total daily output. If workers' output increases in proportion to the decrease in hours, total costs per unit of output are not increased by shorter hours accompanied by the same daily wage. The workers' daily output and daily wage remain the same.

With the same daily wage and daily output per worker, shorter hours would presumably have no effect upon the firm's payroll, profits, or selling prices. If the output per hour failed to increase in proportion to the decline in hours, it is still possible that labor costs per unit of output would not increase, for the decline in daily output per worker might be balanced by a reduction in breakage,

[1] J. E. Cairnes, *Some Leading Principles of Political Economy*, p. 400.
[2] The issue with regard to taxes was discussed in the subsection on taxes and unemployment in Chapter 11. A more extended discussion of the international aspects of higher labor standards is to be found in Chapter 19 *infra*.

defective output, sickness, and accidents due to the shorter hours. In such a case, presumably the former total output of the firm would be maintained, requiring a slightly larger number of employees and hours of employment.

If output expanded more than in proportion to the decrease in hours, a greater quantity would be produced each day by the same labor force and total costs per unit of output would be decreased. For a firm in a competitive industry (horizontal demand curve), this would mean larger profits and therefore more hours of employment provided hourly wage rates were not increased. For the industry as a whole or for a firm with a monopoly (sloping demand curve), employment would increase only if the percentage increase in output exceeded the percentage decrease in hours by enough to offset the decline in marginal receipts with the larger output. In other words, the reduction in variable costs per unit of output would have to be sufficient to cause marginal costs to be less than marginal receipts before an employer would expand employment following a decrease in normal hours.

The case where workers accept lower daily wages for a shorter normal work day is unusual, for generally labor demands the same daily pay with a reduction in full-time hours. Indeed, there are cases where unions have asked for and obtained both a shorter day and an increase in the daily wage. Of course, the earnings of workers may decline when the actual hours worked fall short of the full-time hours. If the workers do accept a smaller daily wage with shorter hours, the results depend upon whether total costs per unit of output are increased or decreased. The effect upon employment, where shorter hours are accompanied by a decrease in unit costs, has just been explained. The case where unit costs are increased will now be discussed.

If the shorter work week leads to higher costs per unit of output, the analysis tends to follow that given in the corresponding subsection of the previous chapter. In case the firm has been "exploiting" labor, an increase in wage rates up to full "marginal productivity," or the rate that would prevail in a perfect labor market, would increase the employees' income without causing the employer to reduce the number of hours of work he hires. Of course, shorter hours, in so far as they reduce the supply of qualified labor and make it scarce, tend to raise the "marginal productivity" of that type of labor so that the same wage rate after decreased hours might involve "exploitation," whereas it did not involve "exploitation" before normal hours were shortened. Furthermore, demand and supply in the labor market may meet at various wage rates or over a range of rates, in which event shorter hours in one firm or industry may result in higher wages and fewer persons employed in the firm or industry, but the volume of unemployment might not increase, because, with a negatively sloping supply curve for labor, the hours of labor offered for sale might decline with higher wages.

As indicated in the previous chapter, it is possible for labor costs to rise at the expense of profits, so that the price of the product is not increased and employment is not decreased. The return to capital-owners may be squeezed with little or no effect on prices and employment because there may be no minimum rate of profits or interest and no equalization of the rate of profit between various firms or industries. Indeed, failure to earn any profits may have no effect upon employment in the short run. Firms continue to operate as long as total receipts exceed total variable costs, so that some balance remains to pay on overhead costs. In the case of firms with a monopoly or with trade-marked products (monopolistic competition), the immediate effect of an increase in labor costs is to reduce the return to capital-owning groups, because the price presumably has been set at the point that yields the maximum profit (or minimum loss). It is possible, however, that a change in labor costs may so change circumstances that the point of largest profit is at a slightly higher price and smaller output.

There is little likelihood that a shorter work day or week would lead to the substitution of machinery for labor, the displacement of men by machines in the firm or industry. With a single shift, shorter normal hours tend to increase capital costs per unit of output, because equipment is less fully used during a year when it is operated fewer hours each day. Under such circumstances, it would require more machines to produce the same volume of output in a year. Perhaps this explains why labor unions are especially interested in gaining increased wages through reduced hours. They tend thereby to reduce the possibility of displacement of men by machines in the industry, because capital costs per unit of output are increased along with labor costs. If a shorter work day causes a change from a single to a double shift in the industry, so that the equipment is operated more hours a day, the capital costs per unit of output may decrease and offset the increased labor costs, when daily wages per worker remain the same while daily output per worker is reduced. In that event, total costs per unit of output would remain the same as before and so, presumably, would the price of the product. As a consequence of the change to a double shift, however, less capital equipment and more employees would be required for a certain volume of output. The demand for capital goods would decrease and the demand for labor would increase.

With no decrease in the weekly wage per worker it is possible, therefore, for the shortened work week to increase payrolls and employment in a firm or industry if the workers formerly were "exploited," if their output increases more than in proportion to the decrease in the normal working week, or if there is a change from a single to a multiple shift so that capital equipment is operated more hours each week. Under such circumstances it is likely that a larger share of the product of industry will be obtained by labor.

General considerations. The usual economic analysis of the shorter work week explains that it will increase unit costs of production because the higher hourly wages increase labor costs and because the greater idleness of capital equipment increases capital costs. Higher total costs per unit of output, it is claimed, will lead to higher prices, which will reduce the demand for the product and lead to less employment. The only recognized exception is the rare case where the demand for the product is absolutely inelastic, but then the rise in price causes a larger proportion of the community's income to be spent for that product so that less can be spent for other products, diminishing employment in other lines of industry.

Some of the weak links in this chain of reasoning were indicated in the foregoing discussion. The shorter working week may not lead to higher unit costs, and higher costs per unit of output, under certain circumstances, may not lead to higher prices. A price rise confined to one firm or one industry would, of course, tend to reduce the volume of sales and employment in that firm or industry. If, however, the work day was reduced by national legislation that increased costs and prices in all industries, there is no assurance that the higher prices would reduce the total volume of sales and total employment. As a matter of fact, a rising price level tends to stimulate the rate of spending, and the total volume of sales in the country might even increase, especially if the money supply increased in proportion to the price rise.[1]

The arguments of "orthodox" economists against shorter hours are generally based on partial analysis and static assumptions, rather than on sequence analysis and dynamic conditions. By attempting to apply partial analysis in reasoning on the effects of a general hours reduction upon the economy as a whole, they commit the fallacy of composition, the mistake of reasoning from the particular to the general. The classical analysis, by concerning itself only with costs and individual prices, fails to allow for changes in aggregate demand, or expenditures, with changes in costs and incomes. Generally, the orthodox economists, in reasoning on the effects of shorter hours throughout industry, have assumed that aggregate demand (total money expenditures) remains constant.[2] Actually it might increase.

As has been pointed out, a more equitable distribution of income tends to speed up the rate of spending and, thus, to increase money incomes. If reduced hours should increase the share of the national income going to the laboring masses and decrease the share acquired by capital-owning groups, total expenditures, income, and employment might expand. Especially would such a result be likely to occur at a time when profits are not being spent or invested.[3]

Furthermore, the rate of spending might be increased if the shorter work week led to a shift in the demand of workers as a result of more leisure and longer week ends. With more free time, workers might buy more automobiles, small homes in the country,

[1] It is difficult to understand how Professor Dale Yoder arrives at the conclusion that the demand for the products of labor is, "on the whole, highly elastic" ("is greater than unity"), so that with higher prices the aggregate demand "will be greatly reduced." (*Cf. Labor Economics and Labor Problems* [second edition], 1939, p. 299.) Apparently he is committing the fallacy of composition mentioned in the next paragraph. The demand for all goods and services cannot be greater than unity for an increase in the price level, unless either the money supply or the rate of spending decrease. With a constant money supply and velocity of circulation, the demand would be unity.

[2] *Cf.*, for example, Professor T. N. Carver's analysis of the universal adoption of a shorter work week, "The Theory of the Shortened Working Week," *American Economic Review*, vol. 26 (September 1936), pp. 456–58.

[3] *Cf.* Emil Lederer, "Economic Effects of Thirty-Hour Week and Stimulation of Industry," *Proceedings of the National Conference of Social Work*, 1936, p. 377.

sports equipment, etc. Economists have argued that a shift in demand only benefits one industry at the expense of others, so that
total expenditures and incomes are not increased. Yet they have
also argued that the development of new products and new branches
of industry during former depressions aided in achieving a quick
recovery. Certainly such a shift in workers' demand might involve
the construction of new factories, new houses, and new equipment,
exactly as the development of a new product does. How significant
such shifting of demand might be is difficult to foretell.[1] This
shifting-demand argument for shorter hours should not be confused
with the naive notion that, if workers had more leisure but no
larger incomes, they would spend more money because they have
not had sufficient free time in the past to spend all their income.

Shorter hours as a recovery measure. The object of a recovery
program is to increase total expenditures and incomes. The possibility that shorter hours may increase workers' incomes and speed
up the rate of spending has already been discussed. That possibility
rests, however, primarily upon mass psychology, which is somewhat
unpredictable. In any program for a general introduction of
shorter full-time hours, the attitude and expectations of employers,
the expectations of workers, the timing of the program, and its execution, all play an important role. There are undoubtedly better
methods for attempting to stimulate economic recovery than a
uniform, all-around reduction in the normal work week. Under
certain circumstances it is even possible that a forced shortening
of work periods might retard recovery. As indicated by the data
on hours and efficiency, a general reduction in the work day below
seven or eight hours is likely to lead to a smaller total output per
worker.

Shorter hours were advocated and widely practiced by employers
as a relief measure in the early 1930's before the New Deal. This
"share-the-work" movement, facetiously called the "share-the-
misery" plan, did not involve a reduction in the full-time work
week but merely a temporary decrease in actual working hours for
each worker with the same hourly wage rates. Thus, labor costs
per unit of output were not affected appreciably. All that occurred
was that more people were given some employment by spreading
or smearing unemployment around more evenly.

[1] For a further discussion of this interesting idea, *cf. ibid.*, pp. 378–81.

GOVERNMENTAL REGULATION OF HOURS

The need for collective action with regard to the hours of labor was indicated in Chapter 2. There it was pointed out that market forces frequently have failed to lead to the most efficient work period and that employers are not, as a rule, interested in the long-run effects of hours upon workers' health, upon their mental and social development, or upon the welfare of the oncoming generation.

Constitutional issues. The constitutional basis for laws regulating the hours of work differs in the case of children, women, and men. Minors are wards of the state, which as guardian protects and educates them. They have no freedom of contract as do adults. Consequently, there is no question of the constitutionality of legal limitations upon the hours of children. Such legislation cannot conflict with clauses of the United States Constitution bearing on the freedom of workers to contract for their services.

Legal regulation of the hours of women and men comes under the police power of the state to pass laws protecting the health, safety, and morals of the workers themselves and the safety of the general public, which might be endangered, for example, if railroad engineers or bus drivers worked such long hours that they tended to go to sleep on the job. The courts have, however, been much more solicitous of the health, safety, and morals of women than of men, arguing that women's health and morals have a closer connection with the well-being of the future generation. It takes more than the United States Constitution to convince judges, in the words of Justice Holmes, "that there are no differences between men and women, or that legislation cannot take those differences into account." In the famous case of *Muller* v. *Oregon* (1908),[1] in which an Oregon 10-hour law for women was upheld, the Supreme Court of the United States declared:

As healthy mothers are essential to vigorous offspring, the physical well-being of women becomes an object of public interest and care in order to preserve the strength and vigor of the race. . . . The limitations which this statute imposes upon her contractual powers, upon her right to agree with her employer as to the time when she shall labor, are not imposed solely for her benefit, but also for the benefit of all.

[1] 208 U. S. 412.

Under the Constitution, the Federal government enjoys certain specific or delegated powers. Federal labor legislation must be based on one of those powers. So far only the power to regulate interstate commerce and the taxing power have been used as the basis for Federal labor legislation, although it is possible that the conditions of labor might be restricted by treaties made with other countries under the treaty power. Federal laws limiting hours have applied either to firms in interstate commerce, to Federal employees, or to the employees of firms contracting with the Federal government. The courts have held that governmental units can stipulate the conditions that shall apply to work done for them under contract.

Although the chief obstacle to the constitutionality of labor legislation is the "freedom of contract," that phrase does not appear in the Constitution. The Fifth and Fourteenth Amendments do forbid the Federal and state governments to deprive any person "of life, liberty, or property, without due process of law." Perhaps workers are being deprived of liberty if they are not permitted to contract for employment no matter what the conditions. It may be that they are also deprived of property by laws which forbid them to sell their services more than a certain number of hours each day. But it is difficult to see how employers are thereby deprived of any liberty or property, since they do not own their employees. Yet it is generally not the workers, but the employers, who are anxious to preserve labor's freedom of contract. As the Supreme Court of Mississippi stated in 1912, "it is rare for the seller of labor to appeal to the courts for the preservation of his inalienable rights of labor; this inestimable privilege is generally the object of the buyer's disinterested solicitude."

State restrictions. The reader will recall that the English Factory Acts, restricting the hours of women to 10 a day by 1847, did not eliminate profits, depress wages, and destroy the export trade, as the employers had predicted. So successful was their operation that states in this country soon followed the English example, first by passing laws limiting the working hours of children to 10 a day and, somewhat later, by also legislating a 10-hour day for women. State laws limiting the working hours of adult women were not effective, however, before 1879 when an amendment to the Massachusetts Ten Hours Law of 1874 made it really

enforceable. In Massachusetts the experience of England was repeated. The manufacturers predicted industrial ruin and lower
wages for the workers. However, an elaborate statistical study in
1880, covering the New England states and New York, showed
"that Massachusetts with ten hours produces as much per man or
per loom or per spindle, equal grades being considered, as other
States with eleven and more hours; and also that wages [in Massa-
chusetts] rule as high if not higher than in the States where the
mills run longer time." [1] The result of this demonstration of the
economic advantages of legal restriction upon the hours of labor was
that Rhode Island, New Hampshire, Maine, and Vermont, which
had opposed such legislation, soon enacted 10-hour laws for women.

In 1940 as many as 43 states had laws limiting the daily or weekly
hours of women in certain branches of industry. Over half of the
states with hours laws for women permit overtime under certain
conditions, but in many states punitive rates must be paid for such
overtime hours. In arguing before the Supreme Court in 1917
against the Oregon 10-hour law for women in factories, the opposition claimed that it was a wages law rather than an hours law,
because it permitted three hours of overtime a day at increased
rates of pay. State hours laws for adult women exempt agricultural
work and, in most states, domestic service.

All but two states restrict the hours of work for children. Three
fourths of the states have laws limiting to eight hours the working
day of children under 16 years of age. Most of them forbid overtime in excess of 48 hours a week. Agricultural work is likewise
exempt from most of these child-labor laws.

The hours of men in private employment are regulated by various
state statutes. Practically all of the states place some restrictions
upon the hours of workers in rail or automobile transportation, and
one third of them limit the hours of men in underground mining
or in smelting, generally to eight a day. Such occupations are considered especially hazardous to the worker owing to the lack of sunlight and fresh air or the presence of intense heat and obnoxious
gasses. One third of the states also have laws restricting the hours
that adult males may work in occupations outside transportation,
mining, and other hazardous work. A number of such state laws
have, in the past, been declared unconstitutional.

[1] Massachusetts Bureau of Statistics of Labor, *Twelfth Annual Report*, 1881, p. 457.

Public servants in two thirds of the states enjoy the eight-hour day by law. In most of these states, the eight-hour maximum also applies to workers employed on public works done under contract and to employees of the various political subdivisions or municipalities of the state.

Federal restrictions. Regulation of the hours of Federal employees began in 1840, when the 10-hour day was put into effect in the government navy yards. By 1912 the eight-hour day was generally effective for persons working directly or indirectly for the Federal government. An act passed in that year required that an eight-hour clause be inserted in all Federal contracts involving the employment of laborers or mechanics. During the first World War the President was given the power to suspend this law "in case of national emergency," with pay at the rate of time-and-one-half for all work in excess of eight hours. The Walsh-Healey Public Contracts Act of 1936 provides for the eight-hour day and the 40-hour week in the manufacture or furnishing of all goods purchased under Federal contracts exceeding $10,000. The Secretary of Labor may permit work on such government contracts in excess of 40 hours in any one week, but the rate of pay for such overtime hours must be at least one-and-a-half times the basic hourly rate.

In order to avoid a nationwide railroad strike in 1916, Congress passed the Adamson Act, providing a basic eight-hour day for employees on interstate railroads. Overtime rates of time-and-a-half were introduced in 1919. The opponents of the Act claimed that it was not really a measure designed to reduce hours but a subterfuge to increase the wages of railroad employees. Recently railroad workers have agitated for a basic 30-hour week by law.

Under the National Industrial Recovery Act of 1933, the Federal government began to extend its regulation of working hours to private employment outside the field of transportation and government contracts. The reader will recall that the NRA codes were to provide an "hours ceiling" and a "wage floor." Codes of fair competition covering half of the affected employees provided for a basic 40-hour work week. Almost another third of the code-covered employees were under codes designating 48 hours as the basic week.[1] The President's Re-employment Agreement stipu-

---

[1] The material on hours in NRA codes is based on Chapter 14 in L. S. Lyon *et al.*, *The National Recovery Administration*, 1935.

lated a maximum work week of 40 hours for white-collar workers and 35 hours for factory and mechanical workers.

The basic-week provisions of almost every code were qualified by exemptions and clauses allowing some elasticity. Most of the codes provided for higher overtime rates for hours in excess of the basic week or beyond eight hours a day, often however with some exemptions or qualifications. The popular overtime rates in the codes were time-and-a-third and time-and-a-half. With actual hours of labor in factories averaging between 35 and 37 a week in 1933, 1934, and 1935, it is not likely that many hours of labor were paid for at punitive rates under the codes of fair competition.

The Fair Labor Standards Act follows the precedents established by the National Recovery Act. Like most of the codes, the Fair Labor Standards Act provides for a 40-hour week after October 23, 1940, for covered employees engaged in interstate commerce or in the production of goods for such commerce. The 40-hour maximum is much shorter than the legal maxima for women or men in most state laws and also is lower than the maximum prescribed by Congress for government employees, railroad workers, and seamen.

The Fair Labor Standards Act permits hours in excess of the 40-hour maximum if paid for at a rate not less than one-and-one-half times the regular rate. This is the most usual overtime rate in trade or union agreements.[1] Further elasticity is provided for in the case of seasonal industries and guaranteed-employment plans resulting from genuine collective bargaining. In an industry declared "seasonal" (the Administrator has ruled that such industries must cease operations completely during off seasons), the maximum work day can be 12 hours and the maximum work week 56 hours for 14 weeks in a year, with time-and-a-half for hours beyond these maxima.

There has been a possibility that employers might make the hours and overtime provisions ineffective by maintaining the same weekly hours and paying the same weekly wage but reducing the regular hourly rate to compensate for the penalty rate for overtime hours. The Act tries to guard against this and similar contingencies by stating that none of its provisions "shall justify any employer in

[1] In the building trades, however, union agreements covering 64 per cent of the total union membership in the 105 cities surveyed on June 1, 1938, specified double time for overtime, compared with 35 per cent covered by agreements requiring time-and-a-half. *Cf. Monthly Labor Review*, vol. 47 (November 1938), p. 1103.

reducing a wage paid by him which is in excess of the applicable minimum wage under this Act." However, the same result could be accomplished by simply not raising regular hourly rates when the general wage level rises, but permitting the overtime hours to increase weekly wages.

The analysis of overtime rates in Chapter 8 indicated that workers were generally receiving less than their full "marginal productivity" (were being "exploited"), when employers pay punitive overtime rates for normal (not emergency) work. Perhaps this conclusion may be modified slightly by the fact that the savings from operating equipment longer each day may help to compensate for the additional cost of the overtime rates. But the experience with overtime work discussed in this chapter would seem to indicate not only that overtime hours are inefficient but also that they reduce the effectiveness of workers during normal hours. Perhaps such forces are stronger when actual hours are in excess of 48 a week than they would be in the case of a 44- or a 42-hour week. The effect of a few hours of overtime in excess of 40 a week would, of course, depend upon the industry, as was explained in the discussion of hours and efficiency. One thing seems certain. Where the practice of paying overtime rates for normal work is widespread, employers are hiring workers on the basis of average, and not marginal, costs.

CHAPTER FOURTEEN

UNEMPLOYMENT AND RELIEF

Unemployment has been and still is the nation's number one economic problem. It is the problem of idle man power, of unused productive capacity, of economic waste, and of human distress.

The previous chapter dealt with the hours of work and labor's demand for shorter working periods. In times of widespread unemployment, however, the actual working hours of many persons are far below normal, and some workers have no working hours at all. Unemployment and underemployment indicate how much actual working hours fall short of full-time hours. A worker may be totally unemployed during a period or he may be partially unemployed, having only part-time employment.

The factors and forces that determine the total volume of employment and unemployment were analyzed in Chapter 11. That chapter discussed the causes; this chapter deals with the effects and with the attempts to relieve persons suffering from those effects. Attention will be concentrated primarily upon the economic and financial phases of the problem, although it is difficult to separate the economic from the sociological and personal aspects of unemployment. The jobless are persons as well as numbers in statistical tables. Involuntary idleness may have adverse effects upon character and personality, upon family life, upon crime and delinquency, etc. Such social consequences are no less real because they, like the human suffering and distress, cannot be measured and run through an adding machine. And in so far as unemployment causes physical and moral deterioration by injuring the health, morale, or work habits of its victims, the nation suffers a real economic loss. Under such circumstances, public expenditures to help conserve our human resources may be a good investment.

368

EXTENT AND INCIDENCE OF UNEMPLOYMENT

The basic material of this section will consist of facts and figures, but the statistics will require some explanation in order to bring out their meaning and their significance. Though facts are said to speak for themselves, they generally require an interpreter to be understood. Especially is this true in the case of unemployment. There is a plethora of data regarding unemployment in this and other countries, but much of it is of questionable value or validity.

Unemployment estimates and trends. During the 1930's, estimating the number of unemployed persons in the country became a favorite pastime for many persons with a statistical bent. There have been literally hundreds of such estimates, some of them differing from others by four or five millions. Differences of definition are partly responsible for such wide variations. Generally, the employable workers are first separated from those who are unable to work because of sickness, injury, or some mental quirk. With this division established, the statistician's problems begin. Should elderly workers who are idle be included as unemployed? Should workers on strike or locked out be counted in? What about persons seeking work but unwilling to take a job except at a certain wage? How about workers who are employed only one or two days a week or who, after losing their jobs, start a petty business like shoe shining or peddling but earn very little money? Should workers with jobs on relief projects be included among the employed or among the unemployed?

Changes in the labor supply are one of the most important sources of discrepancy in unemployment estimates. Married women may begin to seek jobs because their husbands' earnings have been reduced. During a depression, many young persons who have never had a job reach working age and seek employment. Should these married women and new recruits be considered a part of the total volume of unemployment?

The date of the estimates also makes a difference. Because of the normal seasonal variation in employment, there are in prosperous years at least 2,000,000 more workers employed throughout the country in September or October than in January. Consequently, an estimate of the peak of employment in any one year would differ considerably from a figure for the average throughout the year.

Because of such latitude in definition, it is necessary to confine attention primarily to one series of estimates covering a number of years in order to evaluate the year-to-year changes in the volume of unemployment. Indeed, such changes are of much more significance than are estimates of the absolute volume of employment or unemployment on any particular date. Unemployment of very short duration does not create the problems that attend widespread unemployment for long periods of time.

The trend of unemployment in England since 1850 and in this country since 1900 was indicated in Table 16 in Chapter 10. It is evident from the figures in that table that persistent large-scale unemployment has been characteristic of British industry since 1920 and of American industry since 1929. The general trend of unemployment from 1929 to 1938 in 15 important industrial countries combined is revealed by the indexes in Table 21. Judging

TABLE 21.   INDEX NUMBERS OF UNEMPLOYMENT IN VARIOUS COUNTRIES
(1929 = 100) [1]

Year	World (15 countries)	United States	Canada	Great Britain	Australia
1929	100	100	100	100	100
1930	164	177	195	155	174
1931	235	233	295	205	247
1932	291	290	386	213	261
1933	277	296	391	191	226
1934	225	255	319	161	185
1935	196	226	270	149	149
1936	151	162	233	126	110
1937	111	128	189	105	84

from the data in this table, unemployment in the United States corresponded fairly closely with that for the world as a whole, represented by the combined index for 15 countries. After 1932, however, it was somewhat more severe here than abroad. The wage-earners in Canada apparently suffered more from unemployment during the 1930's than they did in this country. Other data tend to substantiate this conclusion.[2]

[1] Taken from the *1938 Year-Book of Labour Statistics*, International Labour Office, pp. 29, 59. These indexes are based primarily upon the proportion of trade-union members unemployed as a percentage of all trade-union members, except for Great Britain, in which case unemployment-insurance statistics have been used. The indexes, therefore, are based on percentages and are not a measure of fluctuations in the absolute number of unemployed workers. As a rule, they do not take account of partially unemployed workers.

[2] *Cf.*, for example, S. A. Saunders, "Nature and Extent of Unemployment in Canada,"

TABLE 22. ESTIMATED AVERAGE EMPLOYMENT AND UNEMPLOYMENT IN THE
UNITED STATES, 1929-1940 [1]

Year	Employment (millions of persons)	Unemployment (millions of persons)	Percentage of labor force unemployed
1929	47.9	0.4	0.9
1930	45.2	3.8	7.8
1931	41.6	8.1	16.3
1932	37.7	12.5	24.9
1933	38.1	12.7	25.1
1934	41.0	10.4	20.2
1935	42.4	9.5	18.4
1936	44.8	7.6	14.5
1937	46.6	6.4	12.0
1938	43.6	10.1	18.8
1939	45.3	9.1	16.7
1940 (6 mo.)	45.9	9.0	16.3

Estimates of the average volume of employment and unemployment in the United States since 1929 are given in Table 22.
They have been compiled by the National Industrial Conference
Board. Estimates of unemployment made by other agencies, such
as the American Federation of Labor and the Alexander Hamilton
Institute, are higher, ranging from 500,000 to 3,000,000 more unemployed during the various years. Such divergence arises partly
from the fact that the Conference Board estimates include workers
on work-relief projects among the employed, whereas the other
estimates include them among the unemployed. All of these estimates omit the partially unemployed; yet the surveys of unemployment in Massachusetts, Pennsylvania, Buffalo, and Philadelphia
in 1933 or 1934, as well as the Federal census of unemployment
in November 1937, show that the partly unemployed have num-
bered almost half as many as the totally unemployed. Consequently,
the loss from unemployment is much greater than is indicated by
the third column in Table 22, showing the totally unemployed as
a percentage of all workers. It has been estimated that as much
as 41 to 47 per cent of all the available hours of labor were lost
because of unemployment during the years from 1932 to 1935
inclusive.[2]

in *Canada's Unemployment Problem*, edited by L. Richter, 1939, pp. 3, 8, 9, and compare
that data with the figures for the United States in Table 16 *supra*.

[1] Taken from National Industrial Conference Board, *Conference Board Economic Record*,
vol. 2 (March 20, 1940), pp. 78 and 84, and subsequent press releases.

[2] David Weintraub and H. L. Posner, *Unemployment and Increasing Productivity*, Works
Progress Administration, 1937, p. 14.

Table 15 in Chapter 10 indicates how the total volume of unemployment was distributed among the major branches of American industry on four different dates. Between 1929 and 1940, the number of employed persons was smallest in March 1933 and largest in September 1937. It is evident from this table that the percentage of unemployment has been greatest in building construction, followed by such industries as lumber, coal and metal mining, street and highway construction, and the railroads. Personal-service industries and agriculture, on the other hand, seem to have suffered relatively little from unemployment. Reasons for such industrial differences in the incidence of unemployment, especially the concentration of depressional unemployment in the capital-goods industries, were discussed in Chapters 9 and 10.

Length of unemployment. Before 1930 the periods between jobs were fairly short for most workers. Labor turnover rates in industry were fairly high, and, consequently, there was a considerable flow into and out of the unemployed group. Such movement and change tended to prevent the formation and growth of a "hard core" or pool of unemployed persons, able and willing to work but gradually becoming unemployable through the debilitating effects of chronic unemployment. Continuous unemployment for three or four years may unfit many workers for regular work.

After 1930 there was a marked increase not only in the total volume of unemployment but also in the length of the period during which individuals suffered from unemployment. Persons once unemployed have experienced increasing difficulty in securing another job. The tendency for unemployment to become prolonged is indicated in Table 23, showing the percentage of all unemployed persons in Buffalo, New York, who had been unemployed for a year or more in November of each year. The second and third columns of the table contain W. S. Woytinsky's estimates of the probable hard-core unemployment in Buffalo on the same dates. In November 1932, two fifths of all unemployed men in Buffalo had been unemployed for two years or over, and half of the Buffalo unemployed were in the two-years-or-over category in November 1933.

Later studies of the duration of unemployment also disclose this tendency for some unemployment to become chronic. An unem-

TABLE 23. PROLONGED AND HARD-CORE UNEMPLOYMENT IN BUFFALO, 1929-1933[1]

Year	Percentage of unemployed who were jobless a year or more	Percentage hard-core unemployed were of	
		total unemployed	all workers
1929	9	8	0.5
1930	21	15	2.5
1931	43	35	8.5
1932	60	50	16.0
1933	68	65	18.5

ployment survey of Bridgeport, Connecticut, in the Spring of 1934 revealed that over half of the unemployed had been out of work at least two years and one sixth of them had been jobless for four years or more.[2] A census of unemployment in the state of Massachusetts in January 1934 showed similar results. At that time one fourth of the employable population of Massachusetts was totally unemployed or employed on relief projects. Almost one half of the unemployed men in Massachusetts had been out of work at least two years, and one seventh of them had been jobless for four years or more.[3] A census of unemployment in Michigan a year later (January 1935) showed that one fourth of Michigan's working population was unemployed and that over one fifth of the unemployed had been jobless for at least four years.[4]

Sample studies of about 4,000 persons (one eighth of the workers) in Lincoln, Nebraska, in November 1933, 1937, and 1939 also indicate the duration of unemployment in that city. The percentage of all workers who were totally unemployed in Lincoln decreased from 25 per cent in 1933 to 14 per cent in 1937 and 1939. The percentage of the unemployed who had been out of a regular job for three years or more increased from 26 per cent in 1933 to 36 per cent in 1937 and 43 per cent in 1939. In other words, almost one out of every two unemployed workers in November 1939 had not

---

[1] Cf. Monthly Labor Review, vol. 38 (March 1934), p. 526; and a preliminary report by W. S. Woytinsky, Recent Trends in Labor Turnover, Their Causes, and Their Effects on the Labor Market, Social Science Research Council, February 1, 1939, p. 9 (mimeographed).

[2] "Unemployment Survey of Bridgeport, Conn., 1934," Monthly Labor Review, vol. 40 (March 1935), p. 630.

[3] Cf. Report on the Census of Unemployment in Massachusetts as of January 2, 1934, Massachusetts Department of Labor and Industries, Division of Statistics, Public Document No. 15, 1935, p. 41.

[4] Cf. Michigan Census of Population and Unemployment, January 14, 1935, State of Michigan, Emergency Welfare Relief Commission, No. 5, "Duration of Unemployment of Workers Seeking Reemployment," March 1937, p. 1.

received regular employment for at least three years. Half of those who were unemployed in 1939 were considered unable or unwilling to work. Only about one out of every nine of those who maintained that they were able and willing to work had been out of a regular job for three years or more. Of the 4,000-odd persons included in the November 1939 sample, 39 per cent had experienced one or more periods of total unemployment between 1929 and 1939, and 14 per cent had been totally unemployed for at least three years during the decade ending in 1939.[1]

The survey of unemployment covering the largest number of years is that for Philadelphia, made during the Spring or Summer of every year from 1931 through 1938, except 1934. The results of this series of sample surveys are indicated in Table 24. The decline in the percentages for 1938 is largely due to the fact that the survey of that year occurred when the 1938 recession reached its depth. Persons thrown out of work in that recession had been jobless for only a short period, which tended to reduce the percentages for the whole group.

TABLE 24. DURATION OF UNEMPLOYMENT SINCE LAST REGULAR NONRELIEF JOB, MALE UNEMPLOYED IN PHILADELPHIA, 1931–1938[2]

Year	Percentage of unemployed who were jobless	
	2 years or more	4 years or more
1931	5.8	1.5
1932	10.8	1.5
1933	25.6	2.9
1935	50.9	20.8
1936	46.5	23.8
1937	61.7	29.4
1938	34.3	19.2

These unemployment statistics indicate that unemployment has been concentrated upon certain workers. In the 1930's, the nation's labor supply was being divided into three more or less distinct groups: one continuously working, one intermittently em-

[1] Statements in this paragraph are based upon Cleon O. Swayzee, *Eight Years of Unemployment in Lincoln, Nebraska, 1932–1939*, University of Nebraska Studies in Business, No. 45 (October 1939), pp. 5, 10–11, 24.

[2] Gladys L. Palmer, *Recent Trends in Employment and Unemployment in Philadelphia*, Works Progress Administration, National Research Project, Philadelphia, December 1937, p. 57; *Employment and Unemployment in Philadelphia in 1936 and 1937, Part II: May 1937*, Works Progress Administration, October 1938, p. 26; and *Employment and Unemployment in Philadelphia, July–August 1938*, University of Pennsylvania, Industrial Research Department, Special Report No. 7, Philadelphia, August 1939, p. 50.

ployed, and one continuously idle. Even if the workers in all three groups were of equal quality at the outset, before widespread unemployment occurred, continuous unemployment would tend to make the third group less and less employable. Consequently, the longer they remain out of work, the more their chances of reemployment diminish. People, like capital equipment, depreciate, and the additional depreciation due to the effects of prolonged unemployment represents a real social loss or cost.

Unemployment by age groups, sex, and race. Two groups are severely affected by unemployment, the young and the old. The incidence of unemployment is lowest among workers from 25 to 55 years of age. Table 25 indicates, by age groups, the percentage of available workers who were totally unemployed in Philadelphia in the Spring of 1931, 1933, and 1938; in Massachusetts in January 1934; in Pennsylvania in the Spring of 1934; and throughout the country in November 1937. It is evident from this

TABLE 25. PERCENTAGE OF EMPLOYABLE WORKERS TOTALLY UNEMPLOYED, BY AGE GROUPS, 1931 1938[1]

Age group	Philadelphia 1931	1933	Massachusetts 1934	Pennsylvania 1934	United States 1937	Philadelphia 1938
All ages	27	47	25	28	20	31
15–19	39	70	51	60	41	70
20–24	32	52	30	36	24	42
25–34	25	43	20	22	16	27
35–44	22	39	20	19	16	25
45–54	23	41	20	22	17	25
55–64	26	44	23	27	20	29
65 and over	34	53	28	34	19	27

table that the new recruits, those between 15 and 19 years of age, have been hardest hit by unemployment. From 1934 to 1939, the unemployment percentage for this youthful group has been twice as high as that for all age groups. On the other hand, the percentage figure for persons 65 or over shows a relative decline following the passage of the Social Security Act in 1935. Presumably its old-age-assistance provisions caused many of the elderly unem-

[1] Gladys L. Palmer, *Recent Trends in Employment and Unemployment in Philadelphia*, pp. 51–54, and *Employment and Unemployment in Philadelphia, July–August 1938*, p. 36; *Report on the Census of Unemployment in Massachusetts as of January 2, 1934*, p. 14; "Pennsylvania Census of Unemployment, 1934," in *Monthly Labor Review*, vol. 41 (September 1935), p. 619; and *Census of Partial Employment, Unemployment and Occupations: 1937*, vol. 4, Washington, 1938, p. 12.

ployed to withdraw from the labor market, so they would not be included as "employable workers."

There are many reasons why young persons in their teens, having left school, did not find regular employment during the 1930's. Many of them lacked job experience and had no special business or vocational training. Failure to find work robbed some of them of initiative, self-confidence, and ambition. Apparently, it paid employers to hire experienced workers or to rehire former employees rather than to take on "green hands" at low wages. This indicates that the low-wage labor of youths may not be cheap and that inexperienced youngsters may not crowd the higher wage adults out of jobs.

As a matter of fact, child labor has been declining in significance during the last four decades. Between 1900 and 1930 the percentage of gainfully employed population represented by youngsters from 10 to 15 years fell from 18.2 to 4.7 per cent. In 1930, as many as 70 per cent of these young workers were in agriculture, so that less than one half of one per cent of the workers in manufacturing establishments were under 16 years of age in that year. Judging by the number of work certificates issued to children 14 and 15 years of age, there was a further decline in the percentage of child workers in industry during the early 1930's.

The charge is frequently made during periods of widespread unemployment that women and children are taking jobs away from the men. The statistics fail to support that claim so far as children are concerned. What story do they tell with regard to the women?

From 1880 to 1910 the percentage of all gainfully employed persons who were women rose from 15 to 21 per cent. By 1930, the figure was 22 per cent, so that, before the depression, more than one out of every five persons working for a wage or for a profit was a woman. In the older industrial countries, the percentage of women employed outside their own homes is higher than in the United States.

With this background, it is interesting to observe what happened to women workers in the depression years of the 1930's. Table 26 summarizes data on the percentage of totally unemployed male and female workers during those years. Judging from this table alone, one would conclude that the men suffered somewhat more from unemployment before 1934 and that the women were harder

TABLE 26. PERCENTAGE OF EMPLOYABLE WORKERS TOTALLY UNEMPLOYED, BY SEX, 1931-1938 [1]

Coverage and date		Men	Women
Philadelphia	1931	27	25
Philadelphia	1932	43	42
Philadelphia	1933	47	45
Massachusetts	1934	27	22
Pennsylvania	1934	27	31
Philadelphia	1935	33	34
Philadelphia	1936	30	35
United States	1937	18	25
Philadelphia	1938	31	36

hit in 1934 and later years. However, the influx of women (many of them inexperienced) into the labor market because of reduced family incomes during the depression partly accounts for the high proportion of unemployed women in the later 1930's. In Philadelphia, for example, the number of women at work or seeking work between 1931 and 1937 increased about 20 per cent more than the number of men; yet the increase in the number of women with full-time employment in the same period was only 6 per cent more than that for men fully employed. On the basis of the Federal unemployment census of 1937, it has been estimated that, of all persons employed or available for employment in November 1937, almost 27 per cent were women. One out of every four of these women was either totally unemployed or working on a relief project, whereas less than one out of every five male workers were so situated.[2]

These statistics indicate that women tended to crowd into the labor market during the depression, but they also show that inexperienced, low-wage women workers failed to displace men on a widespread scale in American industry during the depression years in the 1930's.

As indicated by the discussion of wage differentials, Negro workers are generally a low-wage group. In many localities, especially in the South, they are paid less than white persons working at the same job. Table 27 shows the percentage of white and colored employable male workers in Philadelphia who were totally unemployed each year from 1930 through 1938. This table indicates

[1] *Recent Trends in Employment and Unemployment in Philadelphia*, pp. 51–55; *Report on Census of Unemployment in Massachusetts*, p. 14; "Pennsylvania Census of Unemployment, 1934," *op. cit.*, p. 618; *Census of Partial Employment, Unemployment and Occupations*, vol. 4, p. 12; and *Employment and Unemployment in Philadelphia, July–August 1938*, p. 14.

[2] *Census of Partial Employment, Unemployment and Occupations*, vol. 4, p. 20.

TABLE 27. PERCENTAGE OF EMPLOYABLE MALE WORKERS IN PHILADELPHIA
            TOTALLY UNEMPLOYED, BY COLOR, 1930–1938 [1]

Year	Native-born white	Foreign-born white	Negro
1930	9.8	9.4	12.1
1931	24.3	26.3	36.8
1932	39.3	43.1	59.2
1933	44.4	45.5	61.1
1934	30.0	29.0	49.5
1935	30.5	27.9	54.3
1936	27.5	24.1	50.5
1937	21.5	17.5	43.3
1938	29.6	24.1	51.0

that, compared to the whites, Negroes in Philadelphia suffered
more and more as the depression of the 1930's continued. In 1936
and 1938 one out of every two male Negro workers was unemployed, while only one out of every four white workers was experiencing complete unemployment.

According to the census of unemployment in November 1937,
less than 18 per cent of all male workers available for employment
were totally unemployed or on relief projects, compared with a
figure of over 28 per cent for the Negro and other races.[2] That
census showed that in every geographic division of the country,
except the East Central states (Kentucky, Tennessee, Alabama,
and Mississippi), a larger percentage of Negroes and workers of
other nonwhite races were unemployed, and a smaller percentage
were fully employed, than was true of white male workers. In the
East South Central states, the proportion of male workers fully employed was about the same for both the white and black races.[3]
Such statistics indicate that even in most of the Southern states,
where the wage differential is the largest, Negroes did not displace
white workers during the 1930's, but instead, the low-wage Negro
workers suffered more from unemployment than did the whites.
In the Middle Atlantic and North Central states, where black and

[1] The 1930 percentages have been calculated from unemployment statistics in the
Fifteenth Census of the United States: 1930, "Unemployment," vol. 1, p. 853. The 1934 percentages have been taken from the *Pennsylvania Census of Unemployment, 1934.* For these
and the other percentages, *cf. Recent Trends in Employment and Unemployment in Philadelphia*, pp. 48–49; *Employment and Unemployment in Philadelphia in 1936 and 1937, Part 2*,
p. 54; and *Employment and Unemployment in Philadelphia, July–August 1938*, p. 34. There
are a minor number (less than one per cent) of Mexicans and other races included in
the percentages for Negroes.

[2] *Census of Partial Employment, Unemployment and Occupations: 1937*, vol. 4, p. 39.

[3] *Ibid.*, pp. 90–91.

white workers usually receive the same wage rates on the same job, the percentages of male Negroes unemployed or on relief projects were approximately twice as high as those for white workmen in November 1937.[1]

Work experience of the unemployed. Those who became unemployed during the depression years of the 1930's were, for the most part, average workers who had fallen on evil days. At the time of their disemployment, they differed little from a cross section of those who were fortunate enough to retain jobs. For example, male heads of relief families available for employment in New Jersey in 1934 enjoyed a median annual income of $1,300 from 1925 to 1929.[2] Their annual predepression incomes in each occupational group were close to the general average for all workers in the state. Judging from the few studies that have been made of occupational changes of workers, these heads of relief households also showed a fairly high degree of stability in type of employment before they lost their jobs in the 1930's. One half to four fifths of the relief-family heads in each occupational group pursued the same line of business or an occupation of the same skill during the five years from 1925 to 1929 as they had during the five years before 1925, and these percentages also held true for the five years after 1929.[3] Such statistics do not indicate that the unemployed were unsatisfactory and shiftless workers before they lost their jobs. Their work records seem to demonstrate that satisfactory performance is no guarantee against joblessness and that the unemployed have, in the main, been victims of circumstances beyond their own control.

It is true that there has been a disproportionately large number of unskilled workers in the ranks of the unemployed and that, on the whole, the unemployed have been less well educated than those who did not lose their jobs. A Michigan census of population and unemployment in January 1935, for example, revealed that only 16 per cent of the unemployed had completed 12 grades in school, compared with a figure of 22 per cent for the employed workers.[4]

[1] *Ibid.*, pp. 90–94.

[2] State of New Jersey, Emergency Relief Administration, *Neighbors in Need*, Report No. 1, 1935, pp. 50–52.

[3] *Ibid.*, pp. 40–50; and R. A. Lester, *Some Aspects of Unemployment Relief in New Jersey*, 1936 (unpublished Ph.D. thesis, Princeton University Library), pp. 23–24.

[4] Michigan Census of Population and Unemployment, *Education of Gainful Workers*, First Series, No. 7, March 1937, p. 2.

Nevertheless, schooling has not proved to be a guarantee against unemployment and destitution. Almost every occupation and profession has been represented by those in the ranks of the unemployed or on the relief rolls. A New Jersey survey of 10,000 relief clients in 1934 showed that all sorts of workers had suffered long periods of unemployment, from deep-sea divers and stool pigeons for the police, to chemists with college degrees and former $50,000-a-year executives. The November 1939 study in Lincoln, Nebraska, revealed that more than one out of every six unemployed persons able and willing to work had spent at least one year in college, and about one out of eleven had graduated from college.[1]

The burden of employment shortage was not, however, evenly distributed during the 1930's. As already mentioned, workers in building construction and in the capital-equipment industries have been much more subject to the risk of unemployment and underemployment than workers in the consumers' goods industries. It might be said perhaps that some workers were simply unfortunate in the selection of their lifetime work. Table 28 indicates industries or occupations in which there was a heavy concentration of un-

TABLE 28.   PERCENTAGE OF GAINFUL WORKERS UNEMPLOYED IN SELECTED
INDUSTRIES AND OCCUPATIONS, 1935 AND 1937 [2]

Industry or occupation	Per cent of gainful workers
Michigan, 1935	
Unskilled building workers	58
Construction and maintenance of streets	49
Skilled building workers	47
Unskilled workers in metal mining	41
Agricultural laborers	35
Unskilled workers in forestry	33
All industries	14
United States, 1937	
Construction and maintenance of streets, roads, and sewers	37
Building industry	30
Forestry	26
Independent hand trades	26
Woolen and worsted mills	21
Hotels and restaurants	20
All industries	14

[1] C. O. Swayzec, *op. cit.*, p. 17.

[2] Michigan Census of Population and Unemployment, *Social-Economic Occupational Classification of Workers in Selected Industries*, March 1937, p. 4, and *Industrial Classification of Unemployed and Gainfully Employed Workers*, December 1936, p. 8; and *Census of Partial Employment, Unemployment and Occupations: 1937*, vol. 1, 1938, p. 17.

employment in Michigan in January 1935 and throughout the country in November 1937. New recruits who had not acquired an occupation are, of course, not included in the figures of this table. The percentages for the United States in November 1937 are low, not only because new workers are excluded, but also because not all unemployed persons registered for the 1937 census.

The figures in Table 28 show that in Michigan almost three fifths of the unskilled building workers were unemployed in January 1935, as were about one half of the workers who considered their regular work to be constructing and repairing streets. The high percentage of unemployment among regular street and highway workers, as indicated by the Michigan (1935) and United States (1937) statistics, can be explained only by the fact that during the 1930's much of their work was turned over to relief clients to be done as work-relief projects. Such displacement of regular by emergency-relief employees is discussed at a later point in this chapter.

Unemployment and labor-market policy. During a period of prolonged or hard-core unemployment, the most desirable labor-market policy may be one that conserves the nation's labor forces by preventing deterioration rather than one that provides the most profit or least loss for capital.

The preceding discussion has indicated that certain groups of workers in the community, whether because of age, color, or occupation, were especially hard hit by the depression of the 1930's. Statistics show that there has been little need to fear that low-wage groups would displace family heads, for much of the burden of unemployment has been concentrated upon the shoulders of certain low-wage groups. This has been especially true of youths who were between 15 and 24 years of age.

It has been estimated that in 1936 and 1938 there were from 4,000,000 to 5,000,000 youths between 15 and 24 years of age who were out of school and out of work.[1] Surveys in various cities indicated that, on the average, these youths had been out of school between three and four years. One third of them had never had jobs, and half of them had had no business or vocational training. The intermittent jobs obtained by many of the rest had not been

---

[1] Cf. *Reports on Public Assistance to the Administrator, Works Progress Administration for the City of New York,* March 14, 1939, pp. 185–86.

of a type to afford them satisfactory training from the point of view of their long-run interests.

The nation's labor supply is being increased at a rate of 500,000 a year as the young grow up. What these new additions to the nation's working forces need is work experience and job training for their physical and mental development and to bolster up their morale. Some of them had temporary work in the camps of the Civilian Conservation Corps or had, under the National Youth Administration, jobs on work projects for youth or part-time employment under the student-aid program while continuing their education. However, the CCC and student-aid programs covered only about 300,000 each in the late 1930's, and on NYA projects the average number employed was about 150,000. Despite the student-aid program, the number of college students fell off nine per cent during the period from 1931 to 1935. Strangely enough, at a time when such a large proportion of the resources of industry were idle, the educational equipment of the country was not fully utilized.

Aside from their limited coverage, the chief difficulty with all these programs for the youth has been that, for the most part, they have given the youth a kind of work training for which there is little demand in private industry. Work in the woods under the CCC, for example, is not directly related to the future work careers of most of the enrollees. That, indeed, has been the difficulty with practically all of the work projects devised for the unemployed. Work of a type that would provide a real training for jobs in private industry has generally been condemned and avoided on the grounds that it would be competitive with private industry. The authorities have tried to confine the work-relief projects to "made work"— extraordinary work which normally would not be done. Consequently, there was a shortage of skilled labor in certain lines during the early months of 1937 and 1940. No organization had provided the apprenticeship training for young persons who were unemployed so that they might become skilled workmen. As the Special Senate Committee to Investigate Unemployment and Relief stated in April 1938, such vocational training "would be much more effective and more economical" than to have the youth remain at unskilled work on extraordinary work-relief projects.[1]

---

[1] *Unemployment and Relief, Preliminary Report,* Senate Report No. 1625, 75th Congress, third session, April 20, 1938, p. 14.

Presumably the fundamental purpose of work relief is to provide employment opportunities suited to the skills of the unemployed workers on projects of public usefulness. Yet a *Census of Usual Occupations* of workers on relief in the United States in March 1935 revealed that at least one fifth of those workers had skills which, in the words of the Assistant Administrator of the Works Progress Administration (WPA), were "difficult, if not impossible, to utilize on work projects." [1] As already mentioned, unemployment struck workers in all walks of economic life. There was little possibility of giving relief work at their normal occupations to such unemployed workers, for example, as railroad employees, watchmakers, barbers, bakers, cooks, waiters, miners, farm laborers, elevator and telephone operators, cigar makers, salesmen, machinists and molders, operatives in textile and shoe factories, or machine tenders in other industrial establishments. It was even difficult to avoid giving white-collar workers jobs involving out-of-door, manual labor of an unskilled sort.

As a practical labor-market policy it is highly desirable that workers receive some employment periodically so that they are not continuously idle. From a social point of view, hard-core unemployment is an evil much more grave than the excessive instability represented by high rates of labor turnover. The pernicious effects of chronic unemployment upon the nation's labor resources are so great that it might be profitable for society in the long run, if some program for rotating workers in private employment or a program of government work projects closer in character to private employment were pursued.

In the past it has been argued that the best interests of the nation are served by permitting private employers to hire whatever workers they choose, without regard to the effect of their employment policies upon the nation's present and potential human resources. Employment of workers considered the best for the money and the job, it was claimed, would result in the largest national product and, thus, in the greatest good for society as a whole. Such a doctrine does not apply, however, during periods of widespread unemployment, when part of the nation's normal working force be-

---

[1] *Cf.* Works Progress Administration, *Workers on Relief in the United States in March 1935: A Census of Usual Occupations,* January 1937; and Corrington Gill, "Who Are the Jobless? What Can They Do?" *New York Times,* November 24, 1935, IV, p. 3.

comes a submerged group. Some workers thrown out of jobs and into this submerged class may have been more efficient than employed workers in other lines of business less affected by depressions; the new recruits might prove very able workers with proper training. Furthermore, employed workers, in pursuing their self-interest in an enlightened manner during hard times, may "soldier," so that they do not work themselves out of a job. It is useless to explain to a worker for whose services the demand is inelastic that the interests of society are best served by creating more abundance, when he knows that by increasing his output he may cause his own unemployment. There is evidence, although it is not conclusive and some of it is contradictory, that the productivity per workman decreased slightly during the years immediately following 1929.[1]

The doctrines of laissez-faire economics are based upon the assumption that the nation's economic resources are fully employed or are moving from one employment to another. Such doctrines may not be valid in a society cursed by long-time unemployment on a large scale, which is gradually turning unemployed workers into "unemployables." This whole question of the economics of idle resources is discussed more fully in the next section on relief.

ECONOMIC ISSUES IN UNEMPLOYMENT RELIEF

This section deals with certain economic issues and principles involved in relief programs. It is not, therefore, a tale of shanty towns built in dumps, of homes broken because of destitution and despondency, or of life on a relief budget. Such interesting subjects as "relief racketeering," [2] the fecundity of relief families, and other sociological phenomena fall outside the purview of our analysis. Even the problems involved in administering huge relief organizations, which in the 1930's were the biggest spending and employing units in the states and nation, can be touched upon only inciden-

[1] *Cf.* Harry Magdoff, I. H. Siegel, and M. B. Davis, *Production, Employment, and Productivity in 59 Manufacturing Industries, 1919–36*, Works Progress Administration, National Research Project, Philadelphia, May 1939, Part I, pp. 65–68, and Part 2, pp. 13, 49, 65, 127, 144, and 186; and United States Department of Labor Statistics, *Handbook of Labor Statistics, 1936 Edition*, Bulletin No. 616, p. 719.

[2] Such racketeering took various forms. A survey of one large New Jersey city in the Fall of 1932, for example, revealed that three fourths of the stores, including one run by the mayor, were cheating relief clients by such devices as giving them five per cent less food than their relief orders actually paid for or permitting substitute items forbidden by the relief administration only at extra cost to the relief client.

tally in this discussion of the economic phases of unemployment relief.

The problem of poor or dependency relief is, of course, much wider in scope than that of unemployment relief. Dependency relief consists of providing the essentials of life to persons unable to support themselves for a variety of reasons, such as sickness, injury, old age, mental disability, or lack of work. Only dependency relief to families containing one or more able-bodied members, who are eager but unable to secure work and whose full-time earnings should support the family, can correctly be classified as unemployment relief. Surveys have indicated that from one tenth to one eighth of the families on public relief during the 1930's had no member available for work at the time the survey was made because of sickness, age, death, or family duties. The relief statistics are, of course, affected by this long-time dependency group of families lacking a breadwinner. However, this workerless relief element is fairly stable so that changes in total figures represent primarily fluctuations in unemployment relief. With this reservation in mind, the following discussion is confined to the relief of able-bodied workers whose families have been in need because they have not been able to obtain regular employment.

Relief costs and clients. In 1938 about $2,500,000,000 of public funds were spent for emergency or unemployment relief and well over $3,000,000,000 for all dependency relief. During that year, probably one out of every five persons in the country received some public relief. The Federal government was hiring over 4,000,000 workers under the WPA, CCC, and NYA programs alone in the Fall of 1938 and Spring of 1939. Measured by its clientele or its costs, relief giving was the nation's biggest business from 1933 to 1940—a business that throve the more as other business languished.

The trend of relief costs has been upward for a number of decades. Public expenditures for poor relief in 16 large cities rose from 7 cents per inhabitant in 1911 to 32 cents per inhabitant in 1929—a rate of increase more than double that for all general departments of government.[1] A special survey of all relief expenditures (including mothers' and veterans' aid) revealed a total ex-

[1] Anne E. Geddes, *Trends in Relief Expenditures, 1910–1935*, Works Progress Administration, Research Monograph 10, 1937, pp. 10–12.

penditure of $16,600,000 in the first quarter of 1929 before the depression began, with two thirds of the money coming from public funds.[1] Various estimates of home and work relief indicate that such relief expenditures per capita just about doubled each year from 1929 through 1934.[2] In 1934 approximately $2,000,000,000 were distributed for direct and work relief, with less than one per cent of the funds coming from private welfare organizations. By 1936, total expenditures for emergency relief had exceeded $3,000,000,000 a year and, as has been mentioned, the figure for 1938 was over $2,500,000,000.[3] According to estimates, the average number of persons in all households receiving some form of emergency relief each month in 1934 was around 20,000,000. Although the estimated number of such relief beneficiaries had declined below 12,000,000 in the middle of 1937, the figure rose to about 18,000,000 in the Fall of 1938 and the Spring of 1939.[4]

Of course, not all the unemployed families were on relief. In Philadelphia, for example, it has been estimated that not more than 42 per cent of the city's unemployed population were on relief rolls at any one time.[5] In New Jersey no more than one third of the jobless required relief early in 1932, and at no time was a majority of the unemployed in New Jersey receiving relief.[6] Sample studies show that early in the depression, workers in most relief families were jobless for a year or more before applying for public assistance. During that interval, financial resources and credit were exhausted. It has been estimated that one tenth of New Jersey's relief families had an annual income of over $2,500 in 1929 and another tenth apparently had a 1929 income between $2,000

---

[1] *Ibid.*, p. 92.

[2] *Ibid.*, pp. 38, 41; Social Security Board, *Social Security Bulletin*, vol. 2 (January 1939), pp. 34–35; and Dorothy F. Beck, "Problems in the Compilation of Data on Total Relief and Work Program Expenditures," *Journal of the American Statistical Association*, vol. 33 (June 1938), pp. 353–62.

[3] *Social Security Bulletin*, vol. 2 (June 1939), pp. 44–45. Emergency relief includes direct and work relief but not public works or public assistance under the Social Security Act.

[4] *Hearings before a Special Committee to Investigate Unemployment and Relief*, U. S. Senate, 75th Congress, third session, 1938, vol. 2, pp. 1434–36; and *Hearings before the Subcommittee of the Committee on Appropriations, House of Representatives, on Work Relief and Relief for Fiscal Year 1940*, 76th Congress, first session, 1939, pp. 52–53.

[5] *Cf. Recent Trends in Employment and Unemployment in Philadelphia*, p. 35.

[6] *Cf.* New Jersey Emergency Relief Administration, *An Interim Report*, January 1932, p. 12; and Douglas H. MacNeil, *Seven Years of Unemployment Relief in New Jersey, 1930–1936*, Social Science Research Council, 1938, p. 32.

and $2,500.[1] Such families could, perhaps, live for some time on their savings and other assets. But two thirds of the relief families in New Jersey in the middle 1930's had a predepression income of $1,500 or less. The Brookings Institution estimates for 1929 show that families receiving such low incomes, on the average, had no savings, for they spent more than their total incomes, going into debt for the difference. In many instances it is difficult to understand how such families subsisted as long as they did before applying for public aid.

The fact that relief costs and case loads failed to show a close inverse correlation with employment and payroll indexes during the years prior to 1936 caused some questioning and comment. With a lag between disemployment and application for relief and with less than half of the unemployed on relief, a close relationship between relief and employment could hardly be expected. One upsetting factor was the frequent change in Federal relief programs during those early years. From 1936 to 1940, when the Federal government pursued a steady relief policy, there was a fairly close relationship between changes in employment statistics and yearly movements in relief costs and number of clients.

Despite some $20,000,000,000 spent for emergency relief in the 1930's, there is considerable question whether the relief allowances were adequate to maintain health and decency. From 1933 to 1937, relief expenditures and the estimated nonrelief income of clients in New Jersey covered only 60 to 70 per cent of the calculated cost of minimum maintenance or subsistence.[2] Less than 10 cents was allowed in the state for each adult meal, with only three to seven cents per meal for children on relief; yet food accounted for from 70 to 80 per cent of all direct relief expenditures in New Jersey during those years, compared with about 30 per cent for food in the normal budget of a working-class family.[3] A study of some 2,000 New Jersey families in November 1935 and January 1936 showed that, for families of five or less, the direct relief income was less than 40 per cent, and the wage income on WPA projects

[1] MacNeil, op. cit., p. 32; and Neighbors in Need, New Jersey Emergency Relief Administration, 1935, p. 51.

[2] Cf. MacNeil, op. cit., pp. 100–103; and a statement by Chester I. Barnard, President of the New Jersey Bell Telephone Company and Chairman of the State's Advisory Council on Relief, that the relief given in New Jersey was insufficient to satisfy minimum needs (New York Times, May 2, 1935, p. 14).

[3] Cf. R. A. Lester, op. cit., pp. 59–60.

less than 60 per cent, of the family's average monthly income when the workers in these families were last working at their usual occupations.[1]

Such restricted or inadequate relief for a prolonged period, by reducing clients' vitality and bodily resistance, undermining their health, and making them long-time public charges, may in the end cost the community a sum much larger than the additional amount necessary for adequate relief in the first place. The National Health Survey of 750,000 families in 84 cities during the Fall and Winter of 1935–1936 revealed that the illness rate among unemployed men was over two times that for employed men and that the incidence of disabling illness amongst relief families was 40 per cent higher than in nonrelief families with incomes under $1,000.[2] From the economic viewpoint, the health of a nation is of primary importance, for, in the words of Shakespeare, "sickness doth infect the very life-blood of our enterprise."

A survey of the relief case load in 79 cities during May 1934 revealed that three fourths of the male workers then on relief had not had employment at their usual occupation for two years or more, and almost two fifths of all male relief clients with work experience had not had such employment for at least four years.[3] Such statistics are significant because the average length of unemployment is a rough measure of the chances of reemployment. A study of relief clients obtaining private employment in 13 cities during the Summer of 1935 showed that the reemployment rate of workers who had been unemployed less than six months was 12 times that of persons who had been out of work for two years or more. Relief clients obtaining private employment had been on relief less than half as long as the other relief cases.[4] Other studies have also revealed that the persons out of a job and on relief for the shortest periods of time are the first to leave the relief rolls for private employment.[5] Older and inexperienced workers are at a dis-

[1] MacNeil, *op. cit.*, p. 105.

[2] *Cf. Hearings before a Special Committee to Investigate Unemployment and Relief*, *op. cit.*, pp. 1481, 1486–89.

[3] Gladys L. Palmer and Katherine D. Wood, *Urban Workers on Relief*, Part 1, Works Progress Administration, Research Monograph 4, 1936, p. 44.

[4] Joseph C. Bevis and Stanley L. Payne, *Former Relief Cases in Private Employment*, Works Progress Administration, 1939, p. 11; and F. L. Carmichael and R. Nassimbene, *Changing Aspects of Urban Relief*, Works Progress Administration, 1939, p. 28.

[5] *Cf.* G. L. Palmer and K. D. Wood, *op. cit.*, p. 88.

advantage. The study of 13 cities showed that employers are reluctant to hire untried workers, for the reemployment rate of experienced workers on relief was four times that for workers without a period of experience in private industry during the previous decade.[1]

Recent data on the duration of unemployment amongst relief clients are, unfortunately, not available. A large proportion of the employable heads of relief families had WPA jobs between 1935 and 1940.

Financing of relief. From 1933 to 1940 approximately three fourths of the funds for financing direct and work relief came from the Federal treasury.[2] State and local governments contributed the remaining quarter of the total costs of emergency relief during that period, divided about equally between the states and their subdivisions. For the most part, the actual administration of relief has, however, been in the hands of the state and local units of government.

1. *Federal* vs. *local funds.* Legally, the local units of government are responsible for poor relief in this country. But the incidence of unemployment is so arbitrary and its causes so impersonal that the inhabitants of a community can hardly be held responsible for the burden of unemployment to be found within its borders. The forces determining total employment and unemployment are almost entirely beyond local community control, and responsibility without a measure of control that would make remedial action possible is rather meaningless.

In practice the doctrine of local responsibility would mean the responsibility of real estate rather than the responsibility of industry or income-taxpayers. Practically all the revenues of local units of government are derived from property taxes, whereas the Federal government normally raises about half its tax revenues from income and inheritance taxes. The states stand in between, obtaining only a minor proportion of their funds from either property or income taxes. An important element in the issue of Federal *versus* local relief is whether property-taxpayers or income-taxpayers are to foot most of the relief bills.

---

[1] Carmichael and Nassimbene, *op. cit.*

[2] *Cf.* Arthur E. Burns and Edward A. Williams, *A Survey of Relief and Security Programs,* Works Progress Administration, May 1938, pp. 35, 68–69; and *Hearings before the Subcommittee of the Committee on Appropriations, House of Representatives, Work Relief and Relief for Fiscal Year 1940,* Washington, 1939, pp. 56–57.

It is important to consider the economic effects of various methods of raising revenues for relief. Unlike personal income taxes, property taxes generally are regressive, absorbing a larger percentage of the incomes of the lower than of the higher income groups. That is true largely because the more valuable property is, the more it tends to be underassessed. Furthermore, the financing of relief from local property taxes tends to create a vicious circle. A large volume of unemployment in a locality would mean relatively high relief costs and property taxes. Such higher tax rates would discourage new construction or expansion of existing productive facilities, inasmuch as any improvements would be subject to the higher taxes. Consequently, owners of business firms, in order to lower their assessment and escape the higher taxes, would tend to let their factories depreciate or would try to avoid the locality's taxes entirely by moving their businesses elsewhere. The effect of such activities would be to decrease the volume of employment in the locality, to increase relief costs further, and to raise property taxes still higher, causing additional curtailment of local business operations, etc. Such a vicious circle is likely to occur whenever large relief bills are financed entirely by local revenues.

The circle can be broken by having the state or the Federal government assume a proportion of the local relief costs, thereby spreading the burden over a wider area. Firms are not likely to migrate from the country because of high taxes. Furthermore, these larger units of government can levy taxes that are adjusted to the size of a person's income or the profitableness of a business. Since net income taxes absorb only a percentage of the profit actually made, there is little incentive to curtail business operations or capital improvements for the purpose of reducing taxes. If no profit is made, no tax is paid. Personal income taxes also do not affect business costs.

This discussion raises one question, Does a community injure its business by giving its residents adequate relief? The issue is not one between countries, where price-level and exchange-rate adjustments can offset any temporary increase in production costs in one country. The question concerns one small area within a country, so that currency differences and price-level or exchange-rate changes are not involved. Can a community, under such circumstances, safeguard its labor resources by higher taxes for relief without causing a decline in production and employment within the community relative to such economic activity outside the community?

The answer to that question is not easy. Higher property taxes would tend to reduce the value of land and buildings in the community and to increase the overhead costs of business firms, but such fixed costs may be written down through bankruptcy or reorganization. Higher taxes would, however, discourage new construction. If, after the writing down of capital values, total unit costs of production were still relatively high in the community, existing business firms would, of course, attempt to migrate elsewhere. The foregoing discussion has assumed that labor costs per unit of output have remained constant. It is possible that increased unemployment might reduce wage rates, or that adequate relief, by preserving the effectiveness of labor in the community, might tend to make average labor costs there low in comparison with similar costs elsewhere. Suppose, on the other hand, the community fails to provide adequate relief. What is the effect on labor costs? Either some labor will migrate elsewhere, decreasing the local labor supply, or all labor will continue to remain in the locality, but its effectiveness may be reduced by impaired health. In either case, total costs per unit of output in the community may rise.

High rates of unemployment in a community are, therefore, likely to increase production costs whether the needy unemployed are or are not adequately provided for from the proceeds of local property taxes. Production costs are not affected, however, in so far as the funds for relief are raised by private charity; by taxes on personal property, income, or inheritances; by retail sales taxes; or by other forms of taxation which do not enter business costs or affect selling prices.[1] Nor would employment within the community be decreased if relief revenues were derived from taxes, such as taxes on land alone, which cannot be avoided immediately or eventually by migration to other communities.

2. *Rational grants-in-aid for relief.* Generally, local governments cover too little territory to levy taxes, such as income, inheritance, or retail sales taxes, which do not affect costs of production or distribution. If the vicious circle already mentioned is to be broken

[1] Retail sales taxes do affect selling prices, but may not affect production costs.

and local administration of relief is to be retained, the larger units of government must grant funds to the lower levels of government—the nation to the states and the states to their subdivisions.

Beginning in 1932 the Federal government granted funds to the states for unemployment relief, and most states granted funds to their municipalities for the same purpose. Toward the end of 1935 the Federal government quit the "business" of direct relief and thereafter followed the policy of allocating funds to local project "sponsors" (mostly municipalities) under a work-relief program known as WPA (first Works Progress Administration; later changed to Work Projects Administration).

Both the Federal Emergency Relief Administration and its successor, WPA, were frequently criticized on the ground that the allocation of Federal funds to states and municipalities was determined by personal negotiation rather than by impersonal, systematic methods which the whole country could understand and accept as fair. The allocation of Federal relief funds to states and municipalities presumably should be according to the weight of their relief burdens and the poverty of their economic and financial resources. Yet, under FERA, states with the highest percentages of the population on relief and with the least resources sometimes had smaller percentages of their relief burdens carried by the Federal administration than did relatively wealthy areas with lighter relief loads.[1] Admittedly, relative need and ability are hard to measure and sum up in proper proportions in any formula that is not too complex for the layman to comprehend. But without the use of some uniform principles and standards, the Federal government was open to the charge of allocating to some cities three times as much relief (WPA, CCC, and NYA) money per capita as other cities received, without any apparent "rhyme or reason" for such differences, unless political expediency be considered a reason.[2]

Economics of work relief. Whether wage relief is more economical than direct or home relief has been a moot question during the past decade. The Federal relief authorities and a majority of the citizens have been convinced that relief employment is the

---

[1] Cf. "Rational Grants-in-Aid," *Social Service Review*, vol. 9 (March 1935), pp. 100–102. For a further discussion of this issue, cf. J. Roy Blough, "Equalization Methods for the Distribution of Federal Relief Funds," *Social Service Review*, vol. 9 (September 1935), pp. 423–44; and R. A. Lester, *op. cit.*, pp. 119–42.

[2] Cf., for example, an editorial in the *New York Times*, January 2, 1939.

soundest method of giving relief. A number of state and local relief officials have, however, concluded from their experience that work relief is "not a public economy as against direct relief," that it is "both socially and economically unsound," and that it "should not be continued as a permanent method of meeting the problem of large-scale unemployment."[1]   They believe that any program of public work for the unemployed should be executed in the normal way, with workers hired and fired on the basis of their efficiency rather than their needs, and they condemn the policy of reserving public employment opportunities for those on relief. Past experience with relief employment in England, Germany, and Canada also led to the conclusion that public employment was not in principle or in practice a satisfactory method of doing public work and giving relief to needy persons.[2]   In consequence, this country was the only one that engaged in large-scale programs of work relief during the depression of the 1930's.

The issues in this question of relief employment must be clearly defined. The alternatives are not simply direct relief (the dole) or work relief; public works and the other unemployment programs discussed in the next chapter must also be considered. That idleness is costly and that the wholesale unemployment in the 1930's represented a waste of millions of man-years of labor is evident. Under such circumstances, the government may be able to save by spending—by purchasing products and putting idle men to work. The question concerns the best method of attacking the unemployment problem, and, if government spending is the policy to be pursued, is work relief preferable to a combined program of public works and direct relief? Is it sound social policy to reserve government employment projects for the destitute unemployed and thus to restrict and reduce the employment opportunities of other unemployed persons not on the relief rolls?

[1] Cf., for example, Unemployment Relief in Pennsylvania, September 1, 1932–October 31, 1933, December 1933, App. II, "The Place of Work in Unemployment Relief," by Roger F. Evans, p. 92; Emergency Relief Administration, Unemployment Relief in New Jersey, An Interim Report, January 1932, pp. 32–33; Governor's Commission on Unemployment Relief, Work Relief in the State of New York, A Review of Its Characteristics, Functioning, and Value, August 10, 1936, pp. 108–109; Joanna C. Colcord, "Divorcing Work and Relief," Survey, vol. 71 (June 1935), p. 168; and Paul B. Williams, "No More Sun Porches for Frogs," North American Review, vol. 239 (January 1935), p. 77.
[2] For references, cf. R. A. Lester, "Emergency Employment in Theory and Practice," Journal of Political Economy, vol. 42 (August 1934), pp. 467–68.

The essential difference between public works and work relief is one of method. On public works, especially those done under contract, persons are hired on a competitive basis and are retained only as long as they perform their work in an efficient and competent fashion. On the other hand, work-relief employment is based on need rather than ability or qualifications for the job. Relief employees are generally discharged, no matter how well they have worked, if they no longer need relief. Furthermore, because relief employment is governed by need rather than one's work record, the normal incentives to do good or better work, such as advancement in rank or pay, are usually absent. Likewise, excellent performance on relief projects may be of little assistance in obtaining commercial employment. Indeed, relief clients, in applying for jobs in industry, have often found it best not to mention their past connections with the relief administration. For such reasons, the average efficiency on relief projects has generally been far below the normal operating efficiency under regular employment methods. Various estimates have placed the average efficiency on work-relief projects at 50 to 75 per cent of normal.[1]

The issue of whether direct relief is more economical than work relief boils down to two questions: Are the completed projects worth to the community at least the added cost of work relief over direct relief? Does work on relief projects help to preserve the employability of relief clients so that they are better prepared to resume their regular work than they would be if kept on direct relief? These two questions of benefit to the community and benefit to the client will be taken up in order. Obviously no categorical answer that applies universally can be given to them, for the answer must depend upon the operation of the relief-employment program in each locality. Certain general considerations can, however, be indicated.

1. *Added cost and community benefit.* The additional cost of work relief over home relief depends, of course, upon the nonrelief expenses of the project, such as the costs for materials, equipment, supervision, administration, transportation, and workmen's compensation. Studies indicate that on large programs such nonrelief

---

[1] *Cf.* Lester, "Is Work Relief Economical?" *Social Service Review*, vol. 10 (June 1936) especially pp. 265–66. Much of the material in this subsection on work relief has been taken from this article and the author's unpublished Ph.D. thesis, *op. cit.*, Part 3 on "Relief Employment."

items cause work-relief costs to average about 40 per cent above home-relief costs for the same amount of relief given under comparable circumstances.[1] In comparing this additional cost with the value of the work-relief projects to the community, the effects of the added expenditures upon the general rate of spending will be disregarded, partly because work relief has often resulted in a corresponding contraction of regular municipal expenditures as relief workers took over the jobs of regular public employees.

It is difficult to assess the value to the community of a work project, even a construction project. Values are individual and relative. In the selection of projects, the relief administrations were faced with a dilemma. They wanted the projects to be "value creating" but "noncompetitive," to be "socially useful" yet abnormal in character so that the Federal and state governments would not be subsidizing normal municipal work under the guise of work relief. If municipal functions normally paid for from local appropriations were performed by relief clients, the city officials could and did brag that relief work, by reducing regular budget items or eliminating tax levies for roads, had saved local taxpayers thousands of dollars. Such replacement of normal functions by relief work would, however, lessen the opportunities for regular public employment and put the municipality in the position of hiring employees on the basis of need rather than ability—a questionable principle for public employment. With Federal and state subsidies covering all wage costs and a large part of the nonrelief costs as well, the local officials had every incentive to perform all sorts of work as relief projects. From the local point of view, a relief project was of net benefit to the community if it was worth the 10 or 15 per cent of total costs that the municipality or local sponsor had to meet.

In an attempt to avoid displacement of regular by relief workers, the rules of the Federal Emergency Relief Administration provided that the projects must be "in general, apart from normal governmental enterprises and not such as would have been carried out in due course regardless of an emergency." In short, they were to be extraordinary jobs that would not be done even in prosperous times. Such projects obviously would have been of relatively little value to the community. In practice, most relief work has consisted of regular governmental functions, such as road and sewer

[1] Cf. ibid., pp. 267–68; and *Work Relief in the State of New York*, p. 60.

construction and repair; the construction or improvement of public buildings, parks, and playgrounds; and even the removal of snow, ashes, and garbage. The percentages in Table 28 indicated the reduction in normal employment on streets, roads, and sewers that was caused by concentrating relief work in those lines of public activity. Testifying before a Special Senate Committee in April 1938, Harry L. Hopkins, then Administrator of WPA, stated:

Many cities maintain that we should collect their garbage. We get hundreds of requests that we collect their garbage or sweep their streets. We do not think these are proper projects. . . . There is always a very nice line as to what are normal and what are abnormal city functions. In the main, we do not want to do jobs which the cities ought to do, or to have them let people go, because we are hiring them.[1]

The most useful projects, from the point of view of the unemployed in the community, would have been the production of food, clothing, houses, and other commodities that they so sorely needed. But private industry, claiming squatters' sovereignty in those areas of economic activity, complained loudly when the relief administrators tried to put clients to work making mattresses, shoes, and houses. Consequently, production by relief clients for their own use was confined mostly to agriculture, where it took the form of subsistence gardening. In some states in 1935 and 1936 as much as 10 per cent of all the vegetables raised within the state were grown in relief gardens. Production by relief clients for their own use was no less competitive in farming, so hard hit by the depression, than it would have been in various branches of industry; but the farmers were too numerous and unorganized to enforce any "proprietary" rights to production in their line of business.

Throughout the 1930's the relief administrators struggled desperately to escape an unavoidable dilemma. If relief projects were useful, they were likely to be criticized for competing with private business or regular public employment. If they were so unusual or extraordinary as not to be considered competitive, they were sure to be condemned by the same critics as useless "boondoggling"— a term frequently applied to research and educational projects. The reader can decide for himself whether most educational activity is made work of a "boondoggling" sort. The relief adminis-

[1] *Hearings before a Special Committee to Investigate Unemployment and Relief*, United States Senate, 75th Congress, third session, vol. 2, p. 1369.

trators found, as is characteristic of a competitive society, that there was no middle course between the Scylla of useless or fantastic projects and the Charybdis of competitive work. All commodities and services are competing for the consumers' dollars, and all governmental activities are competing for tax receipts. Failure to face this issue squarely and to recognize that all work worth anything is directly or indirectly competitive resulted in relief projects less urgently needed and, therefore, less useful or valuable to the community.

2. *Conservation of labor resources.* Material resources can be wasted by using them to construct projects of little value. In the same way, labor resources can be wasted not only by permitting them to deteriorate through idleness but also by impairing their effectiveness through misuse on relief projects. Would direct relief be better for the relief client than no work at all?

It is claimed that relief employment maintains the employability of clients by preserving their skills, their work habits, and their morale; that it prevents what has been called human erosion. Whether it does so, however, depends upon the character of the projects, the workers, the supervision, the community's attitude toward the work, and the amount of relief received.

There has been little preservation of skills under relief employment because three fourths of the work was of the unskilled, manual variety. Most of the projects were on roads, streets, sewers, and parks, whereas most of the relief clients normally worked in factories, mines, offices, and stores. Skills are not preserved—they may even be destroyed—if watchmakers, architects, printers, painters, tailors, and electricians are put to work with pick, ax, shovel, and rake. Various sample studies throughout the 1930's indicated that there was little relationship between relief jobs and the workers' normal jobs. A questionnaire survey of work relief in 400 communities in September 1933 showed that in only one city were the relief projects planned with a view to utilizing the existing skills of workers on relief.[1] A sample survey of 13 cities in the latter part of 1935, made by the Federal Emergency Relief Administration, revealed that unskilled, manual jobs were given to about three fifths

---

[1] *Cf. Unemployment Relief Experience for November, 1933,* Family Welfare Association, New York City. M. C. Bristol and H. R. Wright made an interesting study of work relief assignments in Chicago in January 1934. *Cf.* "Some Aspects of Work Relief in Chicago," *Social Service Review,* vol. 8 (December 1934), pp. 628–52.

of the white-collar workers and four fifths of the skilled workers; whereas one tenth of the unskilled workers were given white-collar, skilled, or semiskilled employment on the relief projects.[1] A study of all the employees on WPA in Pennsylvania in the middle of 1936 showed that only one out of every seven was working at his usual occupation.[2] The extent to which skills and training were submerged is indicated by the fact that 70 per cent of all the workers had unskilled jobs on WPA projects, yet only 17 per cent of them were classified as unskilled workers. Because most of the WPA construction activity in Pennsylvania was on roads, about half of the skilled construction workers and three fourths of the semiskilled construction workers found themselves working at unskilled WPA jobs.

Work relief will help to preserve work habits and standards if it is efficiently performed, but will injure such habits and establish low standards of work where employees "loaf" on the job, as was found to be the case on one third of the relief projects surveyed in New York State late in 1934.[3] Work standards were low on many relief projects either because the supervision was lax, because the projects were overmanned, because the work tended to degenerate into pure made work and became unworthy of the workers, or because it lacked the characteristics, disciplines, and incentives of real work. In a few cases relief workers took a negative attitude toward relief employment because they realized it was lessening their opportunities for normal work.[4]

Little reliable evidence exists concerning the net effect of work relief upon morale. It is apparent, however, that workers' morale is not likely to be conserved on projects where the efficiency is low, the discipline is lax, the workers "lean on the handles" of the tools, and the projects are made work, such as "manicuring" the highways and parks. Artificial and fictitious work may only add to the feeling of futility and despair of relief clients.

In considering the full effects of work relief upon the conservation of labor resources and morale, allowance must be made for the

[1] Cf. F. L. Carmichael and R. Nassimbene, *Changing Aspects of Urban Relief*, Works Progress Administration, 1939, Table 76, p. 87.

[2] Cf. Howard M. Teaf, "Work Relief and the Workers," *Survey*, vol. 74 (June 1938), pp. 199–200.

[3] Cf. Governor's Commission on Unemployment Relief, *Work Relief Projects of the Public Works Type in the State of New York*, August 15, 1935, p. 63.

[4] For cases of this, cf. Lester, *Some Aspects of Unemployment Relief in New Jersey*, pp. 193 and 275.

detrimental effects of displacement upon those workers who found their jobs transferred to projects for relief clients. Such displacement is bound to occur whenever need is substituted for efficiency as a basis for public employment.

Assuming that a certain amount of public work is to be done, it is generally more economical to have that work performed as regular work under normal methods of employment. Such a conclusion may need to be modified during periods of prolonged unemployment by having the work rotated or shared. In such an event, however, the unemployed on relief should not be given preference to the unemployed not on relief. Furthermore, made work is not economical. The most needed work must be done first if the nation's material and labor resources are not to be distributed in an uneconomic fashion.

3. *Effects on the labor market.* The employment of between 1,000,000 and 4,000,000 workers under work-relief programs was bound to affect demand, supply, and price in the labor market. Under the Civil Works Administration (1933–1934) and the Works Progress Administration (1935–1940), the wage rates paid were supposed to be no "less than the prevailing rates of pay for work of a similar nature." Actually, under both programs the rates paid certain workers in some localities (for example, building workers in Eastern cities under CWA and unskilled labor in the South under WPA) were well above prevailing rates.[1] Consequently, relief workers, especially the inefficient ones, were overpaid and tended to be satisfied with relief work. The higher relief wage rates also tended to raise wage rates in the community. Under the Federal Emergency Relief Administration's program of work relief (1934–1935), county wage committees decided what the going rates were, but usually the result was arbitrary, county-wide rates instead of an attempt at an accurate determination of prevailing rates.[2] The hourly minimum of 30 cents was above going rates in some localities.

During periods when the cities and the states administered and financed work relief, the wage rates on relief projects were generally kept below "prevailing" rates.[3] From a study of work relief

---

[1] *Cf.* Nels Anderson, *The Right to Work*, 1938, pp. 143–44.

[2] *Cf.* Nels Anderson, "The War for the Wage," *Survey*, vol. 71 (June 1935), p. 164.

[3] For a survey of various wage policies on relief projects, *cf.* Arthur E. Burns, "Work Relief Wage Policies, 1930–1936," *Monthly Report of the Federal Emergency Relief Administration, June 1 through June 30, 1936*, pp. 22–55.

in 26 cities in 1931, Joanna Colcord stated: "I can give you instance after instance where general wage rates have been pulled down by rates set up for relief work." [1] In some states, relief wages were fixed below prevailing rates so that relief projects "would not be in competition with the normal and usual outlets for the employment of labor." The naïveté of this notion soon became apparent as low-wage relief workers began to displace higher paid regular employees at a "saving" for the municipality or state. Low relief wages tended to put a premium on doing normal work as relief projects. The dilemma of valuable yet noncompetitive work cannot be avoided by selecting a certain wage scale for relief employment.

In New Jersey and elsewhere labor-union leaders, especially in the building trades, either forbade members to work at their trades on low-wage relief projects or vigorously complained that it was unfair to do normal work at low relief wages, thereby depriving their members of normal work and putting downward pressure on existing union wage scales. The Director of the New Jersey Emergency Relief Administration admitted that such union arguments were "valid" and confessed that there was absolutely no way by which the state relief administration could protect itself from municipalities which had normal budget items done as relief work. [2] Under the Work Projects Administration, the Federal government in 1939 practically forced project sponsors to pay substandard wages to skilled employees by providing that the hours of all relief employees be raised to a minimum of 130 a month "without substantially affecting the current national average labor cost per person" on work projects, and by stipulating that regional differentials in monthly earnings be no greater than can be justified by differences in the cost of living. The labor unions objected to, and in some cases struck against, this reduction in hourly rates below prevailing commercial wage scales. Generally speaking, workers only gave substandard output for the substandard wages.

The effects upon the labor market and upon normal work and wage rates were more pronounced wherever the work programs were not diversified so that they included the various types and kinds of employment found in normal public and private enter-

[1] "General Principles in Work Relief," *Open Forum Session on Unemployment Relief*, 37th Annual Convention of the American Society of Municipal Engineers, St. Louis, 1931, p. 29.

[2] *Cf.* MacNeil, *op. cit.*, pp. 157, 159.

prise. Unfortunately, fear that "competition with business" would lessen normal work opportunities led the relief authorities to confine relief employment to public, and especially municipal, work, thereby preventing clients from performing the work most needed by themselves and their fellow citizens. Of course, the more relief employment is concentrated upon certain types of projects, such as road construction and repair, the more intense and unfair will be the competition, and the more will opportunities for normal public and private employment in such lines be decreased. By restricting their programs unduly, the relief authorities insisted upon a course of action that was certain to justify their fears.

Relief and self-help production. As already indicated, the relief authorities forced clients to work at productive activities in unorganized occupations, such as shoe repairing, wood chopping, and farming. The authorities recognized that it was most economical to have the unemployed produce food, fuel, and clothing, which were more needed during the depression than were "monumental" public works, "manicuring" programs, or "luxury" relief projects. The argument used to justify such activities was that the products were for the use of the clients and not for sale. It was claimed that, if the clients grew their own vegetables, the money thus saved would be spent by them or by the taxpayers in some other fashion, so that total cash spending would not decrease. But unfortunately for the farmer, the "savings" from relief gardening were probably not spent for agricultural produce of the sort that the unemployed produced for their own use. Producers in other lines gained what the farmers lost. A relief program of production must be well balanced and diversified if demand is not to be shifted or redirected to other products.

Only by pursuing a comprehensive and well-proportioned program can the total amount of employment in a country be increased by the relief authorities without assisting some persons at the expense of others not yet on relief. A general over-all increase in employment and production that is related to the increase in demand arising from that new employment would not mean more intense or unfair competition. Such a general expansion in production and employment occurs with every normal recovery of business. If, however, the expansion in employment is unbalanced in the sense that, compared to the additional demand that develops, it is too concentrated in certain particular lines of economic activity, then competition in those specific lines will be intensified, while other lines will enjoy an increase in demand relative to supply. A relief employment scheme, therefore, cannot emphasize and subsidize certain lines of employment out of proportion to their importance in the existing public and private economy without aiding some private producers while bringing about a relative reduction in the cash demand of other producers, or without causing an uneconomic distribution of public work accompanied by displacement of regular with relief workers.

During the early 1930's, barter-and-scrip production units were organized by the unemployed in various parts of the country, especially on the Pacific Coast. According to estimates, as many as 1,000,000 persons received all or part of their sustenance in 1933 and 1934 from such self-help cooperatives.[1] During the two years following June 1933, as much as $1,500,000 of Federal relief funds was used to buy equipment, gasoline, public-utility services, etc., for such self-help cooperatives, at an estimated saving of over $2,000,000 in relief costs.[2] Through the production of millions of dollars worth of goods and services, such self-help activities reduced relief budgets and eliminated some families from the relief rolls entirely. Wholesale employment of relief clients at high wage rates under the CWA program late in 1933, however, gave these self-help organizations a decided setback, and Federal aid to them ceased in 1935 when the WPA program commenced.

The barter-and-scrip organizations arose from an exchange of goods and services between specialized groups—farmers exchanging food products for the services of barbers, doctors, dentists, entertainers, plumbers, painters, etc., by means of direct or multiple barter or through the medium of scrip money. With decreased spending during a depression, some economic activities are short-circuited from the cash nexus—men are laid off, factories lie idle, and crops are left to rot. The thought naturally occurs, as it occurred to many economists, businessmen, and workers in the 1930's,

[1] Cf. Constantine Panunzio, Self-Help Cooperatives in Los Angeles, 1939, p. 11. Cf. also Monthly Labor Review, vol. 36 (June 1936), pp. 1229–41, and vol. 47 (June 1938), pp. 1–17.

[2] Cf. P. A. Kerr, "Production-for-Use and Distribution in Work Relief Activities," Monthly Report of the Federal Emergency Relief Administration, September 1 through 30, 1935, especially pp. 13–14.

why not bring the idle men, idle factories, and surplus crops together by means of a central exchange (clearinghouse or market for the unemployed) so that the idle people can support themselves without great shifts in their occupational pursuits.[1] In this way the unemployed might become a separate economy of their own for the time being.

Such self-help activities were hampered not only by competition from Federal spending programs of work relief but by the problem of transportation and organization beyond the boundaries of the locality. In addition, as in labor unions, the self-help organizations found that private firms tended to hire away their good executives and leaders. Various plans for establishing regional or national programs of self-sufficing emergency units for production and mutual exchange were proposed, so that the unemployed in large cities might support themselves through a well-rounded program.[2] However, it was only in California that intercommunity exchange by self-help units developed on any scale. Consequently, most self-help organizations were in cities under 50,000 in population, although the major portion of the unemployed were concentrated in large cities, which are the very essence of specialization (involving dependence on a cash market) and which are generally some distance from food-producing areas.

Local self-help activities, because they usually did not develop into general, well-balanced programs, sometimes brought forth criticism and objections from local businessmen, including the storekeepers. It is evident, however, that self-help activities need not curtail total cash spending, because the taxpayers can spend the money saved by reduced relief costs. Nevertheless, some local producers might suffer from a poorly proportioned program, which, without reducing total cash demand, would change its distribution as between certain goods, services, and stores.

---

[1] So far as is known, there was only one case of a cooperative self-help venture during previous depressions. *Cf.* Leah H. Feder, *Unemployment Relief in Periods of Depression*, 1936, p. 153. In 1894 Edward Bellamy outlined an extensive program for self-help employment amongst the unemployed in a statement to the Massachusetts Board to Investigate the Subject of the Unemployed.

[2] *Cf.*, for example, Frank D. Graham, *The Abolition of Unemployment*, 1932; and J. B. Cheadle, H. O. Eaton, and C. A. M. Ewing, *No More Unemployed*, 1934.

CHAPTER FIFTEEN

PUBLIC WORKS
AND OTHER UNEMPLOYMENT PROGRAMS

The previous chapter has explained how practical men, influenced by a fear of government competition with business, have sometimes preferred rather useless and wasteful forms of public expenditure to those which would provide the goods and services most needed by the people. From this point of view, wars and pyramid building would be preferable as public work, because they are certain to be highly wasteful and to be considered "noncompetitive."

This chapter contains a discussion of various programs for stimulating employment either directly or indirectly. They must be examined from the social point of view and judged by their effectiveness in bringing about full and economical employment of the nation's entire resources. Some of these programs involve an expansion in public indebtedness; others might even reduce the Federal debt. Many persons, because they have been schooled in the maxims of individualistic economics, are unduly alarmed about the "financial" burden placed upon the future generation when the government employs people so that they may eat and add to the nation's wealth by constructing roads, bridges, or houses, which posterity will use. How posterity benefits by the alternative, present idleness and undernourishment, is not explained. It would seem as though a "burden" is placed upon posterity whenever the physical and moral quality of the present population is impaired or whenever capital equipment depreciates faster than it is replaced. Certainly, widespread unemployment of men and machines is a waste that is detrimental to the future of a nation. One must look behind the financial forms to the real economic phenomena, to changes in total consumption, in productive capacity, or in the nation's resources. One must also bear in mind that the economic position of the Federal government is entirely different from that of an individual citizen. Unlike the individual, the Federal government owes its own citizens and taxes them to pay off its debts to them. Cancelation of government debt, for example, benefits taxpayers at the expense of the holders of government bonds, but it involves no direct social loss, for the nation's physical resources and productive capacity are not reduced by debt defaults.

The programs discussed in this chapter have been offered by their proponents as a means of reducing the waste of unemployment. Many of these plans have not been tested by experience, and the critical reader will observe that some of them would involve serious administrative difficulties. The economic evil of unemployment is not, however, erased by calling proposed remedies "impractical." The existence of wholesale unemployment constitutes a grave threat to our system of free enterprise, economic individualism, and personal liberty. The dictatorships have demonstrated one way of keeping the population employed, even though at the expense of personal freedom and a relative decline in living standards resulting from an uneconomic distribution of productive resources. Economic systems, as well as individual enterprises, are in competition. If we are unable to solve the problem of extreme unemployment, we may find ourselves consciously or unconsciously following in the footsteps of the Fascist states.

The reasons for equilibrium at underemployment in a "free" economy were discussed in Chapter 10. An individualistic economy is especially ill-suited to boost business from a dead center of general unemployment. No particular firm or industry can alone resume full production, because any expansion in its expenditures will not cause a corresponding increase in the demand for that particular product or products, even though demand in general is somewhat increased. Because they represent such a minute section of the total economy, individual producers cannot singlehanded cause a significant change in general business conditions, or even bring about an increase in the demand for their own products, by expanding employment and production. From the point of view of individual safety and profit, the appropriate policy for each enterprise usually is to swim with the general stream of business rather than against it. Consequently, each firm tends to wait for larger orders before expanding operations. But larger orders for goods and services are likely to come only with an expansion in business operations, which increases the incomes of people so that they can spend more. Employment may fail to expand because everyone is waiting for others to increase their expenditures. Such a stalemate may lead to a chronic state of partial stagnation in an economy that depends primarily upon private spending for its generating power. Such are the difficulties and dangers in relying upon private initiative for recovery in an exchange economy dependent upon individual spending.

This deadlock of delayed spending leading to further delay can, however, be broken by government initiative. The central government is in a much better position to influence and direct the general movement of economic activity than is any single business unit. The government's income is not dependent upon the voluntary spending of individuals; it is derived from taxation rather than sales in a market. The central government's expenditures normally amount to much more than the expenditures of any single firm or industry, and they ordinarily are not restricted by the business test of profit. Furthermore, the Federal administration usually has more influence on the public in general than does the management of any firm or group of firms. Unlike a private company, a state, or a municipality, the Federal government exerts considerable control over the money supply and the price level. The smaller units of government are, in fact, in much the same position as private concerns or branches of industry.

Under certain conditions there may be some conflict between democracy and individualism on the one hand and centralized action to overcome unemployment on the other. The plans discussed in this chapter, however, do not involve a direct limitation on individual freedom. Of course, where the central government owns or exerts control over important sections of the total economy, attempts to stem a downward movement or start an expansion in economic activity by means of governmental action and policies are more likely to succeed than where the operations of the central government play only a minor role in the total economy. That, in part, explains why Soviet Russia has been less afflicted by business depressions and unemployment than have the more democratic, capitalistic countries. Because the expenditures of central governments, especially in democracies of federated states, are but a small portion of total public and private expenditures, some economists suggest that such countries are powerless to prevent a depression and that, therefore, a program of expanded public works should be used only to accelerate recovery after the bottom of a business depression has been reached. Although democratic governments do have some control over the currency and the total money supply, their expenditures are generally too small (not in dollars but in percentage of all expenditures) to have much effect upon the average rate at which the money supply circulates.

PLANNED PUBLIC WORKS AS A REMEDY FOR UNEMPLOYMENT

Public works are substantial construction projects that are operated on a commercial basis. The most efficient and economical methods presumably are used, and workers are hired according to their fitness for the job, and not according to their needs. The cost of materials for the project generally accounts for over half of all expenses on public works. For these reasons, an expansion in the volume of expenditures on public works may have little direct or immediate influence upon relief costs.

The proposal. Variations in public-works expenditures have been proposed as a means of counteracting or offsetting the fluctuations in public spending and as a means of stimulating business recovery. Current expenditures for government services, such as garbage collection, police protection, and school instruction, cannot be postponed; but it is claimed that, with proper advance planning, governments can readily reserve much of their expenditures on capital construction for periods of depression and unemployment. Furthermore, the bulk of the unemployment during business depressions is concentrated in the capital-goods industries, and the large materials expenditures on public works would serve to stimulate those particular industries. If the funds spent by the government on an expanded public-works program would otherwise have remained idle or are new money, the government may increase the volume of spending and the size of incomes in the community. Consequently, the fiscal policy of the government plays an important role in the proposal to use public works as a balance wheel to private business.

On the planned use of public works to combat unemployment, there are two schools of thought. One group, which may be called the "cycle-balancing" school, would expand public works as business activity declines and reduce them as business revives. The cycle-balancing school would not increase the total amount of public-works expenditures over a complete business cycle; but, through advance planning, they would spend more of the total during depression periods and less in periods of prosperity.

The other school has been called the "pump-priming" group. They would expand expenditures for public works during a depression in order to stimulate private business and private spending. In using public works as a lever to lift business out of a depression, they would continue to spend more and more money on public works until industry did revive. Because they do not plan an offsetting reduction in public-works expenditures during prosperity, their program would cause the total amount of public-works construction to expand from decade to decade at a more rapid rate than would be likely under a planned cycle-balancing program. Such a program for a progressive increase in public spending may be based on the economic notion that savings tend to expand faster than industry can absorb them and that increased public works are necessary to prevent economic stagnation.

The Federal government's public-works program, begun in the latter part of 1933, was of the pump-priming variety. Under this program a total of about $5,000,000,000 of Federal funds and over $1,000,000,000 of local public monies had been spent for new construction by the middle of 1939. Table 29 puts these figures in proper perspective and indicates the relative significance of public works.

The figures in this table show that public construction during the 1920's did not constitute one quarter of total construction and that Federal construction accounts for a very, very minor portion of the total national income. Indeed, although it is not indicated by the table, public works did not equal total private construction in any year during the 1930's, and the total of private construction during the New Deal period from 1933 through 1939 was more than double that for all public construction. Consequently, the effectiveness of a public-works program as a recovery measure depends largely upon the timing of the expansion and its effects upon private spending.

Timing of the program. Economists disagree concerning the exact stage in a business cycle at which public-works expenditures

TABLE 29. ROLE OF PUBLIC AND PRIVATE CONSTRUCTION IN THE ECONOMY OF THE UNITED STATES, 1920-1939 [1]

(billions of dollars)

Period	Total national income	Total construction (incl. repairs)	New private construction		New public construction	
			Business	Residential	Federal	Non-federal
Average, 1920–29	70.5	11.6	1.5	3.5	.2	1.8
Average, 1930–39	58.1	7.6	.6	1.1	.8	1.2
1929	82.9	13.4	1.9	3.4	.2	2.2
1930	68.9	11.7	1.5	2.2	.3	2.5
1931	54.3	8.6	.8	1.4	.4	2.2
1932	40.1	5.3	.4	.6	.5	1.3
1933	42.4	4.0	.3	.3	.5	.7
1934	50.3	5.1	.3	.3	.7	.8
1935	55.9	5.5	.4	.5	.8	.6
1936	65.2	8.3	.5	1.1	1.3	.9
1937	71.2	8.8	.8	1.5	1.2	.9
1938	63.6	8.9	.5	1.5	1.0	1.1
1939	69.4	9.7	.5	1.9	1.3	1.3

should be expanded. Their disagreement arises largely from a difference in business-cycle theory. One group believes that depressions are necessary to purge the economic system of its impure elements and that costs and capital values must be deflated before business can recover. According to this group, public works cannot be used to stabilize business because they do not eliminate the causes of depressions. Therefore, such a program only aggravates depressions if it prevents building costs from falling during the early stages of a downswing in the business cycle. How, it is asked, could a public-works program have halted the world-wide deflation from 1930 to 1933, unless this country had abandoned the gold standard? This "depressions-are-necessary-and-inevitable" group believes that a large public-works program should only be initiated after business has definitely begun to revive—an indication that the "necessary readjustments" have been completed. In short, public-

[1] Taken from *Construction Activity in the United States, 1915-37*, U. S. Department of Commerce, Domestic Commerce Series No. 99, 1938, and "Estimates of Construction Activity in the United States," *Survey of Current Business*, U. S. Department of Commerce, vol. 20 (September 1940), pp. 14–15. "Total construction" includes maintenance and work-relief construction as well as new construction; "business" includes "commercial" and "factory" construction; "residential" does not include new construction on farms; and "Federal" does not include work-relief construction.

works programs are of little use except to accelerate a recovery.[1]

The opposite group argues that such a policy would involve expanding public-works expenditures when they were least needed. This "spending-overcomes-depressions" group would apply the stimulus of an expanded public-works program during the early stages of a depression and would not wait until business is prostrate.[2] They claim that deflation is not self-corrective but increases economic maladjustments and leads to a vicious spiral. Increased public-works expenditures, they believe, will change the vicious into a virtuous spiral by raising the prices that have fallen too far, by redistributing income, and by speeding up the rate of spending. Public-works expenditures in their opinion do eliminate the causes of depressions by readjusting prices through reflation, by investing idle savings, and by increasing consumption through increased money incomes.

Other advocates of planned public-works programs as a device for overcoming depressions occupy a middle ground between these two extreme groups. They would start to expand public-works expenditures after building costs have fallen somewhat during the depression but before the bottom of the downswing has been reached.[3]

Financial aspects. The method of financing a public-works program is of major importance in its effects upon private spending. If the increased expenditure is financed from additional taxes, a large part of that tax revenue should come from idle funds. Otherwise, increased public spending would only cause a decrease in private spending.

A number of economists, especially in Sweden, believe that the government should deliberately unbalance the budget during depression periods and spend much more money than is collected by taxes, going into debt for the difference. The Swedish government boldly announced such a policy in 1933, with excellent results.[4]

The government may go into debt by selling its bonds to the public or to the banks, or by borrowing directly from the central

[1] *Cf.* Sumner H. Slichter, "The Economics of Public Works," *American Economic Review*, vol. 24 (March 1934) supplement, pp. 174–85.

[2] *Cf.* J. M. Clark, *Economics of Planning Public Works*, 1935, pp. 66–67.

[3] *Cf.* Arthur D. Gayer, *Public Works in Prosperity and Depression*, 1935.

[4] *Cf.* "Measures to Combat Unemployment in Sweden since 1929," supplement to *Index*, Svenska Handelsbank, June 1938; and R. A. Lester, *Monetary Experiments— Early American and Recent Scandinavian*, 1939, Chapter 10.

bank.[1] If the funds for public expenditures are raised by an expansion of bank credit (banks creating new checking accounts to pay for the government debt), the increased public expenditures will be financed by new money (checking accounts in this case).

The government's monetary and fiscal policies must be coordinated in order to avoid a contraction in loanable funds for private investment with the expansion in public expenditures, and hence to avoid a rise in market rates of interest. For this reason, the government, through the central bank (the Federal Reserve banks in this country) should pursue an expansionist or easy-money policy. In some countries during the early 1930's an expansionist public-works policy was nullified by a deflationary monetary policy, which only aggravated the fall in prices and the unbalance between costs and selling prices.

If a nation on the gold standard vigorously pursues a public-works program while price levels and total expenditures in other gold-standard countries are not increasing, either that nation will be forced off the gold standard or its public-works program will be made relatively ineffective by the contraction in the money supply and the rise in interest rates resulting from the loss of gold to foreign countries. Increased expenditures in one country alone would stimulate gold exports by increasing that country's imports relative to its exports and by raising its price level relative to price levels abroad. The gold standard, by enforcing a common price level upon all countries, serves as a drag upon any national program to expand expenditures and raise prices.

A conference of the International Labour Office in 1937 recommended "the placing to reserve in periods of prosperity of the resources necessary for carrying out works prepared for periods of depression." [2] But what shall the reserve consist of? Dollar bills? Government bonds? Industrial securities? The accumulation of a large cash reserve, by tending to reduce bank reserves by a corresponding amount, would weaken the banking system and cause a contraction of the money supply. If the government wishes to pay for an expanded public-works program with dollar bills, it might

---

[1] Professor E. Ronald Walker has suggested that a public-works program might be financed by interest-free loans from the central banking system. *Cf.* "Public Works as a Recovery Measure," *Economic Record*, vol. 11 (December 1935), p. 188.

[2] "Public Works as a Factor in Economic Stabilisation," *International Labour Review*, vol. 38 (December 1938), p. 733.

as well print new ones as to take them out of hiding in some vault. A reserve of government bonds is also of no particular advantage in initiating the program because the bonds would have to be sold or pledged for bank loans. Presumably newly issued government bonds would serve these purposes just as well. A reserve of industrial securities would also have to be sold or used as collateral in order to raise the funds.[1] Indeed, nothing more is accomplished by establishing such a reserve than could be achieved by a corresponding reduction in the government's debt during prosperous times.

An inventory of current needs, careful planning of the projects to be postponed, and advance budgeting may be of considerable value for a depressional program of public works, but the accumulation of an earmarked reserve in advance serves no useful purpose. Presumably, advance planning of public works by a country on the gold standard should involve a program for concerted action by all gold-standard countries or a plan to abandon gold if such international action is not possible.

Net effects. According to the multiplier principle, expenditures for labor and materials on public-works projects will directly or indirectly stimulate many industries and will increase total expenditures by a sum much larger than the government's total outlay. The U. S. Bureau of Labor Statistics has estimated the amount of "off-the-project" employment resulting from expenditures during the first four years of the Public Works Administration,[2] but it did not attempt to measure all the effects of such expenditures upon individual incomes or employment in an effort to discover a numerical figure for the multiplier. The multiplier theory assumes that increased expenditures spread throughout the economy in a series of waves or cycles which would be self-perpetuating were it not for "leakages." Leakages represent deflationary uses of income received from public expenditures, such as hoarding, the payment of debts to banks resulting in a reduction of the money supply, the purchase of goods from abroad, or other actions that do not increase domestic income and tend to reduce the rate at which money spent for public works is respent. The propensity of persons to consume and of corporations to pay out their receipts is, of course, important

[1] *Cf.* J. M. Clark, "An Appraisal of the Workability of Compensatory Devices," *American Economic Review*, vol. 29 (March 1939) supplement, p. 196.

[2] *Cf. P. W. A. and Industry, A Four-Year Study of Regenerative Employment,* U. S. Department of Labor, Bulletin No. 658, 1938.

in this connection. The speed of transmission is influenced by business and consumers' expectations or "confidence." [1]

Application of the multiplier principle is not confined to public spending. It also applies to private expenditures for investment andco nsumption. As used by some economists it represents partial rather than complete analysis because of a failure to take account of the effects of the public-works program upon all private spending or upon other public expenditures. It is for this reason that the multiplier depends in part upon the method of financing the program as well as the monetary and fiscal policies followed. If the expanded public-works program results in a corresponding contraction of the ordinary expenses of government, the multiplier may really be zero. There is little use of constructing beautiful school buildings with mural paintings on the wall if the municipality, in consequence, has to reduce the budget for teachers' salaries. Under the Federal public-works program in the 1930's there was some displacement of regular by emergency public works. The Federal and local budgets would have provided for some of the PWA projects had the Public Works Administration not been established, so its total expenditures do not represent a corresponding net increase in public spending.

As indicated in Table 29, public construction is but a small proportion of total construction, and total construction accounts for only a small percentage of the total national income. Therefore, the effects of a public-works program upon private spending are of primary significance. If the program causes a relative increase in building costs, weakens the bond market, raises market rates of interest, or causes other changes that tend to reduce private spending, the multiplier may turn out to be a negative figure. Private investment may fall off either because businessmen and prospective home builders fear that increased government debt will mean high taxes in the future, or because business firms are afraid that the

[1] *Cf.* Fritz Lehmann, "The Rôle of the Multiplier and the Interest Rate in Keynes' General Theory," in *The Economic Doctrines of John Maynard Keynes*, National Industrial Conference Board, 1938, pp. 52–62. For an extended discussion of the multiplier principle, *cf.* J. M. Clark, *Economics of Planning Public Works*, pp. 83–104.

Dr. Lauchlin Currie attempted to calculate the investment multiplier for this country in the period from 1919 through 1934. He found that it varied from a minus figure in four years to 21.6 in 1928. *Cf.* "Some Theoretical and Practical Implications of J. M. Keynes' General Theory," in *The Economic Doctrines of John Maynard Keynes, op. cit.*, p. 21.

government will undertake projects, such as slum clearance and water-power developments, which encroach on the vested rights of some private enterprises already suffering from underemployment. Some businessmen brought up on the maxims of individualistic economics feel that during a depression the government should curtail expenditures and throw workers out of employment just as industry does. The very fact that the budget is unbalanced in peacetime may so disturb them that they hesitate to make business commitments, thereby further reducing the rate of business spending.

Some practical difficulties. A program for advance planning of public works in order to overcome business depressions also encounters a number of technical and practical obstacles. Only a limited number of projects can be delayed until a depression arrives. Highways cannot all be constructed or reconstructed at the same time. It takes time to get a program under way, and projects once started may have to be completed regardless of any change in business conditions. All of these factors may interfere with the correct timing of the program and prevent tapering it off promptly at the appropriate date. Political considerations and pressures also make it difficult to execute a program according to an economist's blueprint.

The problem of planning a national program of public works is complicated in this country by the existence of some 180,000 independent spending units of government, including almost 20,000 cities, villages, counties, and townships and about 130,000 school districts. The Federal government must somehow induce these smaller units to plan their finances and public-works expenditures on a business-cycle basis. In order to stimulate local public-works expenditures in the 1930's, the Federal government offered a subsidy in 1933 of 30 per cent, later 45 per cent, of the cost of municipal public-works projects. Although over $2,000,000,000 were spent on non-Federal projects under the Federal Public Works Administration between July 1933 and January 1939, Table 29 shows that there was no increase in non-Federal construction between 1933 and 1935, and the expansion prior to 1939 was not very significant. One reason for the failure of local public works to expand was the financial condition of the municipalities, which the Federal government cannot control; another reason was that many municipalities accepted the Federal subsidy for projects that they would have done without the Federal program. Under any such program of Federal subsidies, some displacement of normal by emergency public works is likely to occur.

GOVERNMENT-GUARANTEED EXPANSION OF PRODUCTION

Business executives and enterprisers are in a strategic position in our kind of economy. By hesitancy, fear, or passive resistance, they can spoil even the best schemes for stimulating economic recovery. A vicious circle may develop under the public-works method of attacking depressions. Because private investment fails to pick up, government expenditures may have to be increased; yet the more the government spends, the more private investors are likely to delay investment of their funds. Under such circumstances, the government's spending program may become prolonged and those who await the return of business "confidence" and recovery, so that the public-works program can be tapered off, may be disappointed repeatedly.

A number of economists have proposed schemes for directly stimulating private production by means of a government guarantee for an expansion in the output of business firms.[1] In essence, their proposals involve the formation of a government corporation to place orders in advance with private industry, expanded production to fill those orders, and storage of the government-ordered products until consumers use the increased money income from the expanded production to buy the added output through normal merchandising channels. One variant of the plan would have all payments connected with the output ordered by the government made in special dated money, in depreciating scrip, or in stamps representing warehouse receipts, so that the government would be certain that purchases of its ordered output would be made through regular channels within a stated interval.

This type of program recognizes that business requires confidence that it can dispose of its output before it will expand. Instead of waiting for orders from individuals to develop that con-

---

[1] This discussion is based primarily upon the following published plans: Frank D. Graham, "The Creation of Employment," *Economic Forum*, vol. 1 (Spring 1933), pp. 144–54; and Mordecai Ezekiel, *Jobs for All Through Industrial Expansion*, 1939. A plan published by Fred I. Kent in the *New York Times*, February 12, 1933, VIII, p. 3, resembles these plans in a number of respects.

fidence, the proposal would have the government give orders for goods, thus permitting industry to produce and pay out the funds with which the additional output could be purchased. In order to insure individual firms against loss from expansion, the government would guarantee each concern that its increased output would be sold. Expansion in each branch of industry would, of course, have to be governed at first by estimates of demand elasticities for different products, although later it could be gauged by the increase of purchases in each line. Unsold surpluses in any particular line could, after a certain period of time had elapsed, be taken over by the government at a stated discount and be given to relief clients or used on government projects. In this way, increased production and employment in each industry would expand incomes and provide markets for the products of other industries.

Obviously, the government would not place orders for personal services, transportation, marketing services, or products made to order, although such services would indirectly benefit by industrial expansion. The plan is also not well adapted for products that are costly to store or that depreciate rapidly with storage, either because of style changes or deterioration. New automobiles, for example, might cause some trouble. Planned expansion through government orders would have to be confined primarily to manufacturing industries. Other branches of the economy would, however, gain with any general increase in buying resulting from the increase in incomes.

Such a program for stimulating industrial expansion on government order and guarantee has a number of advantages over a public-works program of the pump-priming variety. In the first place, it would be much less costly, since possible losses resulting from the government's guarantee would be minor in amount and would not increase the government debt to the same extent that a spending program on public work does. In contrast to public-works and work-relief projects, the goods produced under such industrial expansion would be those that the people most need. Certainly there is little likelihood of a net social loss from the diversified production of more manufactured goods during periods of widespread unemployment. Such an expansion of industrial output takes place in any recovery of business. Consequently, this plan represents a direct attack upon the problem of underemployment in industry.

It puts people back to work in the lines where they must sooner or later find employment, rather than giving them jobs on temporarily expanded public work.

REGULARIZATION OF PRIVATE EMPLOYMENT

The regularization of employment by individual firms was widely discussed as a method of preventing unemployment in the 1920's, before the country was cursed with wholesale unemployment.[1] After 1931 it became evident that any solution to the unemployment problem must involve an expansion in total employment rather than regularization or stabilization at current levels of employment and unemployment.

One firm cannot alone change general market conditions or the general rate of spending. Consequently, a company can do little to increase the total volume of employment. Since all firms are competing for the consumers' dollars, some methods which lead to expansion of employment in one firm are likely to cause a contraction in the sales and employment of other firms. That is true, for example, of cutting prices or branching out into other lines of production. In cases where one firm gains at the expense of others, all firms cannot do what one firm may do, and reasoning from the particular to the general is invalid.

Under certain circumstances, particular firms can spread a given volume of production and employment more evenly during a year or more. However, it is the firms in a monopolistic or semi-monopolistic position through the branding of their products that are in a position to induce customers to buy more regularly. Unless sales can be steadied, a firm can regularize its employment only by producing for stock during certain periods. But many concerns produce on order or provide only services, so they cannot produce for stock. Such a practice is also not possible for firms manufacturing articles that are costly to store or that depreciate rapidly because of style changes, obsolescence, or deterioration.

Generally speaking, only firms or industries that are especially

---

[1] *Cf.*, for example, H. Feldman, *The Regularization of Employment, A Study in the Prevention of Unemployment*, 1925; John R. Commons *et al.*, *Can Business Prevent Unemployment?* 1925; *Employment Regularization in the United States of America*, American Section, International Chamber of Commerce, 1931; and *Possibilities of Business and Employment Stabilization*, Nineteenth Annual Meeting, Chamber of Commerce of the United States, 1931.

favored because of the nature of their product, their nearness to the consumer, or their monopolistic position are able to regularize employment or to guarantee their employees a certain number of hours of work during the succeeding year. The General Electric Company could guarantee employment in its lamp department because the demand for light bulbs is steady and because a bulb, in the words of the company's president, "does not become obsolescent and does not deteriorate" in storage. Furthermore, it is only firms that are in a monopolistic position that can control technological change and prevent technological unemployment in the industry. Monopoly and monopolistic competition are, however, likely to lead to stabilization of employment and production at a low level, especially if the demand for the product is inelastic.

A joint plan for the regularization of employment in the Port of Seattle from 1921 to 1934 has been cited as an example of the virtues of employment stabilization by firms and industries. The Seattle scheme did lead to larger incomes for the longshoremen who were part of that closed-shop arrangement, but such increases were accomplished by a 50-per-cent reduction in the number of longshoremen employed the first year, a further reduction of 8 per cent from 1922 to 1929 when the available work was increasing, and a 21-per-cent cut in the number of waterfront workers during the slump from 1929 to 1933. Those benefiting from this closed-shop scheme for regularizing employment took the attitude that what happened to the employment of others because of the regularization arrangement was not their concern or responsibility.[1]

Such examples show the limitations and disadvantages of employment regularization by particular firms. At best it concentrates the available employment upon a certain group of workers, evens out their yearly incomes and their work hours, and may increase the company's profit. At worst, an attempt to achieve such regularization may increase the instability of other concerns and may raise hopes amongst workers that will be dashed during a depression. One Rochester firm in 1931 bragged: "It has been our policy for years to endeavor to provide continuous employment for the bulk of our employees and our efforts have been uniformly successful." [2]

[1] Cf. F. P. Foisie, *Decasualizing Longshore Labor and the Seattle Experience*, Waterfront Employers of Seattle, February 1, 1934, pp. 5–20.

[2] Cf. R. A. Lester and C. V. Kidd, *The Case against Experience Rating in Unemployment Compensation*, 1939, p. 31.

By 1933 this company had cut its working force by more than 70 per cent.

As a measure to overcome widespread unemployment, regularization by individual firms is ineffective, for single firms can do little to change the total volume of employment in the country. Furthermore, regularization or stabilization of employment at low levels is definitely undesirable when there are as many as 10,000,000 unemployed persons in the nation and the labor supply is increasing at the rate of about 500,000 persons a year.

SUBSIDIES AND INCENTIVE TAXATION

A number of reemployment programs have been proposed, which are based upon a government subsidy or reduction of taxes in order to encourage private employment or private investment.[1] A subsidy or tax credit may be granted an employer for an increase in the number of his employees, in his total hours of employment, or in his total payroll. It may also be granted for an expansion of investment in inventory, in plant, or in equipment. Whether the government grant is given in the form of tax reduction, a tax-credit slip, or a remission of taxes, it represents a subsidy to stimulate expenditures for wages, for production, for machinery, or for the construction of factories and perhaps homes. Tax measures for such purposes have been termed "incentive taxation."

Subsidies for increased employment or investment. Federal subsidies or tax rewards for certain actions represent a "general" type of program, since all branches of business presumably would be affected at the same time. Such a program has the advantage that it directly stimulates all industries to expand together instead of concentrating the initial stimulus upon only a few sections of the economy.

Various methods and mechanisms have been suggested for

[1] For a further discussion of various proposals and the economics of incentive taxation, the reader is referred to the following publications: *Survey of Experiences in Profit Sharing and Possibilities of Incentive Taxation*, Report of a Subcommittee of the Committee on Finance, Senate Report No. 610, 76th Congress, first session, 1939, and *Hearings on S. Res. 215* before the same subcommittee, 75th Congress, third session, 1939; Clarence W. Hazelett, *Incentive Taxation; a Key to Security* (revised edition), 1936; Kenyon E. Poole, "Tax Remission as a Means of Influencing Cyclical Fluctuations," *Quarterly Journal of Economics*, vol. 52 (February 1939), pp. 261–74; Nicholas Kaldor, "Wage Subsidies as a Remedy for Unemployment," *Journal of Political Economy*, vol. 45 (December 1936), pp. 721–42; and Emil Lederer, "Industrial Fluctuations and Wage Policy," *International Labour Review*, vol. 39 (January 1939), pp. 51–53.

schemes of incentive taxation. If the reward is made contingent upon an increase in employment or payrolls, a base period must be selected for purposes of measuring the increase, such as the total of the previous year, the average of the last three years, etc. No matter what base period is selected, some employers will complain that they have been discriminated against because their competitors had poorer employment records in the base year. Employers who made large investments prior to the introduction of the tax-incentive scheme are also liable to complain that competitors are favored by tax rewards for new investment. Similar complaints of unfairness would be made against a tax that varied with the percentage that a firm was operating below capacity. In that case, capacity would be the base.

The incentive-taxation method, although raising many difficult administrative problems, has a number of advantages over a program such as pump-priming by expenditures on public works. The percentage or amount of the tax reward could be varied as the circumstances seemed to require. The problem of timing, which is very important, would be relatively easy, since the scheme could be put into operation at any time, on any scale, and could be stopped at will. No new administrative units of government are required. The existing tax agencies could be used to check on employment records, on payrolls, or on payments to building contractors and equipment sellers. The government does not tend to compete with private business in the form of production projects or self-liquidating public works. If successful, the program puts people to work at jobs in private industry where the expansion is likely to be the most economic and where it must eventually occur. As mentioned in the first section of this chapter, the Federal government during the 1930's subsidized local public works by grants ranging from 30 to 100 per cent of total project costs under PWA, CWA, FERA, and WPA.

The same budgetary deficit and monetary expansion achieved by a public-works program can be obtained by tax reductions under such incentive programs. According to some of the proposals, eligible employers would receive tax-credit slips discountable at the commercial and Federal Reserve banks, so that checking accounts might be increased by a corresponding amount. If the tax subsidy were paid from additional taxes, the increase in taxation need not be as large as the subsidy or credit because the program should save the government some costs by reducing relief expenditures. Financing such an incentive scheme by taxation would involve a tendency to shift the tax burden from active capitalists, who employ labor and invest funds, to passive capitalists whose income comes from previous investment. Such a system of tax rewards would, of course, be just the opposite of the payroll taxes levied under the Social Security Act, which tend to penalize employment.

Unlike suggestions for employment regularization by single firms, incentive-taxation proposals would tend to expand employment and not stabilize it at present levels. As "general" programs, they would operate through changes in total expenditures, incomes, and demand. A subsidy or tax reward for investment should have much the same stimulating effects upon investment as do lower interest rates, and it would operate more directly than interest-rate reductions. The problem of withdrawing the tax subsidy is, in some respects, similar to that of tapering off public works without causing a relapse in private business. However, a subsidy available to all firms would not tend to stimulate some industries disproportionately as a public-works program does, so there would be little need for shifting workers from public to private work as the program was contracted. There would, however, be the same possibility of displacement that occurred under the Federal subsidy for local public works. For example, it would be impossible to determine to what extent investments receiving Federal tax rewards would have been made without such a subsidy.

A tax-incentive plan to increase employment was tried on a small scale and under rather unfavorable circumstances by the von Papen Government of Germany in 1932. If an employer should in any quarter of the year following October 1, 1932 employ on the average more workers than during the quarter prior to September 1, 1932, he would qualify for an "employment-premium" voucher of 100 marks for each additional worker per quarter. These employment-premium vouchers were discountable at the banks and could be used for the payment of certain taxes. Furthermore, employers hiring additional workers were given the privilege of paying them less than the legal wage rates fixed in union agreements. This combination of tax credit and lower wages was designed to reduce the employer's costs for increased production so that he would strive to expand employment, output, and sales. Although the savings in costs from the premiums and wage reductions differed between firms, it was estimated that an employer could, on the average, hire additional workers at only half the prevailing wage rates.[1]

Government experts estimated that, as a result of these privileges, 1,750,000 workers would be reemployed, requiring at least 700,000,000 marks of tax certificates. But the plan failed, and only a part of the certificates had been used when the program was practically liquidated in April 1933. Indeed, the number of unemployed increased considerably after October 1932.

The question arises why so little use was made of the employment premium and its accompanying reduction of wages. Dr. Gerhard Colm claims that the Papen Plan failed because it was based on the postulates of free competition and perfect markets.[2] It assumed that employers, fearing that competitors would take advantage of these privileges, would be forced to produce for inventory, to lower prices, and to compete in other ways for sales, with a result that some enterprises would be operating at full capacity even though others might be forced out of the market. In fact, most markets were imperfect because of personal relationships, product differentiation, and monopolistic elements. Consequently, there was no additional price-cutting and each firm could afford to wait for an increase in orders before expanding, without any fear that other firms might capture most of its markets. Dr. Colm believes that it is better to increase investment and especially expenditures for public works rather than to pursue a recovery program that involves an initial expansion in production for sale. Ordinarily, however, increased employment and incomes would result in an increased sale of goods. If necessary, some form of dated or depreciating scrip could be used to assure expenditure of the increase in incomes.

Hoarding taxes. An idleness tax is another type of incentive taxation, designed to influence or control the rate of private spending. Such a tax might be based on idle capacity or on idle money.

---

[1] Gerhard Colm, "Why the 'Papen Plan' for Economic Recovery Failed," *Social Research*, vol. 1 (February 1934), p. 90.
[2] *Idem.*

One proposal would have money-turnover taxes levied against corporations and persons under the Federal income taxes. A person's or firm's tax would vary with the ratio of average money holdings (cash or checking accounts) to total disbursements for all purposes. If the money-turnover ratio exceeded a certain percentage, the person or firm would be exempt from this particular tax. One advocate of such a tax claims that "the solution of the problem of technological employment is strictly an incentive tax on idle money," [1] which would force the expenditure of any savings resulting from technological improvements.

Most of those who propose to tax idle or loitering money would, however, collect the tax through the banks or would use a special kind of legal-tender currency for the purpose. Proposals for a nonhoardable currency include stamped scrip, to which a tax stamp would have to be affixed by the holder on a certain date,[2] and special dated dollar bills or "calendar currency," which would depreciate a certain number of cents each month or any other period of time selected. The tax, of course, could also be varied in amount from time to time as it seemed desirable to speed up spending. The need for a hoarding tax on checking accounts as well as on all currency is recognized, because about nine tenths of the country's money supply consists of such bank accounts.

There can be no doubt that idle money in an exchange economy means idle men and idle machines. Hoarding, or a decreased rate of use of money, reduces incomes and employment. Although depressions are declared "inevitable" and various recondite reasons are given for the lack of demand, such as loss of confidence and price rigidities, the fact of the matter is that without hoardable money price maladjustments and pessimism could not result in a failure to spend— a "spending strike," as Arthur Dahlberg calls it. With nonhoardable money, general overproduction would not be possible.

Especially during a depression, hoardable money is a good speculation because it increases in value as prices decline and it involves little, if any, carrying costs. Unlike real estate, it is not taxed; unlike commodities, it presents no storage problem. Furthermore,

---

[1] *Cf.* the testimony of C. W. Hazelett in *Hearings on S. Res. 215*, 75th Congress, third session, 1939, p. 269.
[2] *Cf.*, for example, Irving Fisher *et al.*, *Stamp Scrip*, 1933.

money is a liquid asset, representing generalized purchasing power. Consequently, it is not subject to losses in the same way that investments in particular enterprises or commodities are, and it can be used at any time. During depressions, interest rates, the reward for not hoarding, are likely to be low. What a hoarding tax does is to penalize the nonuse of money, making idle holdings have a negative rate of interest.

Recovery programs which call for government noninterference and economy are designed to "lure" holders of money to spend. It is claimed that, if the government will pamper capital, the confidence of capitalists will be restored and private spending will pick up. Government spending programs are supposed to tempt or stimulate private capitalists to follow suit. But hoardable money permits its holders to refuse to be tempted. Liquid capital can continue on a sit-down strike, and those who hold money can decline to spend it until "confidence" is restored by favors, such as repeal or modification of reform legislation that capital-investing groups dislike. A hoarding tax, by forcing money to circulate, helps to maintain demand despite the coyness of business confidence and fluctuations in the rate of profit. It is for this reason that J. M. Keynes, the English economist, believes the idea behind stamped money to be "sound." [1] Others have pointed out that the taxation of stagnant money has "theoretical merit as a means of meeting the problem of secular stagnation" in an economy lacking sufficient inducements to invest.[2]

It is important to note that hoardable money gives capitalists who hold money an advantage over labor. Money is not perishable, whereas labor is. Money has practically no carrying costs, so capitalists can wait for favorable opportunities before employing their money and, incidentally, labor. Labor, on the other hand, has to eat to live. The carrying costs of living may put workers, unemployed because of a decline in money spending, in a weak bargaining position. A tax which penalizes nonworking dollars seems justified because reduced private spending and unemployment increase the money costs of the state in the form of relief expenditures.

The most comprehensive plan for taxing hoarding is contained

---

[1] *The General Theory of Employment, Interest and Money*, p. 357.
[2] Emile Depres, "The Proposal to Tax Hoarding," *American Economic Review*, vol. 29 (March 1939) supplement, p. 228.

in Arthur Dahlberg's book, *When Capital Goes on Strike; How to Speed Up Spending* (1938). He would have the currency consist of a new type of depreciating dollar bills and would levy a monthly tax on average balances in checking accounts above a $300 minimum. Numerous devices and restrictions are also suggested to prevent evading the tax without really spending the money. The controls necessary to plug up loopholes would certainly have to be rather complex and complicated. In order to forestall a shift into foreign money, the country would apparently have to be off the gold standard and perhaps use some form of exchange control. A severe hoarding tax would also stimulate a wholesale shift of funds from checking accounts to savings accounts and other liquid assets, which would sharply contract the volume of checkbook money. Such a liquidation of checking accounts would tend to nullify the plan, because total spending is the product of the money supply times its rate of turnover or velocity of circulation. In order to prevent a reduction in the quantity of money, Dahlberg suggests the adoption of the 100-per-cent-reserve plan for money, which has been endorsed by a number of economists, along with the hoarding tax.[1] Such a plan for full cash reserves would permit a stabilization of the quantity of money and would prevent individuals or banks from reducing the money supply. The 100-per-cent system is mentioned again in the following section on monetary measures.

MONETARY MEASURES

The discussion of the theory of unemployment in Chapter 10 indicated that money and monetary standards play an important part in depressions and in the economics of idle resources. Various kinds of monetary programs have been proposed for combatting depressions and unemployment. Only two types can be discussed here.

Consumers' credits. A program for stimulating demand through subsidies to consumers during depressions has been proposed as a way of increasing consumers' incomes and expenditures without simultaneously increasing producers' costs by wage increases. Consumers' credits is a term that has been used for such a subsidy or grant of new money to consumers who will spend the money within a stated period of time.

[1] *Cf. ibid.*, pp. 85–88, 199–207; and also Irving Fisher, *100% Money*, 1935.

The chief practical problem in connection with such a program is to find a way of making the government's payments to consumers seem just and at the same time sufficient in amount to cause a noticeable increase in demand. The subsidy could hardly be confined to the unemployed and yet be on a sufficient scale, for then the unemployed would be receiving incomes as large or larger than when they were employed. A certain sum could be given to each inhabitant, as was done in Maryland during a depression in 1733 with considerable success.[1] However, it would seem unjust to give the rich the same sum per dependent as was given by the government to the poor. Therefore, J. E. Meade has suggested that the credit per person, which would vary with the volume of "depression" unemployment, be given to all those with an income below a certain level.[2] But such a proposal would also raise many practical problems and result in some anomalies or injustices in borderline cases.

Another problem is to find some method of ensuring that these additional payments would be promptly spent by consumers, and not be hoarded. Payment of the credits might be made by the government in dated money, but even then, there would be the possibility that consumers would use the dated money for cash purchases that they would have made anyway. If the consumers' credits resulted in reduced cash spendings, total demand might not increase.

Professor Jesse H. Bond of the University of Oregon has suggested a rather ingenious device for meeting both of these practical problems. During depressions he would have all retail sellers of goods and services give to each purchaser government credits in the form of trading stamps in amounts equivalent to a certain percentage of the dollar value of customers' purchases. The percentage might be varied with the volume of unemployment. These stamps could be deposited in the banks, and they could also be converted into cash by the government, possibly at the post offices. Such a subsidy measured by total retail purchases would, of course, give greater dollar amounts to the rich than to the poor. With so many retail sellers and sales, it might also be difficult to prevent misuse of the government credit stamps.

[1] *Cf.* R. A. Lester, "Currency Issues to Overcome Depressions in Delaware, New Jersey, New York and Maryland, 1715–37," *Journal of Political Economy*, vol. 47 (April 1939), pp. 208–15.

[2] *Cf.* J. M. Meade, *Consumers' Credits and Unemployment*, 1938, especially pp. 33–36.

The grants of consumers' credits by the government during a depression should be financed from new money, presumably either in the form of increased checking accounts borrowed by the government from the banks or in the form of new currency issues. Meade has pointed out that there is no need for the government to pay interest on these funds because the whole mechanism of interest rates is designed to guide the limited resources available into the most productive uses.[1] In a period of wholesale idleness and failure to utilize resources, the interest mechanism becomes more or less meaningless.

There is some fear that large issues of new money during a depression would lead to price inflation. Such a fear is unfounded. Inflations have not occurred during depressions. They can only arise from increased spending. So long as there are vast unemployed resources of men and equipment, each increase in demand will be met by an increase in supply as idle resources are put to work. Unused resources act as an automatic check to price-level increases. The new money is absorbed by increased output and trade. Price inflation is possible only when most of industry is enjoying full employment.[2] There would be little danger of inflation if the payment of consumers' credits were promptly stopped as soon as "depression" unemployment was eliminated and if taxes were imposed to take some of the new money out of circulation and to retire any government debt incurred under the program. Whether these balancing taxes during prosperous periods should take the form of sales or income taxes has been a debatable question.

A "goods" standard for money. Making our currency convertible into a certain unit composed of standard commodities has also been suggested as a means of increasing the demand for products, stimulating the rate of spending, and stabilizing the price level.

In place of a gold standard, Benjamin Graham suggests a "goods" or "commodities" standard consisting of a composite unit of some 23 storable commodities traded on our organized commodity exchanges.[3] Each commodity would be represented in the composite

[1] *Ibid.*, pp. 48–49.

[2] *Cf.* R. A. Lester, "Is Inflation Possible?" *North American Review*, vol. 239 (January 1935), pp. 14–18; Alvin H. Hansen, *Full Recovery or Stagnation?* pp. 321–22; and Joan Robinson, *Introduction to the Theory of Employment*, 1937, pp. 120–21.

[3] *Cf.* Benjamin Graham, *Storage and Stability; A Modern Ever-Normal Granary*, 1937.

unit according to its importance in our economy during the past decade. There would be free convertibility or exchange between this composite-commodity unit and the dollar; anyone could convert commodity units into dollars or redeem dollar bills in commodity units.

Such a "goods" standard for money would keep the price level of the 23 basic commodities absolutely stable without pegging the price of any single commodity. As long as free convertibility was maintained between the goods unit and the dollar, there would be no possibility of inflation or deflation of the price level, which has been so demoralizing for American business in the past.

The most important advantage of such a goods standard is that it would regulate the money supply in a way that would help to stabilize business and maintain the domestic market for our products. Whenever private demand fell off because of reduced spending, the prices of the 23 basic commodities would tend to decline. As soon as the price of the composite unit began to fall below the conversion price that the government fixed, people would start to exchange commodity units into dollar bills. That would mean an automatic government purchase of the basic commodities, thus supporting the market and preventing general overproduction. As this government market would be a permanent one at the conversion price, businessmen could rely upon it in making their calculations.

Not only would the government's purchases supplement a declining private demand, but the amount of money in private hands would automatically be increased, and this additional purchasing power, along with support for the price level, would tend to stimulate private demand. That expansion of the money supply provides a good stimulant for dull business was proved repeatedly in the Middle Colonies during the first half of the eighteenth century and in various countries during the depression of the 1930's. A system of 100-per-cent bank reserves would be desirable in order to make certain that currency expansion under a goods standard during dull times was not offset by a contraction in checking accounts or bank-made money, as generally has happened during recent periods of reduced spending and declining business.

When private demand revived and prices rose, it would become profitable for people to convert dollar bills into composite units, thus reducing the government's stock of the 23 commodities stored in warehouses, reducing the currency in circulation, and serving as an automatic check to any inflation.

By supporting the market with purchases and by halting price declines or deflationary spirals, such a monetary mechanism would tend to prevent curtailment of production and employment in the midst of want.

GENERAL OBSERVATIONS

It would be possible to apply two or more of these programs at the same time. The "goods" standard of money could, for example, be adopted and used in conjunction with any of them. It would fit in especially well with a program for government-guaranteed expansion of industrial production.

The chief difficulties with some of these programs for overcoming unemployment are practical, administrative ones. For instance, a hoarding tax or the granting of consumers' credits in stamps distributed by retailers would require a rather elaborate system of controls and policing in order to prevent evasion and abuse. Furthermore, the programs must stimulate demand in general by increasing the total volume of spending. Therefore, any program needs general public support to succeed. That is why it should not go counter to principles of justice commonly held. That is also why the success of any anti-unemployment program depends so much on its timing and especially its execution.

It is well to consider the worst that could happen under such programs. Certainly it is difficult to see how increased private production, if well proportioned, could involve much social loss. Individual taxpayers may dislike government spending, even though such expenditures may, in the long run, reduce the total tax burden by eliminating relief expenditures. From a social point of view, however, the important consideration is not the size of the government debt but the size of the total national income that citizens receive in the form of goods and services—their standard of living— with due allowance for capital replacements in order to safeguard future production. In criticizing these programs one ought to bear in mind that the alternative during the 1930's was widespread waste of productive resources with wholesale unemployment and economic stagnation.

CHAPTER SIXTEEN

UNEMPLOYMENT COMPENSATION

Various programs for eliminating unemployment were discussed in the previous chapter. Unemployment insurance was not included in that discussion because it is designed primarily to alleviate the effects of short-time unemployment. Its emphasis is upon benefit payments and protection to workers rather than upon unemployment prevention. It is true, of course, that the payment of benefits may help to sustain total demand by assuring workers a minimum income for a few months should they lose their jobs. Perhaps improvement in the use and services of public employment exchanges under unemployment compensation may also aid in some degree to overcome unemployment, either by providing more adequate data on that economic disease or by directing the unused labor resources to fit the developing demand. Executives in certain large firms have argued that some unemployment would be prevented by levying the tax for unemployment compensation in a way that would encourage employment regularization. How ineffective such an unemployment program would be has been indicated in the discussion of employment regularization in the previous chapter. The subject is discussed further in this chapter under "experience rating."

Unemployment insurance has been advanced and defended as a businesslike method of providing workers some security against unemployment lasting less than half a year. Through systematic premium payments or tax contributions in advance, eligible workers can receive benefits as a right and not as a charitable handout. By relating each individual's benefits to previous contributions and earnings in industry, it is argued that individual incentives and recipients' self-respect are preserved. The unemployed worker is spared the demoralizing influences of pauperization and home investigations, or the uncertainties and paternalism of public or private charity (the dole), while he searches for another job. Unemployment insurance has been called the first line of defense for the disemployed worker. If he is reemployed before his rights to benefits are exhausted, he avoids the evils of destitution and dependency connected with poor relief. That at least is the theory behind unemployment insurance or unemployment compensation, as it has come to be called in this country.

Employment risks and income. A number of industrial risks may cause a worker's earnings to change without advance notice. Such risks include industrial accidents, sickness, and unemployment. Workers are generally not to blame for unforeseen reductions in earnings arising out of these industrial hazards. For the most part, unemployed resources are not responsible for their forced idleness when the volume of spending declines in a specialized exchange economy.

Most workers are not in a position to meet such emergencies as unemployment, injury, or illness out of their own financial resources. Over one third of all nonfarm families had incomes under $1,500 in the prosperous year of 1929, when the average full-time earnings of employed wage-earners were about $1,470 a year.[1] The Brookings Institution estimated that nonfarm families with incomes under $1,500 actually spent more than their incomes in 1929, so that they had no savings.[2] Estimates for 1935–1936 show that over two thirds of all wage-earning families not on relief received incomes under $1,500.[3] In 1939 the full-time earnings of wage workers were about $1,330 a year.[4]

The method of social insurance. Unemployment compensation is not so much a device for eliminating unemployment as a method of distributing an existing burden in a more systematic and provident fashion. Insurance, by spreading an average loss over a large group, diffuses the risk. Individuals who suffer from the hazard are afforded limited protection from funds contributed by all members of the insured group. The incomes of wage-earners, however, are insufficient for them to purchase protection against

---

[1] Maurice Leven *et al.*, *America's Capacity to Consume*, 1934, p. 228; and *Survey of Current Business*, June 1939, p. 14.

[2] Leven *et al.*, *op. cit.*, p. 95.

[3] *Consumer Incomes in the United States, Their Distribution in 1935–36*, National Resources Committee, 1938, p. 26.

[4] Robert R. Nathan, "National Income at Nearly 70 Billion Dollars in 1939," *Survey of Current Business*, vol. 20 (June 1940), p. 10.

such a major economic hazard as unemployment. Therefore, the government must step in and, through the taxing power, compel persons (whether they be workers, employers, or general taxpayers) to contribute funds in advance so that individual workers may have some protection against industrial contingencies such as unemployment. Social insurance resembles private insurance in that the beneficiaries receive their benefit payments as a contractual right; it differs from private insurance in that the government compels persons to contribute to the insurance scheme through taxes, and may itself contribute public funds. It is argued that at least part of the financial support for social insurance should come from nonworker sources because such insurance reduces the costs of public relief and because the various industrial risks to workers are an inherent element in our machine-money economy of capitalism, from which society as a whole benefits. Those risks could be sharply reduced or eliminated only by a radical change in our economic system, such as a return to an economy of local self-sufficiency like the medieval guild system, which knew no widespread unemployment and serious industrial accidents.

In contrast to relief, social-insurance benefits are paid as a predetermined right. The worker is not forced to pauperize himself before he can receive his promised benefits. Relief, on the other hand, is based entirely upon need and, therefore, disregards previous tax contributions and differences in individual resourcefulness or work records. The social-insurance method, by requiring contributions in advance and spreading the risk widely, tends to prevent the vicious circle that arises when relief is financed on a local basis.

It has been said repeatedly that any one state, in adopting such a select method for alleviating the effects of unemployment, would handicap its firms in interstate competition. The reader may wonder why such a social-insurance scheme would not pay for itself, as it is alleged company welfare plans have, by attracting the best workers, reducing labor turnover, improving workers' morale and health, etc. There might, however, be some question whether workers' output would be increased by unemployment insurance as much as the money costs of production would rise, and all firms in a state cannot attract the best workers. Whether a state system of unemployment insurance increases employers' costs depends in large part upon how much the scheme reduces relief expenses and how the funds are raised to finance the insurance benefits. Taxes on workers, on personal incomes or inheritances, or on private homes do not increase the costs of industrial production within a state relative to such costs in other states. Indeed, expenditures for unemployment insurance need be no more burdensome to private firms than other costs of government or business, such as paying for the care of the insane, for useless public jobholders, for needless corporation vice presidents, or for needed sewage disposal.

BACKGROUND FOR AMERICAN LEGISLATION

Trade-union and company plans. With family incomes so insufficient for meeting economic misfortune, there developed privately, both here and abroad, group attempts to spread some of the risk so that the losses from unemployment would not fall with full force upon the individual worker. In all countries, experimentation by trade-unions with unemployment-benefit plans for their members has preceded government legislation on unemployment insurance. Although the first American trade-union plan for unemployment benefits was established in 1831, less than 100,000 union members were covered by unemployment-insurance reserves before the passage of the Federal Social Security Act in 1935, and the number of employees then covered by company unemployment-benefit plans was even smaller.[1]

Company benefit plans have been confined primarily to group life insurance, which is relatively inexpensive, and to company pension plans, which tend to tie the worker to the company during his working life. Unemployment benefits would not only be very costly for most concerns but would be less effective than pensions in anchoring the employee to the firm. Unless the firm had a monopoly, any company benefit program would have to meet the test of profit by paying for itself through reduced labor costs. Some company plans undoubtedly met this profit test by giving the company a nonwage advantage in the labor market. The plans operated as a favorable differential, which helped the company to attract the best grade of workers, to lower labor turnover, and to lessen labor unrest amongst employees. But the more widely such

---

[1] *Social Security in America, The Factual Background of the Social Security Act*, Social Security Board, 1937, p. 8.

plans were adopted, the more the company's differential in the labor market would be reduced, so the profit test tended to prevent general use of such company plans. This is simply another illustration of the economic principle that what a single firm can do successfully, all firms may be unable to do.

Unemployment insurance abroad. European systems of unemployment insurance have been of two sorts: (1) voluntary arrangements established by labor unions and subsidized from government monies, and (2) nationwide programs of compulsory insurance, requiring certain contributions from employers and employees to a state fund. Before our Social Security Act was passed in 1935, a total of 11 European nations were providing subsidies for voluntary programs, which covered about 4,000,000 workers in that year. At the same time, eight European countries had compulsory systems covering around 35,000,000 employees.

Subsidized voluntary arrangements, known as the "Ghent system," had been adopted locally in a number of countries before the first World War and were established on a national basis in France, Norway, Denmark, and Belgium between 1905 and 1908. The first national compulsory unemployment scheme was established in Great Britain in 1911, followed by Italy in 1919 and Austria in 1920. Germany adopted compulsory unemployment insurance in 1927. The compulsory program of Soviet Russia, enacted in 1922, was suspended in 1930 because of a shortage of labor, and it has been in suspension ever since.

Under the Ghent system, employers do not contribute to the funds for benefit payments, which are administered by the unions. Generally speaking, the subsidy from public monies in such European systems amounts to one half of the benefit payments to unemployed workers, although it is considerably higher in some countries for workers with low incomes or large families. Workers' contributions finance the remaining costs for benefits. Under the compulsory schemes, the cost is usually divided among the employers, the employees, and the state, with the government contributing one third, or somewhat less than a third, of the total cost. Total contributions generally range from three to four per cent of the total wages of covered workers, although they were 4.6 per cent in Great Britain and 6.5 per cent in Germany in the 1930's.[1]

[1] *Ibid.*, pp. 22, 29.

Under most European systems, the weekly benefit payments to eligible unemployed workers have varied with the number of dependents in the worker's family. Consequently, they may be as high as 70 or even 80 per cent of the worker's normal weekly wages in some countries. Receipt of such unemployment benefits is usually limited to 15 or 20 weeks in any one year, although they have been granted for half a year in Great Britain.

These facts and figures give an outline sketch of unemployment insurance abroad.[1] It is evident that in European plans the element of need plays an important part. In Great Britain, benefit payments are not related to previous wage rates but are on a flat-rate basis. Although in most other countries benefits are on a percentage-of-wages basis, workers with large families or low incomes are favored. Partly for this reason and partly because of government contributions, there has been a tendency for the dividing line between insurance and relief to become blurred, especially during periods of widespread unemployment. At such times, most European countries have continued benefit payments beyond the legal limit of 15, 20, or 26 weeks a year, usually after a needs test, and have paid for such extended benefits by subsidies or "borrowings" from the national treasury. Such a weakening of the statutory safeguards in order to meet social or relief needs, of course, tended to upset the actuarial soundness of the insurance systems, so that most of the European schemes were technically insolvent for periods during the 1920's or 1930's.[2]

Foreign programs of unemployment insurance emphasize protection rather than prevention. No unemployment-insurance law abroad provides for differential taxes on employers to encourage employment regularization or stabilization by individual firms. England experimented with such incentive-tax schemes between 1911 and 1920, but abandoned them as failures. Schemes of differential tax rates for unemployment insurance were also to be put into practice in Germany, but they proved to be impractical at the outset. In both countries, widespread unemployment prevented

[1] For a more detailed description of the European systems, *cf. idem;* and Barbara N. Armstrong, *Insuring the Essentials*, 1932, Section 5 and Appendix B.

[2] *Cf.* Maxwell S. Stewart, *Social Security*, 1937, Chapter 11; and Arthur H. Reede, "The Actuarial Aspect of Unemployment Insurance: British Experience," *Pennsylvania State College Bulletin*, vol. 30 (July 20, 1936), pp. 1–31.

the adoption of further plans for reducing the taxes of employers pursuing certain employment policies.[1]

American philosophy and patterns.   In the passage of labor legislation, such as factory acts, industrial-accident compensation, unemployment insurance, and old-age insurance, this country has lagged anywhere from 20 to 60 years behind similar developments in Europe, especially in England.   Before the first World War most European countries had established compulsory or government-subsidized systems of health insurance—a type of social insurance not yet adopted in this country.

A number of factors account for our "cultural lag" in such matters as social insurance.   Agriculture, which is highly individualistic, has played a more important role in our economy than in the industrial nations of Europe.   Until 1900, for instance, farmers and farm workers outnumbered industrial wage-earners in America. Our thoughts and our government constitutions have been colored by this individualistic philosophy, which is characteristic of rural and frontier areas and which is opposed to compulsory action by governments.   Not only were there possible constitutional obstacles to overcome in order to establish social insurances in this country but their development was also held back by a fear that a state would handicap its firms in interstate competition by enacting, say, unemployment-insurance legislation.   Although, as previously indicated, that fear was largely uninformed, if not unfounded, it nevertheless played an important restraining role.   Organized labor in America opposed some types of social insurance, especially unemployment insurance, until a few years before laws were passed establishing such insurance systems.   Furthermore, there has been no strong labor party in this country to fight for such workingmen's insurance.   It is worth noting that two progressive Presidents were primarily responsible for the enactment of our first social-insurance laws—Theodore Roosevelt for workmen's compensation and Franklin D. Roosevelt for unemployment and old-age insurance.

Because of our individualistic background and mores, our social-insurance laws provide for more individual differentiation than most foreign legislation.   Benefit rates and contributions are directly

---

[1] For a further discussion of foreign experience with merit rating in unemployment insurance, *cf.* R. A. Lester and Charles V. Kidd, *The Case against Experience Rating in Unemployment Compensation*, 1939.

related to the worker's earnings. Therefore, our social-insurance legislation tends to incorporate the valuations of the labor market. It is claimed that such a relationship is just and is necessary in order to take account of wage differentials and to maintain the solvency of the system without government contributions. However, in following so closely the patterns of private insurance and company benefit plans, administrative problems arise, which make it difficult to extend our compulsory schemes to small employers and to certain groups of workers, such as farm labor and domestic servants. Also unemployment insurance in this country, because its benefits are not related to the number of dependents and other need factors, has had only a minor effect upon relief costs.

Conflicts between private and social purposes have resulted in inconsistent objectives in our social security program. (1) We demand economical administration of social insurance, but at the same time adopt elaborate benefit arrangements providing individualized payments to the last cent, presumably in order to preserve individual initiative. Large firms in stable lines of business demand experience rating so that they may enjoy tax reductions. Both of these features add considerably to the cost of administration. (2) Businessmen insist that social insurance should be self-supporting; yet, by demanding a reduction in the large old-age reserve contemplated in the original provisions of the Social Security Act, they caused the self-supporting features to be eliminated, so that a government subsidy to old-age insurance will undoubtedly be necessary after 1955 or 1960. (3) Some businessmen maintain that industrial hazards, such as unemployment and work accidents, can be prevented if employers are penalized by tax differentials under social-insurance laws. So far they have not claimed that old age can be prevented by that method. Such notions concerning prevention require that all taxes for social insurance be levied on employers and lead to the conclusion that heavy payroll taxes adjusted to company experience are good for business and employment. The same employers have, however, argued that high payroll taxes are bad for business and employment. (4) The Federal government has been attempting to raise wage rates by such legislation as the Fair Labor Standards Act and the National Labor Relations (or Wagner) Act; yet heavy payroll taxes tend to depress wages by penalizing employment and increasing the employer's

tax with each increase in wage scales. A notion of the full significance of payroll taxes on employers under social-insurance legislation in this country may be gained from the following facts: the
Federal unemployment tax on employers' payrolls is three per cent;
the Federal old-age insurance tax on employers' payrolls is one per
cent and is to reach three per cent in 1949; taxes or contributions
under workmen's compensation vary from state to state but average
from one to one-and-a-half per cent of employers' payrolls; proposals for health insurance in this country include suggestions that
part of the funds be raised by a tax on employers' payrolls.

The interests of employers and employees with regard to social
insurance may run in opposite directions, and, as indicated by
illustrations just cited, even employers may find themselves arguing
at cross purposes. In the development of social security in America
there are bound to be some conflicts between the philosophy of individualism and that of social security, between private insurance
principles and social need, and between plans of tax reductions to
encourage prevention and demands for adequate protection for
workers.

ANALYSIS OF AMERICAN LEGISLATION

The Wisconsin Unemployment Reserve Act was the first unemployment-compensation law enacted in this country. Passed in
1932, it became effective in July 1934, a year before the Federal
Social Security Act was put on the statute books. Five other states
enacted unemployment-insurance laws during the first half of 1935
in anticipation of the passage of the Federal Act.

The character of the Wisconsin law affected the Federal legislation. Instead of following European precedents, the Wisconsin law
was patterned after our state workmen's compensation acts, perhaps because those acts had been passed despite fears that firms
would be handicapped in interstate competition. On the premise
that employers would prevent unemployment if taxed for benefits
to disemployed workers, the Wisconsin Act provided for contributions from employers only, for individual employer-reserve accounts,
and for tax reductions or exemptions for employers whose reserves
reached a certain percentage of their payrolls. To base legislation
upon a presumed analogy between unemployment and industrial
accidents was, however, a questionable policy. Industrial acci-

dents result from conditions within the factory, unemployment from conditions outside the factory. The employer has some legal liability for work accidents, but not for unemployment, because it arises for the most part from market conditions over which he usually has little control.

Federal Social Security Act. The provisions of this Act that deal with unemployment do not establish a national system of unemployment insurance. Instead the Act provides for a three-percent Federal tax on the payrolls of employers of eight or more workers in covered lines of employment. This Federal tax on payrolls was derigned to accomplish two purposes: to encourage the states to pass unemployment-compensation laws and to protect employers in states with unemployment-compensation laws from being handicapped in interstate competition. Both of these aims were to be achieved by the tax-credit or tax-offset provisions of the Federal Act, which permit an employer to deduct from his Federal payroll tax all sums, up to nine tenths of the Federal tax, that he has paid during the year into an unemployment fund under a state law approved by the Federal Social Security Board. For example, an employer with a taxable payroll of $100,000 in a certain year would have a Federal tax of $3,000; but his Federal tax could be reduced to $300 (one tenth) if he paid $2,700 (nine tenths) into a state fund during the year. Consequently, most states levy a payroll tax of 2.7 per cent for unemployment benefits, unless the employer's tax is modified by experience rating. The tax-offset provisions of the Federal Act practically force states to finance unemployment compensation by a payroll tax upon employers.

The unemployment-compensation features center around the tax provisions because the sponsors of the Act believed it desirable to permit state experimentation. To facilitate experimentation with tax differentials as a means of encouraging employment regularization, the Federal Act provides for "additional credit allowance" that employers may deduct from nine tenths of their Federal payroll tax. Such additional Federal-tax credit for state-tax exemptions is measured by the difference between the amount an employer actually pays into the state fund during a year and 2.7 per cent of his payroll. Under the merit- or experience-rating provisions of some state laws an employer may be entirely exempt from the state tax. In such a case, an employer with a taxable payroll of

$100,000 would really pay a total tax of only $300, because he could credit his state tax exemption of $2,700 against his Federal tax of $3,000. The one tenth of the Federal tax that is not subject to state tax credits ($300 in this case), is used by the Federal government to make grants to the states, paying for the full costs of administering their unemployment-compensation laws.

As the reader will appreciate, this tax-offset device, with its additional credits for tax exemptions and appropriations to states for administrative expenses, is rather cumbersome and awkward. It was originally adopted not only to facilitate state experimentation, but also for reasons of constitutional law. The Supreme Court decisions upholding the unemployment features of the Social Security Act, however, indicated that other methods, including a system of Federal grants to the states, would have been constitutional.[1] Experimentation under the "additional-credits" provisions obviously eliminates the uniformity of the Federal tax and reopens the whole issue of handicapping employers in interstate commerce by nonuniform state taxes.

The Social Security Act specifies certain standards that state laws must meet if they are to receive Federal subsidies for administration and Federal approval, so that employers in the state may offset their state unemployment-insurance taxes or tax credits against nine tenths of the Federal payroll tax. These standards for state laws include the following financial and labor requirements:

1. All funds collected from state taxes for unemployment compensation shall be deposited in the United States Treasury, and such funds must be used solely for the payment of benefits to unemployed workers.

2. All benefits shall be paid through public employment exchanges unless the Social Security Board grants permission to other agencies, and all persons whose claims for unemployment compensation are denied must be given opportunity for a fair hearing before an impartial tribunal.

3. No worker shall be denied benefits if he refuses a new job where there is a labor dispute, where he would be required to join a company union or refrain from joining a *bona fide* labor organization, or where the wages, hours, or other conditions of work are "substantially less favorable" than those prevailing for similar work in the locality.

The financial provisions are designed to protect the state funds from loss or misuse and to safeguard the country's financial struc-

---

[1] *Chas. C. Steward Machine Co.* v. *Davis* (1937), 301 U. S. 548; and *Carmichael* v. *Southern Coal & Coke Co.*, and *Carmichael* v. *Gulf States Paper Corp.* (1937), 301 U. S. 495.

ture.   A number of state accident-compensation funds suffered
serious losses from investment in municipal and corporation bonds
during the depression of the 1930's.[1]   The requirement that unemployment-compensation monies belonging to the states be deposited
with the U. S. Treasury and invested by the Treasury in securities
of the Federal government prevents a similar loss of unemployment
funds.

The Secretary of the Treasury is given complete control over
the investment and liquidation of state funds so that large benefit
payments may be made without further depressing the security
markets during business slumps and, thus, increasing the tendency
toward deflation.   Collections from state unemployment-compensation taxes average about $1,000,000,000 a year, and the total state
unemployment reserves in the Treasury may reach a total of $3,000,-
000,000 in prosperous periods.   The Treasury may invest these deposited state reserve funds in outstanding Federal bonds, in new
issues of Federal bonds, or in special Federal obligations issued exclusively for this purpose and bearing the average rate of interest
on the total Federal debt.   Without selling any of the Treasury-
held securities in the open market, the Secretary of the Treasury
can liquidate some of these reserve accounts by using the proceeds
from Federal taxes for that purpose or by selling the securities to
the Federal Reserve banks.   It has also been suggested that these
securities be used as collateral for borrowings from the banks.
Pledge of the securities for bank loans or their sale to Federal Reserve banks would tend to incearse the money supply and raise the
price level.   On the other hand, the unemployment funds could be
hoarded by the Treasury in cash or deposited in the Federal Reserve banks, both of which would tend to reduce member-bank
reserves and the money supply and depress the price level.   In order
to take such steps, however, the Social Security Act would have to
be amended, for it requires the Secretary of the Treasury to invest
in Federal obligations all of the funds not needed to meet current
withdrawals.[2]

The second provision, requiring that benefit payments be made

[1] *Cf. Social Security in America*, Social Security Board, 1937, p. 101.

[2] For a discussion of the various ways that unemployment reserves might be used
to facilitate business stability, *cf.* Alvin H. Hansen *et al.*, *A Program for Unemployment
Insurance and Relief in the United States*, 1934, Part 4, "The Investment of Unemployment
Reserves and Business Stability."

at public employment offices or exchanges, enables the unemployment-compensation administration to test the recipient's willingness to work and to make certain that it is impossible for him to find "suitable" employment. Compulsory unemployment-compensation laws abroad also provide that workers must register and report at a labor exchange or clearinghouse for jobs in order to qualify for benefits. Thus, the payment of benefits is related to the more important objective of obtaining jobs for unemployed beneficiaries.

A number of problems arise in administering this second requirement for state laws and also the third one concerning the acceptance of new jobs at rates of pay and conditions not "substantially less favorable" than for similar work in the locality. If a new job is available, should the exchange offer it to the best workers on the list of beneficiaries, or to those who seem less willing to work, or to those who have been unemployed the longest? Furthermore, it has been argued that the facilities of the public exchanges should also be open to relief recipients, who should register there at least once a month. If new jobs are also offered to relief recipients, it may not be possible to test the willingness of insurance receivers to accept "suitable" work by an offer of a new job. Perhaps such a test is not necessary during such short benefit periods as 15 weeks following a waiting period of two weeks.

The employment exchanges must look out not only for the interests of the unemployment-insurance fund and idle workers but also for the interests of employers who use the exchanges in recruiting new employees. If such employers do not receive well-qualified workers through the public employment offices, they may not continue to use them. Indeed, the Federal government and those employers with agreements to hire through the labor unions do not use the public exchanges to obtain many of their workers. Yet the exchanges must have a rather complete and up-to-date picture of wage rates and conditions of work in all lines of employment in the localities under their jurisdiction, if the provisions concerning "suitable" employment are to be administered properly. The chief source of such data is employers. It is easier to ascertain "prevailing" wage rates abroad where union-employer agreements fix the wage rates for most workers. As mentioned in the chapters on wages, studies in this country show a wide range of wage rates for comparable work in the same locality in lines where labor is unorganized.

The test of an offer of "suitable" employment presents other problems. Leaders of organized labor in this country originally opposed compulsory unemployment insurance largely because of fear that the insurance administration would break down wage standards by putting pressure upon unemployment beneficiaries to accept jobs at substandard rates and working conditions. Organized labor distrusts court interpretation of such provisions as the vague phrase "substantially less favorable." If the courts interpret that phrase narrowly, so that workers are not disqualified from benefits for refusing work at nonunion conditions, the bargaining power of labor will be increased and the union wage structure will be strengthened during depressions. If, on the other hand, the courts interpret that phrase broadly, wage standards will receive no support from the unemployment-compensation laws.

A number of British economists have claimed that unemployment insurance in England has increased wage rigidity by strengthening trade-union resistance to wage reductions in periods of depression. Such wage rigidity, they insist, increased the amount of unemployment in Great Britain during the 1920's.[1] This argument fails to allow for the fact that Britain, by returning to the gold standard at prewar parity in 1925, overvalued her currency at the expense of her export trade. It may well be that the price level, wage rates, and interest rates in England were too high for full employment in a country on the gold standard. Our previous discussion indicates that unemployment in certain lines may be caused by wage rates too high relative to the general wage level, but that the whole wage level is not likely to be too high unless the currency is overvalued. In such cases interest rates would also be "too high" for full employment. It is possible that the provision of allowances for dependents may have weakened the incentive for some workers to seek private jobs, because a considerable proportion of the beneficiaries with large families have, under unemployment insurance,

[1] Cf., for example, A. C. Pigou, "Wage Policy and Unemployment," Economic Journal, vol. 37 (September 1927), pp. 355–68; Henry Clay, "The Public Regulation of Wages in Great Britain," Economic Journal, vol. 39 (September 1929), pp. 323–43; J. M. Keynes, "The Question of High Wages," Political Quarterly, vol. 1 (January 1930), pp. 110–24; F. C. Benham, "Wages, Prices, and Unemployment," The Economist, vol. 112 (June 20, 1931), pp. 1315–16; and Leo Wolman, "Wage Rates," American Economic Review, vol. 28 (March 1938) supplement, p. 130.

received as much as, or more than, their normal weekly earnings.[1] That, of course, happens also under unemployment relief but could not happen where, as in our laws, weekly benefits are restricted to roughly 50 per cent of normal earnings.

"Suitable" employment is not only a question of wage rates and antiunion conditions but also concerns the effect of the job upon the worker's health, safety, morals, and ability to secure reemployment in his customary line of work. As the discussion of work relief has indicated, skills may be lost by unskilled work. Because it is difficult for workers to regain a status once lost, society may benefit if skilled workers, such as carpenters and watchmakers, are not forced to accept unskilled jobs just as soon as they become unemployed.[2]

The other provisions that must be embodied in state laws in order to receive Federal grants for state administration are mainly administrative in character. It is, of course, difficult for the Federal government, which foots all the bills for state administration, to control that administration and prevent political abuse.[3] Indeed, the tax-offset device is not well adapted for enforcing high standards in unemployment compensation. So far, Federal approval and subsidies have been granted continuously to all state laws and state administrations.

State legislation. Encouraged by the tax-offset and subsidy provisions of the Social Security Act, every one of the 48 states, the District of Columbia, Hawaii, and Alaska had by 1937 enacted an unemployment-compensation law approved by the Social Security Board. The states were given wide latitude with regard to the type of law they might adopt and the benefits they could pay. Latitude with respect to benefits seemed essential because the rate of compensable unemployment in some states was twice as great as in others during the early 1930's. Experimentation was also considered desirable in order to discover the provisions best adapted to conditions in this country. Consequently, laws patterned after

[1] Great Britain Unemployment Statutory Committee, *Report on the Financial Condition of the Unemployment Fund*, 1938, p. 27.

[2] For a discussion of the British experience with administering clauses defining "suitable employment," *cf.* E. Wight Bakke, *Insurance or Dole?* 1935, pp. 43–52; and *Benefit Decisions of the British Umpire*, Unemployment Compensation Information Service, Benefit Series General Supplement No. 1, Social Security Board, 1938, pp. 63–81.

[3] *Cf.* Bryce M. Stewart, *Planning and Administration of Unemployment Compensation in the United States*, 1938, pp. 478–80.

the Wisconsin Act and laws following European precedents were both permitted. But aside from provisions based on questionable notions concerning unemployment prevention (such as individual employer reserves, guaranteed employment accounts, and experience rating) the state laws are very similar, differing only in minor details. Indeed, the states all promise their employees about the same benefits, despite wide differences in rates of unemployment.

1. *Coverage.* In general, the state laws exempt the employments excluded from the Federal payroll tax. The most important of those exempt employments are agricultural labor, domestic and government service, self-employment, and work for nonprofit organizations. The reasons for such exemptions are mainly administrative and political. Our compulsory systems of unemployment compensation, so closely patterned after private insurance, are not well adapted for including employers of as few as one worker, especially if the worker receives part of his pay in the form of board and room. About half of the state laws, like the Federal tax, apply to employers of eight or more; more than one fifth of the states, however, include employers of one or more in the covered lines of employment. Originally it was estimated that the Federal tax would cover about 50 per cent of all gainfully employed persons in the country. The Social Security Board has since estimated that in May 1938 about 670,000 employers were subject to the state laws and almost 28,000,000 workers (slightly over 50 per cent of the gainfully occupied persons) had earned credits under state unemployment-compensation legislation, although in some cases their credits were too small for them to qualify for benefits.[1]

2. *Type of fund.* As already indicated, the Social Security Act allows states to develop their own unemployment-compensation systems and permits tax credits for contributions to a state-pooled fund, to separate employer-reserve accounts, or to employers' guaranteed accounts. No further mention will be made of guaranteed employment accounts, for they have been abandoned in all but two states, primarily because of administrative difficulties and disadvantages.[2]

The original Wisconsin law represented a pure employer-reserve

---

[1] *Third Annual Report of the Social Security Board*, 1938, p. 48.

[2] For a discussion of these difficulties, *cf.* R. L. Hibbard, "Guaranteed Employment Plans," *Law and Contemporary Problems*, vol. 3 (January 1936), pp. 89–94.

plan. Under it, each employer's contributions were segregated in separate accounts so that the funds were entirely partitioned into more than 7,000 independent compartments. Not only the worker's job but his unemployment-compensation benefits depended on the fortunes of a single employer hiring as few as eight employees. Insurance is based on the principle of spreading an average risk over a large group. Such an employer-reserve scheme concentrates the worker's risk. Some notion of how this segregation of reserves weakened the unemployment-compensation system may be gained by imagining that the reserves of fire, accident, or life insurance companies were split up into thousands of independent parts. If, for example, the reserves of a fire insurance company were segregated by insuring firms or by areas, the insurance company would be unable to fulfill its promises if a fire loss destroyed one firm or one area, for the reserve covering only the insured firm or area would be too small. Because of the certainty that many employer reserves would become exhausted, the original Wisconsin law provided that unemployed workers under such circumstances would not receive their promised benefits. As a number of employer reserves became exhausted in Wisconsin, the law was amended in 1937 to establish a pooled-fund "balancing account" made up of interest earnings and sums saved from the reserves of disappearing firms. The former employees of firms with used-up accounts can draw their promised benefits from this supplementary pooled fund. In case the "balancing account" becomes low, all covered employers in Wisconsin will be assessed an extra tax to increase it.

The laws of six other states provide for separate employer reserves; but all of them, except Nebraska's, which closely follows the Wisconsin law, require that from 5 to 37 per cent of the regular contributions flow into a supplementary pooled fund designed to protect employees of firms with exhausted reserve accounts. Some of these laws provide that in an emergency the supplementary pooled fund shall receive a larger percentage of the total contributions. Apparently no function or purpose is served by such employer-reserve laws with partial pooling that could not be achieved equally well by experience rating with a fully pooled fund. These states did, however, enjoy Federal-tax credits for state-tax reductions in 1940; whereas, under experience rating in states with pooled funds, Federal credit for such reductions is not possible before 1941 or 1942.

A total of 41 states and the District of Columbia follow private insurance principles and the precedents of foreign compulsory laws by providing for a general pooled fund into which all contributions flow and are commingled. Eligible unemployed in such states are assured of benefits as long as the single pooled fund is not exhausted.

3. *Experience rating.*[1] The laws of most pooled-fund states contain merit- or experience-rating clauses, providing state-tax reductions or exemptions for employers with stable employment records. However, the laws of 12 states with almost two fifths of the employee coverage in the country contain no definite arrangements for experience rating, although most of them provide for a study of its feasibility.

As has been mentioned, Britain and Germany found experience rating either impractical or ineffective. Other European nations do not provide for such discriminating tax differentials under unemployment compensation. Experience rating is a product of American philosophy, especially based on the contentions of a group of Wisconsin economists and executives of large firms that were opposed to compulsory unemployment insurance before the passage of such laws in this country. The main arguments for experience rating have been (1) that it would help to prevent unemployment by encouraging firms to regularize their employment and (2) that it would serve to distribute the "social cost" of unemployment in an equitable manner by placing the burden upon those employers or consumers "responsible" for unemployment. Both of these arguments rest upon the thesis that, in some not fully explained fashion, certain individual employers or consumers are "responsible" for unemployment.

The discussion of the theory of unemployment in Chapter 10 casts grave doubt on the notion that individual employers or consumers are to blame for unemployment and will prevent it if they are taxed in exact proportion to their assumed responsibility. The arguments for experience rating are another example of false reasoning from the particular case to general conclusions in economics. It is reasoned that, if each employer was forced by taxes to main-

---

[1] This subsection rests primarily upon R. A. Lester and Charles V. Kidd, *op. cit.* For a discussion favoring such rating, *cf.* Herman Feldman and Donald M. Smith, *The Case for Experience Rating in Unemployment Compensation and a Proposed Method*, 1939. Available statistical data bearing on the issue is indicated in *Current Experience Rating Research*, Employment Security Memorandum No. 7, Social Security Board, April 1940.

tain his working force intact, every working person would be assured of a job. The difficulty with such reasoning is that unemployment is largely a market phenomenon, tied up with the general rate of spending. Individual employers or consumers have no control over that. Furthermore, employment stability at present levels is no solution to the problem of unemployment. As already explained, the total volume of employment must be expanded rapidly if industry is to absorb 10,000,000 unemployed workers and net additions to the labor supply of 500,000 persons a year. The section in the previous chapter on employment regularization by private firms brought out the possible conflict between individual and social advantage, or between profit considerations and social welfare, in such a situation. With the formation of a growing volume of chronic or hard-core unemployment, the rational policy from a social point of view would be to rotate workers and encourage labor turnover rather than to stimulate employers to maintain an identical group of workers and to keep their working forces at a minimum.

An important issue in the problem of experience rating concerns the kind of employment stability that is to be rewarded. Is the stability to be an expanding one, so that the unemployed will be reabsorbed into industry? The reader will recall that the proposals for incentive taxation discussed in the previous chapter all provide for tax reductions or subsidies to stimulate expansion to full employment. Present provisions for experience rating in state laws, on the other hand, place a premium upon stagnant or static stability instead of rewarding employment. Employers who maintain a fixed working force will qualify for the highest rewards in the form of Federal tax reductions. Certainly on social grounds, the incentive-taxation measures mentioned in the previous chapter seem preferable to experience rating—a type of incentive taxation that encourages the status quo in employment.

The question of how an employer's stability should be measured is involved in this issue of social vs. individual objectives. Should stability and "social costs" be measured by total benefit payments to disemployed workers, by the hours of employment offered, by the number of employees retained, or by the number of separations requiring benefit payments? If the objective is an expanding volume of employment, total hours of employment or total payrolls would be the best measure. If maintenance of the same personnel and a stagnant volume of employment is to be rewarded, then compensable separations or total benefit payments to former employees would be the appropriate measure. Benefit payments and compensable separations are the measuring rods for stability in all our unemployment-compensation laws. Consequently, such experience rating will do little to eliminate unemployment.

One of the reasons for substituting the term "experience rating" for "merit rating" was that employers' tax reductions will depend so much upon luck or circumstance rather than merit. With stability measured by benefit payments, employers in industries close to the consumer will have good ratings without any effort on their part, whereas employers in the capital-goods industries are likely to have poor ratings despite all their efforts. Firms located near expanding labor markets may enjoy a good rating despite large lay-offs, because their workers soon receive new jobs and draw no benefits. In company towns and one-industry areas, on the other hand, most laid-off workers will draw their full benefits. Yet advocates of experience rating claim that equity and justice demand such rate differentiation.

The second principal argument for experience rating centers around the idea that unemployment-compensation benefits are "social costs," which should be reflected in the selling prices of the products. Why, it is asked, should one firm have to pay for the unemployment of other firms? Why not charge those to blame for unemployment with the cost of benefits in proportion to their "responsibility"? Why not make irregular buyers pay for their unsteady spending—or is it employers who are to blame?

An examination of this argument reveals a number of holes. What are the "social costs" of unemployment and how have they been met before? Prior to the enactment of unemployment-compensation laws, the bulk of the cost of unemployment was met partly by individual workers and partly from taxes for relief, which were levied either at a uniform rate or at a progressive rate according to the principle of ability to pay. Experience rating reverses that principle by imposing taxes upon the firms most severely affected by unemployment and by charging the highest tax rates at the bottom of a downswing when most firms are least able to pay.

Are relief costs also social costs? If so, the employer who churns his labor force by dropping some workers and adding others from the relief rolls may reduce relief costs more than he increases benefit payments from the unemployment-compensation fund. What should his experience rating be? Under our present state laws he would have a very poor rating and the heaviest tax, because benefit payments are the only criterion used to measure "social costs"; yet such payments extend for only 15 weeks, and unemployment-compensation laws cover only about one half of the working population. To assess employers' policies by their effects upon benefit payments rather than upon total unemployment and relief is, therefore, to view the problem of unemployment from the knot-hole of unemployment compensation.

Disregarding the fact that benefit payments are but a small portion of the total costs of unemployment, it would be necessary to predict such costs with a high degree of accuracy in order to make each employer pay the full costs of benefit payments to his former employees. Various statistics show that each year about one fifth of all firms discontinue business, and special studies in various cities indicate that half of all firms go out of existence within the first four or five years of operation. Although firms do not have any more work accidents after they go out of business, their workers may later draw unemployment benefits. This factor of high business mortality is especially important in view of the fact that experience rating in unemployment compensation is not on an industry basis or confined to very large firms, as is the case in workmen's compensation (industrial-accident insurance). In workmen's compensation, experience rating generally applies in full only to firms paying annual premiums or payroll taxes of $100,000 or more, which means that they have so many employees that the insurance law of averages operates within the single firm.[1] Under unemployment

---

[1] It is interesting to note that the leading advocates of experience rating are executives in large monopolistic or semimonopolistic enterprises such as utilities or corporations like the General Electric Company and the Eastman Kodak Company, which have patent monopolies. The Kodak Company, for example, makes over five sixths of the photographic film produced in this country and reaped an average profit of over 11 per cent on stockholders' total investment (capital and surplus) during the depression decade of the 1930's. Firms that have a large number of competitors, like soft-coal operators, clothing producers, and building contractors, are exposed to more hazards because they cannot control the market for their products. They are generally opposed to experience rating.

compensation, firms with only one employee will be "experience-rated" in a number of states.

The "social cost" argument for experience rating rests upon the notion that those "responsible" for unemployment will be made to pay for such benefits by differential tax rates. The questionable character of notions of individual responsibility for unemployment in an exchange economy has already been indicated. Assuming the impossible—that the full responsibility for unemployment could somehow be allotted to each person or firm, how could one be certain that each would be taxed in exact proportion to his alleged responsibility? Prices are the same for steady and unsteady buyers. There is no certainty that the burden of the payroll tax would rest upon employers or be shifted through prices to consumers, in line with theoretical notions concerning responsibility. Indeed, tax experts are of the opinion that most of the payroll tax will be shifted to employees in the form of smaller wage payments than would occur without the tax. If that is so, very little of the "social costs" of benefit payments will rest upon those charged with the blame.

Organized labor is strongly opposed to experience rating in unemployment compensation, chiefly because it threatens to reduce total contributions and, therefore, total benefit payments to unemployed workers. A number of states provide for complete tax exemption or reduction to almost zero for employers meeting certain qualifications. Many states provide for tax-rate reductions under 2.7 per cent of payrolls but do not provide for tax-rate increases. The Federal government allows credit only for tax reductions, so that states may fear that they will handicap their employers if tax reductions are counterbalanced by punitive tax increases. Consequently, experience rating is mostly in one direction—downward.

It is especially incongruous to include in the same law provisions for experience rating and for the limitation of benefit payments in seasonal industries to stipulated on-season periods. If employers are exempt from benefit charges during off-season peaks, they will increase seasonal unemployment by concentrating unemployment in such out-of-season periods. A combination of experience rating and benefit limitations in seasonal industries, to be found in over one third of the state laws, certainly will not help to prevent unemployment or even to stabilize it.

The expense and difficulties in administering unemployment compensation will be considerably increased by experience rating. In each state, thousands of employer accounts will have to be kept for firms going into and out of business, merging and splitting up. It is argued that experience rating, to have any economic validity, would have to be based on a complete business cycle. Although most state laws rate firms on the basis of a five-year period, the reader can picture the possible problems in charging all benefits to some employer's account. It is also argued that a tax differential of, say, two per cent of payrolls is too small to have any effect upon employers' policies. In that case, the added administrative expense of charging and rating employers would be a pure waste of money. Wider differentials, although more effective, would only emphasize the adverse effects of experience rating upon unemployment. They would mean further stimulus for employers to keep working forces at a minimum, the concentration of more of the taxes upon firms during depressions instead of prosperous periods, and an increase in the relative burden on the capital-goods industry, which is hardest hit by slumps.

A third, minor argument in favor of merit rating is that it would serve to prevent employers from abusing the unemployment-compensation system. It is, however, difficult to see how employers can, with profit, abuse the system. Most alleged abuses turn out to be perfectly valid uses for unemployment compensation. Some rotation of workers and sharing of work may be socially desirable rather than an abuse of the system. Large pools of labor, partly employed, are characteristic of periods of widespread unemployment and present no problem unless they are causing labor shortages elsewhere. The purpose of unemployment compensation is to pay benefits to eligible persons and not to save money for the fund by causing employers to concentrate all the available work upon a certain group of workers.

4. *Contributions.* As a result of the tax-offset provisions of the Social Security Act [1] and the prevention philosophy behind experience rating, most state laws levy taxes only on employers. Only five states have employee contributions, usually one per cent of wages, and the District of Columbia law provides for a government contribution. Had our states followed European precedent

[1] The Federal tax applies to only the first $3,000 of wages a year to each employee.

and provided for a three-way split of the tax amongst employers, employees, and the state, the demand by large firms for experience rating would have been less loud and effective. It is argued that some government contribution is justified because unemployment compensation reduces the burden of relief costs upon the general taxpayer. Employee contributions are defended on the ground that they stimulate workers' interest in the fund, that the workers benefit from the system, that such contributions help to maintain the self-respect of beneficiaries, and that they permit larger or longer benefits. In opposition to employee contributions, it is stated that workers bear most of the burden of unemployment even with a system of compulsory unemployment insurance, that they are not responsible for unemployment, and that the tax on the employer is largely shifted to them. This last claim raises the whole question of the ultimate incidence of a differentiated tax on employers' payrolls.

As previously stated, most economists believe that ultimately the employers' contributions to social insurance in the form of a wage tax will rest principally or largely upon wage-earners.[1] They conclude that such a tax, by increasing the cost of labor to the employer, will cause wage rates to decline or to rise less rapidly than they would without the tax. This conclusion that payroll taxes result in relatively lower wage rates is, however, based on a number of questionable assumptions. It assumes that in the long run there are no limitations, technical or otherwise, upon the substitution of machinery for men. It assumes that the payroll taxes will not increase the cost of machinery in either the short or the long run. The discussion of "the proportion of productive factors" in Chapter 11 indicates how unreal these assumptions may be. This conclusion regarding the shifting of employers' payroll taxes further assumes that the workers were not being exploited prior to the imposition of the tax or that the tax does not effect the degree of worker exploitation. It also assumes that any unemployment caused by the substitution of machinery for men will result in a comparative re-

[1] Cf., for example, H. G. Brown, "The Incidence of Compulsory Insurance of Workmen," Journal of Political Economy, vol. 30 (February 1922), pp. 67–77; A. C. Pigou, Industrial Fluctuations, 1929, pp. 372–73; A. H. Hansen et al., A Program for Unemployment Insurance and Relief, 1934, p. 49; R. Bauder, "The Probable Incidence of Social Security Taxes," American Economic Review, vol. 26 (September 1936), pp. 463–65; and J. K. Hall, "Incidence of Federal Social Security Pay Roll Taxes," Quarterly Journal of Economics, vol. 53 (November 1938), pp. 61–63.

duction in wage rates. Finally, it assumes that social-insurance programs do not increase the output of workers.

An examination of these assumptions indicates that the economists, in asserting that most of the payroll taxes on employers will eventually be shifted to workers through pay envelopes, are reasoning on the basis of the marginal-productivity theory of wages or an equilibrium analysis which postulates complete mobility of the productive factors. They are arguing that payroll taxes cause no significant increase in employers' total costs per unit of output—at least in the long run. Such an increase in unit costs would, however, occur if the price of machinery rose as a result of increased demand due to substitution of machinery for men or if capital-goods producers themselves could not completely shift the tax through pay envelopes. Of course, to the extent that the tax is shifted to workers through wage payments, there is no reason to fear that a state payroll tax for social insurance would handicap that state's firms in interstate competition. Those who maintain that by far the major portion of the tax is shifted in pay envelopes are really asserting that payroll taxes have little effect upon employers' costs of production.

In so far as the payroll taxes for social security do increase employers' costs of production, their effects and incidence resemble those of a tax that varies with the rate of output. The incidence of such taxes has been analyzed by many tax economists.[1] Whether the firms affected by a payroll tax that increases costs are in industries characterized by monopoly, monopolistic competition, or pure competition, such a tax tends to make it profitable for the employer to reduce his output over a period of time. A monopolist or the producer of a differentiated product, for instance, would generally find that, as a result of the tax, his point of greatest profit would be at a slightly higher price and smaller volume of sales and output. Nevertheless, in such a case the employer's total profit would be somewhat smaller than without the tax. In short, if the tax does increase costs it will be partly shifted to consumers through prices, partly shifted to the employees through pay envelopes, and partly borne by employers in the form of reduced profits.

---

[1] *Cf.*, for example, E. D. Fagan and R. W. Jastram, "Tax Shifting in the Short-Run," *Quarterly Journal of Economics*, vol. 53 (August 1939), pp. 566–73 and 578–85; and Joan Robinson, *Economics of Imperfect Competition*, 1934, pp. 76–82.

The proportion that each of these three groups will bear depends on so many factors that only a few can be mentioned here by way of illustration: the elasticity of demand for the product, price policies in the industry (whether prices are relatively rigid because of government regulation, fear of upsetting established relationships, or for purposes of national advertising), and labor conditions, including union agreements and labor's bargaining strength. In the case of unemployment compensation, some of the same economists who argue that payroll taxes on employers are really paid out of the wages of employees also maintain, with perhaps some inconsistency, that unemployment insurance increases the bargaining strength of labor and causes wage rates to to be higher than they otherwise would be.

Differentiated tax rates under experience rating in unemployment compensation and workmen's compensation add a further complicating factor to the problem of the incidence of payroll taxes for social-security purposes. An employer's tax rate may vary from year to year and may be different from that of his competitors. Also, of course, the percentage that payrolls are of total costs varies from industry to industry and from firm to firm in the same line of business. For these reasons, the burden of the taxes for unemployment compensation upon different firms will be far from proportional or uniform. Under competitive conditions, it is difficult for employers to shift any differential elements in their tax. Even uniform taxes are not readily shifted where prices and wages are rigid and fixed.

5. *Benefits.* The Federal Social Security Act contains no requirements regarding the rate or duration of unemployment benefits. Consequently, benefit provisions vary from state to state. All states provide for a waiting period before an unemployed worker begins to receive benefits. This waiting period is generally either two or three weeks of unemployment in a year, or two weeks in any quarter of a year. After such a period, the unemployed worker is eligible for benefits, if he has earned a minimum amount of wages in covered employment or has worked a minimum number of weeks, if he did not quit his job or was not discharged for misconduct, if he is not jobless due to participation in a labor dispute, and if he has not refused to accept "suitable" employment. These provisions are designed to limit benefit payments and prevent abuses.

All state laws relate benefit payments to a worker's previous wages. In general, the state formulas fix weekly benefits for total unemployment at around 50 per cent of the recipient's full-time wage. This 50-per-cent objective is limited, however, by a specified maximum of $15.00 a week in practically all state laws and a minimum of $5.00 in most states, which favors the lowest paid workers. The District of Columbia law, the only one that provides additional benefits for dependents, permits weekly benefits to reach 65 per cent of normal wages. The aggregate number of weeks an employee may receive benefits is generally determined by his previous earnings during a certain period, usually a year. The duration in most states cannot exceed 14 or 16 weeks in a year, which seems short when compared with 26 weeks of ordinary benefits in Great Britain. Such limitations upon the length of benefit payments to one person are necessary to help preserve the solvency of the fund.

In addition to benefits for total unemployment, most states provide benefits for partial unemployment, when lack of work reduces the worker's weekly earnings to below, say, 60 per cent of normal earnings. Of course, unemployed workers are eligible for such partial benefits only after the waiting period is over. In a majority of the states a person's partial-unemployment benefit is determined by the amount that his actual weekly earnings fall short of 60 per cent of his full-time earnings. They must, of course, be less than $15.00. Experience during 1938 and 1939 indicated that checks for partial-unemployment benefits averaged about one sixth as many in number, and around half as much in dollar amounts, as the checks for total-unemployment benefits. Checks for total-unemployment benefits have averaged from $10.00 to $11.00. More than one out of every nine checks for partial unemployment has been less than $2.00 in amount. The value of such small checks is questionable in view of the fact that total cost of administration represented almost $1.50 per benefit payment in 1938.[1]

More than half of the state laws provide for the classification of seasonal industries with a view to imposing special restrictions upon benefit rights for workers in industries with seasons less than a certain number of weeks. The problem of benefit payments in

---

[1] *Cf.* Walter Matscheck and Raymond C. Atkinson, *Problems and Procedures of Unemployment Compensation in the States*, 1939, p. 9.

off-season periods is especially significant in states like Oregon and Washington, whose chief industries are so subject to seasonal fluctuations. If seasonal workers normally are not employed during off-season periods, it is argued that their unemployment is expected and that benefit payments to them during such off-season periods would cause an unfair drain on the fund. The problem of seasonal workers under unemployment compensation is a difficult one to solve equitably and without considerable administrative difficulty and expense.

6. *Actuarial aspects of state laws.* In order to receive Federal approval, state laws had to provide for two years of contributions before benefit payments began. Consequently, Wisconsin was the only state to pay benefits before 1938, and 17 states did not commence benefit payments until 1939. Because of the business slump in 1937 and early in 1938, benefit payments exceeded contributions in one third of the benefit-paying states during 1938. In that year, for example, benefit payments reduced the reserves accumulated during the previous two years by as much as one third in Maine and one sixth in Michigan.[1] From the point of view of the solvency of the state funds, it is fortunate that benefit payments began in most states at about the bottom of the recession of 1937–1938. Starting at such a low point means that there is not likely to be an excess of benefit payments over contributions that will exhaust accumulated reserves until a period of prosperity and reemployment has intervened.

The Federal government is in no way responsible for the solvency of state unemployment-compensation funds, and the Social Security Act lays down no requirements to assure that state laws are actuarially sound. The actuary of the President's Committee on Economic Security estimated that, during the decade from 1924 through 1933, a contribution rate of three per cent of payrolls would have been necessary in order to maintain the solvency of a national insurance system promising benefits of 50 per cent of wages for 11 weeks after a three-week waiting period.[2] Most of

---

[1] Professor William Haber, former relief administrator in Michigan, has stated that "on the basis of a three per cent tax in states with highly seasonal industries like Michigan, insolvency [of the unemployment-compensation fund] is merely a question of time." Cf. William Haber, *Some Current Problems in Social Security*, Bureau of Industrial Relations, University of Michigan, 1938, p. 9.

[2] Cf. *Social Security in America*, Social Security Board, 1937, pp. 76–88.

our state laws promise a maximum of 15 weeks on a contribution rate of 2.7 per cent.

Since 1936 there has been a tendency for the states to reduce contributions and to increase promised benefits. This tendency seems to arise from a belief that the Federal government will be forced to assist states whose funds become bankrupt and from a feeling of undue optimism as reserves have accumulated because benefit payments commenced at the bottom of a depression period. Five states have repealed provisions for employee contributions; in 1939 the Federal government exempted all yearly wages above $3,000 from the Federal payroll tax and the states have followed suit; and beginning in 1941 or 1942 employers' taxes will be further reduced under the experience-rating provisions of most state laws. It is true that about half of the states with experience rating make reductions depend upon the condition of the state fund; but lower tax rates in good times may necessitate large tax-rate increases under emergency provisions during depressions when payrolls are small. Insurance should spread the risk of unemployment over time as well as space.

The actuarial estimate for the decade prior to 1934 assumed a national system, which would be financially much stronger than state systems, because it would spread the risk of unemployment much wider both industrially and geographically. In a few states one or two firms hire as many as 20 per cent of the workers covered by unemployment compensation. In some states unemployment amongst the compensable labor force was twice as severe during the early 1930's as it was in other states. The states with employer-reserve laws subdivide the risk within the state and provide for only a small supplementary pooled fund. All such division and subdivision weakens the financial strength of unemployment-compensation funds.

Experience with unemployment insurance abroad and with private unemployment-insurance plans in this country shows a definite tendency to promise more benefits than the fund can provide during periods of severe depression. Foreign systems, especially the British, have tended to become insolvent because of legislative action granting unexpected and unwarranted extensions of unemployment insurance to ineligible workers who should have been provided for under a supplementary system of relief. In order to preserve solvency, it is necessary to recognize that only a limited amount of unemployment can be handled by the insurance method. Recognizing the need for preserving a long-run balance between contributions and benefits, Great Britain in 1934 established a statutory committee of experts on unemployment insurance to report each year on the financial condition of the fund and to suggest any changes necessary to preserve its solvency. If we are to maintain the present cumbersome and lax method of tax-offset with state laws, some such committee should be established in this country, along with a Federal reinsurance plan to make loans or grants to funds of approved states which are threatened with insolvency.

Relation to relief. In restoring unemployment insurance to an actuarial basis in 1934, Great Britain also provided for a national system of unemployment relief for workers whose insurance rights are exhausted and for those who are not covered by insurance but are available for employment in the insured trades. Previous experience in Britain had demonstrated that persons excluded from unemployment-insurance benefits become pressure groups whose demands for benefits under the system weaken its actuarial basis. It was hoped that such demands could be forestalled by a supplementary relief program financed mostly from national funds, supervised by a central nonpolitical authority, and granting relief according to fairly uniform standards throughout the country after an investigation to determine family needs.

In this country, too, a satisfactory program of unemployment relief will undoubtedly be necessary in order to prevent a similar weakening of the actuarial basis of unemployment insurance. From 40 to 50 per cent of the gainfully employed persons in the United States are not eligible for unemployment insurance, and must therefore depend upon relief if they are out of work and in need. Even workers who qualify for benefits may have to rely upon relief after they have received their 16 weekly insurance payments. A few families whose needs are great have been forced to apply for relief while receiving, or waiting for, insurance benefits. It would aid in protecting the insurance system if its coverage were extended to include more of the wage-earning population and if the length of benefit payments could be increased to 20 or 26 weeks. Despite such measures, many employees would exhaust their bene-

fit rights in a depression of long duration and would be forced to
fall back upon relief.

During the late 1930's, however, the problem in this country was
not so much to protect the insurance program as to prevent it from
suffering in comparison with WPA employment. Workers eligible
for benefits were reluctant to leave WPA jobs, which assured them
larger and longer income payments than they would receive under
unemployment compensation. In Pennsylvania early in 1938, for
example, average unemployment-compensation benefits for the
same group of families were 30 per cent above home-relief grants,
but average WPA earnings were about 30 per cent larger than
such compensation benefits.[1] In some states the unemployment-
compensation agencies advised WPA workers not to leave their
jobs in order to file claims for unemployment compensation. The
exact relationships between unemployment compensation and a
large-scale program of work relief still have to be worked out.
Should persons eligible for unemployment benefits be permitted to
work on relief projects? Should work-relief jobs be considered
"suitable employment" requiring acceptance or forfeit of benefit
rights?

Railroad Unemployment Insurance Act of 1938. In the middle
of 1939, employees on interstate railroads were excluded from the
coverage of state laws, and benefit payments commenced under a
national system of unemployment insurance covering about 1,800,-
000 railroad employees.[2] This system will be much more simple
to administer than our state laws. It calls for a uniform three-per-
cent tax on employers' payrolls instead of experience rating for individual employers. No duplicate state-Federal taxes are required.
Benefits are on a daily, not a weekly, basis, so the problem of partial
unemployment is eliminated. There are six classes of benefits at
25-cent intervals from $1.75 to $3.00 a day. Instead of gauging
benefits to 50 per cent of full-time earnings, they are heavily
weighted in favor of the lower paid workers. The length of benefit
payments is not related to previous wages, so that all workers who
qualify for benefits may receive them for 80 days in a year (roughly

---

[1] Ewan Clague, "The Relationship Between Unemployment Compensation and
Relief from a National Point of View," *Social Security Bulletin*, vol. 1 (June 1938), p. 13.
[2] *Cf.* Murray W. Latimer, "The Security Programs for Railroad Workers," in
Social Security in the United States, 1939, American Association for Social Security, Inc.,
1939, p. 57.

equivalent to 16 weeks of five days). This national system avoids the problems connected with the interstate migration of workers, although there is a problem of interindustry migration and also the problem of the operation of employment exchanges for offering "suitable employment" to beneficiaries or for making placements outside the railroad industry.

The withdrawal of the railroad workers from the coverage of state unemployment-compensation laws further threatens the solvency of some state funds and makes many states still less economic units for administration. This will be especially true in states like Nevada and Montana, where railroad employment represented a sizeable proportion of the total coverage of the state law and the railroads are one of the most steady industries of the state.

Alternatives to the present Federal-state system. In drafting legislation for unemployment insurance in this country, three alternative programs were considered: (1) a compulsory national system; (2) a Federal subsidy, financed by a payroll tax, for all benefits under state laws; and (3) the tax-offset method of credits for taxes paid under state laws, together with a Federal subsidy for state administration. The technical experts and the Advisory Council of the Committee on Economic Security favored the second method of subsidies or grants-in-aid for state benefits, but the tax-offset method was adopted for constitutional and strategic reasons.

Abroad there has been a definite trend toward centralization and the development of national social-insurance systems. A national system of unemployment compensation would have a number of advantages in this country. Like the national program for the railroads, it would not require duplicate taxes and numerous reports under varying state laws for firms operating in many states; it would provide uniform protection for employees in all states; and it would eliminate the troublesome problem of interstate migration of workers. Some migratory workers move so much that they cannot qualify for benefits under any state laws.

A Federal plan would reduce administrative costs, because many states are not economical or distinct units. Seven states alone contain over half the employees covered in this country. A national system would be actuarially sounder because it would spread the risk over the whole country, thereby affording greater protection to workers in small or one-industry states. It would eliminate fears of handicapping firms in interstate competition even with provisions for experience rating. Under present arrangements, states cannot grant workers adequate benefits without levying taxes that may cause fears that some industry will migrate from the state. A national program would also provide more uniformity in judicial decisions regarding claims for benefits or "suitable employment" and would yield comparable national statistics through uniform national standards. Finally, it would facilitate the development of a definite national relief policy so that insurance might be integrated with relief.

A plan of full Federal subsidy under state laws stands midway between a national system and the tax-offset program. It, therefore, enjoys a number of the advantages mentioned for an exclusively national plan. A subsidy or grants-in-aid system would eliminate the duplicate taxes and tax organizations, might help to spread the risk over areas larger than a single state, and would facilitate the maintenance of higher and more uniform standards without fear of interstate competition or migration of industry. Such a system would leave the way open for the use of other sources of revenue than a payroll tax and would permit the establishment of a national reinsurance fund for aiding the states most severely affected by unemployment. On the other hand, it would preserve the inefficient administrative units of the states and might, like the present subsidy for state administration, lead to waste and abuse.

This discussion of the advantages of alternative methods of unemployment compensation really amounts to a criticism of present arrangements. It brings out the basic weaknesses of the present system: failure to provide adequate benefits, lack of sufficient standards, absence of provisions to protect the solvency of insurance funds, cumbersome and costly administrative arrangements, and the pursuit of undesirable objectives under experience rating.

CHAPTER SEVENTEEN

THE OLD–AGE PROBLEM

The effect of age upon earnings is of primary importance to employees who depend upon the sale of their labor for a living. It is important not only to middle-aged and elderly employees but also to young workers who may have to shoulder a large part of a mounting burden of old-age dependency.

The figures for employed workers cited in Chapter 8 from the 1934 census in Michigan indicate that the annual earnings of manual workers begin to decline after they pass 40 years of age, of clerical workers after they reach 45, and of professional workers after 50. For employed women, the peak of earning power was 30 years of age in Michigan. The wage statistics of 30,000,000 workers taxed under the Federal Old-Age Benefits program in 1937 confirm the results of the Michigan census. They show that male workers in the 40–44 age group had the highest median and average wages for 1937 and that female employees in the 30–34 age group enjoyed the highest median earnings, although the 40 44 group had the highest average female earnings.[1] The earnings of male workers in the 60–64 age group were from 15 to 20 per cent below those of workers 20 years younger. Wage statistics for European countries evidence the same general pattern for various age groups.[2] The statistics for earnings at various ages are, of course, affected by unemployment and partial employment, which tend to be more prevalent in the higher age groups.

There is a direct relationship between the problem of old-age dependency and unemployment, for unemployment not only eats up any savings, but also affects older workers more severely than workers from 25 to 40 years of age. That the incidence of unem-

[1] Max J. Wasserman and Katherine D. Wood, "Age and Sex Differentials in Taxable Wages Reported for 1937," *Social Security Bulletin*, vol. 2 (June 1939), p. 11.

[2] *Cf.* "Problem of the Older Worker in the United States and Europe," *Monthly Labor Review*, vol. 48 (February 1939). pp. 264–65.

ployment has been especially high for workers 55 and over was brought out in Table 25. For instance, in this country in 1937 over 22 per cent of the male nonfarm workers in their late 50's were totally unemployed compared with a figure of 14 per cent for workers in their 30's.[1] In this chapter it will be necessary to examine the reasons for this discrimination against middle-aged and elderly workers in the labor market.

At the same time that industrial practices and policies have been reducing new employment opportunities for workers over 45 or 50, the proportion of the population in the upper-age groups has been increasing and will continue to increase for a number of decades. The ratio of persons 65 or over to total gainful workers was about one to ten in 1900 and one to seven in 1935. It is estimated that by 1970 there will be one such aged person to every four workers. Since aged nonworkers must be supported from the product of active workers, the economic importance of our old-age problem is apparent. The increase in the average age of the population and in the length of life of workers constitutes one of the major economic and social problems facing this country.

OLDER WORKERS IN MODERN INDUSTRY

In order to appreciate various aspects of the old-age problem it is necessary to understand the full significance of certain facts concerning our population and the policies of large corporations.

We grow older. A century ago the average length of life in America was less than 40 years. Today it is almost 60 years. Many factors, especially progress in medicine and health protection, are responsible for this advance in longevity. Along with an increase in the average length of life, there has been a decline in the birth rate and a sharp reduction in the number of immigrants, of whom roughly nine tenths were under 40 years of age. Consequently, the median age of the American people has risen from 16.7 years in 1820 to 26.4 years in 1930. Our total population has literally been growing older and will continue to do so for the next 40 years. Although only one eighth of our population was over 45 years of

---

[1] *Census of Partial Employment, Unemployment and Occupations: 1937*, vol. 4, 1938, p. 50. The differential between the percentage of young and of old workers unemployed is greater for men than for women.

age in 1850, it is estimated that by 1980 almost two fifths of all Americans will be 45 or over.[1] In 1850 only 2.6 per cent of the population was 65 or over. By 1930 the figure was 5.4 per cent, and by 1980, according to recent estimates, it will be about 15 per cent. Men who reach 65 live, on the average, 11 or 12 years longer, and women, about 14 years longer.

This age shift in our population is causing more of our economic activity to be directed to meet the needs and tastes of middle-aged and elderly persons. That change in the direction of economic activities has been even more evident abroad where declining birth and mortality rates have resulted in a higher average age for the population than in America. Table 30 shows the percentage of middle-aged and elderly persons in various countries in the early 1920's.

TABLE 30. DISTRIBUTION OF TOTAL POPULATION BY AGE GROUPS IN CERTAIN COUNTRIES [2]

Country and date	Percentage 40 years and over	Percentage 60 years and over
France (1921)	39.1	13.8
England and Wales (1921)	32.4	9.6
Sweden (1920)	31.7	12.2
Germany (1925)	31.3	9.2
Australia (1921)	27.3	7.4
United States (1920)	26.8	7.4

The killing of soldiers in the second World War that broke out in 1939 has undoubtedly raised the proportion of elderly persons in the total population of the warring countries.

Employment problems of older workers. Independent enterprisers, such as farmers, shopkeepers, and artisans, can continue to support themselves until very late in life, because they can work at their own pace. In large-scale industry, however, the machine sets the pace, and workers who cannot maintain that pace may be a liability rather than an asset. Consequently, with the change from a rural, small-scale economy to mass-production industry, the work opportunities for aging workers have been reduced. Although from 1890 to 1930 the median age of the gainfully employed males rose

[1] W. S. Thompson and P. K. Whelpton, *Population Trends in the United States*, 1933, pp. 109–10.

[2] Warren S. Thompson, "Population," *American Journal of Sociology*, vol. 34 (March 1929), p. 965.

from 32.9 to 37.4 years (24.2 to 30.1 years for females), the percentage of all men 65 or over who were gainfully employed dropped from 73.8 to 58.3 per cent during that 40-year period. In short, the working population was getting older, yet the proportion of the population in the 65-and-over group at work declined more than 20 per cent prior to the depression of the 1930's.

Unemployment aggravates the employment problem of older workers, because the hiring-age limit for workers who lose their jobs has been ebbing back into the 50's and even the 40's. A number of recent studies illustrate the plight of the worker past 45 who finds himself unemployed.

Relief statistics reveal that a disproportionate number of the workers from 55 to 64 years old have been on the relief rolls and that reemployment rates for relief clients decrease sharply with the age of the workers. As many as 31.4 per cent of the workers certified for WPA jobs in November 1937 were from 55 to 64 years of age, compared with 25.8 per cent for all gainful workers in the 1930 census.[1] A survey of the reemployment of relief workers in 13 cities during 1935 revealed that the reemployment rates for workers on relief in the 25–34 age group were over twice as high as for workers in the 45–54 age group, and over three times as high as for workers in the 55–64 age group.[2] A study of workers separated from WPA employment in nine areas in 1937 showed that those who found jobs with private industry were, on the average, 10 years younger than the workers who continued on the WPA rolls.[3]

The effect of age on employability is further indicated by statistics of the duration of employment by age groups. The sample survey of unemployment in Philadelphia in 1937 revealed that the median length of unemployment since the last relief job was four years for unemployed workmen in the 60–64 age group, compared with under two years for unemployed workmen in their early 30's.[4] Similar figures for duration of unemployment by age groups in

[1] R. Nassimbene, *Age of WPA Workers, November 1937*, Works Progress Administration, Division of Social Research, 1938, p. 7.

[2] F. L. Carmichael and R. Nassimbene, *Changing Aspects of Urban Relief*, Works Progress Administration, 1939, p. 77.

[3] V. E. Roberts, *Survey of Workers Separated from WPA Employment in Nine Areas, 1937*, Works Progress Administration, 1938, p. 6.

[4] M. W. Bell and G. L. Palmer, *Employment and Unemployment in Philadelphia in 1936 and 1937, Part 2: May 1937*, Works Progress Administration, November 1938, p. 80.

Philadelphia in 1938 were even more unfavorable for older workers.[1] Such long-time unemployment, by tending to decrease employability, served as an additional handicap for older workers in their search for new jobs.

Various studies indicate that changes in industry and in employer policies have made it increasingly difficult for middle-aged men and women to find reemployment, yet it is during the middle years of life that workers, as breadwinners for the family, have the heaviest responsibilities. Indeed, with longer periods of education for children, family responsibilities have been increasing as new employment opportunities for middle-aged workers have been decreasing. The statistics of the United States Employment Service for placements per 100 applicants show that the chances of workers over 40 receiving regular jobs in private industry have been less than half as great as those of workers under 40.[2] Age apparently is a greater handicap in unskilled than in skilled and professional work. Youthful employees seem to be especially required for the manual work of a less skilled nature in large factories. Generally speaking, the downhill road of employability in modern industry seems to begin at about age 45 for men, and five or ten years earlier for women.

1. *Hiring-age limits in industry.* A number of studies have been made of hiring-age limits in American industry. Between 1929 and 1931 a series of surveys in New York, Maryland, California, and Illinois, and also for manufacturing establishments throughout the country, revealed that from 28 to 40 per cent of all employees in the concerns studied were employed by firms having definite maximum age limits above which new employees were not hired.[3]

---

[1] G. L. Palmer, *Employment and Unemployment in Philadelphia, July–August 1938*, University of Pennsylvania, Industrial Research Department, Philadelphia, August 1939, p. 51. A study of workers in 13 cities showed a progressive increase in the duration of unemployment with increasing age. *Cf.* Carmichael and Nassimbene, *Changing Aspects of Urban Relief*, p. 78.

[2] *Cf. Report of Joint Legislative Committee on Discrimination in Employment of the Middle Aged*, State of New York, Legislative Document No. 77, 1939, pp. 24–27; and "Young and Old at the Employment Office," *Monthly Labor Review*, vol. 46 (January 1938), pp. 9–10.

[3] For a list of these studies, *cf.* Solomon Barkin, *The Older Worker in Industry*, Report to Joint Legislative Committee on Unemployment Prepared under the Auspices of New York State Commission on Old Age Security, 1933, p. 225. *Cf.* also Barkin, pp. 190–95; *Monthly Labor Review*, vol. 28 (May 1929), p. 1024, and vol. 35 (November 1932), pp. 1009–10; and Millis and Montgomery, *Labor's Risks and Social Insurance*, 1938, p. 358.

Although the hiring-age limits ranged from 30 to 65, the most common maximum was 45 years for unskilled and semiskilled workers and 50 years for skilled workers. Later surveys show that discrimination against older workers continued throughout the 1930's, although employers were less ready to admit that they had definite maximum hiring ages. For example, some 4,000 answers to questionnaires sent out by the National Association of Manufacturers revealed that 43 per cent of all reporting companies gave preference to workers under 40 in hiring new employees, though less than 8 per cent of all reporting firms admitted that they had established a maximum age limit.[1] These surveys are, of course, subject to the limitation that they depend upon the statements of employers, who may consciously or unconsciously prefer younger job applicants without admitting it.[2]

Age restrictions upon new workers have developed, for the most part, since the first World War; but they were found on the railroads at the beginning of this century. Fixed hiring limits have been especially characteristic of public utilities and large corporations. Age is less likely to be a determining factor in small concerns, where aging workers can often continue on their regular work at a somewhat slower pace. At public hearings on discrimination against older workers in Massachusetts industry in the Fall of 1935, it was found that "complaints of discrimination were least in occupations where there were strong unions and relatively stable working forces," and greatest where the work was seasonal or temporary, so that there were frequent separations and rehirings.[3] Study of individual establishments in Massachusetts disclosed wide variations in the employment of older workers in the same or comparable work, indicating that "apparently adjustments could be made in many establishments without sacrifice of efficiency if they were demanded by public opinion or by seniority regulations of strong trade unions."[4]

[1] *Workers over 40*, National Association of Manufacturers, December 1938, p. 52. *Cf.* also F. Beatrice Brower, *Personnel Policies Governing Factory and Office Administration*, National Industrial Conference Board, 1937, p. 25.

[2] A thorough survey of older workers in Massachusetts in 1935 revealed that "a large number of employers explicitly reported that they used no maximum hiring-age limits, whereas further investigation showed that many of them actually did have such limits, often without realizing it." *Cf.* "Causes of Discrimination Against Older Workers," *Monthly Labor Review*, vol. 46 (May 1938), p. 1139.

[3] Lucile Eaves, "Discrimination in the Employment of Older Workers in Massachusetts," *Monthly Labor Review*, vol. 44 (June 1937), pp. 1362–63.

[4] *Ibid.*, p. 1371.

2. *Reasons for discrimination against older workers.* The various factors that have tended to foster age discrimination in hiring (not in
firing) workers may be grouped under the following four headings:
(1) physical and mental characteristics of older workers affecting
their efficiency and adaptability; (2) promotion and training policies of employers along with lower wages for younger workers; (3)
higher costs of industrial insurance rates under private pension
plans, group life insurance, and workmen's compensation; and (4)
public demand for younger workers in certain occupations. The
importance of these factors varies from one occupation to another
and, as will be indicated presently, some of the reasons given by
employers for preferring younger workers are of questionable
validity.

(1) The physiological efficiency of the average person apparently
begins to decline in the late forties. A series of tests made in Germany on unskilled workers showed that sensory and mental alert-
ness and physical dexterity commence to decline after age 45.[1] On
routine work the output of workmen from 45 to 60 years of age
was equal to that of younger men, but the older workers showed
less adaptability to changes in industrial methods and techniques.
Consequently, it is possible for the worker's productivity to keep
up if he grows old in the same job, whereas it might be low for a
new job. That may be one of the reasons why the period of peak
output apparently continues to a more advanced age for some
skilled workers than for unskilled workers in general.[2]

Without doubt the mechanization of industry has handicapped
the older worker by reducing the industrial value of experience,
good judgment, and quality in output. In some cases, mechanization has also tended to put a premium upon physical endurance,
speed, and ability to stand nervous strain. Middle-aged and aged
workers may be less able to stand the pace set by high-speed machinery, because their reflexes have begun to slow down. This is
likely to be true in large-scale mass production.

(2) In order to stimulate employee morale many firms, especially
large corporations, fill vacancies by promotions within the company whenever possible, leaving for outside job-seekers only the

[1] "Problem of the Older Worker in the United States and Europe," *Monthly Labor
Review*, vol. 48 (February 1939), p. 293.
[2] *Ibid.*, p. 264.

lower paid, elementary jobs which are generally filled by youths just out of school. Where apprenticeship and training are required to fit new employees for their jobs, young workers may be preferred because they have a longer working life ahead of them. Where the job requires agility and manual dexterity, as in the weaving trades, it may be very difficult even to train workers over 30 or 40 years of age.[1] Not only can younger workers usually be trained more readily, but they can generally be hired at a lower wage than older workers, who may have heavy family responsibilities and a training rendered obsolete by technological change.

(3) In the past, employers have frequently stated as an important reason for refusing to hire older workers that they would increase the employer's costs under group life insurance, workmen's compensation, or private retirement programs. At the beginning of 1939 there were over 8,000,000 workers covered by group life policies and about 4,000,000 workers covered by private pension plans. Most of American industry is subject to workmen's or industrial-accident compensation.

A New York committee studying employment discrimination against middle-aged workers found that employers gave "as their reason more often than any other, that compensation rates were increased by the employment of middle-aged persons." [2] Upon investigation the committee found that age had nothing to do with rate-making under workmen's compensation, that "the complaint advanced by employers that the older worker has an undue number of accidents is without foundation," and that the older worker is likely to "prove less expensive from the standpoint of accident cost than the younger men." [3] Various statistical studies here and abroad indicate that the frequency of accidents reaches a maximum between the ages of 20 and 30, apparently because of inexperience, and falls steadily thereafter.[4] The number of severe accidents may, however, be higher among older workers. These opposite trends offset each other so that the net cost of workmen's compen-

---

[1] Cf. "Causes of Discrimination against Older Workers, "Monthly Labor Review, vol. 46 (May 1938), p. 1141.

[2] Report of Joint Legislative Committee on Discrimination in Employment of the Middle Aged, State of New York, Legislative Document No. 77, 1939, p. 29.

[3] Ibid., pp. 30, 33–34.

[4] Cf. ibid., p. 56; "Problem of the Older Worker in the United States and Europe," op. cit., pp. 265–66; and "Age Factor in Industrial Accidents," Monthly Labor Review, vol. 35 (October 1932), pp. 844–45.

sation apparently is about the same for younger as for older workers. Although the belief of employers that the hiring of older workers
would increase their compensation costs appears to be unfounded,
it nevertheless diminishes the employment opportunities of older
workers seeking jobs.

Premiums for group life insurance do vary with the average age
of the working force, but employees generally pay from two thirds
to three fourths of the cost of such group protection, which averages
about one per cent of payrolls, so the employer's share is too small
to have any appreciable effect upon his costs. The effect of private
pension plans upon the hiring of older workers should be of little
significance now that benefits are being paid under the old-age and
survivors insurance program of the Federal government. Employers
with pension plans supplementing the Federal benefits need not
hesitate to hire older workers for fear of being criticized if such
workers are retired at 65 with only a small company pension.
Most older workers will be eligible for a basic Federal pension.

(4) It is claimed that the public prefers younger people for positions such as waitresses, ushers, stenographers, store clerks, and
office workers who meet customers. How strong and widespread
such preferences may be is not known.

The problem of employment for middle-aged and elderly workers
who lose their jobs because of depressions, business failures, or
industrial change promises to be increasingly serious as the average
age of the working population rises and industry becomes more
mechanized and organized along mass-production lines. The trend
seems to be away from the old-line skilled crafts and small independent enterprise, which enabled older workers to make quality
products and, thus, to continue to earn their own way until late in
life.

The premature superannuation of workers in modern industry
is another illustration of the fact that the market may not lead to
the best solution in labor problems. The employment policies of
firms may lead to a conflict between the interests of individual employers and those of society in general. If employers are free to
select workers as they see fit, society may suffer a severe loss from
the permanent unemployment of middle-aged workers whose children are in their high-school or college years. Public officials,
especially in England and America, have recently attempted to

bring to public attention the fact that the discrimination against older workers is largely unjustified and, in the long run, may be injurious to the interests of industry as a whole.

In a report in May 1939, the Committee on Employment Problems of Older Workers, appointed by the Secretary of Labor, concluded that "there is little significant relationship between age and costs, and that the prejudice against hiring older workers rests largely on inadequate and erroneous impressions." [1] The committee went on to say that "employees themselves can help to break down the prejudices against older workers, and that in some instances the problem has been successfully dealt with through [trade] union contracts." [2]

In 1937 Massachusetts passed a law declaring it to be against public policy to dismiss or refuse to employ any person between 45 and 65 because of his or her age. The act relies upon public opinion for enforcement by providing that the names of employers guilty of nonobservance may be published in the press.

OLD-AGE ASSISTANCE

The previous discussion of industrial and population trends indicates the significance of the question of old-age security. The remainder of this chapter deals primarily with methods for meeting the problem of old-age dependency, such as special old-age relief or assistance, including schemes like the Townsend Old-Age Pension Plan, and programs for compulsory old-age insurance financed largely by contributions from employers and employees. The recent political pressure for free public pensions arose in the 1930's largely because many elderly people lost their savings and their jobs in those years and because many firms discriminated against older workers in the labor market.

Extent of old-age dependency. The Committee on Economic Security estimated in 1935, before the Social Security Act was passed, that at least one half of the 7,500,000 people then over 65 years of age were dependent upon others for their support—over 1,000,000 were receiving emergency relief or state old-age assistance; 150,000 were receiving industrial or trade-union pensions; and the

---

[1] *The Older Worker*, Report of Committee on Employment Problems of Older Workers to the Secretary of Labor, May 15, 1939, p. 3.
[2] *Ibid.*, pp. 7–8.

major cost of supporting the remaining 2,000,000 was being borne by children, other relatives, and friends.[1] The Social Security Board estimated that on January 1, 1940 as many as 31 per cent of all persons 65 or over were wholly or partly dependent upon public or private aid, that 27 per cent were dependent upon children and other relatives, and that the remaining 42 per cent were supporting themselves from savings, earnings, annuities, private pensions, or the income of the husband or wife.[2] These figures, however, fail to reveal the unfortunate effects that such dependency can have upon persons who were formerly self-supporting.

State legislation prior to the Social Security Act. That the problem of old-age security has only recently received widespread public recognition is indicated by the fact that the first effective state law for old-age assistance or free pensions to the needy aged was passed in 1923. By 1928 such laws were in effect in six states, but only 1,500 old persons were receiving public old-age assistance at the end of that year. The depression, however, rapidly changed the situation. At the end of 1932 the number of recipients of old-age assistance had increased to over 100,000 in 16 states. The average monthly grant per old-age client in 1932 was $20.78, but the restricting effect of the depression upon state and local budgets caused this monthly average grant to decline to $14.53 per person in 1934, when 235,000 persons were receiving old-age assistance under 27 state laws.[3] In 1934 the average monthly grant in North Dakota was 69 cents, and in Nebraska $1.22, per person. The situation was again changed in 1935 by the passage of the Social Security Act with its provisions for a Federal subsidy to approved state programs of old-age assistance.

Prior to the enactment of the Social Security Act, most of these state laws provided that old-age assistance was available only to persons of 65 or 70 with a record of long residence in the state, without sufficient means to support themselves, and with no children or relatives financially able to support them. Assistance grants were made only after investigation of the means at the disposal of

[1] Committee on Economic Security, *Report to the President*, 1935, p. 24.

[2] *Hearings on H. R. 6635, Social Security Act Amendments*, before the Committee on Finance, United States Senate, 76th Congress, first session, 1939, p. 22.

[3] These figures have been taken from a statistical summary of the development of old-age assistance in "Progress of Old-Age Assistance in the United States, 1936 and 1937," *Monthly Labor Review*, vol. 46 (June 1938), p. 1351.

aged persons and their needs. The grants, financed from general tax monies or from the proceeds of special taxes, might vary from month to month. Such old-age assistance resembled emergency relief. Indeed, in 1935 almost five times as many persons over 65 were receiving emergency relief as were receiving old-age assistance under state laws. The old-age-assistance provisions of the Social Security Act were designed to shift these needy aged from emergency relief to assistance and to encourage some uniformity in such assistance throughout the country. Too much emphasis, however, continues to be placed on cash grants, and too little upon other matters such as medical care and creative or recreational activities.

Old-age assistance under the Social Security Act. As a means of stimulating the desired state legislation, the Social Security Act provides for a Federal subsidy to approved state old-age assistance programs. The Federal government matches state grants to "needy aged individuals" on a 50–50 basis up to $20 a month of Federal money per recipient. The Federal subsidy to state plans is also increased by an additional five per cent to provide funds toward the administrative costs. No special taxes are levied by the Social Security Act to provide funds for this Federal subsidy.

By 1937 all the states were operating plans for old-age assistance that were approved by the Social Security Board. The range in the size of grants and in the number of recipients per 100 persons 65 or over, however, continued to vary widely from one state to another. In 1940 the average monthly grant throughout the country was between $19 and $20 to almost 2,000,000 recipients of old-age assistance. In eight states the average grant exceeded $25 a month, and in eight other states it was under $10 a month. In two states, half or more of the persons 65 or over were receiving old-age assistance, while in three states not one out of ten persons who had reached 65 was receiving assistance grants. Such divergence has in part been due to state and local politics. The Social Security Board, after public hearings, has found it necessary to suspend the Federal subsidy for a period of time in three states because of political or incompetent administration. The provision that after June 1941 the state agency must, "in determining need, take into consideration any other income and resources of an individual claiming old-age assistance" may lead to more withdrawals of Federal funds from offending states.

The present cost of old-age assistance to the Federal government and the states is about $500,000,000 a year. The experience of Canada and European countries indicates that the total of old-age assistance grants tends to expand as the number of aged persons increases and as such assistance becomes more respectable, with more people accepting it. Actuaries have estimated that, without a contributory system of old-age insurance, the total cost of old-age assistance might reach $2,000,000,000 or $2,500,000,000 by 1980.[1] Such a sum would constitute a real burden upon Federal and state budgets and taxpayers. One argument for an old-age insurance system is that it shifts part of this prospective burden to the beneficiaries and their employers.

Comparison with old-age insurance. The Committee on Economic Security, commissioned to draft a program for social security, decided that a part of the threatening burden of old-age dependency could be prevented by a compulsory Federal system of old-age insurance. In establishing such a plan, the Federal government would simply be following the example of a number of private concerns which, for some time, had been operating systems of old-age annuities as a means of safeguarding their retired employees from dependency and poverty. According to the estimates of the Committee's actuaries, such a contributory system of old-age insurance covering half of the gainfully employed persons in the country would, by 1980, cause the old-age assistance burden on the general taxpayer to be less than two fifths the amount it would otherwise reach by that date.[2] This estimated reduction of over 60 per cent in the assistance burden upon the general taxpayer helps to explain why many wealthy persons supported the proposal for a compulsory system of old-age insurance for retired workers. A compulsory system is necessary because private insurance companies cannot hope to sell many annuities to wage-earners on a commercial basis.

Most countries have adopted some combination or mixture of the contributory insurance and noncontributory assistance approaches to the old-age security problem. Generally speaking, a pure contributory plan is too restricted in coverage to meet the entire old-age problem, and an extensive assistance program by

---

[1] *Cf.*, for example, Committee on Economic Security, *Report to the President*, 1935, p. 28.

[2] *Idem.*

itself tends eventually to put too great a burden upon the public treasury. For example, Great Britain in 1925, after 17 years of old-age assistance, found it necessary to establish a plan of contributory insurance. In some countries, like Great Britain, France, and the United States, the two systems exist side by side.

Contributory insurance systems are almost always restricted to employees, often to employees in certain industries. The wage contract simplifies the collection of contributions, the keeping of records, and the calculation of benefits. Under insurance, the monthly benefits, which are related to previously taxed wages, are paid as a matter of right to eligible workers who have reached a certain age. They are paid regardless of the beneficiary's income from other sources. In part, old-age insurance represents a compulsory savings arrangement whereby the employee, his employer, and perhaps the state contribute toward an old-age annuity for the employee.

The coverage of noncontributory assistance is broader, for it is not limited to employees, but is available also to needy aged who have been self-employed, or housewives, or nonworkers. Based on need as gauged by a family or individual budget, it is not related to past earnings and may vary from month to month instead of following a definitely prescribed schedule as insurance benefits do. The liberality of old-age assistance depends upon the determination of need—upon how much of the property and income of the recipient or his relatives is exempt—and upon the adequacy of the grants. When the two systems exist side by side, they are, in a sense, in competition with one another. If old-age assistance grants are as large or nearly as large as the insurance benefits, the contributory insurance system is likely to become discredited and unpopular. If large gratuitous pensions are granted under old-age assistance, subject to no restrictions except age, a compulsory old-age insurance system loses its purpose and becomes ineffectual.

The Townsend Old-Age Pension Plan. At one time in the middle 1930's, the Townsend pension movement apparently had a dues-paying membership of about 3,500,000 persons. The plan they were supporting has, from time to time, varied in its details. Essentially, it involves large monthly pensions for all persons who have reached 60 years of age, to be financed by a Federal transactions tax on every sale of goods, property, or services, including labor services. The goal of the original plan was a pension of $200 a month. In order to qualify for such a pension, the person 60 years or over would have to be an American citizen, to retire from gainful employment, to guarantee to spend the whole monthly pension within 30 days, and, in some versions, to have an income under $2,400 a year. It has been estimated that at least 10,500,000 persons would have qualified for such a $200 pension in 1935, at a total estimated cost of $25,000,000,000 a year.[1] By 1945 the estimated cost reaches $32,000,000,000 because of the increase in the aged population. For pensions of $100 monthly, more than 9,000,-000 persons with incomes under $1,200 a year would have qualified in 1935, at a total cost of around $11,000,000,000.[2]

The economic significance of pensions of $2,400 or even $1,200 a year to persons of 60 or over may be indicated by a few comparative figures. In the prosperous year of 1929 the average income per person was about $750 a year. The national income was around $80,000,000,000 in 1929 and $55,000,000,000 in 1935, so $25,000,-000,000 of pensions a year would mean that 9 per cent of the population would receive a total of gratuitous payments amounting to 31 per cent of the national income in 1929 and 45 per cent of the national income in 1935. Even the yearly total of $11,000,-000,000 for pensions of $100 monthly per person ($200 per couple) is as much as the total receipts or payments of interest and dividends in 1929 and more than the total of interest, dividends, royalties, and net rents in 1935.

The Townsend Plan originally called for a tax of two per cent on each transaction or sale—there might be five transactions in the process of production from raw material to finished product—but it soon became evident that the tax rate would have to be higher in order to raise $25,000,000,000 a year,[3] which is $185 per capita or twice the country's total tax bill in 1929 or 1939. Furthermore, a higher tax rate would be required because the transactions tax would tend to reduce the number of sales by stimulating the

[1] Committee on Old Age Security, Twentieth Century Fund, *The Townsend Crusade*, 1936, pp. 22, 71–72.

[2] *Ibid.*, pp. 26, 71–72. The total expenditures of all government units in this country (Federal, state, and local) amounted to $13,500,000,000 in 1932.

[3] *Cf.* the testimony of Dr. Francis E. Townsend, J. Frederick Dewhurst, and Sumner H. Slichter, *Hearings Relative to the Social Security Act Amendments of 1939* before the Committee on Ways and Means, House of Representatives, 76th Congress, first session, vol. 1, 1939, pp. 603, 789, 877; and A University of Chicago Round Table, *The Economic Meaning of the Townsend Plan*, Public Policy Pamphlet No. 20, 1936, p. 16.

vertical integration of business, by eliminating brokers and other merchandising agencies, and by sharply reducing the amount of trading in security and commodity markets.

The supporters of the plan have argued that it would stimulate prosperity by speeding up the rate of spending. The recipients of the pensions must spend them within a month. However, a transactions tax is a tax on spending and can be avoided by hoarding. It is difficult to understand how a tax based on the rate of circulation of money, which turns over from 12 to 25 times a year,[1] will increase the rate of spending. The pensioners are only required to spend the money within 30 days, and a turnover of once a month is but 12 times a year. The pension money might, of course, turn over more than 12 times a year, but a turnover approaching 25 times a year is most unlikely. Delay between the collection of the tax and payment of the pension would reduce the rate of turnover of the pension money. Also, its spending might permit other members of the family group to hoard or save some of their normal income, which would tend to reduce the average rate of turnover of the total money supply. Furthermore, without dated dollars, it would be difficult for the government to know whether each recipient spent his pension within the time limit.

If the tax were on idle money or if the plan involved an expansion in the money supply, it might increase the total volume of expenditures. But a transactions or gross-sales tax is regressive in the sense that it takes a larger proportion of the income of the lower income groups than of the rich, because the poor spend most of their income and the tax varies directly with expenditures. Based on a tax that bears most heavily upon the low-income groups who are generally rapid spenders, the Townsend Plan might result in a decrease in the rate of monetary turnover.

The Townsend Plan and similar proposals have social as well as economic implications. They involve a public bonus to a special, privileged group to be paid for by taxes levied on the rest of society. Such paternalism in the form of free pensions would undoubtedly weaken, if not destroy, private and social insurance, especially old-age insurance. The aged are only one of the numerous groups in America that suffer from economic insecurity and that are badly in need of a "more abundant" life.

[1] *Cf.* Committee on Old Age Security, Twentieth Century Fund, *op. cit.*, p. 45.

OLD-AGE INSURANCE

As previously stated, compulsory old-age insurance is designed to prevent dependency rather than to relieve the dependent or needy aged. Like other types of social insurance, it relates the benefit payments to previous contributions or taxable earnings, which helps to preserve financial soundness and serves as a safeguard against excessive liberalization of benefits as well as a protection against any reduction of benefits.

Old-age insurance abroad. In 1889 Germany adopted the first national system of compulsory old-age and invalidity insurance. At the time there was strong protest against such insurance, but the opposition soon subsided, giving way to proposals for extending and improving the system. By the time our Social Security Act was passed in 1935, as many as 25 countries were operating compulsory programs of contributory old-age insurance.

These compulsory schemes apply to employed workers, although some countries permit self-employed persons and others to enter coverage on a voluntary basis. Contributions from both employers and the insured workers are required in most of these plans, and the state generally contributes some subsidy. In practically all countries, the monthly annuity payments from, say, age 65 until death vary with the previous contributions of the worker and, in general, amount to around 50 per cent of his average wage before retirement. In most countries, the plan also provides benefits for invalidity before the worker reaches 65 years of age.[1]

Industrial pension systems. For a number of decades before the passage of the Social Security Act, many large firms had had private systems for providing pensions to former employees after their retirement. The motives that led employers to establish such systems have already been mentioned. It was claimed that they paid their way by permitting the company to clear out "old timber" and to advance younger men without incurring public criticism, and by reducing labor turnover, labor unrest, and the possibility of strikes. Generally, the worker had to have 20 or 25 years of continuous service with the company before retirement in order to

[1] For a further discussion, cf. *Social Security in America*, Social Security Board, 1937, pp. 181–86; and Barbara N. Armstrong, "Old-Age Security Abroad: The Background of Titles II and VIII of the Social Security Act," *Law and Contemporary Problems*, vol. 3 (April 1936), pp. 175–85.

be eligible for a pension. Such a provision discouraged unionism, because the employer might interpret a strike as a termination or interruption of the worker's services. In practically all cases the workers had no legal right to the pension—most of the covered workers paid no contributions—so that the pension rested entirely upon the goodwill and financial condition of the company. For these reasons Justice Brandeis of the United States Supreme Court referred to the industrial pension scheme as the "new peonage."

It is estimated that before the Social Security Act was passed there were some 750 voluntary pension plans in effect, covering 3,000,000 or 4,000,000 employees. Over two thirds of these employees were connected with railroads, public utilities, and iron and steel companies. At no time did such private pension plans cover more than 15 per cent of the employees in manufacturing, mining, trade, and transportation.[1] Generally, no more than five per cent of the employees remained with the same employer until they reached the pensionable age and qualified for a pension.[2] The staff of the Committee on Economic Security pointed out in 1935 that "although fully 4,000,000 or 5,000,000 persons have at one time or another probably been employed by railroads with pension plans, less than 120,000 have been awarded pensions."[3] The aggregate funds set aside for pension plans in 1935 were estimated at about $800,000,000.[4] Three years earlier a thorough study revealed that only "about eight percent of the employees in company pension plans were covered by plans in which the guarantees were both actuarially and financially sound."[5]

The old-age insurance system established under the Social Security Act relieved firms of part of the pension responsibilities for which they had failed to make adequate financial provision. A large number of companies, however, decided to supplement the basic Federal benefits with additional pensions for their own employees. Such supplementary schemes proved to be so popular that the volume of private-pension business placed with insurance companies increased after the passage of the Social Security Act.

[1] *Social Security in America*, Social Security Board, 1937, p. 173.

[2] *Cf.* statement by Murray W. Latimer in *Business Week*, April 16, 1930, p. 40; and Latimer, *Industrial Pension Systems in the United States*, 1932, vol. 1, pp. 168–97.

[3] *Social Security in America*, Social Security Board, 1937, p. 176.

[4] *Idem.*

[5] Murray W. Latimer, *Industrial Pension Systems in the United States and Canada*, vol. 2, p. 876.

Old-age and survivors' insurance under the Social Security Act. As a means of reducing future old-age dependency, the Social Security Act establishes a Federal system of old-age annuity payments to covered workers upon reaching age 65 and to surviving widows and dependents in case the worker dies.

1. *Coverage.* At any one time more than half of the nation's gainfully occupied population is included in the coverage of the Federal insurance system, and it is estimated that, as a result of the turnover and migration of labor, 75 or 80 per cent of the working population will eventually build up wage credits under the present coverage provisions of the Act. As under the Federal unemployment-compensation tax, employment on the farm, in domestic service, on the railroads, and by nonprofit organizations is exempt. However, establishments hiring one or more persons in covered employments are subject to the old-age tax.

2. *Contributions.* Two special taxes are levied to finance this Federal insurance system: an excise tax on the payrolls of employers and a tax on the wage income of employees. In both cases the taxes apply only to the first $3,000 paid to one employee in any year. These two taxes are at a rate of one per cent each until 1943, when they are to increase as follows: two per cent from 1943 to 1945, two-and-a-half per cent from 1946 to 1948, and three per cent each (or six per cent combined) after 1948. In France and Germany the combined employer-employee contributions have amounted to about four and five per cent of wages, respectively, and in Great Britain they have represented less than two per cent of the covered workers' wages.

Because the total sum of Federal benefit payments continues to increase each year until 1980, when the system will have been in operation for a generation and will reach maturity, it will probably be necessary by 1970 either to increase the two special taxes or to provide for the deficiency in income through a government subsidy from general taxation. If the subsidy method is used, the government contribution may amount to more than $1,000,000,000 in 1980 and succeeding years, because it has been calculated that the benefit payments after the system reaches maturity will represent almost 10 per cent of taxable wages. In foreign systems of contributory old-age insurance, the government almost universally shares the cost by means of a subsidy. No less than two fifths of the old-age insurance expenditures have been borne by the central government in Great Britain and Germany. It is argued that such a government subsidy is justified by the savings in old-age assistance expenditures resulting from an insurance system.

The extent to which covered employees or their employers are actually paying for the old-age insurance that they eventually receive depends, of course, upon the final incidence of these two taxes. There is little question that the employee bears the tax levied directly upon his wages and, as indicated in the discussion of contributions in the previous chapter, the concensus of expert opinion seems to be that most of the uniform tax upon employers will also be borne by the same employees in the form of decreased wages or deferred wage increases.

If, however, the employer already had an old-age pension system for which the Federal old-age insurance system is at least a partial substitute, it would seem that there would be little shifting of the employer's payroll tax to his employees. Presumably, the employer's payments for old-age insurance or pensions were shifted to his employees at the time that the firm's private pension plan was instituted. Economists who argue that the Federal old-age tax on employers' payrolls is largely shifted to employees apparently would have to apply the same reasoning to private insurance or pension plans unless they could prove that the private plans had a better effect upon employees' efficiency than the Federal plan. The result of such a line of reasoning would be that employer expenditures for any welfare programs whose cost is related to wages are largely shifted to employees through pay envelopes that are smaller than they would otherwise be. In view of the widespread practice of paying the prevailing rate of wages, one may question whether the abolition of private pension plans would have increased employee wages, and one may also question whether abolition of the Federal old-age insurance program would cause a relative increase in the wage rates in covered employments.

3. *Benefits.* The contributions are, of course, related to the promised benefits. Two types of benefits are provided for under the insurance features of the Federal act, monthly old-age benefits to workers from 65 until death, and survivors' monthly benefits to the following relatives of an insured person who dies at any age: his widow 65 or over, his parents 65 or over, his children under 18, and

his widow when caring for his children under 18. In order to qualify for old-age benefits, the worker must not only have reached 65 and have retired in the sense that his or her monthly wages are under $15, but he or she must also have been covered for 40 calendar quarters (10 years) or have been covered during half of the calendar quarters following 1936 or attainment of 21 years of age. In order that the specified relatives of a deceased worker may receive survivors' benefits, the worker must have met one of the requirements concerning length of covered employment just stated or have received at least $50 for work in covered employment during each of six of the 12 calendar quarters preceding his death. It sounds complicated, but such provisions are necessary in order to determine eligibility and to prevent abuses.

Generally speaking, it may be said that the old-age benefits amount to about one half of the average monthly earnings of the worker during the period he was covered by the Act. However, the benefit schedule favors low-wage employees, married workers, and those whose period of covered employment has been relatively short. Such bias is achieved by applying the following formula to the average monthly wages the worker received when covered by the Act: 40 per cent up to $50 plus 10 per cent of the sum by which the average monthly wage exceeds $50. In other words, the beneficiary receives a monthly sum of $20 for the first $50 of average wages and $5 for every additional $50 of average wages in covered employment. In addition, the monthly benefit is increased by one per cent for each year of covered employment. For a wife over 65 or a child under 18, a supplementary benefit is paid amounting to one half the worker's primary benefit. Table 31 shows the old-age benefits that would be received each month by eligible workers who had been paid the selected "average monthly wages" during the specified number of years of coverage. In calculating "average monthly wages," a worker's total wages in covered employment after 1936 or attainment of age 21 are divided by the total number of months included within that period. Months in which the worker received no wages in covered employment, of course, reduce his "average monthly wages."

For a married couple both of whom are 65 or over, the monthly old-age benefit would be one-and-a-half times the figures in Table 31. The survivors' benefits for each dependent parent 65 or

TABLE 31. ILLUSTRATIVE MONTHLY OLD-AGE INSURANCE BENEFITS FOR A
SINGLE PERSON

Years of coverage	Average monthly wage			
	$50	$100	$150	$250
3	$20.60	$25.75	$30.90	$41.20
5	21.00	26.25	31.50	42.00
10	22.00	27.50	33.00	44.00
20	24.00	30.00	36.00	48.00
30	26.00	32.50	39.00	52.00
40	28.00	35.00	42.00	56.00

over and for each dependent child under 18 are one half of the
old-age benefit for a single person. The survivors' benefit for a
wife 65 or over, and for a wife caring for a dependent child of the
deceased, is three quarters of the old-age benefit for a single person.
In case there are no survivors eligible for benefits, a lump sum
amounting to six times the monthly benefit is paid upon the death
of a person insured under the scheme. The total monthly benefit
to a married annuitant or to a worker's survivors cannot exceed
80 per cent of the worker's average monthly wage, or two times the
monthly benefit of a single person with the same wage record. The
total benefits for one worker cannot exceed $85 a month nor be
less than $10 a month.

An examination of the benefit schedule indicates that it has been
drawn up on social-insurance rather than private-insurance principles. The fourfold weight given to the first $50 of average
monthly wages favors the low-wage employee. The use of average
monthly wages instead of total covered earnings or total contributions favors insured workers who will retire in the early years of the
program, so that they will have a short period of coverage before
they are eligible for benefits. The additional benefits for dependents
favor the family unit.

Despite these biases in the benefit schedule, a single person will
receive larger benefits than he could purchase from a private insurance company with his own contributions (not those of his employer), except in the extreme case of a worker covered for 45 years
or more with average taxed earnings of $250 a month, or $3,000 a
year, which is the upper limit of the tax base.[1] It is the employers'
contributions that are being used to redistribute income through

[1] *Cf. Report to Accompany H. R. 6635, Social Security Act Amendments of 1939*, Senate
Report No. 734, 76th Congress, first session, July 7, 1939, p. 16.

larger benefit payments to those retiring in the early years, to low-wage employees, and to workers with dependents than would be paid on a straight commercial basis.

During 1940, the first year of benefit payments, the old-age benefits averaged about $25 a month, which compared favorably, in most cases, with the old-age assistance grants to the needy aged. The estimated increase in total benefits for old-age and survivors' insurance during the first 15 years of benefit payments is indicated in Table 32. "Net tax receipts" is the term used for total contributions minus an item of five per cent representing the estimated costs of administration.

TABLE 32.   GROWTH OF OLD-AGE TAXES, BENEFIT PAYMENTS, AND RESERVE FUND, 1940–1955 [1]

(in millions of dollars)

Year	Net tax receipts	Benefit payments	Interest on reserve	Reserve fund at end of year
1940	501	114	41	1,871
1941	505	298	49	2,127
1942	504	431	54	2;254
1943	919	583	61	2,651
1944	1,067	667	71	3,122
1945	1,078	776	82	3,506
1950	1,751	1,422	136	5,737
1955	1,849	1,930	169	6,871

As indicated in Table 32, it is probable that benefit payments will exceed net tax receipts by 1955. By 1980 it is likely that total benefit payments will be in excess of $3,000,000,000, whereas the yield from the two taxes of three per cent each will probably not be much more than $2,000,000,000. Such estimates are, of course, subject to considerable error because they are based upon a large number of assumptions. For example, a marked change in the level of wages would cause a substantial alteration in both total tax receipts and total benefit payments.

4. *Reserve trust fund.* An amount equal to the full sum of the old-age insurance contributions each year is permanently appropriated to the Federal Old-Age and Survivors Trust Fund, which is held by a board of three trustees. The Secretary of the Treasury, who is a member of the Board, is to invest the funds in obligations of the

[1] *Report to Accompany H. R. 6335, op. cit.*, p. 17. Interest on the reserve has been calculated at 2.5 per cent.

Federal government or Federal agencies. The Secretary must purchase outstanding obligations in the market unless he decides that it is not in the public interest to do so, in which case special obligations can be issued to the Fund, bearing the average rate of interest on the total Federal debt. Table 32 indicates how this Fund may increase until 1956, when, if the estimates prove correct, it will commence to decrease, perhaps disappearing entirely by 1970. The Board of Trustees must report each year on the actuarial status of the Fund, giving estimates of the expected income and disbursements during the ensuing five years. The Board is to make a special report whenever the Trust Fund is "unduly small" or exceeds three times the highest annual expenditures expected in the next five-year period.

The function of social-insurance reserves has been a moot question here and abroad. Before amendment in 1939, the Social Security Act called for a self-financing system of old-age insurance with a reserve sufficiently large to meet two fifths of the old-age benefits after 1980 from interest on the reserve. In that way the system could have been financed with a six-per-cent payroll tax and without a direct government subsidy. In old-age insurance, the problem of financing benefits is concerned not only with an equitable adjustment between young and older workers but also with the steady increase in the total benefits until the system reaches maturity and total benefit payments level off. For example, benefit payments under the present provisions of the Social Security Act will increase from around $100,000,000 in 1940 to over $3,000,-000,000 in 1980. If there is no reserve in 1980 and no government subsidy, the payroll taxes may have to be increased to a combined rate of 9 or 10 per cent, for it is estimated that total benefits will then equal that percentage of total payrolls in covered employments.

The opponents of a large reserve have argued that such reserves are not needed in social insurance as they are in private insurance, because through old-age taxes the government is assured a sufficient number of contributors or customers and because such compulsory systems, once started, have never been terminated. They have also argued that a large reserve would serve no economic function, that it would disturb Federal finances by making a large Federal debt mandatory, and that interest on the reserve would really represent a concealed government subsidy.

A large old-age reserve would really perform an economic function if it were so invested that the nation's productive power was increased in the future, permitting an addition to the real income (goods and services) by the amount of the interest on the reserve. Indeed, some opponents of the large reserve feared that it might be invested in self-liquidating public works and "productive" enterprises, causing the government to expand its economic activities in competition with private business. In certain European countries, old-age reserves have been invested in housing projects and other interest-earning enterprises.[1] If the reserve was invested either in outstanding Federal obligations or in productive enterprise, the volume of savings and investment would be increased, thus tending to reduce interest rates—a development that would be displeasing to private insurance companies.

Some persons were misled by naive analogies with personal finance [2] into believing that it is somehow unsound for social-insurance reserves to be invested in (spent for) government bonds and government productive enterprise. They seemed to feel that the dollar bills received from old-age taxes should be hoarded until paid out in benefits. Such hoarding would, however, have a disastrous effect on the structure of private credit, for it would tend to reduce bank reserves by a corresponding amount. It is necessary to bear in mind that the real burden of old age, represented by the goods and services that nonproducing aged persons consume, cannot be shifted from decade to decade by financial arrangements. The persons contributing now and retiring, say, in 1980 will really be paying for their own old age only if the program and their contributions enlarge the national product in 1980 by the amount that they then consume. The interest on the reserve would represent a government subsidy only if the government wasted the money instead of using it to buy up the outstanding Federal debt, to increase the country's productivity, or to reduce general taxes below the level they otherwise would attain.

The old-age reserve under the present provisions of the Social Security Act has been called a contingency reserve. Such a reserve

---

[1] *Cf. More Security for Old Age*, Twentieth Century Fund, 1937, p. 57.

[2] *Cf.*, for example, John T. Flynn, "The Social Security 'Reserve' Swindle," *Harper's Magazine*, vol. 178 (February 1939), pp. 238–48. The contents of this article offer an excellent illustration of the common fallacy of reasoning from the individual to a general situation, such as that represented by a social-insurance system.

presumably is designed to meet disbursements in excess of income for a few years, without a change in the law or a special congressional appropriation. As was indicated in the discussion of the financial aspects of a public-works program in Chapter 15, a reserve of government bonds, like a new issue of such bonds, must be sold or pledged for a loan in order to raise money. Such a reserve, as that discussion indicated, is little better than the authority to issue new government bonds. Furthermore, a contingency reserve obviously would not be sufficient to meet all contingencies, although it might serve to maintain benefit payments during a business depression, when tax income decreased and benefit disbursements increased as a larger percentage of eligible workers over 65 retired or lost their jobs. Selling the bonds in the reserve during a depression might, of course, present some problems. However, no contingency reserve could withstand a long-time downward trend in the price level. An inflation that resulted in a manifold rise in the price level, such as occurred in Germany in the early 1920's, would also wipe out the reserve and make the promised benefits practically worthless.[1]

Railroad Retirement Acts. As a result of agitation by railroad employees, a railroad retirement act, later declared unconstitutional, was passed in 1934, over a year before the enactment of the Social Security Act. A new act, passed in 1935 and amended in 1937, provides for a special old-age insurance system for the railroads. Unlike other industries, the railroads had adequate wage and service records going back for a number of decades, which can be used as a basis for wage and service credits in calculating benefits under the Railroad Retirement Acts. Furthermore, the proportion of workers 55 or over in the railroad industry in the 1930's was almost double the percentage in all the industries covered by the Social Security Act.

To finance the old-age benefits for retired railroad workers, an excise tax on employers and an income tax on employees are levied on wages up to $300 a month. These taxes amounted to three per cent each in 1940 and will increase by one quarter of a per cent each at three-year intervals until they reach 3.75 per cent each in 1949, or a combined total of 7.5 per cent from then on.

[1] It is estimated that the first World War and the currency inflation that followed resulted in a loss of 4,000,000,000 marks in the reserves of the old-age insurance scheme in Germany. *Cf.* "The Reform of Workers' Compulsory Pension Insurance in Germany: I," *International Labour Review*, vol. 31 (March 1935), p. 399.

Benefits take the form of (1) old-age annuities payable to workers after retirement at age 65 or retirement at 60 after 30 years of service, (2) disability annuities payable to totally and permanently disabled employees who are 65 or have reached 60 after 30 years of service, and (3) death benefits. An employee may elect to have a "joint and survivor" annuity covering his spouse also, in which case the monthly benefits under the double annuity are somewhat reduced. The retiring worker's annuity is calculated by taking two per cent of the first $50 of his average monthly wages, one and a half per cent of the next $100, and one per cent of any balance of his average monthly wages above $150 and multiplying the sum of these three amounts by the number of years of credited service. This formula gives greater weight to years of service or employment, and has less bias in favor of the low-wage employee, than the old-age benefit formula in the Social Security Act. No monthly benefit may exceed $120, and the average annuity payments since 1937, when benefit payments commenced, have ranged between $65 and $70.[1]

Because the benefits are based on wage records going back many years before the Acts were passed, individual and total benefit payments have been large from the beginning. During the fiscal year ending June 1939, total benefit payments exceeded $100,000,000. Consequently, the system will not accumulate a large reserve in spite of the relatively high initial taxes. Under the provisions of the present legislation, it is estimated that total benefits will equal if not exceed the total tax income by 1950.[2] In the meantime the reserve is being invested in government securities to yield three per cent interest. The interest on the reserve is designed to help pay benefits which, it is estimated, will reach a level of $200,000,000 by 1965, representing about 10 per cent of the 1938 payroll of the railroads.[3]

[1] Cf. A. G. Silverman and Joseph J. Senturia, "Retirement Payments for Railroad Workers," Social Security Bulletin, vol. 2 (July 1939), p. 20.

[2] Cf. Murray W. Latimer, "The Security Programs for Railroad Workers," Social Security in the United States, 1939, American Association for Social Security, Inc., 1939, p. 53.

[3] Cf. Annual Report of the Railroad Retirement Board for the Fiscal Year Ended June 30, 1938, 1938, p. 64.

CHAPTER EIGHTEEN

WORK ACCIDENTS AND SICKNESS

Few persons appreciate the tremendous social cost of industrial accidents and sickness. In a year of normal employment it is estimated that as many as 20,000 employees are killed at work, that some 80,000 are totally or partially disabled for life, and that there may be 2,000,000 to 3,000,000 injuries which cause some loss of working time.[1] Indeed, the casualties to American workmen in industry during the first World War exceeded the total casualties of our army in France, and the toll of life and limb exacted by American industry during a decade exceeds the nation's losses in battle from the Declaration of Independence to the present day.[2] The problem is especially serious in this country, where the death rate from work accidents has been about twice as high as in Great Britain, France, or Japan.

Much sickness and fatal disease amongst wage-earners is directly or indirectly due to the nature of the worker's employment. The materials that employees work with may lead to various diseases such an anthrax or lead and radium poisoning. The conditions surrounding the job—air, heat, light, and physical strain—may affect the worker's health adversely. Miners, for instance, are likely to contract asthma, silicosis, and tuberculosis. Various statistical studies show that the health of industrial wage-earners, as a group, compares unfavorably with that of other elements in the population. Table 33 indicates, for example, that the annual death rate amongst unskilled workers is about twice as great as that for professional men, managers, officials, and merchants, and that the death rate from tuberculosis of the lungs, pneumonia, and acci-

---

[1] These figures simply represent rough estimates, since there are no adequate estimates for work accidents for the whole country in any one year. *Cf.* Walter F. Dodd, *Administration of Workmen's Compensation*, 1936, pp. 1–2; and Edison L. Bowers, *Is It Safe to Work? A Study of Industrial Accidents*, 1930, pp. 3–4.

[2] *Cf.* E. H. Downey, *Workmen's Compensation*, 1924, p. 1.

dents is especially high amongst unskilled workers. Agricultural workers, both farmers and farm laborers, show a low death rate from practically all causes of mortality.

TABLE 33. ANNUAL DEATH RATE PER 1,000 MALES 15–64 YEARS OF AGE IN 10 STATES, 1930 [1]

	Tuberculosis of the lungs	Pneumonia	Accidents	All causes
Unskilled workers	1.85	1.36	0.52	14.48
Semiskilled workers	1.02	0.72	0.34	10.09
Skilled workers	0.72	0.60	0.34	8.29
Proprietors and managers	0.43	0.52	0.22	7.93
Clerks and kindred workers	0.66	0.51	0.19	7.75
Professional men	0.26	0.39	0.15	6.71
Agricultural workers	0.47	0.43	0.15	6.23
All gainfully occupied	0.88	0.69	0.30	9.10

Mortality statistics for male workers in England and Wales in the early 1920's follow the same pattern, with a large excess mortality among the laboring classes as compared with merchants, professional men, and other self-employed groups.[2]

The frequency and severity of illness is closely related to the income of the family. The National Health Survey covering 750,000 families in some 80 cities during the Winter of 1935–1936 showed that, in a year, members of families with an income under $1,000 suffer more than twice as many days of disabling illness, keeping them from work, as do persons in families with an income of $3,000 or more a year.[3] Several other studies of the relation between illness and economic status reveal that sickness occurs most frequently among the lowest income groups.[4]

Cost of work accidents and illness amongst employees. The loss of earnings from sickness per employed person in families with incomes below $2,500 has been placed at $30 per person, or a total of $900,000,000 a year.[5] To this total should be added about $400,-000,000 as the annual cost of medical care for such workers. It has been estimated that the wage loss from industrial accidents oc-

[1] *Hearings before a Special Committee to Investigate Unemployment and Relief*, U. S. Senate, 75th Congress, third session, 1938, vol. 2, p. 1491. The death rate is adjusted for the age distribution in each group.

[2] *Ibid.*, p. 1492.　　　　　　　　　　　　　　　　　　[3] *Ibid.*, p. 1486.

[4] A Public Health Service survey of 24 mill villages in South Carolina showed that in families with the lowest income there were 70 cases of illness for every 1,000 persons, while the highest income group had less than 19 cases per 1,000.

[5] *Cf.* I. S. Falk, *Security Against Sickness*, 1936, pp. 13–15.

curring each year runs as high as $1,000,000,000, with the cost of medical care for such accidents amounting to $250,000,000 more.[1] Although there is some overlapping in these figures and they are at best rough estimates, it seems likely that the total cost of work accidents and sickness to wage-earners alone (not their families) amounts to $2,500,000,000 a year. Allowing for an average loss of 20 years of working life for workers killed or permanently incapacitated, the lost working time from work accidents is estimated at one full week of production a year, and the loss from sickness would amount to another week.

Even these figures for dollar cost and loss of potential work hours fail to give a full picture of society's loss from work injuries and illness amongst wage-earners. They do not allow for the effects of sickness and minor injuries upon the employee's productive capacity and length of working life. In the case of industrial accidents, there are additional costs to society in the form of legal expenses, costs of administering industrial-accident insurance, and industrial losses resulting from idle equipment, damage to machinery, and interference with production. Some writers have estimated the total losses from industrial accidents alone at $4,000,000,000 or $5,000,000,000 a year.[2]

Generally speaking, the money value of man does not sufficiently enter into cost calculations in an economy based upon free, rather than slave, labor. The master of a slave permanently disabled while working for another person would attempt to collect damages calculated according to the full economic loss—the present value of the slave's future expected labor plus any added cost in caring for him. But in a free economy, an employer does not own his workmen; he only hires their current labor services. Consequently, unless forced to do so by law, the employer need not treat his workers carefully, because he has little trouble in hiring new workers when the present ones become incapacitated by injuries or ill health. Therefore, society must, in the general interest, legislate to prevent wasteful use of human resources. It has been estimated that as much as half of the present cost of industrial accidents and sickness to wage-earners could be eliminated through proper measures for

[1] *Cf.* H. A. Millis and R. E. Montgomery, *Labor's Risks and Social Insurance*, 1938, p. 188.

[2] *Cf.* Edison E. Bowers, *op. cit.*, p. 5; and *Handbook of Labor Statistics, 1931 Edition*, U. S. Bureau of Labor Statistics, Bulletin No. 541, 1931, p. 315.

prevention.[1] In addition to the problem of prevention, there is the question of how the remaining costs or losses should be apportioned, whether they should be met by social insurance or some other method of collective security.

DEVELOPMENT OF WORKMEN'S COMPENSATION

In this country, programs of social insurance to cover work injuries and occupational disease have come to be called workmen's compensation following the English precedent, although the Continental term, industrial-accident insurance, is more explicit.

The common law. Our common law on work accidents began to take form a century or so ago, when the doctrine of laissez faire was at its zenith and before the Industrial Revolution occurred in this country. Certain judicial decisions around 1840 established a group of special defenses for the employer that made it difficult for an employee to receive any compensation for injuries sustained on the job. It is necessary to appreciate that these special employer defenses grew out of the small-shop conditions existing in most of American industry at that time. Often the journeyman worked in a shop in the master's home. He knew his few fellow workmen from long and close association, and the employer, as a master craftsman supervising their work, also knew them all personally. Because tools and industrial processes were relatively simple and the employees in one workshop were few in number, it was not difficult in many cases to determine whether the employee, his employer, or a fellow employee was responsible for a particular injury. The common law, therefore, came to be based upon the notion of personal fault or negligence on the part of one of these three, and an injured worker could collect damages only by suing for them.

The employer was protected from liability for damages growing out of accidents to his employees by three common-law principles or "defenses." The first of these was the "fellow-servant" doctrine, which absolved the employer of all responsibility if the injury was due to the actions of a fellow workman. The second defense was that of "contributory negligence," which required the employee to prove that no negligence or carelessness on his part contributed

[1] *Cf.*, for example, Bowers, *op. cit.*, Preface; and *Handbook of Labor Statistics, 1931 Edition, op. cit.*

to the accident, regardless of the guilt of the employer. The third possible defense was that no one was to blame for the accident, that it was due to the ordinary risks of the trade which were known to the worker and which he assumed in accepting the job. This "assumption-of-risk" principle was sometimes extended to cover cases where the employee knew that the employer had failed to provide a reasonably safe workshop, and assumed the extraordinary risk in continuing to work.

Employers' liability laws. As industry grew in size and complexity, these special defenses became less and less tenable. With frequent changes in technique, the worker could not possibly know what the risks of the job might be. With thousands of employees in the same firm, workers did not know their fellow employees. It was, for example, rather far-fetched to apply the "fellow-servant" doctrine to the case of a locomotive engineer killed because of a negligent switchman or a defect in the rails. And more and more accidents happened for which no one in particular was to blame.

The injustice of the situation became so apparent that between 1885 and 1910 practically every important industrial state in the country passed statutes modifying or abolishing one or more of the common-law defenses. Although such legislation increased the liability of the employer and improved the worker's chance to collect damages from his employer, he or his survivors still had to prove that the employer was negligent or at fault. That, in many cases, was difficult to do, especially when the worker had been killed by the accident. Fellow workers and foremen would hesitate to testify against the employer for fear of losing their jobs. For the same reason, an injured worker might be afraid to bring suit.

The damage-suit method not only led to antagonism between employer and employee, but frequently involved a long delay before settlement and was very wasteful. Serious accident cases often dragged on for two to six years before being finally settled. Few workers could afford such lengthy and costly litigation. If the case was in the courts, the injured worker received no compensation during the time he needed it most, and, in fatal accidents, his survivors might be left without any support for years. With the passage of employers' liability laws in the 1880's, employers commenced to take out insurance to cover their liability, but the introduction of private liability insurance did not remedy matters. Under the law it did not pay the insurance companies to settle claims without a suit. Consequently, the costs of litigation absorbed a large part of the employer's insurance premium and a large part of the worker's claim, in case he won the suit. Surveys in various states showed that in the first decade of this century less than half of the premiums received from employers by the insurance companies were paid out to injured workers. Ten New York insurance companies receiving almost $25,000,000 of premiums from 1906 through 1908 paid less than 37 per cent of those premiums to injured workmen; the other 63 per cent went to pay attorneys' salaries, claim agents, salesmen's commissions, administrative costs, and dividends. These companies paid compensation for but one claim out of every eight made by injured employees.[1] Such a system was very uneconomical and costly to society, which was called upon to meet a large part of the burden for the care of injured workers and their families.

Shift to workmen's compensation. In 1883 Germany adopted the first compulsory accident-compensation law, and within the next 20 years every country in Europe had followed suit. Although our Federal and state labor bureaus made elaborate studies of European experience before the turn of the present century, the idea of compulsory social insurance for work accidents did not "take" in this country until the Federal government passed such a law in 1908 and President Theodore Roosevelt urged in vigorous messages that the states follow the Federal example.

By 1910 the defects and abuses of liability insurance had become so apparent and flagrant that many employers as well as employees were demanding compulsory compensation legislation as a cheaper and better method for meeting the problem of work injuries. A survey of some 25,000 manufacturers, made by the National Association of Manufacturers in 1910, showed that "more than 95 per cent of those answering were in favor of an equitable, automatic compensation system for injured workers" in place of the "cruel, inefficient, and inequitable system" of employers' liability.[2] A system of compulsory accident compensation was, however, considered by some groups, especially certain insurance in-

---

[1] *Cf.* Walter F. Dodd, *op. cit.*, pp. 21–22. The first chapter of Dodd's book contains a good discussion of the experience in this country prior to the enactment of workmen's compensation laws.

[2] F. C. Schwedtman, "Principles of Sound Employers' Liability Legislation," *Annals of the American Academy of Political and Social Science*, vol. 38 (July 1911), p. 202.

terests, to be "of foreign birth, the outgrowth of socialistic theories," and "an attack on the manhood of employees as American citizens."[1] Some judges adopted a similar attitude. The first compulsory compensation law adopted by New York in 1910 was declared by the State Court of Appeals to be "plainly revolutionary" and unconstitutional, because, in making employers liable without fault on their part, the Act deprived them of property without due process of law.[2]

By 1915 as many as 30 states had enacted workmen's compensation laws in spite of court opposition and employer claims that such laws would undermine the morals of workers by encouraging injuries and would penalize firms in interstate competition with companies located in states without such laws.

The previous liability experience had left labor hostile to insurance companies, so the unions campaigned for state-administered funds rather than insurance by private carriers under the state laws. In a number of European countries, including Germany, Austria, Russia, and Norway, private insurance carriers had been excluded from any part in compensation insurance. Organized labor in Ohio is commonly credited with making that state the pioneer and leader in establishing an exclusive state fund for workmen's compensation.

The first compulsory laws were declared unconstitutional in the state courts. As a result, most states enacted so-called "elective" laws, which permit the employer and employee to choose between the new method of automatic compensation and the old damage-suit procedure. However, an employer rejecting the compensation method was deprived of the common-law defenses in case of suit. In the event the employee chose to sue instead of accepting compensation, the special employer defenses were restored. Consequently, election has been practically unanimous and almost automatic in most states.

In 1917 the Supreme Court of the United States declared an elective law and a compulsory-compensation law both within the police power of the state.[3] It upheld the law of the state of Washington, which taxes employers in order to insure workers in an

---

[1] Walter S. Michols, "An Argument Against Liability," *ibid.*, p. 159.

[2] *Ives* v. *South Buffalo Railway Co.* (1911), 201 N. Y. 271.

[3] *N. Y. Central R. R. Co.* v. *White* (1917), 243 U. S. 188; and *Mountain Timber Co.* v. *Washington* (1917), 243 U. S. 219.

exclusive, state-administered compensation fund. In these decisions the Court stated that the losses from industrial accidents are "an expense of operation, as truly as the cost of repairing broken machinery or any other expense that is ordinarily paid by the employer" and that the method of compensation "is intended as a just settlement of a difficult problem." The Court recognized the advantages of automatic compensation for work injuries not willfully incurred over the method of legal suit, which involved quibbling over the question of fault and also involved the assessment of an unpredictable sum for damages.

The compensation method not only saves society the waste of lengthy litigation, but assures the injured worker of prompt medical attention and financial compensation during the period of injury, when he most needs it, rather than many years after the accident. Such arrangements also are in the interest of the employer because they speed the recovery of the injured worker, improve employer-employee relations, and substitute a certain insurance premium for the uncertain sympathies of a jury. It has also been claimed that the method of compensation tends to stimulate accident prevention.

Provisions of state laws. All states except one (Mississippi) have workmen's compensation laws, but the state laws lack any uniformity and present only a patchwork pattern. Benefit provisions are not alike in any two states. Each state seems to have followed its own inclinations with little regard to the lessons that might have been learned from other states.

In addition to the 47 state laws, there is a Federal law covering longshoremen and harbor workers. Railroad employees are still under the old liability laws because the unions of the railroad workers are not convinced that they would be better off under a Federal compensation law.

1. *Coverage.* It has been estimated that not more than 40 per cent of all gainfully employed workers in the country are actually protected by workmen's compensation laws.[1] The other 60 per cent must still rely upon the damage-suit method. The employments generally excluded from state laws are agriculture, domestic service, and casual work. In half the states, firms employing less than a certain number of employees are also excluded. Such em-

[1] Marshall Dawson, "Coverage Limitations of Workmen's Compensation Laws," *Monthly Labor Review*, vol. 48 (June 1939), p. 1269.

ployment and size-of-firm exclusions generally arise from a demand by employers to be excluded. In some states certain employments originally covered by the law have later been excluded because insurance companies have found that they were "undesirable" or costly risks. Furthermore, evasion of the law by employers is not infrequent. In some states with exclusive state funds, injured workers are eligible for benefits even if their employers have evaded the law and failed to pay premiums.

2. *Method of insurance.* Compensation, in contrast to lump-sum payments collected from damage suits, often involves the periodic payment of benefits over a number of years, perhaps for the rest of the life of a disabled employee. Consequently, security for the payment of compensation must be provided. Three types of insurance are utilized for this purpose: private casualty companies, state insurance funds, and self-insurance. Under self-insurance, employers, mostly large concerns, carry their own accident risks, usually pledging securities to cover the future compensation claims of their employees. Such company payment and administration of compensation has, in a number of instances, led to abuse and is not permitted in seven states.[1] The private insurance carriers may be either stock companies operated for a profit or mutual companies owned by the insuring employers. Eighteen states have state funds or state-operated insurance. In seven of these states private carriers are excluded and employers can insure only with the state fund, while in the other eleven states private insurance carriers compete with the state system for the business. The casualty companies had vigorously opposed the passage of workmen's compensation laws, and the promoters of such legislation had intended that it should be administered by state funds or mutual companies. All the Canadian provinces except Yukon have exclusive state funds, and only Yukon and Quebec permit self-insurance by private employers.

Although no reliable figures are available for recent years, the total compensation costs to employers in this country are probably divided roughly as follows: stock insurance carriers, 38 per cent, mutual insurance carriers, 20 per cent, state funds, 22 per cent,

---

[1] *Cf.* W. F. Dodd, *op. cit.*, pp. 520–21; and Charles F. Sharkey, "Principal Features of Workmen's Compensation Laws, as of January 1, 1940," *Monthly Labor Review*, vol. 50 (March 1940), p. 576.

and self-insurance, 20 per cent.[1] In some states, like Pennsylvania, Virginia, and Montana, as much as 40 or 50 per cent of the total amount of compensation benefits is paid by self-insurers.[2]

In a number of instances during the past decade or two, stock insurance companies and self-insurance arrangements have failed to provide sufficient security for compensation claims. For example, 18 stock companies in New York failed between 1927 and 1935. In February 1935 there were $2,600,000 outstanding claims on insolvent insurance carriers in New York, of which it was estimated $1,727,000 never would be paid.[3] Self-insurers had similar difficulties during the 1930's, and in certain cases employers defaulted on the compensation claims of injured workers. No injured workers have sustained losses from state-owned compensation funds.[4]

Various reports and investigations indicate that exclusive state funds provide insurance at the lowest cost to employers and that insurance with private stock companies is the highest priced of all.[5] The expense ratio for stock insurance companies in the 1930's was around 43 per cent, which means that 43 cents out of every dollar of premiums paid by the employer are absorbed by agents' commissions, claims adjustment, payroll audit, and overhead. The expense ratio for mutual companies was around 23 per cent, much of the difference between stock and mutual companies' expenses being due to the 18 cents for selling costs paid by stock companies out of every dollar of premiums. Some authorities have pointed out that such selling expense is wasteful under a system of compulsory insurance for all employers who cannot become self-insurers. The expense ratio for competitive state funds has been around 15 per cent, and for exclusive state funds as a group less than 10 per cent.[6] In the past, the interest on the invested reserves of the

---

[1] Cf. Dodd, op. cit., pp. 526–27; and Marshall Dawson, op. cit.

[2] W. F. Dodd, op. cit., p. 519.

[3] Ibid., pp. 542–44. Carl Hookstadt stated in 1922 that several disastrous failures of private stock companies had "resulted in hundreds of thousands of dollars in unpaid claims." U. S. Bureau of Labor Statistics, Bulletin No. 301, 1922, p. 18.

[4] The American Federation of Labor has repeatedly endorsed the Ohio or exclusive-state fund as the type of compensation insurance most advantageous to labor.

[5] Cf. Dodd, op. cit., pp. 552–60; and American Medical Association, Medical Relations under Workmen's Compensation, A Report prepared by the Bureau of Medical Economics (revised), 1935, pp. 41–47.

[6] Cf. a Session on "State Funds" in Discussion of Industrial Accidents and Diseases, 1938 Convention of the International Association of Accident Boards and Commissions, U. S. Department of Labor, Division of Labor Standards, Bulletin No. 24, 1939,

Nevada state fund has more than covered administrative costs.[1]

Although indicating the relative cost of each type of insurance, such comparisons are not exactly correct or complete. Some allowance should be made for the fact that state funds pay no taxes and probably give insuring employers less service. On the other hand, the cost of state supervision of private insurance firms, now met by general taxpayers, should be added to the expense of insurance by private carriers. Undoubtedly, the compensation systems of most states involve considerable duplication and waste, which could be eliminated by following the example of old-age insurance and unemployment-compensation laws, and by coordinating workmen's compensation with the other social insurances. Authorities have stated that efficient administration of workmen's compensation should not cost more than 10 to 15 per cent of total contributions.

In any attempt to measure the full cost of workmen's compensation, allowance should be made for court expenses and lawyers' charges to workers, which may run as high as one third of the total damages collected by workers in contested cases.[2] Even at hearings before the compensation authorities prior to appeal to the courts, injured workers often have to be represented by a lawyer.[3] Lawyers and courts still have too much control over workmen's compensation in this country. In the Canadian provinces the courts and lawyers are excluded from the administration of workmen's compensation. Contested cases are simply investigated by a claims agent who reports his findings, and the case is decided by a chief claims officer with appeal to a higher board.[4]

3. *Contributions.* In the first section of this chapter, the working-time loss and medical-care cost of work injuries was estimated at $1,250,000,000 a year. The cost assessed against employers under workmen's compensation, including self-insurance, has been estimated at around $425,000,000 a year,[5] of which a part is absorbed

---

pp. 16–17, 37, 40–41; and John B. Andrews, *Progress of State Insurance Funds under Workmen's Compensation*, Division of Labor Standards, Bulletin No. 30, 1939, pp. 7, 20–24.

[1] "Recent Workmen's Compensation Reports," *Monthly Labor Review*, vol. 28 (June 1929), p. 143.

[2] Marshall Dawson, "Claims Administration in Workmen's Compensation," *Monthly Labor Review*, vol. 46 (June 1938), p. 1339.

[3] *Ibid.*, pp. 1334–45.   [4] *Ibid.*, pp. 1326, 1332.

[5] *Cf.* Marshall Dawson, "Coverage Limitations of Workmen's Compensation Laws," *Monthly Labor Review*, vol. 48 (June 1939), p. 1269.

by administrative expenses and never reaches the injured employees. Consequently, workers themselves bear at least two thirds of the total burden of work accidents.

The cost of workmen's compensation is charged, for the most part, to the employer. In all states except Oregon, which has an exclusive state fund, the full cost of compensation for wage loss is paid by the employer either in premiums, based on his payroll, or as a self-insurer. In Oregon, one per cent of employees' wages is deducted for compensation costs, and in three other states with state funds employees contribute to the medical-benefit fund. A part of the administrative cost may rest on the public in states having state funds.

The incidence of employers' contributions to social insurance, including workmen's compensation, was discussed under "contributions" in Chapter 16, and that discussion need not be repeated here. The general conclusion was that a goodly share of such costs is shifted to workers through pay envelopes, that in some cases a portion of the costs is shifted to consumers through prices, but that, with differentiated rates of contribution under experience rating, at least a part of the tax rests upon the employer. On such grounds it may be argued that the employee really pays for much more than two thirds of the cost of industrial accidents.

There are a number of reasons for levying the full charge for industrial injuries upon the employer. In the first place, he has some legal liability for work accidents. Secondly, it is argued that the bills for industrial accidents are properly a part of the costs of production, because some accidents will happen despite precautions and some industries are more hazardous than others. Thirdly, it is claimed that, if the cost is levied upon the employer under an arrangement for experience rating, it may pay him to introduce safety devices and programs for accident prevention. There is, however, disagreement on this third claim. Some authors believe that the proportion of the total cost of work accidents assessed against American industry is too small to encourage adequate safety measures.[1] With regard to experience or merit rating as a preventive device, an authority has recently stated:

[1] *Cf.* E. L. Bowers, *op. cit.*, p. 163; and *Medical Relations under Workmen's Compensation, op. cit.*, pp. 31–32.

It is difficult to determine the extent to which schedule or experience ratings operate to decrease industrial accidents. The proportionate increase or decrease in premium rate because of merit rating will in many cases be too small to have much effect. Moreover, merit rating hardly touches the small employer who presents the most serious problem of accident prevention.[1]

4. *Experience rating.* In all states, the employer's premium or contribution varies with the estimated risk of accidents in that firm or industry. Each year the previous accident experience in some 700 or 800 occupations, processes, or industries throughout the country is ascertained. This nationwide experience, when adjusted for the state's law and benefit schedule, gives what is called the manual rate for the occupation or trade. In most states, this is the rate that applies to small employers, and it generally is based on the expense loading of stock insurance companies, including their high sales costs.

The manual rate, reflecting the national average for that line of work, would, if used exclusively, tend to favor the mutual insurance companies and encourage self-insurance by the better-than-average risks. In order to combat self-insurance and to take advantage of the safety service of the better stock companies, reductions below the manual rate are permitted under experience rating. Experience rating applies only to large firms, however, so that in some states less than 10 per cent of the total risks are experience-rated.[2] Generally speaking, firms with annual premiums under $600 according to the manual rates [3] are not experience-rated because it would be too costly to rate them, their experience is too narrow for the insurance law of averages to apply, they are less likely to self-insure, and stock carriers are not likely to be interested in such business. In calculating a firm's premium, the manual and experience rates are combined in varying proportions except for firms so large, for example, that their annual premium would be $100,000, in which case the manual is ignored. Self-insurance, of course, is 100-percent experience rating.

[1] Dodd, *op. cit.*, p. 710. Schedule rating, based upon physical conditions in the plant and safety devices, was abandoned by most states after 1933 and was never used by the exclusive-fund states or the Canadian provinces.

[2] *Idem.*

[3] The minimum premium required for experience rating in some exclusive-fund states is much lower. *Cf.* Mark Kormes, *The Experience Rating Plan as Applied to Workmen's Compensation Risks*, Reprint from Proceedings of the Casualty Actuarial Society, 1936, pp. 1, 26, 28.

Experience rating under workmen's compensation differs from such rating under unemployment compensation. There is nothing under unemployment compensation that resembles manual rates and expense loading based on the costs of stock carriers. In practice, experience rating always reduces and never increases the employer's premium in workmen's compensation. Under unemployment compensation, experience rating applies to all firms, big or small. If experience rating were applied in the same way under workmen's compensation there would not be so many "undesirable risks," which no private insurance carriers will voluntarily take at the manual rate. In both kinds of compensation, past experience over a period of from one to five years is used as a basis for predicting future experience. The need for a large sample on which to base experience rating under workmen's compensation is indicated by the fact that a machine shop employing 100 men has an expectancy of one death in 20 years and of one major permanent disability in 15 years.[1]

5. *Benefits.* The benefits under workmen's compensation are of two types: cash to compensate in part for wage losses, and payment for the cost of medical care for the injury. Most states also provide for small funeral benefits in case of death. As already mentioned, the benefit provisions are not alike in any two states, and, in the same state, benefits are likely to be slightly different for the four general classes of injury: death, total or complete disability for life, partial disability for life, and total disability for a temporary period. Furthermore, benefit provisions are frequently amended. Consequently, there are exceptions to many of the following general statements concerning benefits.

Compensation for loss of wages or earning capacity in all except three states is based on a percentage of the average earnings, usually full-time wages, of the injured worker. Weekly benefits vary from 50 to 70 per cent of regular wages, depending on the state, with about half of the states paying disabled workers two thirds of their normal wages. Such benefits cannot exceed $18 or $20 a week in most states, although a few states have maxima as high as $25. In some states, especially if the accident proves fatal, benefits vary with the number of dependents.

Further limitations are placed upon compensation benefits. All states except Oregon provide for a waiting period, generally seven

[1] *Cf.* E. H. Downey, *Workmen's Compensation*, 1924, p. 96.

days immediately following the injury, before benefit payments
begin. If the disability lasts for a certain period of weeks, the payment of compensation is retroactive to the date of injury in a majority of states. Total benefit payments for one injury are also
restricted in most states to a certain period of weeks or to a maximum amount. For example, in only eight or ten states are benefits
paid in fatal accidents for the full period of the wife's widowhood or
the minority of the children. Not half of the states promise to pay
benefits during the rest of the life of a worker who is completely
disabled. In most states, such a worker, completely incapacitated
for life, could not receive more than $8,000 in compensation no
matter what his age at the time the accident occurred. All except
three states limit the total number of weeks of payment for partial
disability for life, and less than a quarter of the states promise to
pay compensation for the full period of incapacity in case of disability for a temporary period.[1]

Various restrictions upon benefits place upon the worker at least
half the cost of work accidents in the most liberal states and three
fourths of such cost in the least liberal states. Each year a Table
of Comparative Benefits is prepared by the National Council of
Compensation Insurance, indicating, in a general way, the relative
cost of benefits for each state in terms of New York State's benefit
scale. The weighted total in this table shows that the benefits in
Vermont, New Hampshire, and Tennessee are no more than two
thirds as large as they are in New York, and that only in Pennsylvania and Wisconsin are the benefit payments higher than in New
York.[2] It is said that the low benefit scales in some states have
acted as a brake upon further development and liberalization in
other states through fear of burdening the state's firms in competition with companies in less liberal states.[3]

Changes in the price level and the cost of living, of course, affect
the purchasing power of social-insurance benefits. It is, therefore,
very important that there be a stable price level or that benefits be
adjusted for price- and wage-level changes in insurances paying
benefits for periods of a decade or more, as is the case under workmen's compensation and old-age insurance. The law in Great

[1] For detailed comparison of state laws, cf. C. F. Sharkey, op. cit., pp. 574–600.
[2] Cf. Marshall Dawson, "Adequacy of Benefits under Workmen's Compensation,"
Monthly Labor Review, vol. 47 (September 1938), pp. 472–73.
[3] Cf. ibid., pp. 463, 471.

Britain provides that the compensation of a worker may be altered for beneficiaries disabled for life whenever the wage rate in the worker's pre-accident occupation increases or decreases more than 20 per cent over a period of 12 months.[1] In some of the Canadian provinces with exclusive state funds a case is never closed, but may be reopened for reconsideration at any time. Such flexibility is difficult to achieve where private insurance companies are permitted to sell compensation insurance on a profit-making basis.

Competition between insurance carriers, and operation for a profit are responsible for many of the troublesome problems in workmen's compensation. Special provision must be made for the "undesirable" risk. In over one fourth of the states it has been necessary to establish a special "second-injury" fund because employers were refusing to employ workers already partially disabled on the grounds that a new injury to such workers would be especially costly to the employer and the insurance company. For example, a worker with one eye would be totally disabled for life if he lost his second eye in an industrial accident; the added cost of compensation for such a worker losing the second eye would be much more than that for a normal worker losing one eye. Some states, in which insurance carriers compete for the compensation business, have found it necessary to set up separate funds or to make supplementary arrangements for benefits to dependents.[2] Another problem in such states is that of relating benefit provisions to the rehabilitation program. Because it generally costs an extra sum to retrain and rehabilitate permanently injured workers so that they may again earn an income, a special fund for rehabilitation is required. Since 1920 the Federal government has been providing a subsidy to rehabilitation programs in 47 states. Under this arrangement some 10,000 workers, crippled by accident or disease, are being rehabilitated each year.

The cost of medical benefits accounts for around one third of the total costs of workmen's compensation. Many state laws contain questionable restrictions upon medical benefits. Only one quarter of the states provide medical and hospital care with no limitation upon the period of time or total amount of money per case.[3] In

[1] Cf. Barbara N. Armstrong, *Insuring the Essentials*, 1932, p. 248.
[2] Cf. Marshall Dawson, *op. cit.*, pp. 447–482.
[3] Cf. "Workmen's Compensation in the United States, as of July 1, 1938," *op. cit.*, p. 583.

all except a few states, the doctor and hospital are selected by the employer, the insurance company, or the state fund, rather than by the injured employee. This power of selection has, in some cases, led to undesirable results, for the profit of stock insurance companies depends in large measure upon the medical bill and how soon the injured worker is returned to work. In many states, employer or insurance-company selection has resulted in the commercialization of medical practice and exploitation of the worker's health through various financial arrangements which make it profitable to give the injured worker the cheapest treatment for the shortest possible period of time.[1]

6. *Occupational disease.* Diseases such as anthrax, lead, and mercury poisoning, silicosis, caisson disease, and the like that are caused by the work materials or unhealthy conditions surrounding the job present a problem similar to that of work accidents. Although none of the workmen's compensation laws as originally enacted provided for disability resulting from occupational disease, about three fifths of the states now provide compensation and medical benefits for disabilities due to certain designated diseases or caused by any occupational disease. Experience in the states with general coverage for occupational disease, like Wisconsin, New York, and California, indicates that the cost of including all occupational diseases is relatively insignificant, amounting to no more than three per cent of the total cost of compensable accidents. In the exclusive-fund state of Ohio, the cost of covering twenty-odd diseases arising out of employment is met by a uniform premium of one cent per $100 of payroll levied on all insurers in the state.

HEALTH INSURANCE

The earning capacity of the worker may temporarily be reduced to zero by sickness or a nonindustrial accident. The burden of the loss in earnings from such causes is distributed unevenly and, as indicated by the figures at the beginning of this chapter, it rests most heavily on workers and those with the lowest incomes. Each year one out of every five workers loses a week or more of employment because of disability caused by sickness or nonindustrial accidents. The wage loss from such causes has been estimated at

---

[1] For a discussion of undesirable medical practices under workmen's compensation, *cf.* Dodd, *op. cit.*, Chapter 10, pp. 408–505.

almost $1,000,000,000 a year. Because that loss is so unevenly distributed amongst workers, a number of countries have adopted programs of social insurance to protect workers and their families against unexpected losses from sickness or nonindustrial accidents. In a sense such insurance is a form of property insurance because the worker may be his family's only earning asset.

Public health insurance, to assist workers through collective arrangements for meeting the economic burden of sickness and nonindustrial accidents, has three purposes: to stimulate the prevention of such losses, to compensate in part for loss of working time, and to provide adequate medical care for beneficiaries. Incapacity to work, as certified by a doctor, is the universal requirement for eligibility to benefits under such sickness-insurance programs. In most countries the compulsory aspects of the programs are limited to employees in specific industries and to low-income groups. In Germany, the health-insurance program, started in 1883, covers three fourths of the wage-earners, and the British compulsory system, begun in 1911, covers four fifths of the wage-earning population.

Although 25 countries with a combined population of over 500,-000,000 people have compulsory health-insurance systems, no American state has yet enacted a health-insurance law.[1] Bills providing for compulsory health insurance were introduced into state legislatures as early as 1915, but they were opposed by private insurance companies, some medical doctors, and by some employers' organizations because, among other reasons, local industry might be handicapped in interstate competition by increased costs in the form of employer contributions. Some officials in the American Federation of Labor also opposed compulsory health insurance around 1920. In its 1935 convention, however, the American Federation of Labor adopted a resolution favoring such legislation.

Compulsory health insurance has been confused with socialized medicine by some persons. Socialized medicine in the sense that we have socialized education, paid for and offered by the state as a free public service, is found only in Russia. Health insurance does not involve the transformation of all doctors into government employees. It is simply a method of pooling contributions in order to finance benefits and to remunerate medical practitioners and

[1] Two Canadian provinces passed such legislation in 1935 and 1936.

hospitals. In connection with health insurance, the fees and services of doctors might tend to be standardized rather than set by the present discriminatory method of charging what the traffic will warrant. However, health insurance can operate fully and satisfactorily with the free choice of doctors and hospitals by patients, as experience in France and many other countries indicates.[1] It is true that in most countries the government provides a subsidy to health-insurance systems as a supplement to the contributions of employers and employees. Such a subsidy may be necessary because it generally requires from four to seven per cent of the total wages of covered workers to finance sickness insurance.

In this country there are various voluntary arrangements for group protection against the risk of ill health and nonoccupational accidents. Many firms have programs of sickness benefits for their employees, including mutual benefit associations and group insurance. As already indicated, such company programs help to tie the employee to the employer because the worker generally loses his benefit rights upon leaving the firm. Probably 2,000,000 employees are covered by mutual benefit associations, which may provide benefits for 13 to 26 weeks of disability in any one year. Over 1,000,000 employees are covered by group accident and health policies taken out with life insurance companies. In both types of program, employees frequently contribute.[2] A few trade-unions have sickness-benefit programs under which $4,000,000 or $5,000,-000 are dispensed each year, and fraternal societies are reported to have sickness-benefit plans covering over 6,000,000 members. Group hospitalization plans have grown rapidly in recent years and include more than 2,000,000 persons. Furthermore, many companies have arranged for group purchase of medical care by their employees.[3] Private life insurance companies also sell accident- and health-insurance policies covering millions of persons, but such policies had a very high lapse ratio during the 1930's, indicating that most people cannot afford to pay for such protection. Experience abroad demonstrates that the health-insurance system should

---

[1] For a discussion of doctors under health insurance, cf. Barbara N. Armstrong, *The Health Insurance Doctor, His Rôle in Great Britain, Denmark, and France*, 1939.

[2] For a discussion of such plans, cf. Eleanor Davis, *Company Sickness Benefit Plans for Wage Earners*, Princeton University, Industrial Relations Section, 1936.

[3] Cf. Leahmae Brown, *Group Purchase of Medical Care by Industrial Employees*, Princeton University, Industrial Relations Section, 1938.

be on a compulsory basis. Even government subsidies to voluntary plans have failed to provide sufficient coverage and adequate benefits.

The suggestion has been made that workmen's compensation laws should be extended to provide a comprehensive health-insurance system for industrial workers, but this proposal has been strongly opposed by most authorities on the grounds that the administration of workmen's compensation has been unsatisfactory and very costly in most states. Foreign experience indicates that the administrative costs of health insurance need not exceed 10 per cent of contributions, compared to 43 per cent for private stock companies underwriting workmen's compensation. Experience abroad, especially in Great Britain and Germany, has also demonstrated that numerous or competing insurance agencies stand in the way of a unified system with uniform benefits at low cost. Indeed, a unified compulsory system of health insurance furnishing broad protection from an exclusive fund could be financed by the percentage—almost six per cent of their income—that workers and their families have generally been paying on some 75,000,000 industrial life or "burial" insurance policies, promising on the average about $200 at the death of the policyholder.[1]

The old-age insurance programs in many countries provide monthly annuity payments to invalid workers completely incapacitated for gainful employment through sickness or injury. Some consideration has been given to the possibility of expanding the Federal Old-Age and Survivors program to include insurance against invalidity.[2]

[1] *Cf.* Maurice Taylor, *The Social Cost of Industrial Insurance*, 1933, p. 193.

[2] For further discussion of health insurance, *cf.* I. S. Falk, *op. cit.;* H. A. Millis, *Sickness and Insurance*, 1937; or Louis S. Reed, *Health Insurance*, 1937.

CHAPTER NINETEEN

ECONOMICS OF LABOR STANDARDS

Standards for wage rates and conditions of work may be established by action on the part of employers and labor unions or of the government. In the chapters that follow, the activities of employers and employees with regard to labor standards will be discussed in detail. One of the main objectives of trade-unionism is to bring about uniform minimum standards throughout a whole trade or industry. This chapter is concerned with the economic limitations to government action on such matters as minimum wages, maximum hours of work, child labor, and the social insurances. These measures and their economic implications have been analyzed separately in the preceding chapters. This chapter discusses the general problem of state and national labor standards in the light of the economics of space relationships. It, therefore, rests primarily upon the theory of industrial location and migration along with the theory of interstate and international trade.

Certain aspects of the issues discussed in this chapter have been briefly explained in the previous chapters. Here these separate explanations are drawn together, integrated, and elaborated. Because this chapter deals in a general way with labor legislation previously analyzed in detail, it serves, in some measure, as a summary and conclusion to Part Two of the book.

BACKGROUND IN FACT AND THEORY

As already explained, it may pay an employer to engage in welfare activities for the benefit of his employees even though such programs do not increase the average efficiency of the total labor supply as much as they increase total labor costs. By affording an employer a differential advantage in the labor market, they serve to aid him in obtaining and retaining the pick of the labor supply. Through feelings of gratitude and good will, or through fear of loss of pension and insurance rights, the employees may hesitate to strike or quit.

When the worker obtains such benefits by means of government rather than employer action, there will not be the same beneficial effects upon company loyalty nor the same restraining effects upon the migration of employees. The differential advantage of the single company therefore disappears, although the cost frequently continues in the form of taxes upon the employer.

It is significant that well-developed welfare programs have been characteristic of large firms with high capital and materials costs relative to labor costs. With labor costs only a small and declining fraction of total costs, it may pay a firm to develop the morale and tractability of its employees in order to obtain efficient and continuous operation of costly equipment. In this respect, legislation raising wages, shortening hours, or providing for social-insurance benefits is not so effective from the point of view of an individual company. Just the opposite is, of course, true for the worker who is, so to speak, partially freed from a particular firm by such state action.

Independent state and national action. Past experience with legislation on working hours, child labor, minimum wages, and social insurance has been surveyed in a number of the previous chapters. In practically every case employers protested that such legislation would hinder them in competition with employers in other areas, and many businessmen predicted ruin for local industry in consequence of establishing higher labor standards by law. As indicated in the chapters on labor history in Part One, some employers in England and America complained that the first child-labor legislation in the nineteenth century would have an "unhappy influence" both upon factory children and upon local industry, which would suffer in international or interstate trade. Experience soon proved those employers to be absolutely wrong. Output was not reduced by restrictions upon child labor, which helped to eliminate the social cost of such labor. By preventing an irreparable loss from defective development and ill health,[1] human resources were conserved for a more productive manhood.

---

[1] For facts indicating a close causal connection between child labor and poor health, cf. *Child Labor Facts and Figures*, U. S. Department of Labor, Children's Bureau, Bulletin No. 197, 1930, pp. 31–32.

The results were similar in the case of hours and minimum-wage legislation. The first English and American laws reducing the working hours of women and children in factories were condemned as weapons for the defeat of local employers in the market place. The reader will recall from the discussion in Chapter 13 that experience in Massachusetts after 1879 failed to bear out the dire predictions of employers and that other near-by states soon followed Massachusetts' example. The first minimum-wage legislation in Australia, New Zealand, England, and America was vigorously opposed by employers on the ground that it would injure local business in competition with firms in other countries or states. How rapidly most employer opposition vanished as experience brought out the beneficial aspects of such legislation was explained in Chapter 12.

Fears of handicapping the nation's business did not prevent Germany from enacting social-insurance laws in the 1880's establishing systems of compulsory sickness, industrial-accident, and old-age insurance, which required that part or all of the contributions be paid by the employer. Later other European countries enacted similar social-insurance measures without any concern as to international reciprocity or fear that they would suffer from competition by the United States, which until 1935 failed to enact any social-insurance laws, except to cover industrial accidents. There is little evidence to indicate that industry in Germany or other European nations suffered from such legislation. In this country the fear of interstate competition, although hindering the passage of laws establishing industrial-accident insurance in some states, failed to prevent over five sixths of all states from independently passing such laws between 1911 and 1920. Of course, compulsory accident insurance did not increase the employer's cost of production by the full amount of his premium payments, for he was already legally liable for work accidents in his shops under certain circumstances.

Why have employers' fears of such labor legislation in the past proved to be largely unfounded? Would experience be the same in the future if a state or nation proceeded to enact further hours, wages, or social-insurance measures? Is there any economic justification for fears that social legislation, which seems to increase labor costs, injures covered firms in competition with companies in other localities, other states, and other nations?

In attempting to answer these questions, it may be well to review briefly some of the reasons why labor legislation seeming to raise costs did not ruin local industry as predicted by some employers. In the first place, many of the employers reasoned on the basis of what would happen to their own business if their costs were increased, neglecting to appreciate that the cost rise would be general and fairly uniform, so that it would affect all employers covered by the legislation in much the same way. Secondly, they failed to allow for the effect of increased costs and increased incomes upon demand in general. In looking at their particular firms they overlooked general effects. Thirdly, they tended, for the same reason, to neglect the effects of such legislation upon the health, energy, and productivity of workers as a whole over a period of time. That was especially true in the case of child-labor and hours legislation. In many instances these measures seem to have increased output about as much as they increased costs, either because of their beneficial effects upon workers or because of their stimulus to management. In the case of the early hours legislation, there is no doubt that many employers had been forcing workers to work longer than the optimum work day of maximum output and efficiency.

Fourthly, labor legislation for social security has in some cases simply provided a new way for shouldering an old burden, so that taxes for workmen's and unemployment compensation, for instance, tended to reduce taxes for relief and lawsuits for damages. In so far as taxes for social security have been shifted to workers through pay envelopes or the Federal old-age insurance programs have relieved employers of some pension obligations, it is even possible that employers' costs have been actually reduced by certain social-insurance measures. Fifthly, labor legislation in some cases may simply have served to reduce or eliminate exploitation of workers by employers who are in a strong market position, especially in mill villages and company towns. In such instances, increased labor costs may have operated to reduce high profits and to squeeze down inflated land and capital values just as increased property taxes sometimes do. The reader will recall the discussion in Chapter 12 pointing out that there may be no normal and necessary rate of profit. Lastly, in the international sphere, the export industry of nations enacting such legislation was not destroyed because of the principle of comparative advantage and the adjustments (gold flows, monetary and price-level changes, or exchange-rate fluctuations), which, as already explained, prevent a nation from being continuously undersold abroad in all lines.   These principles of international trade and finance are discussed more fully in a later section of this chapter.

Labor in location theory.   A large number of factors affect decisions regarding the location of new factories and workshops. The importance of each of these factors varies with the type of business and is constantly changing even for the same industry. Consequently, the best site for a plant or shop may not continue to be the best location with a change in economic conditions. The following list of some important factors in business location indicates how complex the problem is: (1) cheap and easily accessible transportation facilities; (2) accessibility to raw materials; (3) proximity to factories and trading exchanges linked to the industry; (4) accessibility or proximity to selling markets; (5) site cost and availability of existing buildings; (6) taxes and cost of services, including power, water, and fuel; (7) suitability of labor, including its cost, quantity, quality, and tractability.   A survey of business opinion in England early in 1939 indicated that cheap and easily accessible transportation is the factor usually regarded as most important in determining the location of manufacturing establishments.[1]   In the case of mining, access to raw materials would be the primary factor.   In trade and retailing, the most weight would be given to proximity to selling markets.

Labor "is, perhaps, the most complicated of all the principal localizing factors," and "its influence is largely unpredictable," because labor costs and labor conditions change rapidly.[2]   During the last few decades the labor factor has been of declining importance in the location of business. There are a number of reasons for that.   Labor costs have been a declining percentage of the total costs of individual firms as capital equipment per employee has increased. Professor Herman Schumacher states in an article on the location of industry in the *Encyclopaedia of Social Sciences:*

---

[1] *Cf. Report on the Location of Industry in Great Britain*, Political and Economic Planning, March 1939, p. 58.

[2] *Ibid.*, p. 63.

Nowadays local differences in the cost of labor must be very large indeed to induce even a gradual shift in the location of an industry. In fact with the ever increasing "capitalization" of industry as a whole the basis for labor orientation becomes more and more narrowly restricted to preserving continuity of operations and hence to securing tractable labor.[1]

Mechanization has also tended to reduce the relative importance of special skills of workers, which, along with improved transportation facilities, including the automobile, has weakened the strength of local supplies of skilled or special labor as a locational factor. Furthermore, geographical differences in wage rates have been somewhat reduced, and the organization of labor has been extended to areas that formerly were nonunion. With this tendency toward uniformity as labor unions organize entire industries regardless of location, labor differences are somewhat reduced. No longer can employers select business sites on the basis of previous experience indicating that local labor is subdued and will continue to be contented. Finally, the significance of the labor factor in business location has tended to diminish somewhat with the shift of business away from manufacturing toward services, which are closely related to incomes and must be performed in the locality.

The question of labor as a location factor has both qualitative and quantitative aspects. The former covers such matters as skill, training, and adaptability. The latter concerns the available amounts of various classes of labor (male, female, and juvenile) as well as the nature of the competition for labor in the local labor market. A large city affords an opportunity to recruit a working force with little change in wage rates, because it provides a relatively elastic supply of all grades of labor to the individual firm whose demand is a small part of the total local demand. On the other hand, a large company in a small community can exert more control over the labor market and the local government. As a personnel manager in a large rubber company pointed out regarding the company's plant in a small Southern city, it is much easier to organize community sentiment in favor of a company in a small community than in a large one. A small community fears the loss of a large part of the local demand for labor and of the community's income, which would occur if the

[1] Vol. 9, 1933, p. 590.

company should close up its plant or move it to another locality.[1] Some communities are so anxious to acquire and hold new industrial plants that they offer the owners exemptions from property taxes and other special inducements and services, including special protection during labor difficulties.[2]

Factors restricting business migration. Certain forms of investment may be fairly liquid and transferable, but once capital has been invested in plant facilities, located on a certain site, it is fairly fixed. The firm is, so to speak, bound to the community by the investment already sunk in buildings and equipment. The process of shifting the location of such a firm or branch of a firm to another area would be difficult and costly. Of course, investment in new firms or new plants is not so restricted by past commitments.[3] In Chapters 23 and 30 reference is made to a number of firms that moved to certain localities because of special community subsidies.

If a firm only rents its plant and equipment, that firm can readily move to another location, although the plant itself is not moved and may be rented to another concern. With business firms constantly failing or liquidating, some industrial migration may occur without actual migration of the firm but simply by a change of the firms in the industry. Such changes frequently do not, however, involve a migration of the business to other localities. A grocery or clothing store may liquidate and a new concern may rent the same shop or one in the same district.

Study of the factors in industrial location indicates that there are rather rigid limitations to the location of new firms, especially outside the field of manufacturing. Many businesses, for technical and economic reasons, cannot be moved to other localities. A whole group of industries have been called "market bound" because they must be carried on near the point of consumption or sale of the produce or service. That is true of all the service industries, including gas, electricity, telephone service, garages, filling

---

[1] *Cf. Hearings on S. Res. 266 before a Subcommittee of the Senate Committee on Education and Labor*, 75th Congress, first session, Part 8, Anti-union Activities, 1937, pp. 2979, 2983, and 3209.

[2] *Cf.* Chamber of Commerce of the United States, Department of Manufacture, *Special Inducements to Industries*, 1931, 40 pp. *Cf.* also, Jack Hardy, *The Clothing Workers*, 1935, pp. 158, 160; and the discussion of the Brown Shoe Company in Chapter 23 *infra*.

[3] *Cf.* Carter Goodrich *et al.*, *Migration and Economic Opportunity*, 1936, p. 390.

stations, banking, governmental services, movies, and other amusements, as well as professional and personal services such as pressing,
cleaning, laundry, and beauty-shop activities. It is also true of
selling agencies, retail shops, local trade, newspapers, and building construction. It is interesting to note that labor in a number
of these local-market lines, like building, newspaper printing,
and trucking, has been well organized in many localities for a long
time. An explanation of this fact is contained in the discussion
of the market theory of trade-unionism in the next chapter. Here it
is only necessary to point out that such businesses cannot readily
move to avoid labor organization.

Many lines of business are "materials bound" in the sense that
they must be carried on where certain raw materials or natural
resources are located. That is true of extractive industries like
coal and metal mining, oil-well drilling, logging and sawmilling,
farming, canning, and, to some extent, brick and tile manufacture.
Other businesses are largely dependent upon such natural resources as rivers, ports, parks, springs, bathing beaches, and
climate.

Economic activities representing probably four fifths of our
national income are prevented from migrating any great distance
by markets or natural resources. The possibilities of migration
may also be more or less restricted for industries requiring special
skilled labor, like certain kinds of shoe, clothing, and pottery
manufacture. The fact that state and city sales taxes and changes
in local property tax rates seem to have had so little effect upon
the location or movement of business indicates the predominant
influence of the location factors that have been stressed. Indeed,
studies seem to show that "few plants have moved from one type of
community to another during recent years" and that there has
been a "marked stability of locational pattern over the past generation." [1]

It is true that manufacture, agriculture, and the extractive
industries are primary or basic in the sense that transportation,
trade, and consumer markets depend upon such primary economic activities. Therefore, it is possible that secondary activities,
such as retail trade and transportation, may suffer in a locality
if manufacturing firms migrate to another area. It is for this

[1] Carter Goodrich et al., op. cit., p. 344; cf. also pp. 345–83.

reason that localities with industry founded on natural advantages (whether natural resources or natural traffic routes) are much less likely to suffer from the migration of manufacturing concerns than are localities whose manufacturing is based on various subsidies or low labor standards.

Social aspects of industrial migration. Mobility of labor and capital is desirable so that the nation's productive factors may be distributed in the most efficient fashion with changes in transportation facilities, in productive processes, and in available natural resources. To prevent the migration of industry to a more effective location may mean the same bar to progress that is involved in restrictions upon the introduction of improved machinery and technique. Technological change does mean some waste in the form of obsolescence. However, it is more wasteful in the long run to lower labor standards (by accepting lower incomes, lengthening the work day, and permitting child labor) in order to try to halt economic improvement, whether it be new machinery or the relocation of industry. In such cases, a socially desirable and economical change is being held back for a short time at the expense of the best development of labor resources and labor's effectiveness in the long run.

As already indicated, most migration of industry is caused by nonlabor factors like transportation changes, the development of cheaper power, or the exhaustion of natural resources, leaving stranded communities such as the cutover areas in Michigan and Minnesota. Few people claim that it is socially undesirable to move labor and industry from areas made less advantageous by physical and technological change. But when industrial migration is said to result from changes in labor standards, such as minimum-wage, maximum-hours, or child-labor legislation, it is somehow assumed that the migration is socially bad. This assumption largely arises from reasoning on a purely individual basis rather than from a national viewpoint. Of course, owners of real estate in a locality may lose from an emigration of industry and people, while landowners in the locality of corresponding immigration may gain by an equal amount. But such gains or losses are personal and paper phenomena. They do not represent social gains or losses, which can occur only when resources are wasted or are not used in the most effective manner.

Motivated by local pride and profit considerations, local merchants and businessmen may vigorously oppose any emigration of industry and labor, just as skilled workers oppose new machines and methods that reduce the value of their skill. But from a national or social point of view, it is desirable for labor to be highly mobile and to seek out the highest real wage rates so that the country may enjoy the largest or optimum national product per inhabitant.

Labor as a whole gains by the migration of business to locations that prove most advantageous without any lowering of labor standards. Where, however, industry is attracted to an area because labor standards are low and labor is sold relatively cheap, the income of labor as a whole in the country is likely to suffer, unless thereby total employment in the country is considerably increased. A local subsidy to industry in the form of reduced labor standards is on a par with a local subsidy to industry in other forms such as reduced taxes, tax exemptions, or free plant sites and plant buildings contributed by local business and real-estate interests in order to attract manufacturing payrolls from other localities. Such differentials in labor costs within a country can only continue because labor is tied to a locality of low labor costs by certain ties, local preferences, widespread unemployment, lack of funds to pay for the expenses of migration, or ignorance of conditions elsewhere. It is primarily firms manufacturing those products in which labor costs are a large percentage of total costs, such as clothing establishments, shoe manufacturers, and cotton textile concerns, that may be induced to migrate to certain localities by low wages. If, however, the labor used in the low-wage localities would not be paid higher wages in other localities, the migration of concerns to such localities is not open to objections on general economic grounds.

From the point of view of the material standard of living of the whole nation, there is much more justification for regional or national uniformity in the price of a certain grade of labor than there is for regional or national uniformity in the prices of certain products. Regional or national price uniformity is widespread in this country, having been achieved by the methods mentioned in Chapter 5, including the quotation of nationwide prices by firms with branded products, the use of the basing-point system,[1] and

[1] The basing-point system is discussed more fully in Chapter 31 *infra*.

the practice of quoting prices according to the "freight-allowed" method.   Uniform delivered prices mean that the producer's realized net prices from sales to different customers vary with the distance between the seller and the buyer.   Consequently, in terms of realized income, all producers quoting uniform delivered prices are discriminating in favor of the most distant buyers. Such discrimination, whether arising from the freight-allowed method or the basing-point system, is likely to lead to a great deal of cross-shipment, with no buyer (industrial firm or consumer) enjoying the full advantage of a location near the area of production.   Under those circumstances, there is likely to be an uneconomic distribution of the nation's productive resources.

Labor differs from products in that it is not being transported daily from production points in one region to localities of consumption in another region.   Uniform wage rates for the same grade of labor throughout a region or a nation would probably lead to less cross-migration of labor than occurs now.   With a uniform price for a certain grade of labor throughout a territory, migration of labor to the most favorable or most economic localities of production would be forced by unemployment in the least favorable areas.   Through wage differentials between localities, the areas least favored by natural and economic factors may be able to restrain the migration of industry into the most favored areas by offering labor at a cheap rate.   Geographic wage differentials actually tend to lead to an uneconomic distribution of the nation's productive resources, unless it can be demonstrated that such differentials represent a corresponding difference in the cost of living between any two areas or reflect the extent to which workers prefer one area over others as a place in which to live.

Wage standards and regional competition.   As indicated in Chapter 8, the level of real wages in a region largely depends upon the physical productivity of that region and upon the exchange value that its products have in other regions.   The level of money wages in a region within a country must be related to such economic realities.

A state may, however, be a high-wage area without suffering in interstate competition, if it enjoys certain natural and economic advantages.   The state of Washington may be used as an example.

In 1940 the minimum wage for unskilled labor in Washington

was 62.5 cents an hour in airplane manufacture and lumber-and-sawmill operations and 65 cents an hour in cement manufacture and paper-and-pulp operations. These wage rates were as high as the minima for common labor in those lines in any state in the country. Indeed, in no other state were the minimum wages in airplane and cement manufacture as high as they were in Washington in 1938 and 1939. In 1939, average earnings in the pulp-and-paper industry on the Pacific Coast were 80 cents an hour, which was over 20 per cent higher than the average hourly earnings in any other region in the country. As mentioned in Chapter 6, drivers of trucks and delivery vehicles in Seattle have been receiving some of the highest wages for that line of work in the country, and average hourly earnings of longshoremen in the ports of Washington were approximately $1.15 an hour. The earnings of sailors on the Alaska boats, sailing out of Seattle, averaged about $2,250 in 1939, and some of them, by working overtime and doing longshore work, earned as much as $3,500 and $4,000 a year. In fruit and vegetable canning, the highest average earnings in the country in 1939 were 47 cents an hour in western Washington and California. A study by the Wage and Hour Division of the U. S. Department of Labor revealed that the average hourly earnings in fruit and vegetable canning in New York, Illinois, Indiana, Wisconsin, Minnesota, and Iowa in 1939 ranged between 30 and 34 cents an hour.[1]

The various statistics dealing with unemployment, including unemployment compensation and relief, indicate that, despite high wage rates, the state of Washington has suffered no more from unemployment than the country at large. In addition, the population of the state has been expanding, as people have migrated to Washington from the dust bowl and other areas.

What permits employers in the state of Washington to pay high wage rates and still compete with producers in other regions? One large company canning peas in western Washington sold 35 per cent of its pack in New York City alone in 1939. How is it possible for some canning firms in western Washington to sell as much as three fourths of their pack of fruit and vegetables on the Atlantic

---

[1] *Report of the Fruit and Vegetable Canning Industry under the Fair Labor Standards Act,* Research and Statistics Branch, Wage and Hour Division, U. S. Department of Labor, May 1940 (mimeographed), Table 4.

seaboard, where average hourly wages in canning are little more than half those in western Washington? How is it possible for the Pacific Coast pulp-and-paper manufacturers, despite an average hourly wage 25 per cent above that in the East, to reach the Atlantic seaboard markets for pulp and bag paper and to compete with Eastern producers for those markets? How is it possible for employers in Washington to pay average hourly wages of 84 cents in logging operations and 73 cents in sawmill operations, as they did from 1937 to 1940, and yet sell over half of their lumber to markets East of the Mississippi or abroad, where wage rates are much lower? [1] In 1938 and 1939 average hourly wages in sawmills in Washington were from two to two-and-a-half times the average hourly wages in sawmills in the Southern pine region. These three branches of industry (logging and sawmilling, paper and pulp, and fruit and vegetable canning) represent one third of all payrolls under workmen's compensation in Washington and account for more than half of the state's exports to other states and regions.

In the canning of fruit and vegetables and in the production of paper and pulp, wages to workers average but 15 to 18 per cent of total costs. Consequently, other cost items are of more significance. The woods used in Washington are better for making certain kinds of paper and pulp, and the logs are bigger. In the case of fruits and vegetables, the climate helps the Washington farmers to grow certain products of very high quality. As explained in Chapter 8, the output per man-hour in lumber in the West is over twice as great as in the South. The figure for Washington in 1929 (96 board feet of lumber per man-hour) was the highest of any state and was well over three times the average of 28 board feet per man-hour for the Southern states. Despite the high wage rates, the labor costs of logging and milling a thousand feet of Douglas fir in western Washington and Oregon in the first quarter of 1934 were one third less than such costs per thousand feet of Southern pine.[2] The high productivity in Washington is due to

[1] *Cf.* R. V. Reynolds and A. H. Pierson, *Lumber Distribution and Consumption for 1936,* Forest Research Project Report No. 1, Forest Service, U. S. Department of Agriculture, 1938, p. 12.

[2] *Cf.* Peter A. Stone *et al., Economic Problems of the Lumber and Timber Products Industry,* National Industrial Recovery Administration, Work Materials No. 79, March 1936, p. 322.

the degree of mechanization and the horse power available per worker, the average timber stand per acre, and the size of the log sawed. Wages are about one third of the total costs of logging, milling, shipping, and selling Douglas fir lumber in the state of Washington.[1]

Other factors besides productivity per worker and quality of the product help to explain how the state of Washington can produce articles for shipment outside the state despite the high wage levels that prevail in Washington. In the case of airplane manufacture at the Boeing plant in Seattle, not only is the climate favorable for flying throughout the year, but even in 1938 as much as three fourths of all airplane sales were to governments, and government purchases may be distributed on military as well as economic bases. A new plant of the Aluminum Company of America was recently established in western Washington, despite high wage levels, because the cost of electric power is such a large item in the making of aluminum and electric power rates are extremely low in Washington.

The Biennial Census of Manufactures in 1937 revealed that, in important manufacturing lines of the Northwest like pulp, paper, and flour milling, average wages per man-hour were 20 to 30 per cent higher in the state of Washington than the average for 21 Northeastern states, while the average value added by manufacture per man-hour worked in the Washington plants exceeded the figure for Northeastern plants by 25 to 100 per cent.[2] In other words, the regional differential in the value productivity per hour worked in manufacturing was greater than the wage differential. One reason that the value productivity in Washington plants was higher than in Eastern mills was the greater use of mechanical power and machinery per worker.

Under such circumstances, attempts to attract industry by lowering wage rates in Washington might only serve to attract an uneconomic type of industry to that area. The migration to Washington of manufacturing industries using a large amount of hand labor because of reduced labor standards would tend to lower the standard of living of the inhabitants of that state. With

[1] Ibid., p. 15.

[2] Cf. Man-Hour Statistics for 105 Selected Industries, Census of Manufactures: 1937, U. S. Bureau of the Census and U. S. Bureau of Labor Statistics, December 1939, pp. 11, 41–43.

relatively abundant lumber, agricultural, and power resources, Washington should seek only high-wage industries, in which labor is a small proportion of total costs.

STATE AND LOCAL LABOR STANDARDS

The foregoing discussion has indicated some of the important considerations in the economics of local and regional labor standards within a nation. That discussion is continued in this section. The economic aspects of national and international labor standards are explained in the last section of this chapter.

Contrast with international conditions. In discussing state and local labor standards it is necessary to bear in mind certain differences between intranational and international trade. In comparing two areas within a nation, businessmen and workers do not need to take account of exchange rates, price-level changes, monetary standards, or other differences in national policies, including Federal taxation. Within a country there is freedom of movement of capital, and especially labor, to a degree that does not exist between countries. Because economic adjustments between areas within a country cannot be made through exchange rates or through changes in the money supply and the price level, they must occur primarily through the migration of men and business, motivated by the prospect of higher real wages, less unemployment, or greater profits. Between nations, on the other hand, the migration of labor is an adjustment that recently has been almost nonexistent.

Without such spatial adjustments as occur through exchange rates, gold flows, etc., it is possible for nationally advertised products to retail for the same price all over the country, whether they be consumers' goods like chewing gum, magazines, branded foods and beverages, and trade-marked shoes and clothes, or the various kinds of mechanical equipment bearing a single national price. Such national uniformity is possible despite local variations in the cost of labor, delivery service, and rent, because producers can balance lower net returns in some areas by higher net returns in others.

With a fairly uniform price level throughout the country, the question of money costs is of major importance. Business tends to locate where total money costs are lowest and money profits are largest. High labor costs, high taxes, or high transportation costs may force some business to migrate elsewhere within the country, but they would not drive business out of a country in the same way. Within a country, capital may "emigrate" from a locality without increasing the "exports" or products sold by that locality to other localities. Between countries, however, exports of capital mean, sooner or later, a corresponding increase in the capital-exporting nation's other exports and, therefore, in its sales and business. As is explained more fully in the next section, capital investment abroad involves payment in the country's money which foreigners will use to buy goods or services from the capital-exporting country.

Possible effects. The previous subsection reviewing past experience with independent action on labor standards indicates some of the possible results from raising state or local standards. The smaller the area covered, the more likely it is that workers will be attracted from other localities by the differential advantage of higher labor standards. There is also the possibility that such higher standards may improve workers' health and morale and increase productivity, or that the additional cost will be shifted through wages or result in a reduction of taxes so that no net increase in per-unit costs of output occurs.

If money costs are increased and profits reduced, there may still be no tendency for industry to emigrate. As indicated in Chapter 12, firms continue to expand rapidly even when they are failing to earn average profits. There is a definite possibility that higher labor costs might reduce land and capital values without causing an exodus of industry. Indeed, it is very costly and difficult for firms to permit existing plants to depreciate and be abandoned. The overhead costs of abandoned plants, including property taxes, continue. Even should a plant be abandoned by one firm, another one may purchase and reopen it. Answers to a questionnaire by hundreds of British manufacturing executives indicate that the availability of cheap, existing buildings is the primary factor in the location of a large number of firms.[1]

Migration of business and labor, as already explained, is a normal and necessary means of economic adjustment within a country. It is economically desirable when it occurs because labor standards are being raised to the level attained by most areas

[1] *Cf. Report on the Location of Industry in Great Britain*, PEP, March 1939, p. 60.

within a nation. If a state or locality attempts to advance in such matters beyond its neighbors, there is a possibility that its rate of economic expansion may be retarded and the character of its industry gradually changed to adjust to such new standards. But what does a state or locality lose if it restrains industrial expansion by a moderate increase in labor standards?

Taxation as an alternative. It has been argued that taxation for social purposes, such as relief, social insurance, and schools, is a better means of improving the condition of labor than the enforcement of better labor standards, which increase production and business costs.[1] Certain taxes, it is said, do not enhance costs nor reduce business profits until after they have been earned. Net income taxes, which take only a percentage of profits, have been pointed to as having little effect upon the businessman's incentive to expand his output and business.

It must be recognized, however, that most state and local taxes (all except taxes on personal incomes, inheritances, or nonbusiness property) are likely to affect business costs. Even state corporate net income taxes, which do not increase costs, may stimulate manufacturing firms to locate in states not having such taxes. In so far as state or local taxes do increase costs, their effect upon labor's output would generally be less direct than higher labor standards.

NATIONAL LABOR STANDARDS

The economic objection has been made against practically every proposal for national legislation to protect labor that it would injure the country's industry in competition with other countries not having such standards. That notion is even to be found in the 1919 Treaty of Versailles which states that "the failure of any nation to adopt humane conditions of labor is an obstacle in the way of other nations which desire to improve the conditions in their own countries." The activities of the International Labour Office have been based upon the assumption that independent national improvements in labor standards place a nation's industry at a disadvantage in international trade.

---

[1] J. M. Keynes subscribed to this view in an article, "The Question of High Wages," *Political Quarterly*, vol. 1 (January 1930), pp. 110–24, in which he maintained that to squeeze the capitalist "in act of earning his profits is to squeeze him in the wrong place." The international aspects of Keynes' argument are treated in the next section.

Orthodox economists, on the other hand, have long maintained that higher labor standards, taxes, or other costs, if they should affect the cost of producing all goods in equal proportion, would have no permanent influence upon a country's international trade or total exports.[1] A general over-all change in money costs, these economists claim, soon is counterbalanced by offsetting adjustments in exchange rates (if the country is not on an international monetary standard) or through gold flows and changes in the money supply and the price level (if the country is on the gold standard). In short, they insist that a country may not suffer in international trade by abolishing child labor or shortening working hours by law.

Adequate treatment of this issue requires further discussion of the theory of international trade and finance.

International trade theory.[2] Trade arises from a difference in money costs of production, and any attempt by tariffs, taxes, or other measures to reduce cost differences between areas or within an area reduces the volume of trade. On the other hand, measures that spread the range of cost differentials for various products tend to increase trade.

Basically, differences in production costs arise from inequality in natural and human resources. Such inequalities are reflected in variations between localities in the prices of raw materials, in rents, in wage rates, in interest rates, in capital equipment, and in transportation costs. Because of differences in the relative scarcity of various productive factors and agents, the scale of relative costs of producing various products in one country is dissimilar from such a scale in another country. Under those circumstances, a country will export the products which, compared to the cost scales of other trading countries, it is best fitted to produce. This means that a country will tend to specialize in those lines of business which require large amounts of the factors that are relatively abundant, and consequently comparatively cheap, in that country. For example, articles like wool, beef, and wheat, which require large quantities of land relative to labor, are produced in Australia, Argentina, and western United States, where the acreage per

[1] *Cf.*, for example, Sidney Webb and Harold Cox, *The Eight Hours Day*, 1891, pp. 116–17.
[2] For a more complete discussion of this subject, *cf.* P. T. Ellsworth, *International Economics*, 1938, especially Chapters 3 through 6.

capita is high and land is cheap. On the other hand, lace, embroidery, and carving are produced in countries like China, where land is relatively scarce and labor comparatively abundant. Heavy industries like iron and steel are to be found where iron ore and coal are available and transportation facilities are good and cheap. Natural resources like oil, coal, lumber, metals, rubber, and good farming land play a fundamental role in cost differentials between countries. The size of a country's domestic market and the development of its industrial technique are likewise of fundamental importance.

Some of our producers have claimed that they could not compete with low-wage Italian labor, and Italian manufacturers, on the other hand, have complained that Italy is unable to compete with efficient American labor. Who is right? The truth is that the character of our resources, our relative scarcity of labor compared to resources, and our well-developed domestic market have caused American manufacture to specialize in labor-saving machinery such as automobiles, agricultural equipment, and business machines, which require a large market for efficient production. Small countries like Cuba or Denmark could never produce such machines at low cost. Italy, on the other hand, is better adapted for the production of olive oil and wines, because olives and grapes grow well where the land is hilly and dry. In some lines we cannot compete with Italy very well; in other lines she cannot compete with us.

Even if Italy were not especially well adapted for the production of any commodities, she would still have exports. Disregarding transportation costs and assuming no governmental barriers to trade, countries are bound to have exports and imports regardless of their resources, because it is inconceivable that a country would be so diversified in resources and labor conditions that the relative differences in the domestic costs of producing all the commodities it uses would be exactly the same as the relative costs between those commodities in the rest of the trading world. As long as cost deviations from the world average exist in a country, it has a basis for both imports and exports. Such deviations cannot continuously favor either exports or imports. No country can continue to be undersold in all lines of business in world markets, because if all costs were relatively high in a country, the mechanism of international adjustment would operate to reduce the prices of that country's products for foreigners until it did export.

The mechanism of adjustment between countries functions differently for countries having independent currencies than it does for countries on an international monetary standard like gold. The mechanism of adjustment under gold-standard conditions is explained in the following subsection on monetary standards, so only the adjustment under paper-standard conditions will be used here for illustrative purposes.

Assume that it did cost more to produce all commodities in a country than it would cost to buy them from abroad. In that case the inhabitants of the country would begin to make tremendous purchases from abroad and foreigners would buy nothing from the country in question. Barring the use of holdings of foreign currency or foreign securities, the inhabitants of the country could pay for imports from abroad only by selling their money for foreign money. But foreigners would not want to buy the country's money, since they were not making purchases from that country. With many inhabitants striving to exchange the country's currency into foreign money and few foreigners willing to accept the country's currency, its exchange value (the exchange rate) would begin to fall in terms of foreign monies until it became profitable for many foreigners to accept the country's money in order to make purchases there, causing that country to export. As the exchange value of the country's currency falls, the prices of foreign products rise for its inhabitants, so that imports from abroad become more and more costly. Disregarding changes in international investment, the exchange value of the country's currency would decline until its total exports of goods and services equaled, or paid for, its total imports. The exchange rate for countries on independent monetary standards thus serves to equalize the cost levels between countries and to maintain a balance between a country's total outpayments for imports of all kinds and its total inpayments for exports of all sorts. Our initial assumption that the costs of all products in a country were above the world level at the existing exchange rate is really an impossible situation. It could occur only when both imports and exports were prevented by barriers like tariffs and embargoes or where exchange control was combined with export subsidies.

Higher labor standards alone could reduce the proportion of

foreign trade in a country's total trade only if somehow they reduced the differentials between that country's costs of producing
various commodities in international trade and the world's cost
scale. That is not likely to occur. Indeed, higher labor standards
here might increase the cost differentials for this country, because
those now existing are based in part upon our high-priced labor
factor, which causes us to export products requiring proportionately
large capital costs. Of course, some of our industries in which
labor represents a large proportion of total costs might be adversely
affected in foreign trade as our exports of other products from industries with large capitalization increased. The point is that, although the composition of our exports might change somewhat,
there are no grounds for believing that higher labor standards at
home would cause a reduction in the proportion of exports to total
domestic sales, after adjustments had taken place in the exchange
rate or under the gold-standard mechanism.

Perhaps it should be added that there is no economic advantage
in trade as such, whether foreign or domestic. The economic advantages of trade occur because of cost differentials, but no additional gain is likely to result from artificially spreading those differentials between countries, although the economic advantages of
trade are lost by cost-equalizing measures such as tariffs and subsidies.

Labor standards and monetary standards. In the preceding
discussion, the problems of adjustment were minimized because it
was assumed that the country raising its labor standards was on
an independent monetary standard. The problems of adjustment
would have been much more serious and difficult had it been assumed that the country was on the international gold standard.

If the level of costs in a gold-standard country are high compared with the rest of the gold-standard world, the balance between
inpayments and outpayments is restored by the following complicated process: gold is exported to cover the balance; the gold outflow decreases bank reserves and the money supply in the country;
interest and discount rates rise; these steps reduce incomes and increase unemployment, which is supposed to cause a reduction in
the level of costs and prices, thus stimulating the country's exports.
In the other countries receiving the exported gold, the opposite
process of increased money supply and cost level is supposed to

take place, making those countries less desirable ones from which to buy.

The gold-standard method of restoring a country's balance of trade and payments through a reduction in its cost level (including wage rates, interest charges, and rents) is a slow, painful, and wasteful process, involving reduction of incomes, unemployment, strikes, and bankruptcy. On the other hand, restoration of equilibrium with the rest of the world is a relatively simple matter under independent monetary standards. Demand and supply in international trade are brought into balance or equilibrium by one price—the rate of foreign exchange. Under an independent currency, the price of exchange fluctuates freely instead of being fixed or pegged within the (cost of transporting) gold points under a gold standard.

Labor standards and capital movements. It is said that, if labor standards are not applied internationally, the possibility of foreign lending and investment limits the adoption of national standards which reduce the employer's return compared to profits abroad. For example, J. M. Keynes claims that "the extent to which one country can move in these matters, independently of other countries, is greatly affected by the mobility of lending" or of capital.[1] Professor Keynes seems to believe that foreign lending or investment will have an adverse effect upon employment in the lending country regardless of its monetary standard, although he recognizes that "under the gold standard the consequences are much more complicated."[2]

This argument, however, overlooks the fact that foreign lending means a corresponding increase in the lending nation's export balance, no matter what the monetary standard of that country may be. Inhabitants of the lending or investing country are really buying foreign securities and property, which they pay for with their own money in the same manner that they pay for any other exports, whether goods, services, or securities. The lending country's money generally can be spent only within its borders. Consequently, persons in other countries must use the proceeds of the loan or investment to buy from the lending country either products, services, securities, or gold, if the country is on the gold standard. If securi-

---

[1] J. M. Keynes, "The Question of High Wages," *Political Quarterly*, vol. 1 (January 1930), p. 116.
[2] *Idem.*

ties are bought with the loan or it is invested in the lending country, the result has simply been an exchange of indebtedness between the countries involved. Usually only a small part of the proceeds of a foreign loan would be taken in the form of gold exports. If taken in any other form, whether goods or services, employment within the country will tend to be increased. Such a relative increase in a country's exports and employment should not serve to limit the adoption of national labor standards.

The situation within a country is in this respect entirely different from the situation between countries, since loans and investments to another section of the same country are made in the same money. That money can be used to purchase goods, services, or property anywhere in the country and not simply in the locality from which the loan or investment originated. Capital movements between countries generally involve a corresponding movement of goods and services. That is not true of capital movements within a country.

The International Labour Organization. The 1919 Treaty of Versailles, in a section on labor, provided for the establishment of an International Labour Organization. The purpose of this organization has been to encourage and facilitate the adoption of world-wide minimum standards for labor. The treaty implied that labor standards place a burden upon the country that adopts them, so parallel improvement in working conditions in every country is necessary if the industry of an advanced country is not to be placed at a disadvantage in international competition with that of countries less advanced in labor standards. In short, the economic basis of the International Labour Organization has been the century-old objection of employers against factory legislation, namely, that one nation will injure its industry by improving labor conditions within its boundaries if any other nation fails to adopt the same legislation.

The previous discussion of past experience and international trade theory indicates how false is this employer doctrine when applied to the whole industry of a nation. As officials of the International Labour Office state, "experience appears to show that the countries with the most advanced labor legislation are by no means the least successful in the competition for world markets." [1] Al-

[1] *The International Labour Organization, The First Decade,* Preface by Albert Thomas, 1931, p. 30.

though invalid for industry as a whole, previous discussion has indicated that this employer objection may have some validity for particular industries within a country in so far as some of them gain and others lose because the effects of the labor legislation are uneven. Also it may have some validity for gold-standard countries during the period of transition or adjustment to improvements in labor standards, because the mechanism of international adjustment is so complicated and may be so destructive to a country's economy under gold-standard conditions.

Unfortunately, the International Labour Organization has failed to appreciate and apply such distinctions. The employer doctrine of economic injury in international trade from improved labor standards has been fully accepted by the Organization's officials for industry in general as well as in particular, and for countries on independent monetary standards as well as those on gold. As will be indicated presently, wholesale acceptance of such unsound doctrines has weakened the effectiveness of the Organization.

The Organization has never achieved the complete universality that, according to its economic philosophy, is essential for effective international action. Prior to 1934, Russia and the United States were not among its members, while after 1934, first Germany and then Italy and Japan ceased to take any part in its work. Fear of injury from competition by the large nonmember countries prevented some countries from adopting the labor standards recommended by the Organization.

The procedure followed by the International Labour Organization rests on voluntary action by each nation. Prior to 1940, a conference was held each year to which some 50 countries or states sent delegates. At such conferences, each member country is allowed two government representatives, one representative of its employers, and one representative of its employees. These annual conferences make recommendations and adopt "draft conventions," upon approval by two thirds of the delegates. The "draft conventions" specify minimum standards with regard to hours of work, child labor, social insurance of all kinds, night work, minimum wage-fixing machinery, unemployment, and similar subjects. By 1940 over 60 "conventions" had been adopted, most of them applying to industry or agriculture in general, although a number of them refer to particular industries, especially to ocean transportation.

The governments of the member countries must ratify or reject any "draft convention" within a year after it is adopted at an annual conference. The permanent staff of the Organization makes valuable studies of labor conditions in various countries, serving as a center of information and education. Undoubtedly, its recommendations and conventions have helped to establish labor standards which public opinion tends to accept as desirable or normal. In this way, its work may affect standards in a country even though that country refuses to ratify certain "draft conventions." The number of formal ratifications of the 25 draft conventions in effect before 1939 ranges from 11 to 35 out of some 50 ratifying states. The Organization, of course, has no powers of enforcement.

The discussions in the conferences and the statements of officials do not make clear whether all conventions—those eliminating child labor or protecting workers against loss from work accidents and sickness as well as those to reduce the hours of work—are supposed to place a country adopting them at a disadvantage in international trade. With regard to "the regulation of minimum wages as an international problem," the chief of the Organization's statistical section wrote in 1928: "The payment of exceptionally low wages is among the typical cases alluded to in the Peace Treaty in which other countries are prevented from making progress in the improvement of their working conditions by the fact that one country fails to give its workers reasonable conditions of work." [1]

It is against conventions for general reductions in working hours that the employer delegates have used the argument of international competition most extensively and effectively. The first draft convention, adopted in 1919, provides for the eight-hour day and the 48-hour week in all industry, with time-and-a-quarter for overtime. During the following two decades, 23 countries ratified that convention, but four of them made their ratification conditional upon similar ratification by their leading competitors. Consequently, in none of the large industrial countries has this eight-hour convention been in effect.

Many countries gave as their chief reasons for not ratifying, the fear of the competition of countries which did not ratify. Sometimes this fear was expressed as regards the whole economic life of the country as with

[1] Karl Pribram, "The Regulation of Minimum Wages as an International Problem," *International Labour Review*, vol. 17 (March 1928), p. 319.

Belgium and Switzerland; sometimes it is expressed as the fear of a particular industry, as in the case of the Italian silk-spinning industry which competes with the same industry in the Far East, and in the case of the Japanese silk-spinning industry which competes with that of China. Sometimes it has been fear of the competition of the United States. . . .[1]

With regard to the draft convention of a 40-hour working week (adopted by the 1935 conference), the employer delegates charged that it would be "economic suicide" for any country to ratify that convention, because the country would "be cut out of the market at once" and its national economy would "suffer fatal injury."[2] Only one country, New Zealand, had accepted the 40-hour convention by 1940.

Past directors of the International Labour Office have maintained that "the reforms adopted in the more advanced countries had to be protected against unfair competition by other countries which perhaps might not scruple to exploit their workers to the utmost for the sake of commercial advantage."[3] Such statements lend some support to the charge that the ILO is a means whereby rich, prosperous, and advanced countries can impose "on poor and backward states burdens that prevent them from competing in international markets."[4] They also lend support to the arguments of employers against all national labor legislation. The Chamber of Commerce of the United States, for example, used the same argument of the ILO officials against the wages-and-hours bill (now the Fair Labor Standards Act) in stating that it "would affect production for foreign markets and would handicap domestic producers of goods competing generally with imports."[5] With such questionable arguments used so freely by the officials of the ILO and employer delegates to its annual conferences, one would expect that the Organization would at least have made a detailed analysis of the alleged "burdens" or "handicaps" of national labor standards.

---

[1] Herbert Feis, "The Attempt to Establish the Eight-Hour Day by International Action," *Political Science Quarterly*, vol. 39 (December 1924), p. 639.

[2] *Cf. Record of Proceedings, International Labour Conference, Eighteenth Session*, 1934, p. 43; *Nineteenth Session*, 1935, p. 183; and *Twenty-Fourth Session*, 1938, p. 627.

[3] Albert Thomas in the Preface to *The International Labour Office, The First Decade*, p. 11. *Cf.* also Harold Butler, "Introduction," *Annals of the American Academy of Political and Social Science*, vol. 166 (March 1933), p. 3; and *Report of the Director*, International Labour Office, 1938, p. 51.

[4] Ernest Mahaim, "The Principles of International Labor Legislation," *Annals of the American Academy of Political and Social Science*, vol. 166 (March 1933), p. 14.

[5] *Hours-and-Wages Legislation*, Report of Special Committee, Chamber of Commerce of the United States, August 1937, p. 5.

PART THREE

ORGANIZATION AND LABOR RELATIONS

CHAPTER TWENTY

THE GROWTH OF TRADE-UNIONISM

A labor organization may be defined as an association of employees designed primarily to maintain or improve the condition of employment of its members. Although labor organizations may perform social, charitable, or religious functions, they are *labor* organizations only if their primary purpose is to further the economic interests of members as employees. A labor or trade-union is the most common form of labor organization in this country. Such unions generally consist of workers in a certain occupation or industry, associated together for collective action.

The labor movement is a much broader term than labor union. Such a movement presupposes some solidarity between workers in different trades or industries. In that sense, it may be said that the American labor movement began in 1827 when, as explained in Chapter 4, some 15 local unions of skilled craftsmen in various trades established the first "city central" in Philadelphia. Since that date the labor movement in this country has experienced a series of ups and downs.

The significance of a movement cannot, of course, be measured simply in terms of the total number of supporters or members. A strong minority that can exert considerable influence upon nonmembers and sympathizers may be more powerful than a less vigorous majority. The strength of a labor organization depends partly upon the strength of opposing forces and partly upon the territory and sections of industry in which it operates. In spite of such qualifications, however, total membership is perhaps the best available measure of the significance of labor organization in any area or branch of industry. The figures for paid-up membership are generally used to measure the growth and decline of organized labor.

Some reasons for joining and paying dues. Workers join labor unions for a variety of reasons. A worker may, however, be no more conscious of the motive or motives that prompt him to sign a union membership blank than is a person who joins a church or the Elks.

The reasons for acquiring union membership vary with the person, the union, and the circumstances. In some cases the union controls the job through an agreement with the employer, and workers must join the union in order to obtain employment with that firm. In a few cases, employers have even urged workers to join. Sometimes the worker is convinced that union membership is a means of furthering his own economic interests. The union may help to improve wages, hours, and other conditions of work in the firm and industry. It may offer some protection to the individual worker who is fired, or demoted, or has some other grievance. If the union takes up his case, the employer may be more likely to listen and to remedy the matter. A union may also attract some members, especially older workers, through its benefit features, providing old-age, sickness, or strike benefits. Certain younger workers may feel that they can get ahead by becoming officials in unions and making a career for themselves in the labor movement.

Other reasons for joining may be social or emotional. The worker may have a grudge against his foreman or the firm and may look upon union membership as a means of strengthening a group that will curb the employer and his agents. Union meetings may give the worker an opportunity to express his feelings toward the company, to influence the attitude of other employees, and even to convert them to his political and economic philosophy. The individual alone feels especially weak in a world of mass production and mass movements. An organization may give him an opportunity to join others for the achievement of those objectives that he considers socially desirable. Often there is a great deal of social pressure upon workers to become union members. Such pressure may come from parents, relatives, and friends, or from the community at large in a unionized locality. In addition to the threat of social ostracism, there may also be, in certain instances, a fear of personal or property injury if the worker fails to take out union membership. Generally, workers are induced to sign up and pay dues by a combination of such motives— personal gain, social approval, and fear.

DEVELOPMENT OF UNIONISM IN AMERICA

As indicated in Chapter 4, the first labor unions in this country arose early in the nineteenth century as a defense mechanism of skilled workers against the competitive pressure of merchant capitalists. In making purchases, such merchant buyers played producer-employers against one another, forcing reductions in cost through wage cuts and a subdivision of the work so that cheap, unskilled workers might perform work formerly done by skilled craftsmen. The craftsmen organized to resist such reductions in wages and in the demand for their skill. Indeed, labor unions have generally been formed to prevent what workers consider "unfair" competition and "undesirable" conditions in the labor market. Competitive pressure, similar to that which gave rise to labor unionism here, led to the formation of the first craft unions in other countries.

The fact that the world's first "city central" organization of local unions, its first trade-union journal, and its first labor party all arose in Philadelphia in 1827 and 1828 was mentioned in Chapter 4. In many labor-union matters America was first, although this country was soon outranked by almost all other industrial nations. Indeed, it was only in the period after the Civil War, when substantial and continuing unions were established, that trade-union membership in this country exceeded the peak in the 1830's. The total trade-union membership in the five principal industrial centers along the Atlantic seaboard has been estimated at about 300,000 in 1836. Estimates place total union membership in 1872 and 1884 at around 300,000, and in 1897 at 447,000.[1]

Retarding factors. Many explanations have been offered for the delayed development of trade-unionism in America after its early start. A few of the economic, social, and political conditions retarding our labor movement may be mentioned.

The workers in this country have been a very diverse group, belonging to a number of races and speaking a variety of tongues. As new immigrants arrived from abroad, the earlier settlers and native sons tended to become independent businessmen, employers,

[1] *Cf.* John R. Commons *et al.*, *History of Labour in the United States*, 1918, vol. 1, p. 424, and vol. 2, pp. 47, 314; and Leo Wolman, *Ebb and Flow in Trade Unionism*, 1936, pp. 16, 192–93.

or farmers. The population also was moving westward toward free land and the frontier. Consequently, the composition of the labor force in various firms and industries was in a constant state of flux. Industry itself moved readily from one area to another. With such mobility of labor and industry there was comparatively little class stratification. Workers hoped soon to rise out of the wage-earning class. Unionism, on the other hand, can have some permanence only when it is founded on a fairly continuous group of employees.

Free land and frontier conditions gave the country a social philosophy with a distinctly individualistic flavor, which colored our Federal constitution and our state constitutions. This philosophy held sway longer here than in other countries because the population was relatively sparse, the development of the factory system was slow, and agriculture has played such an important role in our economy. Many of our factory workers were recruited from rural areas, where the birth rate is high and rugged individualism is more rife. Workers from rural backgrounds are less likely to join in the collective activities of labor unions.

The size of the country, and therefore the market area for many industries, has also made labor organization more difficult, partly because the industry must be unionized in states with different laws and partly because the employing units are so large. The cost of organizing the whole market area is high in a large country. It is worth noting that, in the past, labor unionism has frequently been most prevalent in local-market lines of business that are less subject to outside competition, such as the building trades, newspaper printing, and service lines of all sorts.

Because industrial wage-earners were comparatively weak in voting strength, they generally joined with farmers and small businessmen in the political movements of the nineteenth century. In the decades before 1870, industrial wage-earners and their families accounted for less than a quarter of the nation's total population, while persons engaged in agriculture and their families represented almost half of the citizenry.[1] Political combinations of groups with such diverse economic interests, however, were very impermanent. They flourished during depressions, when

[1] By 1920 these proportions had been practically reversed.

farmers were suffering from sharp price reductions and labor unions tended to dissolve because of unemployment, wage cuts, loss of membership, lack of funds, and absence of a positive program. With an upswing in business and prices, the farmers became contented and workers tended to join unions as a means of securing wage increases and improvements in working conditions. It has been argued that such fluctuations from political to economic activity and back to preoccupation with politics in the next depression retarded the American labor movement during the nineteenth century.

Period before 1850. The discussion of labor organization in Chapter 4 indicated that, with the rise of prices from 1830 to 1837, labor's first political experiment was discarded and workers turned once more to direct economic action. As many as five national organizations of local craft unions were formed in order to meet attempts by employers to ship the work of the craftsmen from organized to unorganized centers, especially in times of labor strife.

The panic of 1837, however, dealt a severe blow to the unions, and, in the following depression years, union membership declined rapidly as wages were cut and unemployment increased. Workers again turned to political activity. Monopolies and banks were blamed for the depression, while reformers proposed cooperative ventures and utopian socialistic schemes as the solution for the country's economic ills.

Period of national trade-unions (1850-1872). In the early 1850's, prices again rose sharply as the California gold discoveries increased the nation's money supply in the approved fashion. Again prosperity resulted in a shift from the reformist theories of depression days to trade-unionism, as skilled craftsmen began anew to form organizations with which to raise their pay and to maintain a differential above the wage for unskilled workers. In the early 1850's national unions of printers, stonecutters, hat finishers, molders, and machinists and blacksmiths were formed by their respective locals, and trade agreements between unions and employers' organizations were not uncommon. The rapid increase in railroad mileage (over 260 per cent in the decade of the 50's) with the opening of trunk lines brought organized labor more directly in competition with unorganized workers in various regions, demonstrating the need for organization of the craft throughout the whole competitive area. However, an industrial panic in 1857 and the ensuing depression caused the dissolution of many unions and a sharp decline in total membership.

The Civil War at first disorganized labor unions, as many workers and a number of labor leaders joined the army. But the sharp rise in prices which began in 1862 caused such a significant decline in real wages that workers turned to labor unions as a means of maintaining or regaining previous living standards. A trade-union directory shows the growth of local organization in 20 states during the 1860's. It lists 78 local unions at the end of 1863, 270 at the end of 1864, and 300 at the end of 1865.[1] From 1863 through 1865 as many as 12 new nationals were formed, including such important unions as the locomotive engineers; the bricklayers, masons, and plasterers; and the cigar makers— the union of Samuel Gompers, later founder and president of the American Federation of Labor. At the close of the 1860's there were at least 32 national trade-unions in existence. These national unions, which chartered local branches, were sometimes called "international" unions because they had locals in Canada or Mexico. It is estimated that the total trade-union membership during the years from 1869 to 1872 reached a peak of 300,000, or perhaps even 400,000, members.[2] The aggressive trade-unionism of the Civil War and postwar years called forth a no less aggressive organization of employers.[3]

With labor organizing on a national scale and city centrals or trades assemblies in every large city, the time seemed ripe for a federation or consolidation of separate unions for united action on a national scale. In 1866 a National Labor Union was organized after the French pattern, with city trades assemblies and national trade-unions both represented along with, at times, farmers' societies and other political groups. Although many of the existing unions sent delegates to this congress of labor during the first years of its existence, the Union was soon split by dissention between pure trade-unionists and political actionists.

[1] Cf. John R. Commons et al., History of Labour in the United States, 1918, vol. 2, pp. 18–19.

[2] Cf. ibid., p. 47; and Norman J. Ware, "Trade Unions: United States and Canada," Encyclopaedia of the Social Sciences, vol. 15, p. 40.

[3] Cf. Commons et al., op. cit., vol. 2, pp. 26–33.

The leaders of the National Labor Union attempted to promote producers' cooperatives and certain general political reforms, such as land reform, an increase in greenback money, and liberal treatment for Negroes. The cooperative ventures generally failed, and trade-unionists lost interest in the political program. By 1870 the national unions had seceded from the National Labor Union because, as the Cigar Makers' union stated, it had become "an entirely political institution." Thereafter it declined rapidly, and by 1872 had practically disappeared.

The Knights of Labor. During the period of prolonged business depression from 1873 to 1879, the estimated total of trade-union membership fell from 300,000 or 400,000 to 50,000, as wages were reduced and unemployment increased.[1] The number of national trade-unions decreased from about thirty before 1873 to eight or nine in 1877 at the bottom of the depression.[2] The membership of the surviving national unions declined sharply, the Cigar Makers losing almost five sixths of their membership, the barrel makers about four fifths, the Machinists around two thirds, and the printers over one half. With national and local unions disintegrating, labor leaders again turned to political action. During this period, workingmen's parties were active in industrial regions, in some cases joining forces with farmers who were agitating for greenback issues to increase prices. At this time also the socialists appear as active participants in the labor movement in America. Although successful in electing some labor and farmer candidates, the strength of labor-farmer political groups began to wane with the return of prosperity in 1879. Higher prices caused the farmers to lose interest, and more employment caused the workers to turn again to organization for wage increases.

During the depression from 1873 to 1879, employers sought to eliminate trade-unions by a systematic policy of lockouts, black lists, labor espionage, and legal prosecution. The widespread use of black lists and Pinkerton labor spies caused labor to organize more or less secretly, and undoubtedly helped to bring on the violence that characterized labor strife during this period. It was during the years of depression and mass discontent following the panic of 1873 that the Noble Order of the Knights of Labor ex-

[1] *Ibid.*, p. 177.   [2] *Ibid.*, p. 176.

perienced its mushroom growth. The Order was started in 1869 as a trade-union of garment cutters in Philadelphia, although men of all callings were allowed to join, and it maintained its secret characteristics by medieval methods until 1881. "The impenetrable veil of ritual, sign, grip, and password" were adopted "so that no spy of the boss can find his way into the lodge room to betray his fellows."

The national trade-unions had appealed exclusively to skilled workmen. When most of the national unions were disrupted in the 1870's, a number of their surviving locals joined the Knights, which admitted any person who had ever worked for wages except liquor dealers, lawyers, bankers, stockbrokers, and professional gamblers. Although many skilled workers, such as printers, molders, cigar makers, and painters, became members of the Knights, the national unions remained outside. There was no place for national unions as such in the Order, although a few of them were admitted as local assemblies and, after 1883, as national trade assemblies. Membership was direct and not through affiliated independent unions; district assemblies, and even most locals, of the Knights were not made up of workers in a single craft. After the reorganization in 1878, control was centered in the national organization, with much of the remaining power in the district assemblies. The central body could call or terminate strikes and suspend or revoke the charters of local unions. The result was that the Knights of Labor was practically a one-man organization, and that man proved to be too unaggressive and vacillating.

In biology, structure is related to function. The giraffe has a long neck in order to reach the tender shoots high up in trees; the anteater has a tubular nose and long, sticky tongue so that he can collect a meal inside an anthill. The structure of labor organizations also reflects the functions that the organization is designed to perform. It is clear that the Knights of Labor was better adapted for such purposes as education, political action, boycotts, and sympathetic strikes than it was for increasing the wages of skilled workers by means of apprenticeship regulations and other craft restrictions designed to maintain the demand for craft skill. The Order was of most assistance to skilled craftsmen, like newspaper printers and custom shoemakers, who suffered little competition from outside the locality and who could, in case of a strike, be aided considerably by a labor boycott. Of the 196 boycotts in 1885, nearly all supported by the Knights, almost half were against newspapers or clothing manufacturers and dealers.[1]

On the other hand, the wages of certain skilled craftsmen were being subjected to increased pressure as railroad expansion widened the area of competitive production, and the introduction of machinery on an unprecedented scale with factory expansion increased the demand for semiskilled, and even unskilled, labor. Most of the membership of the Knights consisted of these less skilled workers. Because of its motley membership, there was a high turnover, or change in membership, and the total figures fluctuated considerably from one date to another. From a total membership of perhaps 5,000 in 1875, the strength of the Knights increased to 9,000 members in 1878, to 28,000 in 1880, to 52,000 in 1883, to 104,000 in 1885, and to 700,000 in 1886, which was the peak.[2] The successful strike against the railroad lines of Jay Gould and the epidemic of boycotts, both in 1885, were primarily responsible for the sevenfold increase in membership from July 1885 to July 1886. The total membership of all labor unions has been estimated at 200,000 or 225,000 in 1883, at 300,000 in the beginning of 1885, and at almost 1,000,000 in 1886.[3] It is interesting to observe that the depression from 1883 to 1885, which was accompanied by wage cuts and some unemployment, failed to prevent a rise in the total union membership. During that period the membership of the Knights of Labor doubled, and the membership losses of some national unions were offset by the gains of others.

Rise of the American Federation of Labor and decline of the Knights of Labor. The period of prosperity from 1879 to 1882 witnessed a rapid increase in the number of national unions and their membership. By 1884 the national trade-unions had at least 300,000 members in good standing. These trade-unionists were dissatisfied with the Knights of Labor, which tended to disregard craft lines and to direct its energies toward assisting the unskilled rather than the skilled workers.

During the 1880's the national unions were strengthened by changes of policy and by federation. The leaders in the Cigar Makers, Adolph Strasser and Samuel Gompers, brought about reorganization of that union on British lines, with the collection

[1] *Ibid.*, pp. 365–66. [2] *Ibid.*, pp. 199, 339, 343–44, and 381. [3] *Ibid.*, pp. 314 and 396.

of large benefit funds and an arrangement for financial support between locals controlled by a strong national body. Other trade-unions took similar steps to give their organizations more permanence. In 1881 these same leaders of the Cigar Makers were active in forming a Federation of Organized Trades and Labor Unions of the United States and Canada, which had a constitution taken almost verbatim from that of the British Trades Union Congress. This federation was primarily a legislative organization with less than 50,000 members in the affiliated unions in 1884.[1] It gave way in 1886 to the American Federation of Labor, formed by the combined trade-unions of the country after open conflict between the Knights of Labor and the Cigar Makers, in which each side "scabbed" on the other in strikes. The new federation, unlike its predecessor, had economic as well as legislative functions. The national or international (North American) unions were made the basic units of the federation, which in 1886 represented an estimated membership of about 150,000.[2] Samuel Gompers was elected president, a post which he held, except for one year, until his death in 1924.

At the time that the American Federation of Labor was formed, the national trade-unions were more interested in defending themselves from the Knights of Labor than they were in national legislation. The membership of the Knights had increased by 600,000, or sixfold, in the previous year, and the national unions saw the danger in a growing Order which admitted seceding factions of national unions and even boycotted the label of national unions. In 1886, Knights who were members of the Cigar Makers were ordered to withdraw from the national union or forfeit their membership cards to the Knights. The American Federation of Labor really arose from the refusal of the Knights to agree not to interfere with the national unions and not to sign up locals in their trades. In 1885 and 1886 several locals of highly skilled trades had abandoned their national unions to join the Knights. With that refusal, the struggle for the skilled workers broke out into open warfare. The problem of dual unionism and conflict became as acute as it has been recently between the AFL and the CIO.

The Knights of Labor represented the first significant attempt in this country to form one big general union. In the early and

[1] *Ibid.*, p. 377.   [2] *Ibid.*, footnote, p. 410.

middle 1880's, its policies were directed primarily for the benefit of unskilled workers. After most of the workers in large cities abandoned the Knights in the late 1880's, the Order became closely allied with farmers and other middle-class elements for political purposes. The national unions, on the other hand, were interested in trade autonomy. They wanted to use the economic strength of their skill, not to raise the wages of the unskilled, but to improve their own terms of employment through collective bargaining and trade agreements. Their objective was to organize all competing employers in the same line of business or trade in order to establish uniform wage scales and to "equalize" conditions for labor in the occupation or industry throughout the whole competitive area. In the end, both the craft and the industrial unions, like the miners and brewery workers, were opposed to a general labor organization such as the Knights.

The disintegration of the Knights of Labor was very rapid after 1886. A number of employers' associations were formed with the object of eliminating the Order from their branches of business. The lockout, the black list, labor spies, discharge of union members, and "iron-clad" oaths not to join a labor organization, were all used in this antiunion campaign.[1] The trade-unions proved more successful than the Knights in handling strikes and in the eight-hour movement during 1886 and 1887. Furthermore, most of the cooperative schemes fostered by the Knights failed. Finally, the bombing in Haymarket Square in Chicago in 1886 was used to discredit the Knights, although its officials disclaimed any connection or sympathy with that act. The odium attached to the Knights, however, caused some locals of skilled trades to abandon the Order.[2]

The inept and unaggressive leadership of the Knights resulted in a loss of almost 200,000 members, practically all in large cities, from 1886 to 1887. Whereas membership in the American Federation of Labor unions increased from 150,000 in 1886 to 225,000 in 1890, the membership of the Knights declined from 700,000 to less than 100,000 between those two years,[3] so that AFL affiliates had about 60 per cent of all labor-union membership in 1890 compared with about 15 per cent in 1886. In the years from 1894 to 1935 the Federation generally had from 70 to 80 per cent of all

[1] *Ibid.*, p. 415. [2] *Ibid.*, p. 486. [3] *Cf. ibid.*, p. 482.

union membership in this country. By 1900 the Knights had entirely disappeared.

Early decades of the American Federation of Labor. During the 1890's the total membership of the unions affiliated with the AFL showed little increase. The combined membership was 278,000 in 1898 compared with 225,000 in 1890. It is significant, however, that there was little decline in numbers during the depression years from 1893 to 1898. The trade-unions weathered that economic storm very well and gained rapidly in membership during the prosperous years following 1898. As Table 34 indicates, the membership of all labor unions increased fourfold between 1898 and 1904. The total membership of the unions affiliated with the American Federation of Labor in 1904 was six times as large as it was in 1898, and the number of affiliated national and international unions almost doubled during that six-year period, reaching 120. The membership increase was especially marked in coal mining and the building trades which, together with the members in transportation, accounted for over half of the total union membership in 1904.

TABLE 34. TOTAL UNION MEMBERSHIP IN SELECTED YEARS [1]

Year	Total for all unions	AFL affiliates Membership	Per cent of all union total
1898	501,000	278,000	55
1904	2,073,000	1,682,000	81
1910	2,141,000	1,587,000	74
1914	2,687,000	2,061,000	77
1917	3,061,000	2,457,000	80
1920	5,048,000	4,093,000	81
1924	3,536,000	2,853,000	81
1929	3,443,000	2,770,000	80
1933	2,973,000	2,318,000	78
1935	3,889,000	3,317,000	85
1937	7,179,526	3,357,800	47
1939	8,500,000	4,006,354	47
1940	8,700,000	4,237,000	49

[1] Statistics through 1935 have been taken from Leo Wolman, *Ebb and Flow in Trade Unionism*, 1936, and those for 1937 from Wolman, "Union Membership in Great Britain and the United States," *National Bureau of Economic Research, Bulletin 68*, December 27, 1937. The figures for 1939 and 1940 are from the official reports of various labor organizations, and the totals are estimates by the author. In some cases, Professor Wolman's figures represent corrections of the official union-membership statistics. As he points out, unions may, for various reasons, overstate or understate their actual dues-paying membership. Also, there is some variation in the way unions handle unemployed members who are unable to pay dues during their period of unemployment.

During the period of rising prices prior to 1904, many unions succeeded in making trade agreements with employers and employers' associations. An outstanding example was the bituminous-coal agreement of 1898. Strike successes and the sharp increase in membership, however, soon called forth strong employer opposition, which took the form of an "open-shop" drive. Between 1901 and 1903 many employers' organizations, including the National Metal Trades Association and the National Association of Manufacturers, made strong statements in favor of the open shop and absolute employer control of industry. In 1903 some 100 employer organizations formed a federation for collective action on a national scale in order to prevent labor organization and collective bargaining by employees. Citizens' alliances and vigilante groups were active in driving unions from localities so that they would not suffer "untold loss from being unionized," and employers dealing with unions were called "traitors." [1] The anti-union feeling was so strong amongst employers before the first World War that the president of the National Association of Manufacturers declared: "The American Federation of Labor is engaged in an open warfare against Jesus Christ and His Cause." [2] Employers' associations argued that all employers should join and help defray the cost of combatting strikes because "in defending a fellow manufacturer, no matter where located, you are defending yourself, and postponing just so much longer the time when you will be attacked." [3] In declaring that all employers should help bear the burden of the expenses of an organization working for their "direct interest," employers' associations were using the same argument that labor unions have used to acquire membership, namely, that all workers who benefit from the union should belong and pay dues.

The employers' open-shop drive was probably the chief reason that there was little increase in total union membership from 1904 to 1916. In this campaign, employers also used the courts in order to obtain injunctions restraining certain union activities.

[1] *Labor Policies of Employers' Associations, Part 3, The National Association of Manufacturers*, Senate Committee on Education and Labor, Senate Report No. 6, Part 6, 76th Congress, first session, 1939, p. 10.

[2] *Ibid.*, p. 19.

[3] *Labor Policies of Employers' Associations, Part 1, The National Metal Trades Association*, Senate Committee on Education and Labor, Report No. 6, Part 4, 76th Congress, first session, 1939, p. 23.

In two cases in 1908 and 1911, the United States Supreme Court declared general boycotts illegal.[1] In the one case triple damages of $262,000 were assessed against a union under the Sherman Anti-trust Act and paid by the American Federation of Labor. In the other case three top officials of the AFL, including Samuel Gompers, were sentenced to prison by a lower court for refusing to obey an injunction, and, although their sentences were set aside by the Supreme Court, the boycott injunction against the Federation was upheld. Another factor retarding union membership in this prewar period was the series of depressions in 1908, 1911, and 1914. Despite such setbacks for the AFL, it was not seriously threatened by the attempt, beginning in 1905, to establish another rival general union, the Industrial Workers of the World, or the IWW as it was called. Appealing to unskilled and migrant workers, the IWW engaged in strikes, sabotage, and violence. Its ultimate purpose was to eliminate the wage system and to overthrow capitalism. It exerted a strong influence in the lumber camps and metal mines of the West, where working and living conditions were especially bad prior to 1917. Like the Knights of Labor, the membership of the IWW was shifting and very unstable, and probably did not exceed 60,000 or 70,000 paid members in the prewar years.

First-World-War period (1917–1920). By 1916 the boom resulting from the first World War had begun to raise total union membership in this country above the plateau of the previous decade. Toward the end of 1915 prices began the sharp rise that ended in the middle of 1920 with the wholesale price level almost two-and-a-half times higher than its prewar figure. Total union membership increased especially rapidly from April 1917, when this country entered the war, until 1920, when the total stood at 5,048,000 members, or almost double the 1915 membership. The same thing occurred in Great Britain, where the total union membership increased from 4,359,000 in 1915 to 8,346,000 in 1920.[2]

The war strengthened the hand of organized labor in a number of ways. Anxious to avoid labor trouble and work stoppages, the

---

[1] *Loewe* v. *Lawlor* (1908), 208 U. S. 274; and *Gompers* v. *Bucks Stove and Range Co.* (1911), 221 U. S. 418.

[2] *Cf.* Leo Wolman, *Ebb and Flow in Trade Unionism*, p. 31.

Federal government established special labor adjustment boards for such industries as shipbuilding, the railroads, and the maritime industry. In some cases, the decisions of these special boards with regard to wages and conditions of work were binding. For other war industries, a National War Labor Board was established to mediate labor disputes and to help, through advice, in forming what might be called a "labor code" for industry. On these boards, representatives selected by national unions or the AFL had a voice equal to that of employer representatives. Such "recognition" for the leaders of organized labor increased their prestige and influence with workers.

During the war most employers were willing to make concessions to labor, and the antiunion, open-shop drive was suspended, along with the antitrust laws. In many industries, large profits were made as prices rose more rapidly than costs, and government contracts were often on a cost-plus-profit basis so that employers did not need to worry about labor costs. The shortage of labor had strengthened the position of the workers and dulled such employer weapons as discriminatory discharge and the black list. Furthermore, the National War Labor Board, in its advisory capacity, adopted the following principle with regard to the right to organize: "The right of workers to organize in trade unions and to bargain collectively, through chosen representatives, is recognized and affirmed. This right shall not be denied, abridged, or interfered with by the employers in any manner whatsoever." The Federal government, in taking over and operating the railroads, set an example by dealing with the various railroad unions on a national basis.

The war labor boards and their policies remind one of the early years of the New Deal and the NRA (1933–1935). The favorable attitude of the government toward labor organization undoubtedly played a part in the increase of union membership. In addition, workers had little to fear from discharge because, with labor scarce, it was relatively easy to find a new job. As prices and living costs rose faster than wage rates, the pinch of necessity was added to the pull of opportunity for wage increases with large profits. Such an economic situation is favorable to the activities of labor organizations. During the war period, many unskilled and semiskilled workers joined the ranks of organized labor.

The increase in union membership was especially marked in those industries most directly affected by governmental policy, such as the railroads, ocean shipping and shipbuilding, and the metal trades, especially the machinists. Building, metals, and transportation accounted for over half the increase in total union membership during the war years.[1]

FACTORS IN MEMBERSHIP FLUCTUATIONS

The foregoing discussion of the growth and decline in the numerical strength of labor unions until 1920 has indicated how various factors—economic, political, and personal—affect the figures for union membership. Because a number of these factors help to explain the decline in union membership during the 1920's, it may be well to examine that period in connection with a discussion of the factors that play an important role in membership fluctuations.

External factors. Membership figures are affected by internal factors, such as the personnel and policies of the unions, and by external factors in the form of changes in economic or political conditions.

1. *The business cycle.* Union organization and union membership fluctuate with the business cycle. In prosperous periods unions generally wax; in depression periods they tend to wane. For example, trade-unions declined sharply in strength and membership during the depressions commencing in 1837, 1857, and 1873, and their membership increased rapidly during such prosperous periods as that from 1849 to 1854 or from 1898 to 1904.

A large part of the decline of 1,000,000 in total union membership in the United States from 1920 to 1922 was undoubtedly due to the depression and unemployment late in 1920 and in 1921. The decline tended to be most severe in industries like shipbuilding, metals, ocean transportation, and textiles, which had gained so rapidly in union membership during the war. But the period from 1922 to 1929 was considered one of extraordinary prosperity, yet estimates indicate that total union membership declined during each year from 1922 through 1933, except for a one-percent increase in 1927.[2] One must turn to other factors in order to explain the membership decline during the prosperous years of the 1920's.

[1] *Cf. ibid.*, pp. 28, 30.   [2] *Cf. ibid.*, p. 16; also Table 34 *supra.*

2. *Prices and living costs.* The survey of labor organization in the previous section has indicated that rising prices and costs of living, as during the Civil-War and first-World-War periods, stimulate union membership, whereas workers tend to turn from union to political action during periods of falling prices. Of course, declining prices generally accompany a slump in business. But during the period from 1923 to 1929 the cost of living remained practically unchanged in this country and the wholesale price level declined somewhat. Consequently, real wages rose and remained above the prewar level.

3. *Technological change.* As long as the prevailing structure of American unionism was built around craft skill, any changes in technique that increased or decreased the demand for skill of a craft variety were bound to influence union membership. Technological changes in the middle of the nineteenth century tended to develop new crafts—the iron molders, the machinists, the glass blowers, and the railroad crafts. Technological changes during the last quarter of a century, on the other hand, have tended to break down existing crafts. That was especially true in the decade following the first World War.

4. *Attitude of the government.* The policies of the Federal government may encourage or discourage unionism. As already indicated, the friendly attitude of the government as an employer during the first World War, the establishment of labor boards, and the appointment of union officials to high posts in Federal agencies helped to stimulate union membership. Late in 1919 the attitude of the Federal administration toward organized labor changed. At that time, the Federal Attorney General got an injunction against the United Mine Workers, and in 1922 his Republican successor obtained an injunction against the striking railway shopmen that was one of the most sweeping decrees ever issued in a labor dispute. In 1921 the U. S. Shipping Board helped to bring about the defeat and decline of the International Seamen's Union by refusing to let the Board's vessels be used by any operator renewing the agreement with the union. Only with the advent of the Roosevelt Administration and the NRA in 1933 were union leaders granted advisory and administrative positions to an extent that recalled the first-World-War days.

The attitude of the courts toward unionism also has an effect upon membership. The labor injunctions and the Supreme Court decisions against organized labor during the first decade of the present century acted as a retarding influence. Union leaders thought that the Clayton Act of 1914 excluded labor from the antitrust acts, but they soon found that, though the Supreme Court found business combinations, like the U. S. Steel Corporation, "reasonable" combinations, it found in four significant cases (1921–1927) that labor unions may be "unreasonable" combinations in restraint of interstate commerce. Indeed, the Supreme Court upheld injunctions forbidding union organizers to solicit members among employees who had signed "yellow-dog" contracts not to join a union, and some lower court judges issued injunctions against unions and in favor of firms in which the judges had thousands of dollars invested.

5. *Employer organization and policies.* As already indicated, the antiunion campaigns of employers, directed primarily against the Knights of Labor in the 1880's and the AFL in the decade or so before the first World War, had an adverse effect upon union membership. Although employer opposition subsided during the war, it returned with renewed vigor at the expiration of Federal wartime measures protecting and stimulating labor organization. In addition to court cases and injunctions, there was a revival of the open-shop drive, which in the 1920's was called the American Plan. In 1921 an official of the National Association of Manufacturers stated that more than 500 organizations in 250 cities had endorsed the plan, and an American Plan-Open Shop Conference, attended by representatives of some 100 employers' organizations, met semiannually during the 1920's.[1]

Organized employer opposition took various forms in different industries. By united action, shipowners were able to reduce sharply the membership of the Longshoremen's and Seamen's unions after strikes in 1919 and 1921. On the Pacific Coast, rival company unions were established, resulting in closed company-union shops. In certain cities like Chicago, San Francisco, and Cleveland, various financial and merchant groups raised million-dollar funds in the early 1920's in order to weaken the building-

[1] *Cf. Labor Policies of Employers' Associations, Part 2, The Associated Industries of Cleveland,* Senate Committee on Education and Labor, 76th Congress, first session, Senate Report No. 6, Part 5, 1939, p. 12.

trades unions and to introduce the open shop in local construction. The railroads, following their return to private ownership, refused to continue to deal with the shop crafts on a national basis, and many railroads, after the unsuccessful shop-crafts strike in 1922, set up company unions.   In the metal trades, the employers' organization (the National Metal Trades Association) pursued a vigorous open-shop or closed, nonunion shop drive from 1920 to 1924, using such antiunion practices as labor espionage, black listing, mobilization of strike-breakers, and the accumulation of a common defense fund, all of which were effective in defeating a general machinists' strike in Cincinnati in 1920 and in reducing the membership of the Machinists' union from 330,800 in 1920 to 71,700 in 1924.   Other unions, besides the Machinists, railroad shop crafts, and maritime workers, that suffered marked membership reductions during the 1920's were the shipbuilders, the Textile Workers, and the coal miners.   In what appears to have been an antiunion campaign, large buyers of soft coal, like the railroads, put pressure upon union operators to adopt an open-shop policy or suffer a threatened boycott, and coal-mining firms owned by steel companies, railroads, and the Rockefeller interests repudiated their union agreements in order to operate on a non-union basis.[1]

During the 1920's, company-union or employee-representation plans were widely used by large firms in such industries as the metal trades, railroads, rubber, oil, and public utilities.   Although a device for representation rather than for collective bargaining, such plans were sometimes established by the employer as an alternative to national labor unions.   Employee representation really got its start during the first World War when the Federal labor boards, especially the National War Labor Board, in over 125 awards affecting plants where no union was in existence, called for the establishment of some form of employee-representation or works-council plan.[2]   Although the awards of the War Labor Board were not mandatory, strong pressure made it practically impossible to disregard them.   A number of firms also

---

[1] Cf. *The Effect of Labor Relations in the Bituminous Coal Industry upon Interstate Commerce,* National Labor Relations Board, Division of Economic Research, Bulletin No. 2, June 30, 1938, pp. 28, 31–33. Cf. also Chapter 29 *infra.*

[2] Cf. *Collective Bargaining through Employee Representation,* National Industrial Conference Board, 1933, p. 8.

adopted such plans voluntarily, so that by 1919 over 400,000 employees were covered by arrangements for employee representation, and in 1928 the coverage exceeded 1,500,000 workers.[1] Because formal membership and dues were not a part of such plans, their coverage was not comparable with the membership figures of unions. Generally, they were used in connection with a series of employee-welfare measures, such as company benefit plans, group insurance, and recreation programs.

Internal factors. The numerical strength of labor unions may also be affected by the policies of union leaders and the structure of the unions. One can, however, overemphasize the influence of the personality of union officials upon total union membership. Except for the period when the Knights of Labor were supreme, the power and control in organized labor has generally been scattered among the national or local unions and has not been centered in the hands of one or two officials in the national federations of unions.

1. *Union structure.* The development of a new type of labor organization may, of course, cause a rapid expansion in total membership throughout the country. The Knights of Labor, as a general labor union appealing to the unskilled workers, is a good illustration. On the other hand, union membership may suffer if the membership base is confined to a certain class of workers, such as skilled craftsmen, and changes in technique are whittling away at that base. For example, the membership of the AFL craft unions tended to decline in the 1920's as increased division of labor and mechanical improvements broke down existing craft skills without opening up new trades or crafts. Also, craft unions are frequently exclusive in the sense that they try to keep workers out of the trade in order to limit the number in the market, although, to control the supply, they want to have all those who are already in the market join the union.

The mass-production industries were expanding during the 1920's, and the difficulty in organizing the employees of large firms in heavy industry was well illustrated by the campaign of 24 AFL unions to organize the steel industry in 1919. In the great steel strike that followed, the separate craft unions failed to cooperate with one another and, in following their own selfish poli-

[1] *Ibid.*, p. 16.

cies, lost the strike. The AFL campaign to organize the automobile industry in 1927 quickly collapsed because it was given little support by the 17 national unions claiming jurisdiction over certain craftsmen in automobile plants and because it was not vigorously pursued.

2. *Union policies and leadership.* The effect of vacillating and unaggressive leadership upon the membership of the Knights of Labor has already been explained. The legislative and organizing programs of the AFL during the 1920's were also unaggressive and lacking in worker appeal. With a Federal administration largely unsympathetic toward organized labor, no significant labor laws, except for the railroads,[1] were passed in the 1920's. During that period the AFL opposed legislation to establish minimum wages or maximum hours for men or unemployment compensation, and also the Federation apparently was not in favor of legislation for health insurance.

During the 1920's the leadership of the AFL tried to appeal to employers by stressing union cooperation with management as an alternative to company unionism in increasing production and reducing costs.[2] Orgainzing programs by the AFL unions, such as the textile workers' campaign in the South, were attempted on the basis of union-management cooperation and unionism as good business, but they generally failed to appeal to employers, who apparently are more likely to be impressed by economic strength than by the olive branch of conciliation and union co-operation. On the other hand, such nonmilitant, cost-reducing programs lacked the inspirational and dramatic qualities necessary to attract membership, especially amongst unskilled workers. Many employees were suspicious of such programs to help their employers.

THE MARKET THEORY OF UNIONISM

There is a theory about unionism—it might be called the market theory—which explains that labor unions are likely to be

---

[1] Less than half of the union membership in the railroads has been in unions affiliated with the AFL. The four "Big Brotherhoods" in the engine and train service, for example, are independent unions.

[2] For a further discussion of the AFL program of union-management cooperation, *cf.* Jean Carol Trepp, "Union-Management Cooperation and the Southern Organizing Campaign," *Journal of Political Economy*, vol. 41 (October 1933), pp. 602–24. *Cf.* also Chapter 24 *infra*.

most welcome (1) where there are a large number of firms in the industry, (2) where labor costs are a large percentage of total costs, and (3) where the industry is not a new one dominated by the "psychology" of market expansion and is not undergoing rapid technological changes. Under such circumstances, competition is likely to develop extreme price-cutting and cutthroat practices, and the employers in the industry may recognize the value of a national union to equalize labor costs between employers and to stabilize prices in the industry, or in the market area in the case of local-market products or services. On the other hand, unions offer little in the way of market stabilization to the large firms in the mass-production industries, because such firms are able to control their markets either through branding their products with trade-marks or by trade practices that result in price uniformity and price stability, as for example in the steel and automobile industries.

Examination of various branches of our economy shows that the following industries have the three characteristics just mentioned: bituminous coal, building, clothing, the stove industry, and many of the lines of business that are, in some localities, dominated by the Teamsters' union, such as laundry, pressing and cleaning, trucking, garage service, baked goods, etc. Indeed, these industries, along with the railroads and printing and photoengraving, accounted for two thirds of all union membership in 1929 and 1932, before the New Deal administration in Washington encouraged the sharp expansion in union membership beginning in 1933. The railroads and newspaper printing both have peculiar market conditions that make them especially vulnerable to strikes. They have daily and hourly schedules to meet, they cannot move to other localities, and they are very dependent upon public opinion. Unions have generally been stronger in local-market industries that are not subject to outside competition and migration to another locality than they have been in manufacturing industries that can shift their location, as has happened in some cases in the textile industry and the metal trades. Table 35 indicates those branches of industry that have had the highest degree of unionization in terms of total employees in the industry.

The figures in Table 35 show that transportation, building, coal mining, clothing, and printing have been the industries with

TABLE 35. EXTENT OF UNION ORGANIZATION IN VARIOUS INDUSTRIES AND OCCUPATIONS [1]

Industry or occupation	1920	1930	1940
Transportation	57%	28%	60%
Steam railroads	85	55	85
Street railroads	50	58	75
Water transportation	81	30	80
Motor transportation	12	6	20
Building construction	26	39	45
Coal mining	51	33	95
All manufacturing	23	11	25
Clothing	58	36	70
Printing and publishing	50	25	30
Leather and leather products	29	14	30
Tobacco manufacturers	29	15	20
Forest products	18	10	30
Iron and steel	28	9	30
Selected occupations			
Actors and showmen	39	13	24
Barbers	23	19	19
Mail carriers	25	75	80
Molders	43	19	19
Upholsterers	19	20	20
Percentage of all employees organized	17.5	9.3	22

the highest percentage of employees organized. Not one of these is an export industry. On the other hand, manufacturing industries, with the exception of clothing and printing, have been fairly well organized only during periods when Federal protection has been extended to labor organization, such as during the first World War and the administration of President Franklin D. Roosevelt. In Great Britain in 1930 over 35 per cent of all employees in manufacturing were organized, compared with about 11 per cent for this country.[2]

The effects of market conditions upon labor organization in bituminous coal and clothing are discussed in detail in later chapters dealing with collective bargaining in selected industries. Here it is only necessary to state a few facts about the industries mentioned in order to explain how they fit the market theory of trade-unionism.

[1] Figures for 1920 and 1930 taken from Leo Wolman, *The Growth of American Trade Unions*, 1924, pp. 86–88, and *The Ebb and Flow in Trade Unionism*, pp. 116–21, 203, 218–29. The data for 1940 are estimates by the author. They are at best only rough estimates. Wolman's figures under transportation have been adjusted for the various railroad crafts that he included under other categories.

[2] Cf. Leo Wolman, "Union Membership in Great Britain and the United States," *op. cit.*, pp. 11, 16.

Soft coal has been a highly competitive industry. It is produced by thousands of independent operators, no one of which has four per cent of the total output, and at least three fourths of the coal is sold outside the state in which it is mined. During the 1920's the industry suffered from a declining demand and a large excess capacity. Labor costs represent about two thirds of the total costs of mining coal, compared with a figure of around one fifth for other types of mining. As already mentioned, there seems to have been a campaign to eliminate the union from the industry during the late 1920's, with a result that between 1922 and 1929 union membership declined over 50 per cent and average wage rates fell more than 25 per cent. With the union driven from most of the soft-coal fields from 1927 to 1933, repeated wage cuts and severe price-cutting occurred until many of the operators who had opposed the union in 1927 were anxious to have it back again to stabilize the industry. As one operator, who had previously refused to accept the union agreement, explained in 1931:

For the past four years these operators who have dispensed with union agreements have had plenty of time to view the experience of running without any fixed wage scale or without having any labor organization to deal with. It must be admitted that the situation is even worse than when we dealt with the union. Many operators try to keep their properties operating by cutting prices to ridiculous figures, then go back and cut the wages of the miners, and this continues until the level of the miners has been brought down so low in some places as to be a disgrace to the country. Personally, I would much prefer to deal with the United Mine Workers than with these ruthless, price-cutting, wage-cutting operators who are a detriment to the industry.[1]

As indicated in the discussion of collusion between employers' and employees' organizations in Chapter 6, building contractors generally prefer the uniform conditions enforced upon all competitors by the unions to a condition of unregulated competition which tends to lead to wage-cutting, labor strife, poor workmanship, and the bankruptcy of fair and scrupulous contractors. Most of the demand for the open shop in building has come, not from the building contractors themselves, but from manufacturers, bankers,

[1] National Industrial Recovery Administration, *Bituminous Coal Code Hearings*, August 10, 1933, vol. 2, p. 276, quoted in F. E. Berquist *et al.*, *Economic Survey of the Bituminous Coal Industry under Free Competition and Code Regulation*, N. R. A. Division of Review, Work Materials No. 69, March 1936, pp. 184–85.

and merchants who were opposed to unionism. There are generally many employers in building, and it is relatively easy to enter the industry because little capital equipment is required. Without great resources and working within time limits specified in the contract, the average contractor has no desire to wage war with the unions. One strike might ruin him. In bidding on jobs, assurance of stable wages and prices gives the building contractor the same protection against losses that fixed prices for automobiles give to automobile dealers.

In a number of respects, the men's and women's clothing industries resemble the building industry. A large part of the work is done under contract arrangements in a few large metropolitan centers like New York, Philadelphia, and Chicago. The average producing establishment has 40 or 50 workers, so that there are hundreds of small producers in the same producing area. In times past, the industry has been characterized by severe competitive bidding by contractors, miserable wages for piece work, and sweatshop conditions. The union acts as a stabilizing influence by placing a floor under wages. The Ladies' Garment Workers Union in the New York market area, where four fifths of all women's coats, suits, and silk dresses produced in this country are made, has an arrangement with the employers by which competition is severely regulated and limited, union conditions are assured in all shops, and entrance into the industry for both employers and employees is controlled.[1]

The discussion in Chapter 6 of the "voluntary NRA" enforced by the Teamsters' union on the Pacific Coast explained that employers were not displeased with such an arrangement for petty trades, like dry cleaning, baking, trucking, and laundry and garage service, that are highly susceptible to price wars and discriminatory price practices because of the nature of the market for the product, the ease of entrance into the industry, and the large number of small establishments.

The market theory of unionism is perhaps best illustrated by the divergent experience in the two branches of the foundry industry: the stove-plate and the machinery-jobbing foundries.

---

[1] Cf. "Union-Management Relations in the Women's Clothing Industry, New York Industrial Area, 1936," *Monthly Labor Review*, vol. 43 (July 1936), pp. 24–33. Cf. also Chapter 30 *infra*.

The Stove Founders' National Defense Association was formed in 1886 to eliminate the Molders' union from the stove industry, but, beginning in 1891, has negotiated national agreements with the union on a friendly basis. Influenced by the successful joint relations in the stove industry, the National Founders' Association was formed in 1898 to accomplish the same results for foundries manufacturing products other than stove plate, but by 1904 it had become a virulent "open-shop" employers' association.

Professor Russell S. Bauder explains the successful union-employer relations in the stove industry by the fact that the union, by enforcing uniform piece rates, equalized competitive costs and checked a tendency toward cutthroat competition that menaced the industry. Failure of the market for stoves to expand much after 1900 left the industry overdeveloped.[1] In 1904 there were 415 establishments in the stove and furnace industry with an average of about 70 wage-earners per establishment. In 1925 there were 323 establishments averaging 90 workers per plant. Molding of the plate for stoves represents from 40 to 50 per cent of the total cost of manufacturing stoves, and the union has controlled practically all the molders in the industry. On the other hand, Professor Bauder believes that the demand for the products of the jobbing and machinery foundries was expanding so rapidly with the mechanization of industry that any possible market stabilization and cost equalization by the union would have had little positive value to the employers in the industry. The menace of cutthroat competition was less threatening in an industry enjoying such an expanding market. Furthermore, technological change was more rapid in the machinery branch of the foundry industry.

RAPID EXPANSION SINCE 1933

According to the membership claims of the various labor organizations, total union membership increased almost threefold in the first six years of the Roosevelt Administration, from 1933 to 1939. The stated total for 1940 of 8,700,000 members exceeds the previous membership peak in 1920 by almost 3,700,000 members. In no other period of our history has there been such a

---

[1] Cf. "National Collective Bargaining in the Foundry Industry," *American Economic Review*, vol. 24 (September 1934), pp. 462–76.

significant increase in union membership. The advance was especially rapid from 1933 to 1934 and from 1936 to 1938. In this remarkable growth of unionism, the important factors were: (1) the labor policy of the Federal government, (2) general economic recovery, and (3) the rise of a new federation of national unions, founded primarily on an industrial rather than a craft base.

The National Industrial Recovery Act, passed in June 1933, was largely responsible for the sharp increase in membership from 1933 to 1934. The preamble of that Act declared it to be the policy of Congress "to induce and maintain united action of labor and management" and "to improve standards of labor." Section 7a stated the right of employees to organize and bargain collectively through their representatives without interference, restraint, or coercion by employers. Furthermore, union officials were recognized by the Federal administration as the spokesmen for labor generally and, as in the World-War days, were granted an important part in the administration of the Act. The codes of "fair competition" provided for in the law were drawn up by industries, and it is worth noting that the rapid expansion in union membership during the two years of NRA occurred, not in the old craft unions, but in industrial unions like the coal miners, the garment workers, the Textile Workers, the metal miners, the Brewery Workers, the oil-field workers, and in local unions in industries without a national union. Other unions that expanded rapidly during NRA days, like the Teamsters and the Government Employees, were more industrial than craft in character.

From 1933 to 1939, employers did not, however, cooperate with labor organizations in the spirit of the first-World-War days. Employer resistance is indicated by the increase in company unions to evade the real intent of Section 7a and the increase in the expenditures of employer organizations. It has been estimated that early in 1935, before the demise of NRA, there were some 2,500,000 workers covered by company unions, or double the coverage in 1932.[1] Although the annual receipts and expenditures of the National Association of Manufacturers never exceeded $366,000 during the 20 years prior to 1933, in 1935 the Associa-

[1] A. L. Bernheim and D. Van Doren, *Labor and the Government*, Twentieth Century Fund, Inc., 1935, pp. 77–79.

tion's receipts exceeded $600,000 and in 1937 were almost $1,350,-000.[1] During the four years from 1933 to 1937 over $9,000,000 is known to have been spent by 283 firms for labor espionage, strike-breaking, private guards, and industrial munitions.[2]

The National Labor Relations Act, passed in 1935 after the NIRA was declared unconstitutional, had little immediate effect upon union membership, because employers considered the law unconstitutional and continued their antiunion campaigns, with labor espionage and discrimination against union employees. However, the Labor Relations Act, which forbids employers to interfere with unions, to foster company unions, to discriminate against union members, or to refuse to bargain with representatives of a majority of their workers, became an effective factor in the increase of union membership even before the Supreme Court upheld its constitutionality in April 1937.[3] Another factor was the success of labor-supported candidates in the November 1936 elections, especially the overwhelming reelection of President Roosevelt.

Between the Fall of 1936 and the Fall of 1937, the total membership claimed by union officials increased by more than 2,500,000. Most of the increase occurred in the mass-production industries where new unions had been formed since 1933. Unions in the iron and steel, automobile, rubber, oil, and electrical and radio industries accounted for over 1,000,000 new members between 1936 and 1937, and over 500,000 more members were reported in the Fall of 1937 in the new CIO unions formed in that year among such groups as the cannery, wood, shoe, transport, maritime, retail, office, and government workers. Even in the AFL unions, rapid expansion after 1935 occurred, not in the old craft unions, but in such industrial or semiindustrial unions as the Hotel and Restaurant Employees, Retail Clerks, Teamsters, Paper Makers, Pulp Workers, Meat Cutters and Butcher Workmen, Tobacco Workers, the Machinists, Electrical Workers, Govern-

[1] *Labor Policies of Employers' Associations*, Part 3, *The National Association of Manufacturers, op. cit.*, pp. 42, 50.

[2] *Industrial Espionage*, Senate Committee on Education and Labor, 75th Congress, second session, Senate Report No. 46, Part 3, 1937, pp. 79–89.

[3] The constitutionality of the Act was upheld in the following three cases: *National Labor Relations Board* v. *Jones and Laughlin Steel Corp.* (1937), 301 U. S. 1; *N.R.L.B.* v. *Fruehauf Trailer Co.* (1937), 301 U. S. 49; and *N.R.L.B.* v. *Friedman-Harry Marks Clothing Co.* (1937), 301 U. S. 58.

ment Employees, and Teachers. In 1939, membership in craft unions like the building trades, the printing crafts, and the railroad crafts did not exceed the 1929 figure, partly because building had failed to recover and employment on the railroads had been declining. Whereas in 1929 they accounted for almost half of all organized labor, in 1939 union members in building, railroading, and printing represented only about one fifth of all union members. In other words, it was the unskilled and semiskilled workers who accounted for the rapid expansion in membership after 1933. In 1939 the 10 largest national or international unions had approximately 3,500,000 members,[1] and the United Mine Workers, with a membership over 600,000, was the largest union in the world.

The membership expansion since 1933 indicates that market considerations are less important in periods when the Federal administration and legislation favor or protect labor organization. The industries that have been organized since 1933 have not needed nor utilized the unions as a means of stabilizing prices and market conditions, except perhaps in a very round-about fashion in a few instances. The Steel Workers' union has, for example, objected to threatened reductions in steel prices. During the NRA period, from 1933 to 1935, the government itself attempted to stabilize and regulate markets under industrial code authorities, which were more effective than unions could have been. With few exceptions, firms in large-scale industry were organized in the 1930's despite employer resistance to labor unions. After 1933 membership increased because of favorable governmental and economic conditions and the development of new industrial unions, not because American industry conformed more closely to the three conditions that the market theory of unionism states are likely to lead to severe competition and to lessen employer antagonism toward labor organizations.

That general economic conditions were favorable to labor organization between 1930 and 1939 seems to be indicated by Table 36 showing union membership in percentage of the total number of wage and salary employees. In all of the 12 countries listed, except Australia and Germany, there was a relative increase

[1] These unions were: the Mine Workers, the Steel Workers, the Textile Workers, the Automobile Workers, the Teamsters, the Carpenters, the Amalgamated Clothing Workers, the Ladies' Garment Workers, the Electrical Workers, and the Machinists.

TABLE 36. UNION MEMBERSHIP IN PERCENTAGE OF TOTAL EMPLOYEES IN VARIOUS COUNTRIES, 1930 AND 1939 [1]

	1930	1939
Australia	53	50
Canada	13	20
Belgium	36	40
Denmark	37	50
France	10	30
Germany	36	*
Great Britain	26	28
Japan	2	2
New Zealand	22	40
Norway	17	37
Sweden	24	40
United States	9	22

*The German trade-unions lost their independence and separate identity when the Hitler regime came into power in 1933.

in labor organization between 1930 and 1939. Increased class stratification and larger employing units are undoubtedly among the underlying factors in this general expansion in unionism throughout most of the world. In this country, which suffered so severely from the depression of the early 1930's, the economic recovery commencing in 1933 gave labor unions an opportunity to demand and achieve wage increases, and such advances in pay act as a powerful stimulus to union membership. The gain in labor organization from 1930 to 1939 was greater in this country than in any other important industrial nation, with the possible exception of France. The French unions, however, began to suffer a sharp reduction in membership during 1938. Whether the American unions in the future will be able to maintain or increase their membership among unskilled and semiskilled workers remains to be seen. In large measure, the general prospects for union membership are tied up with general economic conditions. It is possible for union membership to increase considerably in this country, for labor here is still not strongly organized compared with the degree of labor organization in Europe and Australasia in 1939.

[1] Sources of data for percentage calculations: 1930 union membership in Wolman, *Ebb and Flow in Trade Unionism*, p. 239; 1939 union membership in *The I. L. O. Year-book, 1938–39*, International Labour Office, 1939, Appendix 6, and sources mentioned in Wolman; total employees in 1930 and 1939 from census figures of total salaried employees and wage-earners in *1938 Year-Book of Labour Statistics*, International Labour Office, 1938, Tables 2 and 3, or estimates based on such census data.

CHAPTER TWENTY-ONE

UNIONS:
ORGANIZATION AND STRUCTURE

The structural pattern of labor organization may appear to be a dull and relatively unimportant subject for discussion. On the contrary, some of the most dramatic conflicts in American labor history have been struggles concerning the structure of unionism, such as the battle between the Knights of Labor and the AFL in the 1880's and between the AFL and the CIO during recent years; and the character and philosophy of a country's labor movement are closely bound up with union forms and structure.

The significance of structure. The bearing of union forms upon total membership was indicated in the previous chapter. The type of organization of unions also plays an important role in such matters as interunion relations, union policies, control of unions, and the possibilities for union reform. Certain types of structure may lead to numerous disputes between unions with conflicting claims to jurisdiction over certain work or groups of workers. Some organizational arrangements may combine workers with such diverse economic interests that the union or aggregation of unions is divided into factions that make concerted action difficult, if not impossible. Comment has already been made upon the close relationship between function and structure in unionism as well as in biology. Generally speaking, smaller and more exclusive unions are likely to be conservative in policy and to pursue restrictive practices. Labor organizations with a large membership base, on the other hand, are more likely to use political pressure to attain their objectives. Presumably the basis of an organization should measure the common interests of its membership. The one-big-union or labor-solidarity concept, upon which the Knights of Labor and the IWW were founded, presumes that wage-earners have more to gain by combined economic and political action as a class than by concerted action as workers in a single craft or industry, or in related crafts and industries.

Not only is knowledge of union structure important for an understanding of union policies and philosophy, but it is also a necessary background for any discussion of reform or improvement. For example, only by a study of the AFL and its affiliated unions can one appreciate the possibilities and problems in any attempt to clean up labor racketeering, or to prevent interunion disputes over jurisdiction, or to mold the form of the affiliated unions so that they are adapted to changed industrial conditions.

Adaptation to the structure of industry. The unit of organization and the distribution of control must be related to the industrial environment if the labor union is to thrive, or even survive. Such industrial factors as the extent of the market for the product, the size of employer units, the occupational characteristics of the work, and the rapidity of technological change have a direct bearing upon union structure. As a consequence of differences in such matters, the industrial problems that are important for one union may be of no significance for another.

The contrast between coal mining and building construction will serve to illustrate how the nature of the industry may affect labor organization. In the soft-coal industry, the product is fairly uniform and its market or competitive area is extensive. Consequently, the union should be large enough to cover the whole competitive area, and control must be centralized in order to keep each local mine in line with the general union standards. In building construction, on the other hand, the market is local and there is less need to worry about nonunion competition from other areas. As a result, authority and financial resources can be decentralized.

If buildings were manufactured in plants and shipped out ready-made to all parts of the country, the whole structural pattern of the building trades would be changed. Strike and financial control would need to be centralized; the building tradesmen in one area would commence to worry about nonunion production in other localities; the change in the technique of production would break down craft divisions by making most of the jobs semiskilled and unskilled work in mass-production factories; and the employers would become a few large firms with heavy capital investment rather than numerous contractors operating on various-sized shoestrings. Under such circumstances, the 20-odd national unions in the building trades would undoubtedly be forced to give up their separate existences and become one industrial union. In mass-production industries, as is also the case in coal mining, the work is not separated into distinct crafts which require a definite training and between which little movement of workmen occurs, but rather there is promotion from lower to higher grades of work.

With the mass production of buildings and one large industrial union it is questionable, however, whether the organization of the workers would have any more economic strength than the separate crafts have today. The separate crafts are strong now, because the employers are so numerous and one small employer can be played against another, because there is no substitute for their craft skill and employers cannot move the work to another locality, and because the craft is a stable and cohesive unit, with all members having invested in the same type of training and all, therefore, vitally interested in furthering the craft. In metropolitan centers, the building crafts are, in reality, divided along industrial or employer lines, since the subcontracting "craft" groups form separate employing units. Mass production would increase the size of the employing units and presumably the size of the workers' organization, but the economic strength of unions is not necessarily in proportion to their size, as the coal miners in the United States and Great Britain learned during the late 1920's. Industrial circumstances, like the size of the product market and the existence of substitutes, may weaken unions with large memberships through failure of the union to control all parts of the competitive area or the work on substitute products. In this connection, it should be noted that many of the building crafts have extended their jurisdictions in order to include helpers and others who might become substitute workers or in order to control potential competition in the form of substitute products. A large organization also raises administrative problems. It may become too vast for effective control, so that autocratic procedures and schisms amongst the membership are the result.

The type of organization suitable for one industry or one stage of industrial development may not be suitable for other industries or industrial circumstances. Consequently, the structure and organization of unionism in a country is continually changing, and the direction of change is not always toward fewer and larger organizations. In the printing trades there used to be one industry-wide organization. Toward the end of the last century, the workers decided that industrial developments made it desirable to break down this all-inclusive organization, and it was gradually split up into five separate craft unions—the compositors, the bookbinders, the photoengravers, the pressmen, and the stereotypers and electrotypers. In the first decade of this century an international union of paper workers divided into an AFL union of paper makers and an AFL union of pulp-and-paper mill workers. Generally, however, the tendency is toward an increase in the size, and a decrease in the number, of national organizations as unions extend their jurisdictions or amalgamate, as, for example, the merger of the carpenters and the woodworkers, or the plasterers and the cement workers. Where such absorption occurs amongst crafts that are peculiar to an industry, rather than amongst crafts that are common to a number of industries, the resulting organization may approach industrial unionism. In all industrial nations during the past few decades, there has been a tendency for separate unions to be combined and for the industrial form of unionism to expand relative to the craft form. Increased mechanization and division of labor have, of course, favored the industrial membership base.

Certain nonindustrial factors also play a role in the organization and structure of unions in a country. For example, there may be separate local unions for women, Negroes, orientals, or persons belonging to different language groups. Often traditional, personal, or accidental factors have some influence upon the way labor is organized. Presumably it is such influences that explain why the coal-miners' union in America covers all employees who work in the mines and practically all of those who work on property owned by the mine operators, including barbers and beauty-parlor operators, whereas in Great Britain the Mineworkers Federation does not include mechanics, firemen, and engineers who work in the mines but have separate organizations; or that explain why the railroad workers in this country are divided into some 20 craft unions, whereas in Great Britain the National Union of Railwaymen has jurisdiction over all grades of railway workers, although probably a majority of the British locomotive engineers, firemen, and clerks are members of separate unions.

If the labor organization is designed primarily to engage in political activity or to change the economic system through revolution or cooperative ventures, the structure of capitalistic industry may have less influence upon the structural form of the organization.

UNION FORMS AND CONTROL

In the labor movement, as in industry and politics, the development during the past century has been toward the centralization of power and control. Basically such centralization has been due to the increase in the size of markets, which has fostered large-scale business. The local unions, which historically came first and which in the early days were jealous of their autonomy, have gradually been forced to give up more and more of their powers to the national unions. Nevertheless, the local union is still, in many respects, the basic unit in labor organization.

Local unions. A local union may be formed by a group of workers in a certain locality—a town, a city or section of a city, a plant or section of a plant. Today there are over 50,000 local unions in America; the organizations affiliated with the AFL alone have over 35,000. Since the formation of national unions by groups of locals, most of the new local unions have been organized and chartered by the national union in the trade or industry.

Historically, the craft was the first membership base for local unions. A craft is a skilled trade or occupation, generally requiring a definite period of training or apprenticeship. It is, therefore, inaccurate to refer to occupations like milk-wagon or taxicab driving, as crafts. Because workers in a craft have a common or identical training, each can perform all phases of the craft work. Some craftsmen, for example, carpenters, molders, and mechanics, may work in many industries; yet their economic interests may be mainly along craft lines—in protecting the investment in their skill—rather than along industrial lines. As indicated in Chapter 4, it was for the purpose of protecting craft skill that the first local unions were formed in this country amongst such skilled workers as shoemakers, printers, tailors, and carpenters in each locality.

Local unions may also be formed around the common interests of workers who are working for the same employer or are producing the same products.   If the boundaries of the industry, not the worker's occupation or trade, are made the basis of organization, the unit is an industrial union.   There is some uncertainty, however, concerning the definition of an industrial union.   Should it include workers having the same employer or group of employers?   Or should it consist of persons working on the same product or group of products?   Or should the material upon which the employees work be the criterion?   The differences that may arise if more than one of these tests are used can be readily appreciated when one bears in mind that the Ford Motor Company operates a railroad, steamships, a steel plant, a foundry, a paper mill, a glass factory, a cement plant, a rubber plantation, and a number of coal mines; and that the General Motors Corporation produces railroad locomotives, electric refrigerators, vacuum cleaners, electric fans, water pumps, electric stoves, air-conditioning units, and power generating plants, as well as automobiles.   The National Recovery Administration (1933–1935) even considered as separate industries the production of mop sticks, powder puffs, and banana bags.   Classification on the basis of a common material would make the United Brotherhood of Carpenters and Joiners an industrial union, for its membership stretches from the growing tree to the finished wood product, including lumbermen, sawmill hands, woodworkers and wood finishers, and box and furniture workers.[1]

Most local and national unions are intermediate types, including workers in a number of cognate trades or occupations, who, in following their economic interests, have combined in various ways.   Where a group of crafts are united, the organization may be called an associated-craft union, and where workers in certain occupations in an industry are joined together, the resulting unit is a semi-industrial union.   In some instances there may be separate local unions for each occupation included within the jurisdiction of one national union.   For example, a well-organized center of the Teamsters' union may have separate locals for ice-wagon, milk-wagon, taxi, laundry, retail-delivery,

[1] In the lumber and logging camps, the Carpenters' union is a full-fledged industrial union, for it claims jurisdiction over all employees regardless of skill.

and produce drivers, to say nothing of garage employees and so-called "general teamsters," who are really general truck drivers. These separate locals may be gathered together into a joint council of locals in the area.

The combination of workers of various occupations into the same local, or into locals of the same national union, generally has occurred through extension of a national union's jurisdiction to new groups of workers or through an amalgamation of two or more national unions. Such mergers and expansion explain some of the long titles of unions, like the United Slate, Tile, and Composition Roofers, Damp and Waterproof Workers of America, or the International Association of Marble, Slate and Stone Polishers, Rubbers, Sawyers, Tile Setters and Terrazzo Helpers. A study of 133 national unions in 1915 revealed that only about one fifth of them could be considered purely craft organizations in the sense that all members were possessed of identical skill and training.[1] Even half of these purely craft unions found it desirable through loose alliances to cooperate with other related trades in the same industry. A number of union amalgamations have occurred since then for such purposes as increasing the strength of the workers' organization, eliminating jurisdictional disputes, and avoiding the undue hardship to workers in an industry resulting from uncoordinated strikes by various craft unions at different times. A study of 85 AFL unions in 1939 showed that only 12 of them, with less than one per cent of the total membership, were pure craft unions.[2]

Many of the local "assemblies" of the Knights of Labor were all-inclusive or general-labor organizations, embracing all wage workers regardless of occupation or industry.

Each local union elects a staff of executive officials, which may include a business agent, who is the paid representative of the union. A business agent may act as representative for more than one local union. In the building trades, where jobs are of such short duration and are scattered all over, business agents have the power to call strikes; but in most unions a strike vote among the members involved is taken before a strike is authorized.

[1] Theodore W. Glocker, "Amalgamation of Related Trades in American Unions," *American Economic Review*, vol. 5 (September 1915), p. 554.

[2] David J. Saposs and Sol Davison, "Structure of AFL Unions," *Labor Relations Reporter*, vol. 4 (May 15, 1939), p. 385.

The authority and power of a local union depend in part upon its financial resources. If the local cannot strike without appealing to the national union for help in paying benefits to striking workers, it will generally await approval of the strike by officials of the national union. If the collection of dues has been sufficient for the local to finance strikes with its own funds, it may be less restricted by higher authorities. Strike, pension, and sickness benefits can be used by the national union to force locals and individual members to comply with the wishes of the national's officials, just as a company may use financial benefits under its welfare programs to influence employees not to strike for fear of losing benefit rights. In addition, the national union may, of course, revoke the charter of the local, which would mean expulsion from the national union.

National unions. In industries producing for an interstate market, the national or international union is generally the most important unit of labor organization. In this country, the national union has customarily enjoyed autonomy and sovereignty. Probably the size of the country and the importance of craft unionism here are largely responsible for the American theory of the sovereignty of the national union, which finds no parallel abroad. Certainly the policies of the American Federation of Labor have helped to maintain the principle of national-union sovereignty, instead of general labor solidarity.

No two national unions are exactly alike. Their differences may be due in part to historical accidents and powerful personalities, but the economic structure of the industry or industries in which they operate has generally been the primary determining factor. For example, the distribution of power between the national unions and their locals is largely dependent upon the nature of the industry and the size of the competitive area. In coal mining, molding, and railroading, which have wide market and competitive areas, the national body exercises most of the authority. On the other hand, in an industry like building, with localized market areas, the national unions exert relatively little control over the locals. In the building trades the local unions generally reserve the right to strike without referring the matter to the national union. Such local freedom is necessary not only because of the nature of building work, but also because the local building trades generally cooperate as a group in strikes and in maintaining a joint closed shop. In many cities, most of the real power is concentrated in the building-trades councils, which in some instances have not hesitated to destroy established locals of national unions or to organize rival local unions.

The determining influence of economic conditions can be seen in the tendency for national unions in most industries to absorb more and more power until in some cases they control such matters as strikes, working rules, negotiations with employers, and signed agreements, leaving the locals little more than administrative and dues-collecting units. The increase in the size of market areas and firms is not alone responsible for this concentration of union power. The fact that centralization helps to strengthen funds for all sorts of benefits by distributing the risk more widely has likewise been a factor. The placing of strike funds in the hands of national officials, for example, gives them great powers. Such powers, however, are often necessary to enforce a common policy, especially when the union is struggling against large corporations whose executives enjoy almost absolute authority because the stockholders have lost practically all real control over the corporation.

Much of the transfer of power from the local to the national has taken the form of an increase in the "taxes" which the locals pay to the nationals rather than any change in the union's written constitution or governmental structure. The national union may assess the local 30 or 40 cents per month for each member in addition to any contributions that members may make to sickness and pension benefit funds. The national may also receive part of each member's initiation fee. The local is generally free to charge members whatever it wishes in addition to the "taxes" levied on it by the national. Some national unions really resemble a big business, with bureaus of accounting, statistics, research, and insurance benefits as well as various credit institutions.

The officers of national unions may also acquire considerable power by political means. The authority to suspend or expel locals, to issue charters to new locals, to hire a staff of organizers and other officials, and to pay out the union's funds, including strike benefits, places a considerable amount of political power in the hands of a few persons at the top. There are, however, various checks upon the authority and power of national officials. All national unions hold periodic conventions to which locals send elected delegates. In such conventions the larger locals are generally given less representation in proportion to their total membership than the smaller locals enjoy. The convention is the supreme legislative and judicial body and also elects officers. In addition, some unions make use of the referendum and initiative in order to obtain a vote by the rank-and-file membership. Between conventions an elected executive council may serve as some check upon the president of the national union. Despite such devices for distributing power, the president of a union may become a little dictator. Between 1929 and 1937 the Carpenters' union failed to hold a convention, and in the 1920's the president of the United Mine Workers did not hesitate to revoke or suspend the charters of local and district organizations or even to overrule a referendum.

Craft versus industrial unionism. A bone of contention in the American labor movement for a number of decades has been the issue of whether national unions should be organized along craft or industrial lines. Organization both ways is likely to lead to conflict unless the craft is peculiar to the industry, such as the printers and pressmen, or the lasters in the shoe industry. The same conflict between the craft and industrial principles has occurred in other countries, but it has not broken out into interunion warfare on a wide scale, as has been the case here since 1935. There has, nevertheless, been a definite tendency in practically all countries for industrial unionism to crowd out craft unionism, the earlier form.

Because recent economic and technical developments have favored industrial unionism, popular opinion is prone to consider craft unionism passé and to overlook the real economic advantages of the craft form for certain classes of workers. Craft unions were flourishing in this country over half a century before industrial unions began to be formed as assemblies of the Knights of Labor. Why, one might ask, was the first industrial union of Carriage and Wagon Workers formed in 1891 and not in the 1820's? Why did groups working on wagons, such as carpenters, painters, blacksmiths, and wheelwrights, form separate craft unions instead of an industrial union of wagon workers? To answer such questions is to state the case for craft unionism.

1. *Economic basis of craft unionism.* One reason for the craft form in the wagon-making industry was that the carpenters and other craftsmen might work in other industries during the year. The same is true of many crafts today. A machinist, for example, may work at his trade in as many as five different industries during one year, especially if the work is seasonal and business conditions are fluctuating. Universal application of the industrial form of unionism would require carpenters or machinists to change unions every time that they moved from shipbuilding to a railroad repair shop, a garage, an automobile plant, or a textile mill.[1] Furthermore, a craft would usually represent a small minority of all the workers in the industry. A majority of the workers, not acquainted with and not particularly interested in the problems of the carpenter or the machinist, would exercise control in a union based on the industrial principle.

Craft problems arise because skilled workers, like carpenters and machinists, face competition from other workers in the craft rather than from other workers in the industry. Craftsmen's wages usually depend more upon the value of their skill than upon the general wage level in an industry. Consequently, common interests in the craft may be stronger for skilled workers than their common interests with other workers in an industry. The craft type of organization on a national scale enables the craftsmen as a group to preserve and enhance the value of their craft skill. This they do in the same manner as lawyers and doctors, by restricting the supply of qualified sellers of the services and by maintaining the demand for their services by preventing outsiders from performing any of the work that they claim as their jurisdiction. For example, a craft union may restrict entrance to the trade by apprenticeship regulations and may prevent reduction in the craftsman's job by working rules which forbid a subdivision of the work or the use of labor-saving devices and machinery. Such craft protective regulations may enable skilled workers to obtain high wages even without collective bargaining, and they are the economic basis upon which craft unionism rests. So strong is this factor of craft protection that, where separate crafts have

[1] It should be pointed out that both these unions have industrial locals in certain industries. The Machinists' union has made agreements with aircraft companies covering all the employees of those companies and the Carpenters' union has done the same in lumber and logging camps.

been amalgamated into a single union, each craft generally insists upon retaining the exclusive right to jurisdiction over employment in its trade, and the movement of workers between the combined trades is jealously guarded.

The economic strength of craft unionism has been underestimated by those who measure power in terms of numbers. Although a craft may be numerically small, its membership is likely to be cohesive, whereas an industrial union with a polygot membership may be split into dissenting factions. Where there is no cheap and suitable substitute for craft skill, it may represent considerable economic strength in the form of monopoly power. Furthermore, the distribution of craftsmen among a number of industries may serve to spread the risk of wholesale strikes and save the union from almost complete annihilation in one contest of strength with employers in the industry. During a craft strike in one industry, employed craftsmen in other industries can supply the union treasury with funds. If combined action amongst unions in the same industry is desirable, craft unions can join together in allied trades' councils or industrial federations, such as the Building Trades, Metal Trades, and Railway Employees Departments of the AFL. In this way the Machinists and Blacksmiths, for example, have acted jointly with the other metal trades and with other shop crafts in the railroad industry, while the Electrical Workers and Sheet Metal Workers have cooperated in collective bargaining with other craft unions in the railroads and in building construction.

2. *Economic basis of industrial unionism.* The arguments for the industrial form rest primarily upon the characteristics of modern large-scale industry. Jobs in large firms, it is claimed, have become so specialized and so peculiar to the firm or industry that comparatively few workers can be considered skilled craftsmen, belonging to a definite and distinct trade cutting across industrial lines. Consequently, organization on a strictly craft basis would exclude from any labor organization most of the workers in the mass-production industries. If the unskilled and semiskilled machine operators in the basic industries are to be organized, it must be along industrial lines. Furthermore, workers in the mass-production industries think along employer or industrial, rather than craft, lines.

The advocates of industrial unionism point out that craft unions have been unable to gain a foothold in any of our basic industries, and that they have flourished only in small-scale manufacturing, in local-market industries like building, or in industries sheltered by public policy such as navy yards, shipbuilding, and the railroads. They point out that the AFL organizing campaigns in steel (1919) and automobiles (1925–1927) failed miserably. That it is easier to organize most workers along industrial lines seems to be indicated by the fact that the AFL has first organized workers into federal labor unions, which are really industrial unions or general-labor unions. Later, in distributing many of the members of such industrial locals in automobiles, rubber, or steel amongst perhaps 20 craft unions, the unity of the organization is shattered.

Organization and action by labor on industrial lines is necessary, it is claimed, because employers and employers' associations are organized mostly upon that basis. Organization of a number of unions in each firm or industry permits employers to play one union off against another, and to take them on one at a time. By signing agreements with some of the separate unions and not with others, employers can cause one group of craft unionists to serve as strike-breakers in the strike of another craft union. That has happened, for example, on the railroads. The shipowners on the Pacific Coast, after signing a two-year agreement with the seamen in 1919, practically eliminated the Longshoremen's union, and then, when the seamen's agreement expired, the owners were able to defeat their strike without any fear of a strike at the same time amongst the longshoremen.

It is argued that industrial unionism offers greater opportunity to bring industrial democracy to industry, and is a better method for combatting company unionism. Furthermore its advocates state that, by including a larger number of workers in its base of organization, industrial unionism can serve to bring greater political pressure to bear upon legislatures.

Finally, it is claimed that jurisdictional disputes between unions would practically disappear if this broader basis of organization were generally adopted. Such a contention is, however, open to question, for the lines between industries are not clear-cut. As has been indicated, automobile firms operate ships, railroads, steel plants, mines, and other factories, and produce all sorts of products. With such intermixing of industries, industrial unions would be contending with one another for control of a certain plant, material, or product. For example, jurisdiction over the agricultural implement industry is claimed by all of the following industrial unions: the United Automobile Workers (both CIO and AFL branches), the Steel Workers Organizing Committee (CIO), the United Electrical, Radio, and Machine Workers Organizing Committee (CIO), and the Farm Equipment Workers Organizing Committee (CIO).

One of the few important industrial unions prior to 1920, the International Union of the United Brewery, Flour, Cereal, and Soft Drink Workers of America, is really an industrial octopus, like certain corporations and holding companies. As its title indicates, it claims jurisdiction over all the employees in a number of industries, which might give rise to considerable interunion conflict if most of American industry were organized on the industrial principle.[1]

Jurisdictional disputes. Disputes between unions over jurisdiction, or the exclusive right to organize workers in a certain section of industry, are bound up with the problem of union structure. Such disputes are more likely to arise where unions are formed on different structural principles and where the same national union may be a craft union in one industry, a semi-industrial union in another industry, and an industrial union in a third industry, as is true, for example, of the Machinists' and Carpenters' unions, which have engaged in a 25-year dispute over the right to install certain types of equipment in breweries.[2]

Jurisdictional disputes arise from a struggle between unions for exclusive control over a certain type of work or a certain group of workers. Unions, like business firms, strive to expand and also to achieve a monopoly. Craft unions attempt to maintain the demand for their skill by marking off certain work for their members. Especially is that true in crafts, like the building trades, where members may be unemployed for periods during a year because of seasonal or business-cycle fluctuations. Consequently,

[1] This union claims jurisdiction over "every brewery, malt, grain elevator, yeast, syrup, vinegar, alcohol, wine, cider, cereal-beverage, soft-drink, and mineral-water worker of good, recommendable character."

[2] *Cf. New York Times*, November 4, 1939, p. 13.

one finds the Painters and the Electrical Workers fighting over the right to paint electric poles and fire alarm boxes, the Carpenters and Plasterers both demanding the right to install plasterboard, and the Carpenters and the Sheet Metal Workers each claiming exclusive right to put metal trim, metal windows, and metal doors in new houses.   The Carpenters argue that hanging doors, laying trim, and installing window casings has always been their work, while the Sheet Metal Workers just as stoutly assert that they have jurisdiction over all sheet metal in building construction.

Jurisdictional disputes may also arise out of conflicting claims to the right to organize workers in a certain branch of industry or in a certain territory.   For example, the Brotherhood of Railroad Clerks and the Teamsters' union both claim jurisdiction over the drivers of Railway Express vehicles; the Brewery Workers and the Teamsters both claim exclusive right to organize brewery-wagon and truck drivers; the Steel Workers' and the Automobile Workers' unions both want to enroll employees in plants making parts for various kinds of machinery; and the men's and ladies' garment unions have come into conflict in the bathrobe and other garment lines.

If the materials and jobs in industry did not change and if there were clear-cut boundaries between industries, with each employer operating in only one industry, probably fewer jurisdictional disputes would arise.   However, there would still be disputes between craft, semi-industrial, and industrial unions claiming overlapping jurisdictions, and certain troublesome questions would remain, such as whether some or all the truck drivers belonged in a separate industry.   Perhaps another reason for jurisdictional disputes is the fact that jurisdictional statements in the constitutions of most unions are in such general terms that they are subject to various interpretations in particular cases.[1] In addition, jurisdictional disputes may arise because two unions are trying to organize in exactly the same jurisdiction.   Such "dual unionism" occurs with a split in the ranks of an existing national union, as the secession of the Amalgamated Clothing Workers

[1] The constitutions of most unions use less than 50 words to describe their jurisdictions. The jurisdiction of the Barbers and Woodworkers is stated in less than 10 words; but the Bricklayers use over 1,300, and the Machinists over 1,600, words for that purpose.

from the United Garment Workers in 1914, or it may exist where two labor centers with somewhat different labor philosophies are competing for control of organized labor, as in the struggles of the AFL with the Knights of Labor, the IWW, and the CIO.

The American theory of the sovereignty of the national unions serves both to increase the severity of jurisdictional disputes and to make them difficult to solve. With the national unions supreme and not subject to any authority except the courts, they are free to disregard any decision by officials of the AFL or an outside arbitrator. Consequently, the disputes may drag on for decades, and never be really settled. As already mentioned, the Carpenters' and Sheet Metal Workers' unions, have, for many decades, engaged in a bitter struggle for jurisdiction over metal trim and doors. In 1909 both unions submitted the dispute to arbitration by a New York judge, who awarded the work to the Carpenters. The Sheet Metal Workers refused to accept the judge's decision. Later in the same year, the new Building Trades Department of the AFL decided in favor of the Sheet Metal Workers. The Carpenters' union refused to abide by the Department's stand, and was suspended from the Department. In 1915 the Department reversed itself in order to hold the Carpenters' union. In 1920 a new National Board for Jurisdictional Awards in the Building Trades Department of the AFL decided the dispute in favor of the Sheet Metal Workers and the obdurate Carpenters were again suspended from the Department. In 1927 the Carpenters were readmitted to the Department, and the Board of Jurisdictional Awards collapsed. The dispute is still unsettled. Jurisdictional disputes have been particularly prevalent and irritating in the building trades, where the 20-odd national unions tread on each other's toes in some locality every day.

Another controversy that has been going on for 30 years is that between the Brewery Workers and the Teamsters for jurisdiction over the drivers of brewery wagons or trucks. The 1913 convention of the AFL reaffirmed the Brewery Workers' jurisdiction "over all workers employed in the brewery industry" by refusing to transfer teamsters handling brewery products to the Teamsters' union. In the 1933 convention of the AFL, however, the brewery drivers were handed over to the Teamsters' union. Since then hundreds of thousands of dollars have been spent for litigation and jurisdictional strikes, and the brewery owners in Oregon and Washington have brought suit against the Teamsters for $3,000,000 in damages arising out of the dispute.[1] In 1939 a Federal district court granted the Brewery Workers' union an injunction restraining the AFL from transferring the beer drivers to the Teamsters' union on the grounds that such a transfer would violate the rights granted to the Brewery Workers' union in its "contract" upon affiliation with the AFL in 1887 and would deprive members of the Brewery Workers' union of property and benefit rights.

Jurisdictional disputes have often been costly for innocent employers caught in the cross fire of such conflicts. They have also proved costly to unions engaged in such internecine warfare. A student of jurisdictional questions in the building trades has stated that "the amount of money spent by the building-trades unions upon jurisdictional controversies, directly and indirectly, represents one of the largest items in their budgets." [2] Furthermore, such disputes have tended to discredit unions and supply ammunition for antiunion drives. The bitter jurisdictional warfare between the United Brotherhood of Carpenters and Joiners (AFL) and the International Woodworkers (CIO) for control of the lumber workers in the Pacific Northwest during 1937 and 1938 led to the passage, by popular referendum, of a stringent antilabor amendment to the Oregon constitution restricting strikes and picketing. The people had become disgusted with the violence, property destruction, and millions of dollars of sales lost because AFL teamsters and carpenters refused to handle or nail lumber cut by CIO woodworkers, and CIO longshoremen threatened to boycott any lumber cut by AFL unionists.

The general importance of jurisdictional disputes has, however, been greatly exaggerated. The classified statistics of the U. S. Department of Labor show that in no year from 1927 to 1940 did jurisdictional strikes account for as much as two per cent of all man-days of labor lost from strikes of all kinds. Strikes caused by disputes between rival unions or factions of a union accounted for less than two per cent of all man-days lost by strikes in 8 of those

[1] *Cf. Report of the Proceedings of the Fifty-Seventh Annual Convention of the American Federation of Labor*, 1937, p. 540.

[2] N. R. Whitney, *Jurisdiction in American Building-Trades Unions*, 1914, p. 126.

13 years, and the figure did not reach nine per cent in any of the 13 years. The years with the highest percentage of man-days lost from interunion disputes were 1933, two years before the CIO was formed, and 1936.

Various systems for settling jurisdictional disputes have been tried, but none has proved entirely satisfactory in practice, partly because there is no one principle that can be consistently applied and enforced. The AFL has favored amalgamation of national unions and settlement "within the family of labor" by negotiation, by the decision of representatives in one of its Departments, or by vote at its annual conventions. However, past experience seems to demonstrate that such methods do not result in final and enforceable settlements of the most important jurisdictional disputes. Arbitration by outside parties and decision by a joint board representing employers and employees have been tried, but the sovereign unions have not hesitated to disregard such decisions. The government may hold elections to let a majority of the workers decide which union shall represent them. Such a procedure has worked well in many dual-unionism cases, although it failed in the Pacific Northwest lumber dispute already mentioned and raises the issue of whether the vote shall be along craft or industrial lines. The Federal government has also brought suit against a union engaged in such a dispute, arguing that it has violated the antitrust acts by conspiring to restrain interstate trade and commerce.[1] Employers and unions are both free, of course, to take such disputes to the courts for a decision and damages.

The settlement of jurisdictional disputes has been rendered especially difficult in this country by the theory of the sovereignty of the national union, which is comparable in rigidity to the theory of the sovereignty of nations, and by the practice of the AFL in granting absolute and permanent jurisdiction to affiliated unions. The constitution of the Federation forbids the granting of a charter of affiliation to any union "if the jurisdiction claimed is a trespass on the jurisdiction of existing affiliated unions, without the written consent of such unions." In Great Britain, on the other hand, the central labor federation (the Trades Union Congress) has consistently taken the stand that no affiliated union has an exclusive right to organize any class of workers. Also, any affiliated union cannot

[1] *Cf.*, for example, *New York Times*, November 4, 1939, p. 13.

accept for membership a member of another union, if that union is engaged in a strike or if the member has unpaid obligations to the other union, and in any case, the other union must be consulted before he is accepted. Furthermore, various unions have arrived at working arrangements regarding their separate jurisdictions, and have established their own agencies for settlement in addition to the disputes committee of the Congress. Consequently, although the Trades Union Congress has over 200 affiliated craft, industrial, and general labor unions, some catering to the same or similar types of workers, Great Britain had far fewer jurisdictional disputes than this country during the years from 1925 to 1939.

In other countries like Norway and Sweden, jurisdictional disputes have been reduced by the adoption of schemes for reorganizing the union structure into fewer national unions conforming more closely to the industrial form.

FEDERATIONS OF UNIONS

Common interests cause unions of various types, whether craft or industrial, to federate along political and geographic lines. Locals of various national unions may form a city central or an allied trades council for combined action on both the economic and political fronts. In each state, union locals and city centrals may join a state federation. The national unions, along with the city centrals and state federations, may be affiliated with a national federation or national union center, such as the AFL or the CIO. There may also be combined action by various unions on a district or regional basis and on an industrial basis, as in the case of the railroad and building-trades unions. The unions affiliated with city, state, and national federations supply the funds and delegates at conventions, in return for which they receive various services and perhaps financial assistance during strikes. The state and national federations are designed primarily for political, educational, and organizational purposes.

City federations. City or county federations of local unions operate under various names in different localities, such as central labor council, central labor union, industrial union council, joint council, and city trades assembly. As mentioned in Chapter 4, the first labor federation formed in this country was a city central established in Philadelphia in 1827. By 1866 there were so many city centrals that an attempt was made to federate them into a National Labor Union, with national unions also represented on an equal basis. As indicated in the previous chapter, this national federation based on city centrals lasted only a few years. By mixing in national politics and pursuing unsuccessful cooperative ventures, it lost its hold on the national unions and also on the city centrals, which were more interested in local politics than in national issues such as greenbackism.

The AFL, as a national federation based upon the notion of the sovereignty and self-government of affiliated national unions, seeks to prevent local central bodies from taking power away from the affiliated national unions, as has happened notably in the building-trades councils of certain large cities, which have gone so far as to destroy locals of affiliated nationals and to organize rival locals. The constitution of the AFL forbids affiliated local central bodies to strike, take a strike vote, support a boycott, or take part in negotiations regarding wages and working rules without notifying the national union concerned and receiving its approval. Actions of the 800-odd city centrals affiliated with the AFL are subject to review by the Executive Council, elected at the Federation's annual conventions. The Executive Council can suspend or expel an offending city central. In order to maintain full control over its city centrals and to prevent any "dual unionism" within the structure of the parent organization, the AFL constitution forbids any affiliated city central from admitting or retaining delegates of any local union that "owes its allegiance" to a national union not affiliated with the Federation. Consequently, it has been necessary for the CIO to establish over 100 state, county, and city industrial union councils or federations, under the direct control of the CIO Executive Board.

The American Federation of Labor. Like the League of Nations, the AFL is a loose federation of over 100 sovereign national unions. Each national union enjoys absolute control over its internal affairs, is free to develop whatever policies and philosophy it wishes, and can leave the Federation at any time for any reason. Samuel Gompers, its president for almost 50 years, once said: "No national or international union is subordinate to the American Federation of Labor. They are sovereign entities in themselves."

The doctrine that the Federation shall in no way interfere with the sovereignty of a national union has sharply limited the central organization's power to improve conditions within national unions that may be embarrassing to the Federation. For example, racketeering has occurred in local-market lines like the building trades where the union business agent has considerable power;[1] yet only the national unions can clean up such abuses, for each union member and local official is a citizen of his national union and not of the Federation. Persons who are members of national unions are represented in the Federation through their national union. Because the Federation officials have considered themselves impotent to intervene constructively in the affairs of national unions, some forward-looking elements have finally revolted against the corrupt or inept leadership of a national union. Even when the insurgents have been supported by more than a majority of the union's membership, the Federation generally continues to recognize and support only the "regular" officers who hold the union's charter and the jurisdiction granted by the AFL. The Federation fought the insurgent Amalgamated Clothing Workers as a dual union to the minority group remaining in the United Garment Workers, only admitting the Amalgamated to the Federation in 1933 after the United agreed to such action in return for the privilege of selling its labels to the Amalgamated at a profit of over $25,000 a year.[2]

Why should a union be willing to pay thousands of dollars to acquire a jurisdiction granted by the AFL? What has kept unions in the AFL, which Gompers called a "rope of sand"? Undoubtedly, the Federation's policy of assuring exclusive jurisdiction to an affiliated union and of combatting any threats to that jurisdiction in the form of dual unionism has served as a powerful lever to force national unions to be members of the Federation. An outside union may at any time find itself confronted by a rival union supported by the Federation and all its subordinate units, including state labor federations and city central bodies. In effect, therefore,

[1] Such racketeering consists of extorting money from employers or employees by means of economic power or position. Racketeering and graft are, of course, to be found in business and government. One can no more say that racketeering is characteristic of labor organization than one can say that embezzlement is characteristic of banking, because some clerks steal from their banks.

[2] Cf. *New York Times*, November 23, 1936, p. 2.

the AFL has served to protect national unions against insurrection or rivalry by forcing local unions to be a part of the national union recognized by the Federation as the one legitimate union in that jurisdiction, or to remain completely outside the Federation's "family of labor," including its state and local union centers. Affiliation not only gives a national union the benefit of a jurisdictional franchise or monopoly, in so far as the AFL can enforce that monopoly, but the national union may also enjoy support in strikes, in selling goods bearing its label, in boycotts, and in organizing new members. Unlike a public utility, the national union does not need to exercise exclusive franchise granted by the Federation in order to retain it. Theoretically, a national union's jurisdiction will be protected by the Federation indefinitely despite the fact that a large part of that jurisdiction is not exercised and, therefore, exists only on paper. No wonder dual unionism is anathema to the Federation! The competition of dual unionism weakens a "rope of sand" based on a monopoly of jurisdiction.

There is one exception to the statement that workers are not members of the AFL but of its constituent national unions. In organizing certain areas, trades, or industries, the Federation may first have the workers join "federal trade unions" or "federal labor unions," which are directly affiliated with the AFL. These locals represent a transitional form of organization, considered necessary because no national union exists with jurisdiction over those workers, or because they are not numerous enough to form separate locals of the national unions having jurisdiction over them, or because such a general or industrial basis seemed the most suitable one to adopt in the campaign to organize those particular workers. Later, presumably, most workers in such federal unions will become members of a national union affiliated with the Federation. Local federal unions also enable Negro workers, who are barred from membership in some national unions, to be organized.

The foregoing discussion has indicated some of the activities of the AFL. Its chief functions may be summarized under the following five headings: (1) jurisdictional—defining and preserving the jurisdictional rights of affiliated unions, including the settlement of jurisdictional disputes; (2) organizational—organizing and assisting federal unions and locals of national unions; (3) legislative—trying to obtain the enactment of legislation favored by the Federation;

(4) educational—attempting to influence public opinion in favor of organized labor through publicity and publications; (5) economic—influencing workers' purchases through the union label or white lists, and supporting strikes of federal unions or national unions. The Federation is officially opposed to sympathetic strikes, which would mean breaking union agreements with employers. In fact, the Federation has no authority to call members of national unions to strike.

Since 1936 the total expenditures of the Federation have ranged between $1,000,000 and $2,000,000 a year, approximately half of which has been spent for organizing purposes. During the last few years, about one third of the revenue of the AFL has been raised by a regular monthly "tax" of one cent per member on national unions and 35 cents per member on local federal unions; a special assessment levy on national unions and receipts from the Federation's monthly magazine have each accounted for between a fourth and a fifth of its total income.

Even before the 10 CIO unions were suspended from the AFL in 1936, less than one quarter of the unions affiliated with the Federation were pure craft unions. About one half of them were associated-craft unions, and more than a quarter were semi-industrial or industrial in character. Despite such a heterogeneous composition and structure, the Federation has been dominated by the craft philosophy because national unions having a majority of the voting strength in the AFL have jurisdictional claims in more than one industry.

Because voting in the AFL convention each year is according to the total membership upon which the affiliated union has paid the membership tax, a few unions can dominate the Federation. In 1935, the 12 largest unions in the AFL accounted for a majority of the total votes, and in 1939 such control was in the hands of the 13 largest unions. In the latter year, the building-trades unions, the printing-trades unions, the Teamsters, the Machinists, and the Musicians together had over 50 per cent of the voting strength. Each year the convention elects an Executive Council of 17 (the president, 15 vice presidents, and the secretary-treasurer), which has been the agency actually controlling the policies of the Federation. It is limited only by the constitution and the annual convention, which the Council may dominate through the control that the 15 vice presidents have over the votes of their own unions.

The controversy of craft *versus* industrial unionism has troubled the Federation for decades. In the 1901 convention a minority of a special committee favored industrial unionism "where practical," and in the 1903 convention a resolution was introduced proposing that a committee study and report on "a plan by which the trades unions can be grouped together on industrial lines." [1] A resolution was introduced in the 1912 convention of the Federation by six delegates of the United Mine Workers, including William Green, who has been the Federation's president since 1924, calling upon the convention to adopt and endorse "the plan of organization by industries instead of by crafts which often divides the forces of labor." This resolution was defeated, although it received 35 per cent of the votes cast, which compares well with the 38-per-cent vote in favor of the minority report for industrial unionism in the 1935 convention. [2]

In the meantime, the experience of certain industrial unions in the AFL had not been particularly happy. The International Union of Carriage and Wagon Workers ("Automobile" was added to its title in 1913) was given an AFL charter in 1893 and claimed jurisdiction over all employees in the construction and repairing of carriages and wagons. Between 1902 and 1913 this industrial union of vehicle workers had jurisdictional disputes with national unions in the following crafts: Blacksmiths, Painters, Upholsterers, Machinists, Carpenters, Sheet Metal Workers, Electrical Workers, Pattern Makers, and Metal Polishers. At the 1913 convention the Carriage and Wagon Workers' union of about 3,000 members was ordered to relinquish jurisdiction over all members coming under the jurisdiction of these craft unions. For refusing to obey that edict, the Wagon Workers' union was finally expelled from the AFL in 1918.

The International Union of United Brewery Workers experienced similar partitioning. This affiliated union was granted jurisdiction over "any person or persons" in the brewery industry by the 1887 convention of the AFL. In a series of Federation actions from 1898 to 1907, the Brewery Workers' union was ordered to relinquish to the craft unions those of its members who were barrel makers, painters, firemen, or engineers, despite the fact that these craft

---

[1] AFL, *Report of Proceedings of 23rd Annual Convention*, 1903, p. 108.
[2] AFL, *Report of Proceedings of 32nd Annual Convention*, 1912, pp. 243, 311–12.

unions had become affiliated with the AFL a number of years after the Brewery Workers' union. Refusing to relinquish such members, the industrial union of Brewery Workers was expelled from the Federation in 1907, only to be readmitted in 1908 with a recognized jurisdiction "over all workers employed in the brewery industry." Despite the claims of the Teamsters' union, chartered in 1899, the 1913 convention and the 1915 report of the Executive Council definitely stated that jurisdiction over the drivers of brewery wagons belonged to the Brewery Workers' union. From 1917 to 1933 the brewery business was sharply curtailed by prohibition. In 1933 the Executive Council and the annual convention of the Federation gave jurisdiction over teamsters, engineers, and firemen in the brewery industry to the respective craft unions.

The final split in the American Federation of Labor over the industrial-union issue came in the 1935 convention when a minority report of the resolutions committee called for industrial unions covering all workers "in those industries where the work performed by a majority of the workers is of such nature that it might fall within the jurisdictional claim of more than one craft union, or no established craft union." [1] Existing jurisdictional claims of national unions were to be disregarded on the ground that changes in industrial methods had so altered the jobs in those industries that they could not have been included in the jurisdictional outlines of charters issued to national unions prior to such industrial changes. This minority report was defeated, as mentioned, by a majority of 62 per cent of the votes cast, and shortly after this convention the Committee for Industrial Organization (CIO) was formed by the officers of seven of the national unions in the AFL that had been active in support of the minority report favoring industrial unionism in the mass-production industries. The Committee for Industrial Organization became the Congress of Industrial Organizations (CIO) at its constitutional convention in November 1938.

Congress of Industrial Organizations. Like the Federation, the Congress of Industrial Organizations is a confederation of 40-odd national or international unions and organizing committees that presumably enjoy autonomy within their own jurisdictions. In fact, the structural patterns and basic provisions of the constitution of the Congress are so similar to those of the Federation that

[1] AFL, *Report of Proceedings of 55th Annual Convention*, 1935, pp. 523–24, 574–75.

there is little need to describe them in detail. The Executive Board of the CIO, like the Federation's Executive Council, directs the affairs of the organization between conventions and controls the affairs of industrial union councils (city or state federations) and of local industrial unions (similar to local federal unions), subject, of course, to appeal 'of its decisions to the annual convention. The Executive Board also makes recommendations regarding jurisdictional disputes between affiliates, and the convention has supreme authority to decide them.

There are, however, a few significant differences between the constitution of the CIO and that of the AFL. Each national union or organizing committee nominates a member to be elected by each annual convention to the Executive Board, so that the Board consists of 40-odd members instead of 17. In addition, each Board member casts the number of votes represented by the membership of his union. Consequently, as few as four national unions, which account for a majority of all votes, can control not only the conventions but also the Executive Board. The monthly "taxes" per member are five cents for each national union and organizing committee and 50 cents per member for each directly affiliated local industrial union.

The CIO is a rival union center or federation, which was originally formed for the purpose of organizing into industrial unions all workers in the mass-production industries. As such, it represented an attempt to break up unused franchises or monopolies in the form of "paper" jurisdictions to certain skilled workers in those industries, claimed by unions affiliated with the AFL. It now includes, however, unions in such crafts as barbering, die casting, and radio telegraphy. In addition to the 10 national unions expelled from the AFL for forming the CIO, the Newspaper Guild, the Quarry Workers', and the Fur Workers' unions withdrew from the Federation to affiliate with the CIO, and the United Electrical, Radio, and Machine Workers seceded from the International Brotherhood of Electrical Workers, an AFL union.

The area of jurisdictional conflict between CIO and AFL unions has been increasing since 1936. The Federation has recently chartered rival unions in coal mining and textile spinning and readmitted one section of the Automobile Workers' union. The CIO has established organizing committees in meat packing, building construction, barbering, liquor distilling, and electrical utilities, which directly challenge the jurisdictional claims of corresponding unions in the AFL. Also there are national unions in the CIO and the AFL that are struggling to organize lumber and furniture workers, government employees, workers in the metal trades, taxicab drivers, and waterfront workers. The situation in the maritime industry is especially confused, with a CIO longshoremen's union and an AFL seamen's union on the West Coast and just the opposite situation on the East Coast. Furthermore, the CIO has local industrial unions of truck drivers, printers, cigar makers, paper makers, laundry workers, and hotel and restaurant employees, although the AFL has national unions in those occupations.

The competition of the CIO has had a stimulating effect upon the AFL and its affiliated unions. Many of the national unions in the Federation have adopted the industrial-union principle by enlarging their jurisdictions to include practically all workers in a plant. The AFL has been spending large sums to organize the unorganized, including unskilled and white-collar workers. In 1939 there were 250,000 workers in the Federation's "federal unions," which, as pointed out, are mostly industrial unions on a local scale. In the rush to organize workers, certain AFL unions are disregarding rigid jurisdictional lines, as telegraph operators in some localities are organized by the Electrical Workers instead of the Commercial Telegraphers' union, and drivers of bakery wagons are to be found in both the Teamsters' union and the Bakery and Confectionery Workers' union. A number of the original CIO unions have also enlarged their jurisdictions, until some of them include workers who can hardly be considered to belong to only one industry. The CIO has still to face the problem of serious jurisdictional disputes because, starting with a clean jurisdictional slate, it could parcel out jurisdictions without stepping on the toes of any one of 100 affiliated unions.

Such increased activity and new policies may be contrasted with the lack of progress and actual decline in membership during the 1920's, when the labor movement was unified instead of being split into rival camps. Contrast such stagnancy, for example, with the organization of over 500,000 white-collar workers since 1935. But the split in the ranks of labor has also been very harmful to the labor movement. Some workers have become disgusted with rival unionists boycotting each other's labels and acting as strike-breakers in interunion conflicts. Those who have lost income or profits as a result of such internecine warfare have also become aroused. Employers have been able to stir up antiunion sentiments by playing unions off against one another. As a result of the ill will engendered by the bitter interlabor struggle, legislation has been passed in some states sharply restricting the activities and rights of organized labor.

Although the rank and file of organized labor may desire peace between the AFL and the CIO, the prospects for such peace or for actual unification of the two groups into one federation have not increased with the passage of time. Not only has the area of possible conflict between rival unions been expanding, but also the number of national unions in the CIO that have rivals inside the AFL has been increasing rapidly. With rival national unions increasing in number and most national unions expanding their jurisdictions, the difficulties of squeezing all of them into a single unified structure become greater and greater.

In addition to serious jurisdictional problems, unification by merging existing organizations would eliminate some union officials from their jobs. The longer the interunion struggle is prolonged, the more such vested interests there will be to oppose consolidation. Above all there is the question of which side would have a majority on the executive council and in the convention of any united labor federation. Should the CIO unionists hold the balance of power, the old-line AFL unions would fear that their jurisdictional monopolies might be curtailed in the same way that past AFL conventions reduced the jurisdictions of industrial unions of Wagon Workers and Brewery Workers.

The structural issue abroad. Because there is no one type of union structure that is superior for all occupations and industries, the issue of craft *versus* industrial unionism has arisen in other countries. Presumably, the best form of unionism in each case is that which permits the group to function most effectively in the pursuit of its objectives. Craft protective regulations under craft unionism may enable a group of skilled craftsmen to obtain higher wages than they could under the industrial form. Yet the unmistakeable trend in all industrial countries is toward industrial unionism rather than the older craft form.

Under pressure by employers' organizations to form industrial unions so that they would need to deal with but one labor organization in each industry, the Swedish Confederation of Trade Unions adopted a scheme of reorganization in 1912, aiming at a gradual amalgamation of the 41 existing unions into 22 industrial unions. A majority of the craft unions opposed this scheme. In 1926 the scheme was modified to permit only one union in each workplace, or a total of 33 unions. Craft unions, which are mostly in building and printing, have been declining in importance and account for less than 15 per cent of all union membership, with most of the remaining 85 per cent in industrial unions.

In 1920 the Norwegian Federation of Trade Unions adopted the principle of federating national unions into "industrial departments." This scheme of reorganization was changed in 1923 to one calling for 10 industrial unions in place of the 32 existing unions. The 1923 plan was opposed by certain craft unions. Nevertheless, through amalgamation, craft unionism has been disappearing in Norway until in 1939 only about 10 per cent of all union membership was in pure craft unions, compared with over 60 per cent in industrial unions. In Denmark, however, the craft union has continued to predominate. In 1939 as many as 45 out of the 67 unions affiliated with the National Trade Union Center in Denmark were of the craft type.

In France, the General Confederation of Labor has admitted only industrial *syndicats* (unions) since 1906, so that craft unions have been of slight importance there. At the formation of the Australian Council of Trade Unions in 1927, approval was given to a method for slowly transforming the Australian trade-union movement of some 350 distinct labor organizations from the craft to the industrial basis.[1]

The question of union reorganization was raised in Great Britain in 1924 by a resolution passed by the Trades Union Congress (the national federation) declaring that "the aim should be, as far as possible, organization by industry," and instructing the General Council of the federation to draw up "(1) a scheme for organization by industry, and (2) a scheme which may secure unity of action without the definite merging of existing unions, by a scientific link-

---

[1] For data and discussion concerning union structure in the Scandinavian countries, France, and Australia, *cf.* H. A. Marquand *et al.*, *Organized Labour in Four Continents*, 1939; and the official yearbooks for these countries.

ing up of same to present a united front." After three years of consultation and investigation, the Council concluded in its 1927 report:

. . . as it is impossible to define any fixed boundaries of industry, it is impracticable to formulate a scheme of "organization by industry," that can be made applicable to all industries. Dealing with the second part of the resolution, which calls for a scientific linking without definite merging, the Council has been compelled to recognize the practical difficulties, and though it has tried to solve the problem and has attempted to draft a scheme on the basis of present-day trade union organization in industry, it has been found impossible to make any definite plan, as the General Council has not been empowered to alter the scope of its affiliated unions, which have divergent policies in regard to organization.

Therefore, the General Council has in this case also come to the conclusion that no general scheme is practicable, though it may be possible for groups of unions which have related industrial interests, and desire closer working, to prepare their own scheme in the light of their own structural, administrative, and industrial circumstances.

Resolutions may be passed, and theoretical contentions advanced, but the fact remains that trade union organization has assumed complex forms which are the growth of generations. Under these circumstances trade union organization will have to be gradually remolded and its present form *adapted*, rather than *transformed*, to meet new conditions.[1]

In short, the General Council decided that any preconceived plan of organization would conflict with too many vested interests to be practical and, with rapid changes in industry, it would soon be out of date. The British Trades Union Congress consists of over 200 affiliated unions, most of which are craft and federated- or associated-craft unions, although two unions of the industrial type (the Mineworkers Federation and the National Union of Railwaymen) and two general unions that take in unskilled workers from all industries and skilled workers from unorganized areas (the Transport and General Workers Union and the National Union of General and Municipal Workers), together contained approximately 43 per cent of the 4,500,000 members in unions affiliated with the Congress in 1938. Union structure in Great Britain is especially haphazard because the Trades Union Congress admits unions based on very different organizational principles and does not recognize one union as having exclusive jurisdiction over any class of workers.

[1] *Report of Proceedings at the 59th Annual Trades Union Congress*, 1927, pp. 102–103.

INDEPENDENT UNIONS

A number of national and local unions are not affiliated with either the AFL or the CIO. The unaffiliated national unions in this country probably have close to 800,000 members made up primarily of railroad craftsmen, post-office workers, and Federal employees. It is impossible to estimate the membership of independent local unions.

The "Big Four" railroad brotherhoods in the engine and train service (engineers, firemen, conductors, and trainmen) have remained outside the AFL since their founding shortly after the Civil War. Although their affiliation with the Federation has at times been urged, the "Big Four" have always refused to join, principally on the ground that their jurisdictional disputes with each other and with railway unions already affiliated with the AFL would be transferred to the Federation's conventions, made up of delegates mostly unfamiliar with the railroad industry. Some of the miscellaneous railroad unions are also independent. In the 1930's the railroad unions cooperated with one another through membership in the Railway Labor Executives' Association comprising some 20 railway unions.

An unknown number of independent unions have sprung up as a result of the outlawing of company-supported unions under the National Labor Relations Act of 1935. As indicated in the previous chapter, there were probably 2,500,000 employees covered by company unions early in 1935. In the various elections held by the National Labor Relations Board prior to July 1940, the independent unions participating polled about 160,000 votes, compared with around 610,000 received by CIO unions and 240,000 by AFL unions. These figures are not representative, however, because CIO unions have taken part in many more of the elections than have AFL or independent unions. Independent unions have won almost half of the elections in which they took part and appeared on the ballot. In general, the independent unions that have been formed since the enactment of the National Labor Relations Act are based on the industrial-union principle. Many of them are revamped company unions or employee-representation plans.

CHAPTER TWENTY-TWO

UNIONS:
ECONOMIC PROGRAM AND POLICIES

Need for collective action in the labor market. As the discussion in Chapter 5 indicated, the need for labor organization arises primarily out of the nature of the labor market. Most labor markets are so imperfect that, without collective action by workers, employers would tend to dominate the market. With highly imperfect markets and employers naming the wage rates, there often is a wide variety or range of wage rates for the same work in the same locality. Such a market condition of plural prices is possible because a relative reduction in the wage offered by an employer does not leave him without suppliers, as would happen in a perfect market. All labor does not desert a wage-cutting employer because at least part of his labor supply, for various reasons, may be immobile. Its immobility may be due to ignorance, to attachments to the locality, to the existence of noncompeting groups, or to ties to the firm in the form of special training, seniority rights, employer good will, or benefit rights. If job changes could be made without a financial loss to workers, they would have no need to worry about the fortunes of their employer or the industry in which they work. A seller in a perfect market does not worry about the fate of any particular buyer.

Without sufficient labor mobility, the supply curve of labor for any particular employer may be very inelastic. As explained in Chapter 5, the negatively sloping supply curve for all labor in an area or a country exerts no upward pressure upon wage rates as a normal positively sloping supply schedule would, but instead tends to support whatever wage rate is established. Collective action by labor unions may, of course, modify the supply schedule of labor for a particular employer and also for employers as a whole. By attempting to induce workers not to offer their services below a certain wage rate, the union is trying to have labor supply curves become horizontal lines at the union wage rates. The union, of course, exerts upward pressure to raise those horizontal supply curves through collective bargaining and collective action.

Wherever one or two firms account for a large part of the employment in a community, the possibility of employer control of the labor market is evident. Where there are many employing firms, they may, through combined action, keep wage rates down and prevent any upward pull on wages by separate employers. The same result may be accomplished if all of them simply follow common practices or conventions, such as the payment of the "prevailing" wage rate or refusal to compete with other employers for individual workers. Collective action on the supply side is often necessary in order to offset such combined action and other monopolistic elements on the demand side of the labor market.

The discussion in Chapter 2 indicated that the market apparatus is not well fitted to settle many nonwage issues that are of vital importance to labor. The length of the working day, for example, is ordinarily determined by personal decision and not by the forces of demand and supply operating in a more or less perfect market. The same applies to other labor issues that affect the health of the worker, such as the speed of operations and conditions in the plant, or the security of his job, which may be jeopardized by arbitrary decisions on the part of the "boss." The market does not prevent the wasteful use of human resources or the discharge of workers for noneconomic reasons. Also it may fail to afford workers some voice in the conduct and government of industry. Collective action on an economic or political plane has frequently been necessary in order that workers might exercise a real influence in the determination of such labor matters.

COLLECTIVE BARGAINING

The economic program of labor organizations has generally been directed toward raising labor standards (wages, hours, and working conditions, including social insurance) and toward achieving some control over jobs within the union's "jurisdiction." Job control and protection may take the form of working rules that affect output or of rules with regard to hiring, firing, lay-off, and promotion, so that workers are less exposed to arbitrary actions by management. Included in such rules may be provisions for the closed or union shop, for lay-off and promotion by seniority of service, and for the establishment of machinery to settle employees' grievances in a more impartial manner. Generally, employers have only relinquished some of their authority and control over labor matters after labor unions have threatened to use economic pressure to achieve the union's objectives.

Nature of collective bargaining. There are two elements in collective bargaining: collective action and representative negotiation. Collective action or the threat to use such action is the power by which the workers' representatives may gain some of their objectives, such as higher labor standards and job control, including protection from injustices on the job.

The advantages to labor from representative negotiation or bargaining are fairly obvious. Not only does it permit the workers to hire a specialist in bargaining whose experience gives him a wide knowledge of the labor market, the industry, and conditions in other firms, but such an expert representative is the employee of the workers' organization and not of the employing firm. Consequently, he is independent in the sense that the employing firm with which he is bargaining has no control over his job, his salary, or his advancement. Employers consider a union representative an "outsider" because he is not in their hire and on their payroll. Employers, of course, likewise use agents or specialists as their representatives in business dealings. Representative dealing and representative government are necessary where the number of persons concerned is so large that it would be impractical to meet *en masse*. We do not all go to Washington to enact laws or abroad to negotiate treaties with foreign countries. Some of us may not like the laws or treaties that our representatives make, but we have to accept the will of the majority. Employers covered by the National Labor Relations Act are required by law to "recognize" and negotiate with the representatives chosen by the majority of their employees.

Collective action is important because the bargaining power of a labor representative is only as strong as the political or economic power of the group that he is representing. The group's economic power depends largely upon the economic injury that the combination of workers can inflict upon the employer by refusing to work for him, by inducing other workers not to work for him, by refusing to buy his products, and by causing other persons not to buy from him. In threatening to injure an employer in the labor market by a strike and in the product market by a boycott, a labor group is, of course, operating through demand and supply. The effectiveness of its collective action would depend primarily upon how indispensable to the employer were the withdrawn labor supply and product demand. It is for this reason that collective action by a relatively large group, or a large proportion of a skilled group, is generally necessary for the achievement of the objectives of the labor organization. Where the area of collective action by workers is wider than the area of collective bargaining with employers, the workers may enjoy a strategic advantage. The printing and the building-trades unions, for example, bargain with employers on a local scale, but they do not permit their national working rules to be one of the subjects of such local bargaining. The national union rules are forced upon individual employers by nationwide collective action on the part of the workers.

Collective labor agreements. Successful collective bargaining results in a collective agreement between the workers' combination and the employer or employers. Unsuccessful bargaining may mean a strike or simply a continuation of the status quo. Agreements arrived at through collective bargaining are also called "trade" or "joint" agreements, and they are generally reduced to writing. Signed agreements may cover such varied matters as wages, hours, overtime rates, working conditions in the shop, working rules, seniority provisions, the closed shop, machinery for the settlement of grievances and review of discharges, provisions for the arbitration of disputes over the interpretation of the agreement, and systems for dismissal wages or unemployment benefits. There are thousands of trade agreements in existence. The International Association of Machinists alone has about 4,500 agreements with individual employers or with employers' associations. Outstanding among the industries almost entirely under written agreements are coal mining, the railroads, breweries, men's and women's clothing, flat glass, and newspaper printing.[1]

Collective labor agreements are not "contracts" in the strict legal sense that they are always enforceable at law. They impose no

[1] For a classification of industries by the prevalence of written union agreements, cf. *Monthly Labor Review*, vol. 48 (March 1939), p. 508.

obligation upon the employer to furnish jobs to the workers nor upon the workers to furnish labor for the employer. They are statements, signed by the representatives of the union and by the employer or representatives of the employers, setting forth the terms and conditions of employment in case workers are hired by the employer or employers whom the agreement covers. One purpose of such agreements is to prevent strikes and wage discriminations or wage undercutting during the life of the agreement.

Until recently the courts generally took the view that collective labor agreements were not enforceable contracts because they lacked sufficient "consideration" mutually given in order to make them binding, or because, in the absence of specific remedies in the agreement, legal enforcement against workers would involve compulsory labor service. Of late, however, in certain states like New York, courts have granted injunctions to employers or to unions when a collective agreement has been broken, and in a few cases damages have been awarded by the courts to employees or employers suffering from the breach of a trade agreement. In some recent instances, parties to an agreement have attempted to improve its legal status by paying nominal sums to one another as "consideration" for making the agreement. Although trade agreements are more and more being enforced by the courts, the cases are so few in number, so lacking in uniformity, and sometimes so contradictory, that no generalizations can be drawn from them. The attitude of the court toward such agreements may depend upon its friendliness toward collective bargaining.[1]

Trade agreements have generally been enforced by the national unions and employers' associations. National unions like the Brotherhood of Locomotive Engineers, the United Mine Workers, and the International Longshoremen's Association have expelled members, fined and suspended local unions, and even voluntarily paid employers for losses sustained from "outlaw strikes" in violation of an agreement. In some unions, proposed agreements are first submitted to a referendum vote of the membership. Employers' associations may also use fines, suspension, or expulsion in attempting to force member employers to abide by a trade agreement.

[1] For a discussion of the enforceability of labor agreements in court, cf. T. Richard Witmer, "Collective Labor Agreements in the Courts," Yale Law Journal, vol. 48 (December 1938), pp. 195–239.

Because unions have generally been most anxious to make and enforce agreements, the record of many well-established unions has been better than that of employers in living up to agreements. That has been true, for example, in the clothing and coal-mining industries. Local "outlaw strikes" are most likely to occur after agreements have first been signed with firms that have vigorously opposed unions.

The area of collective bargaining. Unions strive to make the coverage of their trade agreements extend throughout the whole area of competitive production. They want to equalize labor costs by applying the union scale and working conditions to all employers selling the same class of products in the same markets. For local-market industries, like building and newspaper publishing, the competitive area is practically confined to the city and its environs. But for industries like coal, clothing, and steel, the market may be regional or national. During recent years there has been industry- or trade-wide bargaining on a national scale in anthracite- and bituminous-coal mining, in railroading, and in the pottery and glassware industries, although separate agreements may be signed with each employer after the general terms of employment have been settled by negotiation between the national union and the employers' organization in a national conference. Regional collective bargaining between unions and employers' groups has existed since 1933 in a number of industries, such as the full-fashioned hosiery industry and the silk mills in the Northeast, in trucking and retail meat markets in the Middle West, and in the longshore and paper-and-pulp industries on the Pacific Coast. Most collective bargaining between unions and employers' associations is, however, on a local basis. In 1939 there were probably 5,000 local or city employers' associations throughout the country dealing with various unions, and it is estimated that there were then about 3,500,000 workers covered by agreements negotiated with national, regional, or city-wide employers' associations.[1]

Organized labor in this country has generally attempted to achieve standard or uniform conditions of labor through collective bargaining. Where bargaining with employers' associations is not

[1] *Cf.* Helen S. Hoeber, "Collective Bargaining with Employers' Associations," *Monthly Labor Review,* vol. 49 (August 1939), pp. 303–309.

possible, the unions strive to have all employers in the industry or
the competitive area sign identical agreements. For example, the
agreements of the Steel Workers Organizing Committee (CIO)
with individual companies have embodied practically identical
terms of employment. In trying to extend uniform labor standards
throughout a wide territory, unions, of course, run up against
regional differentials in wages and working conditions, the preservation of which certain employers may believe is important to
their economic interest. National unions, however, strive to whittle
down such differences so that no employer enjoys a competitive
advantage by reason of low labor standards. Local unions in
substandard areas may be encouraged by the national union to
demand better wages and working conditions. If local employers
reject such demands, the local union can strike with assurance of
financial support from the national's treasury.

The standard rate. The downward pressure from a sharp
decline in general business is likely to have the greatest effect upon
prices in highly competitive markets and in markets where the
demand side enjoys a dominant position. Consequently, the chief
task of labor unions is to prevent the undercutting of wage scales.
Like the banks, the barbers, the steel companies, the gasoline
companies, and the automobile firms in the low-priced field
(Ford, Chevrolet, and Plymouth), labor unions strive to confine
competition to quality and service and to prevent any competition
on the basis of price differences. Like local banking associations,
labor unions try to enforce uniform, standard rates as the minimum
for the services of their members.

The difficulty in achieving such price uniformity for labor lies
in the fact that workers have individual differences and that jobs
vary from plant to plant. For such reasons, labor costs cannot be
measured by wage rates or standardized by wage uniformity.
Consequently, if the union is to equalize competitive costs so that
all employers will pay the same price for equal service throughout
the competitive area, it must seek to standardize working conditions, hours of work, and individual outputs, which is what labor
is really selling to the employer. That is one of the reasons for the
numerous working rules that some national unions adopt. Such
rules may involve some restriction upon the economic freedom of
employers and employees, presumably for the good of the whole

group of workers in the occupation or industry. Employers often complain that union working rules limit the worker's freedom of action, but it is usually their restricting effects upon his own operations that displease the employer.

Business itself has working rules and "business ethics," which restrain the individual employer for the sake of uniformity and stability in the industry. The price-cutter is as obnoxious to his fellow businessmen as the wage-cutter or the "scab" is to labor. If a competitor in an industry like gasoline or steel does not stay in line with the common policies, he may be threatened with economic pressure and coercive sanctions by the other firms in the industry or the area.

One should bear in mind that the "standard" or "union" wage rate for a certain kind of work is a minimum, not a maximum, price. Unions do not object if individual workers receive more than the wage rate set forth in the agreement, provided the worker does not violate union standards or speed up output, so that all workers are not receiving equal pay for equal work. In other words, an employee paid by the hour can receive additional compensation for the high quality of his services but not for a greater quantity of output per hour, because such extra output might really mean that he was selling his services at a rate below the union scale for the standard output and would cause competing employers also to speed up their operations in order to maintain competitive equality. The fact that in practice the union's minimum rate usually is the actual rate for practically all workers in the trade indicates how weak in bargaining power the better qualified workers are as individuals. Generally, the labor market is too imperfect to reflect such quality differences between members of the same trade and the same union.

The standard or union rate of hourly wages furnishes a focal point for collective bargaining. The earnings of all union members performing that class of work depend upon that rate, so it serves to concentrate the interests of the union's membership. One difficulty with the payment of labor by the hour, however, is that, although output is really part of the bargain, it is not specified in the wage contract. Consequently, the employer strives to obtain as much in output as possible for his money and the union attempts to see to it that output per worker is not increased without a proportionate increase in wages. Even under nonunion conditions, workers resist the speed-up and try to standardize their outputs.

Standard piece rates. Does adoption of a system of wage payment by the number of pieces or units of output rather than by the hours worked solve the problem of output restriction by stating both the price and the output in the wage contract? What is the attitude of unions toward a piece-rate as opposed to a time-rate system of wage payment? How does piece-rate payment affect collective bargaining by unions?

The piece-rate system of payment can only be used where certain standard conditions apply.[1] It is found in such occupations as the needle trades, cigar making, coal mining, and pottery making. The unions in these trades generally have not opposed piece-rate payment. Some unions have even favored piece rates. Opposition to the piece-rate system arises from the fear that it will stimulate individual outputs, causing the employer to cut the rates as earnings increase. Frequent changes in the job or the product require changes in the rates, giving the employer repeated opportunities to conceal what are really rate reductions. Furthermore, if the jobs are so specialized that only a small percentage of the union's members work at any one piece rate, the union has to bargain on a large number of separate rates, which tends to scatter its forces and weaken its solidarity.

Piece rates generally are acceptable to unions when the industry is so organized that a standard scale of rates can be set that will apply to all shops in the industry. In such a case, single employers may not set their own rates or cut them by separate action. In bituminous-coal mining a general rate is set, to which each mine is adjusted by a system of differential allowances. The interest of all union members is concentrated on the general rate, though disagreements over the differentials may cause dissension and result in favoritism. From the union viewpoint it is desirable not only that the industry be fairly uniform, with few different jobs, but also that those jobs and the products not change much from time to time, so that the rates are not frequently altered. Of primary importance, of course, is the prevention of rate-cutting. That may

[1] A study of 631 manufacturing establishments with over 700,000 employees by the National Industrial Conference Board in 1935 showed that 22 per cent of the employees were on individual or group piece rates. *Cf. Financial Incentives*, Conference Board Studies No. 217, 1935, p. 17.

be done by collective bargaining, where the rates are few, where conditions are rather uniform, and where changes are infrequent. When there are many rates which are constantly changing, as in the men's and ladies' garment industries, the union may insist upon some impartial machinery to review the rates and fix them, so that the employer is not free to make concealed rate cuts with each change in the style of the garment. In the garment industries, appeal can be made to an impartial person or persons in case piece rates cannot be determined by joint employer-union nego-tiation. Often piece-rate workers are assured of a minimum time-rate wage. Where there is no arrangement to prevent employers from cutting the piece rates, there will be collective attempts to restrict output whether the workers are or are not union members.

The strike and the boycott. Where persuasion fails, it may be necessary for the union to threaten to use its economic power in order to overcome the opposition of an employer to its demands. The union may exert economic influence that will affect the em-ployer adversely, in the labor market through a strike, or in his product market by means of picketing and the boycott. The bar-gaining strength of a union depends in large part upon the eco-nomic power that it can exert against an obdurate employer.

A labor strike is the concerted withdrawal of labor from the market in order to reduce the supply of labor available to the employer. In most cases the workers hope to return to their former jobs after winning certain concessions from the employer. There are, of course, other kinds of strikes besides labor strikes. Farmers may refuse to sell milk to distributors or to a certain area, and capitalists may refuse to invest their idle funds. In both cases, the temporary refusal to supply the market is for the purpose of increasing the price or the supplier's return. The boycott, or buyers' strike, is also used by nonlabor groups. Employers may try to influence the policies of other employers or to play favorites through the distribution of their purchases, and the citizens of a country may seek to boycott the goods of countries whose policies they dislike. A sellers' strike or a buyers' strike may, of course, prove costly and economically injurious to those who take part in it.

There are various classes of labor strikes. Employees may strike, not in order to improve their own terms and conditions of employment, but to assist other workers to improve their conditions. Such strikes may take the form of a strike against nonunion materials, a sympathetic strike, or a general strike. For example, the carpenters may refuse to work on lumber purchased from an antiunion firm. Or the truck drivers may, as in San Francisco in 1934, walk out in sympathy with the longshoremen's strike, so that the shipowners could not have the cargo hauled away even if they could get nonunion longshoremen to unload the ships. The supporting strikers, who are not demanding anything for themselves, hope, of course, that someday their favor may be returned. In general strikes, all or most of the workers in an area may join in the strike. Such strikes may be designed to influence governmental policies, but the general strike of 1934 in San Francisco was simply for the purpose of demonstrating the unity of labor to organized employers, who were supporting the resistance of shipowners to the demands of the longshoremen. In the sit-down or stay-in strike, the workers literally sit down on their jobs, which makes it difficult for the employer to fill those jobs with nonstriking workers. In such a strike, the employer or the police have to take the aggressive action that may lead to violence and bloodshed.

Boycotts by laboring groups, designed to curtail temporarily the product market of the employer, may be either primary or secondary in character. Secondary boycotts involve the boycotting of employers or others who deal with the offending employer. Boycotts are likely to be most effective against finished products sold to the consuming public and largely used by workers, although they have also been very effective in the building trades against nonunion materials. Collective action by groups of retail purchasers may be less effective, where the product is sold to manufacturing firms for further processing or where the employer is selling in a nationwide market.

The purpose of a strike is to convince the employer that it is to his self-interest to accede to the demands of the union, to cause him to realize that it is more costly to oppose than to accept the union's program. Essentially a strike is intended to curtail the employer's operations by reducing his labor supply and by erecting barriers to the recruiting of new employees. Especially in prosperous periods, such curtailment of his operations may mean the loss of steady customers for the employer's product or service.

Customers may also be lost through the adverse publicity that may result from the strike and picketing during the strike. Although the loss of customers may be permanent, the loss from idle equipment during curtailed operations may be only a temporary one. A strike may also involve the loss of any investment the employer has made in employee good will and training. To replace the strikers, new employees must be hired and perhaps trained. The employer may have additional costs in the form of wages for company guards, strike-breakers, and police, or expenditures for publicity, munitions, and espionage. As mentioned in Chapter 1, the Republic Steel Corporation incurred almost $2,000,000 of such direct strike expenses in the Little Steel strike of 1937. A stockholder's suit in 1940 alleged that Republic's total losses from the strike exceeded $12,000,000.

On purely financial grounds, weighing the added cost of a strike to the employer against the additional costs of conceding to the union's demands, it might pay the employer to avoid a strike. But the issue is sometimes wider than the question of costs. Although from 1926 to 1940 about three fourths of all days lost as a result of strikes were lost in strikes involving the wages or the hours issue, during certain years in the 1930's as much as one fifth of all mandays have been lost because of strikes involving the issue of union recognition.[1] In some cases, union recognition would presumably have cost the company nothing in the immediate future and might never cause a rise in the labor costs of that firm relative to the labor costs of its competitors. However, recognition of the union might involve giving up some of the authority of the management over job matters and employment. The desire for power and the prestige of authority may be a factor in the refusal of the management to relinquish part of its control over company policies and activities, even though that refusal may cost the stockholders some profits.

The strike strategy of a union may vary with the industrial situation and the financial reserves of the union. Unions try to call strikes at a time when the employers are in a weak economic position. In an integrated industry like automobiles, the strikers

---

[1] For the years 1927–1936, cf. Florence Peterson, *Strikes in the United States, 1880–1936*, U. S. Bureau of Labor Statistics, Bulletin No. 651, 1938, p. 65; and for subsequent years, cf. the May issues of the *Monthly Labor Review*.

may concentrate their energies upon vital operations or "bottle-necks." If possible, the union may use the competition of em-ployers producing the same product or products to weaken the resistance of the "struck" employer. It is not necessary that all the workers be in the union in order to carry out a successful strike. Through picketing and other measures, a union may keep non-unionists away from plants or shops. In large strikes especially, the attitude of the public and governmental officials may be im-portant. The financial resources at the command of the union are also very important in such strikes because unions must spend large sums of money for strike benefits to sustain strikers and for publicity. Even if the strike is eventually lost, funds spent in furthering it may serve as a good investment by showing an em-ployer how costly it is to resist the union's program. The next time the employer may decide that resistance is not worth the additional expense.

Dollar figures are sometimes given for wages "lost" because of the idle hours resulting from strikes. Do such figures measure the net loss to society from labor strikes? If orders are simply held up because of the strike, the firm involved may offer more employ-ment after the strike than it otherwise would have. The customers may shift their orders to other firms, so that the wage losses of the striking employees are offset by the increased earnings of other workers. How much a permanent shift of business away from the "struck" employer would injure the economic interests of the striking employees depends partly on how costly it may be for some of them to find work elsewhere. If the strike is won and the workers receive higher wages as a result, can one say that society gains nothing from such a wage increase?

Picketing. The purpose of picketing is to give publicity to both the existence of a labor dispute and the workers' grievances, and also to persuade other workers and buyers to refrain from working for, or buying from, the offending employer. Such per-suasion may involve social pressure in the community, which con-demns nonstriking employees as "scabs" or "traitors" to the "cause" of labor.

Picketing is an economic device used in connection with a strike or a boycott, and generally occurs on public property near the employer's premises. The methods used vary all the way from a single picket, who walks up and down carrying a sign or distributing handbills, to mass picketing, which involves the use of such a large number of pickets that they may obstruct free access to, or movement from, the plant. The use of mass picketing or of violence in connection with picketing often represents a resort to physical, rather than economic, pressure in order to prevent the company from buying labor and shipping or selling its product. The threat of force by pickets and their sympathizers may intimidate would-be employees and prospective buyers so that they hesitate to do business with the picketed firm. The legality of various methods of picketing is discussed in Chapter 25. Methods that involve simply an appeal to reason or sentiment in order to persuade other workers and buyers not to deal with the picketed firm are generally considered legal by the courts.

Economic possibilities of collective bargaining. The possible advantages to labor from collective bargaining are connected for the most part with the nature of the labor market. By collective action and a standardization policy, the union may prevent employer exploitation of workers and wage discrimination in the labor market. In that way, the union may eliminate wage-cutting and be able to offer strong resistance to competitive pressures upon the labor market.

Collective action by labor increases its economic or bargaining power, enabling a union to achieve wage rates even above those that might prevail in a perfect market. Through collective action the union can threaten the employer with large losses from a strike if he resists its demands. In that way it may even be possible for workers to "exploit" an employer. As indicated in Chapter 5, labor costs can be raised until the firm is earning nothing on its total capital investment and is meeting only its variable costs, yet operations would continue.

Employer "exploitation" by a labor combination would, however, be very difficult to determine. It cannot, like labor exploitation, be defined alone in terms of market conditions—the difference between prices in a perfect and an imperfect labor market. It involves such complex and complicated issues as the correct present value of previous capital investment and the "fair" rate of return on such capital value. Capital values are themselves based on the estimated future return or earnings, discounted by an assumed rate of return. To base capital values on past costs, as has been suggested, is to assume that all past investment was fully justified. The same principle applied to labor would mean to guarantee workers that their earnings would always reflect a certain return on all sums invested in them, including their education and past training. The earning power of particular individuals or of capital investment may be decreased by industrial and other changes. To define "exploitation" in terms of changes in the earning power of a person or piece of capital equipment is to rob the term of all meaning. To define it in terms of a rate of return on new investment is to make some artificial assumption concerning a normal or necessary return on such investment.

By extending its standardization policies throughout the whole competitive area, the union enables workers to obtain higher money wages than would be possible by collective action confined to one firm competing with other firms in the same industry. Indeed, some union officials have proudly pointed out that their policies have helped to "stabilize" industries and to prevent price-cutting and price wars among producers. In so far as union policies tend to maintain the employers' selling prices above what they otherwise would be, the union is also increasing the possibility of higher wage rates for workers in the industry.

Some writers maintain that unions increase the wages of their members at the expense of lower real earnings for other workers. That notion is in direct contradiction to the union idea that the unorganized workers serve as a drag upon the possible gains of union workers, and that labor unions should be interested in organizing the unorganized workers because they are a competitive menace to union standards. It may be true that low wages paid to some unskilled workers put downward pressure upon the wage rates paid to other unskilled workers in a competitive industry. However, the wages paid to unskilled workers, who are unorganized, may not be a competitive threat to the standards of skilled craftsmen who represent distinct noncompeting groups, working in industries that make products for which there are no good substitutes.

The extent to which unskilled workers, who raise their wage rates by organized action, gain at the expense of the unorganized workers depends upon a number of factors. If, for instance, the general supply curve of labor is negatively sloped, higher wages for some workers may not increase the amount of involuntary unemployment, and, therefore, may not put pressure upon the wage rates paid in the unorganized branches of industry. If higher wages stimulate larger outputs, the buying power of the wages of the unorganized workers may not be reduced.   Furthermore, higher wages for the organized may be largely at the expense of profits or fixed-income returns so that selling prices are not increased much.   Such a redistribution of income might tend, at least temporarily, to increase the rate of spending, the aggregate demand, and total employment.

Would those who contend that the gains of organized labor are at the expense of unorganized workers also maintain that complete organization of all workers would leave labor as a whole no better off than if all labor were unorganized? To advance such a doctrine is to overlook completely the nature of the labor market, the connection between wages and output, and the effects of higher wages upon total spending, and to insist that profits and interest must always increase in the same proportion that the level of wage rates is increased. Would the proponents of this doctrine also apply it to profits or to interest, maintaining that higher profits for some employers mean lower profits for others and that higher interest returns for some lenders cause lower interest returns for others?

Certain economists state that labor unions like the building-trades unions and the railroad brotherhoods follow wage policies that may increase the short-run earnings of their members but are definitely injurious to the long-run interests of the union's whole membership because they lead to less employment in the industry.[1] Admitting that such unions can achieve large gains by collective bargaining, these economists claim that present gains will be at the expense of future losses. The future of employment in such industries depends, however, on many factors in addition to wage rates, such as the development of competing forms of transportation or new methods of constructing buildings, the invention and introduction of new labor-saving machinery, population changes, and the size of the total national income and total production.

[1] *Cf.*, for example, Sumner H. Slichter, "The Changing Character of American Industrial Relations," *American Economic Review*, vol. 29 (March 1939) supplement, pp. 131, 133, 136–37.

Furthermore, interest charges play an important role in the total costs of such industries as the railroads and building. Do capitalists also lose in the long run when they hold out for high returns or maintain rigid, monopolistic prices?

It might be foolish for one factor, like labor, alone to accept smaller present returns on the ground that by such singlehanded action it would further its own self-interest. It would be still more foolish for one union in industries like building construction or railroad transportation, where there are about 20 standard craft unions, to act on any such notion concerning the long-run interests of its members. Although one craft union out of many in an industry is less likely to consider the future of that industry than is an industrial union, industrial unions like the coal miners also strive to increase wage rates despite the fact that coal is a declining industry in competition with other sources of heat and power including oil, gas, and electricity. All groups tend to discount the future very heavily, not only because people are optimistic or short-sighted, but because the future of any particular industry is so unpredictable. Furthermore, as indicated by the discussion in Chapter 11, the relationship between wage rates and unemployment, even for a single industry, is very loose and uncertain. Finally, workers may have little to lose by the relative decline of an industry, unless they have a considerable investment in the industry in the form of seniority rights and training that cannot be transferred to another industry, or unless there are other factors that make interindustry movement costly for them.

JOB CONTROL

Property rights in jobs. The notion that people have "vested rights" in their jobs is not a new one. The idea of job tenure is to be found in government, in the schools, and in industry, especially for high-salaried positions. There is a general feeling that the man in the job should not be replaced except for good cause, and that facts, not favoritism, should govern discharges and promotions. Our civil-service laws embody such ideas for government service, and professors employed by colleges and universities demand similar rights. The American Association of University Professors, for example, may black-list a college or university for dismissing and replacing a professor on any other grounds than morals or incompetency, which is to be determined by the testimony of other teachers and scholars. The Association, a sort of union for professors, demands that a university teacher be given "permanent or continuous tenure" after a probationary period not exceeding six years, and that a teacher on tenure receive at least a year's salary after notice of dismissal for any cause except moral turpitude.[1] As employees of the university, professors also exercise considerable control in such matters as promotions and the hiring of new teachers.

Provisions in collective agreements which grant the closed shop, lay-off by seniority, impartial review of discharges, and job tenure tend to protect the jobs of certain workers and to establish property rights for workers in their jobs. Over a period of years, workers employed by the same firm make certain investments related to their jobs. These investments take the form of special training, specialized skills, homes near the work, and obligations acquired on the basis of the job. The worker may also improve the methods of performing his work or conditions surrounding his work. In such fashion, a complex of relationships is built up around the job, gradually leading to the notion that the worker who devotes part of his life to a particular job is entitled to that job unless he is discharged for a just cause. The sit-down strike is, in part, based on the notion of investment and property rights in a certain job. Strikers are not quitting the job but presumably are only ceasing operations pending a settlement of working terms. An employer can hardly fire his striking employees *en masse*, although it is a nice question, as the National Labor Relations Board has discovered, at what date after an unsuccessful strike the defeated strikers whose former jobs have been filled cease to be employees of the firm against which they struck.

Certain employers have tended to recognize the existence of workers' investment or property rights in jobs by granting them dismissal compensation, based on length of service, in case the employees have to be laid off permanently. This practice is becoming rather widespread. In 1936 the railroads, for example, signed a five-year agreement with the 21 standard unions granting railroad employees, who lose their jobs as a result of the consoli-

[1] For the Association's statements of principle regarding job tenure, *cf. Bulletin of the American Association of University Professors*, vol. 25 (February 1939), pp. 27–28.

dation of railroad facilities, certain sums called "separation allowances," which vary with the employee's length of service on the job and amount to a year's pay for workers with an employment record of five years or more on a particular railroad. Practices that involve employer payments to workers deprived of their jobs without fault on their part tend to build up vested rights in jobs.

Unions attempt to achieve some job protection and control in the interest of their membership. Various union controls or rules are incorporated in trade agreements, which serve to increase the job opportunities and job security of union members. In connection with the hiring of employees, a collective labor agreement may provide for an all-union or closed shop. Discharges and other grievances may be subject to review by some joint or impartial body. An agreement may also provide for lay-off and promotion by seniority. Other measures intended to provide job security and employment opportunities for union members include the union label on union-made products, limitations upon the number of apprentices, restrictions upon the use of machinery and labor-saving devices, and control of output to "nurse the job along." These various measures will be discussed *seriatim*.

The union or "closed" shop. Employers may agree to hire only union members or they may seek to exclude unionists from their shops. A "closed shop" may, therefore, be closed either to nonunionists or to union members. What is commonly called the "closed shop" is really a strictly union shop, and so-called "open shops" may actually be open only to nonunion workers.

A workshop is not be to regarded as closed simply because all the workers in the shop at any particular time happen to be union members. Technically, a shop is not closed unless the employer closes it by agreeing to hire only union labor, or unless the union workers are able to exclude all nonunionists by refusal to work in a shop with nonunion employees. Many closed-shop agreements provide that new employees must become union members within a probationary period on the job. One modification of the closed-shop agreement does not compel an employee to join a union but requires that all employees who do join remain members in good standing.

Contrary to general opinion, the closed shop did not originate in America, nor is it a recent phenomenon. Some of the English guilds in the sixteenth and seventeenth centuries forbade journeymen to work with a nonmember, and unions of printers, tailors, and barrel makers had adopted and enforced closed-shop rules in this country by 1820 or 1830.[1] Today closed-shop agreements are much more prevalent in the United States than in England or Sweden. In New Zealand, however, a law passed in 1936 requires that all adult workers in industries covered by the wage awards of the national Arbitration Court, or by trade agreements filed with the Court, be members of a union. In other words, the closed shop is enforced by law.

It is estimated that about 3,000,000 organized employees in the United States were working under closed-shop conditions in 1939. Most of the workers in coal mining, in printing, and in the men's and women's clothing industry were covered by closed-shop agreements, while a majority of the collective labor agreements in building construction, motion-picture production, the fur trade, the brewery industry, and trucking provided for the union shop.[2] In addition it is estimated that in 1939 almost 500,000 workers were employed in "preferential shops," where preference was given to union members in the hiring of new workers, in lay-offs, or in reemployment. The preferential shop has been prevalent in newspaper offices, maritime transportation, and flat-glass manufacture.[3]

Some closed-shop agreements contain a provision for the check-off, which means that the employer serves as a tax-collection agency for the union, deducting union dues from the pay envelopes of union members. Although some locals of about half of the national unions in this country have agreements containing check-off provisions, a number of well-organized unions have never suggested that such provisions be written into their trade agreements, and coal mining and hosiery manufacture are the only major fields of employment in which the check-off is the prevailing practice.[4] The check-off is an American practice that presumably grew out of the custom of deducting from the coal miner's

---

[1] Cf. Frank T. Stockton, The Closed Shop in American Trade Unions, 1911, pp. 17, 23, 25, 27, 33.

[2] Cf. "Closed Shop and Check-Off in Union Agreements," Monthly Labor Review, vol. 49 (October 1939), pp. 830–31.

[3] Ibid., pp. 833–34.   [4] Ibid., p. 835.

pay such items as equipment, company store bills, and company rent. It was granted by the employers in bituminous-coal mining in 1898 (the first Central Competitive Field agreement) so that the union might have sufficient financial strength to organize the nonunion mines in outlying areas. It has likewise occurred in connection with company unions.[1]

The railway brotherhoods have not demanded either the closed shop or the check-off, and both practices are illegal in the railroad industry under the Railway Labor Act of 1926, as amended in 1934. Nevertheless, some of the railway crafts are practically 100 per cent organized. The unions have been able to attract and hold members through their benefit programs—railroading was considered so hazardous that railroad workers were charged especially high premium rates by private insurance companies—and by giving individual employees further protection in case of discharge or grievances and in the enforcement of an employee's seniority rights.

Why do employers grant the closed shop? Do they stand to gain from it?

In the first place, an employer may win the good will of his union employees, for in signing a closed-shop agreement he indicates that he will not attempt to reduce or eliminate the union. Without a closed shop the union may view with suspicion every decision that favors a nonmember instead of a member, and may demand job rules, such as seniority for lay-offs and promotions, in order to curb possible antiunion discrimination by foremen. Where all employees are union members, the union may have less interest in the employer's decisions regarding personnel, because union opposition to a certain promotion or interpretation of seniority rights would mean favoring one member against another. On such grounds, Professor Sumner Slichter argues that "the employer is likely to have more freedom in a closed shop or its equivalent than in one where the union is uncertain of its status," and he found from an examination of some 300 agreements that only 54 per cent of the closed-shop agreements contained restric-

[1] For example, on November 1, 1939 the National Labor Relations Board ordered the Western Union Telegraph Company to refund to its employees all dues deducted from their pay envelopes after July 5, 1935 for the support of a company union, the Association of Western Union Employees. It was estimated that the total rebate of dues collected under the check-off would amount to about $500,000.

tions upon the employer's freedom to make lay-offs, while 86 per cent of the open-shop agreements contained such restrictions upon the employer.[1]

The closed shop may actually serve as a factor to keep down an employer's costs. Without the closed shop, union officials may, in order to hold and attract membership, be forced to make more extreme demands upon the employer and be more stubborn in grievances involving union members. Strife and discontent are more likely to be found in a shop part union and part nonunion. In a closed shop, on the other hand, there may be fewer grievances and strikes because the union can discipline its members and serve as a check upon the abuse of power by foremen.

Employers may grant the closed shop for a number of other reasons. They may desire to use the union's label to aid in the sale of their products. Or they may wish to make the union strong so that it will be able to organize and to "stabilize" the whole industry. If the closed shop pervades the industry, of course, no single employer has a relatively greater burden on that account than his direct competitors. Sometimes an employers' association makes a mutual closed-shop agreement with a union, which practically provides that each organization will deal only with members of the other organization—a sort of two-sided monopoly. Finally, an employer may sign a closed-shop agreement although he may not favor the closed shop. He may decide that the closed shop will be less costly for him than a strike for the closed shop would be.

How costly to an employer the closed shop may prove depends in part upon the extent to which it actually does limit his freedom to hire and, therefore, restricts the supply of labor available to him in the labor market. In many closed-shop agreements the control over hiring is not in the hands of the union, and the employer is free to hire any qualified worker who is willing to join the union. In such cases the closed shop places practically no restriction upon the employer's labor supply. The union itself is made the source of supply where the employer agrees to hire through the union. Generally, the employer can reject workers supplied by the union if they are not competent. A closed-shop

[1] Cf. Slichter, "The Changing Character of American Industrial Relations," op. cit., p. 124.

agreement leads to the greatest restriction upon the employer's access to the labor market when entrance to the union is restricted by a closing of the union to new members, by extreme apprenticeship requirements, or by very high initiation fees. To prevent any closing of the union, some closed-shop agreements provide that the union may not change its membership requirements or refuse to admit qualified applicants during the life of the agreement.

Unionists argue that the closed shop is necessary and desirable for a number of reasons in addition to those already mentioned. They defend the closed shop on the ground that, if a majority of the employees select a certain agency to represent them, the rest should accept that majority decision and assist in paying for the benefits they receive as a group through collective bargaining and the activities of the union. This argument rests on the notion that no employee should be permitted to be a "tax dodger." Union officials also insist that 100-per-cent unionization is necessary if the union is to enforce its working rules, particularly national union rules that may not be embodied in local trade agreements. This argument applies especially in lines like building construction, where jobs change so frequently, where the workers are scattered all over town, and where there are so many rules regarding methods of work, jurisdiction, materials, apprenticeship, etc. In addition, union leaders state that they cannot be responsible for the discipline of all workers in a plant unless all of them are in the union and hence are subject to the union's discipline measures.

Labor officials have also insisted that the closed shop is necessary to prevent discrimination in favor of nonunion men, to prevent competition on the terms of employment, and to win strikes. Such contentions, however, are open to question. Strikes can be won with less than 90 per cent of all the employees organized. Unwilling members may be a positive disadvantage to a union during a strike. Generally, trade agreements are binding upon nonunion employees as well as union members, so a closed shop is not necessary in order to prevent the undercutting of labor standards achieved by collective bargaining. And if the union is strong enough to obtain a closed shop it is generally strong enough to prevent discrimination against its members. Furthermore, such discrimination is illegal in industries subject to the National Labor Relations Act. Sometimes the demand for a closed shop is simply a device for organizing the rest of the shop and consolidating the union's position; sometimes it is merely a means of assuring the prompt payment of union dues, fines, and assessments; in certain cases it is a method of excluding a rival union from the shop or industry.

The closed shop may not be an unmixed blessing to a union and its members. Like the guarantee of an exclusive jurisdictional monopoly, the guarantee of 100-per-cent membership through a closed-shop agreement may cause a union to lose its aggressiveness and may tend to turn it into a sort of bureaucracy that does not adequately represent the interests of the membership. Where a union has had satisfactory dealings with an employer over a period of time and the employer does not oppose the union, where there is joint machinery for the review of discharges and grievances, and where most of the employees will belong to the union simply to protect their job rights and to be eligible for its benefits, the union may gain little, if anything, from the closed shop.

Job seniority. Many collective labor agreements provide that the length of continuous service shall be at least one of the factors in determining the order in which employees shall be laid off and returned to work. Somewhat less common are provisions applying the seniority principle to promotions, granting the person with the most seniority the first opportunity to qualify for a better position. He does not, of course, obtain the job if he cannot qualify.

The purpose of a seniority rule is to provide job security for older workers and to eliminate favoritism and discrimination by the supervisory forces. Under trade agreements, alleged violations of the rule are generally subject to joint review and often such agreements provide for final appeal to an impartial umpire. Even where there is no definite rule regarding seniority, there is a tendency to follow that principle, as is evident in the army, in the university faculty, and in financial institutions. Frequently it is very difficult to determine relative competency. Selection by "merit" is likely to be subject to personal bias and the shortcomings of a foreman's judgment.

Seniority may be determined on the basis of length of continuous service with the company (1) in that occupation, (2) in that department, (3) in that plant, or (4) in any of the company's plants. Obviously, complications may arise where records are not complete, where companies merge, or where some plants are closed. In certain industries like the railroads and printing, the seniority principle is applied rather rigidly to provide job tenure to workers with long service records. In other cases, seniority provisions in agreements may be qualified by a number of factors such as efficiency or ability, family situation, and physical fitness. Those factors being equal, length of continuous service may govern. Often there is equal sharing of the work down to a certain minimum number of hours, perhaps half the normal day, and thereafter lay-offs occur according to seniority. Sometimes certain employees are exempt from the seniority provisions either because they have an exceptional status or because they especially need the work. Applied in such a flexible fashion, there may be little difference between the practice under an agreement with seniority provisions and the best practice under nonunion conditions.

Seniority provisions in agreements are to be found principally in the railroad, printing, automobile, textile, rubber, oil, electrical, steel, metal-smelting, paper, and aluminum industries. Most of these are mass-production industries, which until recently were not unionized, and in practically all of them except printing the closed shop has not been very prevalent. Furthermore, promotion from one grade of employment to another is common. Pure craft unions are not likely to adopt the seniority principle because there is little room for promotion within the craft, and skilled craftsmen have less need to fear that the competition of younger workers will reduce their employment opportunities as they grow older. Seniority is also uncommon in seasonal industries, like building, the garment trades, and coal mining, because it would tend to divide the union too sharply, with one group always bearing the impact of seasonal fluctuations. Such industries are more liable to favor the equal-division-of-the-work principle. A study of some 300 trade agreements negotiated between 1922 and 1929 showed that only about one out of three contained lay-off restrictions, whereas examination of a similar number of agreements signed between 1933 and 1939 revealed that two out of every three embodied such restrictions.[1]

---

[1] *Cf.* Sumner Slichter, "Layoff Policy," in *Addresses on Industrial Relations, 1939,* Bureau of Industrial Relations, University of Michigan, 1939, p. 74.

Seniority provisions in agreements, if fairly flexible, may not have unfavorable effects upon the employer's costs of production. In fact, as already mentioned, the general principle of job preference on the basis of seniority has for some time been favored by most employers. Seniority provisions in agreements help management to eliminate favoritism by foremen, and, to the extent that lay-offs become less haphazard and unfair, the morale and efficiency of employees may be improved. A system of seniority may also force the management to adopt objective ability-rating plans, to be more careful in selecting employees, and to weed out less competent workers before they acquire important seniority rights. Seniority offers no direct protection to inefficient workmen, although it may have adverse effects upon the incentive and initiative of younger workers who are subjected to repeated lay-offs.

Unions demand seniority in order to prevent favoritism, to protect union members against employment discrimination, and to give greater security to long-service employees. Consequently, seniority serves as a check upon early superannuation in the mass-production industries, where there may be a tendency to "burn out" employees by the speed-up and then to discriminate against them in employment. It should be clear, however, that such protection to the middle-aged workers is at the expense of security and job opportunities for younger workers.

Seniority also has its drawbacks from the union's point of view. It may force the union to support the claim of one union member against another and to pass on the competency of various members. The system, if rigidly enforced, may become very complicated and lead to numerous grievance cases. Furthermore, it reduces the mobility of labor and ties the worker to a single firm. If his continuous service may be broken by a strike, he may hesitate to lose such a valuable equity in a job by striking against the employer. Union officials, realizing such problems, have said:

If we weren't afraid of discrimination, I think we'd be better off not to commit ourselves to rigid rules of seniority, not knowing what unforeseen conditions we may face in the future. I'd be willing to throw out this whole seniority system if management would give us a union shop.[1]

[1] Frederick H. Harbison, *The Seniority Principle in Union-Management Relations*, Industrial Relations Section, Princeton University, 1939, p. 34.

We are opposed to rigid or straight seniority. Given the proper treatment by management, a strong union should be able to protect the workers better in the long run by building up effective grievance procedures to check favoritism, bias, or discrimination where they may exist. With assured status and proper leadership, the union is better off to be guided by the general seniority principle, but to decide each case on its own merits.[1]

In some companies, seniority provisions have led to the establishment of a joint body, with representatives of management and the union, to classify and rate employees for the purpose of determining the order of lay-off and to assist in determining promotion. Such steps represent another development in the direction of joint control of employment policies either through regular grievance committees or specially created seniority committees.

Job grievances and discharges. Grievances are disputes or disagreements that arise over the interpretation of a trade agreement, over the application of an agreement, or over any treatment that seems unfair to the employee. Therefore, grievances may involve such questions as seniority rights, wage inequalities, the proper piece rate for a particular job, the application of overtime rates, favoritism in assigning work, abuse from the foreman, or dismissals. They are what might be called secondary disputes in contrast to disagreements concerning broad issues such as wage rates, hours, and working conditions for the whole plant or firm. Because they are mainly personal issues that directly affect only a few persons, the union is usually anxious to settle such differences without a strike. The employer also gains by their just settlement without a suspension of operations.

An arrangement for joint and impartial settlement of grievances furnishes a curb upon any tyranny of the foremen, forcing them to support their actions by facts before a joint union-company body. Frequently, where the various joint committees cannot agree upon a grievance, the agreement calls for appeal to an "outside" or impartial umpire for final decision. Such grievance machinery gives the union an equal voice in the settlement of alleged injustices and helps to prevent discrimination against union members. It is a step in the direction of industrial democracy, giving the workers some measure of authority in job matters. The company,

[1] *Ibid.*, p. 37.

of course, still retains the right to discharge workers for inefficiency or some other good cause.

Under employee-representation plans or company unions, machinery was usually established for settling such grievances. Many employers recognize that arbitrary and unjust actions by foremen are likely to have bad effects upon the morale and efficiency of the working force, that impartial settlement of grievances tends to reduce strife and discontent and serves to stabilize industrial relations.

The union label. Through union labels on products, by shop cards or service buttons, and by white lists, unions attempt to increase the sales of union-made products and of union establishments, thereby increasing the employment and job security of union members. The union label is put on such products as clothing, cigars, and printed matter. The shop card or button may be used for service establishments such as barber shops, hotels, and restaurants. The white list can be used for products to which labels cannot be conveniently attached. It consists of a circular stating the names of firms, say hosiery producers, that operate union shops. All of these devices indirectly function as a sort of boycott against the products of nonunion employers and serve, by affecting purchases, to increase the jobs and employment subject to union conditions.

Other job-protective policies. Unions also attempt to prevent a reduction in the number of union jobs by other measures, such as exclusion or control of new machinery and labor-saving devices, limitations on output and the speed-up, and restrictions upon the number of learners or apprentices. Such protective measures, affecting either the demand for (or the supply of) the labor of a union's membership, are intended to increase the job security of union workers and to maintain the value of investment in the job or in a skill. They are especially characteristic of craft unions.

1. *Machinery and new processes.* Unions may attempt to control or prevent the introduction of machinery, the use of minor labor-saving devices, or the subdivision of the job so that part of it can be performed by lower priced and less skilled labor. Prevention of the use of minor labor-saving devices includes the items that were mentioned in Chapter 6 under policies of employees' organizations affecting supply, such as limitations upon the width of paint

brushes, restrictions upon the use of a stone pick in stonecutting, prohibition of the use by one firm of printing type or matrixes already used by another firm, or the refusal of plumbers to install fixtures already put together. Certain skilled craftsmen, in order to prevent any subdivision or "whittling away" of their jobs, refuse to complete work partly done in a factory. As mentioned in Chapter 6, a local union of painters in one large city threatened to picket the opening of a new ice arena in which factory-made and factory-painted seats were installed, claiming that local painters were thereby deprived of jobs and demanding that the business (and the money) be kept within the community. In order to appease the painters, a number of them were hired at union wage rates to go over the painted seats with dry brushes for a period equivalent to the time that it would take to paint them.

In the case of new machinery, union members may refuse to work on it in an attempt to exclude it from the industry, or the union may attempt to control its introduction into the industry in order to assure union members that they will suffer no loss of employment or reduction in wage rates. Under the "control" policy, the union seeks to have the jobs on the machine given to union members, and, by insisting upon the old wage scale for workers operating the new machine, the union may make the operation of the machine rather costly so that its introduction will be slowed down.

The success of union policies for controlling or excluding new machinery and minor labor-saving devices and for preventing subdivision of the job depend in large part upon the extent to which the employer would be dependent upon the union's members for labor in case he decided to oppose the union's restrictive policies. If the employer would still be dependent upon the skill of union members, the added cost of going nonunion, including the cost of a strike, might not be sufficient to offset the savings that would accompany introduction of the labor-saving method under nonunion conditions. In the case of such restrictions as those upon the width of a painter's brush, the employer may be forced to accept them because he still needs the painter. The same thing was true in the case of the linotype machine producing printing type by lines. When it was first introduced, employers tried to use stenographers to run the linotype machine, but they soon discovered that the training of the printer (his knowledge of spelling, spacing, composition, etc.) was so necessary for efficient operation that even nonunion shops found it profitable to employ printers. Eventually, linotypers were receiving higher wage rates than printers setting type by hand.

In the face of technological changes, a union generally attempts to conserve the available jobs for its own members and to prevent any loss in the value of their skill and training through the obsolescence that may result with the adoption of new production methods. The union's policy may not be unlike that of employers who seek to prevent or control the introduction of new inventions by buying up patents or adopting common restrictive policies. Where the new machine is such, however, that its operation requires none of the skill of the workers under the old method, the union has little opportunity to control the new machine. Glass-bottle blowing by hand—really by lungs—was at one time one of the most skilled and highly paid crafts in the country. However, an Owens bottle-blowing machine was developed which was so automatic that the only labor necessary for its operation was that of a couple of unskilled machine tenders. In such a case the union is powerless to prevent the elimination of the former jobs of its members.

If the union's "control" policies do raise the cost of producing the article or of furnishing the service, the result may be an increase in price that will cause some decline in sales and hence in the employment of union members. Such policies of control or exclusion are most likely to be successful in local-market industries that are not subject to the competition of nonunion producers in other localities or of substitute products or services— in other words, where the local employers enjoy a very inelastic demand for their output.

2. *Restrictions upon output and the speed-up.* As mentioned in Chapter 6, restriction of output occurs among unorganized as well as organized workers.[1] Opposition to the speeding up of operations in mass-production or other industries may be on the grounds that it has bad effects upon the health of the worker, and will shorten the length of his working life by establishing a pace that he cannot maintain after reaching 45 years of age. Such opposition may also be founded on the fear that the speed-up will reduce the hours of

[1] *Cf.* S. B. Mathewson, *Restriction of Output among Unorganized Workers*, 1931.

employment offered to certain workers in that firm.   Unionists claim that any reduction in production costs from the speed-up will eventually be offset by larger relief costs and other disguised expenses to the public, resulting from the adverse effects of the speed-up on the worker's health and employability.

Restrictions upon the units of output per worker in order to "make the job last" are especially characteristic of seasonal industries like the building trades, in which workers may seek to extend the period of their employment during each year.   That helps to explain such restrictions as those upon the number of bricks that a bricklayer can lay, the number of bundles of lath that a lather can tack, and the number of barrels of lime that a plasterer can handle, in any one day.   In nonseasonal lines, however, workers may also try to "nurse the job along," so that they "do not work themselves out of employment."

Economists have been almost unanimous in their condemnation of restrictions upon output, which they claim are based upon a false "lump-of-labor" theory.   According to this theory there is just so much work to be done, so that a particular grade of labor may increase its total hours of employment by reducing the output per worker.

In this matter, the trade-unionists are arguing from the particular to the general and the economists are reasoning from the general to the particular.   Consequently, neither group appreciates the position of the other side.   A trade-unionist, a plumber for example, correctly assumes that the total costs of plumbing are such a small item in the total costs of constructing and maintaining a building that the wage-output ratio of local plumbers will have practically no effect upon total building construction in the locality.   He, therefore, is inclined to take the common-sense view that there is a fixed amount of local plumbing work to be done in any one year and that a rapid pace would result in fewer hours of work for local plumbers.   In drawing general conclusions on the basis of partial analysis and his own limited experience, he is only following the example of the reasoning of certain economists on wages, as was indicated in the section on wage rates and unemployment in Chapter 11.

The economists are correct in insisting that there is no fixed demand for all products or services and that the demand for a particular product or service, though it may be fixed in the short run (for example, after the building contracts have been let), is not fixed over longer periods. But the economists may make a mistake in attempting to apply such general conclusions uniformly to all particular cases, and insisting upon a close relationship between the output of, say, one out of 20-odd building or railroad crafts and the demand for building or railroad service. Small sections of the total labor supply may increase their total real earnings by restrictive practices, even though the real income of the whole community or of other laboring groups is reduced as a consequence.

Business leaders likewise favor restrictive practices that help to maintain prices and prevent any "spoiling of the market." In reasoning that price-cutting is collective suicide because there is only a certain demand for a product or a certain amount of business to be had, they are committing what might be called the "lump-of-business" fallacy. The price policies of employers in many industries seem to be based on the assumption that demand is fixed and that price reductions would not lead to increased sales.

3. *Limitations upon entrance to the trade.* Some craft unions, especially building-trades locals in certain cities, maintain apprenticeship rules, which require that a worker serve a regular apprenticeship of some three or four years before he can qualify for membership in the union and be admitted to the trade as a journeyman. The union may insist upon a certain ratio between the number of journeymen and the maximum number of apprentices or learners in any one shop. And union members may be forbidden to teach their trade to any persons except certified apprentices employed in union shops. Such union restrictions upon the supply of qualified workers may serve to protect union members from too much competition by new recruits. Entrance restrictions that are wholly or partially enforced by the workers concerned or their associations are also found in the professions, like medicine, law, and university teaching. University faculties may insist that all new members have a Ph.D. degree; bar and medical associations may confine the practice of law and medicine to their members and restrict their membership by rigid entrance requirements.

Craft apprenticeship has been of declining importance during the past few decades, because technological improvements have reduced the need for such apprenticeship and because there are many ways in which a trade can be learned besides a formal apprenticeship, such as in nonunion shops, in schools and prisons, or as a helper to a journeyman in a union shop.

Some general remarks. Measures to conserve jobs and markets for members of an organization are not new. The medieval guilds attempted to protect the local market for guild members by apprenticeship rules and by regulations preventing any subdivision of the work and forbidding the use of any new techniques not approved by the guild. Combined action by some workers to further their own interests in the labor market may be called partial monopoly or monopolistic competition, but it is not essentially different from a combination of individuals to form a corporation or the combined action of a group of employers. Craft unions seeking to maximize the lifetime earnings of craftsmen are operating on the same principle as producers of trade-marked articles or owners of patents who seek to maximize their total profits.

It has been argued by some economists that any deviation from perfect markets and pure competition is likely to lead to an "uneconomic distribution" of a nation's productive resources. Labor unions are often opposed because, it is claimed, any group interference with open markets and unrestricted competition will result in a maldistribution of labor resources and a similar misapplication of capital resources. One wonders whether employer discrimination against union members, early superannuation of workers with the speed-up, and exploitation of workers by employer domination of the market do not also result in a warped allocation of economic resources. The trouble with such arguments concerning the use of available resources is that they assume that perfect markets and pure competition always result in the correct distribution of a nation's productive resources, that all labor markets would be perfect markets if labor unions did not interfere, and that all labor is fully employed. Presumably, unemployment itself represents a very wasteful distribution of labor resources.

Whether unions, by restrictive policies that enhance labor costs, increase unemployment is another question to which there is no simple answer. For example, did the hiring of painters to dry-brush the factory-painted seats of that new ice arena increase or decrease total employment in the city and the nation? It did represent a wasteful use of labor resources, assuming that those painters would otherwise have been employed—a most unreal assumption in the middle 1930's. Chapter 11 contained a detailed discussion of the relationship between wage rates or labor costs and unemployment. That discussion indicated that an increase in money wage rates (labor costs) may lead to less unemployment by redistributing money income, increasing the rate of spending, and affecting the labor supply. Certainly, where there has been employer exploitation of labor, the union policy of the standard rate will tend to increase employment by making part of the supply curve of labor a straight horizontal line as in a perfect market. The effect upon employment would be similar to that of a minimum wage. How a minimum wage may increase employment was explained at the end of Chapter 5 and in Chapter 12.

Even the effect of union restrictions and controls upon efficiency is a debatable question. The term "efficiency" itself is vague, and means little unless it is based on total costs per unit of output. Union restrictive practices are probably most prevalent and effective in the building trades; yet Professor Sumner Slichter, who has repeatedly complained that make-work rules and restrictions upon technological change or upon rewards for efficiency keep down a country's standard of living,[1] recently stated:

> The building trades get pretty high efficiency from labor on the whole, though they pay by the hour [according to standard rates]. Labor efficiency in our building trades is the wonder of foreigners familiar with construction abroad.[2]

Why does an employer sign a trade agreement containing union controls and restrictions if they may increase his labor costs per unit of output? As already stated, he may obtain certain advantages from such an agreement, including freedom from strikes and use of the union's label. Why then should he complain if certain disadvantages also accompany the agreement, such as the inability to hire nonunion workers or to substitute college students for regular workers during school vacations? Are seniority provisions

[1] Cf. "The Changing Character of American Industrial Relations," op. cit., pp. 122–23.
[2] Sumner Slichter, "Layoff Policy," Addresses on Industrial Relations, 1939, Bureau of Industrial Relations, University of Michigan, 1939, p. 79.

and the closed shop, for example, to be condemned because they prevent college students, who may work harder, from displacing year-around employees during short, vacation periods? Or because such provisions tend to prevent young workers from replacing older workers? College instructors may believe that the older professors are relatively overpaid and are continued at their salaries, not on purely economic grounds, but because they enjoy tenure and the personal support of their colleagues. Should a university president be free to displace older professors with younger instructors if he feels that thereby the university will get more for its money?

Society definitely gains when the joint settlement of grievances increases total output by improving morale and reducing the number of work stoppages. The use of grievance machinery may also serve as an education in industrial democracy for both the workers and the foremen. There is certainly some social gain in a democracy if workers are not forced to kowtow to the boss in order to hold a job. Unions may even assume some responsibility for supervision of the work, the elimination of waste, and increases in operating efficiency, under schemes for union-management co-operation. Such joint programs for improving production and working conditions are discussed in Chapter 24.

CHAPTER TWENTY-THREE

EMPLOYERS:
ORGANIZATION AND LABOR POLICIES

In forming corporate policies, the management of a firm is influenced by a number of purposes and many pressures. The objective of making large profits may involve the adoption of certain personnel and labor-relations policies, the development of good public relations, and "stabilization" of the industry to prevent price-cutting and similar competitive practices. In addition to the question of profits, there is the question of control of production or operating policies, which the management is prone to consider its special prerogative. Any attempt by workers to gain some control over jobs, employment, and the speed of operations is likely to be condemned and resisted by the managers as "interference" with "their business," even though the corporation's officers or directors may own little, if any, of its capital stock. The policies of the corporation may, therefore, be directed toward maintaining the company's domination over its labor market while preventing labor from strengthening its position in that market through organization. In resisting labor organization by adopting policies that tend to make the worker "loyal" to the company, the management may also increase the efficiency of the working force so that the company is receiving the most in services for each dollar spent for labor.

Some idea of the opposing forces and incentives that may motivate corporate management can be gained from the statement of Owen D. Young that, as chairman of the board of directors of the General Electric Company, he owed an obligation to three groups of people: some 50,000 stockholders who had put their funds into the company, approximately 100,000 people who were putting their labor and their lives into the business of the company, and the millions of customers who purchase the company's products.[1]

[1] Statement quoted in Edward S. Mason, "Price and Production Policies of Large-Scale Enterprise," *American Economic Review*, vol. 29 (March 1939) supplement, p. 68, from John H. Sears, *The New Place of the Stockholder*, 1929.

In addition, the management is interested in perpetuating or improving its own position. How to balance the demands and interests of these four groups, which are likely to conflict at many points, is clearly a difficult economic and governmental problem. An attempt by the management, for example, to improve the company's labor relations by establishing an employee-representation plan raises the whole question of how American industry should be governed and what interests the management and the employee representatives really should, or do, represent.

The attitude of management toward the organization of the company's employees may depend in part upon the nature of the business and the extent to which competing firms in the industry have been organized by the national union. The officers of a firm are most likely to be friendly toward a labor union where the union's economic program appears to coincide with the firm's economic interests. The profits of a company may be less uncertain if the union's program stabilizes the price structure in the industry [1] and equalizes labor costs so that small, fly-by-night concerns cannot undercut older, well-established firms whose policies are more restricted by tradition, public opinion, and past investment in employee good will. Experience in the bituminous-coal industry and the ladies' garment industry in the New York area indicates the advantage to established employers of having a union to enforce standards upon firms that attempt to expand, or to enter the industry, by operating under substandard conditions. The economic program of labor unions may be of advantage to employers in certain industries, such as building, in which it is desirable to have predictable costs. A union may also aid certain firms, such as clothing and printing concerns, whose sales may be affected by the union label.

In many respects, the attitude of the employer or management toward the union determines the character of the union's leader-

[1] The president of the United Rubber Workers of America has pointed to the "stabilization of the price structure" as one of the specific advantages to employers that have resulted from the organization of the rubber workers. He states: "Before the rise of the U.R.W.A. conditions in the rubber industry were chaotic. Price wars were the rule rather than the exception. Millions of dollars were lost by stockholders as a result of bitter struggles between major rubber companies. Since the union became strong there has not been one major price war." Cf. Jacob Baker, "What an Employer Gets from a Union Contract," an address given at Town Hall, New York City, December 6, 1938.

ship and the ability of the union to maintain discipline amongst its membership. If the employer vigorously opposes the union, the workers are likely to select a militant leadership. The negotiation of collective agreements and the settlement of grievances under them, on the other hand, tends to lead to the selection and development of businesslike leaders, such as those in the railroad, printing, clothing, and mining unions. Collective agreements represent an attempt to introduce due process of law into industry, so that the workers are protected from arbitrary managerial actions by procedures designed to ensure decisions on the merits of the case. If the management hires labor spies to oppose and eliminate the union, as a number of automobile companies did in 1936 and 1937 after signing collective agreements with the union, one can understand why labor relations in the industry continued to be disturbed and why alleged violations of the agreement by both sides were frequent. Under such circumstances, each side may be suspicious of actions by the other side, and it may prove difficult for the union to discipline its new members, so that operations will not be interrupted by disagreements and work stoppages.

ORGANIZED RESISTANCE TO UNIONS

The resistance of employers to labor organization may take a variety of forms. Employers may organize so that, through collective action, they can prevent collective action by their employees, or they may resist labor unions singlehanded. Employers' associations and individual employers often use the same methods for opposing organized labor, and antiunion tactics change somewhat with changes in labor laws and public opinion. It is, of course, impossible to discuss all of the various tactics that have been used against labor unions. The discussion here is confined to antiunion practices that have been fairly common and effective. The legal aspects of employers' actions against labor organization are treated in Chapter 25.

The previous chapter has indicated that many American employers have not "fought" labor unions, and that a large number of local employers' associations have signed collective labor agreements. Some employers have never used any of the militant tactics that are described in this chapter, although perhaps most American employers have used one or more of them at some time. That the

practices described in the following pages have been characteristic
of many large firms in this country can, however, be readily appreciated from the statement that in 1939 over 900 manufacturing
plants were members of the National Metal Trades Association,
including plants of General Motors Corporation, Hudson Motor
Company, Curtis Aeroplane and Motor Company, Republic
Steel Corporation, Fisher Body Corporation, and Briggs Manufacturing Company; while 69 companies used the Association's
labor espionage service from 1933 to 1936, including such well-
known concerns as Otis Elevator Company, Wright Aeronautical
Company, a division of the United Aircraft Corporation, Stewart-
Warner Corporation, Hookless Fastener Company, and Yale and
Towne Manufacturing Company.[1]   For some 33 years prior to
1937 the Employers' Association of Akron had paid sums, varying
with the organizational activity of labor unions, to an outside
agency specializing in labor espionage.   The large rubber firms in
Akron supplied most of the income of the Association, three fifths
of which went for the services of the espionage agency in 1936.[2]

Many of the country's best known firms have purchased the
services of espionage agencies directly rather than through an
employers' association.   An incomplete list, compiled by a subcommittee of the United States Senate from its investigations into
industrial espionage in 1937, contained the names of some 1,420
firms and 50 employers' associations that had used detective
agencies for such services as espionage and strike-breaking during
the period from 1933 to 1936.   Among the firms paying thousands
of dollars for labor espionage during those years were the Aluminum
Company of America, Bethlehem Steel Company, Campbell Soup
Company, Curtis Publishing Company, Endicott Johnson Corporation, General Electric Company, Royal Typewriter Company,
and Sinclair Refining Company.[3]   During that period General
Motors Corporation alone paid approximately $1,000,000 for spy
services and had at times as many as 200 labor spies in its plants.[4]

[1] Cf. *Labor Policies of Employers' Associations, Part 1, The National Metal Trades Association*, Senate Report No. 6, Part 4, 76th Congress, first session, 1939, pp. 132–61.

[2] Cf. *Hearings before a Subcommittee of the Committee on Education and Labor Pursuant to
S. Res. 266*, Part 8, U. S. Senate, 75th Congress, first session, 1937, pp. 2954–58.

[3] Cf. *Industrial Espionage*, Report of the Committee on Education and Labor Pursuant
to S. Res. 266, Senate Report No. 46, Part 3, 75th Congress, second session, 1937,
pp. 80–89.

[4] *Ibid.*, p. 23.

Employers' associations. The discussion of employers' associations in Chapter 6 gave some indication of their structure and their activities. They may be local, state-wide, or industry-wide on a national scale. As has been mentioned, it is estimated that in 1939 there were "probably 5,000 local or city employers' associations throughout the country" dealing with various unions.[1] Whether any particular one of the 2,300 state and local chambers of commerce can be considered an employers' association depends upon whether it is primarily engaged in promoting the interests of a group of employers in labor matters. Generally, the titles of employers' associations include such words as Associated Industries, Associated Employers, Industrial Association, or Manufacturers' Association, although employers' associations have also adopted such ingenious titles as Laundry Institute, Industrial Research Bureau, Citizens' Advisory Committee, and Citizens Alliance.

The nation's large employers seek to achieve "a united front" and common opinion on labor relations through the National Association of Manufacturers and its adjunct, the National Industrial Council. The NAM in 1938 had a membership of about 3,000 manufacturing concerns, including most of America's best known firms. Indeed, its membership roll reads like the list of advertisers in popular magazines. As a coordinator of the employer attitude on labor policy, it engages principally in lobbying, propaganda, legal advice, and counsel to members. The Council is a federation of over 200 employers' associations, of which almost half are national associations in various industries and the remainder are state and local employers' associations affiliated with the Council.[2]

In practice, the NAM and the Council that it has "sponsored" are almost the same organization. The chairman of the Council is the president of the NAM. Affiliates of the Council have nine of the 60 or 70 places on the Board of Directors of the NAM. The staff of the NAM makes up the staff of the Council. The NAM furnishes the headquarters for the Council; performs the necessary managerial, secretarial, and clerical services for it; and acts as

[1] Helen S. Hoeber, "Collective Bargaining with Employers' Associations," *Monthly Labor Review*, vol. 49 (August 1939), p. 309.

[2] *Cf. Labor Policies of Employers' Associations, Part 3, The National Association of Manufacturers*, Senate Report No. 6, Part 6, 76th Congress, first session, 1939, especially pp. 68–74.

its "national legislative contact." In turn, the affiliates of the Council cooperate by acting as agents and outlets for the bulletins, the propaganda, and the educational and publicity suggestions supplied by the NAM. In this way, "the interest of national industrial unity" is served and "the cause of industrial unity, to which the NAM is dedicated, is furthered." [1] Generally speaking, the NAM formulates the policies and the Council affiliates carry them to their respective localities and put them into practice. Such an arrangement helps the NAM to unify the opinion of industrialists on matters of labor policy and to extend its sphere of influence to employers who do not belong to the NAM directly but are members of one of the various employers' associations affiliated with the Council. Through such connections with other employers' organizations, the NAM is said to represent between 30,000 and 35,000 manufacturers employing from 4,500,000 to 5,000,000 persons. [2]

1. *Uniform policies.* How the employers' "united front" on labor matters may operate in an industry is illustrated by the policies of the National Metal Trades Association. During the period from 1933 to 1937 as many as 59 firms that were members and contributors of the NAM were also members and contributors of the National Metal Trades Association, and the influence of the National Metal Trades Association upon the National Industrial Council is indicated by the fact that, besides four direct affiliations with the Council, the secretaries or managers of 16 local employers' associations affiliated with the Council were secretaries of their local branch of the National Metal Trades Association. [3]

Each member of the Metal Trades Association had to conduct his business on an open-shop basis under threat of expulsion, which would involve loss of all his contributions to the Association and reimbursement of all monies from the Association's "Defense Fund" spent in his behalf during a labor dispute. In some employers' associations, employer members have even pledged to forfeit as much as $100 to every member of the association in the trade or industry if they sign an agreement with a labor union. [4] The constitution of the National Metal Trades Association also requires

---

[1] *Ibid.*, pp. 256–59.   [2] *Ibid.*, p. 3.   [3] *Ibid.*, pp. 66–67 and 269–70.
[4] *Cf.* Robert W. Dunn, *The Americanization of Labor; the Employers' Offensive Against the Trade Unions*, 1927, p. 86.

that "notice of the expulsion of a member shall be mailed promptly to each member of the Association." This provision is especially significant in view of the economic interdependence of manufacturers of machine tools, automobiles, and automobile parts. In 1936 a Cleveland concern, as a member of the National Metal Trades Association, was ordered, on threat of expulsion from the Association, to modify an agreement with its employees providing that a shop committee of employees would be consulted before lay-offs and reductions in pay were made. The officials of the Association insisted that such provisions were against the Association's principles. In connection with this issue, the president of the Cleveland firm complained

. . . that two Cleveland men had spread stories among the trade that were malicious and false; that his lawyers have told him that he has cause for legal action; that he had no desire to pursue this course but that he would be compelled to do so unless the stories were stopped, as his company had lost much desirable business as a result of the stories.[1]

As a further measure to ensure uniformity of labor policies amongst members, the constitution of the National Metal Trades Association, until revised in 1937 after the Senate investigation, required that a member faced with a strike surrender to the Association full control over the conduct of the strike and over the methods to be used. In short, an outside organization was to run the employer's business as it saw fit during such a period. Furthermore, no member could "make any settlement or adjustment with its employees or their representatives or committee, or with any labor union or representative of such union, without the full knowledge and written assent of the Administrative Council of the Association acting through its Commissioner." For one year after the termination of the labor dispute the member had to conduct its business on the open-shop plan or reimburse the Association for all expenses it had incurred in connection with the dispute. In addition, reports of the labor spies employed by the Association were frequently sent to all the members of one of its local branches so that they would have the same information upon which to base concerted action and a uniform program.[2]

[1] *Labor Policies of Employers' Associations, Part 1, op. cit.*, p. 68.
[2] This paragraph is based on *Labor Policies of Employers' Associations, Part 1, op. cit.*, pp. 41–43, 70–72, 122–23, 126–27.

2. *The Boycott.* Cases of employers boycotting firms that deal with unions have not been infrequent. A number of them were mentioned in the section on employers' organizations in Chapter 6. The Industrial Association of San Francisco, for example, boasted in 1923 that, by means of a buyers' permit system, the boycotting of union employers, the denial of bank credit to employers of union members, and similar methods, it was able in three years to change the conditions of manual work in the city from a situation where over 90 per cent of the employees were in closed, union shops to one where over 85 per cent of them were in open shops.[1] Officials in the International Molders' Union stated that in San Francisco

Foundrymen operating under friendly agreements with Local No. 164 were told that unless they established non-union shops it would be impossible for them to retain their customers. The Industrial Association established a boycott against union shops. Its hired representatives visited buyers of castings and endeavored to have them place their patterns in the non-union association shops. Bankers refused loans to foundrymen employing our members.[2]

During the 1920's it was a common practice for local employers' associations, including the Associated Employers of Indianapolis, the Milwaukee Employers' Council, the American Plan Association of Cleveland, the St. Paul Citizens' Alliance, and the Employers' Association of Detroit, to urge employers to patronize only open-shop producers or retailers with "open shop" show cards in their windows, to refuse to advertise in union-shop newspapers, and to withhold bank credit from union employers.[3] In 1926 the Employers' Association of Detroit, for example, ran the following full-page advertisement in a local newspaper:

The Open Shop has made Detroit a great industrial center.
Detroit needs the Open Shop if she is to continue to advance.
What can Mr. Average Citizen do to promote the welfare of Detroit and incidentally of his fellows, his family, and himself?
The answer is a simple one:
Property owners specify the Open Shop and employ only local contractors who are fighting for progress.
Purchasers of goods buy only from Open Shop producers.

[1] *Cf.* Dunn, *op. cit.*, pp. 49, 52–53.
[2] From an editorial by John P. Frey, *International Molders' Journal*, vol. 62 (October 1926), p. 606.
[3] *Cf.* Dunn, *op. cit.*, pp. 58, 62, 87–88.

If you need printing see an Open Shop printer.
Manufacturers buy patterns and castings from open pattern shops and foundries.
Think Open Shop!
Talk Open Shop!
Yes, and vote for those who support the Open Shop.[1]

In a number of instances in the 1930's, the National Metal Trades Association attempted, through the purchases and sales of its members, to bring economic pressure against individual employers who had signed union agreements. On some occasions, the officers of the Association sought to undermine business officials sympathetic with collective bargaining by communicating with their stockholders and customers.[2] Some iron and steel companies secretly signed closed- or preferential-shop agreements with the Steel Workers Organizing Committee (CIO) in 1939 but denied such action when questioned by other firms in the industry for fear that it would be used against them with their customers.

The effectiveness of business boycotts is further evidence of imperfection in product markets and the economic pressure that certain buyers or sellers can exert in and through the market. Boycotts, black lists, and white lists would presumably be absolutely ineffective in perfect markets with unbranded goods and impersonal operation. And in such markets the threat of a seller or a buyer to move his business elsewhere would have no noticeable effect upon local product or labor markets.

In certain cases, bankers have exerted a great deal of influence upon the labor policies of employers who were dependent upon bank loans to run their businesses. Although the bankers were outsiders, in the sense that they were not hiring the employees concerned, or negotiating with the union, or manufacturing the product, they have frequently been able to induce employers to follow a certain labor program by suggesting that any deviation from the program might result in a reduction or cessation of bank credit to the firm or industry. From experience in local chambers of commerce and in labor conciliation work, one is surprised to find how much power monied persons may exert over labor policies

[1] In *Detroit Saturday Night*, July 31, 1926 (Twelfth Annual Open Shop Number) and quoted in Dunn, *op. cit.*, p. 88.
[2] *Cf.*, for example, *Hearings Pursuant to S. Res. 266*, Part 3, 75th Congress, first session, 1937, pp. 911–14; and *Labor Policies of Employers' Associations*, Part 1, *op. cit.*, p. 113.

in a community, although such persons may themselves hire very few, if any, workers.

3. *Labor espionage.* Since its inception in the 1870's, labor espionage has been a widespread practice throughout American industry. The vice president and general manager of the De Soto Corporation stated in 1937 that labor espionage was "a practice we have grown up with." [1] At the same time the president of a large espionage agency testified that the nature of his business had "changed slightly, but not very much" during the four decades ending in 1937. [2] One spy told a Senate Committee that from 20 years of experience as a labor "stool pigeon" he had "found out there is [*sic*] stools in every union organization." [3] Estimates place the number of labor spies in 1936 at between 40,000 and 135,000 persons, with the minimum expenditures for labor espionage exceeding $80,000,-000 in that year. [4]

Labor spies are hired (1) by employers' associations that offer spy service to their members, (2) by private detective agencies that sell such services to employers, and (3) by corporations that set up their own spy systems, as General Motors did in 1937. [5] Employers' associations may use their spy service as a talking point in soliciting new members. From 1933 to 1936 some 45 employers' associations are known to have been clients of detective agencies offering espionage service, while other employers' associations had their own hired spies. One fifth to two thirds of the income of some employers' associations has been spent for labor espionage. The spies themselves are either professionals who consider that kind of work their occupation or "hooked" men and women who have been recruited by misrepresentation. They may have been told that their spy reports were for the information of the government, the minority stockholders, the bondholders, the insurance company with which the employer is insured, or some similar outside party. When the "hooked" person discovers that he has been serving as a labor spy and that his reports have been going to the employer, he may be forced to continue his spy work under threat of being exposed. An ex-officer of one spy agency admitted that over two out

[1] *Hearings Pursuant to S. Res. 266*, Part 4, 1937, p. 1219.   [2] *Ibid.*, p. 1105.
[3] *Ibid.*, Part 8, p. 2843.   [4] *Cf.* Leo Huberman, *The Labor Spy Racket*, 1937, pp. 5–6.
[5] *Cf. Industrial Espionage*, Senate Report No. 46, Part 3, 75th Congress, second session, 1937, pp. 20–21. This summarizing report contains a great deal of material on the practice.

of three of the 300 operatives in his records were "hooked" men.[1] The professional spies change their names repeatedly in order to avoid detection.

Labor spies join unions and become union officials in order that they may disrupt and destroy labor organizations. Between January 1934 and June 1937, one detective agency had at least 330 of its operatives in 90 different national unions, with as many as 52 in the Auto Workers' union to report on the union drive in General Motors. Of these 330 spies, one was national vice president of the union, 14 were presidents of locals, 38 were secretaries in locals, and 6 were business agents or organizers.[2] Holding such offices, they were in a position to report the names of union members and to reveal the union's plans to the employer, both of which have a demoralizing effect upon the union. Furthermore, they generally create discord or disgust among the membership, by charging some officials with embezzlement or bad faith, by making long speeches, by bickering over parliamentary procedure, or by opposing the program of the officers. They may cause the union to call an untimely strike; they may preach violence; or they may incite the members to riot in order to discredit the union. Often they are able to acquire a following in the union because of their pleasant or vigorous personalities and their free spending on the agency's account.

How a labor spy may disorganize a union is illustrated by the case of a spy supplied by the National Metal Trades Association to one of its employer members in 1934 on the day following a National Labor Relations Board election in which the AFL union received over 95 per cent of the ballots cast. This spy joined the union; became recording secretary; and reported the names of union members to the employer so that they might be discharged. In order to discredit the organizers of the local union before the membership, he brought charges against them alleging embezzlement of union funds. These charges were later disproved as absolutely false. In a little more than a year after he had joined the local, its membership had dwindled to eight members, so that its charter was revoked and the organization disbanded.[3] The Flint local of the Federal Union of Automobile Workers of General Motors plants declined from about 26,000 members in 1935 to 122

---

[1] Huberman, *op. cit.*, p. 53.   [2] *Cf. Industrial Espionage, op. cit.*, pp. 26–28, 75–79.
[3] *Cf. Labor Policies of Employers' Associations, Part 1, op. cit.*, pp. 77–78.

in 1936 through the action of at least 5 spies on its executive board of 13. One spy attempted to undermine leaders of the union by insinuating that they were spies. Another spy who was union secretary was instrumental in having a great number of active union members discharged at the Chevrolet plant, and the union grievance committee, on which there were two spies, refused to take up the cases of the discharged members with the Chevrolet management.[1] In less than a year after a spy became secretary of a federal union in Hartford, Connecticut, in 1935, its membership had dropped from 2,500 to 75.[2]

That labor espionage may prove to be a risky and costly policy for corporate management to adopt is indicated by the experience of General Motors. Both General Motors and Chrysler had their spy service extended to the plants of other companies without notifying them. These other companies included either their own competitors or companies selling materials and parts to their competitors. General Motors spies were even asked to spy on the spies of Chrysler because there was reason to believe that confidential trade secrets were being passed on to Chrysler. Not unnaturally, suspicion fell upon the spies previously hired, so General Motors hired additional spies from another detective agency to spy on the spies already in its plants![3]

The espionage business, of course, expands with labor trouble and strife. Private detective agencies stand to profit most by a maximum of labor disturbance, and the employment of individual spies also rests upon the same foundation. Consequently, they may follow a make-work policy. Spies have frequently been encouraged to doctor up their reports to inflame the imagination of the employer so that he will hire more spies or at least continue to employ those he already has. Spies may even stimulate and incite labor unrest in order to prevent their own unemployment. Suspicion, work stoppages, and even strikes are likely to accompany labor espionage. The bad effects upon employee morale from espionage and the accompanying discharge of union leaders may be a disturbing factor in the company's labor relations for a long period of time.[4]

---

[1] *Cf. Hearings Pursuant to S. Res. 266*, Part 7, 1937, pp. 2318–19; and *Industrial Espionage, op. cit.*, p. 70.
[2] *Cf.* Huberman, *op. cit.*, pp. 21–23.
[3] *Cf. ibid.*, pp. 81–84; and *Industrial Espionage, op. cit.*, pp. 44–48.
[4] *Idem.*

As a result of the Senate Committee's investigation into labor espionage in 1937, the National Metal Trades Association reported that it had abandoned its spy services, and one of the important private spy agencies decided to liquidate its business. As a consequence, more employers apparently have established their own spy services.[1] Testifying before this same Senate Committee in 1938, William Few Long, secretary and manager of the Associated Industries of Cleveland for 17 years and an important figure in the affairs of the National Industrial Council, stated: "It must be remembered that spying always will be an essential part of warfare, and that is true whether it is industrial warfare or warfare between nations and so long as we have industrial warfare, just so long we will have industrial spying in my opinion, regardless of any measures that may be taken to prevent it."[2]

4. *Employment bureaus and black lists.* A large number of local employers' associations, in such cities as Chicago, Cleveland, Denver, Passaic, Indianapolis, and Moline, have established employment bureaus through which members of the association hire their employees.[3] In this way union members may be black-listed and employers may be assured of "loyal" nonunion workers. The constitution of the National Metal Trades Association, for example, requires each of its branches (27 in 1937) "to maintain an Employment Bureau." The names and records of union members or "agitators" are supplied to these Bureaus by spies or by employer members of the Association who send in names to be filed for future "reference." By 1914 the Association had over 400,000 permanent records of workmen.[4] Consequently, the Association, in supplying employers with new workers, could state that they "all are known to be nonunion men."[5] In addition, the Association has issued a great many Certificates of Recommendation to workers who "have proven their loyalty to their employers by having been faithful to them during labor trouble."[6] Such certificate holders were "to be shown favor" and "to be given every consistent preference and advantage by the members" of the Association.[7]

By gaining control of the market place for labor, employers'

[1] *Cf. Industrial Espionage, op. cit.*, p. 74.
[2] *Hearings Pursuant to S. Res. 266,* Part 22, 1938, p. 9457.
[3] *Cf.* Dunn, *op. cit.*, pp. 43, 57, 69, 89–93, 108.
[4] *Labor Policies of Employers' Associations, Part 1, op. cit.*, p. 26. *Cf.* also pp. 82, 104.
[5] *Ibid.*, pp. 102–103.   [6] *Ibid.*, p. 26.   [7] *Idem.*

associations have been able to enforce a boycott against union members and to discriminate in favor of docile nonunion workers. Such discrimination in the labor market has nothing to do with the efficiency or ability of the worker. It is not on the basis of economic merit, but according to the worker's beliefs regarding the desirability of labor organization. Some notion of the effect of such discrimination upon the distribution of labor resources can be gained from the stories of efficient workmen who have been deliberately deprived of opportunity to earn a livelihood in their trade through black-listing.[1] Sometimes workers are black-listed through a system of employment or clearance cards on which the worker's previous employment record is given in full so that the employer can learn from the worker's previous employers whether he is a "reliable" employee.

The importance of control over the central market place for labor is illustrated by the contest that has existed between employers and the unions over the control of the hiring halls for longshoremen and seamen on the Pacific Coast. During the 1920's the Waterfront Employers' Association and the Shipowners' Association of the Pacific Coast established central hiring halls for longshoremen, seamen, marine engineers, and masters, mates, and pilots, in San Francisco and Los Angeles. The owners employed men only through the hiring halls controlled by the employers' associations, and the workers were required to present "grade" books containing their entire work records in order to register and receive employment through the employer-dominated hiring halls. By such control over the labor-supply center, the employers were able to discriminate as a group against former strikers and union leaders. Black-listing was rife. In November 1926, the U. S. Supreme Court declared the practice of requiring that all seamen be hired exclusively through the employers' association bureau was in violation of the Federal antitrust laws.[2] Since 1934 the hiring halls for longshoremen and seamen on the West Coast have been controlled by the unions.

5. *Propaganda and "educational" activities.* Employers' associations have served as agencies for coordinating employer pressure upon the local press, local public officials, and legislatures. They have

---

[1] *Cf.*, for example, *ibid.*, pp. 101–102.

[2] *Anderson* v. *Shipowners' Association of Pacific Coast et al.* (1926), 47 Supreme Court 125. *Cf.* also William S. Hopkins, "Employment Exchanges for Seamen," *American Economic Review*, vol. 25 (June 1935), pp. 250–58.

also functioned as local outlets for the publicity or propaganda campaigns of such national organizations as the National Association of Manufacturers. In 1934, for example, the NAM began a "campaign for the dissemination of sound American doctrines to the public." [1] By 1937 the employer subscriptions for this program amounted to about $800,000 a year, or over half of the Association's total income for 1937.[2] Through the National Industrial Council, local employers' associations were urged to initiate a "united program for community education" under the guidance of the NAM, which supplied leaflets for employees, material for publication or speeches, speakers, sound films for schools, and reprints of articles written by university economists for the "Six Star Service" of the NAM.

The importance of public opinion in labor matters was stressed by the public-relations department of the NAM as follows in 1937:

> Now, more than ever before, strikes are being won or lost in the newspapers and over the radio. The swing of public opinion has always been a major factor in labor disputes, but with the settlement of strikes being thrown more and more into the laps of public officials, the question of public opinion becomes of greater importance. For it is public opinion—what the voters think—that moves those elected to action along one course or another.[3]

With the assistance of local employers' associations, the National Association of Manufacturers was able to carry its propaganda to every industrial community in the country. All means of communication were used, including "payroll stuffers" for employees, letters to stockholders, material for foremen, movies for employees, editorials and news stories for the press, a daily newspaper column by economists (the "Six Star Service"), comic features ("Uncle Abner Says"), "harmony" advertisements under local sponsorship, radio speeches, radio drama (American Family Robinson), radio programs in six languages, movie shorts, newsreels, public speeches at "civic meetings," plant bulletin boards, outdoor billboards, and booklets mailed to professional persons, schools, and libraries. In practically every case, the real source of the material, the National Association of Manufacturers, was kept secret.[4]

The NAM estimated in 1938 that its series of 25 leaflets had been

---

[1] *Labor Policies of Employers' Associations, Part 3, op. cit.*, p. 155.
[2] *Ibid.*, p. 168.   [3] *Ibid.*, p. 158.   [4] *Cf. ibid.*, pp. 160–62.

distributed to over 11,000,000 employees through 79 employers' associations and 1,545 companies. Its movie shorts were seen by "nearly 6,000,000 people" in 1937. The daily newspaper column by economists (the "Six Star Service") appeared in 260 papers with a circulation of more than 4,500,000 in 1936, and reprints were received by more than 300 trade and business papers. The Association's "harmony" advertisements of full-page size appeared in over 500 newspapers. The American Family Robinson was broadcast weekly or semiweekly over 268 radio stations. More than 1,000,000 copies of a series of seven booklets were mailed to persons and schools. The Association's press service was received by 6,252 weekly and small daily papers including 153 foreign language newspapers with a circulation of almost 2,500,000 persons. The president of the NAM estimated that during 1936 alone its propaganda campaign received over $3,000,000 worth of outdoor advertising, newspaper space, and radio time, free of charge.[1]

Some notion of the material distributed in this "educational" campaign to "sell" industry to the public can be gained from articles on labor subjects in the "Six Star Service," written by 11 "outstanding economists" in various universities and paid for by the NAM. About one third of the 500-odd articles in 1936 and 1937 dealt with labor subjects, although not one of these professors taught a subject in the labor field.[2] The professor who wrote the most articles on labor subjects taught only one economics course entitled "classical economic theory." The impression of the labor market conveyed by the articles that appeared in the "Six Star Service" series is revealed by the following quotations:

In order to secure a square deal for all, rich and poor, intelligent and ignorant, the Constitution provides that the value of all services and all commodities sold on the open market must be fixed by one unchanging and unchangeable standard controlled not by men but by natural forces, expressing themselves in natural laws. Bargaining power has no significance on the open, competitive, American market because the value of services, like the value of cotton and eggs and apples, is not fixed by bargains, but by the operation of natural forces.

Bargaining power has significance only when certain groups seek to get more than the market value for their services. This means that they are seeking to exploit other groups by forcing employers to pay them more

---

[1] Cf. ibid., pp. 162–66, 170; and Huberman, op. cit., pp. 134–36.
[2] Cf. Hearings Pursuant to S. Res. 266, Part 35, 1939, pp. 14394–95.

than the market price for their services, and assess the difference on other groups by making them pay it in higher prices. Those who stand for this unethical and indefensible principle pose as the friends of the working man. As a matter of fact, they are preeminently the exploiters of labor.[1]

.   .   .   .   .   .

Wages are fixed by natural forces beyond the control of employers. . . . Competition is so intense in business today that employers cannot afford to permit their competitors to pay less than the market price for their labor.[2]

One cannot help but wonder whether such "classical" economists also believe that natural forces likewise determine the price of each of the 250,000 separate parts that the International Harvester Company manufactures for servicing agricultural implements or the 50,000 prices that the United States Steel Corporation quotes for various forms of its basic products. The quotations from the "Six Star Service" might well be compared with the following statement about markets and equilibrium made by an "outstanding" corporation president, member of the boards of directors of many firms, prominent in the U. S. Chamber of Commerce, and author of books on business management:

I doubt very much the possibility of equilibrium conditions as to wages, *i.e.*, free, unrestricted competition not only between workers but between workers and other factors of production, unless the entire economic system, *i.e.*, all prices, are similarly determined. The possibility of any material reduction in the relative degree of monopoly, oligopoly, and monopolistic competition is remote even without reference to patent monopolies and tariff protection. Any such conception seems to me to involve the abandonment of mass production. Moreover, after a great deal of reflection on the matter, I believe competition, if not limited and regulated to substantial degrees, necessarily destroys internal efficiency of processes and annihilates incentives by the excessive degree of uncertainty which it imposes. That is, both theoretically and practically, it seems to me, there has never been, and there cannot now be, anything approaching an equilibrium mechanism in our prices.[3]

6. *Citizens' Committees.* The citizens' committee is a device for organizing business groups to carry out a campaign against labor organization and the economic program of unions. It is usually a temporary organization, born out of the fear that labor organiza-

[1] *Ibid.*, Part 18, 1938, p. 8087.   [2] *Ibid.*, p. 8093.
[3] From private correspondence dated November 1939.

tions may have adverse effects upon local business, payrolls, and employment. Through such fear it is able to enlist the support of real-estate owners, professional persons, small retailers, farmers, and other nonemploying groups. Often economic pressure in the form of a threat by an employer or employers to move the business to another locality causes local business groups to organize and exert pressure upon local officials and public opinion in order to break a strike or to eliminate labor unions.

During the 1920's, citizens' committees were formed in a number of cities including Chicago, Cleveland, Detroit, and San Francisco. Generally they were formed by employers' associations in order to raise funds, and to secure the cooperation of the nonemploying public, for an antiunion campaign. In Detroit, for example, a Citizens' Committee was formed in 1926 by some 40-odd employers' organizations and trade associations in order to preserve the open, nonunion shop and to prevent the AFL from "injuring" business in Detroit by organizing automobile workers. In Chicago, Cleveland, and San Francisco, citizens' committees, organized by employers' associations, raised millions of dollars to wage a campaign to eliminate the building unions. In such a campaign, building contractors, real-estate interests, and bankers were an important element in enforcing a buyers' and credit boycott against union employers in the industry.

During the 1930's, the citizens' committee was often used as a strike-breaking device. That was true, for example, of the Akron Law and Order League in the 1936 strike of the Goodyear Tire and Rubber Company, the Flint Alliance in the 1937 strike of the General Motors Company, and the Johnstown Citizens' Committee, the Mahoning Valley Citizens' Committee, the Canton Citizens' Law and Order League, the Massillon Law and Order League, and the Warren John Q. Public League, all formed in the Little Steel strike of 1937. Often these citizens' leagues are largely organized and financed by companies facing the strike. For example, the Akron Law and Order League, to which the Goodyear Company contributed "in the neighborhood of $15,000," was formed after a preliminary discussion by Goodyear's president with the presidents of other Akron rubber companies.[1] During the early period of its existence, over 95 per cent of the funds for the Johns-

---

[1] *Hearings Pursuant to S. Res. 266*, Part 8, 1937, pp. 2951–52.

town Citizens' Committee came from the Bethlehem Steel Company. That company paid more than $36,000 to the Citizens' Committee in 1937, most of which was passed on to the mayor of Johnstown to pay salaries and buy ammunition for approximately 500 persons who were sworn in as special police during the strike.[1] A whispering campaign that a long strike would cause the company to move its plants away from Johnstown had frightened merchants and professional men in the area.

As the personnel manager of the Goodyear plant in Gadsden, Alabama, has explained, it is much easier to organize community sentiment in favor of a company in a small community than in a large one.[2] That is true because a small community is so dependent on the company's payroll. In Gadsden, according to the Goodyear personnel director, the community was "100 percent with the company" and against the union largely for the reason that "Gadsden lost an important industry 15 years ago because of labor trouble and the professional men, [and] city and county officials are definitely against permitting agitators to tie up the Goodyear plant."[3] The effectiveness of the threat to move lies not only in putting economic pressure upon small, independent businessmen to oppose the union but in forcing the government officials to side with the company. As the experience of the Remington-Rand Corporation in Syracuse and Ilion, New York, during its 1936 strike indicates, it is easier for a company to sway public officials in small cities than in large ones.

In order to appreciate the contrast in this Remington-Rand case, it is necessary to understand that just before the 1936 strike the union membership included about 80 per cent of the production and maintenance employees in the plants of the company in six localities, and that the company had signed a collective agreement covering those six plants.[4] The union called the strike because the company had acquired a new plant in Elmira, New York, under an assumed name, to which materials and equipment were being transferred from its Ilion plant and to which it was unwilling to

---

[1] *Ibid.*, Part 19, 1938, pp. 8206–9, 8373–74, 8461.
[2] *Ibid.*, Part 8, 1937, p. 2979.   [3] *Ibid.*, p. 2982.
[4] The discussion of this case is based primarily upon a decision by the National Labor Relations Board on March 13, 1937, *In the Matter of Remington Rand*, etc. *Cf. Decisions and Orders of the National Labor Relations Board*, vol. 2, July 1, 1936–July 1, 1937, pp. 626–746.

extend the terms of the union agreement. According to reports, the Elmira plant had been purchased by a group of citizens in Elmira interested in improving business conditions in that town and turned over to the company on the condition that Elmira residents be given preference in employment. Ilion is dependent upon two industrial concerns for its support, with the employees of Remington-Rand amounting to about one fifth of its population. As soon as the strike began, a "For Sale" sign was hung on the Ilion plant, machinery was dismantled and shipped, and a Citizens' Committee was formed of businessmen who were goaded by the fear that loss of the plant would "ruin" their stores, their banks, their loan associations, and their medical and legal practices.

The company had let the local authorities know that it would be influenced in the distribution of its business between localities by the amount of police protection received in the respective communities. Under demand from the Citizens' Committee group to cooperate or resign, the mayor and the chief of police of Ilion were forced to appoint and fully equip about 300 special deputies, after which "law and order" broke loose in Ilion. The mayor explained that, as one of the largest property owners in Ilion, he was afraid of the Citizens' Committee, which included the bankers, because "he could easily be a ruined man and have nothing left but his hat, coat, and pants if these people were to clamp down on him as they were able to do and in a manner which he felt fearful they would do." [1] Some merchants also informed the union members that they feared retaliation by the Citizens' Committee unless they went along with that group.

In Syracuse the story was very different. Despite pressure by a group in the Syracuse Chamber of Commerce, the mayor absolutely refused to provide the large police force demanded by the company for "protection" and display in order to discourage the strikers. The experience of Remington-Rand in Syracuse, with over 200,000 inhabitants, well illustrates that it is much easier to bring economic pressure to bear upon public sentiment, the business elements, and municipal officials in smaller localities where the company supplies most of the demand for labor. The mayor and Citizens' Committee of Middletown, Connecticut, also failed to "cooperate" fully, because they resented the tactics

[1] *Ibid.*, p. 654.

used by the company in attempting to frighten the city. The plants of the company in Syracuse and Middletown were not moved or sold as threatened, but were later reopened and operated. A minority group of stockholders has brought suit against the officers and directors of the company for alleged waste of corporate funds in combatting unionization of employees, fostering a company union, and organizing "back-to-work" campaigns.[1]

Tactics similar to those of the Remington-Rand Company were used during 1935 by the Brown Shoe Company, third largest shoe manufacturing firm in the country.[2] The Brown Shoe Company then operated 14 shoe factories, one in St. Louis and the rest in small towns in the Middle West where the plants had been built with funds subscribed by representative citizens. The typical agreement provided for a certain sum of money to be furnished by the citizens of the town for the erection of the factory, which the company uses free of charge and will later own when it has spent a fixed minimum sum for labor in the plant during a specified period, usually 10 years. Often there is provision for a rebate of all taxes, business fees, and water rates during those 10 years. Approximately one third of the company's machinery is leased from shoe-machinery manufacturers and the rest can be easily moved to another town. Groups of citizens in small towns around St. Louis are constantly seeking to obtain one of the company's plants for their community.

Under such circumstances, the payroll of the company is the town's chief source of income, and the merchants and public officials of the town, many of them subscribers to the fund for the erection of the plant, are deeply interested in keeping it open and in operation. The economic threat to close the plant and move the work to another small town is sufficient to frighten the whole community. It was the closing of the plant, the threat to move, or the actual movement of machinery, that led in 1935 to the formation of citizens' committees in four small Illinois towns where the company had plants. In these towns, pressure was put upon union

[1] *New York Times*, November 30, 1939, p. 23.

[2] Data primarily from *In the Matter of Brown Shoe Company*, etc., *Decisions and Orders of the National Labor Relations Board*, vol. 1, December 7, 1935–July 1, 1936, pp. 803–36. *Cf.* also two articles by Ray L. Kringer, "In the Deep Middle West" and "How to Break a Labor Union," *The Nation*, vol. 141 (November 13, 1935), pp. 569–70, and vol. 142 (January 29, 1936), pp. 131–32.

members by such methods as withdrawal of merchants' credit, solicitation by the citizens' committee of workers' signatures to an agreement to return to work under "any conditions stipulated by the Brown Shoe Company officials," vigilante attacks upon union officials, and the discharge of union sympathizers by local businessmen. Labor spies and corps of special police were also used. As a consequence of such tactics, the union was eliminated from these plants of the company.

The ability of the employer to exert economic pressure upon a community through such methods as the threat to move depends in part upon the nature of his business. As indicated in Chapter 19, most concerns, especially nonmanufacturing firms, are not in a position to migrate because they are "market bound," "materials bound," or "investment bound." Where the community subsidizes the firm through tax concessions or rebates and similar measures, the employer is in an especially strong position to bring pressure upon local businessmen and through them to force the local government to take sides against the union. In order to apply the same tactics, the union would have to threaten to move all of its members out of the community. Such a threat would, of course, prove to be ineffective, which indicates that the employer can often exert more economic pressure than the employees, especially in small communities.

7. *Other features of employers' organizations.* The discussion in Chapter 6 indicated that employers' associations may assist a member, whose employees are on strike, in a number of ways. It may supply strike-breakers.[1] It may have the company's orders filled by other members of the association so that a company with labor difficulties will not lose its customers. Most employers' associations collect "dues" from the members, with which a "defense fund" is built up. Like a union's strike fund, such a defense fund can be used to pay a member company for losses incurred in a strike. With all competitors in the same employers' organization, as all rubber companies in Akron have been in the Akron Employers' Association, it is possible to prevent labor organizations from playing one employer against another. An employers' association, in dealing with a union, can act as a single

[1] For a discussion of strike-breakers and strike-breaking agencies, cf. *Strikebreaking Services*, Senate Report No. 6, 76th Congress, first session, 1939.

unit. If the union asks for "too much," the employers are in a better position to resist because, when one company is shut down, competing firms in the association are also closed. An employers' association can declare an industry-wide lockout (employers' strike) and no employer need fear that he will lose business to his competitors during the lockout.

Employers' associations engage in various kinds of pressure upon legislatures. For example, the executives of nine state employers' associations and seven industry or city employers' associations urged employers to "recruit stockholders, the firms with which you do business, your own staff," in opposition to passage of the National Labor Relations Act.[1] The Associated Industries of Missouri hired a special train to bring 48 Missouri business leaders to Washington "to contact Congressmen personally," and a letter sent to all employers' associations affiliated with the National Industrial Council urged a similar Washington pilgrimage "on a concerted basis" so that as many businessmen as possible might appear personally in Washington to "participate in conferences with Senators and Representatives" from their states in order to prevent passage of such legislation as the National Labor Relations Act and the Social Security Act. Such tactics, however, proved to be in vain in this instance. Generally speaking, employers' lobbying activities are more effective in state legislatures than in the Federal Congress.

EMPLOYER POLICIES AND PRACTICES

Trade is generally considered to be two-sided. Both the buyer and the seller are presumably benefited by a sale. However, there exists a peculiar notion that in the labor market the benefit is mostly one-sided, that the employer is performing a special favor for his employees by hiring them. From this notion of the indebtedness of the employee to his employer arises the demand by some employers that their employees give them unquestioning loyalty without any reciprocal obligation of loyalty on their part. The idea that loyalty should be mostly in one direction, from the employee to the employer, reflects the dependent status of the worker in a wage system, and indicates the weak position of the sellers in most labor markets.

[1] Material in this paragraph taken from *Labor Policies of Employers' Associations, Part 3,* pp. 116–22.

There is no doubt that the employer and his employees have many interests in common. To the extent that the employees have an investment in the firm in the form of money, training, seniority, or good will, they are interested in advancing that firm. An employee's investment in a company may be roughly measured by the loss in earnings that he would experience with a change of employers. It may be that such a loss would generally be small in the case of skilled craftsmen. Certainly craft unions that cut across industrial lines are likely to be less interested in the future of any particular firm or industry than an industrial or a company union would be. Employers are prone to emphasize the mutual interests of management and employees in the fate of the firm, and thus to stress "patriotism" toward the company. Through the company's labor policy, the management may seek to extend that area of mutuality, especially by increasing the dependence of the worker upon the firm, or his attachments to the firm, through such methods as welfare benefits, pension plans, and employee stock ownership.

The motives behind an employer's labor policy may be mixed, and often depend upon the economic circumstances surrounding the firm. It may not be possible to tell to what extent a company's labor policy is motivated by a desire (1) to increase labor efficiency so that the company is obtaining the best results for its money; (2) to prevent the organization of its employees so that the management may have a free hand in determining company policies; (3) to improve the public relations of the company so that it enjoys the good will of customers, legislatures, and public officials; (4) to be fair and decent to its employees on humanitarian grounds. A certain policy may accomplish more than one purpose. For example, welfare programs providing employee benefits may tend to keep a firm's employees from joining a union while at the same time it may reduce labor costs by improving workers' morale, reducing labor turnover, and giving the company the pick of the labor market. Companies with a large investment in capital equipment are generally anxious to obtain high-class workmen so that the output per unit of equipment will be large. Companies subject to government regulation may be much more interested in public good will than are firms located in company towns or selling their products to other employers as raw materials. Some of the companies that have cultivated a reputation for liberality in labor relations have at the same time, however, used such tactics as labor espionage to prevent labor organization, whereby their employees might gain a larger voice in the policies of the company. Of course, companies having signed agreements with unions of their employees are likely to follow very different labor policies from those of firms striving to prevent the organization of their employees or carrying on a campaign to eliminate the influence of a union.

If the labor-relations policy of a company serves as an advertising or publicity device to distinguish the company from others as something special, the effect upon the labor market is similar to that of trade-marked or branded articles in product markets. Such distinctions tend to attract and attach labor or customers to the firm, thereby increasing the monopolistic elements in the market.

Welfare programs. Company programs for employee welfare may serve a number of purposes. They may develop public good will toward the firm. If a company pensions its retired employees, grants sickness benefits to ill employees, arranges for group life insurance to protect their families in case of death, and grants dismissal compensation to employees eliminated from their jobs by technological or industrial change, the company is likely to enjoy "good public relations." Such activities may help to prevent what the management would consider restrictive or unfavorable legislation, and may serve to excuse and explain the high price of the company's products before public bodies. Private welfare programs have also been used to demonstrate that state social-security or relief legislation for the protection of workers was unnecessary. If the company's employees go on strike, the "generosity" of the company may be contrasted with the "ingratitude" of the workers.

The company, of course, is no Santa Claus. Firms have claimed that their welfare programs pay for themselves in the sense that the resulting reduction in production costs offsets the company's contributions to employee welfare plans. It is claimed that welfare activities lower labor costs by reducing labor turnover, by attracting a desirable grade of labor, by improving employee morale and contentment, by forestalling strikes and labor troubles, and by reducing the attractiveness of unions in the eyes of the company's employees. A pension plan permits the firm to retire elderly workers without adverse publicity when they have become a liability to the company. Such retirement also tends to stimulate the younger men by opportunities for advancement. A plan for dismissal compensation may reduce the incentive to restrict output or to prevent the introduction of new machinery, for fear of losing one's job. Company health activities and sports programs may reduce employee sickness or fatigue and also serve to advertise the company.

There is no doubt that such welfare programs also tend to create a greater area of identity of interest between employer and employee, to disrupt the discipline of labor organizations, and to rob labor unions of some of their appeal, especially that of union benefit programs. An employee who has purchased some of the company's stock under an employee stock-ownership plan may hesitate to "strike against his own stock." Collective action by employees may be difficult when the company's pension plan contains such provisions as the following: "Employees who leave the service of their own volition, or under stress of influences inimical to the company, or who are discharged by the company, thereby lose all benefits of the benefit and pension system;" or "Employees who leave the service under strike orders forfeit all claims to pension benefit." [1] The benefits of company welfare programs may thus be limited to employees who "have not engaged in demonstrations detrimental to the company's best interests." [2] Under some plans, the pensioners could be called back as strike-breakers or be forced to forfeit their pensions. Where an employee's pension benefits and the income from his security investments, as well as his job, depend upon the management and fate of one firm, he is likely to be fairly "loyal" to that firm, because he is especially dependent upon it. When in addition the firm offers other benefits that may be withheld or granted at the discretion of the management, there is a possibility for favoritism and the development of a "loyalty" based on subserviency.

The benefit programs of some firms have been designated as "benevolent paternalism," because they have been presented as a generous gesture that the firm will continue as long as the em-

[1] Mary Conyngton, "Industrial Pensions for Old Age and Disability," *Monthly Labor Review*, vol. 22 (January 1926), p. 53. *Cf.* also *Industrial Pensions in the United States*, National Industrial Conference Board, 1925, p. 64.

[2] *Idem.*

ployees are "loyal" and remain "one big happy family." Such paternalism may tend to undermine the independence, and eventually perhaps the self-reliance, of the worker. Where welfare is considered as a gift, rather than a profitable policy or something that the employees really earn, the management may hope that the employees will develop a feeling of gratitude toward the firm and view unions as agents opposed to the company rather than as organizations operating in the interest of employee members.

If the concern is in a competitive industry, it may not be able to afford a large benefit program unless such a program in reality does practically pay for itself. The self-supporting limitations upon welfare activities may be less rigid for firms in a monopolistic or semimonopolistic position. Under such circumstances, corporation managements may, in order to forestall union restrictions upon their control, pay for some unremunerative welfare activities out of funds that would otherwise accrue to the stockholders. It is interesting in this connection to note that the largest corporations with trade-marked products, heavy investment in equipment, and small labor costs per unit of output, like the Standard Oil Company of New Jersey, the American Telephone and Telegraph Company, United States Steel Corporation, the General Electric Company, International Harvester Company, Eastman Kodak Company, and Proctor and Gamble Company, were the leaders in introducing welfare programs. In most of these companies, labor unions had not been a significant factor prior to 1935, and the managements had consistently opposed them.

During the first World War and the postwar period of the 1920's, these large companies carried on what has been called a "welfare offensive." Prior to 1930 it is estimated that three fourths of all employee stock-ownership plans were introduced between 1916 and 1929, and that over three fourths of all industrial pension plans began between 1911 and 1929.[1] The amount of group insurance in force increased from about $13,000,000 at the end of 1912 to almost $10,000,000,000 in 1931.[2] That corporate manage-

[1] Cf. Robert F. Foerster, "Employee Stock Ownership," Encyclopaedia of the Social Sciences, vol. 5, 1931, p. 506; and Murray W. Latimer, Industrial Pension Systems, 1932, vol. 1, p. 42.

[2] Cf. "Group Insurance Experience of Various Establishments," Monthly Labor Review, vol. 24 (June 1927), p. 1228; and Recent Developments in Industrial Group Insurance, National Industrial Conference Board, 1934, p. 24.

ment did not propose to share its control with the workers through employee stock ownership is indicated by a study showing that the average employee holdings in the 13 largest firms having such plans were but 4 per cent of the total stock of the corporation, and that in 20 representative corporations the employees owned only 4.5 per cent of the aggregate stock outstanding.[1] In practice, the influence of employee stockholders upon the management or control of the corporation has been negligible, or better, non-existent, except in a few smaller companies. Even where companies have had plans for sharing profits with their employees, there has been little sharing of the management with wage-earners, although presumably those who receive profits should share in the management and control of the company.

From the employee's point of view, the best types of company welfare are those plans that increase his security by using the insurance principle of spreading the risk, and that give the employee some part in developing, managing, and financing the program so that it has little of the odor of philanthropy or charity. The plans that seem to fit these qualifications best are credit unions, mutual benefit associations, and group insurance. Credit unions are cooperative saving-lending organizations, in which employees buy shares and from which some employees borrow. Employees generally like to be officers and committee members in such associations, and there is little overhead or loss because the employee borrower is well known to his associates.[2] Mutual benefit associations, with employees contributing and serving on committees to pass on benefit claims, are insurance programs covering such contingencies as sickness, accident, and death. Group insurance is an arrangement whereby a company's employees can buy life insurance, and perhaps accident and health insurance, *en masse* from a commercial insurance company without a medical examination and at a low cost, because the company collects the employees' premiums and also generally contributes something toward the cost.

The least satisfactory forms of company welfare from the point of view of employee security are stock-ownership, profit-sharing,

[1] R. F. Foerster, *op. cit.*, p. 508.

[2] For a further discussion of credit unions, *cf.* Helen Baker, *Employee Savings Programs, An Analysis of Recent Trends*, Industrial Relations Section, Princeton University, 1937, pp. 33–37.

and company pension plans where the company fails to set aside funds to make the pension plan financially sound. A thorough study in 1932 showed that only eight per cent of the 2,700,000 workers then covered by company pension plans were under plans "in which the guarantees were both actuarially and financially sound." [1] In addition, employees generally had to be with the firm at least 20 years before they were eligible for a pension, and less than 10 per cent of all factory workers remain with one company that long. Profit-sharing plans have had a high mortality rate in this country, and have generally failed as an incentive to workers or as an answer to the demand for a wage increase.[2] In large firms a wage-earner generally finds it difficult to relate his own efforts directly to the profits of the company. Because profits usually fluctuate, a profit-sharing scheme tends to cause the incomes of employees to fluctuate in the same way, which is likely to increase the economic insecurity of wage-earners.

The record of employee stock-ownership plans has been as bad as that of profit sharing, which it so closely resembles. Of 50 representative plans established prior to 1929 in companies with over 2,000,000 employees, 41 had been discontinued, and only 4 were definitely known to be in existence, by 1940.[3] Out of these 50 companies, comparable price records were available for the period between 1929 and 1933 for 18 preferred and 17 common stocks sold to employees under stock-purchase plans. The median price of those 35 stocks dropped from 115 in July 1929 to 15 in July 1932.[4] As these figures indicate, stocks may be very poor investments for wage-earners. Especially is it undesirable for an employee to invest his funds in the firm with which he is employed, for such a policy concentrates his risks and decreases his security. With all his eggs in one company basket, his attitude toward the company is likely to turn to one of resentment if and when that basket breaks. The losses sustained by employees under stock-purchase plans were large during the 1930's despite the fact that

[1] M. W. Latimer, *op. cit.*, p. 876.

[2] For a further discussion of profit sharing, *cf.* C. Canby Balderston, *Profit Sharing for Wage Earners*, 1937.

[3] For a discussion of these 50 plans, *cf.* Eleanor Davis, *Employee Stock Ownership and the Depression*, Industrial Relations Section, Princeton University, 1933. Recent data on these 50 firms have been supplied to the author by the Section. No data were available on five of the plans for the last seven or eight years.

[4] *Ibid.*, p. 7.

the stock was frequently sold to the employees at a favorable price or with a company contribution toward the cost of the stock.[1]

Some idea of the significance of various company welfare and personnel programs may be gained from Table 37, which summarizes the data gathered from 2,452 establishments with over 4,500,000 employees in 1935. From the employer's point of view, plans that increase the dependence of the employee upon the company may be definitely desirable as a way of reducing labor turnover and tying the employee more firmly to the company. Programs for sickness or accidents, which demonstrate their value to the employee by paying him benefits a number of times, may be especially good for developing employee "loyalty" to the firm. Death benefits or dismissal compensation, on the other hand, can only "pay" their way if they favorably affect the morale of the remaining employees rather than those directly receiving the benefits.[2]

TABLE 37. PREVALENCE OF WELFARE AND PERSONNEL ACTIVITIES, 1935[3]

Activity	Percentage of reporting firms
Medical program	65
Group insurance	59
Loans to employees	44
Athletic teams	41
Pensions	37
Mutual benefit association	28
Savings plan	16
Dismissal compensation	13
Credit union	11
Relief fund	11
Stock-purchase plan	7
Profit sharing	5
Time and motion study	27
Suggestion system	23
Job analysis	18
Rating systems for wage-earners	12

On the whole, the enactment of the Social Security Act in 1935 and the Federal relief programs in the 1930's tended to reduce the importance of company welfare programs and the amount of

[1] For a review of recent experience with employee stock ownership, *cf*. Helen Baker, *op. cit.*, pp. 24–29.

[2] For further discussion of dismissal compensation, *cf*. Everett D. Hawkins, *Dismissal Compensation: Voluntary and Compulsory Plans Used in the United States and Abroad*, 1940.

[3] Data from *What Employers Are Doing for Employees*, National Industrial Conference Board, 1936, Appendix.

company welfare work in certain lines.   Because public welfare programs do not "pay" the company in the form of publicity and employee "loyalty," large corporations have favored company welfare and "paternalism" rather than state welfare and "paternalism." Organized labor has, of course, preferred public programs because they increase labor mobility between firms, decrease the control of the employer over his employees, and make the employees more independent.   Benefits under public programs are not related to length of service with one firm or to the depth of the employee's loyalty to a company. Labor also prefers public "handouts" to private "handouts" because they are more certain, if not more adequate.   The program of Federal Old-Age and Survivors Insurance Benefits has restored some company pension plans to solvency and caused many firms to insure their plans with insurance companies in a way that will give their retiring employees supplementary benefits in addition to those they receive under the Federal program.

Employment regularization.   A company with trade-marked products or in a monopolistic position may seek to influence the purchases of dealers and consumers of its output so that it is able to offer steadier employment to its employees.   It is especially easy for firms producing stable, storable articles for direct consumption, like soap or electric light bulbs, to regularize employment.   Fairly stable employment for individual employees may have a favorable effect upon employee morale or "loyalty" and help to keep the firm's working force intact.   Since all firms are competing for the consumer's dollar, however, more security for some employees may mean less security for others unless somehow all buyers of both consumption and capital goods are induced to distribute their expenditures more evenly over a period of time.

Among the devices that an individual firm may use to stabilize its employment are: (1) changes in purchasers' buying habits by such means as advertising, new styles, or the establishment of direct retail outlets by a manufacturing firm in order to eliminate the speculative purchases of middlemen; (2) production for inventory, or the construction of capital improvements, during slack periods; and (3) the development of side lines or "fillers" in order to reduce the seasonal variation in sales.   Obviously, many firms cannot stabilize employment by such devices.   A company in a

competitive line of business, like bituminous-coal mining or contracting for building construction, cannot change customers'
buying habits or foretell what percentage of the total business in
that line the company will have from time to time. Firms in
service lines and companies producing on order or manufacturing
products that depreciate rapidly because of style changes or deterioration cannot produce for inventory. A company may reduce
the seasonal variation in its sales by offering other articles with
opposite seasonals, such as a coal company selling ice or a manufacturer of farm and garden implements producing sleds; but,
though the introduction of the "filler" article may help to stabilize
the operations of one firm, it is likely to unstabilize or upset the
business of firms that are already offering the article as their chief
product. Indeed, there are numerous cases in which regularization by some firms or industries would accentuate the irregularity
of others.

It is a question whether employment regularization by private
firms is socially desirable, especially during periods of widespread
unemployment. Obviously, from the point of view of the individual
firm and the employees enjoying more stable employment, regularization may be a distinct benefit. A particular company has
little interest in the conservation of labor resources except those
that it employs. An actual case may serve to illustrate possible
differences between individual and social viewpoints in employment regularization.

A plan of employment regularization or "longshore decasualization" through central registration and dispatching was put into
operation in the port of Seattle in the middle of 1921. It involved
strict limitation upon entrance to the occupation, so that the
available work could be conserved for the registered men. The
number of longshoremen registered under the scheme was gradually reduced from 722 in 1922 to 664 in 1929, despite the fact that
"work picked up" and that there was "increased cargo" to handle
during that period.[1] Because the labor supply had been decreased,
the earnings of practically all Seattle longshoremen before 1930
ranged from $1,300 to $2,500 a year. From 1929 to 1934, when

---

[1] The data and quotations dealing with this Seattle plan have been taken from
F. P. Foisie, *Decasualizing Longshore Labor and the Seattle Experience*, Waterfront Employers
of Seattle, February 1, 1934.

the joint plan terminated, no replacements were permitted as men quit or died, with the result that the number of registered workers declined to 525 in 1933 and their employment continued to be fairly steady. The plan was criticized in Seattle on the ground that it did "nothing to relieve the general problem of unemployment" but instead aggravated that problem. The operators of this closed-trade arrangement and the registered workers benefiting from it, however, adopted the attitude that what happened to "outsiders" whose employment opportunities were reduced by the closed employment doors at the waterfront was not their responsibility. In short, they were not concerned with the social effects of a plan that was to their personal benefit.

Employee representation. The top management of large corporations has used employee representation as a device to improve workers' morale and interest in the business, to facilitate the exchange of information between management and the working force, and to increase operating efficiency and the "loyalty" of the employees. In some cases, representation plans have also been a concession by corporate management in order to avoid genuine collective bargaining with the employees. These objectives were to be achieved by having the employees elect representatives who would meet periodically with representatives of the management to settle employees' grievances, to discuss the company's business, and to make suggestions for improving working conditions and production methods.

Election of employee representatives and joint conferences with management representatives may help to interest employees in the problems of the management and give them a feeling of participation in the affairs of the firm in which they may spend their working lives. Through representative negotiation, employees may enjoy some voice in the determination of company policies, even if the employee representatives serve only in an advisory or consultatory capacity. Settlement of complaints and claims of inequality or discrimination in joint conferences gives the employees an opportunity to obtain a hearing for their grievances from persons higher in authority than their foreman. The elimination of friction and misunderstanding, of course, has a favorable effect upon employee "morale." The recommendations from employee representatives or those received through a suggestion system may help to abolish waste, to lower production costs, and to improve safety and health conditions within the plant. In addition, the employee-representation system may serve as an "educational" device whereby the management can keep the employees better informed about the conditions and facts of the business.

From this discussion of the objectives and advantages of employee representation, it is evident that such plans served to restrict the complete authority of the foremen by requiring them to defend their actions before joint committees. Employee representatives and employee suggestions might "show up" a foreman, and, therefore, tended to stimulate the supervisory force to do a better job. It is easy to understand why foremen frequently lacked enthusiasm for employee-representation plans and why they have sometimes been lukewarm toward union-management cooperation, which is discussed in the next chapter and which in many respects resembles employee representation. Lack of foreman cooperation has often proved the stumbling block for employee-management cooperative ventures.

The companies adopting employee representation have generally been large integrated corporations with relatively low labor costs per unit of output. In such firms, there is little personal relationship between the top officials and the common employees, and the continued efficient operation of the plant and equipment is an important factor because of heavy overhead costs. A survey in November 1932 showed that three fourths of the workers in employee-representation plans were under plans covering 10,000 or more employees.[1] Indeed, there has been a definite tendency for companies to change from individual dealing to employee representation with an increase in the size of the firm. A survey in May 1934 of labor-relations procedures in about 3,000 firms in manufacturing and mining with over 2,500,000 employees showed that in establishments with less than 200 wage-earners approximately 79 per cent of the workers were dealing with their employers individually, 13 per cent through employee representatives, and 8 per cent through labor unions. For establishments with between 200 and 10,000 wage-earners the figures were: 55 per cent of all wage-earners dealing individually with their employers, 30 per

---

[1] *Cf. Collective Bargaining through Employee Representation*, National Industrial Conference Board, 1933, Table 2, p. 17.

cent through employee representatives, and 15 per cent through labor unions. In establishments with over 10,000 wage-earners, only 14 per cent of all employees were dealing individually and 4 per cent through trade-unions, compared with 82 per cent operating under employee-representation plans.[1]

Generally speaking, the employee-representation plans established prior to 1933 were not found in isolation but were part of a group of industrial-relations policies, including various welfare programs. It was sometimes said that the gains to the company from employee representation were shared with the employees through the company's contribution to the various welfare plans. It is worth noting that there were few attempts to share those "gains" in the form of increased wage rates, for such action might cause other companies either to object or to raise their rates by the same amount, thus establishing higher "prevailing" wage rates.

There were but few scattered instances of employee-representation plans in this country before the first World War. The National War Labor Board promoted the establishment of employee committees in various firms and industries, but many of the shop committees established under the awards of the Board disappeared after its power ceased, following the Armistice in 1918. A series of surveys made by the National Industrial Conference Board show that the number of workers covered by employee-representation plans increased from about 400,000 in 1919 to 1,241,000 in 1924 and 1,548,000 in 1928.[2] With the enactment of the National Industrial Recovery Act in June 1933, promising workers freedom to organize and bargain collectively through their chosen representatives without employer interference, the number of employee-representation plans increased until by April 1935 it was estimated that 2,500,000 workers were covered by such plans.[3] A November 1933 study of some 650 companies, with representation plans covering more than 1,000,000 employees, showed that over three fifths of the plans had been established within the five months following the enactment of the National Industrial Recovery Act.[4]

---

[1] Calculated from data in *Individual and Collective Bargaining in May, 1934*, National Industrial Conference Board, 1934, Table 2, p. 13.

[2] *Collective Bargaining through Employee Representation*, p. 16.

[3] A. L. Bernheim *et al.*, *Labor and Government*, Twentieth Century Fund, 1935, p. 79.

[4] *Individual and Collective Bargaining under the N.I.R.A.*, National Industrial Conference Board, November 1933, Table 6, p. 24.

The advocates of employee representation have been wont to refer to it as "collective dealing," "collective negotiation," or the "collective expression of employee opinion" rather than as collective bargaining. As a bargaining device, such plans have many shortcomings. The employee representatives usually are not specialists in bargaining; they know little about conditions elsewhere; and, as employees of the firm, they cannot be too aggressive for fear of discrimination by the management. An employee-representation plan or company union[1] cannot send organizers to low-wage areas and force backward employers to adopt the labor standards of more reputable firms. Because such plans cannot prevent competition in labor standards, they are unable to equalize labor costs throughout the whole area of competitive production unless the company itself enjoys a monopoly. The limited membership base of company unions thus sharply restricts the possibility of using them to raise wages or to shorten hours. If a company union went on strike, as some of them did, it would generally be without strike funds, the expert advice of experienced strike leaders, and the moral or financial support of workers in other firms or industries. Indeed, the company union cannot effectively use such weapons of organized labor as the boycott, the label, craft protective regulations, or limitations upon learning the trade, although it is true that some company unions have enjoyed the closed shop or a check-off arrangement with the employer. Consequently, the company union lacks effective control over the labor market. Furthermore, such organizations have no political or social program and do not have legislative agents to press for laws favorable to labor. Obviously, the company union is defective as a means of equalizing bargaining power between wage-earners and employers.

Prior to 1935 the managements of companies generally drafted, introduced, and lent financial or other support to, employee-representation plans, and also retained final authority over all matters covered by the plan. However, by the 1934 amendments to the Railway Labor Act and by the National Labor Relations Act, employers in interstate commerce are forbidden to interfere with, support, or dominate a labor organization used for collective

[1] These two terms are used interchangeably and refer to the same general pattern of employer-employee relationships.

bargaining on rates of pay, hours, or other conditions of employment. Consequently, former employee-representation plans have either been abandoned or converted into "independent" unions or employee associations, which have a constitution and bylaws, are generally financed by the collection of dues from members, and may have a collective labor agreement with the plant, company, or companies included in their coverage. As indicated at the end of Chapter 21, a number of these revamped company unions have been designated as collective-bargaining agents after winning employee elections held by the National Labor Relations Board.

In this country, organized labor has opposed employee representation as company unionism designed to restrict the growth of "genuine" labor unions. Organized labor has not, however, objected to shop committees when they were not used to undermine the unions. In England and other European countries, works councils or joint councils have been established by the managements of individual firms, not in opposition to labor unions, but as a sort of supplementary device for large companies in dealing with problems outside the scope of collective labor agreements. Such machinery for joint consultation at regular intervals has performed some of the advisory functions of employee representation in this country. In England, for example, it has been used to settle grievances, to make suggestions for improving work methods, to consider questions of safety and employee welfare, and to provide a channel for explaining to the employees the problems of the management and the condition of the business.[1] A plan that was strictly confined to such functions would not run counter to the National Labor Relations Act in this country.

Scientific management. Attempts have been made to solve some labor problems by "scientific" methods, such as job analysis, time-and-motion study, and rating systems for wage-earners. Through research and the "analytical approach" of scientific management, certain groups, especially industrial engineers and "efficiency experts," have hoped to establish "objective" standards of job performance, which would determine the way that the work should be done and the exact amount that each worker should

---

[1] Cf., for example, J. Henry Richardson, *Industrial Relations in Great Britain*, International Labour Office, 1938 (second edition), pp. 155–70.

accomplish in a certain period. Employers have introduced such "scientific" methods into their plants in order to obtain more for their payroll dollars through increased efficiency.

Unfortunately for the advocates of scientific management, there is no "scientific" formula for determining the exact wage rate that should be paid for each job done according to the "standard of performance." Scientific management still leaves the wage issue wide open to dispute. Furthermore, scientific management cannot, through research, determine how much voice in the operation of industry wage-earners should enjoy. It does not solve the problem of industrial democracy. Employees may be even more efficient under a discipline they help to impose upon themselves than under one handed down from on high. Finally, scientific management is unable to fix a standard of performance that will have no effect upon the length of working life. The speed-up reduces the lifetime earnings of workers not only because it may have bad effects upon the worker's health but also because it may reduce the job opportunities of older workers who cannot maintain the pace. It may cause a reduction in the firm's demand for labor. In short, scientific management cannot settle many "human" problems in industry which involve personal judgment and social values. Are increased efficiency and output socially desirable if they can be achieved only at the expense of making workers into mere industrial automatons?

Other practices. Individual employers may resort to other antiunion practices such as "yellow-dog" contracts, in which employees agree not to join a union as a condition of employment; or discrimination against union members, including the use of black lists; or court injunctions to enforce yellow-dog contracts or to prevent threatened actions by unions; or control of local public officials and the police, especially in company towns; or closure of the plant in a lockout of employees for the purpose of discouraging labor organization; or movement of the business to a nonunion locality; or wage increases to stimulate employee "loyalty" to the company. In case of a strike, the management may hire strikebreakers and guards,[1] pay high wages to employees leading back-

---

[1] The type of persons who become professional strike-breakers or guards and who, in some cases, have been deputized by the local police in order to preserve "law and order," is indicated by an episode that occurred during the 1936 elevator strike in New

to-work movements, offer sums to employees if they merely enter the plant, and carry on a publicity campaign against the strikers. The legal restrictions on such antiunion practices are discussed in Chapter 25.

The reader himself can further explore and analyze the social implications of the various policies and practices pursued by employers and employers' associations. Undoubtedly some mal-distribution of economic resources may be involved (1) in expenditures for labor espionage, "educational" or publicity campaigns, and welfare offensives; (2) in such practices as the black-listing of workers, discrimination against union members, or employers' boycotts against firms failing to follow antiunion labor policies; and (3) in the migration of industry for the purpose of avoiding certain labor standards or some measure of democracy in industry.

York City. As several hundred guards were being hired in a New York "fink" agency, word got around amongst the waiting horde of applicants that each man was to be fingerprinted. In the stampede for the exit, two men were severely injured.

CHAPTER TWENTY-FOUR

UNION–MANAGEMENT COOPERATION

This chapter deals with a number of experiments in cooperation between unions and management for the benefit of both labor and capital. Stockholders were to benefit through the elimination of waste, the conservation of materials and mechanical energy, and a reduction in labor costs from more economical methods of manufacture. Labor was to gain by improved working conditions, larger earnings, and more stable employment for the firm's working force. The significant cases of union-management cooperation in this country have arisen from a desire to convince the employer that the union is to his advantage. In a sense, such plans for cooperation have represented the answer of organized labor to employer schemes for employee representation, employee suggestions, and scientific management. Union-management cooperation has been designed to accomplish through union channels some of the objectives of such management schemes.

Admittedly the programs have often been somewhat vague, but they deal primarily with production problems.[1] They generally do not give the union representatives any voice in price or selling policies, nor do they deal with hours and wage levels. Under union-management programs the workers do, however, obtain some additional voice and influence with regard to operating methods and conditions within the workshop. The workers make suggestions for improving production, and scientific methods of management may be introduced under the joint auspices of the union and the management, so that the union has some influence or control over the way that changes are made in production techniques. In practically all instances, however, the company officials retain the power to veto any suggested changes for reasons of expense or managerial policy.

[1] Cf., for example, M. L. Cooke and Philip Murray, *Organized Labor and Production, Next Steps in Industrial Democracy*, 1940.

The discussion in the previous chapter indicated that unions are likely to resist scientific management and time-and-motion study if it is imposed upon the workers in an autocratic manner, not in order to encourage the worker to think about his work and to suggest ways of improving it, but so that the employer may obtain more labor service for his payroll dollar by speeding up operations in his plant. As the president of a national union has said, employees ask of industrial programs, that claim to promote progress or efficiency in a "scientific" manner, such questions as the following:[1] Who will benefit? What effect will it have on our health, jobs, and earnings? Does it increase the chance for creative self-expression and the exercise of intelligence on the job or does it rob the work of its interest and meaning? Their work has an important effect upon employees who spend most of their active hours in industry. The social aspects of industry, especially the effect of work on workers, were stressed by Gerard Swope, former president of the General Electric Company, when he said at a recent meeting of the American Society of Mechanical Engineers: "Although management must stand for efficiency, this is not the factor to be considered. Since industry is part of democracy and a democracy is made up of human beings, the development and education of these human beings, to provide for their growth, happiness, and well being, must be sought." [2] In short, human costs and human considerations are more important than money costs and mechanical efficiency.

Unions must, and do, recognize that, though many of the interests of labor and management are not identical, most of them are interdependent. With such dependency and overlapping of interests, an injury or a benefit to one productive factor in any particular firm is likely to affect the other factor in the same direction, if not to the same degree. For instance, larger sales mean more employment as well as a larger return on capital investment; lower costs and improved quality may result in both higher wages

[1] *Cf.* Spencer Miller, Jr., "Labor's Attitude toward Time and Motion Study," an address delivered before the Society for the Advancement of Management and the Management Section of the American Society of Mechanical Engineers, December 6, 1937, printed by the *American Federationist*, official journal of the American Federation of Labor.

[2] Quoted in Ordway Tead, "Joint Management Research as an Aid to Collective Bargaining," *The Society for the Advancement of Management Journal*, vol. 4 (May 1939), p. 71.

and larger profits. On the other hand, inefficient operations and poor output, especially if the firm is in a competitive industry or is manufacturing branded products having an elastic demand, are likely to mean low wages and bad working conditions. Because employees may be so dependent for their livelihood upon efficient operation of the firm, it is only natural that they should be interested, and want some voice, in the affairs of the enterprise. Pointing out that industry is generally operated on autocratic rather than democratic principles, a report of the British Liberal Party on industry says of the worker:

> While, as a citizen, he has an equal share in determining the most momentous issues, about which he may know very little, in regard to his own work, on which he has knowledge, his opinion is seldom asked or considered, and he has practically no voice in determining the conditions of his daily life, except insofar as trade-union action has secured it. Indeed, where management is inefficient and autocratic he is frequently compelled to watch waste and mistakes of which he is perfectly well aware, without any right of intervention whatever. And this despite the fact that when these errors issue in diminished business for the firm concerned, he and not the management will be the first to suffer, by short-time working or complete loss of employment.[1]

Unions are also interested in output and production problems because the rate of operations is really a basic consideration in any attempt to bargain collectively for the sale of labor services. Output is part of the bargain. As one author has expressed it,

> . . . the labor contract has this curious characteristic, that labor is hired without any precise definition of just what is being bought. A man is hired by the day. But exactly what he shall do in that day, how quickly he shall work, how much he shall produce—these are questions left to a tussle between himself and his foreman. So clumsy an arrangement naturally provokes the worker to conceal what he could do if driven, and management to try and find out.[2]

In an industrial situation open to labor exploitation, workers will strive to guard against selling their labor cheaply by giving more services for the same pay.

The interdependence of labor and management also appears in the question of operating efficiency. Efficiency depends in part

---

[1] *Britain's Industrial Future, being the Report of the Liberal Industrial Inquiry*, 1928, p. 148.
[2] J. Raymond Walsh, *C.I.O., Industrial Unionism in Action*, 1937, pp. 231–32.

upon the attitude of workers toward their work, especially where the job involves some handwork and where workers are not paced by machinery. Advocates of union-management cooperation state that it elicits a morale that makes for efficiency, and that workers can contribute to improvements in operating methods through the knowledge and experience they gain from handling the machinery and materials. Pointing to the relationship between efficiency and consent, they maintain that there are two types of discipline: discipline by authority or dictatorship, under which orders from the top are to be accepted and followed without question; and the discipline that arises out of consent and cooperation. The latter type necessitates some sort of representative system, whereby workers can help to establish standards of work and suggest methods of operation. The proponents of union-management cooperation insist that a worker will want to live up to work standards that he himself helps to set and agrees with. They also explain that the union itself can serve as an agency for disciplining the workers where the employer accepts the union and deals with it in a friendly fashion.

It is claimed that union-employer cooperation reduces employee resistance to changes in industrial methods. Employees are naturally suspicious of sudden changes which they do not understand and concerning which they have not been consulted. With no opportunity to participate in a discussion of proposed changes or to cooperate in introducing new methods, workers may fear that their interests will suffer from the change. In some cases of union-management cooperation, on the other hand, the unions have relaxed their rules and protective regulations designed to safeguard the security of individual workers. The problem of employee security is, however, fundamental in any plan for cooperation between management and the union for the purpose of improving efficiency and eliminating waste. Workers will not be interested in labor-saving methods that are likely to result in elimination of their jobs. Economic insecurity, especially mass unemployment, causes workers to react against labor-reducing methods and devices. Why should workers worry about minutes wasted in the plant when, outside, millions of man-years are going to waste because of unemployment? The problem of securing trade-union cooperation to improve efficiency in production depends not only upon trade-union policy and employers' attitudes toward unionism but also upon provisions for economic security for individual workers.

Practically all of the experiments here discussed were started during the prosperous years of the 1920's, when certain AFL unions tried so hard to interest employers in cooperation. During the depression years of the 1930's there was a lull in the enthusiasm for such cooperative programs. Economists pointed out the need for nationwide programs, explaining that individual-firm or one-industry attacks upon such labor problems as unemployment rested upon too narrow a base. With specialization and the interdependency of firms and industries, improvements in efficiency confined to a single occupation, firm, or industry may work to the disadvantage of the participating workers by reducing their hours of employment. Where a group of workers faces an inelastic demand for its collective services, only a cooperative program on a wide scale can prevent a reduction in employees' earnings as a result of increased efficiency under union-management cooperation. So far all experiments with such cooperation have been on a one-firm basis; none of them have been on a national or even an industry-wide basis. In the outstanding cases of union-management cooperation, the employees concerned have faced fairly elastic demand schedules for their services because of the nature of the competition from nonunion employers.

In considering union-management cooperation it is necessary to bear in mind a number of facts. In the first place, labor is not responsible for many kinds of inefficiency and waste, such as bad scheduling, faulty design, misjudgment of markets, excessive overhead, or similar forms of mismanagement. Indeed, a committee of 15 engineers named by Herbert Hoover in 1921 found, from a statistical study of some 200 plants in six industries, that "over 50 per cent of the responsibility" for waste in those plants lay at the door of management and "less than 25 per cent at the door of labor," while the amount chargeable against the public, trade relationships, and other outside factors was smaller still except in textile manufacturing.[1] Those six industries included

---

[1] Committee on Elimination of Waste in Industry, *Waste in Industry*, Federated American Engineering Societies, 1921, p. 9. One may wonder how these engineers were able from their field studies to allocate the responsibility, part of which must have been psychological, between productive agents, but the general proportions they give are probably fairly correct.

building and printing, both of which were highly unionized. In the second place, cooperation between management and labor is occurring in various branches of industry all the time without any formal plan. Economic circumstances and employer attitudes are generally more important than written agreements in fostering such cooperation. In the third place, successful cooperation between the union and management is impossible as long as the union leaders distrust the management and fear that it may try to undermine the union. Cooperation requires good faith on both sides.

Finally, it is necessary to recognize that the interests of labor and capital may conflict on certain matters, so cooperation in production problems does not eliminate the need for collective bargaining to settle such issues as the level of wages, hours of work, and the speed of operations, which cannot be decided by "scientific" tests or formulas. The union must strike a balance between cooperation and bargaining. If the union officials become too management-minded, they may fail to represent and protect the interests of their constituents, and consequently be repudiated and replaced by more radical leaders. A case in which that very thing happened is discussed in the following sections dealing with the experience with union-management cooperation in certain industries.

On the railroads. Between 1923 and 1926, plans for union-management cooperation were introduced on four American railroads (the Baltimore and Ohio Railroad, the Canadian National Railways, the Chicago and North Western Railway, and the Chicago, Milwaukee, St. Paul and Pacific Railroad) having about one sixth of the total combined railroad mileage in the United States and Canada. In each instance, the program was started in the shops of the maintenance of equipment department where cars and locomotives are repaired or rebuilt. Later the "B. and O." plan was extended to the maintenance-of-way and transportation (train) departments of the Baltimore and Ohio, and in 1929 the Canadian National's plan was expanded to include the employees of the maintenance-of-way department—the fellows who one wag claims spend their time getting on and off the tracks and watching the trains go by.

There are special reasons why cooperation started in the railroad repair shops at that particular time. The defeat of the railroad shop crafts in the 1922 strike had left many railroads with company unions and had put the seven shop-craft unions in a frame of mind especially favorable to the adoption of union-management cooperation, which could serve as a countermove to employee-representation plans. Work efficiency had become so low in some shops that many railroads during and after the strike "contracted out" much of the repair work on their rolling stock rather than having it done in their own shops. Such practices, of course, increased the insecurity or irregularity of employment of the members of the shop-craft unions. In short, they were facing the competition of the company union, and their members were facing the competition of repair work in factories which were likely to be nonunion. It is interesting to note that the "Big Four" Brotherhoods in the engine and train service, which did not face those two forms of competition and had not been party to the 1922 strike, took only a passing interest in the cooperation plans advocated by the shop-craft unions.

Not only were the workers in the railway shops anxious to obtain steady employment with the companies, but the railroads, with considerable investment in repair-shop facilities, were, of course, interested in restoring efficiency in shops disorganized by the strike. Expenses for maintaining equipment were accounting for about one fourth of the railroads' total operating expenses. The Chicago, Milwaukee, St. Paul and Pacific Railroad was especially anxious to remedy the laxity of discipline and friction between men and management, which were obstructing output in some of its shops, because the system had just gone into receivership.[1] In the case of the government-owned Canadian National Railways there was a special need to obtain the political support of organized labor for this experiment in railroad nationalization.

Programs of union-management cooperation on the railroads have been influenced in their development by a trained engineer, Otto S. Beyer, who, as technical adviser first to the Machinists' union and then to the Railway Employees' Department of the AFL, helped to establish union-management cooperation on all of the railroads mentioned except the Chicago, Milwaukee, St. Paul and Pacific. He introduced the technique of joint em-

[1] Louis A. Wood, *Union-Management Cooperation on the Railroads*, 1931, pp. 100–101.

ployee-management committees for discussing constructive suggestions submitted by workers and management. He was insistent that these joint committees deal only with practical plant operating methods, concerning which both sides might have common interests, and not with employee grievances or with terms of employment. The situation in the first shop in which union-management cooperation was tried early in 1923 has been explained as follows by Beyer:

> . . . basically two things were wrong: (1) the shop, for better or worse, had got the reputation of not being efficient. Consequently, whenever economy was in order, that was the first place shut down, despite the fact that the railroad company had a good many million dollars invested in it. The shut-downs harmed management-employee relationships. (2) the other troublesome thing, more fundamental in nature than the first, was that the local management looked upon the union and the union [grievance] committee as a nuisance which it had to put up with. Under those circumstances the management decided to give the union no more than it had to.[1]

In proposing union-management cooperation, the union leaders hoped to convince the management that the union was to its advantage.

Experience with union-management cooperation on the railroads since the middle 1920's has indicated that both the companies and the workers may benefit from it. The plan in most cases improved the quality of the work and also managerial efficiency by stimulating officials to make improvements in order to forestall worker suggestions that would reflect upon them. It also generally resulted in a great reduction in the number of grievances, by affording workers a chance to call attention to unsatisfactory conditions before they became grievances. There is no doubt that the suggestions of the workers resulted in considerable savings to the companies, although often the gains could not be measured and some of them might have been achieved without the plan. Many of the suggestions were fairly technical. For example, it was suggested that air-operated jacks be substituted for hydraulic ones, which saved enough labor to reduce

[1] Otto S. Beyer, "Collective Cooperation by Management and Labor," in *Collective Bargaining and Cooperation*, Bureau of Industrial Relations, University of Michigan, Bulletin No. 8, 1938, p. 56.

lifting costs by $12 to $30 per car undergoing repairs.[1] A suggestion that the bands supporting the air drums of locomotives be hinged also saved several hours of labor in certain repair operations.

That union-management cooperation has brought forth a large number of suggestions from employees, especially the committee members, is indicated by the statistical record for the various railroads. During the first 12 years that the plan was in operation in the B. and O. shops, 9,089 meetings were held on company time and a total of 28,248 suggestions were made, of which 86 per cent were adopted and the rest were dropped as impractical or were postponed because the expense involved was not deemed justified at the time.[2] During the first five years of the plan on the Canadian National Railways, over 13,000 suggestions were made, of which four fifths were brought up by employees and about 82 per cent were adopted.[3] Figures for the shops of the Chicago and North Western Railway tell a similar story. A report of the maintenance-of-way section of the Canadian National shows that, during the first nine years of the "cooperative movement" (1930–1938), a total of 15,714 suggestions were offered, of which 77 per cent were proposed by the employee representatives and two thirds were adopted.[4] The record shows a steady decline in the number of suggestions from 4,017 in 1930 to 1,432 in 1936, after which the yearly total tended to level off.

The railroad employees gained from the cooperative plan in a number of ways. Many of their suggestions resulted in more wholesome working conditions within the shops and reduced the hardships connected with their work. By encouraging the management to bring more work into the shops, the yearly earnings of the men were increased and their employment became more regular or steady. The Chicago and North Western Railway for the first time began to build an order of new cars in their own shops and, as the general foreman stated, the employees were determined to

---

[1] L. A. Wood, *op. cit.*, p. 203.

[2] "B. and O.'s Famous Cooperative Plan Is Twelve Years Old This Year—And Still Going Strong," *Baltimore and Ohio Magazine*, vol. 22 (October 1936), p. 9.

[3] *Studies on Industrial Relations III*, International Labour Office, Studies and Reports, Series A, No. 38, 1935, p. 15.

[4] *Seventh Annual Report* and *Ninth Annual Report*, Canadian National Railways, Union-Management Co-operative Movement, Maintenance-of-Way Section, May 17, 1937 and August 16, 1939 (mimeographed).

build those 600-odd cars as cheaply as they could have been constructed in a factory. The Canadian National Railways decided to give the cooperating shopmen a supplementary wage of two cents an hour. When the Canadian Pacific Railway Company vigorously objected to such a separate wage increase, the Canadian National, in order to avoid having to withdraw from the Railway Association of Canada, dropped the supplementary-wage plan and granted its shopmen in Canada one week's vacation with pay—the first vacations with pay ever given on a North American railroad.[1] Recognition of the workers' importance on the job and the consideration given to their ideas about operating the shop had, in some cases, significant effects upon their morale and self-respect. The union shop committee in several B. and O. shops took such an interest in operations that discipline in those shops was left largely to the union, and the managements of all the railroads adopting the plan were less concerned with administering discipline. The shop-craft unions gained from their preferred positions, so that they encountered fewer difficulties in organizing the men and union membership received a great stimulus.

The cooperative programs on the railroads also met with apathy and hostility. Local bosses, accustomed to absolute authority in the shops, often regarded suggestions from the employees both as a threat to their prestige or power and as a reflection upon their foremanship. Such foreman opposition was sometimes accompanied by a lack of interest on the part of the employees and nonattendance of committee members at joint meetings. In time the list of suggestions tended gradually to diminish in size,[2] perhaps because the workers feared that reduced employment might follow labor-saving improvements during a depression or because, as one union leader on the B. and O. said, some of the "fellows feel that cooperation is purely and simply a movement to benefit the management."

The problem of how to share the gains from cooperation in a fair manner continued unsolved. The workers were convinced, and railroad management was generally ready to admit, that the companies received more of the economic benefits flowing from the suggestion-technique of cooperation than did the men.[3] Especially on the B. and O. were the employees disappointed and

[1] Wood, *op. cit.*, pp. 240–41, 248–49.   [2] *Cf. ibid.*, p. 313.   [3] *Ibid.*, pp. 235–37.

resentful because the high hopes of financial benefits, raised by prophecies of the large gains to be shared, failed to materialize. The Canadian National was the only railroad system that unequivocally acknowledged that a surplus had accrued through cooperation, a share of which should go to the employees.[1] Wages on the railroads practicing cooperation were no higher than on other roads, partly because of combined and uniform action by railroads on wages and partly because even the shop-craft unions desired to keep the system of cooperation outside the area covered by collective bargaining, including wage rates and other craft issues.[2]

In clothing and textiles. Certain industries, like men's clothing or textile and hosiery manufacture, consist of a large number of small producing units that are widely scattered geographically and are all in competition with one another. In such highly decentralized and competitive industries, the unions are often forced to become interested in problems of production and management in order to meet competition in the form of products made in nonunion shops.

1. *The Amalgamated Clothing Workers.* This union has a dozen or more technical experts who advise with the management on problems of organization, operations, and quality of product. The president of the Amalgamated said in 1938: "We maintain a large research bureau and a technical staff that is constantly at the service of employers. We have helped many manufacturers to introduce efficiency methods because, in doing so, we knew we were helping our members by enabling their employers to stay in business on a competitive basis." [3] A few cases will illustrate how the union has increased its organization of the industry by assisting union employers and inducing other employers to accept the union in order to enjoy the benefits of its knowledge of the industry.

In 1925 the A. Nash Company of Cincinnati invited the union to organize its employees because it wanted the Amalgamated to reorganize production methods and improve the quality of the product, which had fallen off with the rapid growth of the company's business and the inefficiency that had developed. In an

---

[1] *Ibid.*, p. 242.   [2] *Ibid.*, p. 239.
[3] Charles B. Coates, "The Union of Tomorrow," *Factory Management and Maintenance*, vol. 96 (September 1938), p. 45.

article published in the Fall of 1927, the president of the company stated that "the Amalgamated brought experts from various markets and have rendered a service which can never be figured in dollars and cents in raising to a high quality and standardizing the production of this company." [1]

The chairman of the board of directors of one of the country's largest and most respected clothing houses stated in 1939 that he would never want to return to the open shop that had existed in his firm until 1934. Pointing out that the relations between the management and the union had been most harmonious, he added that on one occasion the union sent its technical adviser for consultation with the company on a problem of production and the service rendered by this technician had been most valuable to the company.[2]

In a number of other cases in various cities, the union has been active in discovering sources of waste and in reducing costs, always insisting that "unnecessary overhead, exorbitantly high salaries, undue selling expenses, excessive cost of supervision, unnecessary clerical expense, must be found and reduced." [3] In one instance, when a firm was refused further credit by its bank because of its financial condition, one of the union's banks came to the company's rescue with a substantial loan that was later repaid.

The Amalgamated Clothing Workers of America in 1924 entered a cooperative agreement, known as the X-Construction Plan, with the clothing factories of the Hart, Schaffner and Marx Company of Chicago. Under this plan, which remained in force for several years, the union assumed responsibility for the major part of the production process, namely, the tailoring of the garments from the cut cloth. Collective bargaining involved only the price of the finished product, so that the union itself determined the various piece rates and shared in the control of industrial and business policies, which relieved the company of considerable responsibility for certain normal managerial functions. Under joint labor-management auspices, production costs were reduced by a more minute subdivision of labor, the substitution of machine for hand operations, improvements in routing material through the plants,

---

[1] *Handbook of Labor Statistics, 1929 Edition*, U. S. Bureau of Labor Statistics, Bulletin No. 491, 1929, p. 488.

[2] From the files of the Industrial Relations Section, Princeton University.

[3] *Handbook of Labor Statistics, 1929 Edition, op. cit.*, p. 487.

and a reduction in the number of styles, all of which enabled the company to meet customers' style requirements at smaller costs for labor. Substitution of team methods and machine work for costly handwork required that the employees relinquish certain customs and rules restricting output. In return, they expected to be compensated by a gain in the volume of available work and in employment security, as a result of increased sales from lower costs and selling prices for the product. Regarding experience under the plan, the editor of the union's weekly paper has written:

The larger objective of the experiment was to stabilize employment by supporting a large-scale industrial enterprise against the reckless competition of non-cooperating employers. Yet the union could not logically withhold its cooperation from other manufacturing concerns, however keen their competitive practices, if they agreed to deal with labor on a union basis. Hence only one objective, stabilization of employment conditions, was met, and that only in part; the major objective, that of defeating reckless competition, was not achieved.[1]

2. *The Naumkeag Steam Cotton Company.* This Massachusetts firm produces a fine quality of bed sheets and pillow cases, and it employed about 2,500 workers in 1927. After a strike in 1919, the company accepted the closed shop and joint settlement of grievances, and later agreed to provisions for departmental seniority. An industrial union, a local of the United Textile Workers of America (then AFL), covered all workers except those in a small well-knit craft union of loom fixers, which consistently refused to participate in the joint cooperative program. Working conditions at the company's mills had been exceptionally good, and wages had long been well above the average level for the industry. The company's plant and equipment were highly efficient, but its operating methods and the working rules of the union had tended to result in fairly high labor costs.[2]

By 1927 increasing competition had impressed the management with the need for operating economies. In that year the union agreed to carry on a campaign to sell the company's union-made products and to "cooperate in effecting economies in manufacturing." Periodic conferences were held between the union

---

[1] J. B. S. Hardman, "Labor-Capital Cooperation," *The Encyclopaedia of Social Sciences,* 1932, vol. 8, p. 628.

[2] Most of the material in this subsection has been taken from R. C. Nyman and E. D. Smith, *Union-Management Cooperation in the "Stretch Out,"* 1934.

officials and the management to discuss policies.   Nevertheless, from 1927 to 1928 the company's sales fell off sharply and its profits declined from 14.5 to 3.6 per cent on the stockholders' equity in the firm.[1] In the face of such figures, the management proposed to follow the policy of other textile firms and reduce costs by "stretching out" the number of looms per weaver from an average of 13 to 24, which would have meant the dismissal of about 250 persons.

This proposal brought on a crisis, in which a strike was averted only by an agreement in February 1929 providing for research by an outside engineer, who presumably was to help both sides to discover the proper number of looms per weaver on the basis of scientific management. This engineer and his staff were to work under the direction of a joint committee of the management and the union. Final acceptance of the results of the engineer's research was left to collective bargaining. In this way, the union hoped to control the change, and it was assured that discharges would be confined as far as possible to "temporary" workers and that all demotions would be according to seniority. At a mass meeting, the workers voted to accept the "stretch-out" on the basis of such an arrangement for "factual analysis" and "joint research." The management accepted the proposal only out of friendly feelings toward the union and a desire to avoid labor trouble. The operating executives were frankly opposed to the arrangement, fearing that the engineering studies might "show them up," and disliking the idea of "outsiders" coming in to upset the methods to which they were accustomed.

At the end of a year of joint research, although the research staff felt that definite action would still be premature, the union and the management decided that sufficient data had been accumulated to indicate that a 20-loom standard would not "overburden" the weavers if they followed the standard operating methods laid down by the engineers. By May 1930 most of the weavers were on a 20-loom average, and by May 1931 the average number of "sides" for most spinners had been increased from 9 to 17. When the stretch-out was fully effective in weaving and spinning departments in the Fall of 1931, it reduced the total number of workers there from 757 to 558. Despite slightly higher average earnings

[1] Financial data on the company in *ibid.*, Appendix, pp. 196–97.

for the remaining workers, joint research was saving the company a sum estimated at $200,000 to $300,000 a year.[1] Both sides seemed well satisfied with the way the change had been accomplished, and the "Naumkeag experiment" was hailed in the press as a major advance in the art of management.

During 1931 discontent with the results of the stretch-out spread among the workers and also the management. The union had been unable to get the company to adopt a plan, suggested by Otto S. Beyer, for a number of subordinate joint committees to educate the foremen and the workers generally by active participation in the plan, as was the case on the railroads. The cooperative activities were mostly confined to a few top persons in the union and the company, so the employee body as a whole did not understand the basis for the changes. As a result, although the workers were at first well pleased under the stretch-out, the foremen failed to insist upon maintenance of the precise standard of operating practices, which had been left largely to their care. Because the standard methods were not fully understood and consistently followed, the work began to seem excessively burdensome. Though worker dissatisfaction grew, it was not aired in union meetings or reported through the existing grievance machinery, because the national-union and the local-union officials had become so strong in their support of the plan—it was being used as part of a textile organizing campaign in the South and had received wide acclaim. Consequently, action was not taken to correct the conditions that were arousing the workers' resentment.

With the industry suffering from price and wage cuts and the general depression, the management found the results of "joint research" too slow and meager to avoid deficits, which occurred in each year from 1930 through 1933. The loss in 1930 was the largest, amounting to 5.6 per cent of the stockholders' investment. Dollar sales in 1931 were little more than half the 1927 figure. In the search for economies, the management, knowing that competing mills were operating on schedules calling for a far larger number of machines per man, felt that the compromise on 20 looms per weaver had been too small. Also, competing mills throughout the cotton textile industry had made two drastic wage reductions, while the Naumkeag Company had maintained its

[1] *Cf. ibid.*, p. 75.

high rates. As the depression deepened, however, operations were curtailed to four days a week, and in January 1932 the company cut wage rates by 10 per cent, which still left Naumkeag's rates perhaps the highest in the industry.

The union had accepted the wage cut only on the condition that "joint research" be discontinued in the mill. Apparently the union leaders sensed the workers' fear that further "stretch-out" research would lead to more unemployment, demotions, and excessive job burdens. The abandonment of joint research caused the workers to suspect that the union leaders had been deceived in accepting it in the first place. If it were not a tool of the management, why were the union officials so anxious to get rid of it? Furthermore, in May 1932 the management asked that the workers accept another 10-per-cent wage cut and the resurrection of joint research. Increasingly adverse economic conditions and price-cutting in the industry were continuing to undermine the competitive position of the company with its high-quality product. A vote of the union members favored a strike rather than acceptance of joint research in addition to a wage cut, which alone went into effect in June 1932. Unfortunately, the company made the mistake of refusing to have the executives share in the wage cut.[1]

Conditions in the industry, however, continued to grow worse. The union officials saw the need for further cost reduction in view of the fact that the company could not help itself without some industry-wide agreement to prevent wage- and price-cutting, which the union had proposed but which was not possible until the passage of the National Industrial Recovery Act in June 1933. Unfortunately, the workers had not been educated to appreciate the real situation, so the union officials actually were closer to the management than to the workers whom they were supposed to represent. The workers felt, especially after the union permitted the introduction of joint research in the company's bleachery in January 1933, that the union was not protecting their interests, and some of them began to accuse the union leaders of "selling out" to the management.

In March 1933 the company proposed the restoration of joint research in the weaving and spinning departments and the adop-

---

[1] *Cf.* Francis Goodell, "Joint Research under a Collective Bargaining Agreement," in *Collective Bargaining for Today and Tomorrow* (ed. by H. C. Metcalf), 1937, p. 70.

tion of 28 looms per weaver. Officials of the national union were called in, and they agreed to a 24-loom standard and the resumption of joint research, with the assurance that no more than 100 workers would be laid off as a result. The union had reversed itself again on the issue of joint research, and the workers struck in defiance of the union and the company. The national union refused to support the strike as a violation of the union's agreement with the company, and radical elements took over the leadership of the strike.

Fortunately for the striking workers, a Code of Fair Competition for the Cotton Textile Industry was adopted in July 1933 under the NIRA, prohibiting further stretch-outs without approval of the code authority and raising wages in the industry so that the competitive pressure for cost reductions at the Naumkeag mills was relieved. In addition, orders for the company's products increased sharply. After the adoption of the code, the two-months' strike was settled on the existing basis of 20 looms per weaver and an agreement to postpone additional stretch-out research for a period of two years. Following the strike, most of the workers resigned from the local of the United Textile Workers and formed a new, independent union. Although recognizing the new union, the management refused to resume relations with it on the cooperative basis formerly accorded to the old union. Union-management cooperation had ended.

This Naumkeag experience indicates the difficulties facing any cooperative program between a union and a company for the purpose of saving labor without some means for protecting the job security of the workers. With the industry suffering from depression and harassed by wage- and price-cutting, it is questionable whether any company-wide cooperative venture to increase output per worker would have worked out satisfactorily for both sides unless somehow the company's sales could have been maintained. Unfortunately, in the Naumkeag case, the plan of cooperation did not involve discussions between workers and minor executives in order to bring them into close touch with the company's problems and to ensure maintenance of the standard operating procedures. As it was, the union officials seemed to the workers to have become so management-minded that the workers sought other leadership. Some errors of judgment by both the union leaders and the management helped to increase the workers' suspicion that the union had become a tool of the company and was no longer an effective agency for collective bargaining.

With the Naumkeag experiment as an example, the United Textile Workers in January 1930 began a campaign to organize the nonunion textile mills in the South.[1] The keynote of the campaign was the AFL policy of union-management cooperation. Federation President William Green made numerous speeches in the South, while a consulting engineer held over 200 conferences in 1930 and 1931 with Southern cotton-mill executives to explain to them the principles of union-management cooperation as they had been worked out in the Naumkeag mills and to offer his assistance in establishing similar plans in their plants after recognition of the union. The net result was that three small firms in Georgia with a total of about 80 employees signed a cooperative union agreement copied directly after the one in effect at the Naumkeag Company. These three firms, none of them in the cotton-textile industry, signed such agreements in order to have the advantage of union support for the sale of their products to workers.

The campaign was successful in obtaining a friendly public opinion for the union, but the Southern millowners failed to see how they could benefit from union-management cooperation, which at Naumkeag required three years to increase the number of looms from 12 to 20 per weaver, whereas they had increased the number from 24 to 48 and 72 per weaver overnight. Union cooperation to them represented a check upon their ability to reduce costs as they pleased. On the other hand, few employees were attracted by the campaign. A program stressing economies and cost reduction was not dramatic and militant enough to appeal to the workers. They feared that under such a plan the union might merely become another agency of exploitation, working hand in glove with the employer.

In coal. Like clothing and textiles, bituminous coal has been a highly competitive industry. Union-management cooperation was tried in this industry in the late 1920's and early 1930's as a means of combatting nonunion competition and providing the coal miners with more job security.

---

[1] Material for this and the following paragraph has been taken from Jean Carol Trepp, "Union-Management Cooperation and the Southern Organizing Campaign," *Journal of Political Economy*, vol. 41 (October 1933), pp. 602–24.

1. *The Rocky Mountain Fuel Company.* Following a strike in which five strikers were killed, Josephine Roche obtained a majority of the stock in this second largest coal company in Colorado, which had been a leader in the opposition to the union. With majority control, Miss Roche reorganized the board of directors and executive departments of the company in March 1928, making John R. Lawson, an officer of the United Mine Workers and president of the Colorado State Federation of Labor, a director and vice president of the company and making Edward P. Costigan, an attorney for the union and later U. S. Senator, general counsel of the company. After urging its employees to join the union, the company signed an agreement stating that the company and the union would undertake "to stabilize employment, production, and markets through cooperative endeavor and the aid of science," to which in 1930 the following clause was added: "recognizing the principle that increased productivity should be mutually shared through the application of equitable considerations to the rights of workers and to economic conditions affecting the operations and business of the company." [1] An attempt was made to induce other coal operators in the state to join in the cooperative movement, but all of them refused to give up their antiunion policy, so the Rocky Mountain Fuel Company was the only union coal operator in Colorado between 1928 and 1933.

The company produces a form of subbituminous coal, which is a clean and easily ignitible fuel well suited for use in homes. A considerable part of its market, therefore, is domestic and highly seasonal. Over 300 coal mines were operating in Colorado in 1931, and during the following depression years competition was sharpened by the opening of many new small mines Because the company's product is, for the most part, consumed locally, it was possible for organized labor in Colorado to carry on a sales campaign, which helped to maintain sales during the depression. Union groups attempted to persuade small businessmen, coal retailers, and public officials to purchase the company's coal, in some cases arguing that the taxpayers had an interest in the company's cooperative labor policy, since they were still paying

---

[1] *Cf.* Mary Van Kleeck, *Miners and Management*, 1934, pp. 248–49. This discussion of cooperation in the Rocky Mountain Fuel Company rests in large measure upon this book.

interest on state bonds issued to defray the cost of putting down a strike. The sales of the company also began to increase on the Pacific slope after three California unions took up the campaign of the Colorado workers. Partly as a result of such sales efforts, the company's share of the total coal tonnage produced in the state increased from 6.5 per cent in 1928 to 11.5 per cent in 1932.[1]

No definite machinery of joint committees was estabished for cooperation at the company's five mines, except for two temporary experiments in 1930 and 1932. The workers did, however, make some suggestions for improving output, and company officials helped to keep them informed about the business. The union officials discussed with the men such matters as the quality of the output. In 1928 the company increased its basic daily wage from $6.77 to $7.00 and agreed to maintain a 23-cent differential above the basic daily wage paid by other operators in the state. These provisions were repeated in the 1930 agreement, although the $7.00 basic rate for day work was higher than that then being paid by any coal mines in the country outside of Montana. In order that the company could continue to pay such wages, the union and the company mutually agreed "to justify the payment of the differential in the wage scale by cooperative effort and increased efficiency." [2] The union promised not to "obstruct or hinder in any way" increased mechanization of the mines or changes in mining methods.[3] Indeed, the union was willing to permit unprecedented flexibility in the application of rules, and it allowed Sunday work to meet nonunion competition.

Some of the results of the cooperative experiment are indicated by the company's production figures. From 1928 to 1930 its output per worker increased from 5.27 tons a day to 6.49 tons, compared with 4.7 tons per worker for all Colorado coal mines in 1930. The company's 1932 output was also much higher per worker than that for the other mines. Administrative and selling expenses were reduced by more than a third between 1928 and 1932. The labor policy of the company helped to stimulate sales by allowing it to guarantee the delivery of coal against interruption by strikes, a promise which nonunion mines did not dare to make. As an indication of how the company stabilized employment, its records show that the percentage of all miners working during

---

[1] *Ibid.*, p. 351.   [2] *Ibid.*, p. 263.   [3] *Ibid.*, pp. 261–62.

each month of the year increased from 12 per cent in 1928 to 64 per cent in 1931.[1] Whereas the average number of days worked by the company's employees in 1928 had been 178 (compared with 188 for all Colorado mines), by 1932 the company's average figures had increased to 192 days (compared with 128 for the whole state). From 1928 through 1932, the average number of men employed by the company remained about the same, and the average earnings of its employees were around $1,660 in both of those years.

This record is all the more remarkable in view of the fact that in the middle of 1931 the nonunion mines began a price war in what was considered an attempt to render the company unable to meet October interest installments on its $3,000,000 debt. The union-recognizing, high-wage policy of the company had aroused the animosity of nonunion interests in the state, resulting in some attempts to have the company boycotted by retail coal dealers. When the company publicly expressed opposition to price-cutting, secret discounts, and wage reductions in the Summer of 1931, as futile acts leading only to a vicious spiral of deflation, the hostility of employer groups in the state was again aroused. The union employees, convinced that an intensive effort was being made by nonunion interests to break the company's agreement with the union, voluntarily offered half of their wages during three months in 1931 as a loan to the company so that it might make the interest payments on its bonded debt issued in 1913. The company accepted this loan of nearly $100,000 from its employees, and later repaid them. During this period other operating companies in the state were forced into receivership, including the largest coal operator in Colorado. In 1931 the workers also accepted a reduction in the basic rate of wages from $7.00 to $5.00 a day, which represented a differential of 25 cents above the wages paid by the company's competitors. Average daily earnings in the company's mines in 1932 were $6.79, compared with $7.97 in 1929 and with $3.00 and $4.00 in many nonunion mines in Colorado.[2]

The passage of the National Industrial Recovery Act in 1933 and the rapid spread of union organization in coal mining thereafter completely changed the competitive situation for the Rocky

[1] *Ibid.*, p. 359.
[2] *Cf.* John R. Lawson, "History of Industrial Struggles in Colorado Coal Mines," *Colorado Labor Advocate*, December 31, 1931, p. 1; and the *Annual Reports* of the company.

Mountain Fuel Company. By the Fall of 1933, practically all of the coal mines in Colorado were unionized, and all of the operators competing with the company had signed agreements with the union, raising their wages to the company's levels.

It was nonunion competition and the friendly attitude of the company toward organized labor that provided the stimulus for union-management cooperation. With the disappearance of its wage differential and its unique position as the only union operator in the state, the company also lost the competitive advantage of labor's active assistance in consumer sales. Organized labor could no longer carry on a campaign to cause buyers to discriminate in favor of the company's product, nor could the union refuse to cooperate with other operators. In this case, as in so many others, the particular firm lost certain advantages when its policies became generalized through adoption by competing companies. That loss was, of course, accompanied by certain competitive gains, such as relatively higher wages for other operators.

Recent examples. In 1938, following the Little Steel strike of the previous year, the Steel Workers Organizing Committee (CIO) proposed that the union employers enter into a program of union-management cooperation as a means of meeting nonunion competition and enabling the union to concentrate upon efforts to organize nonunion employers—also perhaps as a way of getting back at those steel companies whose working forces were disorganized by the strike arising out of refusal to sign written agreements with the union. By 1939 almost a third of the 541 employers having signed agreements with the union were reported to have "concluded or begun negotiations to put into effect in their plants the program" of union-management cooperation outlined by the union in a pamphlet on *Production Problems.*[1] Agreements for union-management cooperation in the steel industry were to contain the following provisions:

1. The union agrees to cooperate with the management in order to reduce costs, enlarge sales, improve quality and in general to advance the interests of the industry.

2. The management agrees to share equitably with the union any benefits so obtained, in the form of increased employment, better work-

[1] *Cf.* Harold J. Ruttenberg, "The Strategy of Industrial Peace," *Harvard Business Review*, vol. 17 (Winter 1939), pp. 175–76.

ing conditions, increased wages or decreased hours. Reduction in seasonal unemployment through employment-regularization methods is suggested.

3. Nobody is to lose his job as a result of any improvement that is installed. If ways are discovered to do more work with less labor, they are to be put in gradually, and then only with the consent of the union. They must be installed in such a way that no discharges are necessary—as, for instance, at a time when sales and output are increasing or when the rate of "quits" or retirements permits staff reductions.

4. The research must be truly joint in every respect.[1]

The union statement goes on to explain that separate research committees should be set up to receive suggestions but not to handle grievances. Factual analysis and standards of work set by joint understanding and democratic procedure should replace arbitrary decisions. Emphasis is placed upon the need to have the workers on the job participate in the discussion of suggestions, so that the improvements will be understood and accepted by the workers concerned. It is also interesting to note that the steel companies themselves recognized the need for educating their foremen in democratic methods and joint procedures. Practically all of the major steel companies with union agreements had provided special training classes for their foremen in 1938 or 1939.[2]

In 1940 this cooperative program was in effect in about a dozen small steel concerns which, with two exceptions, accepted the program under the pressure of economic adversity that left no alternative except bankruptcy.[3] The managements of these firms were induced to cooperate by the company's financial plight. In one case, the recommendations of the union research committee are reported to have resulted in a net saving of $166,200 for the firm during the first year of union-management cooperation.[4]

In December 1938, all branches of the American Stores and Acme Markets in Philadelphia established a joint research board in collaboration with two AFL unions—the Retail Clerks and the Meat Cutters. The plan provides for constructive suggestions from employees, for joint study of various ways to eliminate waste and

[1] *Production Problems*, Steel Workers Organizing Committee, Publication No. 2, 1938, p. 5.

[2] Ruttenberg, *op. cit.*, p. 169.

[3] *Cf.* Harold J. Ruttenberg, "The Fruits of Industrial Peace," *Harvard Business Review*, vol. 18 (Spring 1940), pp. 291–92; and R. R. R. Brooks, *As Steel Goes*, 1940, pp. 213–14.

[4] Philip Murray, "Labor and Responsibility," *Virginia Quarterly Review*, vol. 16 (Spring 1940), p. 273.

improve efficiency, and for "friendly, two-way cooperation." In the same year, the Photo-Engravers' union opened a research department for technical information and study, which offered its services to union employers as well as union members. In some respects, it resembles the engineering service offered by the union of Printing Pressmen to some 500 newspapers published in union shops. At the union's headquarters these newspapers are scanned for defects, and the union may send technicians to correct the trouble without cost to the publisher of the paper. A number of individual firms in various industries have also tried union-management cooperation during the past two decades.

General remarks. Union-management cooperation has never been tried on an industry-wide basis or by a firm with an inelastic demand for the labor of the cooperating employees. Why should a union that has the whole industry organized be anxious to cooperate in joint research to reduce costs, including labor costs? Practically without exception, such labor-capital cooperation has been adopted by individual firms with a fairly elastic demand for labor either because of competition within the industry or because of the practice of contracting out for work. In cases where the firm's labor demand is of such a flexible character, union-management cooperation may furnish employees with larger earnings and more job security. It may also serve as a means of combatting nonunion competition. In such cases, the security of the cooperating workers may be gained largely at the expense of more job insecurity for other workers. Indeed, the stimulus for union-management cooperation has been the competitive individualism of capitalism, and unions have proposed such cooperation when it serves to further their own self-interest.

Strangely enough, successful cooperation is difficult to accomplish. Not only do workers fear that their job security may be reduced by labor-saving methods and that the union may no longer serve their interests in collective bargaining, but foremen generally oppose such plans. Management as well as labor may prevent successful cooperation. Craft unions, of course, would oppose any cooperation that would lead to labor economies by splitting up the craftsman's job. For this reason, the industrial form of unionism lends itself more readily to changes in techniques and methods of production under joint programs.

This discussion of experience with union-management cooperation should have indicated that more is necessary for the success of such programs than the mere desire to cooperate. A program of labor-capital cooperation in production economies is likely to succeed only under certain industrial circumstances and under favorable economic conditions.

CHAPTER TWENTY-FIVE

THE GOVERNMENT IN LABOR RELATIONS

The community as a whole has an interest in industrial relations and labor disputes. Strikes and lockouts may inconvenience many persons by stopping the flow of essential services, such as transportation and electricity, or of essential commodities, like foods and fuel. Work stoppages may also cause the whole community to suffer a large economic loss, while an accompanying boycott may result in economic injury to persons or firms not directly involved in the dispute. Presumably, the government should afford some protection to third parties and prevent the dispute from degenerating into industrial anarchy.

Both sides appeal to the community for its support through business patronage, economic influence, and political pressure upon public officials. Strikes are fought by political as well as economic means, as each group tries to sway public opinion and to obtain favorable action from the governor, the mayor, the police, and the courts. The voting public should presumably be interested in making certain that government officials act with fairness and in the general interest of the community.

Exactly what role the government and the courts should play in economic disputes is still, however, an open question. Although there are laws fixing minimum wages and maximum hours, the final settlement of labor conflicts is left largely to the opposing parties themselves. The courts generally do not attempt to settle the economic issues involved, to decide what wages and hours are fair. The law simply sets limits within which the parties may use their powers of persuasion and economic pressure to gain their objectives. The police and the courts presumably act as a referee in the economic conflict, making certain that both sides obey the law and deal no foul blows, such as acts of violence, breach of the peace, trespass, misrepresentation, fraud, or intimidation.

In attempting to limit the area and methods of economic conflict it is not clear, however, whether the law should seek to equalize the economic strength of both parties in the industrial conflict so that neither side enjoys a decided advantage over the other, or should "simply designate certain economic weapons or actions as illegal in industrial disputes. Some courts seem to be arguing for the equal-balance-of-power theory, for example, in condemning the closed shop because it concentrates excessive and monopolistic power in the hands of those who control the union; yet courts, in deciding labor cases, do not condemn large corporations because they involve a concentration of economic and monopolistic power. Generally, the law and the courts declare certain means and certain ends or purposes to be illegal, regardless of the effect of such legal limitations upon equality of economic and bargaining power. Therefore, "equal protection of the law" for both sides in labor conflicts may be of the sort that Anatole France called attention to when he said that the law forbade both the rich and the poor to sleep under bridges. In industrial disputes, legal restraint upon one side may give positive aid to the other side in the economic contest.

The interest of the community in the continued operation of industry has led the government to establish conciliation services to aid in preventing or shortening strikes. Some laws have aimed at eliminating certain causes of strikes, and other laws have placed restrictions upon the right to strike or to picket. The dramatic character of strikes has, however, given most people an exaggerated notion of their relative importance in our economic life. Statistics show that the apparent loss from strikes and lockouts during the period from 1930 to 1938 was less than one per cent of the economic loss from unemployment during those years.[1] The annual loss from work accidents or sickness of wage-earners is 10 times as large as the apparent loss from strikes in years of greatest industrial strife and unrest. The economic loss, both direct and indirect, from strikes and lockouts is, of course, impossible to determine. The sales of firms not subject to the strike may increase as a result of it, or buyers may simply postpone their purchases so

---

[1] Cf. "Extent of Waste from Depression Unemployment," *Monthly Labor Review*, vol. 49 (November 1939), p. 1076; and Florence Peterson, "Review of Strikes in the United States," *Monthly Labor Review*, vol. 46 (May 1938), p. 1066.

that monthly sales after the strike are larger than they would otherwise have been. On the other hand, industries and firms are so interdependent that a strike in a key industry may slow down operations in other plants and industries or even paralyze economic activity in various communities. Large work stoppages can, therefore, start a cumulative contraction of business.

In some countries, the prevention of work stoppages has been considered so important that economic conflict in the form of strikes and lockouts has been outlawed, and the conflicting economic issues between labor and capital are settled by political, rather than economic, means. That has been true in dictatorships like Germany, Italy, and Russia, and also in those democracies providing for compulsory arbitration or court decision on economic issues in industrial relations, as is the case in Australia and New Zealand. In the other democracies, the employers and unions have desired to settle the economic issues in labor disputes without political decisions or control.

LEGAL LIMITATIONS ON UNION PRACTICES

In a discussion of organized labor and the law, a distinction should be drawn between the substantive law (both common and statutory law), which defines the rights of persons or property, and remedial law, which provides for legal protection through injunction or damage suit in case there has been a violation, or is a threatened violation, of those rights. Labor's complaint against the law has three aspects: its objections to the substantive law, its opposition to the injunction, and its claim that judges in general have a bias in favor of employers.

The economic background of most judges is upper class. Generally speaking, their social contacts are mostly with employing and professional groups. Their incomes as lawyers and later as judges are usually sufficient to make them satisfied with existing economic arrangements. Most of the judges in higher courts are appointed for life, rather than elected, so that they do not need to please the electorate in order to hold their positions and receive their steady incomes. As investors, they are interested in preserving profits—indeed, in some cases judges have granted injunctions against unions in favor of firms in which they themselves had thousands of dollars invested.

Legal training and language also tend to prejudice judges against unions, whose legal status has improved with time. Judges, who have been taught to revere precedents, are not likely to have an evolutionary view of society and to modify their decisions according to changes in the development and organization of industry. The attitude of courts in general toward labor unions is also affected by the body of concepts and principles that comprise what might be termed the "verbal law" and that stem from an early period. A legal writer says of this "vocabulary of vague vituperation":

One cannot read many decisions on this subject without receiving the impression that the average court begins the consideration of a case with something akin to a prejudice in favor of the employer. . . . The continued use of such terms as "intimidation" and "threats" to describe ordinary economic pressure, "conspiracy" in referring to a combination of workmen, and "primary intent to injure" in speaking of the objects of labor action, indicates a tendency to look with disfavor upon labor's cause before it is pleaded. The most concrete manifestation of this attitude is the persistence of the "prima facie" theory of tort applied in these cases [the theory that presumes an employer is entitled to relief on showing that he has suffered or will suffer economic injury from economic pressure by a union, with the burden of proof upon the union to justify its action in the eyes of the court].[1]

Substantive law on economic pressure by labor. There is a surprising lack of uniformity in the court decisions regarding the legality of various devices for economic pressure, such as the strike and the boycott, which are used by labor to induce employers to accede to the workers' demands. Because court decisions on labor law are so confused and inconsistent, it is difficult to make general statements regarding "the law" on any particular point, and it is also difficult for workers to know whether their economic activities are in violation of the law.

Various factors help to explain the state of confusion with regard to labor law. The common law, evolved from court decisions, has experienced striking changes as the social and economic philosophy of the courts has been modified with the passage of time. The first court cases, as indicated in Chapter 4, declared all strikes illegal and condemned group action by workers to improve

---

[1] Bernard Eskin, "The Legality of 'Peaceful Coercion' in Labor Disputes," *University of Pennsylvania Law Review*, vol. 85 (March 1937), pp. 481–82.

wages as a punishable crime. In referring to the fact that the courts had gradually reversed themselves concerning the legality of certain actions by labor, Justice Brandeis said in 1921: "The change in law by which strikes once illegal and even criminal are now recognized as lawful was effected in America largely without the intervention of legislation. This reversal of common-law rule was not due to the rejection by the courts of one principle and the adoption in its stead of another, but to a better realization of the facts of industrial life." [1] On the legality of such matters as the yellow-dog contract, minimum-wage laws, and discharge for union activity, the U. S. Supreme Court has either reversed itself or completely changed its position over a period of years.

Not only has the attitude of the same court changed from time to time, but different courts vary in their attitudes, so that court decisions in a single state often seem irreconcilable. In addition, the statutory law varies from state to state; Federal statutes differ from state statutes; and municipal ordinances regarding certain types of strikes, picketing, or other union activities permit further jurisdictional and territorial differentiation. In few cases are the facts exactly alike. Even the industry in which the union activity occurs may have a bearing upon its legality. Courts are less likely to approve strike actions by employees in essential public utilities; there are special labor laws covering employees on interstate railroads and at sea; and the employees of the government presumably have no right to strike at all. Consequently, few generalizations can be made from the court decisions on the economic activities of unions, and those few generalizations are as subject to exceptions as the rules in a German grammar.

1. *Strikes.* The legality of a strike depends upon (1) the primary purpose of the strike or the nature of the concession desired by the workers, and (2) the methods used in conducting the strike. A strike may, therefore, be illegal because of its objective or because of the way in which pressure is brought to bear upon the employer. If the purpose of the strike is obnoxious to the court, it is illegal regardless of the methods used in conducting it.

To be legal in most jurisdictions, a strike must concern the strikers' wages, hours, or working conditions; its primary purpose must involve a direct and immediate benefit to them. In the case

---

[1] *Duplex Printing Co.* v. *Deering* (1921), 254 U. S. 443.

of strikes for the sole purpose of strengthening labor organization through demands for the closed shop or the check-off, the courts are likely to consider the economic benefit too indirect and remote to justify the strike. From the legal viewpoint, a labor dispute involves a conflict between the right to strike or cease work and the right to carry on a business. The courts recognize that economic struggles result in some economic loss and injury to both sides. It is therefore necessary for the courts to balance one right against another and to determine whether a particular purpose justifies injury to an employer or to third parties with no direct interest in the struggle. If the primary aim is to advance the economic position of the strikers, the courts may consider the effects on others as unavoidable and incidental.

In the case of strikes for the closed shop, strikes against an employer for use of nonunion materials, sympathetic strikes to assist other strikers, and general strikes, the courts are wont to consider the effects on third parties too important to overlook. A strike for the closed shop would generally involve the demand that any non-members be discharged. In order to preserve economic individualism, the courts attempt to protect the right to pursue one's calling without restraint from third parties. The benefit to the strikers from a closed shop is considered too "remote" to justify direct injury to nonmembers by economic pressure to force their discharge.

Strikes against the use of nonunion materials and sympathetic strikes are not considered to be for the direct gain of the striking employees but are what might be called "billiard shots." A second employer's workers put economic pressure upon him by striking in order to affect his dealings with another employer. They strike for the purpose of inducing their employer to exert pressure upon the producer of the nonunion materials or the firm in which the strike began. Even though the sympathetic strikers or workers striking against nonunion materials are in the same national union as the employees of the firm in which the dispute originated, the courts have construed their action as primarily intended to injure a third party (the employer not involved in the original dispute). The courts have not been impressed with the economic argument that working conditions throughout the whole competitive area are of primary economic interest to each local union and that injury to one local is of direct economic significance to other locals of the same national union. Personal bias can, of course, have a marked influence upon a judge's decision concerning the purposes, motives, or intentions of workers who strike or threaten to strike—the threat may be just as unlawful as the act.

General strikes are an extended form of sympathetic strikes and may have the added objective of putting pressure upon the government. They are of questionable legality, for their primary purpose is well outside the bounds of the area of employees dealing with their own employer on their own terms of employment.

The question of the legality of the methods used in conducting a strike is also not clear-cut. Attempts to enlist the sympathies of third parties by peaceful persuasion, including argument or appeal to their sense of fair play, are lawful. But the use of economic pressure or a threat to use economic pressure in order to influence the actions of third parties is often called "coercion" or "intimidation," which are considered illegal. The exact limits to the use of economic pressure by withdrawal of labor or patronage are, however, vague and indefinite. Tactics such as violence, criminal acts, and physical damage to property are, of course, unlawful regardless of the purpose or the occasion. The sit-down strike, in which the workers literally sit on their jobs, is also considered illegal by the courts because they do not recognize the right of a worker to any particular job.

The employer's weapon that corresponds to the strike is the lockout. Prior to the passage of the National Labor Relations Act there was practically no legal limitation upon the lockout, presumably on the grounds that it does not directly involve economic pressure upon, or injury to, third parties. Such an assumption is, however, open to question. As indicated by the Remington-Rand, the Brown Shoe, and other cases discussed in Chapter 23, employers often attempt to gain their objectives in labor disputes by putting economic pressure upon other businessmen and workers through lockouts and a threat to move the business. Pressure is also brought to bear upon the local government in the same manner. Late in 1934 the Great Atlantic and Pacific Tea Company (the A. & P.) temporarily closed its 293 Cleveland stores, locked out 2,200 employees, and began to move warehouse stocks to its other 14,800-odd stores, in retaliation for a Teamster strike against the

company and the "wholly inadequate police protection" afforded
the company by the mayor of Cleveland. Some dozen years earlier
the company abandoned its warehousing operations in Jersey City
when the employees threatened to organize. What was the primary
intent of the A. & P. officials in locking out all the Cleveland employees, most of whom were not parties to the strike? Was the
lockout aimed at "coercing" the non-striking employees, the
public, and the local government by economic pressure and the
threat to withdraw the company's patronage from Cleveland?
Company threats to move may have more influence on local
governments than general strikes.

During the 1930's the three large tire manufacturers in Akron,
Ohio, repeatedly threatened to move their businesses away from
that city unless "labor conditions" there were altered in line with
the desires of the officers of the rubber companies. The threat to
inflict economic injury upon Akron unless the companies were
given more control over labor represented an attempt to coerce
not only the Akron rubber workers but the entire city, especially
the municipal government.

2. *Boycotts.* It is generally legal for employees to boycott their
own employer and, "by peaceful means," to persuade the employer's customers to refrain from dealing with him. But economic
pressure on third parties by a threat to withdraw patronage in
order to induce such third parties not to deal with the offending
employer is considered to be a "secondary boycott" and illegal.[1]
The courts look upon it as another form of the "billiard shot."
Yet in modern industry, it may be very difficult for workers and
their sympathizers to discriminate against an offending employer
in their purchases without affecting the business of third parties,
for few manufacturers produce finished articles and sell them
through their own retail outlets.

The economic reasoning in the court cases on "secondary
boycotts" is often of questionable validity, and frequently one
case is not consistent with another. The judges fail to explain why
it is lawful to persuade dealer-customers of the employer to withdraw their patronage by arguments and appeals to sympathy,
and yet not lawful to use the workers' combined purchases as a
means of achieving the same objective. Generally people are free

[1] *Cf. Duplex Printing Press Company* v. *Deering* (1921), 254 U. S. 443.

to distribute their purchases or dollar votes as they wish, and combined action by consumers' organizations is not similarly restricted by the courts. The highest courts in some states have held the "secondary boycott" by labor to be legal on the grounds that what individuals have a right to do when acting singly, they may legally do when acting as a group.[1]

The discussion in Chapters 6 and 23 contained numerous examples of attempts by employers' associations to carry on boycotts against employers because they were dealing with unions or were operating closed shops. The courts have not declared such concerted action by employers to be "coercive" and illegal. There are court cases in which employers operating company stores have forced employees by threat of discharge to refrain from patronizing competing stores, yet such economic pressure was not declared to be illegal "intimidation." It is not at all clear to the layman why courts allow employers' organizations to bring economic pressure on other employers to affect their relationships with unions or permit employers to put economic pressure upon patrons of their competitors, while condemning similar economic pressure by workers as illegal. That such apparent inconsistency has also puzzled lawyers is indicated by the following quotation from a legal periodical:

> While the great weight of authority condemns the use of pressure against third parties by laborers, the judicial attitude is by no means the same in the cases involving the same type of economic coercion exerted by entrepreneurs against competitors. When business men, singly or in combination, seek to cause a cessation of business dealings between a competitor and his patrons and suppliers by the exertion of economic pressure upon the latter, the weight of authority allows the activity, provided it is carried on by business men to advance their trade interests. It is difficult to reconcile this result with the numerous decisions condemning the use of similar pressure by combinations of workmen. . . . Is the desire of an entrepreneur to strengthen and advance his business a matter in which society has a greater stake than in the desire of workmen to improve their economic condition, so that the first type of interest might justify conduct which is not justified by the latter? If the advancement of both is equally favored by society, can it be said that the entrepreneurs need such a device as the "pressure boycott," in order to achieve their aims, more than workmen need it? [2]

---

[1] *Cf.*, for example, Francis B. Sayre, *A Selection of Cases and Other Authorities on Labor Law*, 1923, pp. 427, 458.

[2] Bernard Eskin, *op. cit.*, p. 464.

There is a definite need for further study and judicial recognition of the use of economic power by employers to "coerce" other employers, employees, and the government. A thorough comparison of the methods of economic pressure used by both sides would, without doubt, lead to more equity in the law.

The black list is another type of employer boycott, and when operated by an employers' association is clearly a "secondary boycott." Over 30 states have statutes forbidding or restricting the use of black lists; yet, despite common and statutory law against the practice, there have been few cases in which black-listed workers have secured any redress in the courts.[1] The laws have, for the most part, been ineffective.

This practice well illustrates the practical disadvantages that workers experience even when the law, in principle, is really impartial. The employers can operate secretly and are, therefore, less open to legal attack. Workers' actions involve so many persons that secrecy is almost impossible in many cases. One of labor's weapons, picketing, is based on publicity. The injury to single employees is often too small to warrant a legal suit. That, however, is not likely to be true of injury to large employers. Furthermore, the courts consider the employer's right to do business a property right, which means that a firm may collect damages for illegal economic pressure by workers that reduces sales or the "going-concern" value of the firm, based on its business relationships.

3. *Picketing.* The use of picketing in strikes and boycotts has already been explained in Chapter 22. Only the legal issues in picketing will be discussed here. So long as the strike or boycott itself is legal and mild methods of persuasion are used by the pickets, the practice is not likely to violate the law or municipal ordinances. However, it is illegal for pickets to intimidate others by threats of personal injury and physical damage to property, or to engage in mass picketing in such large numbers as to obstruct the free passage of persons or vehicles. Also, they are not permitted to misrepresent the facts of the case or to abuse the privileges of free speech.

Whether workers can legally picket retailers who sell the products of an "unfair" firm or who advertise in an "unfair" newspaper is still unsettled, and seems to depend upon the legal jurisdiction,

---

[1] *Cf.* Edwin E. Witte, *The Government in Labor Disputes,* 1932, pp. 214–15.

the personal attitude of the judge, the methods of picketing used, and the type of appeal made to the public by the pickets.[1]

4. *The antitrust laws.* In Canada, labor unions are exempt from the law of criminal conspiracy and from the antitrust laws. In England, labor organizations were exempt from the law of criminal conspiracy in 1875 and from civil conspiracy in restraint of trade in 1906, after the Taff Vale decision of 1901, which held a union responsible for damages to an employer and which led to the formation of the British Labour Party. Though Canadian and English unions are not subject to suit under antitrust laws, the most important cases against unions in this country have been prosecutions under the Federal antitrust laws (the Sherman Act of 1890 and the Clayton Act of 1914). These laws provide that the injured party shall be paid triple the actual damages sustained from restraints of interstate trade or commerce.

It is questionable whether Congress in passing the Sherman law ever intended to have it apply to labor organizations.[2] Nevertheless, the courts soon began to apply this legislation to acts of labor unions that affected interstate trade; and in 1902 a hat-manufacturing firm in Danbury, Connecticut, brought suit against the United Hatters for damages sustained from a successful boycott of retail dealers throughout the country, following a strike in the Danbury shop. The U. S. Supreme Court in 1908 declared this "secondary boycott" a conspiracy to restrain the company's interstate trade, allowed the company triple damages, and concluded that the 250 members of the union were all liable and could each be sued for the damages.[3] The company finally collected $234,000, most of which was paid by the AFL. In 1911 the Supreme Court upheld an injunction against the Molders' union and the AFL in connection with a nationwide boycott of stoves produced by the Bucks Stove and Range Company.[4] The Federation had placed

---

[1] *Cf.* Goldfinger v. Feintuch (1937), 276 N. Y. 281; and Albion G. Taylor, *Labor Problems and Labor Law*, 1938, p. 502.

[2] A thorough study of the subject concludes that the Act was not intended to apply to labor organizations. *Cf.* Edward Berman, *Labor and the Sherman Act*, 1930. For an opposite view, *cf.* A. T. Mason, *Organized Labor and the Law*, 1925.

[3] *Loewe* v. *Lawlor* (1908), 208 U. S. 274 and (1915), 235 U. S. 522.

[4] *Gompers* v. *Bucks Stove and Range Co.* (1911), 221 U. S. 418. The publicity in this case was so unfavorable to the company that its sales continued to decline after the injunction. Within three years the company, under new management, made its peace with the union.

the company on its "We Don't Patronize List," and, when some of its officers continued to give publicity to the boycott in defiance of the injunction, they were given jail sentences for contempt of court. However, the sentences were never served.

The consternation that these cases caused in labor circles led to a campaign by organized labor to obtain relief from the Sherman Act. The Clayton Act, passed in 1914, provided "that the labor of a human being is not a commodity or article of commerce" and that labor organizations shall not "be held or construed to be illegal combinations or conspiracies in restraint of trade under the anti-trust laws." Although this Act was hailed as the "Magna Charta" of labor and some labor leaders contended that it excluded unions from the antitrust laws, succeeding court decisions showed that the judges were unable to perceive that this Act made necessary any change in the application of the antitrust laws to labor.

In 1921 the U. S. Supreme Court upheld an injunction against the Machinists' union in a "secondary boycott." [1] The union had signed agreements with three out of the four manufacturers of newspaper printing presses but had been notified that it would have to organize the Duplex Company in Michigan and enforce union standards there, including the 8- instead of the 10-hour day, or the other three firms could not continue their union agreements. Members of the Machinists' union and other unions began an elaborate boycott of the company's product in and around New York City, following a strike caused by the refusal of the Duplex Company to accept a union agreement. It was this boycott that the Supreme Court enjoined as a conspiracy to restrain the company's interstate trade. In another case decided in 1925, the Supreme Court held that coal miners in Arkansas, members of the United Mine Workers, had intentionally interfered with interstate commerce, and thus violated the Sherman Act, in destroying mining properties and coal destined for interstate trade during a clash with detective-agency guards and strike-breakers, following company termination or breach of the union agreement. [2] The coal company finally collected $27,000 from the union in a compromise settlement out of court.

Finally, in 1927 the Supreme Court upheld an injunction

[1] *Duplex Printing Company* v. *Deering* (1921), 254 U. S. 443.
[2] *Coronado Coal Company* v. *United Mine Workers* (1925), 268 U. S. 295.

against the Stone Cutters' union for a boycott of the products of some quarries in the Bedford-Bloomington District of Indiana that had gone on a company-union basis after refusing to renew agreements with the Stone Cutters' union.[1] Members of the union in other states, in line with the union's constitutional requirement not to work on stone cut by nonmembers, refused to handle the Bedford stone in construction work. In upholding the injunction, the Supreme Court declared the union guilty of violating the Sherman Act. In a minority decision, Justices Holmes and Brandeis pointed out that "it has long been settled that only unreasonable restraints are prohibited by the Sherman Law" and that the restraint of trade in this case could hardly be regarded as unreasonable. Union members could not work on stone cut "by men working in opposition" to the union without aiding and abetting "the enemy."

In the decisions of various antitrust cases, the economic sympathies of the judges seem to have played an important part, for the "rule of reason" has generally been applied to employer restraints of interstate trade, whereas in the cases of labor restraints the judges have based their decisions largely on the presumed "intent" of the accused labor organization. In corporation cases the courts have permitted "reasonable" restraint of trade if such restraint was considered to be in the public interest. The monopolistic practices of large corporations, like the U. S. Steel Corporation and the United Shoe Machinery Company, were upheld by the U. S. Supreme Court as "reasonable" restraints of interstate trade that were not socially harmful despite their direct effects or the "intent" of the company officials. It was stressed that as "good trusts" they had tended to increase stability in the industry.[2] In 1925 the Court upheld the trade-association activities to maintain the prices of hard wood flooring and cement with the argument that price uniformity serves the public interest by tending "to stabilize trade and industry, to produce fairer price levels, and to avoid the waste which inevitably attends the unintelligent conduct of economic enterprise" [3]—the very objectives that labor

[1] *Bedford Cut Stone Company et al.* v. *Journeyman Stone Cutters' Association* (1927), 274 U. S. 37.

[2] *United States* v. *United States Steel Corporation* (1920), 251 U. S. 417; and *United States* v. *United Shoe Machinery Co.* (1918), 247 U. S. 32.

[3] *Maple Flooring Manufacturers Association et al.* v. *United States* (1925), 268 U. S. 563; and *Cement Manufacturers Protective Association et al.* v. *United States* (1925), 268 U. S. 588.

unions claim as their purposes and that, in the Duplex case, were clearly the aims of the union. The reader may recall the antitrust case discussed in Chapter 6, which involved a permit system aimed at eliminating the building unions in San Francisco and which was also decided by the U. S. Supreme Court in 1925. Various employers' associations were accused of interfering with the free flow of building materials between states by conspiring not to sell materials to union employers and by boycotting and black-listing contractors who were not in the combination. The Court refused to condemn this employers' combination on the grounds that the "motive for conspiracy" was monopolistic control of the local market, the restraint of interstate commerce being "purely incidental." [1] It is difficult for the layman to understand why the restraint of trade in the Bedford case, decided two years later, was not also "purely incidental" to the self-preservation of the union or to the control of labor conditions in the local Bedford district.

It would seem as though the social consequences of labor's restraint of interstate trade are as observable as the social effects of similar restraint by employers, so that the "rule of reason" could be applied to labor combinations as well as to business combinations. Certainly the stabilizing effects of unions upon prices and working conditions have as much economic and social merit as stabilization achieved through trade-association action or the formation of giant corporations by mergers.

Injunctions. As already mentioned, injunctions and damage suits are remedial actions based on the substantive law as laid down in statutes and court decisions. Injunctions are orders issued by courts of equity requiring a person or persons to do, or to refrain from doing, certain acts. The theory behind such court injunctions is that they are necessary in certain instances in order to prevent irreparable damage—injury to property that could or would not be fully repaired by the payment of compensation following a damage suit. Since market relationships and opportunities are considered by courts as property, labor injunctions are generally designed to protect the business relationships and expected profits of employers by enjoining strikes, boycotts, and picketing, which might cause "irreparable" damage to the employer's position in the labor or commodity markets. It is an equity principle that

[1] *Industrial Association of San Francisco et al.* v. *United States* (1925), 268 U. S. 64.

injunctions should not be issued when the injunction would result in a loss for the defendants (the workers, in strike cases) greater than the injury that the complainant (the employer) would sustain without the injunction. The loss that workers might suffer from an injunction against a strike would, however, be difficult to estimate.

From the point of view of employers, injunctions have generally been preferable to damage suits. Injunctions can be obtained quickly, and the effectiveness of a strike often depends upon timely action. They tend to give the public the impression that the strikers are running afoul of the law and help to undermine the morale of the workers on strike. In addition, they serve to forestall injuries that might lead to suit against the firm's employees. Damage suits are likely to have a bad effect upon the firm's public relations and labor relations. Even injunctions may cause harmful publicity, as is indicated, for example, by the experience in the Bucks Stove and Range case. Many damage suits apparently are started to bluff the workers or to tie up union funds during strikes, for a large proportion of them are dropped after the strikes end.[1]

Injunctions in labor disputes were apparently first issued in this country in the early 1880's, and their use increased steadily until in the 1920's over 900 injunctions were granted to employers in labor disputes.[2] In England, on the other hand, the practice of issuing injunctions in labor disputes is practically unknown, and the few injunctions granted in the past to English employers were annulled, reversed, or severely critized by the courts. In this country, labor unions have also applied for injunctions to restrain the operation of black lists or to prevent violations of workers' statutory rights.

Labor's objections to the use of court injunctions in industrial disputes have been directed primarily against (1) the procedure in issuing temporary injunctions without a fair hearing of both sides or an opportunity for prompt appeal, (2) the sweeping character of such "judge-made" orders or law, and (3) the denial of a fair trial for those accused of violating the injunction.

[1] Professor Witte lists 66 cases in which damages were recovered from labor unions or their members following successful damage suits. *Cf.* E. E. Witte, *The Government in Labor Disputes*, 1932, pp. 139, 345–48.

[2] Definite references to 1,845 injunctions issued on application of employers between 1880 and 1930 have been collected by Professor Witte. *Cf. ibid.*, p. 84. In the strike of the railway shop crafts in 1922, nearly 300 injunctions were granted although only 12 were officially reported.

In almost half of the labor injunction cases prior to 1932, temporary restraining orders were issued *ex parte*, simply on the basis of the employer's complaint without an opportunity for the workers to present their side of the case.[1] Such temporary injunctions often forbade action that was perfectly lawful, including discussions and meetings. In most instances the temporary orders were the only injunctions issued in the case, and in the remaining cases, full hearings usually occurred months after the temporary restraining orders were issued.[2] Some injunctions, as those in the 1919 coal strike, prohibited union officials from calling a strike or paying strike benefits, or directed them to call off the strike. Of course, workers could not be ordered to work, as that would be a form of slavery. The difference between labor and commodities in that regard is evident.

Labor injunctions seem to have become more sweeping prior to the enactment of the Norris-LaGuardia Anti-Injunction Act in 1932. Many of them were dragnet decrees with "blanket" clauses extending broad and vague prohibitions to "all persons whomsoever." Failure to obey an injunction is contempt of court, and the accused person was usually tried before the judge who issued the injunction and without the benefit of a jury. Consequently, many labor injunctions were, in effect, judicial legislation enacted, interpreted, and enforced by a single judge. They placed "the power of the state upon one side of a complicated social struggle in advance of, and frequently altogether without, that careful ascertainment of fact which is the traditional protection of the innocent."[3]

The Clayton Act of 1914 and various state laws patterned after it were designed to remedy abuses in the issue of injunctions in labor cases. However, subsequent court interpretation or condemnation of these acts robbed them of all effectiveness, so that labor was not granted relief from the "evils" of injunctions until further legislation was passed in the early 1930's.

1. *Anti-injunction laws.* Preceded by Wisconsin, the Federal government in 1932 passed the Norris-LaGuardia Act limiting the issuance of labor injunctions by the Federal courts. About half of

---

[1] *Ibid.*, p. 90.   [2] *Ibid.*, p. 93.
[3] Felix Frankfurter and Nathan Green, "The Labor Injunction," in *Encyclopaedia of Social Sciences*, 1932, vol. 8, p. 655.

the states have also enacted anti-injunction laws curbing the power of state courts to issue injunctions in labor disputes. These acts, it should be noted, do not change the substantive law.

The Norris-LaGuardia Act prohibits the Federal courts from issuing injunctions against paying strike benefits or giving publicity to the facts of a labor dispute. Except in unusual circumstances, when temporary restraining orders may be issued for five days upon sufficient testimony under oath, the Federal courts are forbidden to issue temporary or permanent injunctions in labor disputes without a hearing and an opportunity for cross-examination in open court. Prompt appeal to higher courts is provided for in labor injunction cases, as well as a public trial by jury before another judge in cases of contempt of court occurring outside the courtroom.

Employers can, of course, still obtain injunctions against labor. Furthermore, in the Federal courts and in the courts of about one half of the states, unions can be sued as entities or through representative members. Employers have claimed that one reason that labor injunctions are so necessary is that unions are irresponsible and each member must be sued separately for damages. It is a mistake, however, to believe that incorporation of labor unions would increase their financial responsibility or prevent racketeering in labor organizations. Incorporation is designed to limit liability, and racketeering is to be found in both financial and industrial corporations and the governments of incorporated cities or villages. Labor leaders object to the compulsory incorporation of unions because unions would then enjoy less freedom in their internal affairs. At present they are treated as fraternal organizations under the law, which permits them to control membership and to expel members (including suspected spies) with few legal difficulties. Employers' associations also are not incorporated, and usually less is known of their activities and financial affairs than is generally known concerning most labor unions.

LEGALITY OF EMPLOYER TACTICS

The legal aspects of certain employer tactics—the lockout, the black list, and the boycott of employers by employers' associations or organizations—have already been discussed in the preceding section. The following discussion deals with statutory legislation regarding other employer methods of opposing labor unions or strikes.

Antiunion agreements. Contracts not to join a labor union during employment with a firm, or to refrain from striking, are commonly called "yellow-dog" contracts. State and Federal legislation prohibiting such nonunion contracts has been declared unconstitutional by the United States Supreme Court,[1] and in 1917 the Court upheld an injunction restraining attempts by the United Mine Workers to organize workers who had signed such agreements.[2]

The Norris-LaGuardia Act of 1932 declares such promises or contracts "to be contrary to the public policy of the United States" and not enforceable in any Federal court either by injunction or by damage suit. Similar legislation has been enacted by almost half of the states. The National Labor Relations Act of 1935 clearly forbids the use of such antiunion contracts by firms in interstate commerce.

Importation of strike-breakers. The Brynes Act of 1936, as amended in 1938, makes it unlawful to transport over state lines any person employed for the purpose of interfering, by force or threats, with peaceful picketing in a labor dispute involving conditions of employment, or with the exercise of labor's rights of self-organization and collective bargaining. Some states have laws prohibiting the importation of armed guards from another state or prescribing residence requirements in the county for special police officers.

Labor espionage. A few states and some cities have attempted to regulate industrial espionage by a statutory requirement that private detective agencies register or obtain a license. In actual practice, however, such laws have been violated[3] or have been ineffective.

In a number of cases the National Labor Relations Board has held that the employment of labor spies to inform the employer of union activities is a violation of the rights guaranteed to em-

[1] Cf. *Adair* v. *United States* (1908), 208 U. S. 161; and *Coppage* v. *Kansas*, (1915) 236 U. S. 1.

[2] *Hitchman Coal and Coke Co.* v. *Mitchell* (1917), 245 U. S. 229.

[3] Cf., for example, "Industrial Espionage," *Report of the Committee on Education and Labor Pursuant to S. Res. 266*, Senate Report No. 46, Part 3, 75th Congress, second session, 1937, p. 13.

ployees in the National Labor Relations Act. The Act itself, however, does not outlaw labor espionage.

Many other antiunion activities, such as the establishment of company unions or discriminatory discharge of union members, are violations of the broad provisions of the Railway Labor Act or the National Labor Relations Act and will be mentioned in the general discussion of those laws.

Railway Labor Act. Limits to the labor policies of railroad and airplane carriers in interstate commerce are defined in the Railway Labor Act of 1926, as amended in 1934 and 1936. The amended Act provides that neither the carriers nor the employees shall interfere with, influence, or coerce the other party in matters of self-organization or in the choice of representatives. Presumably, that provision forbids such employer practices as labor espionage or discriminatory discharge for union membership. The majority of any craft or class of employees determines the representatives of the craft or class for the purpose of collective bargaining, so the employer cannot play one group of employees against another group in the same line of work. A carrier is forbidden to deny or to question in any way the right of its employees to join a labor organization, and it is unlawful for a carrier to interfere in any way with the organization of its employees, including the contribution of funds or other support to the workers' agency for collective bargaining. Such provisions serve to eliminate the yellow-dog contract and the company union from railroad and airplane transportation, where the carriers operate between states. The Act also makes illegal the closed shop and the check-off in employments covered by its provisions.

National Industrial Recovery Act of 1933. Drawing upon the wording of the declaration of public policy in the Norris-LaGuardia Act, Section 7a of the National Industrial Recovery Act stated that every code of fair competition for an industry should provide:

That employees shall have the right to organize and bargain collectively through representatives of their own choosing, and shall be free from the interference, restraint, or coercion of employers of labor, or their agents, in the designation of such representatives or in self-organization or in other concerted activities for the purpose of collective bargaining or other mutual aid or protection; that no employee and no one seeking employment shall be required as a condition of employment to join any company union or to refrain from joining, organizing, or assisting a labor organization of his own choosing. . . .

Although this section of the Act was subject to various interpretations, it implied that yellow-dog contracts were prohibited, that the use of labor spies and discrimination in employment to discourage unionism were illegal, and that employer attempts to promote company unions were unlawful if they interfered with the workers' rights to self-organization. Nevertheless, the number of employees covered by company unions increased rapidly— almost doubling during the year following the passage of the Act, to judge by sample studies.[1] In order to have some kind of collective-bargaining agency, firms that had hitherto opposed collective bargaining established company unions as a substitute for trade-unionism.

To interpret Section 7a and to settle disputes arising under it, a National Labor Board was established by Presidential order in August 1933. In addition to Senator Robert Wagner of New York as chairman, the Board had an equal number of employer and employee representatives. Without statutory authority, the Board had to rely upon its prestige, or upon the Recovery Administration and the Department of Justice, for enforcement of its orders. There was some conflict between the Board's function as a mediator to settle labor disputes by finding some middle ground of agreement between disputants and its function as a judicial agency to hand down decisions upon appeal from its 20 regional boards. Decisions tended to impair the diplomatic or mediatory function of the Board. In order to determine who the employees' representatives were, it was also necessary for the Board to hold elections.

By November 1933, the National Association of Manufacturers had attacked the Board, and in December of that year certain large firms challenged the Board's authority by refusing to permit it to hold elections among their employees. In line with the application of the Railway Labor Act, the Board had gradually come to adopt the majority rule (that representatives elected by a majority vote should be the exclusive representatives of the workers covered

---

[1] *Cf.* National Industrial Conference Board, *Individual and Collective Bargaining under the N.I.R.A.,* November 1933, and *Individual and Collective Bargaining in May 1934,* 1934, as well as A. L. Bernheim *et al., Labor and the Government,* 1935, pp. 78–80.

by the election), and had interpreted Section 7a to mean that the employer had to negotiate or bargain in good faith with the representatives of the majority of his employees. In March 1934 President Roosevelt helped to undermine the prestige of the Board by establishing a separate labor board for the automobile industry on the principle of proportional representation rather than majority rule.

In July 1934 the National Labor Board was replaced by a new National Labor Relations Board of three public representatives, established under a recently enacted Public Resolution No. 44. This new Board, with definite powers to conduct elections, was authorized to investigate issues arising under Section 7a. Although it was better fitted for judicial decisions than its predecessor, the new Board enjoyed no additional powers to enforce its decisions. Consequently, some employers brought successful injunction suits against enforcement of this Board's orders and its attempts to hold employee elections. The President also helped to undermine the prestige of this second Board by holding that it had no power to act in some seven industries having special labor boards. Furthermore, after the Board had heard and decided a case, the whole case was retried *de novo* when it reached a court. This second Board ceased to function when in May 1935 the United States Supreme Court declared the whole National Industrial Recovery Act unconstitutional. In July 1935 the National Labor Relations Act (commonly called the Wagner Act) was enacted by Congress on the basis of the experience of the previous two Boards in interpreting and enforcing Section 7a.

National Labor Relations Act of 1935. This statute is ostensibly designed to eliminate certain causes of industrial strife and unrest that obstruct interstate commerce, and it applies to all firms whose activities affect or burden interstate commerce except the railroads. The preamble of the Act states that "the inequality of bargaining power" between employees who do not possess full freedom of association and employers who are organized in corporate or other forms of association "tends to aggravate recurrent business depressions, by depressing wage rates and the purchasing power of wage-earners in industry and by preventing the stabilization of competitive wage rates and working conditions."

A National Labor Relations Board of three members is established (1) to certify the representatives of a majority of the employees as exclusive bargaining agents after deciding the appropriate bargaining unit and conducting an election in that unit if
necessary, and (2) to prevent employers from engaging in certain
"unfair labor practices" specified in the Act.   It is necessary to
discuss these unfair labor practices in some detail, for they include
various antiunion tactics by employers, which the Act is designed
to eliminate.

1. *Unfair labor practices.* According to the statute, it is an unfair
labor practice for an employer

(1) to interfere with, restrain, or coerce employees in the exercise of
their rights of self-organization and collective bargaining.
(2) to encourage or discourage union membership by discrimination
in regard to hire or tenure of employment or condition of work, except
such discrimination as may be involved in a closed-shop agreement with
a *bona fide* union.
(3) to dominate or interfere with the formation or administration of
any labor organization or contribute financial or other support to it.
(4) to refuse to bargain collectively with the representatives of his
employees.
(5) to discharge or otherwise discriminate against an employee for
filing charges or testifying under the Act.

These provisions are designed both to prevent an employer from
discriminating against union members or from interfering with
the self-organization of employees and to force the employer to
bargain exclusively with the union representing a majority of the
employees.

In its decisions, the Board has interpreted the unfair-labor-
practice provisions of the Act as forbidding an employer to engage
in such antiunion (not antistrike) activities as the following:
spying on union activities, discriminatory discharge, favoritism
between rival unions, campaigns to secure pledges of employee
"loyalty" and promises not to strike, employer-conducted elections
to discredit a union, or antiunion statements designed to discourage
organization.[1] In a number of cases the Board has held that antiunion statements are a violation of the Act, especially when

---

[1] *Cf. Third Annual Report of the National Labor Relations Board*, 1939, Chapter 7, "Principles Established," pp. 51–126; and *Fourth Annual Report of the National Labor Relations
Board*, 1940, pp. 57–73.

coupled with a threat to close or move the plant if the employees join a certain union or select certain representatives.[1] It is evident that a wide variety of employer practices may be considered in violation of the broad provisions of the Act concerning interference with employees' self-organization, discouragement of union membership, or refusal to bargain with the representatives of the majority, which the Board has interpreted to mean that the employer must negotiate and try in good faith to reach an agreement with such representatives. The provision that makes it an unfair labor practice for employers to dominate or support the bargaining agency of the workers practically outlaws company unions from employments covered by the Act.

2. *Enforcement procedure.* The procedure of the Board in hearing and deciding on unfair labor practices has received the approval of the United States Supreme Court. It is the procedure used by the Federal Trade Commission, the Interstate Commerce Commission, and the Securities Exchange Commission. When a complaint is received it is investigated by the office of the regional director for the area. If such preliminary investigation seems to indicate that an unfair labor practice has been committed, a formal hearing is scheduled before a trial examiner. After the hearing, the evidence, together with the trial examiner's recommendations, is forwarded to the Board, which may review the case. If the Board decides the case, an order may be issued which can be enforced only by a Federal court. There is no punishment for contempt of the Board's orders before they are validated by a Federal court, so such orders cannot be enforced without court approval and support. At any stage in the procedure, the employer may agree to comply with the Act and avoid further proceedings. If the employer agrees to cease the unfair labor practices complained of before a court makes part or all of the Board's order the court's decree, there are no penalties for violating the Act except such compensation as reinstatement in their former jobs with lost-time pay for workers discharged for union activity. In addition to reinstatement with back pay, the Board may order employers to disestablish company unions or to negotiate in good faith with a *bona fide* union representing a majority of the employees.

Having complaints investigated by special expert boards, which

---

[1] *Cf. Third Annual Report of the National Labor Relations Board*, pp. 59–61.

are not restricted by the rules of evidence for jury cases, seems a better way to obtain the facts than court proceedings, and also prevents the courts from being cluttered up with numerous cases, most of which can be settled outside of court. Less than five per cent of the complaints filed with the National Labor Relations Board during the first five years ever reached the courts. The rest were eliminated on the way by withdrawal, dismissal, settlement, or compliance.

During 1937 and 1938 the Board was highly successful in the decisions handed down by the Supreme Court. Prior to the 1938 elections, the Board's orders were fully sustained in all 12 Supreme Court decisions and in three out of every four decisions of the circuit courts. During the next two years, approximately equal numbers of the Board's orders were fully sustained, modified, and set aside by various Federal courts. Up to February 1941, the Supreme Court had given the Board 23 victories, 5 partial victories, and only 2 defeats. It is to be expected that the court record of the Board will be more unfavorable in the future, for various principles have already been established by past Supreme Court decisions, so only cases involving new matters and new issues will come before the Supreme Court for decision.

3. *Elections.* The Act states that representatives chosen "by the majority of the employees in a unit appropriate" for collective bargaining "shall be the exclusive representatives of all employees in such unit for purposes of collective bargaining" on terms or conditions of employment. Often the Board must hold employee elections to determine who are the exclusive representatives of the workers. In connection with such elections, the Board has held that the agency receiving a majority of the votes cast in the appropriate unit shall be the exclusive bargaining agency. The Board itself is authorized to decide whether "the unit appropriate for the purposes of collective bargaining shall be the employer unit, craft unit, plant unit, or subdivision thereof." The Board has held that for longshoremen the whole Pacific Coast is the appropriate bargaining unit, and for Pennsylvania anthracite coal the Board adopted an industry-wide unit.

The administration of this provision of the Act has been severely criticized by AFL officials since the AFL–CIO split, which occurred some months after the passage of the Act. It is claimed that

the Board has favored industrial rather than craft bargaining
units, although the statistics of the Board's decisions in cases
involving a disagreement between CIO and AFL unions over the
appropriate unit do not seem to support such a claim.   Indeed,
because AFL unions have been expanding their jurisdictions
recently, as explained in Chapter 21, unions affiliated with the
Federation have frequently requested industrial units or some unit
wider than that desired by the opposing CIO union.   It is unfortunate, perhaps, that the National Labor Relations Board's
decisions in election cases are not directly subject to court review
as is true of similar cases decided by the National Mediation Board
under the Railway Labor Act.   Court review of the National
Labor Relations Board's decisions regarding bargaining units and
elections is possible only in cases that also involve other provisions
of the Act.

4. *Difficulties in administering the Act.* The language of the National Labor Relations Act is fairly simple and its purposes are
clear. Nevertheless, its administration raises a number of questions
and problems because decisions under it involve the motives for
employer actions and the conflict of various rights.

If an employer makes a certain statement, is his purpose to
discredit a labor union?   If he follows a certain business policy,
is he trying to influence the organization of his employees?   To
be more specific, suppose that a firm with many plants decides
upon a relative reduction in the rate of operations in the most
unionized plant or decides to move the machinery in that plant to
another locality.   Is the employer's motive to discriminate against
the union, to make more profits (possibly to reduce losses), or
both?   How are the Board and the courts to determine what was
the main motive behind such business decisions?   In one case in
which a company allegedly moved its plant to avoid the union,
the Board ordered the company to pay moving costs for those
unionists who wished to move to the new location of the
plant.[1]

The Supreme Court has ruled that the evidence to support
charges of employer violation of the Act should be sufficient to
afford "a substantial basis of fact from which the fact in issue"
might be "reasonably inferred."   In other words, the evidence in

[1] *Cf. Decisions and Orders of the National Labor Relations Board*, vol. 2, p. 949.

a case must be of such a character that a "reasonable mind" would accept it "as adequate to support a conclusion." [1] In the Board's evidence, a group or series of actions on the part of the employer is presented to indicate his attitudes and intentions toward the union. Consequently, it is not always possible to say whether a certain action, if taken alone without accompanying antiunion activities, would be considered by the courts in violation of the Act. Furthermore, it may be possible for the employer to conceal his purposes in such a way that it is impossible to prove by evidence that certain actions were primarily intended to weaken the union.

What limitations upon the employer's freedom of speech are permitted under the Act to prevent him from interfering with the self-organization of his employees or from arousing employee fear of discrimination for joining a union? When does the employees' right to organize collectively without employer interference supersede the employer's right of freedom of speech? The Federal courts have held in a series of cases that an employer violates the Act when, among other actions, he asserts to his employees that union organizers are not to be trusted; that unions are made up of reds, radicals, and communists; that the union will injure the employer's business and diminish employment; that unions are valueless and unnecessary in securing improvements in wages and working conditions; or that it is unwise to join unions.[2] Some or all of these statements may be true of a particular local union. So far as the Act is concerned, however, the issue is whether the employer made these statements to influence the organization of his employees. Freedom of speech has, of course, also been curtailed by labor injunctions and limitations upon picketing.

In attempting to prevent employers from interfering with the self-organization of employees, other rights of employers may also be limited. For example, employers may not be free to spend their money for the commodities and services of other employers in a way that will conflict with the rights guaranteed in the Act. The Board has held that employers have discriminated against unions by refusing to renew a contract with an independent contractor

---

[1] *Consolidated Edison Co. et al.* v. *National Labor Relations Board* (1938), 305 U. S. 197; and *National Labor Relations Board* v. *Columbian Enameling and Stamping Co.* (1939), 306 U. S. 292.

[2] *Cf. Fourth Annual Report of the National Labor Relations Board,* 1940, pp. 135–36.

because the contractor had assisted a union or by bringing pressure on stores to have them stop extending credit to union members or strikers.[1] If the courts uphold the Board in such cases, it will mean that employers cannot use the boycott as an antiunion weapon. One must always bear in mind that it is the Federal courts, and not the Board, that enforce the Act and ultimately determine what is legal or illegal under the Act.

How far can an employer go in assisting a labor union and in working with a union so that it will be strong enough to discipline the workers and prevent rival factions or rival unions? When does an agreement become a "collusive" agreement through which an employer favors one of two rival unions? Under the Act, an employer can sign a closed-shop agreement with a union if that union represents a majority of his employees in the appropriate bargaining unit, although such a closed-shop agreement may involve discrimination against nonmember employees and may interfere with the self-organization of some employees. In a number of cases the Board has, however, set aside closed-shop agreements where there was evidence that the employer's motive was to force some employees to join a certain union. Usually employers have favored AFL unions, although in one case the Board invalidated an agreement with a CIO union on the ground that the employer had apparently preferred it to an AFL union, which probably had a majority of his employees.[2] The employers who have preferred AFL unions have often been producers of building materials, such as lumber and electrical equipment, and their preference has been based on a boycott or threatened boycott of their products by members of the AFL building-trades or Teamsters' unions. Is limitation upon the use of boycotts by unions one of the remedies for employer favoritism? In a case in 1939 a company contended that it was unable to comply with a reinstatement order of the Board, adopted by a Federal court, on the grounds that a union of AFL teamsters would not permit the company to reemploy two CIO teamsters. The court issued a warning that anyone interfering with the execution of the court's order would be put in jail for contempt of court.[3]

[1] *Decisions and Orders of the National Labor Relations Board*, vol. 10, pp. 108–12.

[2] *Ibid.*, vol. 8, pp. 1155, 1162.

[3] *Eavenson and Levering Case*, C.C.A.–3, reported in *Labor Relations Reporter*, vol. 4, pp. 543–44.

Another issue that complicates the administration of the Act concerns the status of strikers. Must an employer who has not committed an unfair labor practice rehire strikers following an unsuccessful strike which caused the firm to lose money? The Supreme Court has held that an employer cannot refuse to re-employ strikers under circumstances that indicate discrimination against them for union membership or activities.[1] For purposes of the Act, strikers remain employees as long as the strike is "current" and operations have not returned to normal. If the strike has been caused by an unfair labor practice, the Board has ruled that the strikers continue to be employees not only during the strike but after the strike has ended. Unless they obtain "equivalent employment" elsewhere, such strikers are eligible for reinstatement at normal wages extending back to the date that the strike began. The Supreme Court has ruled that employees who engage in a sit-down strike and resist efforts of police officers to dislodge them thereby lose their status as employees under the Act and are no longer protected by its provisions.[2] The Federal courts have, however, held that strikers do not lose their employee status under the Act by engaging in disorderly conduct, by disturbing the peace, by disobeying an injunction against violence on the picket line, or even by committing assault and battery.[3] The Board has refused to reinstate strikers in their former jobs because they committed serious crimes during the strike; but the Board has usually ordered reinstatement of strikers where their misconduct was not grave (was a misdemeanor rather than a felony) and the employer's conduct was such as to indicate that the strikers in question were not reemployed because of their union activities rather than their misconduct.

One further problem in interpreting and applying the Act will be mentioned. The Act makes it an unfair labor practice for the employer to refuse to bargain with the exclusive representatives of his employees. When is an employer negotiating or bargaining in good faith? Must he continue to bargain during a strike, regardless of what the union representatives say of him or regardless of the way the strike is conducted?

[1] *National Labor Relations Board* v. *Mackay Radio and Telegraph Co.* (1938), 304 U. S. 333.
[2] *National Labor Relations Board* v. *Fansteel Metallurgical Corp.* (1939), 306 U. S. 240.
[3] *Cf. Fourth Annual Report of the National Labor Relations Board*, 1940, pp. 135–36.

It is clear that under the Act the employer must meet with the representatives chosen by a majority of his employees and must make a *bona fide* effort to reach an agreement with them. He need not accept any particular demand of the union; but he must offer counter proposals. Also, he is not required to continue to bargain if all possibilities of achieving an understanding through the bargaining process have been exhausted, so that further negotiations would plainly be futile. However, if both sides reach an understanding on terms and conditions of employment, the Supreme Court has held that the employer fails to accept collective bargaining in good faith if he refuses to sign a written agreement with the union, embodying the accepted terms.[1] Only after numerous court decisions will it be possible to say what sorts of conduct constitute bargaining in good faith and what positive actions the Board can require an employer to take in order to fulfill the requirement in the Act that he bargain with the representatives of a majority of the employees. The Supreme Court has held that the employer is not required to bargain with employees who have engaged in a sit-down strike or who have violated a collective agreement with the employer.[2]

This discussion of the problems involved in the administration of the Act indicates why its administrators are likely to be accused, and have been accused, of unduly protecting the interests of unions and of fostering collective bargaining. The Act itself was designed to protect unions and encourage collective bargaining. Unions are also favored because the public hearings give unfavorable publicity to the employer; the government, as a third party, takes action only against employers under the Act; and the unions are generally free to select the time for a Board election that best suits their purpose.

5. *Proposed amendments.* Employers have complained that the National Labor Relations Act is one-sided and that it fails to emphasize the settlement of labor disputes. It is true that, in light of the experience of the previous labor boards under Section 7a, all the unfair labor practices in the Act represent restrictions upon the tactics of employers, and that this particular Federal statute

[1] *H. J. Heinz Co.* v. *National Labor Relations Board* (Jan. 6, 1941), U. S. 73.
[2] *National Labor Relations Board* v. *Fansteel Metallurgical Corp.* (1939), 306 U. S. 240; and *National Labor Relations Board* v. *Sands Manufacturing Co.* (1939), 306 U. S. 332.

places no limits upon the practices of employees. The Act is based on the notion that such employer restrictions are necessary in order to equalize bargaining power—in order to balance both the existing legal restrictions upon economic pressure by employees and the advantages the government has given to employers by permitting incorporation and other forms of association.

In suggesting amendments to "equalize" the Act, however, employer groups have not proposed that the employer restrictions simply be matched by exactly the same employee restrictions (for example, that employee representatives be required to bargain collectively in good faith) nor that their suggested "employee" unfair practices be enforced by the same procedure of Board orders to cease the practice, following a series of steps and hearings. The National Association of Manufacturers and other employer organizations have proposed that the Act contain totally new and one-sided restrictions upon unions, not matched by comparable restrictions upon employers or employers' associations; and instead of the existing enforcement procedure, they wish to allow the employer to be free to violate any of the Act's unfair labor practices whenever representatives of the employees commit one of the suggested unfair labor practices for employees.

Amendments have been proposed that would favor the craft unit for collective bargaining by requiring that the craft, single plant, or single firm must be the bargaining unit if the majority in the craft, plant, or concern so desire. Other proposed amendments would make a complete segregation of the judicial from the administrative activities carried on under the Act. Such a proposal is designed to prevent the same board from prosecuting cases and handing down decisions in those cases. Another suggested amendment would permit court review of Board decisions concerning the appropriate bargaining unit and the representatives of the majority in that unit.

In June 1940 the House of Representatives passed a bill embodying the three amendments mentioned in the previous paragraph. This bill also contained provisions that would permit an employer to express opinions on any subject if they were not accompanied by acts or threats of coercion or discrimination, that would deny reinstatement to employees suffering from a violation of the Act if those employees had engaged in willful violence or destruction of property, that would limit the Board's back-pay orders in favor of employees discharged for union activity to a period of not more than a year prior to the order, and that would require the filing of charges of unfair labor practices within six months after the date when such practices are alleged to have been committed. This House bill also stipulated that the rules of evidence applicable to the Federal district courts be followed in proceedings before the Board "so far as practicable."

The suggested amendments do not follow the pattern of the Railway Labor Act. Undoubtedly, the Railway Act represents a more advanced stage in labor legislation than the National Labor Relations Act. Based on the assumption that employers in the industry are recognizing and dealing with unions, the Railway Act emphasizes the duty of both sides to negotiate and maintain agreements, provides for the settlement of disputes by mediation or by arbitration of differences arising under agreements, and limits the right to strike or change terms of employment during a period of investigation by an emergency board. The National Labor Relations Act, on the other hand, may be looked upon as legislation designed to bring about the conditions upon which the Railway Labor Act rests, and, therefore, it does not limit the right to strike nor provide for arbitration or mediation of disputes—a function left to the United States Conciliation Service, discussed later in this chapter. The National Labor Relations Act may, however, reduce strikes by fostering written agreements and by enabling unions to settle disputes by filing charges with the Board as a substitute for striking. The Act also tends to eliminate strikes arising from the issue of union recognition. On the other hand, the Act may at first have tended to increase strike activity by strengthening unions in industrial areas, such as steel and newspaper offices, where they were weak prior to 1935. Increased union strength in such cases was undoubtedly a factor in subsequent strikes.

State labor-relations acts. In order to cover intrastate employments, six states have passed labor-relations laws more or less modeled after the National Labor Relations Act. The New York, Pennsylvania, Wisconsin, and Utah acts, as passed in 1937, only prohibited unfair practices by employers. The Massachusetts Act, adopted the same year, declares in addition that the sit-down strike is an unfair labor practice which can be proceeded against in the same manner as unfair labor practices by employers. The Pennsylvania Act as amended in 1939 contains three unfair labor practices by employees, including the sit-down strike. The Minnesota Act and the revised Wisconsin Act, which date from 1939, declare a whole series of employee actions to be "unfair labor practices," including the seizure of property (the sit-down strike), attempts to compel employees to join a labor union, mass picketing, or striking in violation of the terms of a collective agreement. The Minnesota law requires that a majority of the pickets be employees of the firm, and the Wisconsin statute makes it an unfair labor practice for employees to engage in a "secondary boycott" or to help in a strike, in a boycott, or in picketing, unless a majority of the employees in the collective bargaining unit vote by secret ballot to call a strike.

Like the Railway Labor Act, the Minnesota statute contains a positive "duty" on both sides to "endeavor in good faith to reach an agreement"; limits the right to strike by requiring 10 days' notice of an intention to strike or lock out; provides that, if an emergency commission of three is appointed to investigate and report on a labor dispute in an industry "affected with a public interest," neither party shall change the situation until 30 days have elapsed or the commission has reported; requires that whenever a craft exists it shall be the recognized unit for collective bargaining; and is enforced directly by the courts rather than through a special expert board. In line with an amendment proposed by employers for the national act, the Minnesota Labor Relations Act provides that "any employer, employee, or labor organization who has violated any of the provisions with respect to any labor dispute shall not be entitled to any of the benefits of this act respecting such labor disputes."

In 1938 the voters in the State of Oregon adopted, as an initiative measure, a statute forbidding picketing or boycotting except in disputes directly involving wages, hours, and working conditions (which excludes picketing in sympathetic strikes, jurisdictional disputes, or secondary boycotts) and also approved by a majority vote of the employees. There is considerable doubt about the constitutionality of such statutory limitations upon the right to picket or to strike in industries not "affected with the public interest" like the railroads and public utilities. In October 1940 the Oregon Supreme Court declared the 1938 antipicketing statute unconstitutional. The following section discusses a state law that was declared unconstitutional by the U. S. Supreme Court because it limited the right to strike in nonessential industries.

MACHINERY FOR SETTLING LABOR DISPUTES

This section deals with positive efforts by the Federal and state governments to aid in settling labor disputes. It is concerned with the government as a peacemaker rather than as an umpire or a policeman.

Methods and terms. Government intervention in industrial disputes may take various forms, the most common of which are mediation, arbitration, and investigation. The government may induce or force the disputants to accept one of these methods for the settlement of the disagreement, or it may establish agencies to perform such services upon request.

Mediation is a term commonly used interchangeably with conciliation. It refers to a type of industrial diplomacy whereby a neutral party, without using any force, seeks to find some middle ground for an agreement that will be accepted by both sides. A mediator must, therefore, be tactful and never take sides or argue the merits of the dispute. Each side must have confidence in him so that he may know the utmost concessions that the respective parties are willing to make.

Arbitration is the judicial method. Whereas a mediator should never render a decision, an arbitrator's function is to make awards. Arbitration may be voluntary in the sense that the disputants are free to consent or refuse to submit their differences to the decision of a third party, board, or court. Under compulsory arbitration, the disputants are compelled to submit a dispute to an outside person or board for arbitration. During the process of arbitration, the parties generally must refrain from engaging in a strike or lockout. Often both parties are bound to abide by the decision unless it has been agreed in advance that compliance with the arbitration award is voluntary.

The difficulty with arbitration is that there are no accepted principles for deciding what are "fair" wages or profits. Consequently, the decisions are likely to be influenced by prejudice, public opinion, and expediency, with resulting compromises that are unsatisfactory to both sides.

Under *compulsory investigation* an outside agency or board investigates a labor dispute without consent in advance from the parties directly concerned. Such investigations are for the purpose of discovering the facts. They generally result in a written report and sometimes in a decision on the dispute. The published reports or decisions are effective only through their influence upon public opinion. While the investigation is taking place there is usually an enforced waiting period during which employers cannot make changes in conditions of employment and employees cannot strike.

A distinction should be made between *primary* and *secondary* disputes in industry. Primary disputes concern major issues, such as wages, hours, and working conditions. They may arise in the absence or at the expiration of a labor agreement. Secondary disputes involve differences concerning the interpretation or application of the terms of an agreement in a particular case. It is evident that secondary disputes lend themselves more readily to adjudication. Many labor agreements provide for the arbitration of secondary disputes.

Experience seems to indicate that it is unwise to have the same persons engaged in mediation, which is diplomatic, and in arbitration, which is judicial. It may be well for persons engaged in mediation or in the arbitration of secondary disputes to be on permanent appointment so that they may become well acquainted with their work and with labor relations in certain areas or industries. There are advantages, however, in a changing personnel on boards that render decisions on primary disputes under voluntary arbitration or compulsory investigation. With a constantly changing board there is little opportunity to criticize its personnel and to accuse it of partiality by pointing to past decisions.

Mediation and arbitration services. A number of states provide for some agency that is authorized to assist in the peaceful settlement of labor disputes by making available services for mediation or voluntary arbitration. The Conciliation Service in the United States Department of Labor employs some 50 "commissioners" who offer to assist in mediating disputes all over the country. Because they have no compulsory powers, these commissioners can intervene only when the parties to the disputes are

willing. Nevertheless, they have been successful in settling a large
number of disputes. High public officials, like governors or presidents, may also intervene in an attempt to mediate an important
labor dispute.

Under the Railway Labor Act, as amended in 1934, a National
Mediation Board of three members was established in order to
help, by mediation, to settle primary labor disputes on interstate
railroads. In case its mediatory efforts fail, the Board is instructed
to try to induce the parties to submit the controversy to arbitration.

This country has been far behind England in providing machinery and personnel for the voluntary arbitration of industrial
disputes. Many American employers are somewhat doubtful of
the impartiality of persons employed by the U. S. Department of
Labor. The British Industrial Courts Act of 1919 provides flexible
machinery for voluntary arbitration by establishing a panel of
independent persons, employer representatives, and worker representatives, from which boards may be selected for the arbitration
of a dispute upon request by both disputants.

Beginning in 1888, the Federal government passed various
legislation providing machinery for the voluntary arbitration of
labor disputes on interstate railroads. Under the present Railway
Labor Act, as amended in 1934, the National Mediation Board
endeavors to have both sides agree to submit their controversy to
arbitration and, in case the arbitrators named by the disputants
are unable to agree upon the selection of one or two additional
arbitrators, the National Mediation Board has the duty to name
such remaining arbitrator or arbitrators.

Compulsory investigation in the United States. Unless compulsory investigation is confined to service industries like the railroads and public utilities in which there is little opportunity to
produce for stock, prohibition of a strike during a waiting period
while the investigation is proceeding may give the employer an
advantage by allowing him more time to prepare to meet the strike.
Often the effectiveness of strikes depends upon their timeliness,
and a compulsory waiting period may interfere with the correct
timing of a strike.

1. *On the railroads.* Under the Transportation Act of 1920, a
Railroad Labor Board of nine members, representing equally
workers, employers, and the public, was empowered to investigate

disputes on the railroads and to hand down decisions which, however, could be enforced only by public opinion. The Board commenced to function during a trying period because the railroads had just been handed back by the government to the private owners and many troublesome problems had accumulated. Unfortunately, the chairman of the Board was openly critical of labor; only one of the three labor members appointed was nominated by the unions; and the Act itself had been passed over labor's opposition. With no enforcement powers, the Board was unable to stop the shop-crafts strike in 1922 or the establishment of company unions in violation of its orders. The partisan character of the Board's personnel led some members to attack others on personal grounds in dissenting opinions. In time the Board lost not only the confidence of labor but also that of employers and the public. By 1925 the carriers and the unions agreed to try to draft a new measure, which developed into the Railway Labor Act of 1926.

If a labor dispute on the railroads is not adjusted through mediation or resort to arbitration, the President may appoint an emergency board made up of persons not interested in any employee organization or any carrier. Such a board of public representatives, appointed only for one emergency, is to investigate and report its findings. Emergency boards must report to the President within 30 days after their appointment. During that period and for 30 days after such a board has submitted its report, neither side is to make any change in the conditions out of which the dispute arose, except by mutual consent. This compulsory waiting period allows sufficient time for the report to influence public opinion.

2. *In Colorado and other states.* The Colorado Industrial Commission Act of 1915 provides for a 30-day waiting period after notice of intention to strike, to lock out workers, or to change the terms of employment. During that waiting period a fixed commission of three members investigates the dispute and may make a public report or decision. The Act covers all employers in industries affected with a public interest, namely, public utilities, intrastate railways, and mines. During the 30-day waiting period, the employer can make all sorts of strike preparations, including production for stock and the replacement of aggressive employees.

There has been a wide difference of opinion regarding the success of this Colorado law.[1] There have been a number of illegal strikes and many legal ones, for the Commission's awards are not binding. The Commission has been forced to make a number of difficult decisions on short notice and without adequate data on which to make a judgment. Profit considerations seem to have been the important factor in many of its awards. When the disputes have been interstate or nationwide in character, such as bituminous-coal strikes, it has been difficult to handle them under a state law. For strikes in violation of the waiting-period provisions of the law, union leaders and strikers have been sentenced to jail.

As indicated in the previous section, the Minnesota Labor Relations Act provides for a "cooling" or waiting period of 10 days after notice of an intended or desired change in conditions of employment and another 10-day waiting period after notice of intention to strike or to lock out employees. The latter waiting period may be for 30 days if the Governor appoints a commission to investigate and report on a dispute in an industry "affected with a public interest." A 10-day notice of intention to strike is also required under the Wisconsin Labor Relations Act for employees harvesting or processing farm and dairy products, which a strike might cause to deteriorate.

Compulsory arbitration in the United States. In this country, compulsory arbitration has not been widely used, in part because it is of questionable constitutionality in industries not directly affected with the public interest, such as public utilities.

1. *In secondary disputes on the railroads.* The Railway Labor Act, as amended in 1934, practically provides for the compulsory arbitration of disputes arising out of grievances or the interpretation or application of agreements. Upon petition by either party, such a secondary dispute may be appealed to the appropriate one of four divisions of the National Board of Adjustment, composed of equal numbers of employer and labor representatives. In case of a deadlock, a neutral third party is selected either by the division or by the National Mediation Board. The awards of a majority in a division of the National Board of Adjustment can be enforced through suit in the Federal courts.

---

[1] *Cf.*, for example, C. E. Warne and M. E. Gaddis, "Eleven Years of Compulsory Investigation of Industrial Disputes in Colorado," *Journal of Political Economy*, vol. 35 (October 1927), pp. 657–83; and E. E. Witte, *op. cit.*, pp. 253–55.

2. *The Kansas Industrial Relations Court* (*1920–1925*).   After a nationwide coal strike, the state of Kansas passed an Industrial Relations Court Act in 1920, which forbade strikes, lockouts, boycotts, and picketing in industries declared to be "affected with a public interest," including public utilities, railroads, mining, and food and clothing.   In these industries a special Court of Industrial Relations, composed of three judges, could intervene in case of disputes and hand down binding decisions fixing wage rates, hours, and working conditions or rules.   In making its compulsory awards the Court was to see to it that labor received "fair," "just," and "reasonable" wages and working conditions; that capital received "at all times a fair rate of return"; and that consumers were charged "fair" prices.   One was reminded of the days of the medieval guilds with their "just" wage and "just" price doctrines.   Willful violation of the orders of this special Kansas Court were punishable by fine or imprisonment.

Organized labor vigorously opposed the Act because it forbade workers to use their various means for exerting economic pressure (strike, boycott, and picketing) while depriving employers of only the right to lock out their employees, and because it prevented Kansas unionists from participating in nationwide railroad, meat-packing, and coal strikes during the early 1920's.   Some union leaders in Kansas served jail sentences for violating the Act in such strikes.

Many employers in Kansas also objected to the Act, partly because they disliked the Court's decisions or awards.   A packing company, backed by the Associated Industries of Kansas, carried one of the Court's awards to the U. S. Supreme Court, and the Supreme Court held in two decisions in 1923 and 1925 that the manufacture of food products was not sufficiently affected with a public interest to justify the state in authorizing a court to fix wages and hours of work.[1]   In another case in 1923 the U. S. Supreme Court also held the Act's provisions unconstitutional for coal mining.[2]   In 1925 the Kansas Court of Industrial Relations was abolished by the legislature.   Although the Industrial Relations Act is still in existence and presumably could be applied to

---

[1] *Wolff Packing Company* v. *Court of Industrial Relations* (1923), 262 U. S. 522, and (1925), 267 U. S. 552.

[2] *Dorchy* v. *Kansas* (1923), 264 U. S. 286.

disputes on the railroads or in public utilities, it has remained inoperative since 1924.

Employers and employees in this country have generally objected to having the government decide what wages should be paid and what hours should be worked in various industries. They have preferred to rely upon voluntary methods and economic strength rather than upon compulsory methods and political strength. On the other hand, Australia and New Zealand have had compulsory arbitration for a number of decades, as was indicated in Chapter 12. Their experience with that method of settling labor disputes is discussed in the next chapter.

CHAPTER TWENTY-SIX

LABOR RELATIONS ABROAD

This chapter represents a sort of Cook's tour of labor relations and labor legislation in 10 democratically governed countries just before the outbreak of the second World War in September 1939. It was originally written early in 1940, and the tense of the verbs has not been altered to take into account the kaleidoscopic changes in Europe beginning in April of that year.

The 10 important industrial countries discussed in this chapter are Canada, Great Britain, France, Sweden, Norway, Denmark, Holland, Belgium, Australia, and New Zealand. Many of these "democratic" countries became part of the battleground of the war during 1940. What permanent changes in labor relations and labor conditions will occur in various areas in Europe following the war cannot be predicted, but presumably past experience will afford the basis for future peacetime measures concerning labor in those countries that retain democratic forms of government. Certain phases of labor conditions in some of these countries have been mentioned in previous chapters. Important labor legislation is national in scope in all of them except Canada and Australia, which have federal systems of government and in which state or provincial legislation is of importance.

Obviously, it will not be possible from such a Cook's tour to obtain more than an outline view of conditions in each of these countries at the outbreak of the war in September 1939. But such an over-all view of labor conditions in the important democratic nations should give the reader some notion of broad outlines and general trends in labor matters in the democratic sections of the world during peacetime. It helps one to see the forest from the individual trees and to distinguish between temporary adjustments and long-time trends, which may be especially desirable during a time when labor laws and conditions in various countries are undergoing certain changes, largely necessitated by war needs. Presumably, the accumulated experience of democratic countries with various methods for settling labor disputes is reflected in their labor laws and in the provisions that they have made for the peaceful solution of differences between employers and employees.

In most of these countries, organized labor has had a stronger political position than it has enjoyed in the United States. The Labour Party has been a significant factor in Australian politics since the late 1890's, and in the 1930's labor parties were in power for various periods in Great Britain, Sweden, Norway, Denmark, Australia, and New Zealand. It is true that the labor governments in the Scandinavian countries needed the support of the agricultural parties in order to obtain a parliamentary majority, because agriculture is such an important element in the economy of the Scandinavian countries,[1] but the significant fact is that labor parties and the labor press have been so important in many democratic countries. The General Council of the federation of trade unions in Great Britain has control over a daily newspaper with a circulation of 2,000,000 copies; the labor party in Denmark publishes a newspaper that has a larger circulation than any other Danish newspaper; and in Sweden, Norway, and Australia, labor newspapers represent a large section of the daily press. In Sweden the names of strike-breakers are printed in the labor press.

The important role played by labor parties and the labor press in these foreign countries finds no counterpart in this country. As was explained in Chapters 4 and 20, although the labor movement got an early start in America in the 1820's, it failed to develop much during the ensuing 70 years. Some of the factors retarding its progress were discussed in Chapter 20. In a recent survey of *Organized Labour in Four Continents*, H. A. Marquand, a British professor of industrial relations, states that in the United States "organized labor in the past has encountered more hostility from the law and the State than in any other country maintaining a democratic form of government."[2]

A glance at Table 36 in Chapter 20, showing the percentage of workers organized in various countries, indicates that, with regard

[1] In Sweden, for example, 39 per cent of the gainfully employed population is in agriculture, compared with 54 per cent in industry and trade, part of whom are employers or independent businessmen.
[2] H. A. Marquand *et al.*, *Organized Labour in Four Continents*, 1939, p. xi.

to labor organization, the United States, Canada, and France were well behind the other democratic nations in both 1930 and 1939. The situation of organized labor in Canada has been very similar to that in the United States, many of the large "international" unions having locals in Canada as well as in this country. Indeed, unionism in Canada is so closely tied up with organized labor in the United States that the national union center, the Trades and Labour Congress of Canada, suspended the CIO unions in Canada from the Congress in January 1939.

Among the factors retarding the French labor movement have been the predominantly rural character of France and a wide split in the labor movement that persisted from 1922 to 1936 and severely weakened the French trade-union movement. With a relatively large rural population in France, the formation of a labor party, dominated by trade-unions, has seemed out of the question. Rank-and-file demand for unity finally resulted in an amalgamation of the two factions of the labor movement into the General Confederation of Labor in 1936, and the electoral triumph of the Popular Front political parties in the same year led to the formation of a government under socialist direction. Such successes were followed by an unprecedented increase in trade-union membership in France from about 1,000,000 in 1935 to well over 5,000,000 in 1938,[1] although thereafter union membership began to decline with the fall of the Popular Front government.

Unions and employers' organizations. Table 36 indicates that in 1939 about 40 or 50 per cent of all employees in Australia, Sweden, Denmark, New Zealand, and Belgium were union members, compared with a figure of around 20 per cent for the United States and Canada. In Denmark, farm laborers and domestic servants are well organized, while in Sweden not only are farm laborers and government employees organized, but some 40 municipalities have formed an employers' association to negotiate collective agreements with their organized workers.[2] In France, the Civil Servants' Federation forms a large section of the national federation of organized workers.

---

[1] *Cf.* Andre Philip, "France," in Marquand *et al.*, *op. cit.*, p. 33; and *The I. L. O. Year-Book, 1938–1939*, International Labour Office, 1939, p. 409.

[2] The Royal Social Board, *Social Work and Legislation in Sweden*, 1938, p. 48.

The structure of labor unions abroad was briefly discussed in Chapter 21, where it was pointed out that there has been a definite trend toward industrial unionism. In Belgium, for example, industrial unions have recently tended to displace craft unions. In Sweden the organized employers put pressure upon the unions to amalgamate into industrial units so that the employers might replace a number of separate and different agreements with a single agreement in each industry. The central federations of unions in Belgium, France, and the Netherlands have generally been formed along religious or political lines.

In the Scandinavian countries, trade-unions are not required to incorporate or to register under any law or to account for their funds; but there has been no question of their legal responsibility, and racketeering in trade-unions is unheard of in those countries. English law forbids labor unions to incorporate, but they can register if they wish to obtain certain benefits and assume certain obligations. The salaries of the heads of British labor unions have averaged around £400 or £500 (about $2,000) a year, and none of the officials of Swedish national unions or the Swedish labor federation receives a salary of more than $2,000 a year.[1] In the Netherlands, unions find it advantageous to register in order to be invested with a legal personality. In Belgium, registration is also optional; while in France, unions must register their bylaws. Some Canadian provinces have recently made union registration compulsory, although it is voluntary under the national law.

Under a law passed in 1936, the New Zealand unions may be registered with the national Arbitration Court, and no new union can be registered for the jurisdiction of an existing union unless a majority of the workers in that jurisdiction approve. All employees subject to any of the Court's awards or to an agreement filed with the Court must be members of the appropriate registered union, and it is unlawful for a covered employer to hire a nonunionist if a union member is available. In return for this closed shop by law, the unions must accept all workers who apply for membership and must limit their dues to one shilling a week unless a majority

---

[1] *Cf.* Marquis W. Childs, *This Is Democracy: Collective Bargaining in Scandinavia*, 1938, p. 15. By way of contrast, the general range of salaries for presidents of national unions in this country is from $5,000 to $8,000, and a few receive salaries as high as $20,000 and $25,000. Of course, differences in living costs and standards tend to modify this contrast.

of the membership votes to accept a higher rate of dues.[1] Some of the awards of arbitration courts in Australia grant union labor preference in employment, in which case the employment of nonunionists is illegal.

In the European countries under discussion, with the exception of France, employers' associations have generally negotiated with unions instead of seeking to destroy them. Far more than in the United States, the European employers' associations have tried to enroll the small employers, so that the unions and employers' associations may negotiate single national agreements covering all employers in an industry or a certain competitive area. In Great Britain and the Scandinavian countries, practically all the employers are included in employers' associations that are federated into a central employers' organization. Even before the first World War, the General Federation of Danish Employers, which includes virtually all Danish employers, made a declaration to the effect that "the main basis for the regulation of conditions of work is no more the individual labor contract . . . but the collective agreement negotiated and accepted by employers' and labor organizations."[2] Where, as in the United States and France, employers' associations have been belligerent and antiunion so that they are not engaged in negotiating agreements with labor organizations, there is less need to enroll all eligible employers, and the employers' associations are not closely knit into a central federation, which may exercise a considerable degree of control over individual members.

The President's Commission on Industrial Relations in Great Britain, in its report of August 25, 1938, stated that in England

Labor and employer organizations have been further strengthened by the frequent support and encouragement which they render to each other. Repeatedly employers and representatives of employers' organizations stated to us that they preferred strong unions to weak ones, because the strong union is better able to secure the fulfillment of agreements and is better able to bring competitors up to the wage and hour standards of the industry, as set by the agreements. Repeatedly labor representatives stated to us that they preferred strong employer organizations to weak

---

[1] *Cf.* E. J. Riches, "The Restoration of Compulsory Arbitration in New Zealand," *International Labour Review*, vol. 34 (December 1936), pp. 754–55.

[2] Halvard M. Lange, "Scandinavian Labour 1920–1937," in H. A. Marquand *et al.*, *op. cit.*, p. 239.

ones, because the stronger the organization the fewer the units which remain outside to undermine industry standards.[1]

In Sweden, also, labor unions have tried to force unorganized employers to join the employers' association so that collective bargaining might be more orderly and all-inclusive and that national agreements covering the whole competitive area might be negotiated between unions and employers' associations. It is reported that some Swedish unions have helped to force unorganized employers into employers' associations by demanding that nonmembers pay wage rates above those stipulated in the union's agreement with the association.[2]

In some European countries, employers' associations exercise considerable power and control over employer members. In Sweden, for example, the centralization of financial power and authority in the hands of the Swedish Employers' Federation has gone to far greater lengths than it has on the labor side, where separate national unions are still fairly autonomous. Each employer member of the Federation is required to post a bond, from which fines or damages may be collected for violations of the Federation's bylaws. An affiliated employer or employers' association is forbidden to make any collective labor agreement or to declare a lockout without definite approval from the executive board of the Federation. The Federation has the authority to order a lockout, in which case every member in the industry affected is bound to obey the order "on pain of damages" and of forfeiting his rights in the Federation.[3] In Sweden, as in Denmark, the Employers' Federation has a "war chest" from which employers engaged in an approved strike or lockout may receive daily compensation, just as union members on strike receive strike benefits from union funds.

In Great Britain, employers' associations usually forbid member firms to negotiate directly with a union, and require that all differences or disputes with a union be referred to the association. Member firms are generally forbidden to employ workers of other member firms during a strike or lockout in those other firms.

[1] Mimeographed copy of report, dated August 31, 1938, paragraph 82, p. 18.
[2] M. W. Childs, *op. cit.*, p. 26.
[3] *Report of the President's Commission on Industrial Relations in Sweden*, mimeographed release dated September 22, 1938, paragraph 9, p. 4.

Authoritative information concerning the activities of the National Confederation of Employers' Organizations in Great Britain, which included 266 industry-wide employers' organizations in 1936, is meager. Although "exercising great authority and wide influence," the National Confederation "seldom comes into the open," "usually avoids publicity," and "publishes no general reports on its activities." [1] Its member organizations are reported to include firms normally employing fully 7,000,000 workers. In Australia, employers' associations not infrequently make private investigations of firms suspected of undercutting the awards of the courts under compulsory arbitration; and where such undercutting is discovered, steps are taken to stop it. [2]

Collective bargaining in many European countries has been between national unions and industry-wide employers' associations so that a large percentage of all workers are covered by national collective agreements. In Sweden, for example, there were about 760,000 members of unions in 1935, and collective labor agreements covered almost 720,000 workers, of whom over a third were included under national agreements. A similar situation has prevailed in Great Britain and Denmark, where a sizeable proportion of all workers have been subject to collective agreements on a national or regional basis.

The President's Commission on Industrial Relations in Sweden and in Great Britain reported in 1938 that it found no collective agreements in Sweden providing for either the closed shop or the check-off, and that in Great Britain closed-shop agreements were exceptional and the check-off was very exceptional. Where employers do not strive to weaken or eliminate labor unions, the closed shop is less likely to be a significant issue.

Legislation on labor agreements and standards. Various countries adopted legislation in the 1930's to extend the area over which terms of employment were determined by collective bargaining. In Great Britain, France, the Netherlands, Belgium, New Zealand, and in various states of Australia and provinces of Canada, the terms of collective agreements entered into by representative or majority groups in an industry may be made legally

[1] Cf. J. Henry Richardson, *Industrial Relations in Great Britain*, International Labour Office, Studies and Reports Series *A*, No. 36, 1938, pp. 84–85, 91–92.

[2] Cf. W. Rupert Maclaurin, "Compulsory Arbitration in Australia," *American Economic Review*, vol. 28 (March 1938), p. 74.

binding upon all persons in the industry or in a particular region. Such extension of agreements tends to encourage employers and employees to join the organizations negotiating agreements, since they are likely to be blanketed under the resulting agreements.

The breakdown of wage standards in the British cotton-textile industry, that began in the unorganized sections of the industry and spread to some organized employers, led to the passage of the Cotton Manufacturing Act of 1934, under which the wage rates agreed upon by collective bargaining between the unions and the organized employers were made legally binding upon all manufacturers in the weaving section of the industry. There has been some question of following the same procedure in the retail grocery and clothing trades in Great Britain.[1]

In 1936 France passed legislation making it possible for the Minister of Labor to transform collective agreements into a legalized code for a whole industry or trade in a defined area. The legalization and extension of collective agreements must be requested by both parties to the agreement, who must be the most representative bodies of employers and employees in the industry and in the area. This procedure was rapidly applied in France in the late 1930's, because business in large cities, which were well unionized and had good labor standards, was suffering from the competition of small towns and rural areas where labor standards were lower.[2]

A law enacted in the Netherlands in 1937 authorized the government to declare the terms of a collective agreement binding upon an entire industry or branch of industry, if the agreement had been entered into by a majority of the workers in the trade or industry. During the first six months of 1938, for example, an agreement covering 66 Dutch footwear factories with some 65 per cent of all workers in the industry was made the common rule for the entire footwear industry in Holland, because wage- and price-cutting were jeopardizing labor standards. A 1936 law in Belgium empowered the government to make the hours provisions of a collective agreement binding upon an entire industry.

In New Zealand, under the system of wage-fixing by a national court of arbitration, collective agreements affecting a majority of workers in an industry may be made binding upon all employers

---

[1] *Cf.* H. A. Marquand *et al.*, *op. cit.*, p. 182.　　　　　[2] *Ibid.*, p. 41.

in the industry, and the court may extend one of its awards so as to make the award binding upon any labor union or employer in the industry. In this way, it is possible to achieve national uniformity in labor standards. In three Australian states (Queensland, South Australia, and Western Australia), voluntary collective agreements and awards by the court of arbitration may be extended by the court and thus be made binding upon all employers or employees in that industry within the state.

Four Canadian provinces (Alberta, Ontario, Saskatchewan, and Quebec) adopted legislation in the 1930's, by which the labor standards in collective agreements may be made legally enforceable for every employer or employee in an industry or a district within the province.

Most democratic countries have laws for the establishment of minimum wages or maximum hours of work, especially for industries not well organized. The legal provisions for minimum wages in Great Britain, Australia, and New Zealand were discussed in Chapter 12. The British minimum-wage boards and the courts of arbitration in Australia and New Zealand fix normal working hours as well as wage rates. An act passed in 1936 provided that the New Zealand court establish the 40-hour week in all covered lines of industry except where employers could prove that it would not be practical to operate the industry on the 40-hour week. The 40-hour week was also established by law in France in June 1936, but the law was modified (not repealed) by various special decrees in November 1938, March 1939, and April 1939, which permitted longer normal working weeks, especially for work connected with the national defense. The French Forty Hour Law also provided for a legal vacation of 15 days for one year's work. A Swedish law passed in 1938 assured workers (including domestic servants) who had worked 180 days in a 12-month period of a vacation of at least 12 days with full pay.

By the end of 1937 all the Canadian provinces except Nova Scotia had enacted general minimum-wage laws applying to men as well as women, and most of these laws empowered the minimum-wage boards to fix maximum hours also.

Law on strikes, lockouts, and other practices. In a number of democratic countries, strikes are prohibited in certain industries, or before a certain waiting period has elapsed, or before a certain procedure has been followed. In the Netherlands, strikes are forbidden on the railroads and in public service. In Norway, also, public employees do not have a right to strike; while in Belgium the right of certain classes of government employees to strike has been recognized. According to the British Trades Disputes and Trade Unions Act of 1927, a strike or lockout is illegal if it has an object other than the furtherance of a labor dispute within the industry in which the strikers are employed *and* is designed or calculated to coerce the government, either directly or by inflicting hardship upon the community. However, in Great Britain and Canada, as already mentioned, labor unions are freed from any liability under the common law of conspiracy in restraint of trade. Trade-union contracts in restraint of trade are legal in Great Britain, and British unions cannot be sued for any tortious acts by members.

Both Australia and New Zealand outlaw all strikes or lockouts in industries covered by court awards or by collective agreements filed with the arbitration courts. In the state of Queensland, a strike must also be authorized by a vote of the members of the union. Nevertheless, there have been a number of illegal strikes in Australia during the last two or three decades, especially in coal mining.

The laws of Sweden, Norway, and Denmark forbid strikes and lockouts in industries covered by collective agreements during the lifetime of the agreement. In Sweden the law requires that a notice of strike be given seven days before a strike is actually called. In Denmark the law requires a two-week notice before a strike is called, and during that period the union inquires of the Industrial Court whether the strike would be legal. In Canada, employers and employees in public utilities and mining are required to give at least 30 days' notice of changes that they plan to make in the conditions of employment, during which period strikes and lockouts are prohibited. Some 650 strikes in violation of this Canadian law, most of them in coal mining and shipping, occurred during the 28 years ending in March 1935.[1]

Some foreign countries place strict limitations upon secondary

---

[1] *Cf.* B. M. Selekman, *Law and Labor Relations: A Study of the Industrial Disputes Investigation Act of Canada*, Business Research Studies No. 14, Harvard University Graduate School of Business Administration, March 1936, pp. 8–9.

boycotts, sympathetic strikes, and picketing activities. In 1936, for example, Norway passed a law outlawing seven specific types of boycott, mainly the secondary boycott or "billiard shots" by buyers. In Denmark and Sweden there is only one exception to the ban on strikes and lockouts during the term of a collective agreement. In those countries, sympathetic strikes or lockouts are permitted in support of another legal strike or lockout. Both employers and employees wish to retain the power to take such sympathetic action under a collective agreement. There are no special laws with regard to picketing in Sweden because strikes there have not been violent, both sides realizing the value of friendly relations after the dispute is ended.

Under an Act of 1927, sympathetic strikes are illegal in England when they are extended beyond a given industry and also have as an object to coerce the government, either directly or by inflicting hardship upon the community. This Act undoubtedly outlaws general strikes, but has apparently had little effect upon the number of sympathetic strikes involving more than one industry, because most of them are not designed to coerce the government. The same Act states that picketing must not be carried on in a manner calculated to intimidate any person, or to obstruct movement to and from a place, or to lead to a breach of the peace. The President's Commission on Industrial Relations in Great Britain reported in 1938 that "in the case of strikes involving at the outset enough workers to make continued operation of a plant impractical, employers almost invariably shut down their plants and do not attempt to operate until the controversy has been settled by negotiation" and that, even in lines where labor organization is not extensive, "there is a general feeling among workers and employers that 'the job belongs to the man' and that it is not right for men to take, or to be asked to take, the jobs of their fellows." [1]

Foreign countries also have legislation containing provisions similar to those in the Wagner or National Labor Relations Act, dealing with such matters as discrimination against unionists, bargaining in good faith, and the majority rule. Such restrictions are, however, less necessary in most foreign countries because, generally speaking, they are at a more advanced stage in the

[1] Mimeographed Report, *op. cit.*, p. 10.

development of union-employer relations. In Great Britain, for example, discrimination against strikers and their leaders is reported to be of little significance, because both sides desire "to effect a resumption of work under circumstances as free from bitterness as possible, so that future strife may be avoided." [1] The labor spy, hired by employers, is practically unknown abroad.

In Sweden, the right of association is guaranteed to workers, and both sides are definitely obligated to enter into negotiations, to attend joint meetings, and, where necessary, to make "proposals supported by reasons for the settlement of the question concerning which negotiations were instituted." [2] If either of the disputing parties fails to fulfill this obligation to negotiate, the Labor Court can, at the request of the other party, order the offending party to negotiate in good faith under penalty of a fine.

Between April 1937 and April 1938, seven out of the nine Canadian provinces passed legislation dealing with labor organizations and labor relations. All of these provincial acts grant employees the right to organize for lawful purposes without employer interference and also require employers to bargain with the representatives of a majority of the employees. Employers who refuse to bargain may be fined $500 in Alberta and British Columbia and $100 in Nova Scotia. In some provinces, fines may also be levied against an employer who tries to prevent his workers from joining unions by such means as intimidation, discharge, or threat of loss of employment or position. In addition, the Dominion government passed legislation in 1939 penalizing, by a fine up to $1,000, employers who discriminate against unionists. In connection with elections to determine who are the representatives of the "majority," there is no provision for separate representation by crafts. Two provinces require that trade-unions and employers' associations file their constitutions, a list of officers, and financial reports for the government's confidential use. [3]

---

[1] *Report of the President's Commission on Industrial Relations in Great Britain*, dated August 25, 1939 (mimeographed), p. 11.

[2] *Report of the President's Commission on Industrial Relations in Sweden*, dated September 19, 1939 (mimeographed), p. 8.

[3] For a more detailed discussion of this Canadian legislation, *cf.* H. Fabian Underhill, "Recent Canadian Labor Relations Legislation," *Journal of Political Economy*, vol. 48 (June 1940), pp. 357–73.

Methods of settling labor disputes.[1] Provisions for government intervention in labor disputes range all the way from compulsory arbitration in Australia and New Zealand to conciliation in England, where there has been a complete absence of any government compulsion, where there is no enforcement of collective agreements, and where usually both parties are even free to disregard decisions resulting from an appeal to voluntary arbitration.

Compulsory arbitration in Australia and New Zealand, with strikes and lockouts outlawed in the covered industries, has had its drawbacks. As already indicated, it has not prevented a number of strikes from occurring in those countries in violation of the law. A major weakness of the method has been its tendency to encourage lengthy litigation, including long briefs containing tenuous arguments, which has congested the courts. Because the judge is rarely well acquainted with conditions in the industry subject to the dispute, arbitration tends to become a battle of wits between opposing lawyers.[2] In some of the Australian states, machinery for conciliation has been tried as a method of forestalling some litigation and relieving the courts. In New Zealand, councils of conciliation may try to bring about an agreement between both sides or may make a recommendation, either of which the national court of arbitration can make binding. Failing settlement in that fashion, the court can make its own decisions, which are binding upon both parties.

Compulsory arbitration has been tried at times in Great Britain, Sweden, and Norway. A Parliamentary committee in England reported in 1918 that "the experience of compulsory arbitration during the war period has shown that it is not a successful method of avoiding disputes and in normal times it would undoubtedly prove even less successful."[3] England abandoned compulsory arbitration after the first World War, and in 1938 the President's Commission on Industrial Relations in Great Britain found that both organized labor and employers were definitely opposed to compulsory arbitration of industrial disputes.[4] Norway also tried compulsory arbitration during the first World War and again from 1927 to 1929

[1] A good factual discussion of this topic is to be found in Margaret H. Schoenfeld, "Industrial-Relations Machinery in Democratic Foreign Countries," *Monthly Labor Review*, vol. 49 (November 1939), pp. 1050–74, from which some of the material in this chapter has been drawn.

[2] *Cf.* W. Rupert Maclaurin, *op. cit.*, pp. 67–69.

[3] *Report of the President's Commission on Industrial Relations in Great Britain*, p. 7.

[4] *Idem.*

during the gold-parity depression in that country. In both cases
the employers and labor opposed compulsory arbitration, and during the second period the law was simply disregarded and remained
unenforced.[1] Sweden experimented with compulsory arbitration on
private railroads and in the municipal enterprises of the three
largest cities during the period from 1909 until 1923, when that
method of settling primary disputes was completely abandoned.
"In Sweden both workers and employers want to avoid compulsory
arbitration; they want to limit the state to its present role of voluntary umpire." [2]

The existence of compulsory arbitration in New Zealand and
Australia has tended to cause the adoption of temporary measures
for compulsory arbitration in Denmark. Danish bacon, butter, and
other agricultural products compete in the English market with
similar products from Australasia, where compulsory arbitration
helps to prevent labor stoppages. The Danes have been afraid that
a labor stoppage, temporarily preventing shipments of such products as bacon to England, might cause a permanent lowering of the
Danish quota on imports into Great Britain. Furthermore, Denmark, with few natural resources such as the other Scandinavian countries enjoy, simply has to import certain products, so it is
essential to prevent an interruption of her exports such as might
result from a widespread strike.

In 1933 Denmark enacted a law forbidding strikes and lockouts
for one year, and in 1936 a law was passed enforcing compulsory
arbitration for one year. A law passed in 1934 for the purpose of
reducing strikes requires that all employers and unions in an industry abide by proposals of the public conciliator (called arbitrator), if
they are accepted by a majority vote of workers in all the unions
involved and a majority of the capital of all employers concerned.
Upon failure to settle disputes in three separate industries, occurring
in 1937, 1938, and 1939, the proposed settlement of the public conciliator was enacted into law. In 1938 compulsory arbitration was
also established by law to settle disputes in three Norwegian industries, which it had not been possible to settle by voluntary methods. Special boards were given powers of compulsory arbitration in

[1] M. W. Childs, *op. cit.*, p. 47; and Finn Moe, *Does Norwegian Labor Seek the Middle
Way?* League for Industrial Democracy Pamphlet Series, June 1937, p. 20.
[2] Childs, *op. cit.*, p. 30.

those industries, although such arbitration was not established for Norwegian industry in general.

Denmark, Norway, and Sweden have adopted compulsory arbitration for secondary disputes—disagreements concerning the interpretation of collective agreements adopted voluntarily. In case of a breach of such a collective agreement, including strikes or lockouts in violation of the agreement, the Industrial Court in each of these countries has the power to assess damages against the offending party. In these courts, action is quick because it is not hampered by legal rules or procedures, and, generally speaking, the decisions are not subject to appeal.

The procedure for settling labor disputes in France changed considerably in the 1930's. The arrangements from 1936 to the outbreak of war in 1939 were somewhat unusual and might be called compulsory resort to conciliation and arbitration with freedom to strike or to lock out employees. Unlike most countries, France draws no distinction between primary and secondary disputes, and both are subject to the same procedure. In case both parties fail to agree upon a new collective agreement, the arbitrator may make an award that is binding upon both parties until they do sign an agreement. In determining the wage rates to be imposed in such temporary awards, the arbitrators "have taken account of minimum standards of living, variations in the cost of living, comparable rates of wages in other industries in the region, possibilities of making profits, and general economic conditions." [1] Although recourse to arbitration and acceptance of the arbitrator's decision are compulsory, the law at the same time preserves the right to lock out or to strike. Prior to November 1938, sanctions for disobeying the awards of arbitrators were limited to the moral pressure of public opinion or to damage suits in the ordinary courts against parties violating the awards, on the grounds that their actions involved abusive exercise of property rights or the right to strike. In November 1938, however, a decree established penalties for failure to comply with the terms of arbitration awards.

Compulsory investigation has sometimes been used for important disputes in Great Britain and the Netherlands, and has been in force on a wide scale since 1907 in Canada. In disputes of major public interest, the Minister of Labour in England may appoint a

[1] H. A. Marquand *et al.*, *op. cit.*, p. 48.

Court of Inquiry to make an investigation. Under the law, the appointment of a Court (of which there were 20 in the 18 years prior to 1938) does not operate to stop or to postpone a dispute; the purpose is to expose the facts and to bring public opinion to bear upon the merits of the conflict. In Holland, also, the Minister of Labor may, in a dispute seriously affecting the public interest and likely to involve at least 300 workers, appoint a special committee of inquiry to investigate and report on the dispute. The decisions of such committees may be published in order to influence public opinion, but there is no compulsion on either side to accept their findings.

The Canadian Industrial Disputes Investigation Act, passed in 1907 and amended at various times, requires that employers and employees in the covered industries give at least 30 days' notice of changes which they contemplate making in conditions of employment. If protest is made, such changes cannot occur, nor is a strike or lockout permitted, until after both parties have received the report of a special three-man board appointed under the Act to investigate the dispute. Statistics indicate that, on the average, it takes from two to three months for an appointed board to investigate and make its report.[1] The findings of a board are not enforceable, but strikes, lockouts, or changes in terms of employment before and during a board's proceedings may be penalized by fines. The Act includes in its coverage employment in coal or other mines, railways, shipping, telephone and telegraph lines, and power works employing 10 or more persons. The Act may be extended to include other industries if employers and employees request it, and all the provinces except Prince Edward Island have delegated to the Dominion government the power of compulsory investigation of disputes in covered industries entirely within their boundries. In addition, five provinces adopted legislation in the 1930's, giving local authorities much the same powers in disputes as the Dominion has under the Industrial Disputes Investigation Act.

From March 1907 until March 1935, a total of 638 disputes were referred to boards under the Canadian Act, and in all but 49 of them a strike was averted. In 15 of those 49 cases, illegal strikes occurred either before or during board proceedings. On the other hand, a total of 657 illegal strikes or lockouts in violation of the

[1] B. M. Selekman, *op. cit.*, pp. 39–40.

Act occurred during the same period from 1907 to 1935, of which 469 were in mining and shipping.[1] Because those administering the Act have emphasized its conciliatory rather than its compulsory features, the Dominion government has in no instance brought persons violating the Act before the courts in order to punish them. Indeed, in only 19 out of the 657 cases of violations have private parties brought action in the courts.[2] Furthermore, because of the policy of furthering conciliation instead of using compulsion, publicity of board findings has rarely been utilized to bring public opinion to bear upon recalcitrant parties to a dispute.

Most of the decisions or recommendations of these special boards of conciliation and investigation have concerned wages, although in recent years some boards have also recommended union recognition, the holding of employee elections, the payment of back wages by a company breaking a collective agreement, and even reinstatement with back pay for a worker unjustly discharged.

Although Canadian labor opposed the Industrial Disputes Investigation Act from 1907 until 1918, since then labor has favored an extension of the Act to cover all industries. This legislation has proved an aid to the unions both in securing recognition from employers and in affording union representatives an opportunity to meet and bargain with employers in connection with the procedures followed under the Act. The Act has operated to protect workers from sudden wage reductions, and employers have little opportunity to prepare for a strike by producing for stock during the waiting period, except in mining, where most of the strikes in violation of the Act have occurred. In addition, a kindly administration has not attempted to enforce penalties against workers for violating the Act.

Canadian employers were also generally hostile to the Act from 1907 until 1912, and, although they later came to favor it, they have consistently opposed all attempts to extend its provisions to other industries not affected with a public interest. Employers have been somewhat less favorable to the law since 1925, when penalties were written into it for changes in working conditions during the 30-day waiting period and before a board reports.

Legislation recently enacted in five Canadian provinces (Alberta, British Columbia, Manitoba, New Brunswick, and Quebec) follows

[1] *Ibid.*, p. 9.   [2] *Ibid.*, p. 10.

the Dominion Industrial Disputes Investigation Act by providing
for conciliation and special boards of investigation consisting of
three members to deal with intraprovincial labor disputes. Like
the Federal Act, these provincial laws prohibit strikes or lockouts
during waiting periods varying from a minimum of 20 days to well
over 60 days in some of the provinces. Generally speaking, Canadian labor organizations do not seem to object to such postponement of strikes, although it may be to their disadvantage when it
is applied to seasonal industries or in industries where production
for storage is possible.[1]

In all of the countries here discussed, the government provides a
staff or panel of persons who may act as conciliators or as arbitrators
in industrial disputes. Perhaps the facilities for conciliation and
voluntary arbitration are most highly developed in Great Britain,
where the Ministry of Labour maintains a staff of full-time trained
conciliators and a panel of qualified and experienced citizens who
are willing to serve as arbitrators. In addition, there is a permanent
Industrial Court to decide controversies submitted to it by the
Minister of Labour, upon consent of both parties, after all existing
joint machinery has been tried without success. Unless otherwise
agreed to by both parties, the Court's awards are not binding; but
they are generally accepted. English employers and workers prefer
to be free of legal compulsions, both groups believing that collective
agreements should rest upon mutual understanding and good faith
rather than upon legal sanctions.

Government conciliation and arbitration procedure in the
Netherlands closely resembles that of Great Britain. The government provides public facilities for conciliation and arbitration, and
there is no compulsion to accept the findings of official agencies
unless arrangements have been made in advance to do so. Provisions for the settlement of disputes in Belgium, also, are similar to
those in England, except for a unique feature involving penalties for
causing a stoppage of work before an attempt is made to settle the
existing difference under the prescribed procedure.

The type of machinery for settling labor disputes in each country
must be related to the traditions, institutions, and conditions in
that country. The situation in the United States has been very
different from that in countries where employers' associations desire

---

[1] For further discussion of this Canadian legislation, cf. H. F. Underhill, op. cit.

well-organized unions, where there are no company unions or hired labor spies, or where there is little, if any, violence in strikes. Despite such differences, the experience of foreign nations has some lessons for us, especially as we seem to be following in the footsteps of some of those countries, although we are still some distance behind them in the development of labor and employer organizations and of industrial relations.

Foreign strike statistics. The significance of strikes and lockouts is probably best measured by the number of working days lost as a result of such work stoppages. Table 38 contains figures for the working days lost in terms of each 100 employees in the

TABLE 38. AVERAGE NUMBER OF DAYS LOST EACH YEAR FROM STRIKES AND LOCKOUTS PER 100 EMPLOYEES IN THE WORKING POPULATION IN VARIOUS COUNTRIES DURING THE DECADE 1929 TO 1939 [1]

Country	Days lost
Norway	140
Sweden	66
Australia	61
Belgium	38
United States	36
Denmark	35
Great Britain	23
Netherlands	23
France	21
Canada	12
New Zealand	8

country's working population. It is impossible to avoid giving undue emphasis to one bad year in such strike statistics, although a 10-year average does present a more correct picture than would the figures for a single year. Elimination of the year 1931 from the Norwegian statistics would, however, reduce the average to 45 days, and the Danish yearly average would drop below nine days with the year 1936 omitted. As indicated in the footnote to the table, the figures for France and Belgium are too low because statistics are not available for 1936 in those two countries. Furthermore, the 1930's were years of unusual labor changes in the United

[1] Table calculated from data in the *1939 Year-Book of Labour Statistics*, International Labour Office, 1939, pp. 4–16, 208–10. Statistics for days lost from strikes and lockouts in France were missing for the years 1936 through 1938, in Norway and Sweden for the year 1938, and in Belgium for the year 1936. In France in 1936 there were over four times as many workers involved in strikes or lockouts as in any of the previous seven years, and in Belgium during the missing year 1936 over three times as many workers were involved in strikes or lockouts as in any of the seven previous years.

States, because of the rapid increase in union membership and the split in the ranks of labor. Such variations in conditions within this country certainly affected its strike statistics for the period.

The International Labour Office, which compiles these statistics for strikes and lockouts, explains that the completeness of the data varies from country to country because small disputes may be excluded in some countries, because workers indirectly affected are included in some cases with those directly involved, and because the methods of calculating the number of working days lost differ from country to country. Nevertheless, it is believed that the data "make it possible to compare in a general way fluctuations in the extent and importance of disputes within the various countries." [1]

It is interesting to note from Table 38 the high figure for days lost in Australia, where there is compulsory arbitration of labor disputes, and in Norway and Sweden, which have had compulsory arbitration for secondary disputes. On the other hand, New Zealand with compulsory arbitration and Canada with compulsory investigation have the lowest figures for days lost in the whole group. Great Britain and the Netherlands, which have not relied upon compulsion at all, also stand well in the list.

Of course, successful labor relations cannot be measured by strikes and lockouts alone. Psychological aspects of the matter cannot be overlooked. Neither are such statistics the sole test for determining the success of various methods or government systems of settling labor disputes. A particular method may be valuable because it helps to educate the workers and the employers in labor matters. If any conclusion can legitimately be drawn from these statistics of days lost, perhaps it is that no particular system for settling labor disputes is best. A system that seems to work well in one nation may not operate so successfully elsewhere.

[1] *Ibid.*, p. 207.

States, because of the rapid increase in union membership and the shift in the ranks of labour. Such variations of conditions within this country certainly affected its strike statistics for the period.

The International Labour Office, which compiles these statistics for strikes and lockouts, explains that the comparisons of the data vary from country to country because small disputes may be excluded in some countries, because workers indirectly affected are included in some cases with those directly involved, and because the methods of calculating the number of working days lost differ from country to country. Nevertheless, it is believed that the data make it possible to compare in a general way fluctuations in the extent and importance of disputes within the various countries.

It is interesting to note from Table 35 the high figure for days lost in Australia, where there is compulsory arbitration of labor disputes and in Norway and Sweden, which have had compulsory arbitration for secondary disputes. On the other hand, New Zealand with compulsory arbitration and Canada with compulsory investigation have the lowest figures for days lost in this whole group. Great Britain and the Netherlands, which have not relied upon compulsion at all, also stand well in this list.

Of course, successful labor relations cannot be legislated by statutes and by-laws alone. Psychological aspects of the matter cannot be forecasted. Neither can such attitudes as those that for determining the success of efforts to induce a government by means of settling labor disputes. A particular method must be valuable because it induces in either the workers and the employers in labor matters. If any conclusion can legitimately be drawn from these statistics of days lost, perhaps it is that no particular system for settling labor disputes can... that it is that seems to work well in one country can... be adopted successfully elsewhere.

PART FOUR

COLLECTIVE BARGAINING IN CERTAIN INDUSTRIES

CHAPTER TWENTY-SEVEN

THE INDUSTRY IN INDUSTRIAL RELATIONS

Experience with labor relations and collective bargaining has differed from industry to industry. For example, labor relations in the railroad industry have evidenced a marked contrast to labor relations in steel or in maritime transportation; the labor situation in clothing has not been similar to that in the newspaper industry; and labor experience in the lumber industry (logging and sawmilling) has presented a sharp contrast to experience in the paper-and-pulp industry, which obtains its raw materials from the lumber industry.

Industrial differences and labor. Various factors account for these differences or contrasts in industrial relations. On the railroads and in paper and pulp, for example, employment is fairly steady and employees do not change employers frequently. In marine transportation and lumber, on the other hand, labor turnover is very high and employment fluctuates widely—partly because of seasonal variation. In the past, a large percentage of the loggers have lived in camps operated by the employer and were, to a considerable extent, migratory workers. Seamen may change employers with each sailing, and the jobs of longshoremen often last less than six hours, so that a waterfront worker may work for a number of employers in a single day. The type of worker who cuts trees or loads vessels for a living generally would not be well adapted for work on a newspaper or in a clothing factory. Conditions in the industry partly determine the kind of employees in that industry as well as the attitudes of employers and workers toward one another.

Labor relations are affected by the nature of competition in the industry and the market for the industry's product. Competitive pressures may lead to antiunionism and labor troubles, unless the employers, the union, or both together are able to reduce such pressures by "stabilizing" the industry to prevent wage- and price-cutting. Price competition, for example, tends to be much more severe among building contractors or the thousands of clothing manufacturers than it is in the railroad industry, where competition in prices has been outlawed and a single railroad often has all the business between two cities. In addition, clothing firms can easily migrate to another locality to take advantage of cost and other competitive differentials, whereas railroads and coal mines are confined to their present locations. The customer market has much more influence on labor relations in newspapers, which are sold largely to workers, than it does in steel, which is sold mostly to other employers.

The influence of competitive and seasonal factors is especially marked in agriculture. One of the reasons for labor troubles when agricultural laborers attempt to organize is that the farmer is often selling a staple product in a perfect market, in which he may be competing with farmers in various regions and nations. Persons can start up in the farming business almost anywhere. Under such competitive pressures, farmers in a certain locality are likely to oppose the organization of farm laborers, because it will raise their costs but not the selling price of their products, for the labor organization will not cover all producers of that crop. Agricultural labor problems are also, of course, tied up with the seasonal nature of agricultural employment, which requires workers to migrate and to lead unsettled lives, often in poor living quarters. Migratory workers, moving from camp to camp or town to town, are not able to establish a legal residence so that they can exercise political power through the ballot.

A mature industry is more likely to have stable labor relations under union agreements than is an industry that is experiencing rapid expansion and technological change. In this connection, a comparison might be drawn between the automobile and railroad industries. The railroad workers were organized into some 20 "standard" craft unions during the first two decades of this century. In the same period, the automobile industry, which experienced the sharp rise and change characteristic of a new industry, remained unorganized.[1] It is difficult for a union, especially a craft

[1] For a discussion of labor in the automobile industry, cf. William H. McPherson, *Labor Relations in the Automobile Industry*, 1940.

union, to adjust its economic program and structure to an industrial situation that is changing rapidly.

The nature of the industry also influences the character of the labor organization or organizations in that industry. A labor union must adjust to the special industrial environment in which it operates. The problems that face a union tend to determine its program, policies, and leadership. In certain industries, the employers have been so large in number and so diversified in interests that competition, unless restrained and regulated, would lead to wage- and price-cutting. Under such circumstances, the employers themselves have often been unable to "stabilize" the industry. Bituminous coal, clothing, building, laundry, trucking, and cleaning and pressing might be cited as examples. In those industries, the unions have found it necessary to regulate competition and to discipline erring employers, so that high wages might be paid and stability and order might characterize labor relations in the industry. Often the unions in such industries have aided in the formation or development of strong employers' associations. It is interesting to note that most of the industries in which collective bargaining is generally carried on with employers' associations are industries or trades having a large number of competing firms such as building, clothing, soft coal, hosiery, shoes, hats, the maritime industry, canning, fishing, cleaning and pressing, textiles, laundries, trucking, barbering, retail trade, printing, and hotels and restaurants.[1] In general, the mass-production industries, characterized by a limited number of large firms, do not deal with labor unions through employers' associations that cover most of the industry or the whole competitive area.

The industry as an economic unit. The union program of equalizing labor costs for competing employers involves the fixing of labor standards that can be enforced upon all employers in the industry who are producing for the same market. If a product or service enjoys a nationwide sale, unions strive to have collective bargaining on an industry-wide basis so that any resulting agreement will cover the whole competitive area. Collective bargaining on an industry-wide or national scale has characterized the railroad, coal, stove, and pottery industries, and, to some extent, the

---

[1] Cf. Written Trade Agreements in Collective Bargaining, National Labor Relations Board, Division of Economic Research, Bulletin No. 4, November 1939, p. 267.

men's clothing industry, the flat-glass industry, and the glass-bottle industry. Other industries, like building, newspapers, cleaning and pressing, and other service trades, are local-market lines, in which the locality constitutes the whole competitive area. The NRA, with its industry codes, encouraged collective dealing and bargaining on an industry-wide basis.

Both the practice of nationwide or even regional bargaining on an industrial basis and the organization of labor on an industrial basis tend to make labor industry-minded rather than class-minded. The Longshoremen's union strongly supports ship-subsidy bills; the coal miners oppose government projects to develop cheap electric power, which competes with coal; the Steel Workers' union opposes price reductions in steel; and various unions support the tariff on the products their members make. As indicated in Chapter 21, numerous craft unions have expanded their jurisdictions, especially since the founding of the CIO, until now most unions have an industrial orientation. Also, various craft unions, like the railroad and the building crafts, have joined together in federations for purposes of collective bargaining and unified action on an industrial basis.

Because industries differ so widely in labor matters, an understanding of labor relations can best be obtained through industry studies. Such an approach enables one to appreciate the economic and practical problems in labor relations. A knowledge of an industry's economics and past experience with labor relations are necessary in order to understand its present labor policies and attitudes. Furthermore, such a background of economic and historical facts furnishes the only sound basis for judging the prospects of industrial peace in that branch of the economy.

In the chapter that follows, the sharp contrast between labor relations in railroad and maritime transportation during the 1920's and 1930's is explained in the light of the characteristics and past experience and attitudes in both industries. The marked difference between labor relations in the West Coast lumber and pulp-and-paper industries can also be cited as an example of the influence of industrial factors upon labor relations.

Contrast between lumber and pulp-and-paper industries. The pulp-and-paper industry on the West Coast has never experienced the violent strikes, the radical unionism (especially the

IWW), and the bitter jurisdictional battles that have characterized the lumber industry in the Northwest. Although employing less than 10 per cent of the gainfully occupied population, the lumber industry accounted for over half of the days of idleness from strikes in Washington and Oregon between 1927 and 1940, and it accounted for over two thirds of the employee complaint charges filed in those states with the National Labor Relations Board from 1935 to 1940. In the pulp-and-paper industry, with about one fourth as many employees as lumber, there were no work stoppages from labor disputes between 1934 and the middle of 1940, and not one employee complaint was filed with the National Labor Relations Board during those years. One corporation and its officers, through control of two other concerns, dominates the West Coast pulp-and-paper industry, accounting for more than half of the production capacity and employees in both pulp and paper. Partly because of enlightened management, partly because of the influence of the National Industrial Recovery Act of 1933, and partly perhaps because of repeated Federal charges of monopolistic practices in the West Coast branch of the industry, this corporation did not oppose the organization of its employees after 1933. Under its leadership, the officials of the employers' association covering all West Coast pulp-and-paper manufacturers met in a conference with the representatives of the two old-line AFL unions in 1934, and since then the association has negotiated uniform agreements applying to the whole industry. After 1935, hourly earnings in this industry on the Pacific Coast averaged from 25 to 30 per cent above the hourly earnings of employees in the same industry in the rest of the country.

Whereas employment in the pulp-and-paper industry on the West Coast expanded throughout the 1930's, employment declined 65 per cent in lumber in the Northwest from 1929 to 1932, when the average wages of lumber and sawmill workers fell below 40 cents an hour, and a number of them received less than 30 cents an hour. The West Coast lumber industry has been well organized in employers' associations which cooperate closely with one another, so that the employers have been able to "stabilize" the industry, probably better than the unions could. For fully two thirds of the lumber production on the West Coast, detailed cost data are submitted to the trade association for the area as a basis for determining costs and adequate prices. Through an employers' organization, a fair degree of uniformity in retail prices is maintained for that third or fourth of the Northwest lumber output that is retailed within the region. The large producers and large brokers, who own ships and other equipment, confine their sales primarily to the Eastern markets, and one of these large firms alone controls a fifth of the total output of logging and sawmill operations in Washington and Oregon. Those two states supply about 95 per cent of the nation's output of Douglas fir, and large Northwest operators tend to specialize in Douglas fir, which enjoys a distinct advantage over other soft woods because it is especially desirable for structural purposes.

Past excesses in labor matters help to explain recent labor troubles in lumber in the Northwest. As stated by a committee appointed by the President to mediate the 1917 strike, the bitter and uncompromising attitudes of the employers helped to foster the IWW in the Northwest lumber camps, where its ideology still persists. Through a strong employers' organization, the operators defeated the 1917 strike, which centered around the workers' demand that the 10-hour day give way to an 8-hour day, as had happened in practically all large industries on the Coast. The 1935 strike, in which the National Guard was called out in Washington and Oregon, followed the refusal of employers to recognize and negotiate with the union. Complaint against the conservative leadership of the AFL union in the 1935 strike led to a split of the workers into two organizations, one CIO and the other AFL. The jurisdictional or organizational battles between these two labor factions were very bitter during the late 1930's, although the CIO union had a majority of the workers in logging during that period. Even in 1940, many employers in the Northwest lumber industry were still hoping to eliminate the unions and return to the "good old days." Their opposition has undoubtedly been one cause of the strikes, the labor unrest, and the radical unionism that have characterized the Northwest lumber industry.

Subsequent chapters. In addition to the following chapter contrasting labor relations in rail and water transportation, the labor experience of certain other industries is discussed in the chapters in this part of the book. The particular industries chosen for discussion represent different market situations and a variety of experience with collective bargaining. These other industries are bituminous coal, clothing, steel, and newspapers.

Bituminous coal is a highly competitive industry having a long experience with collective bargaining on a regional and national scale. Nonunion competition in the 1920's almost destroyed the union, and since 1933 the Federal government has helped to regulate the industry and to enforce fixed prices for coal.

In terms of competition and the number of firms in the industry, clothing resembles bituminous coal. Experience with collective bargaining in clothing prior to 1933 was somewhat similar to that in coal, but the unions, in collaboration with employers' associations, have recently "stabilized" the clothing industry by means of an elaborate system of private regulation, which restrains competition.

The iron and steel industry was the first industry in the United States to have collective agreements with unions, and such agreements were fairly common in the iron industry from 1865 to 1900. However, mergers changed the competitive situation in steel, and, during the period from 1900 until the CIO organizing campaign began in 1936, steel was an antiunion stronghold. Since 1936, collective bargaining and agreements have been the practice in a large part of the steel industry.

Newspaper publishing is a local-market industry, having a long experience of collective bargaining with the printing trades. More recently, the white-collar newspaper workers have organized and have bargained collectively with newspaper publishers.

CHAPTER TWENTY-EIGHT

RAIL AND WATER TRANSPORTATION

The contrast between labor relations on the railroads and in the maritime industry during the 1920's and 1930's was almost as sharp as that between the lumber and pulp-and-paper industries on the West Coast. While the maritime industry suffered from a number of severe strikes between 1934 and 1937, and from hundreds of work stoppages during the late 1930's, labor relations were very stable in the railroad industry, with no violation or abrogation of agreements and practically no strikes. A number of issues, including wage rates and dismissal compensation, were settled by national collective bargaining between the railroad unions and the employers during the decade of the 1930's.

THE RAILROADS

Railway workers were among the first wage-earners to form lasting trade-unions. The locomotive engineers organized in 1863, the conductors in 1868, the locomotive firemen in 1873, and the trainmen in 1883. These "Big Four Brotherhoods" in the engine-and-train service have always been in a strong position for collective bargaining because their services are required to operate the trains safely and on schedule. Because of their strategic advantages, they have often bargained singly and have refused to join the AFL. These railroad labor unions were at first primarily insurance organizations, formed because the hazards of railroad work were so great that private insurance companies were not interested in insuring the lives of railway employees.

The unions. The four brotherhoods, the seven "shop-craft" unions, and the ten "miscellaneous" craft unions make up the 21 "standard" railroad unions. The shop-craft unions are in the Railway Employees' Department of the AFL and have always acted as a unit in collective bargaining, as if they were one union. Their members work in railroad construction and repair shops, and most of them, such as the Machinists, Electrical Workers, and Sheet Metal Workers, have the bulk of their membership in other industries. The miscellaneous crafts include the unions of such workers as the telegraphers, signalmen, clerks, marine craftsmen who work on railroad wharves or boats, and maintenance-of-way employees who work on the rails and roadbed. In addition to the 21 standard unions, there are a number of others, including the unions of the train porters (red-caps), sleeping-car porters, cooks, waiters, etc.

In contrast to the situation in this country, railroad workers abroad have generally shown a preference for industrial unions. Attempts to establish industrial unionism on American railroads in 1893 and 1911 failed. In 1926 the presidents of the 21 standard railway unions formed the Railway Labor Executives' Association for cooperative action on legislation and in negotiating agreements. In certain cases, this association has been effective in handling negotiations on a national scale.

Employers' associations. The carriers do not have a national organization dealing exclusively with labor problems. In the past, the Association of American Railroads, representing 96 per cent of the railroad mileage in North America, has at times carried on negotiations with regard to labor legislation and labor conditions, but the collective agreements are signed by the individual carriers. Before the first World War, some of the bargaining was on a regional basis between the "Big Four Brotherhoods" and the three territorial organizations (northeastern, western, and southeastern), established by the railroads originally for the classification of freight and similar problems.

Nature of the industry. The railroads do not need labor organizations to "stabilize" the industry. The Federal government has done that. The Interstate Commerce Commission, especially since 1910, has fixed railroad rates, so the same price is charged for freight or passenger service on all railroads between any two cities. Price competition is nonexistent, except for such competition by other forms of transportation (air, bus, or truck), whose rates and operations between states are also regulated by the Interstate Commerce Commission.

The fact that the railroads have been so subject to Federal legislation and control has made them especially susceptible to public

and congressional opinion. Consequently, the railroad unions have
been able to use the threat of appeal to Congress to assist them in
gaining their demands in negotiations with the employers. The
fact that employment on railroads fell from 2,000,000 workers in
1920 to about 1,000,000 following 1931 has helped to make the
public and the Congress sympathetic toward the problems of railway labor. This decline in employment has played a part in the
enactment of full-crew laws and the stress on seniority in railroad
agreements. Seniority is also to be explained by the differences in
the desirability of jobs open to the same class of employees, such as
the different runs for locomotive engineers.

Trains operate all hours of the day and night on a strict schedule.
Consequently, the industry would be severely affected by a strike,
especially of the skilled workers who operate the trains. It was in
the great railroad strikes of 1877, largely in the freight service, that
the Federal troops were called out for the first time to prevent
further violence and property damage in a labor dispute.

During the 1880's a number of railroad strikes occurred. Many
of them were shopmen's strikes, led by members of the Knights of
Labor. In 1885, the threat of a general strike against Jay Gould's
railroads for the discharge of union members was effective. In the
Pullman strike of 1894, Federal troops were again called out. In
contrast to these early decades in railroad history, strike statistics
show that there were only 15 small strikes on the steam railroads
of this country from 1927 to 1939. During those 12 years, less than
70,000 man-days of idleness was caused by strikes among the
1,000,000 or 1,500,000 railroad workers employed during that
period.

Federal legislation. The early strikes led to the passage of a
Federal act in 1888 providing for voluntary arbitration on the
railroads and the appointment of an investigating commission by
the President. Such a commission proved ineffective in the Pullman strike of 1894. In 1898 the Erdman Act was passed by Congress, covering only employees actually engaged in operating the
trains. This law provided for voluntary arbitration and mediation
upon request of either party. From 1906 to 1913 some 60 controversies were settled under the Erdman Act, but dissatisfaction with
the Act increased, partly because the workers were not pleased
with the results of arbitration that took into account the ability of

the railroads to pay increased labor costs. In 1913 Congress passed
the Newlands Act, which also covered the operating employees
and provided for a permanent board of mediation that could offer
to mediate on its own initiative. However, labor became increasingly dissatisfied with arbitration, and in 1916 the machinery of the
Newlands Act proved inadequate to settle the controversy over the
eight-hour day demanded by the "Big Four." The unions had rejected arbitration of the issue and had called a general strike, which
was averted only by the passage of special legislation (the Adamson
Act) granting the eight-hour day to railroad workers by law.

Prewar bargaining. The demand for the eight-hour day was
the first concerted action by the "Big Four" on a national scale.
During the previous decade, collective bargaining in the "running"
trades had been on the regional basis of the three "territories."
Often the conductors and trainmen, and sometimes the engineers
and firemen, had acted together in this early regional bargaining.
The terms reached in such regional negotiations were incorporated
in agreements with the roads in the region. The "Big Four Brotherhoods" had agreements with individual roads dating back to the
1890's, the 1880's, and even the 1870's in some cases. By 1917 the
"Big Four" had enrolled roughly 80 per cent of the railroad employees in the engine-and-train service, whereas it is estimated that
less than 30 per cent of the employees in other service branches
were members of unions. Efforts of the shop crafts toward regional
bargaining were successful in one territory in 1917.

Federal operation. The railroads were taken over by the
Federal government in 1917, when this country entered the first
World War. The Federal Railroad Administration, as a single
employer, dealt with all the railroad unions on a national basis,
whether the unions were weak or strong. This meant that wage
increases, working rules, and other conditions of employment were
standardized on a national basis through "national agreements."
The Railroad Administration also established bipartisan adjustment boards, on which the unions were represented. These boards
were *national* boards for the settlement of secondary disputes.
Furthermore, the Federal Railroad Administration removed all the
former obstacles to membership in labor unions so that from 1910
to 1920 the membership of all railroad unions nearly tripled. It
has been estimated that in 1920 over 90 per cent of the employees

operating the trains were organized, while perhaps 80 per cent of the employees in the other railroad occupations were union members.[1]

Experience under the 1920 Act. In returning the railroads to their private owners in 1920, the question of the machinery for the settlement of labor disputes arose. At this time the unions favored government operation and ownership. The prewar machinery for settling disputes had proved inadequate to solve the issue of the eight-hour day. The shippers were requesting compulsory arbitration. As a compromise, which the unions did not favor, the Transportation Act of 1920 provided for a tripartite Railway Labor Board to mediate and to engage in compulsory investigation, but the Board had no power to enforce its findings or recommendations.

Any permanent board would have had troubles under the circumstances, because the railroads were determined to return to prewar labor conditions with regard both to working rules and to the unit and methods of collective bargaining. The unions, of course, preferred national dealings and bargaining because that gave them a strategic advantage in both economic and political power. It tended to reduce the influence of any particular road and caused railroad workers throughout the country to be interested in any change in wages or rules.

In the second decision handed down by the Board, it granted wage increases ranging from 12.5 to 26.2 per cent. When prices began to fall in 1920 and 1921, the railroads appealed to the Board for wage decreases instead of attempting to negotiate with the unions on a national basis. After obtaining a general wage reduction averaging 12 per cent in 1921, the railroads soon appealed in the depression of 1921–1922 for another reduction that would wipe out the previous 1920 increases. The "Big Four Brotherhoods" threatened a strike. The Board, explaining that it was swamped with cases, postponed the wage case involving the "Big Four" but awarded another decrease effective July 1, 1921, for the other railroad workers. This second wage decrease brought on the shop-crafts strike in 1922 and resulted in a split of the united front of railway labor. Thereafter the "Big Four" disregarded the Board and negotiated directly with the railroads, sometimes on a regional

[1] *Cf.* H. D. Wolf, *The Railroad Labor Board*, 1927, p. 59.

basis as they had before the war. The miscellaneous crafts accepted the second wage cut without a strike. The railroad workers came to feel that the Board was prejudiced in favor of the carriers and that its decisions were based too much on the railroads' "ability to pay."

In the 1922 strike of 400,000 railroad-shop craftsmen, the Federal government obtained a sweeping injunction which forbade practically all the traditional strike activities of unions. In the course of this dispute, a large number of company unions were established by the carriers, partly at the recommendation of the Board that steps should be taken to form some sort of organizations to represent shop-craft employees before the Board.[1] In addition, the Supreme Court decided that the Board was powerless to enforce an award directing the Pennsylvania Railroad to deal with the national railroad unions rather than its own company union. After the shop crafts lost their strike, all the unions began to deal directly with the roads and to disregard the Board.

Labor relations under the 1926 Act. Some new machinery for the settlement of railroad labor disputes was needed if the carriers and the unions were to avoid compulsory arbitration by law. In 1925, official conferences were held by the executives of certain railroad unions and a committee of the Association of Railroad Executives (merged into the American Association of Railroads in 1934). As a result of these conferences, a bill was drafted, approved by both parties, and passed by Congress in substantially the same form as drafted originally. This Railway Labor Act of 1926, as amended in 1934, was discussed in Chapter 25. A Supreme Court decision in 1930 indicated that the Act outlawed all company unions sponsored, dominated, or financed by the employer.[2] It specifically places a "duty" on both sides "to exert every reasonable effort to make and maintain agreements" and to settle all disputes. For the purpose of making and maintaining agreements, three steps are to be followed: (1) direct negotiation, (2) mediation by the National Mediation Board, and (3) voluntary arbitration. This is the prewar pattern. If those steps should fail to settle the controversy, a special fact-finding or

---

[1] *Cf. Hearings on Railway Labor Act Amendments*, Committee on Interstate and Foreign Commerce, House of Representatives, 73rd Congress, second session, pp. 154–55.

[2] *Texas and New Orleans Railway* v. *Brotherhood of Railway and Steamship Clerks* (1930), 281 U. S. 548.

emergency board appointed for that dispute by the President shall make recommendations, which can be enforced only by the pressure of public opinion.

Since the passage of the Railway Labor Act, there have been no major strikes on the railroads. Officials of the carriers had come to realize that they would have to deal with the national unions, that the unions could not be eliminated. During the late 1920's, railroad revenues were sufficient to provide wage increases. By 1931, however, revenues had declined so much that the Class I railroads proposed a joint national conference on wages with the 21 standard railroad labor unions represented in the Railway Labor Executives' Association. The roads wanted to obtain a wage change more rapidly than would be possible under the steps provided in the Act. The unions accepted this procedure, and the precedent for negotiating nationally on wage rates and labor conditions has since been followed on numerous occasions. Under a national agreement, effective February 1, 1932, the unions accepted a 10-per-cent "deduction" from their wages for a year. By national bargaining between the unions and the roads, this horizontal deduction was continued each year until 1935.

In 1936 the 21 standard labor unions, through the Railway Labor Executives' Association, negotiated directly with a committee of the American Association of Railroads for the continuation of protections to railroad employment and pay contained in the expiring Emergency Railroad Transportation Act of 1933. A bill for that purpose had also been introduced in Congress. The railroads were willing to bargain out of these legal protections to workers adversely affected by railroad coordinations or consolidations. An agreement, virtually national in coverage, was signed in May 1936. It provides for dismissal compensation and "coordination allowances" for railroad employees who suffer reduced pay or unemployment as a result of the unification of the facilities or operations of two or more railroads. The agreement runs for five years. During that time, no worker's pay shall be reduced because of demotion resulting from consolidation or coordination, and a worker who is forced to move as a result of coordination must be reimbursed by the carrier for moving expenses and any loss suffered in selling his home. Monthly "coordination allowances" of 60 per cent of previous average monthly earnings are granted to workers who become unemployed through coordination. The length of such monthly allowances increases with the worker's length of service, being five years for unemployed workers with 15 or more years of service prior to their displacement by coordination. If the worker so deprived of employment prefers, he can resign from the railroad and receive a lump-sum "separation allowance," amounting to a year's pay if his length of service has been five years or more.

In 1937 the national railroad unions again conducted wage negotiations on a national basis. This time the five "operating" unions (including the switchmen) negotiated separately from the "nonoperating" unions. Both received a five-per-cent wage increase, though the effective date of the "operating" group's agreement was two months later than that of the "nonoperating" group. The relationship between railroad rates and wages is indicated by the fact that early in 1938 the Interstate Commerce Commission permitted an increase in freight rates partly on the grounds of "increased labor costs." Later, in 1938, the roads requested a 15-per-cent wage reduction because revenues had declined. In the negotiations on this issue the 20 unions in the Railway Labor Executives' Association again acted together, dealing with the railroads on a national basis. In this instance, as explained in Chapter 1, no agreement resulted; an emergency board was appointed by the President as provided in the Railway Labor Act; and the board recommended that the carriers drop their proposal for a wage reduction, which they did.

On June 30, 1939, there were a total of 4,061 agreements on the railroads in this country, 87 per cent of which were with national unions. Under these agreements, the "Big Four Brotherhoods," the Clerks' union, and the Telegraphers' union represented the eligible employees on railroads having from 96 to 99 per cent of the total railroad mileage in the country; the Brotherhood of Maintenance of Way Employees had agreements in force on 92 per cent of the total mileage; and the seven shop-craft unions had agreements covering from 71 to 81 per cent of the total railroad trackage.[1]

[1] *Cf. Fifth Annual Report of the National Mediation Board for the Fiscal Year Ended June 30, 1939*, pp. 18, 25.

THE MARITIME INDUSTRY

Labor relations in water transportation have been in sharp contrast to such relations on the railroads during the past two decades. From 1927 to 1939 there were over 500 strikes in water transportation, resulting in a total of approximately 5,500,000 man-days of idleness for workers. In other words, the total of days idle because of strikes in the railroad industry was only about one per cent of the total for the maritime industry during those years, although there were three or four times as many workers employed on the railroads as there were working on the waterfront or on ships.

In 1937 and 1938 a number of writers suggested that the Railway Labor Act be extended to cover water transportation as it had been extended to air transportation in 1936. During the same period a number of bills were introduced in Congress, designed to apply many of the provisions of the Railway Labor Act to the maritime industry. The United States Maritime Commission and most employers favored such a measure, but the spokesmen of the maritime unions were opposed to any attempt to apply the Railway Labor Act to the maritime industry and to exclude the industry from the jurisdiction of the National Labor Relations Board. They pointed out that the maritime unions were still struggling to make collective bargaining effective and to achieve recognition, whereas in the railroad industry the practice of collective bargaining was deep-rooted and the unions had long enjoyed recognition of their basic rights. From 1921 to 1934 collective bargaining was practically nonexistent in the maritime industry, for employers in certain ports had suppressed unionism by means of company unions, employer-controlled hiring halls, and the black-listing of union members. The major issue underlying the important maritime strikes from 1934 to 1939 was union recognition. In view of the immaturity of maritime labor relations, the union leaders contended that emphasis should be placed upon guaranteeing and developing collective bargaining instead of placing restraints upon union activities and the right to strike by establishing elaborate settlement procedures (a mediation board, waiting periods, compulsory arbitration of secondary disputes, etc.), which might be appropriate at a more advanced stage in the development of labor relations.[1]

[1] *Cf. Report of the Maritime Labor Board*, March 1, 1940, pp. 46–52. Much of the

Nature of the industry. Maritime transportation is subject to government regulation of competition and enjoys a variety of government subsidies. Intercoastal trade (between American ports) is reserved for American ship lines and the rates are uniform for such interstate trade, being controlled by the Interstate Commerce Commission. Consequently, price competition is nonexistent in intercoastal shipping and there is no need for unions to stabilize the industry. Indeed, strong employers' organizations have been able to control the industry in the past. It is true, of course, that the seas are open to all ships, whereas a railroad roadbed is used exclusively by one railroad.

In the deep-sea trade between countries, American ships are in competition with foreign lines. An attempt is made through various "shipping conferences" to prevent price-cutting and other kinds of competition in foreign shipping, but such conference control may be upset through nonconference competition or internal dissatisfaction. Because of the relatively high cost of constructing and operating American ships, the Federal government subsidizes American vessels through mail contracts, construction subsidies, and other means, so that we may have a merchant marine. In this way, the Federal government practically furnishes the profits made in foreign trade by American ship lines that otherwise could not compete with, say, the ships of Norway, where mass-production industries are not bidding up the price of labor. The Federal government, through the threat to alter the subsidy, can and has put pressure upon ship operators to follow a certain labor policy. The Federal government itself owns a number of the commercial vessels.

Maritime transportation is subject to seasonal fluctuations and to changes in the business cycle. It is, of course, affected also by tariffs, trade treaties, wars, and the nation's policy regarding the merchant marine. Consequently, employment is unsteady and uncertain. Employment is made still more unstable by the practice of hiring seamen for a single round trip only, and of hiring longshoremen only for the period required to load or unload a particular ship. The separation rate of seamen in deep-sea shipping, for example, is five times the average rate in manufacturing. The

discussion in this section on maritime labor is based upon this report of the Maritime Labor Board.

U. S. Maritime Commission has advocated an arrangement for
the continuous employment of seamen instead of having them
hire on and off after each voyage.

Characteristics of employment.   Special laws govern seamen
while at sea, where the "master" is supreme and strict discipline
and loyalty are required.   That is one of the reasons for the hard-
bitten individualism that seems so characteristic of ocean transportation.   The seaman lives an abnormal life, subject to various
risks on board ship.   He is unable to participate in the social life of
a particular locality, and frequent absences from home make him
politically impotent.   While on ship he cannot change employers,
and the ship operator provides the sailor's food and living quarters,
much as does the employer who runs a camp for migratory workers.
The seafaring employees are divided into unlicensed seamen and
the licensed personnel, like masters, mates, pilots, and engineers,
who hold government licenses for their occupations.

The longshoremen, who load and unload the ships, are mostly
unskilled workers, although some skill is required to operate
winches and to place cargo properly in the ship's hold.   The work
is hard and the accident rate is high.   In 1932 the rate of accidents
per million man-hours worked was 25.5 in the maritime industry
(95 for longshoremen in San Francisco) compared with 13.2 accidents per million man-hours for all industry.   In 1936 the accident
frequency rate was 17.6 among longshoremen compared with 13.6
for all industries.   Some accidents are caused by employer pressure
to speed up operations, because dock fees and charges mount
rapidly and the time required to load and unload a ship is considered waste time.   It has been estimated that, in shipping, loading
and unloading costs average about a third of total operating or
variable costs.[1]

Longshoremen are hired to load or unload a particular ship and
are dismissed when that job is finished.   Consequently, some longshoremen may change jobs or employers every day, which has
afforded employers a good opportunity to discriminate amongst
employees and to black-list union leaders.   Furthermore, the
frequent change of jobs tends to cause workers who are squeezed

---

[1] *Cf.* Paul Eliel, "Labor Problems in Our Steamship Business," *Yale Review,* vol. 26
(March 1937), p. 513; and Federal Coordinator of Transportation, *Hours, Wages, and
Working Conditions in Domestic Water Transportation,* vol. 1, September 1936, pp. 17–18.

out of other industries to crowd into longshore work. A large surplus of longshore labor in a port also increases the power of the employer to exert pressure upon workers by giving most of his work to "favored" gangs. Longshore workers also lose much working time because the going and coming of ships is uncertain and irregular. Boats carrying freight dock at all hours of the day or night, so that the work is unpredictable and may be concentrated around certain days of the month. All of these factors (repeated change of jobs, large surplus of available labor during most periods, and irregular demand and earnings) tend to place the employer in a strong position in the labor market. Employer domination in the longshore labor market has been responsible for the prevalence of the "kick-back," whereby employees under pressure have secretly returned part of their wages to the employer for the privilege of working.

Longshore hiring methods on the West Coast differ from the practice in most East Coast ports, where the "shape-up" method generally prevails. Under this method, all longshoremen in search of jobs line up in a semicircular "shape" at each pier at the time the hiring occurs. In New York City, for example, there is one "shape" for the morning's work, another for the afternoon's work, and still a third if work is to be performed overtime. If a longshoreman gets a job in the morning shape, and wishes to work throughout the day, he must take part in the afternoon shape. In this way, each pier constitutes a labor market with only one bidding buyer but many competing sellers. It has been estimated that there are usually from three to five times as many men as there are jobs at the waterfront in New York City.[1] With the employer so dominating the market, there are great possibilities for abuse of power and for exploitation of workers.

The central-hiring-hall method on the Pacific Coast tends to eliminate much of the labor competition in the shape system and to reduce the power of the employer or his hiring agent. Under the hiring-hall method, all employers must employ longshoremen through a central hall. A union dispatcher, not the employer, chooses the men to fill the employer's order from a list of longshoremen "registered" at the hall. Restrictions upon registration tend to prevent any undue surplus of longshore labor. In 1939 the

[1] *Cf. Report of the Maritime Labor Board*, p. 141.

average yearly earnings of longshoremen in Seattle and Portland were $1,750, or almost twice as large as the $900 average in New York City in 1938.[1] The dispatcher is required to distribute the jobs amongst the registered workers in a way that will tend to equalize their earnings. Under such a method, there is little possibility of the "kick-back" or of employer discrimination and favoritism.

Labor organizations. There are a dozen different labor organizations, claiming a total of more than 200,000 members among the seafaring personnel or longshore workers on both coasts. Five of these unions have CIO charters, five hold AFL charters, and two are independent. The situation on the East Coast is entirely different from that on the West Coast. To an outsider, therefore, labor organization in the maritime industry seems confused and confusing.

On the East Coast, the International Longshoremen's Association (AFL) has jurisdiction over longshoremen, claiming a membership of 66,000 in 1939. On the West Coast, the longshoremen are organized almost 100 per cent in the International Longshoremen's and Warehousemen's Union (CIO), claiming a membership of 33,000. The ILWU resulted from a vote to abandon the conservatively led ILA in 1937, although the longshoremen in some Puget Sound ports in Washington have continued as members of the AFL union.

On the East Coast, most of the unlicensed seamen are members of the National Maritime Union (CIO), formed in 1937 as the result of a revolt against conservative leadership in the International Seamen's Union (AFL). Its seagoing membership was reported at about 51,000 in 1939. A new AFL union has been chartered, which also claims jurisdiction over all unlicensed seafaring personnel, but it had considerably less than 5,000 members on the East Coast in 1939. On the West Coast, the unlicensed personnel are distributed amongst three unions: the unlicensed deck personnel are represented by the Sailors Union of the Pacific (AFL), with a claimed membership of 8,000; the marine cooks and stewards are represented by a CIO union; and the unlicensed engine-room workers are represented by an independent union.

---

[1] *Cf. Longshoremen: Pacific and Atlantic,* International Longshoremen's and Warehousemen's Union, Seattle, 1940, pp. 9–13; and Elizabeth Ogg, *Longshoremen and Their Homes,* New York City, 1939, p. 31.

With regard to the licensed personnel, an AFL union claims jurisdiction over the masters, mates, and pilots; a CIO union claims jurisdiction over the marine engineers; and an independent union claims jurisdiction over both classes of ship personnel. An AFL union and a CIO union are both organizing radio operators on ships. According to an estimate in 1939, about 25 per cent of the licensed personnel and 85 per cent of the unlicensed seamen were members of unions.[1]

Employer organizations. There are over 40 employers' associations in the maritime industry. Only a few of these associations, however, bargain on a coast-wide or regional basis. The American Merchant Marine Institute, which contains the major lines in the Atlantic and Gulf areas engaged in international, intercoastal, or coastwise shipping, bargains on a coast-wide basis with the union of the unlicensed seamen, the National Maritime Union. Bargaining on the East Coast for licensed personnel and longshoremen is on a port-by-port basis or by individual companies.

On the Pacific Coast the employers have more readily joined together for united action in the past. The following three employers' associations are coast-wide and negotiate coast-wide agreements for their members: the Pacific American Shipowners' Association, the Waterfront Employers Association of the Pacific Coast, and the Shipowners' Association of the Pacific Coast. These three associations have many duplicate members, especially the first two, which have the same president. The Waterfront Employers Association and the Shipowners' Association also cooperate very closely on labor policy, both signing the same coast-wide agreement with the Longshoremen's union. The Pacific American Shipowners' Association negotiates agreements with licensed and unlicensed seafaring personnel for its 20 members operating in foreign, intercoastal, and intracoastal trade. The Waterfront Employers Association with 33 members negotiates a single agreement with the Longshoremen's union, covering all its members in all West Coast ports. The Shipowners' Association, consisting of the operators of steam schooners carrying lumber and general cargo, negotiates both with the unions of seagoing personnel and with the Longshoremen's union. The agreement

---

[1] *Cf.* U. S. Social Security Board, *The Maritime Industry and Unemployment Compensation*, 1939, p. 102.

with the longshore union contains a special paragraph permitting sailors to perform longshore work on steam schooners where that has been the practice. The Waterfront Employers Association of the Pacific is composed of four regional waterfront employers' associations, for which it is authorized to negotiate longshore agreements. All large companies, and practically all small companies, that use longshore labor are members of one or more of these regional associations.

Experience with collective bargaining. The earliest written agreement with an employers' association in the maritime industry was secured by the seamen on the West Coast in 1902. The Pacific Coast has always tended to lead the East Coast in both union organization and collective bargaining. Unions of seamen were formed in the 1870's and early 1880's. Employers' associations, to combat the new seamen's unions, were formed in 1885 by employers on the Great Lakes and on a coastwise basis for the Pacific Coast. Following the Pacific Coast strike in 1886, the Shipowners' Association of the Pacific Coast opened a hiring hall to be operated on a nonunion basis and issued to seamen a continuous discharge or grade book containing the seaman's work record.[1] These books were useful in barring union members from employment. Shipmasters refused to hire anyone unless he came through the hiring hall and had his grade book. These same devices, by which shipowners could control maritime employment, were widely practiced on the Pacific Coast again in the 1920's.

After having resisted the unions since 1885, the Shipowners' Association of the Pacific Coast signed an agreement with the Sailors' union in 1902. This agreement was soon followed by other agreements with the three seagoing unions, so that the principal West Coast lines were covered by written or verbal agreements following 1902. These agreements, which were renewed without interruption until 1921, provided for hiring through a union representative in all ports and contained detailed wage schedules. In 1913 the longshoremen secured written agreements with two employers' associations in the Puget Sound region. The next year the employers in San Francisco formed the Waterfront Employers' Union to discourage the growth of the Longshoremen's union,

---

[1] Material on West Coast maritime labor before the first World War has largely been taken from Paul Taylor, *The Sailors Union of the Pacific*, 1923.

which the employers refused to recognize officially. In 1916, the Longshoremen's union was defeated in a two-months' strike in San Francisco.

In the East, the employers' association on the Great Lakes began in 1900 to require each seaman to carry a welfare membership book similar to the grade books introduced on the West Coast in 1887. By 1903 the seamen on the Great Lakes had secured an agreement with an employers' association composed of contract and private carriers closely allied with the steel industry through the great ore traffic. However, the agreement was not renewed after 1907, when the association announced a return to an openshop policy. A U. S. Steel subsidiary, controlling about one third of the freight vessels on the Great Lakes, dominated the labor policy of the employers' association and discharged union men, whose membership frequently was discovered through a spy system.[1] On the Atlantic Coast, collective bargaining had not developed to any extent before this country entered the first World War in 1917.

1. *The war period.* During the war, the Federal government's labor policy largely determined the character of labor relations in the maritime industry. Controlling about 300 vessels, the government overshadowed the private operators. To assure an unbroken flow of commerce, the government adopted for the first time a policy of collective bargaining and collective agreements in the maritime industry. On the Atlantic Coast, the U. S. Shipping Board, with jurisdiction over vessel personnel, arranged for the collective bargaining conferences that led to the "Atlantic Agreement" of 1917, the first written agreement ever made between the Seamen's union and the Atlantic operators as a body. On the Great Lakes, the Shipping Board was able to eliminate the use of continuous discharge books and exclusive use of employer-controlled hiring halls, but was unable to arrange a signed agreement between the Seamen's union and the employers' association. On the Pacific Coast, the Board simply accepted the terms of the existing agreements, which were renewed in 1918 and 1919 with wage increases commensurate with those of the East Coast.

A National Adjustment Commission, composed of representatives

[1] *Cf.* H. E. Hoagland, *Wage Bargaining on the Vessels of the Great Lakes*, 1917, especially pp. 60, 87, and 95.

of the Longshoremen's union, the employers, and the government, was created in 1917 to act as an arbitration tribunal of last appeal in disputes between the longshoremen and their employers. Subordinate local boards were established in most of the major ports, further indicating recognition of the union and the use of collective bargaining. However, the San Francisco employers, organized in the Waterfront Employers' Union, refused to deal with the Longshoremen's union, and the arbitration system did not function in San Francisco. After the war, the local tribunals ceased to operate and the National Adjustment Commission lost its power to make binding decisions.

With this encouragement by the Federal government, the maritime unions expanded rapidly. The membership of the Seamen's union increased from 16,000 in 1915 to 103,000 in 1921. Of the unlicensed ship personnel, 90 per cent on the Pacific Coast, 70 per cent on the Atlantic Coast, and about 50 per cent on the Great Lakes were organized in 1921. The Longshoremen's union expanded from 25,000 members in 1916 to a peak of 74,000 in 1920. Following the maritime strikes from 1919 to 1922, however, the membership of the Longshoremen's union declined to 34,000 and the Seamen's union to 18,000. By 1933 the Seamen's union had only 8,000 members.[1]

2. *The doldrums of the 1920's.* After the war, the shipowners began a movement to return to "normalcy" or prewar conditions for longshore work. In a 16-week strike on the Pacific Coast in 1919, all the war gains of the longshoremen were wiped out. As a means of eliminating the union, the waterfront employers in California ports set up company unions with discharge books and hired longshoremen only from an employer-controlled hall. Under this closed-shop arrangement, employment was restricted to members of the "blue-book" union. During the 1920's, discrimination was prevalent and grievances smoldered in the minds of men who had little opportunity to present grievances or complain against "gyp" practices. In some Washington and Oregon ports the Longshoremen's union continued to exist without employer recognition or agreements. As indicated in Chapter 6, the shipowners with headquarters in San Francisco were able to enforce changes

[1] Membership figures from Leo Wolman, *Ebb and Flow in Trade Unionism*, 1936, pp. 184–89.

throughout the West Coast by playing one port against another and threatening not to send ships to ports that failed to conform to the orders from San Francisco.

On the Atlantic Coast the longshoremen were able to continue their agreements after 1921 in a few ports, especially New York City, so that organization there was stronger than on the West Coast prior to 1934. On the Great Lakes there was complaint of discrimination in the 1920's through a practice equivalent to the discharge book.

The longshoremen have generally been aggressive and have occupied a key position in the industry. Before the West Coast strike of the longshoremen in 1919, the employers renewed their agreement with the Seamen's union at an increase in wages. In this way, the employers could play the nonstriking seamen against the longshoremen in the 1919 strike, and the seamen's strike in 1921 could receive no support from the Longshoremen's union defeated in 1919.

One reason for treating the seamen well in 1919 was that they were needed to help bring the troops back home as rapidly as possible. By 1921, however, when the seamen's agreement expired, the shipping industry was suffering from the postwar slump and the government was trying to withdraw from direct participation in the industry. Over two months before the seamen's agreement was to expire, the American Steamship Owners' Association unanimously decided to discontinue agreements with the union. In an effort to find a solution, the Shipping Board announced a sharp wage cut and a new set of working rules, which all operators using the Board's vessels were required to follow. This action precipitated the 1921 seamen's strike. The Shipping Board obtained injunctions against the strikers, and both the Board and the Steamship Owners' Association refused to arbitrate the strike. In 1922 the Association instituted another wage cut, which reduced seamen's wages to 30 or 35 per cent below the wage scales in 1920.

Except for a few isolated instances, no agreements were signed with the Seamen's union from 1921 to 1934. Collective bargaining had ended. In California the employers' associations were able to suppress unionism by the exclusive use of employer-controlled hiring halls for the employment of seamen. In addition, "grade" books were required for seamen, and company unions were established for the licensed personnel. As in the case of the long-shoremen, the seamen became resentful and bitter under the reduced labor standards and the employment control exercised by the employers. "The unredressed grievances and the unexpressed hatreds of these years go far towards explaining the chaotic out-bursts and the hotly contested strikes of the period after 1934." [1] Under employer control, the average monthly wages of seamen in intercoastal trade did not increase during the boom period from 1924 to 1929, for shipping did not prosper, and by 1933, average wages for able seamen reached the low figure of $47 a month.[2]

3. *The New Deal period.* The passage of the NRA in 1933 served to revive the maritime unions after a decade of quiescence, during which collective bargaining was almost nonexistent for the seamen and most of the longshoremen. However, none of the 27 proposed shipping codes, except the one applying to the New York Canal system, was adopted, so that maritime labor did not enjoy the full benefits of Section 7a of the NIRA. [3] The workers accused the shipowners of "stalling" and, especially on the Pacific Coast, began to take matters in their own hands.

When the Waterfront Employers' Union of San Francisco rejected the demands of the Longshoremen's union for union control of the hiring halls, a six-hour day, wage increases, and a coast-wide agreement, a strike on the whole West Coast ensued in May 1934. Up and down the Coast the strike was joined by the seamen, the licensed personnel, the teamsters, and other unions in a united front. The four West Coast regional employers' associa-tions also formed a Coast Committee for united employer action. For three days there was a general strike in San Francisco following an attempt by business groups in the city to open the port by the use of strike-breakers. Finally, both sides agreed to present the strike issues for arbitration by a board appointed by the President. This board handed down a coast-wide decision granting the 30-

[1] Paul Elmo Hohman, "Maritime Labor in the United States: II," *Internationa. Labour Review*, vol. 38 (September 1938), p. 381.

[2] *Cf.* William S. Hopkins, "Employment Exchanges for Seamen," *American Economic Review*, vol. 25 (June 1935), p. 252; and *Merchant Marine Statistics, Fiscal Year 1937*, U. S. Department of Commerce, Bureau of Marine Inspection and Navigation, 1938, p. 69.

[3] Federal Coordinator of Transportation, *Hours, Wages, and Working Conditions in Domestic Water Transportation*, vol. 1, September 1936, p. 203.

hour week, an hourly wage of 95 cents with $1.40 for overtime, joint support of the hiring halls with actual administration by a union-selected dispatcher, and the establishment of a bipartite labor-relations committee in each port for the settlement of grievances. These provisions are still the basic conditions in the longshore agreement covering the West Coast.

The Seamen's union was designated as the official bargaining agency for the entire coast, following a vote conducted by the President-appointed board that arbitrated the 1934 strike. Issues that could not be settled by negotiation were arbitrated by a special tribunal. The seamen obtained control of hiring by refusing to take jobs except through the union hall.

On the Pacific Coast the period between 1934 and 1936 was characterized by unrest and distrust. The employers complained about the "left-wing" leadership of the Longshoremen's union, the low output, and the repeated work stoppages in violation of the agreement. The union blamed the antiunion actions of employers for such "quickie" strikes, and pointed to the fact that certain employers waited many months after final appeal was denied before paying the workers several hundred thousand dollars of retroactive overtime granted them under an arbitration award. In 1936 another strike occurred when a new agreement could not be negotiated. The employers wanted penalties for violation of agreements and actual joint control of hiring halls. The Maritime Federation of the Pacific, formed in 1935 and then consisting of 13 affiliated unions, wanted material advances for its seagoing organizations and refused to arbitrate the provisions of the 1934 longshoremen's award. For three months there was virtually no water-borne commerce along the entire Pacific Coast. This time no serious attempt was made to use strike-breakers, so little violence occurred.

As a result of the 1936 strike, the Sailors' union obtained wage increases, the eight-hour day with punitive overtime rates, union preference in hiring, employment through union halls, and joint committees for settling grievances. The new longshoremen's agreement retained the 1934 gains and provided for preferential hiring of union members. For a year after the Longshoremen's union on the Pacific Coast voted in 1937 to affiliate with the CIO, the Waterfront Employers' Association refused to recognize the union under its new name, so it was necessary to obtain a decision from the National Labor Relations Board designating the union as bargaining agency for the whole Pacific Coast.

On the Atlantic Coast, labor relations have been more satisfactory during the last decade. Over four fifths of the man-days of idleness caused by maritime strikes from January 1936 through June 1939 occurred on the Pacific Coast. During the 1920's the Atlantic Coast employers did not engage in all the antiunion practices so systematically carried out on the Pacific Coast. Prior to 1934 the Longshoremen's union on the Atlantic Coast maintained agreements in certain cities and was relatively stronger there than on the West Coast. The leadership of the Longshoremen's union on the East Coast has remained conservative and in a strong position.

In December 1934 the Seamen's union on the Atlantic Coast signed an agreement with 28 steamship companies, which gave the seamen increased wages, employment preference for union members, and machinery for settling grievances. This agreement was stimulated by an intimation that the continuance of the government's mail subsidies might depend upon observance of the National Industrial Recovery Act by the East Coast shipping companies.[1] Nevertheless, the conditions of the Atlantic agreement, including wages and hours, were less favorable to the seamen than those in the Pacific Coast agreement—a fact that caused considerable discontent, especially when the union leaders renewed the Atlantic agreement in 1936 with some increase in wages but without elimination of all the differences. Rank-and-file groups on the East Coast began to challenge the leadership of the Seamen's union and eventually, following an outlaw strike and elections by the National Labor Relations Board, the new National Maritime Union (CIO) practically displaced the old Seamen's union, which has since been reorganized and renamed the Seafarers' International Union. In 1937 the National Maritime Union signed an agreement with the American Merchant Marine Institute covering 43 per cent of the shipping on the Atlantic Coast.

In June 1939 as much as 74 per cent of the total tonnage of the U. S. merchant marine in coastal or foreign trade was under collective agreement at least for some classes of ship personnel.

[1] Hohman, op. cit., p. 388.

All of the unlicensed personnel was covered by collective agreements with regional or national labor unions on 65 per cent of the total salt-water tonnage. The corresponding figure for all licensed officers was 38 per cent. About one third of the tanker tonnage, mostly tankers operated by the large oil companies, was under agreements with employee-representation plans.[1] On the Great Lakes, collective bargaining is less well developed and the unions are weaker.

The process of collective bargaining is further advanced among longshoremen than among seamen. Virtually the whole labor force of longshore workers on the Atlantic Coast is covered by agreements in effect at 26 East Coast ports and 16 Gulf ports. The agreements between the Longshoremen's union and the New York Shipping Association practically determine the longshore labor standards in the North Atlantic ports as far south as Hampton Roads, because each port follows the practice of basing local agreements on the terms accepted by the organized waterfront employers in New York. South of Hampton Roads the terms of agreements are not uniform from port to port and they are inferior to the North Atlantic standards. On the Pacific Coast, practically 100 per cent of all water-borne tonnage is loaded and unloaded under the terms of a single agreement covering the whole coast. Regional agreements are negotiated for auxiliary longshore workers such as weighers, checkers, and talliers.

In 1936 the U. S. Maritime Commission replaced the Shipping Board. The Commission has insisted that the crews working on vessels forming part of the fleet operated directly for the Commission's account have the status of government employees. Therefore, the Commission has refused to sign agreements with the maritime unions and has hired its unlicensed personnel from the registers of U. S. commissioners in various ports rather than through union hiring halls. In 1938, Congress passed a law establishing a Maritime Labor Board to mediate disputes in the industry, to encourage the practice and procedure of collective bargaining, and to propose a permanent Federal policy for improving maritime labor relations.

[1] Data in this and the following two paragraphs have been taken from the *Report of the Maritime Labor Board, op. cit.*, pp. 42–43, 101–103, 112–16.

Summary of contrasts. Although labor unions began to appear almost as early in the maritime industry as in the railroad industry, labor relations in these two industries have been in marked contrast, especially since the first World War. The railroads were easier to organize because the employees live settled lives and the labor turnover is comparatively low. Furthermore, the railroads are much more vulnerable to the economic and political pressures of unionism. Trains must run on schedule, and the operating crafts, such as the engineers, are skilled workers who cannot be readily displaced by strike-breakers. On the other hand, workers can easily be recruited for the jobs of unlicensed seamen and longshoremen. These maritime occupations have generally been overcrowded.

The railroads have been more affected by public opinion than the ship operators. The customer market for railroad service has been different from the market for water transportation, which has been used largely by employers who ship freight. More people use the railroads, more people work on the railroads, and the Federal government has regulated railroad transportation and labor relations for a longer period of time and more strictly. In the 1920's and 1930's the attitude of the various Federal agencies toward the respective unions was more favorable in the case of the railroads than in shipping, where both the Shipping Board and the Maritime Commission had sharp and repeated conflicts with the maritime unions.

Water transportation has been more competitive than rail transportation because the seas are open to all ships. Shipowners have, however, formed strong employers' associations, especially on the Pacific Coast, that were able to play one port against another and one union against another, because the employers' organization had a wider base and was more inclusive than the organization of either the longshoremen or the seamen. The shipowners' associations practically eliminated the unions in marine transportation from 1921 to 1933—a feat that the railroads could not possibly have accomplished. Consequently, during that period the practices of the employers and the attitudes of the employees differed widely in the two industries. The railroad managements realized that they had to live with and deal with the unions.

In the maritime industry, much bitterness was engendered during the 1920's and the early 1930's by the practices of the employers, especially on the California Coast. The violent opposition of the shipowners bred a militant and radical leadership in the workers' organizations. It has been said that, generally speaking, employers get the kind of union that their policies tend to foster. Even in the late 1930's, the shipowners, especially on the West Coast, had not reached the stage where they were ready to deal with the unions as permanent organizations in the industry. Some employers were awaiting an opportunity to eliminate the unions as had been done in the 1920's.

One result of suspicion and hostility between employer and employee organizations on the West Coast has been the tendency for workers to resort to direct action instead of relying upon the arbitration machinery provided in the agreements for settling secondary disputes. On the Pacific Coast between February 1937 and June 1939, there were 209 work stoppages by longshoremen and 144 by workers in one of the six seafaring unions, all 353 stoppages in violation of existing agreements, which forbid strikes, lockouts, or stoppages of work for any reason during the life of the agreement.[1] The arbitration of secondary disputes naturally works better on the railroads, where employees do not change employers frequently; but the attitudes of both parties, and not the nature of the industry, are largely responsible for this poor record in water transportation.

[1] Cf. Report of the Maritime Labor Board, op. cit., pp. 156, 165, 168, 172–73, 179–81, 184–85, 194.

CHAPTER TWENTY-NINE

BITUMINOUS COAL

The soft-coal industry in this country has had a long and varied experience with collective bargaining. During part of that experience, bargaining between the union and groups of employers' associations has been on a regional or national scale, while at other times it has been confined to local negotiations and agreements, with most of the industry operating under nonunion conditions. Since 1934, collective bargaining in bituminous (soft) coal has been practically on a national basis, with over 70 per cent of the nation's output represented at the negotiations leading to collective agreements, and with 95 per cent of the workers in the union. The United Mine Workers of America, with a membership of over 600,000 employees in both hard and soft coal, is the largest single union in the world. Experience in the anthracite (hard) coal industry in this country has, during most of the last three decades, offered some interesting contrasts with the situation in soft coal.

All over the world, coal has been a "sick" industry since the first World War, suffering from a declining market and excess capacity.[1] In some countries, such as England and the United States, the industry has experienced long periods of bitter price competition, with prices below the full costs of production, because the thousands of firms in the industry were unable to cooperate. During the last two decades various countries have resorted to government regulation of coal production and prices in order to "stabilize" the industry. In 1937 England finally turned to government ownership (with private operation) of the country's coal resources.

Collective bargaining alone has not solved all the industry's difficulties either here or abroad. Has such bargaining, however, helped in some measure to cure the "sicknesses" from which the

[1] *Cf. The World Coal-Mining Industry*, vol. I, International Labour Office, Studies and Reports, Series B, No. 31, 1938.

soft-coal industry in America has suffered? Has it improved earnings and employment for the American workers who depend upon this industry for a livelihood?

Economic conditions in the industry. The discussion of the market theory of unionism in Chapter 20 indicated that the bituminous-coal industry well exemplifies the conditions under which employers are most likely to welcome a labor union as a stabilizing influence: a large number of firms in the industry, labor costs representing a large portion of the total costs of production, and the industry no longer expanding rapidly in terms of sales. Consequently, it is not surprising to find an expert newspaper reporter stating that in 1933 shopkeepers in the former nonunion coal areas in West Virginia "hailed the union organizers with an almost evangelical fervor, supplied them with gasoline for their shabby cars, and gave them a lift in the work of organization" and that the employing coal operators this time "offered no resistance" to the organization of their employees.[1]

1. *The mines.* Bituminous coal is mined commercially in over 6,000 mines in 30-odd states. The thickness, the depth, the slant, and the character of the coal veins varies considerably between mines and even within the same mine, so that it is not feasible to try to undercut some soft-coal veins by machinery. In addition, mines vary in the distance between the mine and the consumers. Such nonuniformity between mines has given rise to thin-vein, machine, and freight differentials in wages, as a means of offsetting the natural handicaps of certain mines. More will be said about these wage differentials at a later point.

By way of contrast, practically all of the nation's hard-coal deposits are concentrated in ten counties of Eastern Pennsylvania, so that anthracite coal is, in a sense, a "natural" monopoly.

2. *Operators.* There are about 4,000 operating companies in the soft-coal industry. The largest producer accounts for only about three per cent of the total output, and the largest 200 firms control no more than about one third of the total production. Some of the largest producers of bituminous coal are the so-called "captive mines," which are owned by coal consumers such as steel and railroad companies and which account for about one fifth of all soft-coal production.

[1] Louis Stark, "The American Federation of Labor," *Atlantic Monthly*, vol. 155 (April 1935), p. 489.

ECONOMICS OF LABOR

For purposes of bargaining collectively with the union, the operators are organized into a number of state, regional, and local employers' associations. However, the competitive interests of the operators in different areas have been too diverse to permit them to organize into a national association as the workers have done. With such a lack of cooperation, it has not been possible for the soft-coal operators to combine in restraint of interstate trade, which would be necessary if they were to apply monopolistic restrictions, since about three fourths of all soft coal is sold to consumers outside the state in which it is mined.

In the Pennsylvania anthracite industry, on the other hand, eight or ten companies own or control over nine tenths of the available coal deposits, and some of these companies have been closely interrelated through banking interests such as J. P. Morgan and Company. In the 1920's, the miners complained that the monopoly in hard coal afforded large returns to investors but low wage payments to workers.

3. *The miners.* Between 400,000 and 500,000 workers were employed in and around the soft-coal mines during the 1930's, and some 100,000 more were working for anthracite-coal operators. Two thirds of these workers were on piece rates, for those who actually do the mining are paid by the tons of coal they mine, while the others who work in and around the mine are paid by the day. Coal miners are used to working at their own pace with little supervision.

In this country, coal miners have represented a great variety of nationalities, and as late as 1910 about half of them were foreign born. Many coal miners live in isolated mining communities, in which the houses, stores, and the land are owned by the coal company. About half of the coal miners employed in 1930 were working in essentially one-industry counties.[1] Consequently, the supply of labor in soft-coal mining is generally fairly inelastic. Through control of real estate, retail trade, and local government, the company may be able to charge excessive rents and prices and to suppress freedom of speech.

The life of a coal miner is not an easy one. Coal mining is a hazardous occupation, with an average of about 2,000 workers

[1] W. C. Trapnell and R. Ilsley, *The Bituminous Coal Industry, with a Survey of Competing Fuels,* Federal Emergency Relief Administration, 1935, pp. 5–8.

killed on the job each year. (The death toll per 1,000 full-time workers is much lower in German and English mines.) Furthermore, the average number of days worked per year in the 1930's ranged from 146 to 199 in bituminous coal. Statistics show that between 1899 and 1934, freight-car shortages, mine breakdowns, and other causes of lost time accounted for 12 times as many days of idleness for soft-coal miners as did strikes and lockouts.[1] Chronic underemployment was characteristic of bituminous-coal mining even in the 1920's, when the industry averaged but 188 days of work a year. With one pay envelope and one year's earnings varying considerably from the next, coal miners know what economic insecurity actually means.

4. *Prices and costs.* The price structure in bituminous coal has been extraordinarily flexible. Not only have prices fluctuated widely, but on a certain day the price at the mine for a given grade of coal frequently has varied between customers and markets. For example, the minimum price for a certain grade of lump coal in a group of mines in the Clearfield district of Central Pennsylvania on January 1, 1935 was $2.50 for buyers in two market areas, $2.90 for those in two other market areas, and $2.85 for the remaining market areas.[2] Such variations result from allowance for differences in the freight rates to various markets, from partial absorption of freight rates by mine operators, from differences in the competitive situation in various market areas, etc. In the past, before minimum prices were fixed by government agencies under the NRA of 1933, the Bituminous Coal Conservation Act of 1935, and the Bituminous Coal Act of 1937, it is claimed that the bargaining power of various consumers had a marked effect upon the price structure, that the prices of soft coal for industrial and railroad users were forced well below the cost of production, while prices for coal commonly used for domestic fuel by householders was relatively too high.

Most buyers of coal pay more to the railroad companies than to the mine operators, for the railroads each year receive a larger

[1] F. E. Berquist *et al.*, *Economic Survey of the Bituminous Coal Industry under Free Competition and Code Regulation*, Office of the National Recovery Administration, Division of Review, Work Materials No. 69, March 1936, p. 48.

[2] *Report of the Committee on Prices in the Bituminous Coal Industry*, National Bureau of Economic Research, 1938, pp. 10–11.

total revenue from bituminous coal than the mine owners. In 1938, for instance, the mine owners received an average of about $1.90 a net ton for soft coal at the mine, while the average freight charge per net ton hauled was $2.27, and the average retail price in 38 cities was $8.61 a ton.[1] Freight rates have represented a rigid item in the delivered cost of coal to the buyer. Although the average price of bituminous coal per net ton f.o.b. at the mines fell from $2.68 in 1923 to $1.27 in 1932 (a drop of over 50 per cent), the average freight cost per net ton of bituminous coal hauled was $2.30 in 1923 and $2.26 in 1932.[2]

In soft- and hard-coal mining, wages or labor average about two thirds of all costs, while in other types of mining, wages generally constitute around one fifth of total costs. With wages such a large proportion of total expenses, a considerable reduction in costs in coal mining is bound to involve a cut in wages. Certain other costs can, of course, be reduced, as, for instance, interest and other fixed costs, royalties, and charges for depletion, which together may account for as much as one sixth of all coal-mining costs.[3] Indeed, it has been a common occurrence during the past two decades for soft-coal companies to go through bankruptcy, with the mines continuing to operate under new management and under greatly reduced capital charges.

5. *Demand.* The demand for bituminous coal is largely a demand for power rather than for fuel, and the chief consumers are the nation's great industries. In the early 1930's about 75 per cent of the primary energy used by manufacturing industries and by public utilities, and over 80 per cent of the locomotive power used by the railroads, came from bituminous coal. Manufacturing plants account for over a third, railroads for over a fifth, and electric utilities for over a tenth, of the total consumption of bituminous coal. Consequently, the demand is in large measure determined by the volume of industrial production and varies with the business cycle.

The demand for bituminous coal, especially over a short period

[1] *Cf. Minerals Yearbook, 1939,* U. S. Department of Interior, Bureau of Mines, 1939, pp. 770, 786–87.

[2] F. E. Berquist *et al., op. cit.,* p. 32. Of all the coal sold in 1935, as much as 86 per cent was loaded at the mine for shipment by rail.

[3] For cost statistics, *cf.* Waldo E. Fisher, *Economic Consequences of the Seven-Hour Day and Wage Changes in the Bituminous Coal Industry,* 1939, especially p. 39.

of time, is not likely to be modified much by price changes at the mines.[1] In most industries consuming soft coal, its price is but a very small part—usually well under 10 per cent—of the total cost of manufacturing the product, so that changes in the cost of coal would have little effect upon the prices of the final products of industries using coal for power or fuel. Indeed, almost half of the bituminous coal mined is consumed by railroads, public utilities, and steel companies, which have rigid price structures. Furthermore, mine prices are less than half the delivered price to industrial consumers and less than one fourth of the retail price. Consequently, mine prices must be changed substantially in order to have much effect upon the delivered prices of coal to its consumers. From 1923 to 1929 the average selling price at the mine dropped from $2.68 to $1.78, or about 34 per cent, yet the consumption of coal in the United States was no greater in 1929 than in 1923. Average mine prices again dropped 29 per cent during the depression years from 1929 through 1932, yet consumption declined 40 per cent to a figure of 307,000,000 tons in 1932—the lowest figure since 1905.

Power is essential to production, and shifts to substitute fuels require time. It is generally too costly to discard existing equipment used to burn coal or to try to adopt it for the use of substitute sources of energy like oil or gas. Yet there has been a definite tendency since the first World War for other sources of power (oil, natural gas, and hydroelectric) to displace coal, although the amount of direct displacement may be difficult to determine. Since 1918 the energy supplied by each of these three substitute sources of power has increased about 200 per cent, while that supplied by bituminous coal has actually declined.[2] As a result, bituminous coal now supplies less than half of the total energy used in this country, compared with two thirds of the total in 1920. In addition, increased efficiency in its use has permitted the railroads, steel companies, and public utilities to obtain the same results with from 20 to 50 per cent less coal than was necessary in 1920. These are some of the factors in the declining demand for soft coal.

[1] For a further discussion of the demand for soft coal, cf. John P. Miller, "The Pricing of Bituminous Coal: Some International Comparisons," in *Public Policy*, edited by C. F. Friedrich and E. S. Mason, 1940, especially pp. 148–49.

[2] Statistics from annual volumes of the *Minerals Yearbook*.

6. *Supply and excess capacity.* Because it disintegrates rapidly, bituminous coal cannot be stored for any length of time after it is mined. For this and other reasons, soft coal is generally sold before it is mined, which means that potential, not actual, output is peddled in the market. The practice of selling unmined coal has tended to depress prices because the industry, especially since the first World War, has suffered from excess capacity. Even during the year 1929 it operated at 29 per cent under capacity, and in the peak year of 1937, operations averaged 37 per cent below capacity—26 per cent below if calculated on the basis of a five-day week.

Various factors have been responsible for such excessive capacity in the industry. Capital investment in mining property and equipment (excavation of the shaft, hoisting machinery, ventilating systems, undercutting machinery, etc.) represents a permanent investment of a highly specialized character. Neither the equipment nor the property can be used for other kinds of business. And mines once opened may deteriorate rapidly if unused for long periods of time. Meanwhile, taxes, insurance, and interest on the investment continue.

Through lower ton-mile rates for long hauls, by the extension of railroad facilities to new coal lands, and in other ways, the railroad companies have stimulated overcapacity and the opening of new mines. The system of distribution of coal cars under the Interstate Commerce Commission has also contributed to overdevelopment in coal. Where a shortage of freight cars occurs in the peak season, the cars are arbitrarily prorated to each mine on the basis of the physical capacity of the mines to load coal, without regard to the cost of production, distance from the market, or other economic criteria.

The union policy of "competitive equality" through wage differentials has likewise helped to keep submarginal mines in operation. Under this policy, relatively low wage rates are permitted in mines handicapped by geological disadvantages or poor location. Natural disadvantages that raise costs are partly absorbed by the miners in the form of low rates per ton of coal mined. Probably no collective agreement covering a large part of the whole competitive area could have been reached on the basis of a uniform wage scale for all operators, because that would have

resulted in putting the mines in certain districts out of business.
The principle of "competitive equality" represents a compromise
that has not, however, been consistently applied.   Operators
favored by nature or location have been permitted to retain some
of their advantages. Miners in thin veins are paid more per ton
than those in thick veins, but the rate is not high enough to compensate them fully for the disadvantage of mining in a thin vein.
The union has also maintained that producers using machines for
mining should share with the miners the gains from machine operation, because of the necessity of preserving a competitive relationship between machine producers and operators forced to mine
their coal by pick.

In practice the principle of "competitive equality" has represented a mixture of uniform standards and differentials.   The
union has demanded a uniform work day and uniform rates of
pay for "day men," who are not on a piece-rate basis. It is only to
miners on tonnage rates (roughly two thirds of all workers in the
industry) that the system of differentials from the "basing-point"
rate for the area is applied, the differentials allowing for variations
(1) in the width of the coal seams, (2) in mining methods, or (3)
in freight costs from the mine to the market. Some wage differentials are, however, simply historical hangovers, which are perpetuated because investments, capital values, and jobs are based
upon them.   Part of the blame for irregular employment and
earnings in bituminous coal rests upon this system of "competitive
equality," which, along with the other factors fostering excess
capacity, has helped in times past to produce ruinous nonunion
competition and price wars.

Largely because of increased mechanization of the mines, the
average output per man per day increased from four net tons in
1920 to over five net tons in 1932, the low year in total production.
In the late 1930's output per man averaged about 4.7 net tons a
day. With the downward trend in demand during the last two
decades, the number of men employed in the industry has declined
from a peak of over 700,000 in 1923 to around 470,000 in the late
1930's.

Regional bargaining.   The first local union of coal miners
came into existence in 1849, and in 1870 the first wage agreement
with an association of coal operators was signed in the anthracite

field.[1] In those early years, however, the fortunes of unions, including those of the miners, changed rapidly. Although a Miners' National Association had 35,000 members in some 12 states in 1875, it disappeared the next year and only in 1885 was a new national organization, the National Federation of Miners and Mine Workers, formed. The next year (1886) this national federation of miners met in a joint conference with certain operators from Pennsylvania, Ohio, Indiana, Illinois, and West Virginia, and signed an interstate agreement with them, which fixed a scale of wages at basing points in those five states and established a bipartisan board to handle interstate disputes arising under the agreement. This was the first experiment with interstate collective bargaining in bituminous coal. Its purpose was to adjust prices and to standardize wages in order to avoid labor disputes, wage- and price-cutting, and low returns for operators.

By 1889 this first attempt at interstate collective bargaining and agreements had broken down. It was understood that the miners would enforce the wage scale upon the other operators in these states. That, however, proved difficult to do. In 1887 only 60,000 miners were union members out of a total of 280,000 mine employees in the country. Many operators who had not participated in the joint conference, along with some who had signed the agreement, refused to pay the adopted wage scale. First the Illinois operators in 1888, and then the Indiana operators in 1889, withdrew from the joint conference, claiming that they were suffering from competition in unorganized areas. In addition, there was bitter internecine warfare between the National Federation of Miners and an assembly of the Knights of Labor formed in 1886 to organize the coal miners. Although these two unions tried to cooperate in the joint conferences, conflicts arose because the Knights of Labor tried to undercut the union scale in certain areas in order to gain recognition. This first experiment with regional collective bargaining in the central states broke down because of nonunion competition and the conflict between rival unions.

The failure of the joint conference and the disastrous results of local strikes in 1889 caused the two rival unions in 1890 to combine

---

[1] For more detailed historical material, cf. Arthur E. Suffern, *The Coal Miners' Struggle for Industrial Status*, 1926; and David J. McDonald and Edward A. Lynch, *Coal and Unionism: A History of the American Coal Miners' Unions*, 1939.

into the United Mine Workers of America, within which the two unions (the former National Federation of Miners, then affiliated with the AFL, and the miners' assembly of the Knights of Labor) maintained some autonomy until the Knights' assembly was dissolved in 1898. The United Mine Workers had 21,000 paid-up members when it was formed, but by 1897 the membership had fallen below 4,000. During the years prior to 1897, competition had resulted in extreme price- and wage-cutting in bituminous coal. In Illinois, for example, the average wages of coal miners declined almost 50 per cent between 1895 and 1896, and in 1897 the average wage rate in coal mining was about 13 cents an hour.[1]

As a result of this deterioration in labor standards, the United Mine Workers convention decided to call a strike in 1897, which was joined by 150,000 miners and lasted for 12 weeks. The miners refused to settle the strike except by joint conference with the operators in the entire Central Competitive Field, consisting of Illinois, Indiana, Ohio, and Western Pennsylvania. At such a joint conference in 1898 an agreement was reached, establishing a pick-mining rate of 66 cents a ton at Pittsburgh, compared with 40 cents a ton in a union agreement for the previous year, and laying the foundations for a system of collective bargaining that continued for almost thirty years.

1. *Collective bargaining in the Central Competitive Field (1898-1927).* The Central Competitive Field Agreement of 1898 covered mines producing about one third of the total output of soft coal at that time. In addition to wage increases, it granted recognition to the union and the eight-hour day. The union, in turn, agreed to give the employers, who signed the agreement, all possible protection "against unfair competition resulting from a failure to maintain scale rates" of wages as designated in the agreement. To place the union in a financial position to call strikes against operators refusing to pay the wage scale, it was understood that the operators would "check off" or deduct union dues from wages when authorized to do so by individual miners.

Except for three minor interruptions, the Central Competitive Field agreements were renewed throughout the period from 1898 to

---

[1] *Cf. History of Wages in the United States from Colonial Times to 1928*, U. S. Bureau of Labor Statistics, Bulletin No. 604, 1934, p. 332; and Paul Douglas, *Real Wages in the United States*, 1930, pp. 152, 350.

1927. Tonnage rates of wages were fixed at basing points on the principle of "competitive equality," and day rates were established on the principle of uniformity for all mines. The interstate joint conferences were followed by state and district conferences, which attempted to apply the terms of the general agreement to component areas by raising or lowering wage rates to the same degree that they were changed for the basing point in the district. These district joint conferences, following the general conference, were necessary because the widely varying natural and competitive conditions in the industry made it impossible to fix wage rates for each mine in a general, interstate conference. During the two-year periods (1906–1908, 1910–1912, and 1914–1916), when the joint conference for the whole Central Competitive Field failed to reach an agreement, settlements were made by state and district joint conferences. Probably the chief cause of friction in the interstate and district conferences was the question of wage differentials or inequalities. At the Hearings on the Bituminous Coal Code in August 1933, John L. Lewis, president of the union, said: "the established differentials in many instances have been the source of continued discord among miners and operators alike." The wage differentials between various districts and mines have been influenced by local bargaining power and the competition of other fuels as well as the miners' demands for more uniform earnings.

With the steady increase in tonnage and day wages under the collective agreements for the years 1898 to 1903, the paid-up membership of the United Mine Workers increased from under 4,000 in 1897 to 115,000 in 1900 and 247,000 in 1903. In 1902 the president of the United Mine Workers would not allow the bituminous miners to aid the striking anthracite miners by joining the strike, on the grounds that collective agreements must be observed so that the union would be respected as "a responsible body with which to deal." Finally, after the strike had continued for almost half a year, the President of the United States intervened in the great anthracite strike of 1902 and, following a conference with Mr. J. P. Morgan, the operators agreed to accept voluntary arbitration of the strike. Under the arbitration award the miners received a 10-per-cent increase in wages and the operators were to deal with representatives of their employees. Although the union only obtained full recognition from the anthracite operators in 1920 and although the anthracite wage negotiations first began to take on the semblance of a joint conference in 1912, the union's membership in the anthracite field began to increase following the 1902 strike. Except for a voluntary wage cut accepted by a union vote of the bituminous miners in 1904, the wages in soft coal continued to increase under the collective agreements. By 1913 the union had a total paid-up membership of 378,000, or about two thirds of all coal miners in the country.

With the rapid increase in prices following 1915, the union obtained wage increases in 1916 and 1917 on the grounds that the cost of living and profits were rising faster than wages. After the United States entered the war in 1917, an act was passed creating a Federal Fuel Administration to fix coal prices. Early in 1918, following a joint meeting under the auspices of the Fuel Administration, the union accepted an agreement to run for the duration of the war but not beyond March 1920. This "Washington Agreement" gave the miners a wage increase and contained an "automatic penalty clause" providing that $1.00 a day be deducted from the miners' wages for violations of the agreement. This penalty clause is still contained in collective agreements in the coal industry. In return for signing this agreement, the Fuel Administration granted the operators an increase of 45 cents a ton in the price of coal, thus permitting low-cost operators to put from 20 to 22 cents of extra profit in their pockets.[1] One result of this price and market situation was that between 1916 and 1919 the number of commercial mines in operation increased over 50 per cent and the production of bituminous coal in 1918 amounted to 579,000,000 net tons, the highest yearly figure on record in this country.

In the 1917 convention of the union, the delegates from states outside the Central Competitive Field threatened to break up the Interstate Joint Conference. They objected to the system of regional bargaining by which operators and miners in the Central Competitive Field states established the basic rates that were then applied nationally to other regions in the North, South, and West. A compromise was worked out whereby union representatives of outlying districts were permitted to sit in with the miners at the Interstate Joint Conference and to speak on questions affecting their districts. However, the operators in the Central Competitive

[1] Arthur E. Suffern, *op. cit.*, p. 97.

Field steadfastly refused throughout the whole period of the Inter-state Joint Conferences to permit operators outside the Central Competitive Field to take part in the collective bargaining which fixed the basic rates. The Central Competitive Field operators wished to make the changes in basic rates, which would then be forced upon their competitors in other regions by the union. It was this peculiar arrangement for setting national wage rates by regional bargaining that broke down in the late 1920's because of competition from nonunion operators in states outside the Central Competitive Field.

In the Fall of 1919, a year after the Armistice was signed and after the Federal Fuel Administration had ceased to function, the bituminous-coal miners demanded a wage increase. Their wages had remained fixed for a year and a half, while retail prices had been increasing. In anthracite coal, the operators had granted the miners a 40-per-cent increase effective November 1, 1919. But the bituminous operators and the Federal administration refused to consider a request for increased wages in soft coal, arguing that the agreement really ran until April 1920, and that any strike to force wage increases before then would be a violation of the existing collective agreement.

The United Mine Workers called a bituminous-coal strike on November 1, 1919; but the Federal Attorney General obtained a court injunction forbidding the officers of the union to promote the strike by the payment of strike benefits and directing them to withdraw the strike order. The injunction was based upon the allegation that the Federal legislation creating the Fuel Adminis-tration was still in force, for technically we were still at war with Germany because the United States had not as yet signed a treaty of peace. Although the acting president of the union complied with the court injunction, many workers continued to strike, and a large number of union representatives were cited for contempt of court in disobeying the injunction. Finally, in December 1919, the miners accepted a temporary wage increase and the appoint-ment of a Presidential Commission to arbitrate the matter. This Commission granted the miners a 27-per-cent increase in tonnage rates and an increase of a dollar a day for men on day rates. The result was that, at the basing points in Western Pennsylvania and Ohio, pick-mining rates were $1.12 a ton, machine rates were 94 cents a ton, and the rate for inside day labor was $7.50 a day. A collective agreement was signed, based on the Bituminous Coal Commission's award, and these 1920 rates were maintained in union agreements negotiated for the following seven years.

During the war, prices and wages had been fixed by the Federal Fuel Administration for both union and nonunion fields. The production and consumption of bituminous coal had also increased; the paid-up membership of the United Mine Workers had expanded beyond 440,000 by 1921; and the Central Competitive Field states (Pennsylvania, Ohio, Illinois, and Indiana) continued to produce about 70 per cent of the nation's total output of soft coal until 1921. The postwar demand for bituminous coal, however, began to fall off with the depression of 1921, leaving the industry with a large volume of excess capacity. The result was resort to price- and wage-cutting, especially in the nonunion coal fields of Kentucky, West Virginia, and Virginia.[1] More and more of the nation's total output of soft coal came from these three nonunion states until in the late 1920's they were supplying more tons of bituminous coal than the four states of the Central Competitive Field.

Because the employers refused to meet to negotiate a new agreement as provided in the 1920 agreement, a bituminous-coal strike was declared on April 1, 1922. The anthracite agreement expired on the same date, so some 158,000 anthracite miners went on strike at the same time. The operators in both branches hoped to achieve a wage reduction. In anthracite not a pound of coal was mined during the five months of the strike, but in bituminous only about 450,000 out of 640,000 miners remained on strike during the four and a half months before an agreement was signed, continuing the 1920 wage level for soft coal in the Central Competitive Field. The invasion of the markets of the struck mines by the nonunion coal, which continued to be produced during the strike, finally forced the bituminous operators to capitulate. The collective agreements signed in 1922 covered about 70 per cent of the country's output of soft coal.

In 1923, following an investigation by a United States Coal

[1] During the war the Southern mines were about 50 per cent organized, but the union was unable to complete the organization after the war because of yellow-dog contracts, injunctions, the antagonism of employers' associations, etc.

Commission, the 1920 level of wage rates was reaffirmed and certain inequitable differentials in various districts were readjusted. At the Jacksonville conference in 1924 the union was able to induce all the districts in the Central Competitive Field to sign an agreement, renewing the 1920 scale for a three-year period. However, this last Central Competitive Field agreement was broken by many of the operators long before it expired on April 1, 1927.

2. *Collapse of regional bargaining from nonunion competition.* Shortly after the Jacksonville Agreement was signed, most of the nonunion operators, especially in the South, began to reduce their wage rates. The nonunion coal fields were then paying about $5.00 a day for day workers, compared with a standard of $7.50 for union fields. Table 39 indicates the course of average wage rates per hour for all workers (day and tonnage rates combined) in the four Central Competitive Field states (Pennsylvania, Illinois, Ohio, and Indiana) and in three important Southern states (West Virginia, Kentucky, and Virginia). Wage reductions in 1923 and 1924 were accompanied by price-cutting, so that the average price of coal at the mine in the nonunion field of Western Kentucky was about 30 per cent below the average price in the neighboring state of Indiana, its union competitor.

TABLE 39. AVERAGE HOURLY EARNINGS IN BITUMINOUS COAL, 1921–1937 [1]

Period of survey	Central Competitive Field states		Three Southern states		All states		
	Dollars	Index	Dollars	Index	Years	Dollars	Index
Oct. 1, 1921–							
Feb. 15, 1922	0.894	100.0	0.819	100.0	1933	0.495	100.0
Last quarter, 1924	0.885	99.0	0.699	85.3	1934	0.679	137.2
Nov. 26, 1926–							
Mar. 22, 1927	0.860	96.2	0.670	81.8	1935	0.712	143.8
First quarter, 1929	0.707	79.1	0.616	75.2	1936	0.745	150.5
First quarter, 1931	0.662	74.0	0.552	67.4	1937	0.862	174.1
Feb. 1933	0.458	51.2	0.374	45.7			

Wage- and price-cutting in the nonunion fields led to a shift in the production of bituminous coal. In 1919 the Central Competitive Field states produced 58 per cent of the country's total

[1] Data from the U. S. Bureau of Labor Statistics, and taken from F. E. Berquist *et al., op. cit.,* p. 75; and from W. E. Fisher, *Economic Consequences of the Seven-Hour Day and Wage Changes in the Bituminous Coal Industry,* 1939, p. 92. The figure for October 1921–February 1922 includes only two Southern states as data for Virginia are not available.

output, compared with a figure of 25 per cent for the three Southern states already mentioned. By 1927, however, these three Southern states, with 44 per cent of the United States total, had surpassed the four Central Competitive Field states. Between 1919 and 1927 the tonnage produced by West Virginia and Kentucky doubled.

It is not surprising, therefore, that union operators began to break their union agreements and to operate on a nonunion basis within a year after they had signed the Jacksonville Agreement. In the Fall of 1924 and early in 1925 a number of large coal companies, controlled by Rockefeller, Bethlehem Steel, and railroad interests, repudiated the collective agreement and abandoned the Jacksonville wage scale. The union charged that such repudiation was part of an attempt by large buyers of coal, especially the railroads, to eliminate the union from the industry. Several railroad companies shut down their own "captive" mines to purchase coal from Southern producers, expecting thereby to force their miners to accept nonunion working conditions. During the ensuing strikes between 1925 and 1927, when the last Central Competitive Field Agreement expired, many buyers refused to purchase union coal and even threatened to boycott operators who signed agreements with the union.[1] Some Northern operators substantiated the union's claim that certain railroads tried to force an open-shop policy upon operators in the North by threatening to buy permanently in the South.

Operators in the Central Competitive Field insisted that nonunion competition broke down the whole system of regional collective bargaining in the 1920's, that wage- and price-cutting in nonunion fields robbed them of their markets, making it impossible to maintain union standards. They claimed that severe competition forced all but one per cent of the coal companies in central Pennsylvania to break the Jacksonville Agreement before it expired.[2] However, the union maintained that it was unable to organize nonunion fields in the South partly because a number of companies that operated under union agreements in the North employed mine guards to drive the union out of existence in the South.[3] Even the Brotherhood of Locomotive Engineers operated

---

[1] *The Effect of Labor Relations in the Bituminous Coal Industry upon Interstate Commerce*, National Labor Relations Board, June 30, 1938, pp. 31, 38.

[2] *Ibid.*, p. 39.   [3] *Cf.* D. J. McDonald and E. A. Lynch, *op. cit.*, p. 170.

its New Rivers Collieries in West Virginia on a nonunion basis, insisting in 1924 that it would be unable to meet nonunion competition if the union wage scale were paid.

3. *Period of local collective bargaining (1927–1933)*. The termination of the interstate agreement in 1927 was followed by a strike of almost 200,000 union miners in soft coal. However, the flood of nonunion coal from the South and from Northern mines that had previously broken the Jacksonville Agreement rendered the strike ineffective. In addition, the strikers were restricted by a number of extreme injunctions forbidding meetings or discussions.[1] After a stubborn struggle for 16 months, the union admitted defeat, permitting each district to negotiate agreements as best it could.

From the middle of 1928 to the middle of 1933, the only important areas under union agreements east of the Mississippi River were Illinois and part of Indiana. Some local agreements were negotiated in Pennsylvania and Ohio, at wage rates slightly above those paid in nonunion mines. It is estimated that in 1933 no more than 15 per cent of the total output was produced under union agreements.[2] In 1930 and 1931 the union's dues-paying membership in soft coal was only about 100,000. From 1928 to 1933 there was an open revolt against the leadership of John L. Lewis, which led to revocation of the charter of the Illinois district and to the formation of the Progressive Miners of America in addition to the National Miners' Union organized by the communists.

Generally speaking, wage rates and the mine prices of bituminous coal declined about 20 per cent from 1924 to 1929 and over 45 per cent from 1924 to 1932. Wage- and price-cutting during this period resulted in low earnings and bankruptcy in the industry. In the early 1930's some coal operators were reported to have joined miners on the relief rolls and in the bread lines.[3] The miners began to join rival and radical unions to such an extent that in 1931 and 1932 some companies are alleged to have signed agreements with the United Mine Workers in order to counteract "left-wing" tendencies among the miners. By then, mine owners who had gone nonunion in the 1920's were admitting that the situation was much worse than when the union was strong enough

---

[1] For example, at Rossiter, Pennsylvania, a judge issued an injunction banning all meetings and songs on a lot that was more than a quarter of a mile from the struck mine of a coal company in which the judge admitted he had $6,000 invested.

[2] Berquist *et al.*, *op. cit.*, p. 6.   [3] Louis Stark, *op. cit.*, p. 489.

to enforce some wage stability in the industry. Operators who had sworn in the 1920's that they would never deal with the union were ready by 1933 to welcome the union organizers and to sign a new interstate agreement.[1] In a number of respects, conditions in the industry during the years prior to 1933 resembled the situation prior to 1898.

4. *Collective bargaining in the Appalachian region following government intervention (1933 to date).* No union took more advantage of Section 7a of the National Industrial Recovery Act of 1933 than did the United Mine Workers. Within a few months after the passage of that law, the miners' union had tripled its membership and had organized more than 90 per cent of the workers in the industry. Many of the former nonunion mines in the Southern states were organized under the legal protection of Section 7a.

In drawing up the NRA code for the industry, it was recognized that the Central Competitive Field was no longer the competitive area and that stabilization of the industry required joint solution of the North-South competitive relationships. With the signing of the bituminous-coal code in September 1933, the Appalachian Mountain area, extending from Pennsylvania to Alabama, became the bargaining unit in the industry. Including Pennsylvania, Michigan, Ohio, Maryland, West Virginia, Virginia, and parts of Kentucky and Tennessee, the Appalachian region accounts for more than 70 per cent of the nation's output of bituminous coal.

Under this code, wage rates and prices were fixed and government support was given to the wage scales established by collective bargaining so that nonunion operators enjoyed no wage advantages. When the NIRA was declared unconstitutional in 1935, the Bituminous Coal Conservation Act of 1935 was passed, empowering boards to fix prices and giving legal authority for the extension of the hours and wages provisions in collective agreements to all operators in the various districts. In 1936 the Supreme Court declared the Bituminous Coal Conservation Act unconstitutional, and in 1937 a Bituminous Coal Act was passed, which provides for the fixing of coal prices. In short, beginning in 1933 the government has helped to enforce price stabilization in the industry, and from 1933 to 1936 the government, by fixing minimum wages in

[1] *Cf. idem;* and *The Effect of Labor Relations in the Bituminous Coal Industry upon Interstate Commerce,* National Labor Relations Board, June 30, 1938, pp. 44–46.

coal, enabled the Appalachian operators to conclude union agreements granting higher wage rates to their employees. The Federal government has granted the industry some of the advantages of monopoly, such as price-fixing, presumably because the union and collective bargaining alone were not sufficient to "stabilize" the industry by preventing wage- and price-cutting.[1]

The Appalachian Joint Conference establishes the wage rates for pick and machine mining in thin or thick veins for certain districts and localities in the Appalachian states. These regional agreements form the basis for subsequent agreements in the outlying districts. Under the first Appalachian Agreement in 1933, the basic day wage for inside skilled labor was $4.60. Under the fifth Appalachian Agreement signed in 1939 and in effect until April 1941, the same worker is paid $6.00 a day. The Southern territory has enjoyed a 40-cent-lower day rate since 1933, which means that, relatively speaking, the Southern differential has been reduced as wages have increased. Since 1933 the proportion of the total production of the Central Competitive Field states has increased slightly at the expense of the Southern states, but there has not been the violent shifting of production between states that characterized the decade before 1933. Wage differentials between the North and the South and between producing fields within both territories are, however, still a troublesome problem.

The first four Appalachian Agreements each granted some increase in wages, and the fifth one provides for the union shop. The United Mine Workers argued that the existence of a rival AFL union made a closed shop necessary in order to enforce employee discipline, if the penalty clause for outlaw strikes was to be continued as part of the collective agreement. Since the second Appalachian Agreement, the miners have enjoyed a seven-hour day and a 35-hour week with time-and-a-half for overtime beginning in 1937.

A study has been made of the economic effects of the second Appalachian Agreement, which provided for wage increases and a reduction in hours to seven a day and 35 a week.[2] Comparison of the months before and after the agreement took effect on April 1,

[1] For a critical discussion of the coal program of the Federal government and some international comparisons, cf. John P. Miller, op. cit., especially pp. 169–75.

[2] Waldo E. Fisher, Economic Consequences of the Seven-Hour Day and Wage Changes in the Bituminous Coal Industry, 1939.

1934, indicates that it raised the average hourly earnings of all workers in bituminous coal about 22 per cent (from 58.4 to 71.4 cents).[1]   Data from mines accounting for approximately two thirds of the nation's total output indicate that total mining costs per ton increased about 14.5 per cent (labor costs rose 18.5 per cent) following the wage and hour changes.[2]   However, the increase in prices, fixed by the Code Authority with the support of the Federal government, was more than sufficient to offset the rise in costs, so that operators' margins or returns on investment more than doubled after the second Appalachian Agreement.

Whether the increases in coal prices that accompanied the wage increases caused a relative reduction in the volume of coal sold thereafter is difficult to determine.   For reasons already explained, the demand for bituminous coal may not be affected immediately by price changes.   Shifts to substitute sources of power and fuel take time.   Furthermore, during the years following 1933 there was an upswing in the business cycle so that the consumption of bituminous coal increased over 30 per cent between 1933 and 1937.

General remarks.   With the assistance of price regulation by the Federal government, the union has been successful in securing wage increases and shorter working hours.   It has not, however, been successful in increasing the average number of days worked in a year above 200.   Consequently, the earnings of many miners are still low because of unemployment.

Collective bargaining and government regulation have eliminated the extreme price- and wage-cutting that led to demoralization of the industry.   They have not, however, been able to bring about a significant reduction in the excess capacity of the industry either by eliminating a large number of mines or by increasing the demand for the product.   Abolition of the various wage differentials would, of course, help to close many uneconomic mines, but would also result in the permanent lay-off of many employees in some areas.

Higher wage rates seem to have stimulated the mechanization of mining and the increased use of machines for loading coal.   Such mechanization appears to have more than offset the increase in the number of workers employed as a result of the reduction in the work week to 35 hours.   Consequently, the problem of surplus labor and underemployment continues to plague the industry.

[1] *Ibid.*, p. 10.   [2] *Ibid.*, p. 38.

Recent experience in bituminous coal presents an excellent example of the limitations of collective bargaining even when the Federal government assists in maintaining a stable price structure. Modification of competition within the industry cannot stop the competition of substitute products, and higher prices have not helped to prevent the relative decline in the demand for the product. Although collective bargaining may prevent demoralization within the industry and preserve good labor standards, it cannot cause an increase in the volume of sales of bituminous coal. It cannot help to increase employment in the long run, although it may prevent the exploitation of the workers in a declining industry, especially where many of the workers live in company towns. In short, collective bargaining is not a cure that will bring about the recovery of a sick industry.

CHAPTER THIRTY

CLOTHING

The public has always had a special interest in the garment workers, because a large number of women work in the industry, because the industry has tended to breed unsanitary sweatshops, and because it is concentrated in large cities. More than one third of the manufacturing employees in New York City are clothing workers, most of whom are women. It was estimated that in the middle 1930's over half of all organized women workers in the country were in one of the clothing unions.

The two outstanding unions in the needle trades, one of men's and the other of women's garment makers, each has a total membership in excess of 250,000 workers, and each has had 25 or 30 years of experience with collective bargaining. During the 1920's the clothing unions engaged in various experiments involving union-management cooperation, joint schemes for unemployment insurance and dismissal compensation, low-cost housing projects, and labor banks. Likewise they are well known for their educational, cultural, and recreational activities, which have included Broadway "hits" and summer schools. The presidents of the clothing unions, who have had socialistic leanings, have been especially interested in national issues and programs for national planning and industrial stability.

The clothing unions have applied programs of industrial stabilization to their own industry. To some extent they have reorganized the structure of the industry in order to limit competition and prevent wage-cutting. Today both the men's and women's branches of the clothing industry are subject to an elaborate machinery of private control and regulation, enforced jointly by the unions and the employers' associations. In addition, the clothing unions are famous for the private machinery they have established for the settlement of labor disputes, especially the institution of an impartial chairman who has the power to hand down binding decisions. Labor relations in men's and women's clothing production were fairly peaceful during the 1930's, when many other industries were experiencing widespread strikes and labor "growing pains."

In 1939 the Amalgamated Clothing Workers of America in men's clothing and the International Ladies' Garment Workers' Union in the women's branch of the industry included in their membership about 90 per cent of the workers producing men's and boys' suits, coats, and pants and women's suits, coats, shirts, dresses, and blouses. In 1937 the Amalgamated concluded its first national agreement covering 85 per cent of all the men's coat-and-suit production in this country. Since 1935 the ILGWU has had a joint collective arrangement with employers, which covers 95 per cent of the women's coat-and-suit industry and is designed to maintain working standards and fair trade practices.

The industry. The clothing industry is divided into various branches. Largely on the basis of capital requirements and scale of operations, these may be classified into two main groups. One group, which is favorable to operations by small-scale contractors because considerable handwork is required, includes men's and boys' outer garments, women's dresses and outer garments, fur goods, and hats and other headgear. The other group, which is less favorable to subcontracting and small establishments because machinery is more widely used, consists of men's shirts, collars, and cuffs; underwear and nightwear; men's garters, suspenders, and neckwear; corsets; men's overalls and work clothes; etc. Another possible grouping of the various branches of the industry is that indicated by the jurisdictions of the unions in the needle trades: (1) men's clothing except workclothes, (2) women's clothing, (3) hats and other headgear, (4) furs, (5) gloves. In addition to factory or ready-made clothing, there is custom tailoring and dressmaking.

1. *Style.* In clothing, especially women's clothing, style plays a very important role. Every year there are some 300,000 different styles and types of women's clothes. Style tends to determine the size of producing units, keeping them small and "exclusive." By fixing limits to the use of machine processes, it restricts capital investment. It is an important factor in causing the industry to be

concentrated in large Eastern cities, especially in New York which is considered "the market."

Style also influences merchandizing practices. Wholesalers or jobbers, not working on orders, must stimulate sales. Especially in women's clothing, nothing stimulates sales as much as changes in style, so the jobber strives to have "something new" almost every week.

The seasonal nature of the industry is tied up with changes in fashions. Style, therefore, helps to ordain when certain clothing workers shall be unemployed and for how long. In part it is also responsible for the high rate of mortality of firms in the industry. With ever-changing style patterns, especially in certain kinds of women's clothing, competition is keen, and firms may lose large sums in the form of rapidly depreciating inventories.

Fashion helps to cause small contracting firms to flourish in certain branches of the industry, especially in New York City. In a market dominated by style and seasonality, merchandizing considerations may be more important than improvements in the technique of production. Contracting for the production of his stock of garments enables the wholesaler or jobber to conduct his operations with a minimum of risk, because he knows his production costs in advance and can avoid the overhead cost of idle equipment during off-season periods. In a market dominated by style and seasonality, there is some advantage in a contracting system that permits flexibility and expansion or contraction of operations with little responsibility or risk.

2. *Fluctuations in employment and sales.* The clothing industry is greatly affected by seasonal factors and swings in the business cycle. Of 24 industries studied for the period from 1923 through 1931, women's clothing evidenced the greatest seasonal variation in payrolls and men's clothing ranked sixth.[1] In percentage terms, the seasonal fluctuations were over twice as great in women's clothing as in the men's branch of the industry. In a normal year during the 1920's, the full weeks of employment in women's clothing in the New York market ranged from 25 to 40 weeks a year. The Brookings Institution study of *America's Capacity to Produce* contains an estimate that the average clothing worker probably had from 30 to 36 full weeks of employment out of 52 in

[1] Simon Kuznets, *Seasonal Variation in Industry and Trade*, 1933, pp. 414–15.

1929.[1] In clothing there are two distinct seasons, with employment reaching one peak in February, March, or April and another peak in August, September, or October. The peaks are a month or two earlier in men's clothing than in the women's branch.

In the past, seasonal variation in the industry enabled employers to reorganize their shops in slack periods, to discharge employees with whom they were displeased, and to beat down wages through competition for the declining employment. Because even in the best years the average clothing worker rarely works more than 45 weeks a year, the problem of periodic spells of unemployment has occupied a place of importance in the programs of the unions in the needle trades. In order to prevent discrimination against union members in slack periods, the unions have insisted upon the rule of equal division of the work wherever feasible.

An interesting development occurred in the sales of various kinds of clothing during the 1920's. It could be called "the decline of man." Whereas in 1919 American consumers spent almost as much for men's as for women's clothing (the difference was only five per cent), by 1930 American families were spending twice as many dollars for women's wearing apparel as they were for men's clothing.[2] This two-to-one ratio persisted throughout the 1930's. The 20-per-cent decline in retail expenditures for men's clothing from 1923 to 1929 was accompanied by a drop of over five per cent in employment in the men's branch of the industry.[3]

That the clothing industry is severely affected by business depressions is indicated by the experience from 1929 to 1933. During that period payrolls and the value of the product of both the men's and women's clothing industries declined more than 50 per cent.

3. *Location and organization of production.* The clothing industry is concentrated in large cities, close to the market. Within each city, clothing producers tend to locate in certain areas. About three fourths of the ladies' garment industry and around one third of the men's clothing industry is located in New York City. In both branches of the industry, Chicago is next to New York in importance and Philadelphia follows.

[1] Edwin G. Nourse *et al., America's Capacity to Produce,* 1934, p. 218.
[2] "Our Clothes Budget: Part 7 of the American Consumer Market," *Business Week,* June 8, 1932, p. 17; and *Biennial Census of Manufactures.*
[3] *Biennial Census of Manufactures,* 1931, p. 309.

The women's garment industry is highly concentrated in New York City because style is so important and a large supply of women workers is required. For cheaper goods, where fashion is less important, a larger percentage of the production is located outside New York City. For example, about four fifths of all women's coats, suits, and silk dresses are produced in or around New York City, but less than one half of all women's underwear and only one fifth of all house dresses are produced in the New York area.

More than one half of all men's clothing, except work clothes, is produced in New York, Chicago, Philadelphia, and Rochester, and around 70 per cent of all employees in that branch of the industry are in 10 cities having the largest output. Men's clothing production is more scattered than women's clothing production partly because fashion changes are less frequent and significant. In both ladies' and men's clothing, the establishments in New York City are small compared with those outside the New York area. That is because small contracting shops are characteristic of New York and because, in men's clothing, the New York shops produce cheaper clothes whereas the Rochester, Cleveland, and Chicago shops specialize in quality, trade-marked goods and have from three to ten times as many employees per establishment.

The clothing industry is characterized by a large number of small firms, most of which are proprietorships, partnerships, or closed corporations. In men's clothing there are between 2,000 and 3,000 firms, and the women's branch of the industry contains between 4,000 and 5,000 separate establishments. The average number of wage-earners in 1937 was 38 in shops manufacturing women's outer clothing and 62 in establishments making men's suits and coats, compared with an average of 128 wage-earners in shirt factories and 168 wage-earners in factories producing men's underwear. In the ladies' garment industry, the six largest firms together do not employ four per cent of all the workers in that branch of the clothing industry, and in men's clothing no one producer has more than three per cent of the total volume of sales.[1]

[1] *Cf.* J. W. Hathcock *et al.*, *The Men's Clothing Industry*, Office of the National Industrial Recovery Administration, Division of Review, Work Materials No. 58, March 1936, p. 34.

A number of factors explain why clothing is produced on a small scale. Changes in fashion and seasons, along with the desire for "exclusiveness," tend to operate against mass production. In the making of a man's suit, for example, there are hundreds of operations to be performed, which vary with the style and the quality of the materials used. Much of the work must be done by hand or on a sewing machine. The technique of production of outer garments has not changed much since the beginning of this century. Census figures show that all manufacturing plants use more than 10 times as much horsepower of mechanical energy per worker as do men's clothing establishments, and over 20 times as much power per worker as do women's clothing establishments. All that is needed to start a clothing shop is a few sewing machines, which can be rented and placed in a rented room. The jobber furnishes the materials, so that contractors can begin as clothing manufacturers with as little as $100 of capital. As a result, the number of firms in the industry varies considerably from time to time, with fly-by-night manufacturers often in the business only at the peak of each season.

Contract shops are generally smaller than the manufacturing shops—called "regular," "legitimate," or "inside" shops—that are operated by the firm selling the garments, whether a manufacturer, a wholesaler, or a jobber. About one half of the workers in shops making women's dresses, coats, suits, and shirts work in contract shops, while approximately one third of the employees in men's clothing are employed in contract establishments. The contractor's expenses are largely for wages, since the cut material is generally consigned to the contractor by the jobber or wholesale house, which frequently operates one or more "inside" shops. Before union agreements regulated the jobber-contractor relationship, the jobbers had the numerous contractors bid competitively for the work. Such competitive pressure upon contractors, whose expenses were largely for wages, often led to wage-cutting, especially in the slack seasons. Structurally, financially, and strategically, the contractors were the weak link in the chain of production and distribution; while the manufacturers and jobbers, who were able to play one contractor against another and were more permanent, had no responsibility for conditions in contract shops. The contract shops, the irresponsible element in the industry, were frequently unsanitary "sweatshops" in tenement houses, operating for long hours and at low wages. The greatest irregularity in employment and the largest number of labor troubles occurred in the contract shops.

In addition to the contract shops, there are submanufacturers, who differ from contractors in that they normally perform the cutting operation and go through the form of buying the material from, and selling the finished product to, the wholesale house or jobber. They are not, however, independent of the jobber, since they are working on his orders.

Some large and influential buyers, like department stores and retailing combines, have at times acted as their own jobbers by contracting for the production of their clothing stock.[1] These retail distributors, by virtue of their size and sales, may be in a strategic economic position. For example, department and chain stores account for over two fifths of all dress sales, while specialty shops account for about one third of the total.

4. *Costs*. The biggest items of expense in the manufacture of clothing are first materials and then wages. Taking all manufacturers of men's and women's outer garments as a group (including contractors, submanufacturers, and regular manufacturers), materials and wages represent from 80 to 90 per cent of the total value of the product. Wages alone are around one third of the total costs of production. Most workers in these branches of the clothing industry are on piece rates, although minimum hourly rates are often established.

Studies indicate that even under union conditions, wage rates are highest in the large cities (New York and Chicago) and lowest in small cities and rural areas. For instance, during the last half of 1934 average hourly wages in men's clothing in the 10 most important cities were 71 cents, compared with 53 cents per hour in cities with less than 50,000 inhabitants.[2] Nevertheless, in New York City under the contract system, costs of production are often lower than they are outside of New York.

The workers. Women constitute about half of the workers in men's clothing factories and almost three quarters of the em-

---

[1] *Cf.* Jack Hardy, *The Clothing Workers, A Study of the Conditions and Struggles in the Needle Trades*, 1935, p. 165.

[2] *Hathcock et al., op. cit.*, p. 84.

ployees in shops producing women's clothing. In New York City, four fifths of the dress workers are women, and female employees constitute over nine tenths of the workers in shirt factories. Many of these female workers are between 16 and 24 years of age; most of them do not remain in the industry for long periods of time. A study by the Women's Bureau in 1932 revealed that one fifth of the female employees in the sewing trades in Connecticut were under 18 years of age.[1] According to the U. S. Census, workers between the ages of 10 and 17 constituted about 10 per cent of the workers in the industry in 1930, and almost half of the female employees then in clothing were married, widowed, or divorced. As an indication of the shifting character of the labor supply in the clothing industry, one author states that it was once estimated that the membership in the New York local of dress workers completely changed every four years.[2]

Inexperienced female workers have been widely used because most of the work in the industry, especially in ladies' garments, can be learned in a very short time. The chief crafts requiring special skill and years of training are the designers, who create fashions, and the pattern makers, graders, markers, and cutters, who represent the various stages in converting new designs into the cut cloth. Thereafter, relatively little skill is necessary except when the garment requires a large amount of hand tailoring. The skilled work is mostly done by men, whose strength is also generally required to operate the pressing machines.

A large percentage of the clothing workers—about 40 per cent in 1930—are foreign-born immigrants who speak a wide variety of tongues and have very diverse backgrounds. This fact helps to explain the emphasis that the clothing unions have placed on educational programs. Jewish and Italian workers tend to predominate, and the common religion of the Jewish workers and employers has helped to draw them closer together than in other industries. Many of the leaders in the clothing unions are Jews. Recently a number of Negro workers have entered the industry.

Labor and employer organizations. There are five principal unions in the clothing industry. The International Ladies' Gar-

[1] Women's Bureau, U. S. Department of Labor, *The Employment of Women in the Sewing Trades of Connecticut*, 1932.

[2] Elsie Glück, *Introduction to American Trade Unionism*, 1935, p. 160.

ment Workers' Union has jurisdiction over all branches of ready-made women's and children's garments. In 1938 this union had organized from 85 to 95 per cent of the dress, coat-and-suit, shirt, blouse, and neckwear branches of the industry but had organized only about one third of the workers in the larger and more scattered factories manufacturing infants' and children's wear, underwear and nightwear, and corsets and brassiers. The Amalgamated Clothing Workers, with jurisdiction over the manufacture of men's and boys' clothing, also has affiliates in gloves, neckwear, shirts and cotton garments, cleaning and dying, and laundry establishments. In 1936 the Journeymen Tailors Union became affiliated with the Amalgamated. The United Garment Workers of America likewise claims jurisdiction over men's clothing, but its membership is confined mostly to factories producing overalls, work clothing, and raincoats. The union label is its chief source of strength, and the principal employers' association with which it deals is entitled the Union Made Garment Manufacturers' Association. The jurisdictions of the remaining two unions, the United Hatters', Cap, and Millinery Workers' International Union and the International Fur Workers' Union, are indicated by their titles.

All of these clothing unions are industrial in form except the United Garment Workers, which is affiliated with the AFL and might be called a union of associated craftsmen. Among the factors explaining why the industrial rather than the craft form has been adopted by the clothing unions are the following: the large number of unskilled workers in the industry, the large number of crafts peculiar to the industry, the isolation of immigrant clothing workers in large cities, the common religion of the Jews, and the socialistic-intellectual outlook of the leadership. Nevertheless, within the general industrial structure of these unions, the locals, especially in New York City, are organized separately on the basis of craft, language, or sex. The crafts are much the same in both men's and women's clothing, and they include cutters, pressers, sample makers, machine operators, finishers, tailors, and basters.

In each city the separate locals are combined into a joint board, to which the locals send delegates. The joint board is the main center of authority in each city, so the employers in each market have only one agency to deal with. In women's clothing in New

York City there are two joint boards, one for locals in the dress branch and the other for the coat, suit, and shirt branch. The executive board of the national union attempts to achieve some uniformity in agreements and to equalize labor costs between the several markets.

The clothing industry has been too divided in interests and too scattered in location to permit organization of the employers in one all-embracing employers' association. The economic interests of the contractors are often opposed to those of the manufacturers or jobbers. Under the NRA, for example, the contractors frequently sided with the unions against the jobbers or manufacturers. Also the employers in certain cities are in sharp competition with employers in other cities or rural areas. Consequently, there generally are two or more employers' associations in each city or market area.

In men's clothing, each city usually has an employers' association of manufacturers and another separate association for contractors. That, for example, is true in New York, Chicago, Philadelphia, Rochester, and Baltimore. Within each city the employers' association may include all or a majority of the men's clothing manufacturers or contractors, so that the union and the employers' association can negotiate a city-wide agreement for that market.

In women's clothing, the employers' associations are also divided functionally, with the membership of each association composed chiefly of either regular manufacturers, or jobbers, or contractors. Consequently, in the New York area there are three employers' associations in the coat, suit, and shirt branch of the industry—one for "inside" manufacturers, one for jobbers, and one for contractors. In the dress branch, there are four associations. The dress jobbers have two, one of which includes jobbers handling only low-priced dresses.[1]

Both the Amalgamated Clothing Workers' union and the International Ladies' Garment Workers' Union have taken steps to encourage the formation of employers' associations. The president of the ILGWU has said: ". . . even the organizing of employers into trade associations has become an integral part of our program

[1] *Cf.* Helen S. Hoeber, "Union-Management Relations in the Women's Clothing Industry, New York Industrial Area, 1936," *Monthly Labor Review*, vol. 43 (July 1936), p. 25.

as a union." [1] His predecessor stated in 1929 that the employers' associations had accepted the union's "proposition" that each association join with the union to stabilize the industry, to maintain exclusive control in each field, and to exclude nonmembers.[2] Employers' associations have also helped the unions to organize workers.   Employers' associations have signed agreements with the ILGWU stating that "the parties hereto recognize the necessity of unionizing the entire industry" in the New York area and that the employers' association "will cooperate with the union" for such purposes.

Of the 2,535 firms having agreements with the Amalgamated in 1926, only 413 were covered by agreements made with employers' associations.[3]   In 1939, the agreements of the ILGWU covered 8,640 firms in the United States and Canada, of which 7,320 were included under the union's agreements with 62 employers' associations.[4]

Experience with collective bargaining. In order to avoid confusion, it seems desirable to discuss the rise and growth of labor unionism in women's clothing and in men's clothing separately. Because the ILGWU was formed before the Amalgamated, union experience in the ladies' garment branch of the industry will be treated first.

1. *Women's clothing.* The decades of the 1880's and 1890's were the period of "seasonal unionism" in the ladies' garment industry. Unions rose and disappeared in rapid succession, with fluctuations in business conditions, unsuccessful strikes, internal rivalries, and struggles between dual unions.   During this period, wages were low; hours of work ranged from 60 to 70 a week, although they were often indefinite during busy seasons; and working conditions, in many cases, were indescribably bad.

In 1900, delegates from cloak-and-suit unions in four cities met to form the International Ladies' Garment Workers' Union, chartered the same year by the AFL. The new union's membership remained around 2,000 until the successful strike of some 20,000 shirtwaist makers in New York City in 1909 and the "great revolt"

[1] Cited in Herbert Harris, *American Labor*, 1939, p. 216.
[2] Benjamin Schlesinger, "Rehabilitation of the Cloak-Makers' Union of New York," *American Federationist*, vol. 36 (December 1929), p. 1434.
[3] *Cf.* C. E. Zaretz, *The Amalgamated Clothing Workers of America*, 1934, p. 176.
[4] *Cf.* Harris, *op. cit.*, p. 217.

of 55,000 coat-and-suit workers in the same city in 1910. The latter strike, lasting seven weeks, finally resulted in the signing of the famous "Protocol of Peace," which was the first collective agreement between a union and an employers' association covering an entire large industry in New York City. This protocol, largely conceived and formulated by interested citizens including Louis D. Brandeis, contained principles that have since guided labor relations in the clothing industry. In addition to the preferential union shop, the 50-hour week, wage increases, and price committees for fixing piece rates, it provided for a Joint Board of Sanitary Control to assure safe and sanitary conditions in workshops and a joint Board of Grievances to settle disputes and proposed changes in working conditions, with final appeal to a Board of Arbitration serving as a supreme court for the coat-and-suit industry. Relying upon this machinery for settling differences, the protocol expressly prohibited strikes and lockouts, and "perpetual peace" was expected to ensue.

The protocol did not mention contractors who, not being parties to the agreement, were creating a competitive situation that was undermining labor standards in the New York market. Consequently, in 1911 and 1912 the Boards established under the protocol ruled that it was in violation of the spirit of the protocol to send work out of the city and that all contractors working for members of the employers' association should register with the union so that the latter could enforce union standards in all contract shops. These rules represented the first recorded measures designed to regulate contractor-jobber relationships.

In New York City the preferential shop led to the organization of 90 per cent of the workers in the cloak-and-suit trade—1,796 shops with 49,000 workers were covered by agreements.[1] In 1913 a successful strike in the dress branch of the industry in New York forced manufacturers into the employers' association and resulted in an extension of the protocol provisions to the dress branch of the industry. In the same year, protocol agreements were signed by the Boston dress manufacturers and Boston cloak-and-suit manufacturers. In 1913 the union had about 90,000 members, four fifths

---

[1] Statistical and historical material in this section is largely based on Louis Levine, *The Women's Garment Workers, A History of the International Ladies' Garment Workers' Union*, 1924.

of whom were under protocol agreements. In 1915, an agreement covering practically all the cloak-and-suit production in Chicago was signed after an arbitration award. Like other protocol agreements, it prohibited strikes and lockouts and provided for a board of arbitration and a wage committee with an impartial umpire or price adjuster.[1]

The protocol machinery did not, however, operate smoothly during the years prior to 1916. Most employers were not ready to accept joint regulation and "industrial democracy." In New York, submanufacturing was tried in order to avoid the protocol provisions as interpreted by the Boards. Employers tended to disregard the provisions for a preferential union shop, and the workers engaged in illegal stoppages of work. When the New York employers' association in cloak-and-suit production disliked a Board decision regarding the preferential shop, its members locked out their employees, and the union countered by calling a strike that lasted for 14 weeks during 1916. Public sentiment favored the strikers. The agreement that terminated the strike abolished the joint machinery established under the protocol. Soon thereafter the protocol machinery was eliminated in other cities, giving way to collective agreements of the traditional type.

Dissatisfaction with the protocol arrangements for settling piece rates caused the union in 1919 to demand and obtain payment by the week in all important cities. Postwar prosperity enabled the union in its 1919 strike campaign to achieve wage increases, the 44-hour week, and various limitations upon contractors, such as registration of contractors, the union shop, a minimum of 10 sewing machines per contractor, equal division of the work between contractors, and no additional contractors unless those already engaged were busy. However, competitive pressures in the industry after 1920 led to widespread violation of certain provisions of the collective agreements with the union.

a. The 1920's. In the 1920's the coat-and-suit trade, always the bulwark of the union, suffered a steady decline in production and employment as consumers' tastes shifted to fur coats and the lighter products of the dress factory. From a paid-up membership of over 100,000 in 1920, the union declined to 75,000 members in

[1] For material on the union in Chicago, *cf.* Wilfred Carsel, *A History of the Chicago Ladies' Garment Workers' Union*, 1940.

1923 and to 32,000 in 1929. With sales reduced, the employers' associations in various cities launched a concerted, though unsuccessful, campaign in 1921 to reintroduce piecework and to cut wages. The union has generally used the organizing device of striking against all employers in the market and then signing agreements on new terms. This method puts pressure upon nonunion employers to sign an agreement in order to avoid further strike difficulties and calls public attention to the dispute. In 1922 the union brought the New York cloak manufacturers into line by obtaining an injunction restraining them from violating their agreement with the union. Generally, however, injunctions have been used against the union. In the 1924 dress strike in Chicago, for example, a series of sweeping injunctions helped the manufacturers to defeat the union, 53 strikers having to serve jail sentences for contempt of court.

During the 1920's the "fugitive" shops that moved out into small towns for the purpose of evading the union presented a real problem. Local business or community organizations, in order to attract new firms, would offer to pay the costs of moving the machinery and training the workers, and sometimes would offer to meet part of the costs of renting premises or furnishing power and materials.[1] If the union succeeded in organizing the clothing firm in its new location, the employer might move again, leaving the union to face the angry charges of unemployed workers and local "boosters." In view of the migration of firms and widespread unemployment in the industry, it is not surprising that many workers tried to "help" their own employers to meet competition by secretly accepting wages below the union scale or by working overtime at straight pay.

From 1923 to 1929 the union was weakened and almost wrecked by an internal split. A communist faction gradually increased its power within the union until it had gained control of the New York Joint Board in 1925 and the Chicago Joint Board in 1926. When the agreement in the New York cloak-and-suit trade expired in 1924, the employers' association refused to accept the union's demands and a deadlock occurred. The Governor of New York intervened to prevent a threatened strike and appointed a fact-finding commission to make recommendations that would serve as

[1] *Cf.* Wilfred Carsel, *op. cit.*, pp. 134, 238–40.

a basis for negotiating a new agreement. In its preliminary reports in 1924 and 1925 and its final report in 1926, the Governor's commission proposed wage increases, an arrangement for an unemployment-insurance fund, and the limitation of contractors to those with 14 or more machines, but it ignored the other union demands such as a 40-hour week and a guarantee of 32 weeks of employment a year. The international officials of the union favored the commission's report as a basis for negotiating a new agreement, but the communists in control of the New York Joint Board opposed it and rejected the Governor's offer to arbitrate. A 26-week strike followed, which cost the union $3,500,000 and ended in an agreement less favorable to the union than the terms recommended by the commission. With the union heavily in debt and the morale of the rank and file low, the influence of the communists began to wane until they had lost control of the New York Joint Board by 1928. Under the left-wing administration in Chicago the joint unemployment-insurance fund established by agreement in 1926 was altered and practically eliminated. Although the radicals were ousted from the Chicago Joint Board in 1926, the problem of dual unionism continued for a number of years.

In the late 1920's probably 75 per cent of all ladies' garments were produced under nonunion conditions. Although some agreements were signed with the several employers' associations, both the associations and the union were too weak to enforce them. In the small contract shops, piecework prevailed generally as a bootleg method and other provisions of the collective agreements were also disregarded. With little limitation or control of contractors and submanufacturers, the industry became so demoralized by severe competition that even the jobbers had become interested in labor standards by 1929 and were anxious to combat the growing menace of "sweatshops." However, little was accomplished in "stabilizing" the industry or jobber-contractor relations between 1926 and 1933 because of the disorganization of the union, whose membership averaged only about 45,000 during that six-year period.

b. After 1932. In 1933 the National Recovery Administration provided the regulation and limitation of contractors that the union had been unable to achieve. Under both the coat-and-suit code and the dress code approved in August and October 1933, jobber-contractor relations were controlled in order to limit competition and to eliminate competitive bidding. Under these codes, a contractor could accept work only from the jobber designating him; jobbers could not change contractors without permission; jobbers were required to distribute the work equally among designated contractors; and the prices paid by jobbers to contractors were determined, in the presence of an expert and a union representative, on a "unit system" of labor cost plus an additional sum for the contractor's overhead.[1] After obtaining such competitive restrictions and minimum wages in the codes, the union was willing to accept piece rates, which it had opposed for 15 years. Agreements signed in the Fall of 1933 were based on the code provisions, including the 35-hour week. By 1934 the membership of the union had increased to 200,000, or five times the 1932 figure.

Collective agreements in the coat-and-suit branch were renewed in 1935 and 1937. The New York dress agreement was renewed in 1936 and 1939. The 1937 cloak-and-suit agreement in New York limited the number of contractors and forbade a change in the number of machines in a shop without agreement by all parties concerned. When the National Industrial Recovery Act was declared unconstitutional in 1935, the union and the employers' association established a National Coat and Suit Industry Recovery Board, designed to stabilize the industry and to maintain standards through the use of a Consumers' Protection Label affixed to garments produced by member firms, which constitute about 95 per cent of the entire industry. In 1938 the average hourly earnings in union shops in the coat, suit, and shirt branch were about $1.25 and in the dress branch about 80 cents.[2] In 1939 full-time hours in the industry were further reduced to $32\frac{1}{2}$ a week.

2. *Men's clothing.* Before the Amalgamated Clothing Workers was established, the men's clothing industry was troubled by periodic stoppages, and spontaneous strikes were so frequent that they were regarded as a necessary evil in the industry. Concessions

---

[1] *Cf.* Sherman Trowbridge, *Some Aspects of the Women's Apparel Industry*, National Recovery Administration, Division of Review, Work Materials No. 44, March 1936, pp. 19–23.

[2] Max D. Danish, "The International Ladies' Garment Workers' Union," *Labor Information Bulletin*, vol. 6 (August 1939), p. 3.

won by workers during busy seasons quickly disappeared during slack seasons. By way of contrast, relations between the union and the Hart, Schaffner and Marx clothing concern have not been broken by a strike or lockout since the signing of the first agreement in 1911. In 1910, 1911, and 1912, before any of the men's clothing markets were organized, earnings throughout the industry averaged 23 cents an hour, with 24 cents the average in New York City and Chicago. Full-time hours averaged 55 a week, although actual hours were often as high as 60 and 70 a week because overtime at regular rates was very common. Throughout the industry the average wage in 1938 was 77 cents an hour for a full-time week of 36 hours, with hourly earnings in New York City and Chicago averaging about 85 cents an hour.[1]

The United Garment Workers, a federation of clothing locals, had been founded in 1891 with an AFL charter. Gradually, however, the more radical rank-and-file workers in the large cities became dissatisfied with the conservative and conciliatory leadership of the United Garment Workers, especially its unaggressive policy in the Chicago strike of 1910 and the New York City strike of 1913. An attempt to exclude from the 1914 convention of the union a large number of delegates from clothing centers like New York City and Chicago led to the formation in that year of the Amalgamated Clothing Workers, which left the United Garment Workers with about 20,000 members, mainly in the work-clothes branch of the industry. In this split and the ensuing rival union conflict, the AFL officials backed the United Garment Workers, declaring the Amalgamated Clothing Workers a dual union. The Amalgamated, with 40,000 members at the time of its founding, did, however, have the sympathy and support of the International Ladies' Garment Workers' Union, whose membership, point of view, and tactics were very similar to those of the Amalgamated. It was not until 1933 that the Amalgamated was granted an AFL charter.

The 18-week strike in Chicago in 1910 had led to an agreement

---

[1] For wage and hour data prior to 1933, *cf. Wages and Hours of Labor in the Men's Clothing Industry: 1932*, U. S. Bureau of Labor Statistics, Bulletin No. 594. Later data, based on surveys and statistics gathered by the union, have been taken from George Soule, *Sidney Hillman, Labor Statesman*, 1939, pp. 229–31; and Gladys Dickson, "The Amalgamated Clothing Workers of America," *Labor Information Bulletin*, vol. 6 (June 1939), p. 1.

with Hart, Schaffner and Marx, which, as an employer of 6,000 workers, was the largest clothing establishment in the world. Sidney Hillman, president of the Amalgamated since its founding in 1914, was a leader in this Chicago strike, which ended with but one signed agreement. This first Hart, Schaffner and Marx agreement was influenced by the Protocol of Peace, for it prohibited strikes or lockouts and established a permanent Board of Arbitration to settle all differences. In 1912 a subordinate Trade Board, corresponding to the Board of Grievances in the New York Protocol, was established with the added feature of an impartial chairman. The impartial chairman is a professional adjuster, paid by both sides, who understands the problems of the industry and can render decisions promptly. In addition to being a court of final appeal, the Board of Arbitration was given the power to adjust wages and to fix piece rates. In 1916, special piece-rate committees were established, with a third impartial member acting when necessary. The provisions of the early Hart, Schaffner and Marx agreements became the pattern for subsequent agreements in the industry.

Following a strike in 1915, an agreement providing for a closed shop and a permanent arbitration board was signed with two New York City employers' associations. In 1919 the Hart, Schaffner and Marx procedure and union conditions, including the 44-hour week, were extended to practically all men's clothing manufacturers in New York City. Complete organization of the whole Chicago market and establishment of the union's machinery for settling disputes occurred in 1919 after violent employer opposition and strikes in 1915 and 1916. The Rochester Clothiers Exchange, formerly an antiunion employers' association, also signed an agreement with the Amalgamated in 1919 following arbitration of a strike. The Amalgamated was aided in its organizing campaign by the War Department, which enforced certain standards of work in the manufacture of army uniforms. In Philadelphia, for example, the threat to withdraw lucrative government contracts was used in order to force employers to grant their workers the right to organize and in order to maintain the labor standards prevalent in other markets.[1] By 1920 the membership of the Amalgamated had

[1] *Cf.* Charles E. Zaretz, *The Amalgamated Clothing Workers of America, A Study in Progressive Trades-Unionism*, 1934, p. 124.

reached 177,000, which was three times the 1917 membership figure.

a. The 1920's. During the 1920's the union's membership declined, as did employment and sales in the men's branch of the industry. As part of a general open-shop campaign, employers and employers' associations in New York City, Boston, and Baltimore instituted a lockout in 1920 in opposition to the union and the arbitration system. The New York market had been upset during the inflation of 1919 and early 1920, because the employers had ignored the machinery for fixing wages in the agreement, as thousands of firms bid up wage rates. The New York City lockout occurred after the union refused to allow abolition of the joint machinery, including the impartial chairman for the market, established in 1919. The 1920 lockouts involved 60,000 workers and cost the union over $2,000,000 in New York alone. In the end the union obtained a new agreement, but the New York City employers' association was so weakened that it had to be replaced by a new one in 1924, following a trade-wide strike in that city. Experience in New York from 1920 to 1924 indicated how necessary to the union's program are strong employers' associations. In contrast to the lockouts in the three Eastern cities, the union accepted wage cuts determined by the processes of negotiation and arbitration in Chicago, Rochester, and other cities. The Rochester market returned to the piece-rate method as a necessary measure to reduce labor costs. It was during the 1920's that the union experimented with union-management cooperation and production standards to reduce costs.

Internal difficulties within the union prevented full enforcement of the 1924 agreement in New York, which provided for an unemployment-insurance fund first established in 1928. The 1926 agreement in New York provided for regulation of contractors. Each jobber was required to register, with the impartial chairman, the contractors he expected to use. Any change in contractors by a jobber had to receive the approval of the union and the employers' association. At that time it was estimated that 75 per cent of all men's clothing was produced under closed-shop agreements with the union.[1]

Relations between the union and the employers' association

[1] Zaretz, *op. cit.*, p. 211.

continued unbroken in Chicago during the 1920's. In 1924 the first unemployment-insurance benefits were paid in Chicago from a joint fund established by an agreement. Philadelphia, the only remaining major nonunion center, was organized in 1929 by a very clever union campaign conducted without publicity. The arbitration machinery that had been introduced in the other large markets by 1920 was established in Philadelphia in 1930.

From the union's point of view, it was fortunate that the Philadelphia shops were organized before the depression of the early 1930's, which tended to destroy union standards and to depress wages. The problem of runaway employers had plagued the union in the 1920's. The migratory problem was particularly troublesome in New York City because the contractors were not organized into a strong employers' association. During the depression, union agreements were ignored by firms in New York and other clothing centers. In the midst of widespread unemployment, work standards were disrupted, wage cuts occurred in all markets, and the evils of the sweatshop reappeared. Shops were moved to nonunion areas and work was farmed out to nonunion contractors, many of whom migrated out of the cities, especially to rural areas in New Jersey and Pennsylvania. Average hourly earnings in Eastern Pennsylvania and in some nonunion shops in Baltimore fell to 21 cents in 1932, which was even less than the average in the Chicago market 20 years earlier before the Amalgamated was formed. Hourly earnings were highest in Chicago, where they averaged 90 cents in 1930 and 65 cents in 1932. The wide differential between an average of 58 cents an hour in New York City and 21 cents in Eastern Pennsylvania in 1932 indicates how nonunion competition was tending to undermine the whole structure built by the union.[1] Throughout the industry, average weekly earnings per year dropped from $22.84 a week in 1929 to $13.70 in 1932.[2] The membership of the union declined from 100,000 in 1930 to 70,000 at the beginning of 1932.

b. *After 1932.* Under the NRA, with its minimum wages, maximum hours, and Section 7a, the Amalgamated made a rapid recovery. In 1934 its membership stood at 135,000, and by 1935

---

[1] Earnings statistics taken from *Wages and Hours of Labor in the Men's Clothing Industry: 1932, op. cit.,* p. 7.

[2] *Cf.* J. W. Hathcock *et al., The Men's Clothing Industry,* National Recovery Administration, Division of Review, Work Materials No. 58, March 1936, p. 81.

the union had organized practically all of the men's clothing industry. Under the code of fair competition, the government regulated the industry so that wage-cutting and sweatshop conditions were practically eliminated. Jobber-contractor relationships were also controlled, as they were in the ladies' garment industry under the dress and coat-and-suit codes.

In 1937 a national agreement granting a 12-per-cent increase in wages to workers in the men's coat-and-suit industry was announced in the form of a joint press release. This negotiated increase represented the first bargaining on a national scale in the industry. A study of the Amalgamated agreements in 1937 revealed that practically all of them provided for the closed shop and that a majority of them contained check-off provisions. Either piece-rate or time-rate methods of payment were permitted, but where the piece-rate system is followed, weekly minima are generally stipulated and the piece rates are established by joint committees. When style changes require that new piece rates be fixed, time studies are conducted so that fair rates will be established. Several agreements prohibit employers from moving outside the city during the life of the agreement, and a number of them require that contractors be registered and that any change of contractors by a jobber must receive the union's sanction.[1]

In June 1939, following the signing of a two-year agreement with the New York Clothing Manufacturers Exchange whose members have 40,000 employees, the president of the Amalgamated promised the New York City employers that no manufacturer with an Amalgamated agreement outside of New York would pay less for labor than employers were required to pay in New York. At that time, the Amalgamated had agreements with nine tenths of all employers in the industry. The president stated that the "general organization" of the union was supervising the whole rate structure throughout the industry so that the union could guarantee employers in the various cities that labor costs for a similar operation on a comparable garment would be the same in all markets.[2]

The union adopted this stabilization plan because the inter-

[1] Helen S. Hoeber, "Collective Bargaining by Amalgamated Clothing Workers," *Monthly Labor Review*, vol. 45 (July 1937), pp. 24–28.

[2] "Contract and Wage Stabilization," *Labor Relations Reporter*, vol. 4 (August 21, 1939), p. 918.

national office of the union was gradually losing control over wage agreements as joint boards in the various cities competed with one another to aid local employment under the pressure of declining demand. The plan, involving the classification of garments into certain grades so that labor costs can be made uniform for each grade in all localities, comes into conflict with prevailing wage differentials and is complicated by variations in garments. Moreover, the further limitations upon employers that the plan requires may raise questions as to its legal status.

Industrial regulation under collective agreements. The leaders of the clothing unions, practically from their founding, have recognized that high wages and reduced hours could not be attained without strict regulation of competition in the industry. Unless contractors were limited and competitive bidding abolished, average earnings of $1.25 an hour, a full-time work week of $32\frac{1}{2}$ hours, and joint unemployment-insurance funds would not be possible.

Limitations upon competition and employers' freedom of action under agreements in the clothing industry are numerous. In both the men's and the women's branch of the industry, jobbers must designate their contractors, and a jobber cannot change, release, or increase his contractors without consent from the union and the employers' association, or permission from the impartial chairman for the market. With certain exceptions, jobbers must distribute their work equally among their contractors. Competitive bidding by contractors is eliminated. Jobbers must pay contractors a sum sufficient to meet union wage scales plus an additional amount to cover overhead and reasonable profits. Jobbers must guarantee that union standards will be observed in the shops of their contractors, and they are made financially responsible for any failure of their contractors to maintain such union conditions. The impartial chairman, designated by the union and the employers' association, can examine an employer's books and can make final decisions on any complaint, grievance, or dispute. His decisions are binding, and work stoppages are forbidden. In New York City the decisions of the impartial chairman, by the terms of the collective agreements, are deemed awards in accordance with the Arbitration Law of the state. Upon the filing of such a decision in a court of law, it becomes a judgment upon which execution may be issued.[1]   According to agreements in both men's and women's clothing, an employer cannot move beyond the five-cent fare limit on the subways in New York City, or the 10-cent fare limit in Chicago, during the life of the agreement without permission from the union or the impartial chairman.

Joint control and private regulation of the industry have been even more extreme in the women's clothing industry in the New York area.[2]   Agreements in the dress and the cloak-and-suit branches of the industry in New York provide for joint regulation of the introduction and use of new machinery. Both the employers' associations and the impartial chairman can impose fines on employers violating the agreement, and discharged workers may be reinstated with back pay.   In the cloak branch, the impartial chairman prescribes a uniform method of bookkeeping for the industry. The union and the employers' association can examine the books of members to make certain that they are complying with the agreement.   In the dress branch of the industry, each department of a shop must be on either a weekly wage or a piece-rate basis; while, in the cloak branch, certain occupations must be paid by the week. Uniform piece rates are fixed at a meeting of the representatives of the union, the jobber, and his contractors. If the jobber and the union cannot agree, the impartial chairman sets the rate. All overtime is prohibited and only one shift is allowed.

In a U. S. Supreme Court decision in 1937, Chief Justice Hughes quoted the following statement in praise of the Amalgamated Clothing Workers:

Today the Amalgamated has collective agreements with clothing manufacturers and contractors employing the greater number of clothing workers in the United States. These collective agreements have brought peace to that portion of the industry that has entered such agreements. . . . The President of the New York Clothing Manufacturers Exchange, Inc., has stated that the "organization of collective bargaining machinery, the establishment of an impartial tribunal, and the founding of unemployment insurance are the outstanding achievements" in the industry and that the Amalgamated Clothing Workers "has been perhaps the largest single

[1] *Cf.* Sol A. Rosenblatt, "The Impartial Machinery of the Coat and Suit Industry," *The Arbitration Journal,* vol. 3 (July 1939), p. 226.

[2] Material for this paragraph has been taken from Helen S. Hoeber, "Union-Management Relations in the Women's Clothing Industry, New York Industrial Area, 1936," *Monthly Labor Review,* vol. 43 (July 1936), pp. 24–33.

contributing factor to the lasting peace and harmony that have characterized those clothing markets where the Amalgamated Clothing Workers of America was the other contracting party to the collective agreement." [1]

The Chief Justice did not give his opinion of the methods used by the union and the employers' associations to regulate the industry and to eliminate certain forms of competition. There may be some question whether such restraints upon competition are legal under the Federal antitrust laws.

[1] *National Labor Relations Board* v. *Friedman-Harry Marks Clothing Co.* (1937), 301 U. S. 58, 73.

CHAPTER THIRTY-ONE

IRON AND STEEL

The iron and steel industry presents a sharp contrast to industries like bituminous coal and clothing, with thousands of employers, no one of which controls even four per cent of the total output of the industry. Productive capacity in iron and steel is concentrated in a few large concerns, upon which most of the other firms in the industry depend for materials. These few giant corporations serve as leaders in establishing price and wage policies for the industry. Unlike the clothing and soft-coal employers, the employers in iron and steel are able to cooperate or to enforce uniformity. The large steel companies do not need assistance from labor organizations or the government to help them to stabilize prices and to control trade practices. The economics of the iron and steel industry in large part explains why steel was the "citadel of antiunionism" prior to 1937.

The industry. There are various stages in the conversion of iron ore into automobile bodies, steel rails, tin plate for containers, or some other finished steel product. The successive processes tend to divide into (1) the production of pig iron in blast furnaces, (2) the production of steel ingots out of pig iron by means of the open-hearth or Bessemer processes, and (3) the production of finished steel products out of steel ingots in rolling mills. The large integrated companies perform all of these successive stages, whereas the smaller firms generally specialize in one stage, or manufacture certain special finished steel products such as tools.

1. *Location.* The manufacture of iron and steel products is concentrated in a few areas. Between 85 and 90 per cent of all the industry's capacity is to be found in six states, and within those states it is concentrated in certain districts: in the Pittsburgh-Youngstown region, in the Chicago-Gary area, around Buffalo, New York, and around Birmingham, Alabama. About half of the

industry's capacity is to be found in the Pittsburgh, Chicago, and Youngstown areas.

The availability of a cheap supply of iron ore and coal, both of which are bulky, is the important location factor. Consequently, transportation, especially by water, is of considerable significance. Over one fifth of the employees in the industry work in communities with less than 10,000 inhabitants, and almost one half of them work in communities with a population under 25,000. The company-controlled town, the company store, and company-owned houses for employees are found where steel plants are located outside the large cities. It has been estimated that 60 per cent of the iron and steel companies rent or sell houses to some of their employees and that about 15 per cent of the wage-earners in the industry live in company houses. Perhaps 20 per cent of the companies, especially in the South, operate stores either directly or through agents.[1] Even in the Pittsburgh area, one large firm was reported in the early 1930's to have had a large proportion of its employees in debt to the company's stores.[2]

2. *Concentration of control.* A few large firms dominate the industry. Although there are some 200 companies manufacturing iron and steel products, the U. S. Steel Corporation alone accounts for almost two fifths of the industry's productive capacity. The five largest companies own over two thirds of the nation's total iron and steel capacity, while the 10 largest companies control all but one fifth of the nation's capacity. The large companies are integrated concerns, whereas the small firms are generally dependent upon the few giants for supplies of materials such as pig iron, steel ingots, etc.

Limitations upon competition are, however, much greater than these figures indicate. In the case of a number of finished steel products, there are less than five producers, perhaps because costly special equipment is necessary to manufacture the article. For example, only three or four firms produce armor plate and heavy steel rails. In the case of these products, as well as tin plate, orders have been allocated amongst the few producing firms with no pretense at competition.

[1] *Cf.* C. R. Daugherty, M. G. de Chazeau, and S. S. Stratton, *The Economics of the Iron and Steel Industry*, 1937, pp. 185–86.
[2] Horace B. Davis, *Labor and Steel*, 1933, p. 144.

3. *Costs.* The iron and steel industry is characterized by high overhead costs. A single steel plant may represent an investment of at least $60,000,000,[1] and it is estimated that capital investment in plants and machinery in the industry amounts to approximately $10,000 per worker.

In the production of pig iron, overhead costs are double wages costs, which are around five per cent of total costs. Materials and fuel are big items. In the production of crude steel and finished steel products, wages for all firms are about one third of total costs, and are roughly equal to overhead costs and the cost of materials and fuel. However, for nonintegrated producers the cost of materials is a much larger proportion of total costs than labor costs. For the combined concerns in the integrated U. S. Steel Corporation, wages and salaries are more than double overhead costs, and account for about 45 per cent of total costs.

4. *Demand.* Steel products are bought primarily by firms in other industries, which use steel for equipment or as material for their products. Normally, the automobile industry, the railroad industry, and the industrial users of metal containers account for approximately half of all purchases of finished steel products. A single industrial group alone will buy from 50 to 95 per cent of the output of many finished steel products.

For the most part, finished steel products, especially rolled articles, are sold direct to industrial customers on order and not through middlemen. Product specifications often prevent production in advance for a general market. Direct sales to large customers normally account for over two thirds of all sales. It has been estimated that in 1934 at least 42 per cent of the total tonnage of steel sold was shipped to less than 100 companies.[2] In 1936 two companies alone are reported to have purchased two thirds of all production of tin plate. In such cases the conditions of sale, including the price, are matters of agreement (sometimes also bargaining) between the executives of the selling and buying corporations.

Much of the demand for steel is inelastic because good substitute products are not available and because steel represents a relatively small percentage of the value of the products manufac-

---

[1] Even a small nonintegrated mill may represent an investment of at least $5,000,000.
[2] Daugherty, de Chazeau, and Stratton, *op. cit.*, p. 51.

tured by industries consuming steel. As mentioned in Chapter 11, only about $80 worth of steel goes into the average automobile. Steel rails, nails, and metal containers represent but a small percentage of the total costs of the railroad industry, the building industry, or the food and packaged material encased in metal containers. The fact that the demand for steel is derived from the demand for products like automobiles and building, or from the demand for services offered by railroads and public utilities, all of which are characterized by price rigidity, is of fundamental importance to an understanding of price policies in the industry. A study of the demand for the products of the consumers of steel helps to explain why steel executives insist that the demand for steel is affected primarily by general business conditions and very little by changes in the prices of steel products. Inelasticity in the demand for steel products also explains why officials of the union have at times supported price maintenance in steel.

5. *Pricing policies.* Since about 1900, the basing-point system of pricing finished steel products has been used as a means of obtaining price uniformity and preventing price-cutting. Under the basing-point system, all producers, regardless of the location of their mills, quote prices to customers as if the product were sold to the buyer at one of the selected basing points, as if each basing point were an organized market for steel products. The prospective buyer is quoted a delivered price calculated by adding to the basing-point price the hypothetical cost of shipping the product from the basing point to the buyer's premises. On the other hand, pig iron, semifinished steel (ingots and billets), and steel rails are generally sold at the mill on a f.o.b. basis, not on a delivered-price basis involving basing points and hypothetical shipping charges.

With the demand for most steel products relatively inelastic, producers as a group would not gain by cutting prices. Furthermore, each producer is fairly certain that he will not be able to increase his share of the total business by price-cutting, because competitors will follow suit. "Secret" price concessions seldom remain secret. Consequently, it is to the self-interest of competitors to maintain high prices, and the basing-point system, by fostering price uniformity on a national basis, has helped to "stabilize" the industry. Various trade-association activities and the leadership of the U. S. Steel Corporation in past periods also help to explain why quoted prices may not change for months or years, why price changes are generally identical and on the same date at two or more basing points, and why the price differentials between basing points have evidenced little direct relationship to the freight rates between those points.

6. *Employment.* Steel has been an expanding industry. In the five years from 1935 to 1940, over $1,000,000,000 was spent for new equipment and capital construction in the industry. Despite labor-saving devices, the total number of workers in the industry has continued to increase, reaching a peak of close to 500,000 wage-earners in 1937.

Although the long-time trend of employment in the iron and steel industry has not been downward, the employees have suffered from widespread unemployment or underemployment during depressions, for iron and steel are primarily producers' goods, subject to considerable price inflexibility. From 1929 to March 1933 and from the peak in 1937 to the low point in 1938, employment in the industry declined 50 and 32 per cent respectively. Payrolls in the latter period decreased 50 per cent.

In addition to cyclical swings, employment in the steel industry is subject to seasonal fluctuations and unpredictable shutdowns and lay-offs. The annual earnings for all workers in the industry for the period from July 1932 to June 1933 were $560; for workers given some work during each of the 12 months during that period average annual earnings were $690, compared with $1,700 in 1929. It was estimated that in 1939 the firms most efficiently managed would commence to make profits when operations began to exceed 50 per cent of capacity.

7. *Wages.* Although there is a North-South differential of almost 30 per cent in iron and steel wages, there has been a high degree of uniformity in the rates paid for common labor within the several districts of the industry, and general wage changes customarily occur at the same time, with most firms following the leadership of a few large companies. Wage scales in steel are, however, highly complex, and it has been estimated that well over half of the wage-earners in the rolling and finishing mills are paid on a piece-rate basis.

8. *The employees.* According to statistics for June 1933,[1] plant

---

[1] Figures in this paragraph taken from Daugherty, de Chazeau, and Stratton, *op. cit.*, vol. 1.

workers comprised about 83 per cent of all employees in iron and steel, and 46 per cent of the industry's employees were in jobs classified as unskilled. Presumably because much of the work in the plants requires endurance and ability to stand high temperatures, the industry had a larger percentage of its workers in the age groups from 20 to 44 than was true for industry in general. In 1933 the industry also had a high proportion of foreign-born workers—34 per cent of all employees. The large number of employees per plant is indicated by the fact that 82 per cent of all workers were employed in establishments with over 500 employees and 42 per cent in establishments having more than 2,500 employees.

Collective bargaining in the premerger period (1865–1892). As early as 1865, a system of regular annual conferences and joint agreements regarding wage rates and conditions of work was introduced in the iron mills of Western Pennsylvania. This first system of written agreements, negotiated between a committee of the iron manufacturers and the United Sons of Vulcan (a union of iron puddlers formed in 1858) lasted in the Pittsburgh area until 1874, when, following a strike over the issue of a wage reduction, all agreements were negotiated with the manufacturers individually. From the beginning, the agreements in the iron industry provided for a sliding-scale system, whereby the wages paid iron workers would vary directly and automatically with changes in the price that manufacturers received for standard iron billets.

In 1876 the Sons of Vulcan, then one of the strongest unions in the country, joined with a national union of iron and steel heaters and rollers and with a national union of iron and steel roll hands to form a skilled iron workers' union called the Amalgamated Association of Iron, Steel, and Tin Workers of the United States. This union negotiated many agreements, especially in the iron branch of the industry. In 1882 and 1889 the Amalgamated had a membership of 16,000, and in 1891 its membership reached a peak of 24,068, or about one fourth of the eligible workers employed in the iron and steel industry. In 1891, just before the famous Homestead Strike, it is estimated that the union had slightly under 50 per cent of the steel workers in the Pittsburgh district, and in the Illinois area the steel workers were somewhat better organized than around Pittsburgh. The main strength of the union, however, lay in the craftsmen in the iron branch of the industry.

It was the failure of the union to establish itself in the rapidly expanding steel branch of the industry that proved its undoing. Beginning in 1892 with the unsuccessful strike at Homestead, one of the best organized of the steel mills, the union began to decline in power and prestige. The decline of the Amalgamated followed the rise of large steel combinations associated with such names as Andrew Carnegie, Henry Clay Frick, and Elbert H. Gary.

The open-shop drive (1892–1910). Until the 1890's there had been a considerable degree of competition in the iron and steel industry, despite some attempts at pools and gentlemen's agreements. Under such circumstances, the system of agreements with sliding-scale wages that was generally used in iron and partly used in steel during the 1880's helped to stabilize wages and prices. Because Pittsburgh at that time enjoyed certain natural advantages, enforcement of the union wage scale helped Carnegie to drive competitors out of business or to absorb them, as he did in 1882 and 1890. After 1890, Carnegie Steel was in such a strong position in the industry as a result of mergers that it was able to challenge and defeat the union. In short, unionism in the iron and steel industry was accepted and even encouraged until the competitive situation changed in the 1890's and one firm became dominant in the industry.

The steel operators had complained about the restrictions placed by the union upon mechanical improvements, and the union's resistance to the three-shift day. The union was not particularly interested in reducing hours below 12 a day because most of the skilled workers were on a tonnage basis. With the steel industry experiencing an expanding market and a rapid rate of technological change, the operators became anxious to eliminate the union that they had tended to favor in the 1880's. The Carnegie Company used the defeat of the union at Homestead in 1892 to eliminate unionism entirely from its plants. In 1897 the Jones and Laughlin Steel Corporation, the largest independent steel producer in the Pittsburgh district, expelled the union. Indeed, between 1894 and 1900 the union was dislodged from practically all the steel mills and most of the iron mills in the Pittsburgh district. It retained its hold only in the iron mills west of Pittsburgh, in the steel mills in

Illinois, and in most of the tin and hoop mills. In the late 1890's the membership of the union fell to 10,000.

In 1901 the United States Steel Corporation was formed by the merger of the Carnegie Company and a number of other firms in the industry. At the time of its formation, the Corporation controlled 43 per cent of the pig-iron production and 66 per cent of the steel-ingot and castings production in the country. In certain steel products the new Corporation enjoyed a complete monopoly. The ultimate authority on labor questions was concentrated in the executive committee of the Corporation.

The union realized that, through the U. S. Steel Corporation, the antiunion policy of the Carnegie Company might be spread throughout the industry. The Corporation's executive committee had gone on record as "unalterably opposed" to any extension of unionism in the mills of its subsidiaries. Following an attempt by the union to extend its agreements to cover all the mills of three of the Corporation's subsidiaries, a strike was called, which soon became a general strike against all of the mills of the U. S. Steel Corporation. As a result of defeat in this strike, the union was forced to concede that 14 mills formerly under agreement would henceforth be considered nonunion. From 1902 to 1909 the union was dislodged from one mill after another in the U. S. Steel combine, and, following defeat in a strike against placing the only remaining union-recognizing subsidiary on a nonunion basis in 1909, the Amalgamated was entirely eliminated from the mills of the Corporation.

Shortly after its formation, the U. S. Steel Corporation established its employee stock-ownership plan and instituted an extensive system of espionage to aid in discharging and black-listing union members. Labor espionage had been used as early as 1892 by the Carnegie Steel Company. The Corporation extended its antiunion policy to its coal and ore mines and to its railroad and shipping lines. Other steel companies followed the leader's policy of refusing to recognize labor unions or to confer with union officials in their official capacity. Refusal of Bethlehem Steel Corporation's officials to recognize or deal with a machinists' union led to an unsuccessful strike against the company in 1910.

The period of nonrecognition (1910–1936). Although the union had been eliminated from the large iron and steel plants and survived only in a few small bar, sheet, and tin mills, strikes continued to occur. Strikes took place in Youngstown, Ohio, and Braddock, Pennsylvania, in 1916, in which five strikers were killed and six squares of the business district of Youngstown were burned to the ground. Between 1916 and 1932 a total of almost 400 strikes occurred in the iron and steel industry. In many cases they were spontaneous strikes and guerilla warfare, in which the Amalgamated took no part. They arose from grievances against arbitrary treatment and from complaints against the 12-hour day, which was the normal working day for over two fifths of the workers in steel in 1910, 1914, and 1919. Indeed, through espionage and control of steel towns, the companies were able to combat the Amalgamated so that its membership only increased from about 7,000 in 1913 to around 16,000 in 1918. This was the war period during which most unions expanded rapidly.

In 1918 and 1919, union organization was in the air. Perhaps to forestall organization of their workers, the Bethlehem Steel Corporation, the Youngstown Sheet and Tube Company, and the International Harvester Company introduced employee-representation plans into their steel mills during those years. At its 1918 convention, the AFL had adopted a program for organizing the steel industry, and a joint committee of 24 craft unions having jurisdiction in iron and steel was established.

The organizing campaign began in Chicago and Pittsburgh late in 1918. Despite the fact that union meetings were forbidden in certain steel towns—one mayor said that "Jesus Christ himself could not speak for the AFL" in his town—the joint committee reported a membership of 100,000 in June 1919. The officials of the U. S. Steel Corporation refused to meet with the union officials to discuss an agreement. Following mass discharges of union members, a strike was called, and soon 350,000 steel workers had quit the mills. During the strike, thousands of Negroes were imported from the South as strike-breakers; two outside labor-spy agencies were hired to supplement the espionage service of the U. S. Steel Corporation; twenty strikers were killed; and full-page advertisements appeared in newspapers implying that Huns, anarchists, and the Bolsheviks were behind the strike. In the end the strike was lost, partly because the 24 craft unions contributed little money and fought with one another concerning jurisdictions.

Defeat of the union in the 1919 strike caused its membership and influence to decline in the 1920's. The number of companies having agreements with the Amalgamated declined from 41 in 1920 to 25 in 1929 and 13 in 1932.[1] One of these agreements was with a plant of the Republic Steel Corporation at Warren, Ohio, where the Amalgamated cooperated with the company in 1932 to defeat a strike called by a communist-controlled union, the Steel and Metal Workers Industrial Union. In the first quarter of 1933 the Amalgamated's membership in good standing was reported at the low figure of 4,800. From 1920 to 1933 its membership never represented as much as 10 per cent of the nation's steel workers, and the members were concentrated among the craftsmen in small tin-plate, sheet-steel, and wrought-iron companies, rapidly becoming obsolete with the new technological advances in the industry.

Following pressure from public opinion, including a request by President Harding, the American Iron and Steel Institute in 1923 reluctantly agreed to strive to abolish the 12-hour shift in the industry. In addition, the steel companies extended their "welfare" programs in the 1920's. These programs included accident prevention, employee stock ownership, pensions systems, mutual benefit associations, group life insurance, recreation facilities, and so forth. No new employee-representation plans (company unions) were established in the large steel companies, however, from 1921 to 1933.

The New-Deal period (1933–1940). In order to understand the developments in steel labor following 1933, it is necessary to appreciate the effects of the depression upon steel workers. In 1929 as many as 435,000 employees in the iron and steel industry were receiving an average hourly wage of 63.5 cents and average annual earnings of $1,620. During the 12 months of July 1932 to June 1933, when the National Industrial Recovery Act was passed, average wages were 48.5 cents an hour and average annual earnings had dropped to $560—less than $11 a week. Although the work had been spread until there were two and a half employees for every full-time job, the number of employees had declined to 213,000 in March 1933, or half the number in March 1929. During late 1932 and early 1933, the steel mills of the country were operating at only 15 or 20 per cent of capacity.

[1] Daugherty, de Chazeau, and Stratton, *op. cit.*, p. 944.

In addition to lack of income and employment, the workers frequently found themselves completely dominated by the company both on the job and in the community. Systems for labor espionage and for exchange of information between companies concerning "agitators" and "undesirables" had put the fear of economic punishment into the hearts of workers. The total trade-union membership in iron and steel in the year prior to the NRA did not exceed two per cent of the workers in the industry. About 20 per cent of the workers employed in the industry were in seven company unions, of which the Bethlehem Steel Corporation's employee-representation plan was the most important. The remaining employees, averaging about 700 to a plant or mill, were supposed to make their complaints individually at the front office or perhaps to the president of the corporation. That this arrangement was working none too well is indicated by the fact that strikes and lockouts caused over 375,000 man-days of idleness in iron and steel in 1932, the largest figure for any year in the 1920's and 1930's except 1937.

1. *Under the NRA (1933–1935).* Company-initiated and company-sponsored unions were established in most of the steel industry immediately following the passage of the National Industrial Recovery Act in June 1933. By the end of 1934 there were 93 employee-representation plans covering from 90 to 95 per cent of the workers in the iron and steel industry. Although these plans were under company domination, they represented a distinct advance over the one-sided system of individual labor dealings. That advance was indicated by the opposition of foremen and superintendents, and by the growing independence of the officers of some of the company unions. Although open revolt in the company unions occurred after the Supreme Court terminated the NRA in May 1935, the plans did afford many workers some experience in collective dealing on an industrial basis during the NRA period.

The Amalgamated Association of Iron, Steel, and Tin Workers attempted to take advantage of Section 7a of the NIRA through an organizing campaign. Although the union's paid-up membership did increase from 4,800 in the middle of 1933 to 19,000 in the middle of 1934, it had dropped below 10,000 toward the end of the NRA period. The craft outlook, uninspired leadership, internal factionalism, and past defeats of the union prevented it from taking full advantage of the organizing opportunities. In addition, most of the steel companies and the American Iron and Steel Institute formed a united antiunion front while favoring employee representation. In 1934, for example, the Republic Steel Corporation refused to renew written agreements for three of its plants that had been under agreement with the Amalgamated for a period extending back to the years before they were merged with Republic. In the Fall of 1933, the coal miners' union met stern resistance from the steel companies in attempting to organize the "captive" mines, and even in 1934 the steel companies, although signing agreements covering their coal mines, refused to recognize the union as such. In a case involving Section 7a, a Federal judge handed down a decision in February 1935, stating that the company-union plan of the Weirton Steel Company complied in all respects with the Recovery Act and refusing to grant the government an injunction to restrain the company from interferring with the self-organization of the employees. Despite Section 7a, the large steel companies dismissed many workers for union activity. Under such circumstances, the Amalgamated was unable to establish or reestablish collective bargaining and written agreements in the steel industry.

During the NRA period, two wage increases restored wage rates to about the 1929 level, and full-time hours were further reduced. In addition, thousands of grievances were brought to the attention of the top management through the new employee-representation plans. From 1934 to 1936 a total of 36,709 questions were settled under the employee-representation schemes, of which 70 per cent were decided in favor of the employees.[1] Nevertheless, it was difficult for companies with newly formed plans to develop the management spirit and technique worked out by Bethlehem Steel and the American Rolling Mills Company over a period of many years. Many foremen tended to oppose the new method of settling grievances because they felt that it "short-circuited" them and undermined their authority.

2. *The Steel Workers Organizing Committee.* The National Labor Relations Act was passed in July 1935. Within a few months the steel workers in various plants of U. S. Steel subsidiaries, especially

---

[1] *Cf.* Frederick H. Harbison, *Labor Relations in the Iron and Steel Industry, 1936 to 1939* (unpublished Ph.D. thesis, Princeton University Library), 1940, p. 17.

in the Chicago and Pittsburgh areas, were demanding wage increases and were attempting to establish central employee councils for company-wide dealings. In a few instances, attempts to establish independent unions were made. In January 1936, eighty representatives from seven of the nine plants in the Carnegie-Illinois Steel Corporation in the Pittsburgh-Youngstown district formed a "central committee" to press for company-wide recognition and compulsory arbitration of unsettled grievances. By May 1936, there was organized unrest in practically all of the plants of the Carnegie-Illinois Corporation, which, following a merger in 1936, employed about half of the workers in the entire U. S. Steel Corporation, and nearly one fourth of all steel workers in the country.

The convention of the Amalgamated Association of Iron, Steel, and Tin Workers in the Spring of 1936 forced its officers to accept the CIO proposal to contribute $500,000 toward a program to organize the iron and steel industry. When the Steel Workers Organizing Committee (SWOC) was formed in June 1936, it was apparent that the organizing drive should be concentrated in Carnegie-Illinois, where unrest and dissatisfaction with employee representation was so widespread. The SWOC program involved an attempt to discredit employee representation while capturing its personnel.

Shortly after the SWOC campaign began, the president of the U. S. Steel Corporation stated that the management was convinced that the vast majority of the employees "resent the idea of paying tribute for the right to work" and that, therefore, the management stood "squarely on the principle of the open shop." [1] The corporation continued to support the plan of employee representation as "the fairest method of collective bargaining." However, it hesitated to grant the various demands of employee representatives, including increased wages and the 40-hour week. Only after the 1936 election, which was interpreted as an overwhelming victory for the New Deal, was a wage increase granted. Furthermore, the corporation established a precedent by signing agreements with employee representatives, embodying the new wage scale. In November 1936, the SWOC filed a complaint with the National Labor Relations Board charging that the Carnegie-Illinois Corporation had

[1] *U. S. Steel News*, July 1936, p. 1.

dominated and supported the company union and had coerced employee representatives into signing the wage agreement.

Collective bargaining (1937–1940). A number of circumstances led the top officials of the U. S. Steel Corporation to sign an agreement with the SWOC in March 1937 and to withdraw recognition from its employee-representation plans. Early in 1937 there was a boom in steel, with plants operating at almost 90 per cent of capacity. The employee-representation plans were tending to disintegrate as many representatives joined the SWOC and others made various demands upon the management. At the time the agreement with U. S. Steel was announced, the SWOC had about 150,000 signed membership cards, but the collection of dues had been suspended from November 1936 to April 1937. In addition, the political situation, both in Pennsylvania and in Washington, D. C., favored the union.

Although the Carnegie-Illinois agreement with the SWOC only recognized the union as the representative for its own members, it did grant the demands of the SWOC and employee representatives for wage increases, the 40-hour week, and final appeal of grievances to arbitration by an outside umpire. Only a few small companies had signed agreements with the SWOC before the Carnegie-Illinois agreement in March 1937. Two months later, the SWOC claimed 110 signed agreements with companies employing about 300,000 workers.

The Carnegie-Illinois agreement became a sort of standard agreement for the industry. The experience of the top officials of the SWOC had been in the United Mine Workers' union, so they had originally aimed at establishing collective bargaining in steel on an industry-wide basis between the union and an association of the principal steel producers. They had in mind a sort of "Appalachian Agreement" for iron and steel. The Carnegie-Illinois agreement meant the abandonment, at least temporarily, of industry-wide collective bargaining and the substitution of separate agreements with individual concerns.

The industry-wide program of the union received a setback when, in a contest for the presidency of the American Iron and Steel Institute in May 1937, the candidate of U. S. Steel was defeated by Tom Girdler of Republic Steel, the candidate of the antiunion group later called "Little Steel." This "Little Steel" group included the following six companies with a total of about 186,000 employees: Bethlehem Steel, Republic Steel, Youngstown Sheet and Tube, National Steel, Inland Steel, and American Rolling Mills. The Jones and Laughlin Steel Corporation had signed an agreement with the union following a 36-hour strike and an employee election in May.

The SWOC had made little progress in Bethlehem Steel, American Rolling Mills, and National Steel, for employee-representation plans were strongly entrenched in these firms. However, the union had made considerable headway in Republic Steel, in Youngstown Sheet and Tube, and in Inland Steel. It was against these three companies that the union called a strike on May 26, 1937, following their refusal to recognize or negotiate with the union. In addition, Republic Steel had helped to bring on the strike by discharging union members and closing down certain plants that were strongly organized. During the strike, Inland Steel and Youngstown Sheet and Tube closed their plants, but Republic Steel attempted to operate several mills. In addition, a plant of the Bethlehem Steel was later drawn into the strike when two railroad operating unions struck for a signed agreement. Throughout the strike, officers of these four firms refused to recognize the union and insisted that they would under no circumstances make an agreement with it.

In the "Little Steel" strike of 1937, the union was defeated. The National Guard limited "picketing" activities and gave the protection necessary for a successful back-to-work movement. Following this defeat, the union pressed charges against all six of the "Little Steel" companies on the grounds that they had violated the National Labor Relations Act by fostering company unions or by committing some other "unfair labor practice." The companies against which the "Little Steel" strike was waged are among the most profitable ones in the industry. They exert considerable influence and control in the communities where their mills are located, and they have enhanced the prestige of the leaders of "independent" unions or former company unions by granting them favorable treatment in grievances and other matters. The SWOC even has grievance committees in several of the plants of these firms. In addition, some of the "Little Steel" group offer their emloyees better wage rates, vacation periods, or welfare programs than the principal companies under agreement with the SWOC.

Although industry-wide collective bargaining has not been achieved, it must be recognized that the terms of the SWOC agreements establish the level of labor standards in the whole industry. It is the SWOC that is largely responsible for the fact that the average earnings of workers in steel plants in 1939 were approximately 83 cents an hour, which is from 25 to 30 per cent above either the 1929 figure for steel or the 1939 average for all manufacturing industries.[1]   The SWOC was also largely responsible for preventing wage cuts in 1937 and 1938.

In the last four months of 1937, steel production dropped from 83 to 25 per cent of capacity and employment was almost cut in half. With this "recession" continuing into the Spring of 1938 and price cuts impending, the U. S. Steel officials informally requested the union to accept a wage cut in the new agreement to be signed. Not only did the SWOC spokesmen refuse to accept a wage cut, but they advised against price cuts and put pressure on Washington in June 1938 to delay a monopoly investigation of the steel industry at a time when increased competition might have caused price and wage cuts. Pointing to "the terror-stricken condition of the steel industry brought about by a system of cut-throat competition," the chairman of the SWOC said in October 1938: "If the steel corporations cannot put their own house in order, it is the avowed purpose of the organized steel workers in this nation to promote a constructive legislative program that will adequately protect the interests of the industry and its workers." [2] In the absence of stabilization by industry-wide collective bargaining, the SWOC leaders have used political pressure to prevent price reductions, which might result in wage reductions.

In the Spring of 1940 the SWOC had some 650 agreements, of which over 70 were in the basic iron and steel industry and covered about two thirds of the industry's total working force. The other agreements were in 25 different industries closely related to steel, including companies producing such articles as cash registers, refrigerators, lawn mowers, bedsprings, agricultural machines, hardware, stoves, steam shovels, sash weights, steel railroad cars,

[1] Harbison, *op. cit.*, p. 9.
[2] Statement of Philip Murray in Cleveland, October 13, 1938, *SWOC press release.*

steel rolling-mill equipment, and heavy machine tools.   Union officials estimate that at least 2,000,000 workers are employed in the various industries where the SWOC has one or more signed agreements.[1] The membership of the SWOC at the beginning of 1940 has been estimated by various authors as "probably close to 225,000 paid-up members" and as an average dues-paying membership in steel of about 100,000 with the total membership in the basic steel industry amounting to 300,000 or 350,000.[2]

It is claimed that the union by 1940 had some 75 closed-shop agreements with small firms employing a total of 13,000 or 14,000 workers.[3]   Other companies have, "as a matter of policy," persuaded workers to belong to the union and pay their dues.   The SWOC leaders have insisted that such complete "recognition" of the union helps to ensure the responsibility and discipline of a labor organization.   Strong discipline may be difficult for a new union to achieve, although the chairman of the board of directors of the U. S. Steel Corporation stated in April 1938:

The union has scrupulously followed the terms of its agreement and, insofar as I know, made no unfair effort to bring other employees into its ranks, while the corporation's subsidiaries, during a very difficult period, have been entirely free of labor disturbances of any kind.[4]

Centralized authority within the SWOC is maintained through administrative and financial control.   Almost three fourths of the funds collected from members are placed in the national treasury of the union.   All agreements must be approved in advance by the national office, and no strike is to be called without approval from the national office.   A local union engaging in an unauthorized strike will receive no support from the national treasury.   The entire administrative staff of the SWOC has been appointed rather than elected, and all the national officers and regional directors received their union training outside the steel industry, especially in the United Mine Workers.   Such "outside" control is considered a transitional stage, partly to be explained by the fact that the SWOC may have received as much as $2,500,000 from the CIO

---

[1] R. R. R. Brooks, *As Steel Goes*, 1940, p. 172.

[2] *Ibid.*, p. 162; and Harbison, *op. cit.*, p. 104.

[3] Brooks, *op. cit.*, p. 169.

[4] United States Steel Corporation, *Report of Annual Meeting of Stockholders*, 1938, p. 43.

unions, especially the coal miners.[1] After a period of experience, presumably the present provisional administration will be replaced by steel workers and more rank-and-file control.

The experimental or provisional period for the union in steel promises, however, to be a long one. In 1940, union recognition was still the important issue. Collective bargaining with the union had not been accepted as a permanent feature of the industry by many employers. The cleavage between union and nonunion firms was so great that the American Iron and Steel Institute and the union were scarcely on speaking terms. The "Little Steel" companies had not budged from the position that they took in 1934 against signed agreements, although any antiunion activities on their part were, of course, curbed by the National Labor Relations Act. Employer opposition accounts for the fact that, up to 1940, the SWOC had filed 692 complaints and 286 petitions for elections under the National Labor Relations Act.[2]

By means of an organizing campaign in Bethlehem Steel, the SWOC has been attempting to break through the "Little Steel" group. In "Big Steel" the union has made few gains since 1937 because of an attempt to limit collective bargaining mostly to wages and the settlement of grievances. The large firms apparently want a weak union so that their own personnel and welfare programs will play a significant role in labor relations. In 1940 the local branches of the SWOC in the U. S. Steel plants were, generally speaking, weak and far behind locals in other firms under union agreements.

Except for the Jones and Laughlin Steel Corporation, the union's relations were best in the small companies, which were not in a strong position to resist the union's demands and which looked upon the union as a possible stabilizing influence in the industry. Although the small companies generally seemed willing to grant the closed shop, while all large companies were opposed to it, many of the small firms were hesitant to take such action openly for fear of reprisals from antiunion customers and competitors. Of the Jones and Laughlin Steel Corporation, the chairman of the SWOC said in 1940 that, following the short strike in 1937,

---

[1] Cf. R. R. R. Brooks, op. cit., p. 160.   [2] Harbison, op. cit., p. 67.

The company abandoned its anti-union policy and embarked upon a sincere experiment in labor relations. As a result the Jones and Laughlin Steel Corporation is enjoying a period of harmonious labor relations. There are no "excesses" at the plants of this company. Indeed, labor relations here have become a model for the entire industry.[1]

[1] M. L. Cooke and Philip Murray, *Organized Labor and Production*, 1940, p. 260.

CHAPTER THIRTY-TWO

NEWSPAPERS

The rise and growth of the American Newspaper Guild since 1933 provides the first example in American experience of widespread union organization among workers usually classified as professional or "white-collar" employees. The Guild has become the collective-bargaining agency for the editorial and commercial workers of newspapers in a large number of cities throughout the country. In the mechanical or printing end of the newspaper business, collective bargaining and collective agreements have been the common practice since 1900.

Nature of the business. Today newspaper publishing, like the steel, automobile, and banking industries, is a big business, operated on a commercial basis. In the peak year of 1929, the receipts of newspapers from advertising and sales exceeded $1,000,000,000, and in the late 1930's newspaper revenues again approached $1,000,000,000 a year. In the early part of the last century, newspapers were personal journals containing few, if any, advertisements. Nowadays newspapers derive at least two thirds of their revenue from advertising. In that earlier period, newspapers were operated without business offices. Today they are run primarily for a profit and are likely to be owned by a wealthy businessman, or a holding company, or a large organization operating a whole chain of newspapers. Newspaper chains account for almost half of the nation's newspaper circulation, which exceeds 40,000,000 papers each day. The six largest chains alone distribute more than one out of every four daily newspapers and one out of every three Sunday newspapers sold in this country.[1]

News is gathered by reporters who work for a single newspaper, a group of newspapers, or a wire-service association. Most newspapers obtain nonlocal news from wire services like the Associated

[1] *Cf.* Alfred McClung Lee, *The Daily Newspaper in America*, 1937, p. 216.

Press, the United Press, or the International News Service, although newspapers with a large circulation will have their own correspondents in key cities within the country and abroad.

While the news contained in the daily paper comes from all over the world, the paper (the product) is always identified with some city or locality, and its circulation is largely confined to the local area. In a very real sense, the market for newspapers is a local market. Newspapers in one city do not compete, to any extent, with the newspapers published in distant cities. That is not true of books or magazines.

The market for newspaper service has other peculiarities. It is very steady in terms of total newspaper circulation, but total sales of advertising fluctuate widely with business conditions. Between 1929 and 1933, for example, the advertising receipts of all newspapers declined almost 50 per cent, compared with a decrease of only around 10 per cent in the circulation of all daily papers.[1]

In the publishing and selling of news, time and regularity are important. Because various editions of the paper must be ready at certain hours of the day, a modern newspaper office, like a railroad, operates on a time schedule. Any delay or interruption in the service is likely to irritate readers and to cause a sharp decrease in the newspaper's circulation. Therefore, a newspaper publisher's losses from a strike or a labor dispute are likely to be large. Furthermore, newspapers are sold directly to persons of all classes, and the sales of any paper may be affected considerably by changes in public opinion, especially if there is a competing paper in the same locality. A newspaper's sales of advertising space may also be affected by the attitude of the public toward the paper.

Employers and employers' organizations. There are approximately 2,000 daily newspapers and between 5,000 and 6,000 weekly newspapers in this country. Two or three daily newspapers have a circulation that approaches or exceeds 1,000,000, and some of the newspaper chains have a total daily circulation of 2,000,000 or 3,000,000, so that the 10 largest newspapers or newspaper chains probably account for fully one third of the daily newspaper circulation and close to one third of the employees in the industry. The number of employees on large metropolitan papers ranges from

[1] Statistics on circulation and receipts from advertising or sales are available in the *Biennial Census of Manufactures.*

1,500 to 4,000, and the largest chains have over 10,000 employees. Of the wire services, the Associated Press alone has about 7,500 full- and part-time correspondents.[1] In the newspaper chains and the wire services, the management and labor policies are generally determined at the central office.

Trade activities and labor policies in the newspaper industry are coordinated by publishers' associations, of which the most important is the American Newspaper Publishers' Association. The newspapers with membership in that Association represent about four fifths of the total circulation of daily newspapers and employ about four fifths of the employees of daily newspapers throughout the country.[2] In addition to this national association, there are state and regional publishers' associations.

The American Newspaper Publishers' Association has influenced the labor policies of publishers through its Special Standing Committee, its Open-Shop Department, and its special bulletin on labor. The Special Standing Committee, created in 1900, assists employers in negotiating union agreements and has been a party to national agreements with the printing unions, providing for the arbitration of labor disputes. With the general movement for the open shop in the 1920's, some fifty members of the American Newspaper Publishers' Association were largely instrumental in having an Open-Shop Department formed within the Association in 1922. It included Association members who were interested in maintaining and extending the nonunion shop. Newspaper publishers enrolled in the Open-Shop Department pledged themselves to supply employees to a member experiencing labor difficulties or a strike. For example, in 1933 labor crews ranging from 10 to 300 men were sent into 10 cities to aid publishers in strikes.[3] The pressure to reduce wage scales in the early 1930's caused a number of newspaper publishers to drop their collective agreements at that time in order to change to the open shop.

Employees and labor organizations. There are probably about 200,000 employees in the newspaper industry, of whom almost half are in the printing or mechanical trades and about 30,000 are

---

[1] *Collective Bargaining in the Newspaper Industry*, National Labor Relations Board, Division of Economic Research, Bulletin No. 3, October 1938, p. 3.

[2] *Ibid.*, p. 53.

[3] Report of the Open-Shop Department, *Editor and Publisher*, vol. 66 (April 29, 1933) p. 66.

in the editorial and reporting branch of the business. Employees in the printing trades are, of course, skilled craftsmen who have inherited a union tradition. Local printers' unions were among the first unions formed in this country, and the present national union of printers was founded in 1850. Technological change created several distinct crafts within the printers' union, so that in 1889 and subsequent years four crafts—the pressmen, the stereotypers and electrotypers, the bookbinders, and the photo-engravers—left the parent typographical or compositors' union to form separate national or international unions.

The relative numerical importance of the various mechanical trades in newspaper, book, and job printing combined is indicated by the following statistics for 1930: 183,632 compositors, linotypers, and typesetters in the United States, of whom 40 per cent belonged to the Typographical union; 42,143 pressmen and plate printers, of whom 87 per cent were union members; 19,437 engravers, of whom 44 per cent were organized; and 7,824 stereotypers and electrotypers, of whom 97 per cent were in the union.[1] The pressmen and the stereotypers have been very highly organized since the beginning of the century.

In the editorial and reporting branches of the business, the individualistic "white-collar" spirit of the employees prevented any organization prior to 1891, when the printers' union began to charter local newswriters' unions. Although the printers' union chartered 38 locals between 1891 and 1905 and another 15 locals in 1919, practically all of them passed out of existence within a few years after they were established. Newswriters were prone to consider their occupation a profession, or a prelude to a high-salaried position or a publishing career, rather than a trade that needed the economic protection afforded by collective action. The newspaperman's independence defeated early organizing efforts, and it was only when the depression of the early 1930's demonstrated the price that the newspapermen paid for their individualism in the form of relatively long hours, job insecurity, and low wages, that they were successfully organized into a separate national union. In 1937 the newswriters' union (the American Newspaper Guild) changed from a craft to an industrial base when it abandoned the AFL to affiliate with the CIO. Its juris-

[1] Leo Wolman, *Ebb and Flow in Trade Unionism*, 1936, pp. 215, 222.

diction was expanded to include the employees in the business branch of the industry, such as advertising solicitors, cashiers' clerks, and office boys, as well as reporters and subeditors. In some newspaper offices, the employees in the business branch outnumber the editorial employees. Also, the Guild has been extending its jurisdiction into the field of magazine publication.

Collective bargaining in the mechanical trades. Prior to 1880, the bargaining between the printers' unions and the publishers was on a local basis, although the local unions tried to achieve uniform wages for newspaper compositors in each city. The unions not only met with opposition from some individual publishers, but in New York State, Chicago, and elsewhere, the publishers combined into associations in order to resist the activities and demands of the local unions.[1] Many publishers of daily newspapers, however, favored written labor agreements as a means of assuring uninterrupted service and the profitable operation of their business. It has been customary for a number of newspapers in a city or locality to deal as a unit with each specific union.

During the 1880's and the 1890's, the national union of printers (the International Typographical Union) began to exercise more power and control over the activities of its locals. The locals were required to consult with the international before signing agreements; all strikes had to receive the sanction of the international, which controlled a newly created central strike fund; and the international was given the power to discipline locals, including the power to replace printers striking in violation of their agreements. Through centralized authority and standardization of agreements and union practices, the bargaining strength of the union was increased.

Following the introduction of the power press, the printing pressmen established a separate organization in 1889. Jurisdictional disputes between the Typographical union and the Pressmen's union were ended by an agreement in 1894, and similar agreements were made by the Typographical union with the seceding unions of bookbinders, stereotypers and electrotypers, and photoengravers between 1894 and 1903. Allied printing trades

[1] *Cf.* John R. Commons *et al.*, *History of Labour in the United States*, 1926, vol. 2, pp. 60–61.

councils were established both locally and nationally as a means of coordinating the efforts of the separate national unions in the mechanical trades of the industry.

The advantages of employer unity in dealing with unions led to the creation of the Special Standing Committee on Labor in the American Newspaper Publishers' Association. As early as 1899, the Association had discussed plans for industrial arbitration as a means of eliminating strikes and lockouts. In 1900 the International Typographical Union and the American Newspaper Publishers' Association concluded a national arbitration agreement providing for compulsory arbitration of all disputes that might arise in newspaper departments covered by local agreements containing provisions for arbitration. In other words, the arbitration agreement and procedure covered not only secondary disputes involving the interpretation and application of existing local agreements, but also primary disputes concerning the terms and conditions of employment to be embodied in new local agreements. The presence of nonunion publishers in the Newspaper Publishers' Association made it impossible to have a national system of collective bargaining and collective agreements. Under the arbitration agreement, local arbitration boards were established with appeal to a national board, whose decision was final. Work operations, at the terms of employment in effect before the dispute, were to continue pending the arbitration award. If either of the parties to a local agreement containing arbitration provisions should engage in a strike or lockout in violation of the agreement, or should refuse to accept an arbitration award, the appropriate national organization was to withdraw all aid and support from the defaulting member.

In 1901, the American Newspaper Publishers' Association also made arbitration agreements with the International Printing Pressmen and Assistants' Union and the International Stereotypers' and Electrotypers' Union, both modeled after the arbitration agreement with the International Typographical Union. In 1905 a similar national arbitration agreement was made with the International Photo-Engravers' Union. Because the international unions assumed responsibility for the enforcement of local agreements, they required that all local agreements receive approval in advance from officials of the international union. Several times the Pressmen's union proposed to the Publishers' Association that arbitration be made binding upon all members of each organization, but the Publishers' Association, with many nonunion members, refused to adopt such a measure.

Following the national arbitration agreements, the membership of the unions and the number of newspapers subject to collective agreements increased rapidly. In 1900 a total of 200 newspaper publishers, employing about 20,000 persons, were reported to have had agreements with the unions in the mechanical trades.[1] By 1912 the Typographical union had 264 local arbitration agreements with newspapers in the Publishers' Association, the Pressmen's union had about 160 such agreements, the Stereotypers' union had 108, and the Photo-Engravers' union had 44.[2] The membership of the combined printing unions rose from about 40,000 in 1900 to around 80,000 in 1912. During this period the Pressmen's union on two occasions paid publishers thousands of dollars in cases where locals struck in violation of local arbitration agreements, in one case replacing the strikers with other union workers.

In 1912 a dispute arose between the Pressmen's union and certain newspaper publishers in Chicago that resulted in the termination of the pressmen's national agreement with the Publishers' Association. In 1911, the two Hearst newspapers in Chicago, under the national arbitration agreement to which they were a party, obtained a wage decrease and an increase in hours under an arbitration award. The next year these Hearst papers refused to arbitrate an issue involving a reduction in the number of pressmen, and the International Pressmen's Union supported a strike against Hearst papers throughout the country on the grounds that they had violated the national arbitration agreement in Chicago. The union then refused to renew the national arbitration agreement with the American Newspaper Publishers' Association because the Chicago local of the ANPA had supported the Hearst management.

In 1919 the Pressmen's union again accepted a national arbitration agreement with the American Newspaper Publishers' Association, which has been renewed periodically and continues to operate. In 1940 the Special Standing Committee of the Publishers'

---

[1] David Weiss, "History of Arbitration in American Newspaper Publishing Industry," *Monthly Labor Review*, vol. 17 (July 1923), p. 18.

[2] *Ibid.*, p. 24; and *Collective Bargaining in the Newspaper Industry, op. cit.*, p. 92.

Association reported that, of its 400-odd members, 159 had written, and 26 had verbal, agreements with the Pressmen's union. Of the written agreements, 154 contained arbitration provisions.[1] During the 1920's, the Pressmen's union continued to suspend locals engaging in outlaw strikes, paying thousands of dollars to reimburse injured publishers. As indicated in Chapter 24, the Pressmen's union, under a program of union-management cooperation, offers some 500 newspapers a service that includes technical research, assistance from consulting engineers, and examination of copies of those papers for defects.

In 1920, after 20 years of experience under national arbitration agreements, the International Typographical Union had some 344 local arbitration agreements with publishers who were members of the Publishers' Association. Nevertheless, in 1922 this national arbitration agreement was terminated, and there has not been a national arbitration agreement between these two organizations since 1922. Refusal of the national union to submit its rules to arbitration was the reason given by the publishers for terminating the national arbitration agreement in 1922. As early as 1902 the Publishers' Association had requested that the national union's rules be made subject to arbitration. The Association especially objected to the union rule preventing the exchanging or borrowing of printed matter between newspaper establishments, so that all advertisements and features would have to be set up separately in each newspaper office, and the union rule requiring foremen to be union members, so that the union could more readily prevent antiunion discrimination in the shop.

Despite the absence of a national arbitration agreement, it was found that, of the 435 publishers in the American Newspaper Publishers' Association in 1935, there were 321 members operating their composing rooms under an agreement with a local of the Typographical union and 51 others operating on a union basis although without any agreement. These 372 union establishments were publishing 455 daily and 192 Sunday newspapers and were employing 23,868 members of the Typographical union.[2] The Special Standing Committee of the Publishers' Association reported

---

[1] *Editor and Publisher*, vol. 73 (April 27, 1940), p. 20.
[2] "Collective Agreements in Newspaper Composing Rooms," *Monthly Labor Review*, vol. 42 (January 1936), p. 170.

in 1940 that members of the Association had 330 written agreements with the Typographical union, of which 310 provided for the arbitration of primary or secondary disputes.[1]

A study of the wages and hours of 35,000 union printing tradesmen employed by newspapers in 72 cities showed that in June 1939 their average wage was about $1.35 an hour and their average hours were 38 a week, so that their average weekly earnings exceeded $50.00.   Photoengravers received the highest average hourly wage ($1.70), and stereotypers the lowest ($1.24).[2]   During the depression of the early 1930's the wage rates paid union members in the printing trades continued to increase from 1929 to 1931, and the decline from 1931 to the low year of 1933 was less than seven per cent.   In 1939 the wage rates paid to union printing tradesmen were the highest then on record, averaging 11 per cent above the 1929 level.[3]   In the printing trades, the closed shop is generally found in newspaper establishments in large cities.

Collective bargaining by the Newspaper Guild.   As indicated in a previous section, there was little collective bargaining in the editorial, reporting, or business branch of the newspaper industry prior to 1934.   Of the 60 newspaper writers' locals chartered by the Typographical union between 1891 and 1919, only two were in existence in the 1930's.   In 1923 the Typographical union voluntarily surrendered jurisdiction over the newswriters to the AFL. However, the Federation chartered only nine local unions of newswriters during the following decade.   Agreements were signed between newswriters' locals and the publishers' associations in certain cities, but the publishers, who had shown little hostility before the first World War, began to place obstacles in the way of organization by the newswriters after 1918.   In addition to fear of publisher reprisals, the newswriters were still too individualistic for organization on a national scale.   They were prone to consider themselves, not as a group of employees, but as members of a profession, who might sometime become employers.

Certain economic changes, however, caused newswriters to realize that they were only employees whose economic interests

---

[1] *Editor and Publisher*, vol. 73 (April 27, 1940), p. 20.

[2] "Union Scales of Wages and Hours in the Printing Trades, June 1, 1939," *Monthly Labor Review*, vol. 49 (December 1939), pp. 1485, 1496, and 1507.   Union "mailers" are excluded.

[3] *Ibid.*, p. 1487.

needed the protection afforded by organization. The purchase of newspapers by chains and the consolidation of papers, as indicated by their double-barreled titles, caused many editorial employees to lose their jobs or to feel that they were but a small element in a large commercial business, run by the publisher in his own interest. When advertising revenues began to decline in the early 1930's, the editorial employees were the first to feel the pinch of economy in the form of wage cuts, long hours, and staff reductions. For example, the average weekly earnings of editorial employees on 31 newspapers declined more than 15 per cent from April 1930 to April 1933, during which time the number of editorial employees was reduced more than 10 per cent.[1]

The wages and hours for the unionized mechanical trades and the individualistic newswriters presented an interesting contrast in the early 1930's. Surveys in the Spring of 1930 showed that the average working week for the mechanical tradesmen on newspapers was 45 hours, with none of them working more than 48 hours a week, whereas over 16 per cent of the editorial employees surveyed had a full-time work week in excess of 50 hours.[2] The average wage for the printing trades in 1930 was $1.24 an hour or about $56.00 a week on newspapers, compared with a weekly average of $59.30 for deskmen, $43.60 for reporters, and $40.00 for photographers.[3] Between the Spring of 1930 and the Spring of 1933 the average wages of printing tradesmen on newspapers were reduced less than 7 per cent, while the average wages of editorial employees were reduced more than 15 per cent, some reporters suffering wage cuts as high as 40 per cent. In the first part of 1934 the American Newspaper Guild made a nationwide survey which disclosed that the average salary for a reporter after 20 years of service was $38.00 a week, and that almost half of all reporters received less than $32.00 a week. In New York City, one third of the editorial employees included in this Guild survey were receiving $35.00 a week or less, whereas union printers and pressmen in New York were averaging from $46.00 to $55.00 a week, with all of them receiving more than $35.00 a week.

[1] "Salaries and Working Conditions of Newspaper Editorial Employees," *Monthly Labor Review*, vol. 40 (May 1935), pp. 1138, 1141.

[2] *Ibid.*, p. 1144; and "Union Wage Rates in Time-Work Trades in 1930," *Monthly Labor Review*, vol. 31 (November 1930), p. 1221.

[3] *Idem.*

Under such conditions, the newswriters were anxious to establish a newspaper code under the NIRA in order to improve and stabilize wages, hours, and working conditions in the editorial departments of newspapers. But without any organization, they had little authority or influence in the establishment of a newspaper code. Especially when the publishers opposed a code for themselves while advocating codes for other industries, the newswriters began to see the need for organization under Section 7a of the NIRA. In Great Britain, the British Institute of Journalists and the Union of Journalists, founded in 1890 and 1907 respectively, have made the newspaper editorial rooms there virtually closed shops.[1]

The first proposed code submitted by the American Newspaper Publishers' Association in August 1933 practically disregarded editorial employees, for it designated newswriters earning $35.00 a week or more as "practitioners of a profession" to whom the wages and hours provisions of the code were not applicable. This proposed code was rejected by the Recovery Administration, but the newspaper code finally approved by the President on February 17, 1934 did not differ materially from the one submitted by the Publishers' Association. The President did, however, request that editorial workers be put on a five-day, 40-hour week. In the meantime, dues-collecting guilds of newspapermen had been formed in some 42 cities during the last four months of 1933, and at a national convention in December 1933 they combined to form the American Newspaper Guild. The name "Guild" was adopted to indicate a status mid-way between a trade-union and a professional organization. Refusal to admit that they were workingmen and to identify themselves with wage-earning groups prevented the Guild journalists from affiliating with organized labor as the stage and screen actors had done many years before. The success of the Actors' Equity Association offered an example of what labor unionism could accomplish for a widely diversified group of professional, white-collar workers.

According to the constitution of the new Guild, its purpose was "to preserve the vocational interests of its members and to improve the conditions under which they work by collective bargaining."

[1] Cf. Estelle Muraskin, *Newswriters' Unions in English-Speaking Countries*, U. S. Works Progress Administration, New York, 1937 (mimeographed).

Local unions in metropolitan or municipal areas were divided into shop units. In addition to the national organization, there were also state and regional units. In April 1934 a Guild local signed its first collective agreement with a publisher, and in June 1934 the Guild reported a total membership of 8,000. Observing that the Guild was moving toward collective bargaining, William Randolph Hearst remarked that he had "always regarded our business a profession and not a trade union," while Roy W. Howard of the Scripps-Howard chain asserted that journalism was a "profession" that could "no more flourish and develop in the strait-jacket of trade unionism than an orchid on an iceberg." [1] During the latter part of 1934 the Guild became involved in some important strikes. In the *Newark Ledger* strike, the American Newspaper Publishers' Association supported the publisher while local and national labor organizations assisted the Guild. The Guild used mass picketing, a boycott of the paper, and a secondary boycott of advertisers in order to win the strike. Even before the Guild's affiliation with the AFL in 1936, the printing-trades unions, the Teamsters, and other labor organizations assisted Guild locals in carrying on strikes.

The newspaper code provided for a bipartisan Newspaper Industrial Board to settle disputes. The four labor representatives on this eight-man Board were national officers of the printing-trades unions. In the middle of 1934 the publishers voted overwhelmingly against a plan of the Recovery Administration to enlarge the Board so that the Guild might have a representative. The Guild was able to obtain a place on the Board only through an arrangement whereby the representative of the Pressmen's union resigned. As the Newspaper Board was unable to select a panel of impartial chairmen until a few days before the Supreme Court declared the Recovery Act unconstitutional, the Board deadlocked on practically all important cases.

In December 1934 and January 1935, the National Labor Relations Board, established under Public Resolution No. 44, handed down two decisions ordering the Hearst *San Francisco Call-Bulletin* to reinstate Dean S. Jennings, found to have been forced to resign from the paper because of Guild activities. The publishers of the nation, in protest against this decision, arranged a meeting to

[1] *Editor and Publisher*, vol. 67 (June 2, 1934), p. 8; and *Guild Reporter*, June 1934.

consider withdrawal *en masse* from the newspaper code. As in their
initial protest against a newspaper code, the publishers insisted
that the decision in the Jennings case threatened the "freedom of
the press," since all such matters should be decided by the Newspaper Industrial Board. The President finally gave in to the
publishers, who then called off their scheduled meeting. As the
Guild expressed it, the "publishers cracked down and the President
cracked up." The Newspaper Industrial Board, because of a
deadlock, never settled the Jennings case. Such experience taught
the Guild to cease relying entirely upon government action. Its
officers had discovered what organized labor learned long ago,
that economic strength is more powerful than political action or
legislation. Because the Guild considered columnist General Hugh
Johnson hostile to labor as NRA administrator, the Washington
local barred him from Guild membership under the constitutional
provision that "no person whose interests are deemed to lie with
the employer as against the employees shall be eligible."

Publisher resistance and opposition gradually converted the
Guild into a trade-union with increased centralization of power.
At the 1937 convention, the Guild's executive board was given the
power to suspend locals signing agreements that failed to include
the minimum bargaining terms stipulated in the Guild program.
The national organization has signed agreements on a nationwide
basis with the Associated Press and the United Press, covering
all their editorial employees in this country, and with the Newspaper Enterprise Association, a newspaper syndicate. In dealing
with major newspaper chains, the Guild has adopted a chain
council plan of organization, by which the entire weight of the
national organization can be used in chain negotiations. In five
cities the Guild has also engaged in collective negotiations on a
city-wide basis with local publishers' associations, following the
procedure used in the mechanical departments, so that the resulting
agreements will cover the whole competitive area. Locally, the
newspaper business may be highly competitive, so some publishers
may refuse to make concessions to the Guild unless rival publishers
grant the same terms of employment. In some cities, Guild locals
have signed city-wide agreements.

In 1940 the Guild had a membership of around 20,000, representing over half of those eligible for membership from the editorial

departments and about one fourth of the remaining newspaper employees within its jurisdiction.[1] It had branches in over 500 newspaper shops, and over 120 signed agreements covering some 140 newspapers, wire services, radio stations, and news magazines. About a fourth of the agreements provided for the closed or Guild shop, and most of them provided for special compensation to dismissed workers. The minimum terms of the Guild's bargaining program also call for the 40-hour week, vacations with pay, sick leave, advance dismissal notices varying with length of service, and a minimum-wage scale increasing with length of service and type of work. The 1939 agreement with the *Seattle Post-Intelligencer*, for example, covers all skilled and unskilled workers in the editorial and business branches of the firm, contains 6 wage classifications for editorial-department employees and 20 for business-office employees, and provides a dismissal indemnity ranging from 2 weeks' pay in cash for regular employees with between one half and one year's continuous service to 28 weeks' cash severance wage for employees with $12\frac{1}{2}$ years or more of service. Dismissal pay is guaranteed to employees in practically every Guild agreement.[2]

Unlike the unions in the mechanical trades, the Guild has strongly opposed arbitration as a means of fixing the terms of new agreements. Such arbitration the Guild considers to be premature before it has the industry well organized and the belligerence of the publishers' associations subsides. (In the middle of 1937 the publishers' associations met in Chicago to organize their resistance to the Guild.) The Guild has, however, been willing to establish arbitration machinery for the settlement of secondary disputes. Nevertheless, only a small percentage of all agreements signed with the Guild provide for arbitration of unsettled disputes arising under the agreement, and Guild agreements also do not contain clauses prohibiting strikes or lockouts during the life of the agreement.

By 1939 the American Federation of Labor, which the Guild abandoned in 1937, had 10 federal local unions of newswriters and some 20 federal local unions of business-office employees and newspaper carriers, the latter split up on craft lines. Through a Labor Newspaper Organization Council comprising all craft

[1] "Collective Bargaining by the American Newspaper Guild," *Monthly Labor Review*, vol. 50 (April 1940), p. 826.

[2] For a summary of the provisions of 78 agreements signed with the Guild, *cf. ibid.*, pp. 827–42. *Cf.* also *Editor and Publisher*, vol. 73 (April 27, 1940), p. 94.

unions in the various newspaper departments, the AFL is attempting to coordinate the collective-bargaining activities of its craft locals and to negotiate a single agreement with a publisher, covering all his white-collar employees. With the Guild and the Federation both attempting to organize workers in the editorial and business branches of newspapers, a number of jurisdictional controversies have occurred. There has also been considerable disagreement and strife between the left-wing and the more conservative groups within the Guild itself.

The Guild has been very effective in improving wages, hours, and working conditions for newswriters and even employees in the business branches of the industry, who have accounted for less than one fifth of the Guild's total membership. It has established standards for wages, hours, dismissal notification, and severance pay that many newspaper publishers have decided to adopt even though they refuse to deal with the Guild or have only been willing to post informal, bulletin-board agreements. Through this organization, a well-educated, middle-class group has been able to improve its economic status by following typical trade-union methods.

The Guild has demonstrated its ability to bring strong economic pressure to bear upon publishers through strikes, boycotts, and pressure upon advertisers to cancel their space. Most of its strikes have been won, for few newspaper publishers can long resist a union in the face of sharply diminished circulation and advertising revenue or of complete interruption in the publication of the paper. Advertising aims to gain good will, not ill will, for the advertiser. Consequently, a merchant is likely to cease advertising in an offending newspaper if such advertisement involves picket lines around his establishment and the listing of his firm in the *Guild Reporter*, weekly organ of the American Newspaper Guild, as one of the advertisers who continue to use anti-Guild newspapers. The legality of Guild picketing of firms advertising in offending newspapers seems to vary somewhat with the economic philosophy of the judge and the methods of picketing employed, but few advertisers want to prosecute labor organizations in the courts in order to establish their right to advertise in a certain newspaper without being picketed as a result. Advertisers generally are too dependent on retail sales to go out of their way to offend labor organizations.

PART FIVE

CONCLUSION

CHAPTER THIRTY-THREE

CLOSING REMARKS

Many of labor's economic problems arise out of conflicting interests and desires in a capitalistic system based on individual purchases and sales in markets. In a business civilization motivated by individual self-interest, private aims are often in conflict with social goals; personal profit may be at the expense of human welfare and social values; freedom to spend or not to spend money may result in unemployment and economic insecurity for workers. Labor's economic problems involve such issues as the proper balance between incentive and economic security, between co-operation and bargaining in industry, and between industrial democracy and discipline.

Individualism may not operate to the advantage of society when sellers are confronted with inelastic demand curves so that it pays them to restrict the supply they offer for sale, or when markets are dominated by large economic units, whether business corporations or labor organizations. Fundamentally, individualism is based on the objectivity and fairness of markets, which means that they must approximate the old-fashioned economist's ideal of a perfect market. The whole theory of the economic distribution of resources under individualism assumes the existence of perfect markets and the nonexistence of unemployment. It assumes furthermore that local interests will not attempt to attract manufacturing plants by such subsidies as tax exemptions, free plants and plant sites, or low labor standards and earnings that may cause a deterioration of the human resources in the locality, an increase in local welfare costs, and perhaps some curtailment of local sales. The unreality of such assumptions in our modern economy is evident. The business and real-estate interests in many communities try to attract and hold new concerns by various lures and subventions. Buyers and sellers generally strive to dominate the market and to control market prices by the exercise of economic pressure, even though their efforts are not always successful.

The importance of economic pressure in determining prices and market conditions could be eliminated only by somehow converting all markets into perfect ones. That would mean the atomization of business units so that no buyer or seller would account for more than a very small percentage of the total purchases or sales in any local market. In order to establish perfect markets, all products would have to be standardized so that there would be a large number of firms making and selling each and every article. The tendency for a number of decades has, however, been in the opposite direction—toward larger business units which sell trade-marked and nationally advertised products.

Business produces not only goods but widespread unemployment and surprising economic inequalities as well as industrial injuries, disease, dissatisfaction, and old-age dependence. Many of these human costs business is able to avoid, so they rest upon individual workers or the community at large in the form of higher relief costs, larger medical costs, or more crime.

Costs as income. In an individualistic economy, analyses of labor problems tend to be on an individualistic plane. People reason from a particular instance to the general situation, and individualistic economics supplants political economy. One woman writer recently said: "Most women, I am convinced, think from the particular to the general, and not from the general to the particular. . . . It is significant, I think, that there has been no John Maynard Keynes, no Stuart Chase, no Marx, no Adam Smith among women." [1]

Individualistic reasoning leads to an undue emphasis on the cost rather than the income and demand aspects of payrolls. Wages are both a cost and an income, just as debt and credit are the same thing looked at from different angles. Yet during the early 1930's, the very people who complained that the prevailing depression was caused by too much debt were arguing that what was needed to overcome the business slump was an expansion in credit! Much the same thing applies to arguments about wages. The same people may argue both that costs, especially payrolls, must be

[1] Dorothy Dunbar Bromley, "The Future of Eleanor Roosevelt," *Harper's Magazine*, vol. 180 (January 1940), p. 137.

reduced and that workers' incomes must be increased so that demand may expand.

When certain income changes affect wide areas in the economy, even individual manufacturers begin to appreciate the importance of the income aspects of costs. For example, an employer may come to support systems of unemployment compensation or relief, which help to maintain the market for his products, even though he may dislike the taxes levied to finance them. The cost aspects are less troublesome to an employer when a condition is generalized, when his competitors must meet the same cost changes or labor standards because they occur uniformly over the whole competitive area.

It has been said that factories and workers become unemployed because employers ask too much for their products and because workers ask too much for their labor. According to the traditional theory, the existence of idle equipment and excess capacity is a clear indication that prices are too high, that the employers are refusing to produce in order to enforce a certain price policy. In the same way, some writers have argued that, if workers remain unemployed, it is largely because they are unwilling to accept lower and lower wages.[1]

Although such economic dogma may be correct for a barter economy, it is likely to be incorrect for a money economy with large business units. Declining prices (price reductions), by causing people to withhold expenditures and hoard money, may increase the amount of idle economic resources. A large number of factors, some of which are noneconomic, affect the rate at which people spend money. When expenditures are declining in a country or community, many workers cannot find employment even though they may be willing to work for very low wages. Factories do not operate at 50 per cent of capacity because wages or other costs are too high; costs per unit of output generally decline as manufacturers increase their operations up to full capacity of the plant. It is lack of demand, not high costs, that explains why General Motors, Ford, and other large firms lay off thousands of

---

[1] "When leading economists in the field of labor problems say that 'wages are out of line' at the present time and that 'this is holding up the return of prosperity,' they are speaking through the closed iron visor of a particular set of economic folkways and a particular, historically-dated theory of 'marginal productivity.'" Robert S. Lynd, *Knowledge for What?* 1939, p. 145.

workmen and will not hire a larger number of workers at any wage during a slump.

Difficulties in labor economics. The traditional economics attempted to find answers to labor's economic problems by adopting static assumptions and applying partial analysis based on the individual firm. But individual-firm analysis is especially ill-adapted for finding answers to general problems involving employment, unemployment, wage levels, cost levels, labor standards, and the business cycle. For an explanation of such phenomena, a general or monetary analysis, based on changes or developments over a period of time, is much more appropriate, although it may yield less simple and certain answers. Variations in the rate of spending with economic change may depend in part upon social psychology, which may be somewhat unpredictable and concerning which economists may not qualify as experts.

Unfortunately for those who seek easy answers in labor economics, the whole may not be the sum of its parts. The simple maxims of mathematics may not apply. For example, the labor supply curves or schedules for most employers are positively sloped, yet the general supply curve of labor appears to be negatively sloped. Individual supply curves cannot be summarized because they apply to separate markets and because they are based upon the assumption that conditions in all other markets do not change, which assumption is violated as soon as any summation is attempted. The same thing holds true of the demand for labor. In the building trades, for example, the demand for most types of skilled labor (plasterers, plumbers, bricklayers, etc.) is undoubtedly very inelastic, which means that a reduction of wage rates for one of the 20-odd building crafts alone would result in lower weekly or annual earnings for the members of that craft. Therefore, a summation of the demand schedules for all the separate crafts would presumably give a very inelastic and incorrect curve, for a wage-rate reduction affecting all building workers at the same time would have a much greater effect on new building than the same percentage reduction confined to a single craft.

Certain economists have argued that the demand for building-workers' services and for other labor is elastic, so labor's annual earnings would increase if it would be willing to accept wage cuts. Such general assertions may be absolutely incorrect for certain kinds of labor considered separately or for most labor during, say, the downward phase of the business cycle. Some of these economists have qualified their conclusions by saying that the elasticity of demand would increase or develop with the lapse of a short period of time. When the element of time is introduced, however, the assumptions of the analysis are no longer valid and a process or sequence analysis must be followed rather than the straitjacket method of demand and supply schedules, which rest on the assumption of instantaneous change while other things remain the same.

Professor Sumner Slichter, in an address before a meeting of the American Economic Association in December 1939, stated that the demand for short-term loans was inelastic, that the demand for investment funds (long-term loans) seems to be fairly inelastic during most phases of the business cycle, and that labor unions underestimate the elasticity of demand for labor, especially over a period of several years.[1] How the elasticity of the general demand for capital and labor was discovered, to what phase of the business cycle his remarks applied, and why the elasticity of demand for capital is assumed to be less than that for labor, Professor Slichter failed to explain. Unfortunately, economists seem to have widely varying notions concerning the demand for labor.

Labor in modern capitalism. In an economy of large buying, selling, and producing units, economic competition differs widely from that in the economic theorist's make-believe world of perfect markets, pure competition, and full employment. Corporations, by means of their collective strength, are able to dominate markets and to control the prices of their products. Under such circumstances, labor must combine if it is to protect its economic interests through collective action and collective bargaining. Business corporations are really combinations of capitalists who bargain collectively through the corporation. Individual workers are especially dependent in our modern economy because of extreme specialization, employer practices, and the nature of labor markets. With labor markets so imperfect and so subject to control by

---

[1] *Cf.* Slichter, "The Impact of Social Security Legislation upon Mobility and Enterprise," *American Economic Review*, vol. 30 (March 1940) supplement, pp. 54–55, 58. *Cf.* also, Slichter, "The Changing Character of American Industrial Relations," *American Economic Review*, vol. 29 (March 1939) supplement, pp. 127, 129, and 134. Money represents generalized purchasing power, so one would expect the demand for money to be more elastic than the demand for many particular goods or services.

monopolistic elements, both the buyers and the sellers of labor
strive to drive good bargains by using their economic strength to
further their own interests. Industry-wide trade agreements
and labor standards set by law restrict competition by helping to
prevent single employers from driving better bargains with labor
than their competitors do.

Collective action by labor and collective labor agreements do
tend to reduce the wide range in individual outputs and individual
wage rates that occurs without the organization of labor. Some
uniformity in wage rates and some standardization of individual
outputs may be necessary in order to prevent concealed undercutting of the wage. Wherever sellers attempt to achieve standards
and uniformity in prices, such collective restrictions tend to occur.
They are found among unorganized as well as organized workers.

Labor unions do not object to the payment of wages above the
union rate to workers because of the high quality of their services,
their long length of service with an employer, or their all-around
ability. But labor organizations do take steps to prevent price-
cutting by means of a speed-up in output without a corresponding
rise in wage rates. The kind of competition one finds in unionized
industries is similar to that between local banks that have identical
charges, between steel, lead, and cement companies that quote
identical prices, or between the manufacturers of the three popular
low-priced cars (Ford, Chevrolet, and Plymouth), who quote substantially the same prices. It is a competition on the basis of
quality and personal friendships rather than on the basis of price,
and the social implications of "administered" prices and restrictions upon price competition in the labor field are the same as
they are in the field of business.[1]

In a competitive society, labor organizations seek to advance the
economic interests of their members and sometimes come into
conflict with one another regarding such matters as jurisdiction or
failure to cooperate in strikes. In a free-for-all capitalism, it is not
surprising to find that self-interest causes the Steel Workers Organizing Committee to support high steel prices, the United Mine
Workers to oppose the projects of the Tennessee Valley Authority

[1] For a discussion of the social implications of administered prices, cf., for example,
H. S. Dennison and J. K. Galbraith, *Modern Competition and Business Policy*, 1938;
C. F. Ware and G. C. Means, *The Modern Economy in Action*, 1936; or *Price Behavior
and Business Policy*, Monograph No. 1, Temporary National Economic Committee, 1940.

because they produce competing fuel, or the National Brotherhood of Operative Potters to support a higher tariff on pottery products. Indeed, the pottery manufacturers (the U. S. Potters Association) first began to negotiate with the union after union representatives pleaded for a higher tariff before a Congressional committee and after an understanding was reached that the tariff increase should lead to a wage rise if the union would help to maintain uniform selling prices for pottery products.[1]

Labor unions, both craft and industrial, may join hands with employers in order to gain at the expense of the rest of society, or they may oppose social improvements if such improvements might lead to a reduction in the union's membership or in employment within the union's jurisdiction. Programs of "decasualizing" and regularizing longshore employment in various ports have involved limitations upon entrance into the occupation through refusal to permit an increase in the number of workers registered at the central hiring hall, controlled by the union or by the union and the employers. Such programs, on the Pacific Coast for example, have increased the annual incomes of longshoremen until they average from $1,700 to $1,800 a year, or almost double the average for New York City, where "decasualization" has not occurred.[2] The relatively high incomes of Pacific Coast longshoremen may only be possible because other workers are excluded from employment at the waterfront.

Answers to labor problems. Unfortunately, there are no easy solutions to labor problems. The market does not solve them satisfactorily in many cases, partly because a perfect labor market and pure competition in labor are not possible. There is little likelihood that the buyers of labor (employers) will be broken up into atomistic units selling only standard (not trade-marked) products. Yet, if the answer is not supplied by the market, it will be obtained by personal or political decisions or by a test of economic strength.

In the past, labor has feared political decisions on its economic problems because of the possibility that repeated political decisions might lead to government dictatorship over labor and to the

[1] *Cf.* David A. McCabe, *National Collective Bargaining in the Pottery Industry*, 1932, pp. 90–91.

[2] *Cf. Longshoremen: Pacific and Atlantic*, International Longshoremen's and Warehousemen's Union, Seattle, 1940, pp. 9–13.

suppression of the activities of labor unions, as has occurred under dictatorships abroad. Like most employers, labor objects to compulsory arbitration because it means solving labor's economic problems by the personal decision of some "outsider" instead of through the market and economic forces. There is no scientific formula that an arbitrator can apply in order to find correct solutions to labor disputes; he must rely upon his own judgment and conscience to guide him.

Reliance upon economic factors and pressure for answers to labor issues means that at times conflicts of economic force will break out into economic warfare—strikes and lockouts. Perhaps such industrial disputes are part of the price that must be paid for the benefits of industrial freedom and individualism, just as the economic waste connected with business failures and unwise investment is part of the cost of operating a system of free private enterprise. Individualism has been defended as the system under which dumb fools can do the least damage, because no one person has control over a large section of the economy. As corporations and other organizations increase in size and economic significance, however, such a defense of capitalism begins to lose its validity.

If perfect markets and pure competition are impossible, there is the question of how to prevent large business units or labor organizations from obtaining complete domination of markets and using them for selfish, rather than social, purposes. For an attack upon certain labor problems, such as unemployment, it may be necessary to prevent individualism from injuring the general interests of society, the common welfare.

Unselfish phrases and pious hopes are of little help in finding solutions to labor problems. As was pointed out in the chapter on union-management cooperation, such programs are likely to fail except under certain rather special economic circumstances. Correct answers to labor problems require some understanding of the economic factors and underlying forces, some understanding of the nature of markets in general and the labor market in particular. Unfortunately, we know surprisingly little about labor markets, where the economic forces affecting labor converge. Yet such a knowledge is necessary for a correct formulation of governmental policies regarding labor, for intelligent legislation on labor issues, and for wise judicial decisions in labor cases. An understanding of the character of labor markets is necessary in order to decide what labor problems should be left (1) to decision by the market and economic forces, (2) to legislative action by government and to governmental programs, and (3) to court decisions. As it is, no such functional division has been made, and the law on labor activities and methods is not only changing but uncertain.

Issues in industrial relations. The first labor unions in this and other countries were formed by skilled craftsmen to protect members from the effects of competitive forces. Historically, it was the competition of the merchant capitalist, who as a middleman played employers against one another, that led to the rise of trade-unionism as a protective device. Ever since the formation of those early craft organizations, unions have generally sought to eliminate competition on labor standards by making labor costs uniform for all competing employers. Unions, especially industrial unions, have also attempted to "stabilize" the industry or industries over which they claim jurisdiction, so that the prices received by employers may be sufficient to permit them to pay union wage scales.

In the past, employers have generally opposed unions in industries where the employers themselves could "stabilize" the industry without the assistance of a labor union. That has been true, for example, in the mass-production industries, like steel, automobiles, oil, rubber, etc., or in banking and the professions where competition on the basis of price is considered "unethical." However, in highly competitive lines, like bituminous coal, clothing, building, laundry, and cleaning and pressing, employers are so numerous and have such diverse interests that they have not been able to form a single trade or employers' association covering the whole industry. Consequently, they have been unable to "stabilize" the industry without the assistance of a labor organization. Under such circumstances, a majority of the employers in the industry may be willing to have the unions help to regulate that industry and enforce standards, so that certain forms of competition can be outlawed. In such highly competitive industries, the unions must "stabilize" the industry and eliminate nonunion competition in order to achieve substantial gains for their members. Private regulation of industry by unions, usually in collaboration with employers' associations, is similar, in certain respects, to the regulation of industry under the medieval guilds. It lacks, however, the moral force of the religious scruples that the guildsmen had.

The regulation of industry by union methods is illustrated by the clothing unions and the Teamsters' union on the West Coast. The joint regulation of the clothing industry in the late 1930's was more extreme than it was under the NRA from 1933 to 1935. The clothing unions have not only eliminated the sweatshop and given their members the benefits of cultural and educational activities along with unemployment-insurance and low-cost-housing programs, but they have also conferred certain benefits upon employers in the industry by eliminating competitive bidding and fixing uniform prices for the production of garments in contract shops. In bituminous coal, the Federal government has, by law, granted employers the benefits of price-fixing, because unregulated competition in soft coal led to certain evils, including the breakdown of labor standards, prior to 1933. On the other hand, the bankers, the steel producers, and the manufacturers of sulphur, gasoline, photographic film, tin cans, bottles, typewriters, light bulbs, razors, tooth paste, sugar, crackers, cereals, cigarettes, and 1,001 other articles, have been able to eliminate practically all price competition through such means as the basing-point system, price zones, branding and patenting, and price quotations on a "freight-allowed" basis. Despite the partial monopoly enjoyed by producers of trade-marked articles, the Federal and state governments have passed resale-price-maintenance laws, which legalize vertical price-fixing from manufacturer to consumer and which prevent price-cutting by forcing all sellers to sell at the price stipulated by the producer. Indeed, such "fair-trade" laws are designed to make price-fixing mandatory.

Presumably private regulation of business by unions and employers' associations is primarily in the interest of the employers and workers in the industry. Unions are generally guided by the economic interests of their members. As experience under the NRA indicated, union-employer cooperation to regulate competition in an industry may operate to the disadvantage of the consumer. Although we are all consumers, it is always to the economic advantage of any group to increase its money income, even if that involves an increase in the price of its product or service.

Unfortunately, there is no way to determine scientifically,

whether wages or selling prices are too high or too low. The economists formerly tried to use as a test the price that would prevail if the market were a perfect one. But, since wages and prices can only be too high or too low compared with other prices, all markets would have to be perfect markets before such a test would be a valid one. As already stated, perfect markets are so rare as to make that test impractical and impossible. People generally criticize prices or wages on the basis of previous price and wage relationships or such relationships in other areas. But such a method naïvely assumes that these earlier or more distant relationships are correct. Wages in the men's clothing industry tripled from 1911 to 1924. Were wages too high in 1924 or too low in 1911? Are average wages of $1.25 an hour in the coat-and-suit branch of the ladies' garment industry too high in view of the seasonal unemployment in the industry, the skill involved in the work, and a work week of 32½ hours? There is no scientific answer to such questions.

Some economists have argued that a vigorous enforcement of the Federal antitrust laws against unions and employers' organizations would at least prevent prices and wages from being "too" high. Unfortunately, strict enforcement of the antitrust laws would not make imperfect markets into perfect ones and would tend to prevent uniform standards or "stabilization" in those industries that are in the weakest economic position because of the large number of employers in the industry who are competing with one another. Enforcement of the antitrust laws to prevent union-employer arrangements for stabilizing the industry would tend to make competition more severe in lines where it has been the most severe in the past and would have little effect in industries where price competition has been negligible, such as automobiles, agricultural implements, electric motors, oil, utilities, banking, railroads, etc. Undoubtedly, some government control over monopolistic elements in labor and product markets is desirable, but how much and by what methods the government should regulate industry and labor is a question concerning which much has been said and written since the Supreme Court invalidated the NIRA. To date, economists, business executives, labor leaders, and government officials hold widely varying views on the whole problem of the relationship of government to business. The learned economic journals have recently been full of articles expressing conflicting opinions on the subject.

Past experience in the field of industrial relations has demonstrated that the signing of written agreements tends to restrict the area of friction and to reduce the number of strikes or work stoppages. Collective agreements help to preserve industrial peace through mutual understanding and machinery for the settlement of grievances and disputes. The bitterest and most costly battles in American labor history have been fought when employers have refused to recognize or deal with labor unions and have, consequently, declined to sign any agreements with them. Employer opposition to unions, of course, tends to foster militant, radical, and irresponsible leadership in labor organizations. When their organization is struggling for its very existence, workers tend to select fighting leaders. On the other hand, the business of bargaining, of negotiating agreements, and of enforcing agreements tends to develop responsible and businesslike leadership in labor organizations. Such official responsibility tempers radicalism and causes union officials to consider the economics of the industry in which their members are employed. Labor leaders like Samuel Gompers and Sidney Hillman were socialists who firmly believed in the class struggle before they became "labor statesmen" engaged in the business of administering a union or a federation of unions.

In labor relations and labor legislation, developments in this country seem to be following in the general path of experience abroad, but with a lag of a number of decades. In Europe, unemployment and old-age insurance laws were enacted from 20 to 50 years before the Social Security Act was passed in this country in 1935. The democratic countries in Europe and Australasia passed through the stage of active employer opposition to the existence of labor unions a number of decades ago. In England, for example, there were no campaigns to eliminate labor unions during the 50 years prior to 1940. Since 1900, open-shop campaigns have been known as "the American Plan"; labor espionage and company unionism have also been largely American phenomena.

Within this country, various industries have reached different stages in the development of labor relations. In certain industries, labor relations have been more advanced than in others. The antiunion phase of labor relations had practically ended by 1926 in the railroad industry. Since then written agreements with unions have been the standard practice, and strikes have been practically unknown on the railroads. The maritime industry, on the other hand, was beset by a number of major and minor strikes in the 1930's, and the maritime unions, faced with employer opposition and hostility, continued to struggle for their existence. In short, labor relations have been in a much more formative and immature stage in ocean transportation than in rail transportation. On the Pacific Coast, labor relations in the pulp-and-paper industry had, by 1940, reached a much more advanced stage than they had in the lumber industry, which furnishes the raw materials for paper and pulp.

Widespread strikes and unrest have occurred during periods when labor unions were expanding rapidly in membership and employers were attempting to prevent such expansion. That was true from 1900 to 1904, from 1916 to 1920, and from 1933 to 1937. Open-shop campaigns, such as those following 1900 and 1920, have also given rise to strikes, lockouts, and labor troubles. A number of industries that were organized during the first World War became nonunion during the "American-Plan" or company-union period of the 1920's. The maritime industry, the railroad shops, the building industry in cities like Chicago and San Francisco, and, to some extent, the textile, coal, and clothing industries, might be cited as examples. However, the losses of union membership in the 1920's were more than recouped during the 1930's.

There have been cycles in labor relations just as there have been cycles in business activity. A chart of the number of workers involved in strikes or of total union membership resembles the fever chart of business, with peaks and recessions. Fluctuations in labor relations from union dealings and agreements to open-shop or company-union conditions and back to union agreements again have been costly to consumers and upsetting to American business. The cyclical swings from union shop to open shop every decade or so have not only been wasteful but have tended to prevent the development of stable relationships, mutual understanding, responsible organizations, and machinery for the settlement of labor difficulties by peaceful methods. Stable labor relations are an essential part of a stable economy.

The question of industrial democracy. A democratic society must be interested in the government of its industry because political developments are so directly affected by economic conditions. A nation's politics tends to be shaped by its industrial background. Students of government have maintained that industrial dictatorship has a close bearing upon political dictatorship.

The problem of industrial democracy grows more important as it becomes more difficult for individuals to set up in business for themselves and to gain a measure of economic independence by selling to a market made up of many buyers. Labor's dependence is great not only because of the minute division of labor and the specialization of economic functions, but because generally the worker sells his services to but one buyer and must deliver his services by working most of the day or night on the buyer's premises under the discipline of the buyer or his agents. Such a condition of dependency and dominance may be accepted with little grumbling when industry is functioning smoothly; but, when there is widespread unrest, let us say because of prolonged and extensive unemployment, labor is likely to lose faith in the rulers of business and to demand a greater voice in the affairs of industry. Such a period of questioning took place during the 1930's, which helps to explain why workers so readily joined labor unions during that decade.

The struggle for influence and authority is a never-ending one. The attempt of workers through organization to gain a larger voice in industrial affairs has been resented and opposed by many employers. Labor agreements, grievance machinery, and labor-relations laws may deprive employers of some of their vested rights. Men who rise to high posts, both in business and labor unions, are generally determined and domineering persons, accustomed to fighting for what they want or want to keep. They are not likely to relinquish, without a struggle, the power that has accompanied ownership or position.

Labor economics and economic interests. Labor problems are human problems that involve selfish interests, vested rights, personal concepts of justice, and social standards of value. The extent to which labor unions, employers' associations, and employers' labor policies should be restricted by law is a political question to which the economist can give no objective and conclusive answer. The economist can explain the probable economic effects of various labor measures and laws. He can indicate how a certain program may affect total employment, total production, and profits. He can point to the lessons of past experience. But the people must decide the results that they desire—whether they are willing to restrict freedom of spending in order to obtain more employment, whether business should be taxed to provide unemployment and old-age benefits for workers, whether the work day should be shortened, whether the bargaining power of labor should be increased and there should be more democracy in industry, or whether employer control of the labor market is preferable to collective bargaining and collective agreements.

A study of the economics of labor helps one to understand the economic consequences of certain labor legislation or policies. It should enable the student to see through superficial arguments and to detect errors in popular reasoning on labor problems. It provides a basis for correct analysis and a background for sound judgments. In short, it should make the student intelligent. But a study of the economics of labor issues may fail to make a person less selfish and more social-minded. Education and intelligence cannot change a person's economic interests, whether he is a wage-earner, a corporation president, or a large stockholder. Despite extensive study, a person is likely to continue to pursue his own interests, although perhaps in a more intelligent fashion.

In an exchange economy ruled by the money motive, different economic groups strive to improve their economic position and to increase their economic power by obtaining some degree of monopoly or market control. Consequently, selfish interests come into conflict, and some persons improve their economic status partly at the expense of others. As has been repeatedly pointed out in this book, the pursuit of personal gain may lead to antisocial actions, so one cannot reason from self-interest to the social good. With labor constantly pressing for more economic advantages and capital-owning groups striving at least to maintain their economic power and to prevent a relative reduction in their living standards, it is clear that labor problems grow out of a basic diversity of economic interests. That diversity is likely to continue as long as most of the people must live by selling their services to employers, who own or control the productive facilities, the patents and trade-marks, and the various market rights and relationships that enhance one's economic power in a capitalistic economy.

INDEX

Abbe, E., 350n.
Abbott, E., 79n., 80n.
"Acceleration" principle, 240, 241, 270
Accident prevention, 501, 502
Accident rates, by industrial groups, 491; in maritime industry, 778
Actors' Equity Association, 866
Adair v. *United States*, 716n.
Adams, T. S., 344n.
Adamson Act, 365, 771
Adkins v. *Children's Hospital*, 44, 332
Administered prices, 878
Age, relation to earnings, 463
Age restrictions upon new workers, *cf.* Hiring-age limits
Aggregate demand, 267ff.
Agricultural Adjustment Administration, 32
Agricultural labor, *cf.* Farm workers
Agriculture, production in, 253; unemployment in, 254; unionism in, 762
Air transportation, Railway Labor Act extended to, 776
Akron Employers' Association, 656
Akron Law and Order League, 652
Allied trades councils, 580
Amalgamated Clothing Workers of America, 583, 589, 684–86, 814, 821, 822, 828ff.; union-management cooperation by, 684–86
Amalgamation of unions, 572, 575
American Association of Railroads, 773, 774
American Association of University Professors, 616, 617
American Family Robinson, 649
American Federation of Labor, 588–93; and boycott cases, 552; and industrial-craft controversy, 592, 593; conflict with Knights of Labor, 548; control of, 591, 592; formation of, 548; functions, 590, 591; income and expenditures, 591; membership of affiliates, 550; stimulated by CIO, 595

American Iron and Steel Institute, 846, 848, 850, 854
American Merchant Marine Institute, 781, 782
American Newspaper Guild, 856, 859, 864ff.
American Newspaper Publishers' Association, 858, 861, 862, 863, 865, 866; Open-Shop Department of, 858; Special Standing Committee of, 858, 861, 862, 863
American Photo-Engravers' Association, 147, 148
"American Plan," the, 129, 884, 885
American Rolling Mills Company, 848, 851
American Shipowners' Association, 136
American standard of living, 226ff.
American Steamship Owners' Association, 785
American Stores and Acme Markets in Philadelphia, 696
American Telephone and Telegraph Company, 129
Anderson, B. M., Jr., 287, 288n.
Anderson, N., 399n.
Anderson v. *Shipowners' Association of Pacific Coast et al.*, 648n.
Angell, J. W., 216n.
Answers to labor problems, 879-81; economics more important than good will for, 880
Anthracite coal industry, 793, 794; labor relations in, 799, 802, 803, 804
Anti-injunction laws, 714–15
Antitrust laws, application to labor, 147, 709–712; not apply to unions in Canada and Great Britain, 709, 747; union-employer collusion and, 836, 883
Antiunion agreements, *cf.* Yellow-dog contracts
Antiunion campaigns, 556, 557, 673, 869
Antiunion practices, *cf.* Espionage, labor; Black lists; Boycotts, by employers;

National Labor Relations Board, functions of, 720–22; success in the courts, 722; under Resolution No. 44, 719, 867

National Labor Relations Board v. Columbian Enameling and Stamping Co., 724n.

National Labor Relations Board v. Fansteel Metallurgical Corp., 726n., 727n.

National Labor Relations Board v. Friedman-Harry Marks Clothing Co., 836n.

National Labor Relations Board v. Mackay Radio and Telegraph Co., 726n.

National Labor Relations Board v. Sands Manufacturing Co., 727n.

National Labor Union, 544, 545, 588

National Maritime Union, 780, 781, 788

National Mediation Board, under Railway Labor Act, 723, 733, 735, 773

National Metal Trades Association, 130, 135, 137, 138, 551, 557, 640, 641, 643, 645, 647

National Miners Union, 808

National regulation, of industry, *cf.* Tudor regulations

National Resources Committee, 223, 227n., 230n., 233n.

National Steel Company, 851

National unions, increased power of, 577; operations of, 576–78; sovereignty of, 576, 586, 589

National War Labor Board, 553, 557, 669

National Youth Administration, 382, 385, 392

Natural resources, the market and, 41

Naumkeag Steam Cotton Co., 686–91

Negro workers, efficiency of, 206n.; union restrictions on, 206; wages of, 205ff.

Netherlands, compulsory investigation in, 753; extension of collective agreements by law in, 745; limitations on right to strike, 747; organized labor in, 741; strikes and lockouts in, 756, 757

Neuberger, R. L., 150n., 152n., 153n.

New York Clothing Manufacturers Exchange, 833, 835

New York Labor Relations Act, 24, 25, 729

New York Shipping Association, 789

New Zealand, compulsory arbitration in, 750; extension of collective agreements by law in, 745, 746; 40-hour week in, 746; limitations on strikes and lockouts, 747; minimum wages in 304ff.; strikes and lockouts in, 756, 757

Newark Ledger strike, 867

Newcomer, M., 232n.

Newlands Act, 771

Newspaper code, under NIRA, 866, 867

Newspaper Enterprise Association, 868

Newspaper Industrial Board, 867, 868

Newspapers, collective bargaining in, 767, 860–70; labor organization in, 862, 868, 869; labor relations in, 761, 762, Chapter 32; nature of market for, 857

Newswriters' unions, before formation of the Guild, 859ff.; chartered by AFL, 869, 870

Noncompeting groups, 207

"Normal" profits, exploitation and, 127

Norris-LaGuardia Anti-Injunction Act, 714, 715, 716, 717

Norway, compulsory arbitration in, 750, 751, 752; craft *vs.* industrial unionism in, 597; limitations on boycotts in, 748; strikes and lockouts in, 756, 757

Nourse, E. G., 816n.

Nyman, R. C., 686n., 687n., 688n.

Occupational differentials, in wages, 207

Occupational disease, 490, 506

Ogg, E., 780n.

Ohlin, B., 261n.

Old-age and survivors' insurance under the Social Security Act, benefits, 482, 483, 484, 485; contributions, 481, 482; coverage, 481; explanation of, 481ff.

Old-age assistance, 472ff.; contrast with old-age insurance, 475, 476; state legislation for, 473, 474

Old-age dependency, 463, 472, 473

Old-age insurance, abroad, 479; in the U. S., 479ff.

Old-age insurance reserve, 437, 485–88

Old-age problem, Chapter 17

Old-age relief, *cf.* Old-age assistance

Old persons, percentage of population, 464, 465

Older workers, employment problems of, 465–72; reasons for discrimination against, 469, 470, 471

Oligopsony, 97

Oliver, H. M., Jr., 121n., 301n.

One-big-union concept, 569

Open shop, campaigns for, 551, 556, 557, 831, 885; in steel, 849

Oregon antipicketing law, 730, 731

Organizational disputes, 595, 596

Organized labor, influence on prices, 295

Organizing campaign, AFL in steel, 845

Osborn, F., 211n.

Output restrictions by unions, *cf.* Union restrictions upon output